Britain 1981

An official handbook

SURREY COUNTY LIBRARY

London: Her Majesty's Stationery Office

Her Majesty's Stationery Office

Government Bookshops
49 High Holborn, London WC1V 6HB
13a Castle Street, Edinburgh EH2 3AR
41 The Hayes, Cardiff CF1 1JW
Brazennose Street, Manchester M60 8AS
Southey House, Wine Street, Bristol BS1 2BQ
258 Broad Street, Birmingham B1 2HE
80 Chichester Street, Belfast BT1 4JY

*Government publications are also available
through booksellers*

Obtainable in the United States of America
from Pendragon House Inc.
2595 East Bayshore Road
Palo Alto
California 94303

£11·00 net

ISBN 0 11 701004 9

Contents

	Page
Introduction	ix
1 The Land and the People	1
The Physical Background	1
The Demographic Background	6
The Social Framework	13
2 Government	19
General Survey	19
The Monarchy	20
Parliament	24
The Privy Council	35
Her Majesty's Government	36
Government Departments	40
The Civil Service	56
Local Government	60
The Fire Services	68
3 Overseas Relations	70
Membership of the European Community	72
The Commonwealth	77
International Peace and Security	81
Britain and the United Nations	83
Other International Organisations	86
Development Co-operation	86
4 Defence	93
Policy	93
Planning and Control	93
Deployment	94
The Armed Forces	96
Civil Defence	100
Defence Procurement	100
5 Justice and the Law	102
The Law	102
Criminal Justice	102
Civil Justice	121
Administration of the Law	125
6 Social Welfare	130
National Health Service	130
Personal Social Services	140
Social Security	143
Voluntary Services	150
Equal Opportunities for Women	152
Race Relations	153
7 Education	155
The Youth Service	171

Page

8 Planning and the Environment 174
Control of Pollution 182
Voluntary Organisations 188

9 Housing 190

10 The Churches 196

11 The National Economy 200
Economic Development 200
Economic Management 203
National Income and Expenditure 204
The External Position 207

12 The Framework of Industry 210
Organisation and Production 210
The Government and Industry 222
Competition Policy and Consumer Protection 230
Company Law 233

13 Manufacturing and Service Industries 234
Manufacturing 234
Construction 255
Service Industries 256

14 Energy and Natural Resources 262
Energy 262
Non-fuel Minerals 280
Water 281

15 Agriculture, Fisheries and Forestry 285
Agriculture 285
Fisheries 297
Forestry 300

16 Transport and Communications 302
Inland Transport 302
Ports 312
Shipping 314
Civil Aviation 318
The Post Office 322

17 Employment 326
The Working Population 326
Manpower Policy 327
Employment Protection Law 332
Pay, Hours of Work and Holidays 333
Industrial Relations 335
Health and Safety at Work 341

18 Finance 346
The Public Sector 346
Financial Institutions 357

19 Overseas Trade and Payments 368
Overseas Trade 368
Balance of Payments 376

		Page
20	Promotion of the Sciences	381
21	Promotion of the Arts	397
22	The Press	412
23	Television and Radio	420
24	Sport and Recreation	428

Appendix	438
Currency	438
Metric Equivalents for British Weights and Measures	438
Bibliography	440
Index	463

Diagrams

United Kingdom population changes and projections	8
The Royal Family: genealogical tree	22
Functional analysis of defence expenditure 1980–81	94
Functional analysis of defence personnel 1980–81	97
Personal income and expenditure 1979	206

Maps

Britain	*inside back cover*
The Assisted Areas	224
Proposed Assisted Areas	225
Oil	266
Gas	269
Coal	272
Electricity	276
Some minerals produced in Britain	282
Main railway passenger routes	310

Photographs

The Humber Bridge	*facing page* 38
Computer Services	*between pages* 38 *and* 39
Robot	*between pages* 38 *and* 39
Infrared Telescope	*facing page* 39
Equipment for the Disabled	*between pages* 134 *and* 135
New cars	*facing page* 294
Technological Research at Universities	*between pages* 294 *and* 295
Aircraft	*facing page* 295
Covent Garden	*facing page* 390
New Agricultural Equipment	*between pages* 390 *and* 391
Sport	*facing page* 391

Acknowledgement is made for photographs to:
Brian Bell for IRAS aerial dish (between pp 38 and 39); *BP Oil* for Invashrew invalid car (between pp 134 and 135); *Rolls-Royce Motors* for Silver Spirit (facing p 294); *Mather & Platt* for sprout harvester (between pp 390 and 391).

The theme for the cover design is computer software. Britain is a world leader in software systems and services.

Introduction

Britain 1981 is the thirty-second official handbook in the series; it has been prepared and revised by Reference Division (now Reference Services, Publications Division) of the Central Office of Information. The handbook is widely known as an established work of reference and is the mainstay of the reference facilities provided by the British Information Services in many countries. It is distributed overseas in a limited free edition and is on sale by Her Majesty's Stationery Office throughout the world.

Britain 1981 is primarily concerned to describe the machinery of government and other institutions. It also provides some general background, but does not attempt an analytical approach to current events. The text, generally, is based on information available up to September 1980.

Care should be taken when studying British statistics to note whether they refer to England, to England and Wales (considered together for many administrative and other purposes), to Great Britain, which comprises England, Wales and Scotland, or to the United Kingdom (Great Britain and Northern Ireland) as a whole.

The factual and statistical information in *Britain 1981* is compiled with the co-operation of other government departments and agencies, and of many other organisations. Sources of more detailed and more topical information (including statistics) are mentioned in the text and in the Bibliography towards the end of the book.

Reference Services
Publications Division
Central Office of Information, London

1 The Land and the People

THE PHYSICAL BACKGROUND

Britain, also known as the United Kingdom of Great Britain and Northern Ireland, constitutes the greater part of the British Isles, a group of islands lying off the north-west coast of mainland Europe. The largest islands are Great Britain (comprising the mainlands of England, Wales and Scotland) and Ireland (comprising Northern Ireland and the Irish Republic). Off the southern coast of England is the Isle of Wight and off the extreme south-west are the Isles of Scilly; off north Wales is Anglesey. Western Scotland is fringed by numerous islands and to the north-east are the Orkneys and Shetlands. All these have administrative ties with the mainland, but the Isle of Man in the Irish Sea and the Channel Islands between Great Britain and France have a large measure of administrative autonomy and are not part of England, Wales, Scotland or Northern Ireland.

TABLE 1: Area of the United Kingdom

	Total		Land		Inland water	
	square km	square miles	square km	square miles	square km	square miles
United Kingdom[1]	244,108	94,251	241,001	93,051	3,107	1,200
Great Britain	229,988	88,799	227,518	87,845	2,470	954
England	130,438	50,362	129,702	50,078	736	284
Wales	20,769	8,019	20,640	7,969	129	50
Scotland	78,781	30,418	77,176	29,798	1,605	620
Northern Ireland	14,120	5,452	13,483	5,206	637	246

[1] Excludes the Isle of Man, 588 square km (227 square miles), and the Channel Islands, 194 square km (75 square miles).

The latitude of 50° North cuts across the southernmost part of the British mainland (the Lizard Peninsula) and latitude 60° North passes through the Shetland Islands. The northernmost point of the Scottish mainland, Dunnet Head, near John o' Groats, is in latitude 58° 40′. The prime meridian of 0° passes through the old observatory at Greenwich (London), while the easternmost point of England is nearly 1° 45′ East and the westernmost point of Northern Ireland is 8° 10′ West. It is just under 1,000 km (some 600 miles) from the south coast to the extreme north of mainland Britain and just under 500 km (some 300 miles) across in the widest part. There are numerous bays and inlets and no place is as much as 120 km (75 miles) from tidal water.

The seas surrounding the British Isles are shallow—usually less than 90 metres (50 fathoms or 300 feet)—because the islands lie on the continental shelf. To the north-west along the edge of the shelf the sea floor plunges abruptly from 180 metres (some 600 feet) to 900 metres (about 3,000 feet). These shallow waters are important because they provide breeding grounds for fish. The North Atlantic current, the drift of warm water which reaches the islands from across the Atlantic, spreads out over the shelf and its ameliorating effect on the air is thus magnified. The effect of tidal movement is also increased by the shallowness of the water.

Geology and Topography

Despite its small area, Britain contains rocks of all the main geological periods. In general, the oldest rocks appear in the highland regions in the north and west, and the youngest in the lowland areas in the south and east. This is mainly the result of persistent slow sinking over many millions of years in the south and east accompanying the formation of the deep North Sea and English Channel sedimentary basins.

Beneath the lowland areas in the south and east of England lie the younger rocks. The harder chalk and limestone formations stand out as ranges of low, grass-covered hills (rarely reaching 300 metres, 1,000 feet, above sea level) separated by clay vales of rich farm land. These younger formations rest on an old volcanic foundation present at a depth of a few hundred metres under much of central England. This volcanic foundation, containing the oldest British fossils, comes to the surface as craggy hillocks in north-west Leicestershire. At greater depths beneath southern England lies the continuation of the older rock formations of Belgium and the Rhineland.

The south-western peninsula of England, mainly the counties of Devon and Cornwall, is composed of very old slate and sandstone formations into which has been forced a large mass of metal-bearing granite whose outcrops now form most of the high ground such as Dartmoor.

Still older rocks form most of the mountainous and hilly terrain in Wales, the English Lake District, the southern uplands of Scotland and the southern border counties of Northern Ireland.[1] These rocks were subjected to compressions 400 million years ago which folded the strata and turned muddy sediment into slate. In Wales and the Lake District thick volcanic formations, eroded by rivers and Ice-Age glaciers, form spectacular mountain scenery.

Carboniferous limestone formations form the Mendip Hills, south of Bristol, and the Pennines in northern England. In Scotland similar strata of a partly volcanic character underlie the midland valley. These and other carboniferous strata contain the coal measures which were the foundation of British industrial expansion. The outcrops and shallow seams of coal which have now largely been exhausted were found on the edge of the plains and up the valleys leading to the high land. Most of the present deep coal workings lie underneath the fertile lowlands. The continental shelf under the North Sea contains large, exploitable quantities of oil and natural gas.

The Scottish Highlands are built from very thick formations of crystalline rock, now deeply eroded, which was deposited between 1,000 million and 500 million years ago. Far older rocks, including the oldest in Britain, emerge from beneath the Highlands on the north-western seaboard of Scotland and in the Outer Hebrides, forming barren and rocky land. On the mainland of Scotland a cover of red sandstone between 800 million and 1,000 million years old has been partly eroded, leaving imposing isolated peaks.

Extensive areas in Antrim in Northern Ireland and in the islands of the Inner Hebrides are composed of volcanic lava flows which erupted 50 million to 60 million years ago when the North Atlantic Ocean was in the process of opening

---

[1] The highest peaks are: in Scotland, Ben Nevis, 1,342 metres (4,406 feet); in Wales, Snowdon, 1,085 metres (3,560 feet); and in England, Scafell Pike (in the Lake District, Cumbria), 978 metres (3,210 feet). The highest peak in Northern Ireland is Slieve Donard, 852 metres (2,796 feet).

out. The lavas and the roots of the volcanoes which fed them are deeply eroded into wild mountain scenery.

The landscape of Britain is mainly the result of cycles of uplift and erosion in the past 25 million years, culminating in the last Ice Age. Around 750,000 years ago great glaciers built up in the mountainous areas of Britain and Scandinavia and spread out as ice-sheets into the lowland areas. The mountains and the valleys were formed by the glaciers while the ice sheets deposited a thick blanket of boulder clay, gravel and sand over the lowlands north of a line from Bristol to London. Large lakes of meltwater held back by the ice gradually dried up, leaving deposits of sand and silt. Throughout much of the country the blanket of glacial debris affords soils of great fertility.

Britain's complex geology is one of the main reasons for its rich variety of scenery and the stimulating contrasts found within short distances, particularly on the coasts. The ancient rocks of the highland area often reach the coast in towering cliffs; elsewhere the sea may penetrate in deep lochs, as along much of the west coast of Scotland. Bold outstanding headlands are notable features in other parts of the varied coastline: the granite cliffs of Land's End; the limestone masses and slates of the coast of south-west Wales; the red sandstone of St. Bees Head on the coast of Cumbria; and the vertically jointed lavas of Skye and the island of Staffa in the Inner Hebrides. Even around the lowlands there are striking contrasts. In some parts the soft, white limestone—the chalk—forms white cliffs as at Dover and in the Needles off the Isle of Wight; while other parts of the south and south-east coastline have beaches of sand or shingle. The eastern coast of England between the Humber and the Thames estuary is mostly low-lying, and for centuries some stretches of it have been protected against the sea by embankments.

The marked tidal movement around the shores of Britain sweeps away much of the sand and mud brought down by the rivers and makes the estuaries of some British rivers[1] valuable as natural harbours.

Climate

Britain has a generally mild and temperate climate. The prevailing winds are south-westerly and the weather from day to day is controlled mainly by a succession of depressions from the Atlantic. The weather is subject to frequent changes but to few extremes of temperature. Although the winds are largely determined by those of the eastern Atlantic, occasionally during the winter months easterly winds may bring cold, dry, weather which, once established, may persist for many days or even weeks. During the summer months the Azores high pressure system usually extends its influence north-eastwards towards north-west Europe, and the depressions take a more northerly course, often passing entirely to the north of the country.

Winds

South-westerly winds are the most frequent, and those from an easterly direction the least; such winds occur about one-third as often as south-westerlies although easterly winds are appreciably more frequent in the spring than at any other time of the year. In hilly country, wind direction may differ markedly from the general direction owing to local topography. Winds are generally stronger in the north than in the south, stronger on the coasts than inland, and stronger in the west than in the east. The strongest winds usually occur in the winter; the average speed at Lerwick, Shetland Islands, varies

---

[1] The longest rivers in England—the Severn and the Thames—are only about 354 and 338 km (220 and 210 miles) long respectively; those in Scotland (the Tay and the Clyde) are about 188 km and 170 km (117 and 106 miles) long.

from about 29 km/h (18 mph) in January to about 19 km/h (12 mph) in August, while at Kew Observatory, on the western outskirts of London, the average speed varies from about 15 km/h (9 mph) in January to about 12 km/h (7 mph) in August. The stormiest region is along the north-west coast with over 40 gales a year; south-east England and the east Midlands are the least stormy, with gales occurring on about two days a year inland and on some 10 to 15 days on the Channel coast.

Temperature

Near sea level in the west the mean annual temperature ranges from 8°C (46°F) in the Hebrides to 11°C (52°F) in the extreme south-west of England; latitude for latitude it is slightly lower in the east. The mean monthly temperature in the extreme north, at Lerwick (Shetland), ranges from 3°C (37°F) during the winter (December, January and February) to 12°C (54°F) during the summer (June, July and August): the corresponding figures for the Isle of Wight, in the extreme south, are 5°C (41°F) and 16°C (61°F). During a normal summer, the temperature occasionally rises above 30°C (86°F) in the south, but temperatures of 32°C (90°F) and above are infrequent. Minimum temperatures depend largely on local conditions, but −10°C (14°F) may occur on a still, clear winter's night in inland areas. Lower temperatures are rare.

Rainfall

Britain has an annual rainfall of about 1,100 mm (over 40 inches), while England alone has some 830 mm (about 33 inches). The geographical distribution of annual rainfall is largely governed by topography and exposure to the Atlantic, the mountainous areas of the west and north having far more rain than the lowlands of the south and east. More than 4,000 mm (roughly 160 inches) of rain fall on the summits of Snowdon, the Lake District and north-west Scotland during the average year, whereas some places in the south-east of England record less than 550 mm (about 22 inches). Rain is fairly well distributed throughout the year, but, on the average, March to June are the driest months and October to January the wettest. A period of as long as three weeks without rain is exceptional, and is usually confined to limited areas.

Sunshine

The distribution of sunshine shows a general decrease from south to north, a decrease from the coast inland, and a decrease with altitude. During May, June and July (the months of longest daylight) the mean daily duration of sunshine varies from five hours in northern Scotland to eight hours in the Isle of Wight; during the months of shortest daylight—November, December and January—sunshine is at a minimum, with an average of half an hour a day in some parts of northern Scotland and two hours a day on the south coast of England.

Visibility

In fine, still weather there is occasionally haze in summer and mist and fog in winter. Fogs have become less frequent and less severe as a result of changes in fuel usage and the operation of clean air legislation. In London, for example, the frequency of dense fogs in winter is about half what it was 20 years ago.

Soil and Vegetation

Many parts of the surface of highland Britain have only thin, poor soils. These stretches of moorland are found over the Highlands of Scotland, the Pennines, the Lake District, the mountains of Wales and in parts of north-east and south-west England. In most areas the farmer has cultivated only the valleys and the plains where soils are deeper and richer; villages and towns are often separated by uplands with few if any habitations.

With the exception of a few patches of heath and forest, almost the whole of lowland Britain has been cultivated, and farmland covers the area except where there are urban and industrial settlements. Elaborate land drainage has been developed through the centuries to bring under cultivation the fertile soil of the low-lying fenland of Lincolnshire and part of East Anglia.

With its mild climate and varied soils, Britain has a diverse pattern of vegetation. When the islands were first settled, oak forest probably covered the greater part of the lowland, giving place to extensive marshlands, forests of Scots pine on higher or sandy ground and perhaps some open moorland. In the course of the centuries the forest area was progressively diminished and, in spite of planting by estate owners in the eighteenth and nineteenth centuries and the establishment of large forests by the Forestry Commission in the past 60 years, woodlands now occupy only about 9 per cent of the land area. The greatest density of woodland occurs in northern Britain, in some parts of south-east England and on the Welsh border. Yet much of Britain appears to be wooded because of the numerous hedgerows and isolated trees. The most common trees are oak, beech, ash and elm and, in Scotland, pine and birch. The number of elms, however, especially in southern England, has been severely reduced since the late 1960s by 'Dutch' elm disease.

There are various types of wild vegetation, including the natural flora of woods, fens and marshes, foreshores and cliffs, chalk downs and the higher slopes of mountains; the most widespread is that of the hilly moorland country, which consists mainly of heather, grasses, gorse and bracken, with cotton grass in the wetter parts. Nearly 80 per cent of Britain however is used for agriculture (including rough grazing land and woodland on agricultural holdings) with most of the prime farming land in England. The amount of land in urban use is less than a tenth of the agricultural land.

Farming land is divided into fields by hedges, stone walls or fences and, especially in the mixed farms which cover most of the country, presents a pattern of contrasting colour. The cool temperate climate and the even distribution of rainfall ensure a long growing season; streams rarely dry up, grassland is green throughout the year with many wild flowers from spring to autumn; in most years there is scarcely a month without some flowers in hedgerows and woodlands.

Fauna The fauna of the British Isles is, in general, similar to that of the rest of north-western Europe, though there are fewer species. Some of the larger mammals, including the wolf, the bear, the boar and the reindeer, have become extinct; but red deer, protected for sporting reasons, flourish in the Scottish Highlands and on Exmoor in the counties of Devon and Somerset, roe deer are found in Scotland and in the wooded areas of southern England, and fallow deer (which are probably not indigenous) have been introduced into parks and are wild in some districts. The badger, a nocturnal animal, is rarely seen; there are foxes in most rural (and increasingly in urban) areas. Common and grey seals may be seen on parts of the coast, though not usually in the same localities. Smaller mammals include mice, rats, voles, shrews, hedgehogs, moles, squirrels (the imported grey much more numerous than the native red), hares, rabbits, weasels and stoats. Less common species include the otter, the pine marten and the polecat. Species which have established themselves in the wild after escape from captivity include the muntjac, coypu and mink.

About 460 species of birds have been recorded in the British Isles. Some 200 species breed; the rest are regular migrants to, or pass through, the country, or are casual stragglers. Visitors to Britain are often struck by the abundance, variety and tameness of song birds in towns and villages. The pigeon, blackbird and chaffinch are widely distributed but sparrows usually predominate near houses. London and some other large towns have huge flocks of starlings which congregate to roost on buildings, especially in winter. Most species of birds have maintained their numbers over the last few decades, owing to their success in adapting themselves to man-made surroundings, and in London there has been an increase in the number of species breeding as a result of the improvement in the environment brought about by anti-pollution measures. Some birds, however, particularly some of the larger species have tended to decrease, but several species, such as the osprey and the ruff, have re-established themselves after disappearing from Britain in the nineteenth century.

Many species of gulls and other sea birds nest around the coast, and gulls may regularly be seen feeding far inland; some nest in inland sites such as gravel pits and sewage farms. The drainage and reclamation of marshlands have diminished the natural habitat of ducks, geese and other aquatic birds, but the survival of such species is largely assured on the nature reserves and bird sanctuaries which have recently been established on an increasing scale. Nearly all British wild birds are protected; the principal exceptions are those considered injurious to agriculture and game birds shot for sport in the open season (these are protected when breeding by a close season).

About 30 kinds of freshwater fish are found, salmon, trout, pike, roach, dace and perch being widely distributed. Stocks of trout, rainbow trout (an introduced species), carp, tench and roach are frequently supplemented by specially bred introductions for angling. In a number of rivers measures to control pollution have resulted in fish becoming more numerous; in the Thames in London, where pollution levels have been reduced to a quarter of those in the 1950s, nearly 100 kinds of fish have been found, compared with only one in 1958.

Reptiles and amphibians are few. The former are represented by three species of snakes, of which only the adder is venomous, and three species of lizards, including the snake-like slow-worm. The amphibians are represented by three species of newts and five species of frogs and toads. Most British reptiles and amphibians are indigenous but at least one, the marsh frog, has been recently introduced from continental Europe. Ireland has no snakes.

There are more than 21,000 different kinds of insects. Among the largest are the rare swallowtail butterfly (8–10 cm, 3–4 inches) and the stag beetle (6 cm, $2\frac{1}{2}$ inches). The insect fauna is less varied than that of continental Europe and lacks a number of common European species. With modern methods of pest control, extensive insect damage to crops or timber and serious outbreaks of diseases spread by insects are not common but there is some anxiety that chemical protection against insects may be reducing the population of creatures which feed on them, and of their predators in turn. These and other effects of agricultural chemicals on wildlife are the subject of special government safeguards supported by the agricultural chemicals industry.

THE DEMOGRAPHIC BACKGROUND

The people who now inhabit Britain are descended mainly from the people who inhabited the area nine centuries ago. The last of a long succession of invaders and colonisers from Scandinavia and the continent of Europe were the Normans, a branch of the Norsemen or Scandinavian Vikings who, after settling in northern France, intermarrying with the French, and assimilating their language and customs, crossed the Channel to England and conquered it in 1066.

Obviously it is not possible to estimate the relative importance of various early peoples—pre-Celts, Celts, Romans, Anglo-Saxons and the Norsemen, including the Danes—in the ancestry of the present English, Scots, Welsh and Irish. Over most of England and the lowlands of Scotland the language which soon came to predominate was English, mainly a marriage of Anglo-Saxon and Norman-French, while the use of Celtic languages persisted in Wales, Cornwall, the Isle of Man, the highlands of Scotland and in Ireland.

The available records do not enable any precise estimates to be made of the size of population or of the extent or direction of population movement until the beginning of the nineteenth century. It is believed, however, that at the end of the eleventh century the population of Great Britain was about 2 million, while at the end of the seventeenth century reasonable contemporary estimates put the population at about 6½ million. The main factor in this gradual growth of population was a slow natural increase, with high death rates and, in particular, very high infant and maternal mortality. Immigration from the continent of Europe has been an influence at certain times as, more recently, has immigration from Commonwealth countries.

Statistics and Censuses

From the beginning of the nineteenth century there is relatively plentiful and reliable information about the British people—their number, sex, age, geographical distribution, births, marriages, deaths, occupations, language, and family structure. Most of it comes from two main sources: the regular flow of statistical information based on compulsory registration of births, marriages and deaths, and the periodic censuses taken regularly every ten years since 1801 (because of war there was no census in 1941). The last census was in 1971; the next will be held in 1981.

Numbers

Britain's estimated mid-1979 home population was 55,883,000 (see Table 2). The populations of the Isle of Man, Jersey, and Guernsey and associated islands are about 60,500, 74,500 and 54,400 respectively. In the period 1975–78 for the first years since records began (other than in war) the

TABLE 2: Populations 1901–79[a]   *thousands*

		1901 census	1931 census	1961 census	1971 census	1979 mid-year estimate
England	Males	14,714	17,839	21,012	22,355	22,605
	Females	15,795	19,520	22,448	23,663	23,791
	Persons	30,509	37,359	43,461	46,018	46,396
Wales	Males	1,014	1,294	1,292	1,328	1,345
	Females	1,004	1,300	1,352	1,404	1,430
	Persons	2,019	2,593	2,644	2,731	2,775
Scotland	Males	2,174	2,326	2,483	2,515	2,490
	Females	2,298	2,517	2,697	2,714	2,678
	Persons	4,472	4,843	5,179	5,229	5,167
Northern Ireland	Males	590	601[b]	694	755	765
	Females	647	642[b]	731	781	781
	Persons	1,237	1,243[b]	1,425	1,536	1,545
United Kingdom	Males	18,492	22,060	25,481	26,952	27,204
	Females	19,745	23,978	27,228	28,562	28,679
	Persons	38,237	46,038	52,709	55,515	55,883

[a] Differences between totals and the sum of their constituent parts are due to rounding.
[b] Estimates.

population fell slightly, although it began to recover in 1979. The decline, common to much of western Europe, was mainly the result of a sharp fall in the birth rate (see below). Births in 1979 out-numbered deaths but the direction of net migration, as in other recent years, was outward.

The total population of New Commonwealth and Pakistani ethnic origin (including children born in Britain and children with only one parent of such ethnic origin) was 1·9 million in 1978, about 3·6 per cent of the total population of Great Britain.

Projections for the future suggest that population growth will take place at a much slower rate than was expected a few years ago. Britain's total population is expected, on 1979 estimates, to be 56·4 million in 1986, 58·4 million in 2001 and 60 million in 2019.

The country as a whole has a population density of about 236 people to the square kilometre (611 per square mile), but in England the figures are 355 people to the square kilometre (920 per square mile), and in Greater London 4,378 people per square kilometre (11,347 per square mile).

Birth Rates

Annual births have fallen by some 30 per cent since the mid-1960s. The birth rate declined from 17·8 live births per 1,000 people in 1966 to 11·6 in 1977, an unprecedentedly low figure. The most recent information suggests that the fall in the birth rate has come to an end; births in England and Wales rose in 1978 for the first time since 1964. In 1979 there were 638,000 live births (compared with 849,823 in 1966), of which over 10 per cent were illegitimate, and the birth rate was 13.

Several factors may have contributed to the fall in the birth rate. Family planning, particularly the use by women of the contraceptive pill, has become

United Kingdom population changes and projections

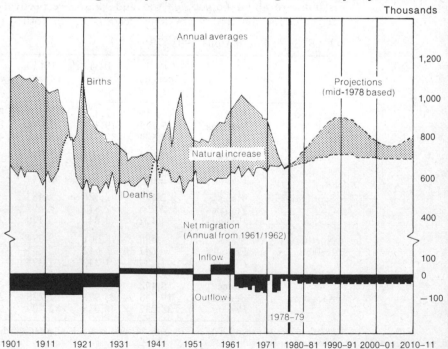

Thousands

more widespread, and sterilisation of men and women has also become more common. An appreciable proportion of pregnancies (nearly 40 per cent of those conceived outside marriage and about 8 per cent for those conceived within marriage) are ended by legal abortion.

There are indications that the proportion of childless marriages may be increasing a little, and for marriages which do produce children there is a continuing tendency for the interval between marriage and the first birth to be longer. The numbers of third and later children born have fallen substantially. The biggest falls have been in the births of third and later children to manual workers, but proportionately the pattern is broadly similar for all social classes.

The fertility of women born overseas, particularly those from the Irish Republic, the West Indies and the Indian sub-continent, was shown in the 1971 census to be higher on average than that of the indigenous population, but has since been falling. The population of New Commonwealth and Pakistani ethnic origin contains a larger proportion of young people than the indigenous population and so contributes disproportionately to the number of births.

Mortality

At birth the expectation of life for a man is just over 69 years and for a woman it is just over 76 years. The corresponding expectations in 1901 were 48 years for men and 52 years for women. The improving health of the population has had the effect of increasing young people's chances of reaching the older age groups. Life expectancy in the older age groups has increased relatively little.

The general death rate has remained about the same for the past 50 years, at about 12 per 1,000 population, reflecting the gradual ageing of the population since there has been a considerable decline in mortality at most ages, particularly among children and young adults.

The causes of the decline in mortality include better nutrition, rising standards of living, the advance of medical science, the growth of medical facilities, improved health measures, better working conditions, education in personal hygiene, and the smaller size of the family, which has reduced the strain on mothers and enabled them to take greater care of their children.

Mortality from tuberculosis is a tiny fraction of what it was in the mid-nineteenth century, and mortality from acute infectious diseases in infancy has virtually been eliminated. The infant mortality rate (deaths of infants under one year old per 1,000 live births) was 13·3 in 1978; neonatal mortality (deaths of infants under four weeks old per 1,000 live births) was 8·8; and maternal mortality was 0·1 per 1,000 live births.

The mortality from each major cause often reflects factors directly linked to occupation and the wide variations between the life patterns and living standards of the different social classes.

Migration

Traditionally Britain has a net outflow of people to the rest of the world (net loss by migration between 1871 and 1931 for instance was about 4 million) though there have been exceptional periods—in the 1930s when there was a considerable flow of refugees from continental Europe, and in the late 1950s and early 1960s, mainly the result of a large influx of people from the West Indies and the Indian sub-continent.

The traditional pattern of migration in Britain has been maintained in the past few years.

Between 1969 and 1979 Britain lost nearly half a million people by migration: 2·4 million emigrants and 2·0 million immigrants; in both totals about a third of the people were returning to their country of origin.

Sex Ratio

There are about 6 per cent more male than female births every year. Because of the higher mortality of men at all ages, however, there is a turning point, at about 45 years of age, at which the number of women exceeds the number of men. This imbalance increases with age so that there is a preponderance of women among the elderly. In the population as a whole there are more than 105 females to every 100 men.

Marriage and Divorce

Marriage trends since the 1930s have been towards a higher proportion of people marrying and an earlier age pattern. The proportion of the population of Great Britain who were or had been married rose from about 52 per cent in 1939 to 60 per cent in 1978, while the proportion of single persons (in the population aged 15 years or over) fell from 33·3 per cent to 23·8 per cent. Wide-ranging changes in family life appear to have occurred in the 1970s and include a record decline since 1945 in rates of first marriage, particularly among teenagers; later starts to family building; and a continued rise in the proportions of people divorcing, including those divorcing for a second or subsequent time, and of people marrying for a second or subsequent time. In 1978 just over 11 decrees of divorce were made absolute for every 1,000 married people in England and Wales, compared with 2 in 1961; some 85 per cent of divorces in England and Wales in 1978 occurred among couples both of whom were in their first marriage. The average age of people at the time of divorce in England and Wales is about 38 for men and 36 for women. Remarriage rates among younger divorced people are high, and births in remarriage are likely to become a more important component of total births in the future.

Age Structure

The estimated age distribution of the British population in mid-1979 was roughly as follows; under 15 years, about 21 per cent; 15–64, 64 per cent; and 65 and over, 15 per cent. Some 17 per cent of the population were over the normal retirement ages (65 for men and 60 for women).

The changing age structure has for the time being produced a balance between those who are primarily producers of resources and those who are primarily consumers that is more unfavourable than at any time since the early 1930s. This 'dependency ratio' of children and older people to the size of the population of working age is, however, projected to fall from 67 per cent in 1976 to 58 per cent in 2001. This will be the result principally of the decreasing proportion of children in the population.

Perhaps the main feature of the changing age structure is the increasing number of elderly people, reflecting birth patterns in the early years of this century and the final decades of the nineteenth. Between mid-1970 and mid-1979 the number of people over the normal retirement ages rose by 9 per cent. Proportionately there was a particularly large increase in the number of people aged 85 and over, 25 per cent over the same period.

Distribution of Population

The population of England is, and has been for centuries, greater than that of all other parts of Britain. The distribution of the British population by country is shown in Table 2 on p 7.

The standard regions of England, sub-divisions of the country used for most statistical and economic planning purposes, have the following populations (provisional mid-1979 estimates): East Anglia 1,863,200; East Midlands 3,765,800; Northern 3,087,400; North-West 6,476,100; South-East 16,857,500; South-West 4,315,700; West Midlands 5,152,200; and Yorkshire and Humberside 4,878,200.

TABLE 3: Size and Population of Some of the Main Urban Areas, Mid-1979

	Area		Population estimate (provisional)
	square km	square miles	
			(*thousands*)
Greater London	1,580	609·7	6,877
Birmingham	264	102·0	1,034
Glasgow	157	60·5	794
Leeds	562	217·0	724
Sheffield	368	141·9	544
Liverpool	113	43·6	520
Manchester	116	44·9	479
Bradford	370	142·9	462
Edinburgh	135	52·0	455
Bristol	110	42·3	408
Belfast	140	54·0	354[a]
Coventry	97	37·3	339
Cardiff	120	46·3	282

[a] Population in mid-1978.

Table 3 gives figures of some of Britain's largest urban areas. About half the population lives in a belt across England with south Lancashire and West Yorkshire at one end, and the London area at the other, having the industrialised Midlands at its centre. Other areas with large populations are: the central lowlands of Scotland; north-east England from north of the river Tyne down to the river Tees; south-east Wales; the Bristol area; and the English Channel coast from Poole, in Dorset, eastwards. Less densely populated areas are the eastern fringes of England between the Wash and the Thames estuary, and the far south-west. The seven major metropolitan areas which have been denoted as 'conurbations' in successive population censuses accommodate a third of Great Britain's people while comprising less than three per cent of the total land area. They are: Greater London, Central Clydeside, Merseyside, South East Lancashire, Tyneside, the West Midlands and West Yorkshire. Most of the mountainous parts including much of Scotland, Wales and Northern Ireland and the central Pennines, are very sparsely populated.

These differences in average density between different regions have been widening. There has been a geographical redistribution of the population from Scotland and the northern regions of England to East Anglia, the South-West and the East Midlands. The proportion resident in Greater London and most of the metropolitan counties of England has recently been falling. People, particularly the young and skilled, have tended to leave city centres and conurbations, although such migration may not necessarily mean a change of job but rather an increase in the distance of travel to and from work. In other cases it has been a consequence of falling employment in city centres, a trend which has led to special measures, worked out for each city, to attract small industries back there.

Language   In England, Wales, Scotland and Northern Ireland, English is the language predominantly spoken. In Wales, however, Welsh, a form of British Celtic, was spoken by 21 per cent of the population (some 542,000 people) aged three years and over at the time of the 1971 census. The Welsh Language Council, an official body, promotes the use of the language. The Welsh Language Act 1967 affirms the equal validity of Welsh with English in the administration of justice and conduct of government business throughout Wales. The number of bilingual schools is increasing. In Scotland some 88,000 persons in 1971, mainly in the Highlands and western coastal regions, were able to speak the Scottish form of Gaelic. A few families in Northern Ireland still speak the Irish form of Gaelic. The Cornish variety of Celtic is no longer effectively a living language, although there is a revival of cultural interest.

Some of the country's ethnic minorities have their own languages, normally as well as English. Among the Asian community, for example, the most usual languages are Punjabi, Gujarati, Bengali or Urdu.

Immigration Control and Nationality

Immigration into Britain is controlled by the Immigration Act 1971 and administered according to rules made under it. The Act confers a right of abode—and exemption from control—on citizens of the United Kingdom and Colonies who are connected with Britain by birth, adoption, naturalisation or registration or are children or grandchildren of such persons, on citizens of the United Kingdom and Colonies from overseas who have been resident in Britain for a continuous period of five years, and on Commonwealth citizens with a parent born in the United Kingdom. Those having this right of abode are known as 'patrials'. In general, others wishing to enter Britain for employment must hold work permits. Exceptions include Commonwealth citizens with a grandparent born in Britain, certain permit-free categories, and nationals of European Community countries. The dependants of work permit holders and of those who may enter without work permits may also be admitted, as may the wives and children of men already settled in Britain and certain other categories. A number of changes in the rules took effect in 1980.

Under the British Nationality Act 1948, people born in the United Kingdom, the Channel Islands, the Isle of Man, a ship or aircraft registered in the United Kingdom, or a territory which is still a colony, are, with insignificant exceptions, citizens of the United Kingdom and Colonies by birth. Citizenship may also be acquired: by descent from a father who is himself a citizen otherwise than by descent and, in certain specified circumstances, from a father who is a citizen by descent only; by registration, for citizens of Commonwealth member countries or of the Irish Republic, for minor children and for women married to citizens of the United Kingdom and Colonies; in consequence of a United Kingdom adoption order; and, for aliens, by naturalisation. The requirements for naturalisation include five years' residence in the United Kingdom or a colony, good character, a sufficient knowledge of English and the intention to reside in the United Kingdom or a colony. The requirements for registration are similar except that most Commonwealth and Irish citizens settled in Britain by 1973 have the right to be registered after completing five years' ordinary residence without satisfying any other requirement. In 1979, 24,600 people acquired citizenship by naturalisation and registration.

A citizen of the United Kingdom and Colonies does not forfeit his citizenship by acquiring or possessing the nationality or citizenship of another country (although he can lose it automatically if the territory from which he derives it becomes independent); nor does a woman who is a citizen of the United Kingdom and Colonies lose her citizenship by marriage to a foreign national. Indeed, a citizen cannot be deprived of his citizenship against his will except in very exceptional circumstances (for example, if he has obtained naturalisation or registration as a citizen by fraud). Any man or woman who is a citizen is, however, at liberty to renounce citizenship if he or she possesses or acquires the nationality or citizenship of another country. Citizens of the other independent Commonwealth countries are, in United Kingdom law, British subjects or Commonwealth citizens and, as such, enjoy full political and civic rights if resident in Britain.

A Government White Paper, published in 1980, contains proposals for replacing the present nationality law with new legislation.

THE SOCIAL FRAMEWORK

This section gives some points of general interest about household structure and social characteristics in Britain as a background to the information given in later chapters. It deals with topics in very broad and informal terms and many exceptions apply to the generalisations.

The way of life of the people of Britain has been changing rapidly throughout the twentieth century. As in many other countries underlying causes include two major wars, a lower birth rate, longer expectation of life, a higher divorce rate, widening educational opportunities and technical progress, particularly in communications and transport and a better standard of living. One of the features of the change in social attitudes has been the development of a more informed tolerance of others' behaviour and an unwillingness to penalise individuals with particular problems. Relationships between the generations, too, are changing, and young people are more ready to criticise traditional values and institutions and to seek greater influence in shaping society.

The following account applies primarily to Great Britain. Many of the same factors are at work in Northern Ireland but their effect is modified by both the Province's history and the emergency of recent years.

Homes and the Environment
The majority of people (some 97 per cent) live in private households (in families or on their own). The remainder include residents in hotels, and people in the armed services and in educational or other institutions. In 1978 eight out of ten people lived in a family unit headed by a married couple. Of these nearly half contained one or two dependent children and a fifth had no children. Only 2 per cent of people lived in households containing more than one family, a proportion which has been falling as fewer young married couples live with their parents. One in ten people lived with no family and 8 per cent lived in a one-parent family.

The average size of households has continued to fall progressively, from over four persons in 1911 to 3·1 in 1961 and 2·7 in 1977 and 1978 largely reflecting increases in the numbers of people living alone and the trend towards smaller families. It is estimated that in 1978 22 per cent of households in Great Britain consisted of one person only, 31 per cent of two, 17 per cent of three, 18 per cent of four and 12 per cent of five or more. The number of one-parent families has been increasing rapidly.

Three British households out of four live in houses rather than flats. Terraced housing, most of it built in the early years of the present century, still provides accommodation for over a quarter of all households. In inner urban areas, which have increasing priority in the Government's housing and planning policies, slum clearance and redevelopment have been major features of post-1945 public housing programmes, but, with help from public funds, the modernisation and conversion of sub-standard housing has increasingly been encouraged as an alternative to clearing and rebuilding. Emphasis in new building is on low-rise, high density layouts, often incorporating gardens or patios. Nearly half of Britain's housing stock has been built since 1945.

The main housing development of the past 50 to 60 years, however, has been suburban. Many families now live in houses grouped in small terraces, or semi-detached or detached, usually of two storeys with gardens, and providing two main ground-floor living rooms, a kitchen, from two to four bedrooms, a bathroom, and one or two lavatories. Many such houses, built in the 1920s and 1930s, are located in 'ribbon development' along main roads, but recent patterns have involved housing estates set back from the main thoroughfares with amenities such as health and community centres.

Housing standards are continually improving; some 94 per cent of households in Great Britain have exclusive use of a bath or shower, and 94 per cent sole use of an inside lavatory—high percentages by international standards. Most housing built nowadays is centrally heated, and just over half of all households now have central heating. About 57 per cent of British households have a telephone, 57 per cent one or more cars, 91 per cent a refrigerator, 75 per cent a washing machine, 32 per cent a deep freeze and 3 per cent a dish washer.

Over half of all families now own their own homes, though more than half of these home owners still have further repayments of mortgages to make. Most of the other households rent an unfurnished house or flat either from a local authority or housing association (an increasing trend) or from a private landlord (a falling trend). People in unskilled manual jobs are more likely to live in rented accommodation, particularly local authority housing, than people in non-manual occupations. One-third of all families move house every five years.

An important influence on the planning of housing and services has been the growth of car ownership. Greater access to motorised transport and the construction of a network of modern trunk roads and motorways have resulted in a considerable increase in personal mobility and changed leisure patterns, as well as changes in the design of housing and shopping areas. Most detached or semi-detached houses in new suburban estates have garages, and out-of-town shopping centres, frequently including large supermarkets, are often specially planned for the motorist and offer an alternative to shopping in the centres of older towns. The 32 new towns and the 'expanding towns' (generally seen as one of the most successful achievements of British planning since 1945) have set high standards in accommodating people and traffic.

The growth in car ownership has brought very great benefits but also a number of problems, notably, in many towns and cities, increased congestion, noise and air pollution. Public transport, too, has been affected, and many services have been reduced or eliminated, especially in rural areas. The people without access to a car include those among the poorer sections of the community, or the elderly or infirm; mobility allowances help the disabled. Restrictions on bus licensing are being relaxed in order to make it easier for new services to develop, and the Government is encouraging car-sharing on journeys such as those to work. In a densely populated modern industrial society there is much scope for conflict between the need for communal facilities and the desire to preserve existing beauty or places of historic interest, and between potential users of a new service and people whose way of life is threatened by the need to accommodate it. As a result the activities of the established amenity societies, such as the National Trust and the Council for the Protection of Rural England, are supplemented to a growing extent by those of groups formed expressly to safeguard the amenities of a particular area and to publicise the views of the people they represent.

There has been a steady reduction of the main atmospheric and fresh water pollutants that have been of concern in the past, producing dramatic improvements in, for example, the quality of the air in cities and the condition of the river Thames. Long-established problems have not yet been entirely eliminated, however, and controls are still necessary. There is also general recognition of the need for more research into and monitoring of newer problems, such as pollution from traffic, which are more difficult to control. Advice is provided by the standing Royal Commission on Environmental Pollution and the Noise Advisory Council. Voluntary societies include the National Society for Clean Air, the Noise Abatement Society, the Keep Britain Tidy Group, Friends of the Earth, and the Council for Nature.

The Economic and Social Pattern

Marked improvements in the standard of living have taken place during the twentieth century. Nonetheless considerable inequalities of income and wealth, among them regional disparities, remain. The gap between social classes in such matters as infant mortality rates, educational progress, working conditions and ill-health remains wide and is increased by high unemployment such as that accompanying the economic recession in the industrialised world which began in 1979. There has, however, been a long-term tendency to a reduction in the proportion of semi-skilled and unskilled workers, and an increasing number of people in professional or managerial occupations are children of manual workers. One study showed that in each year between 1961 and 1978, in every 100 jobs, one manual job was supplanted by more highly paid work.

The working population comprises nearly half the total population. For a long period an increase in real earnings was a principal factor in British working and social life. Between 1950 and 1974 real personal disposable income[1] more than doubled to £74,916 million (1975 prices). It fell in 1975, steadied in 1976 and fell again in 1977 but rose in 1978 and again in 1979 to £82,289 million.

The difference between average earnings of men in different occupations has become less in the course of the present century. Income before tax of the self-employed is more unevenly distributed than total income, largely because of the very large incomes of a small number of people, mainly professionals such as lawyers, accountants and some doctors. In the last 30 years, there has been little change in the distribution of pre-tax income between the top and bottom halves of the population. Successive falls in the share received by the top 10 per cent have been retained largely in the upper half of the distribution. Since 1949 the share received by the top 10 per cent fell from 33·2 per cent of total pre-tax income to 26·2 per cent in 1977–78. The combined effect of the tax system and the receipt of transfer payments and direct and indirect benefits in kind is to redistribute incomes on a more equal basis.

There is very little knowledge about long-term trends in the distribution of wealth, but such estimates as there are show a substantial fall in the share owned by the richest people in the community. In 1976 about 25 per cent of personal wealth was owned by the top 1 per cent of the adult population (compared with over 30 per cent in 1966 and about 60 per cent in 1923). Between 1966 and 1976 the share owned by the lowest 90 per cent increased from 32 per cent to 40 per cent. The inclusion of state and occupational pensions as a form of wealth lowers the share of the top 1 per cent by nearly a half and nearly doubles the share of the bottom 80 per cent. The proportion of personal wealth held in the form of physical assets rose from less than a third in 1960 to just under 50 per cent in 1976, reflecting especially the increasing importance of dwellings. There has been a marked decline in the relative importance of company securities in the composition of personal wealth.

---

[1] Total personal income less taxes on income, national insurance contributions, transfers abroad (net) and taxes paid abroad, adjusted to take account of inflation.

The volume of consumer spending in Britain, after allowing for inflation, decreased in 1977 but rose in 1978 and again in 1979. Over the period 1970–79 there were some significant changes in the pattern of expenditure. The shares spent on food, clothing and footwear and tobacco fell while those spent on housing and on alcoholic drink, particularly wines and spirits, increased substantially. A large increase in spending on radio and electrical goods was mainly due to people buying music centres and other audio equipment, colour televisions (well over half the television licences are issued for colour), and more recently, video tape recorders. Expenditure on television rental, too, more than doubled, while that on admission to cinemas, theatres, spectator sports and the like increased by more than 38 per cent in real terms.

Some 12·5 million visitors to Britain in 1979 spent a total of £2,764 million. More overseas visits than ever before were made by British residents, 15·5 million, 15 per cent higher than in 1978. Visits for holidays were the main reason for this, undoubtedly helped by large reductions in some air fares; visits for other reasons also increased but not as substantially. Following the pattern of recent years, overseas visitors to Britain spent at a higher average rate per visit than did British residents visiting overseas.

The general level of nutrition is high. The movement towards a greater use of convenience (including frozen) foods, and imported foods, in the 1960s has been partly offset by a reversion to a slightly less expensive diet. Other trends include the continuing popularity of health foods and slimming products, an increase in the number of meals eaten away from home, either at work or in restaurants, and a growth in consumption of food from 'take-away' and 'fast food' shops. The last 20 years or so have seen a gradual decline in total food supplies per person, which is regarded as consistent with reductions in physical activity and the greater proportion of less active people in the population. The trend is common to most developed countries.

Over the period 1968–78 total estimated consumption of beer (Britain's most popular alcoholic drink) rose by more than 25 per cent a head; that of wine by 55 per cent (consumption of wine has, however, fallen by nearly 12 per cent since 1976); and that of spirits by 93 per cent. A notable development in the 1970s was the large increase in consumption of lager, now estimated to account for a quarter of the beer consumed.

The Role of Women

The greatest social changes have probably been in the economic and domestic lives of women. Almost all theoretical sex discrimination in political and legal rights has been removed.

The changes have been significant but, because tradition and prejudice can still handicap women in their working careers and personal lives, major legislation to help to promote equality of opportunity and pay was passed during the 1970s.

At the heart of women's changed role in society has been the rise in the number of women at work, particularly married women. As technology and society permit highly effective and generally acceptable methods of family planning there has been a decline in family size. Women as a result are involved in child-bearing for a much shorter time and, related to this, there has been a rapid increase, which is still continuing, in the number of women with young children who return to work when their children are old enough not to need constant care and attention.

Since 1951 the proportion of married women who work has grown considerably, to more than half of those under 45 and three-fifths of those between 45 and 60. The proportion of the total workforce accounted for by married women increased from 4 per cent in 1921 to an estimated 27 per cent in 1979. Compared with their counterparts elsewhere in the European Community, British women comprise a relatively high proportion of the workforce, about two-fifths (only Denmark has a comparable percentage). There is still a significant difference between women's average earnings and men's, but the equal pay legislation which came into force at the end of 1975 appears to have helped to narrow the gap between women's and men's basic rates. During the 1970s women's wages rose proportionately more than men's but remain relatively low because women tend to work in lowly-paid sectors of the economy, they often work in predominantly female workforces, and they work less overtime than men.

Women's average hourly earnings, exclusive of overtime (for full-time employees), increased from just under two-thirds of those of men in 1970, to about three-quarters in 1980.

As more and more women joined the workforce in the 1960s and early 1970s there was an increase in the collective incomes of women as a whole and a major change in the economic role of large numbers of housewives. Families have come to rely on married women's earnings as an essential part of their income rather than as 'pocket money' or a means of buying 'extras'. At the same time social roles within the family are increasingly being shared.

Ethnic and
National
Minorities

Britain has a long history of accommodating minority groups and in the last hundred years or so a variety of people have settled in the country, some to avoid political or religious persecution, others seeking a better way of life and an escape from poverty.

Many Irishmen have made homes in Britain, and comprise the largest single minority group. Many Jewish refugees started a new life in the country towards the end of the nineteenth century and in the 1930s, and after 1945 large numbers of other European refugees, Poles in particular, also came to settle. The large communities from the West Indies and the Indian sub-continent date from the 1950s and the early 1960s. There are also sizeable groups of Americans, Australians, Chinese and various European communities such as Greek and Turkish Cypriots, Italians and Spaniards. Most recently, refugees from Indo-China have found new homes in Britain. In the last generation British society has therefore become more multi-racial as ethnic minority groups from almost all parts of the world have made a permanent home in the country. Although a small proportion of the total population, they represent a significant element in certain areas.

The minority communities tend to live mainly in the urban centres, especially the largest towns, and in particular areas within these centres. The most recent immigrants, such as the West Indians and the Asians, are usually concentrated in the poorer inner city areas, whereas earlier arrivals have tended to move out to the suburbs.

Most minorities share a way of life that is broadly similar to that of the British community as a whole, though some of the newer arrivals, mainly from Commonwealth countries and sometimes with a poor command of the English language, may face problems of limited employment opportunities and inadequate housing. Many have, however, opened small family businesses such as general stores and restaurants which widen the range of choice and services for local communities. In areas with large and fairly recently-arrived immigrant populations arrangements are made in schools and elsewhere to enable host and minority communities to understand each other's traditions better and to help immigrants who need special language training.

Leisure Trends　Most people have considerably more free time, more ways in which to spend it and higher real incomes than had previous generations. Agreed hours of full-time work are usually from 35 to 40 hours a week, although many people actually work somewhat longer (about 45 on average for manual workers) because of voluntary overtime work, while the hours worked by women and girls average somewhat less. Most employees work a five-day week.

Almost all full-time employees are entitled to a paid holiday each year in addition to public holidays and in practically every case the minimum period is three weeks.

The number of holidays (of four or more nights) taken in Great Britain by British residents was 44 million in 1979 compared with 31 million in 1966. More than two holidays in five in Great Britain are spent at the home of a friend or relative, and a quarter involve camping or caravanning. Holidays abroad in 1979 numbered 9·9 million, compared with 5·5 million in 1966, and well over half involved 'package' arrangements. Spain is by far the most popular destination, and receives well over a quarter of all British holiday-makers abroad. A third of the population each year, however, takes no holiday away from home.

Leisure patterns generally are determined by age, sex, social class, income, access to a car and education. The most common activities are home based, or social, with television-watching the most popular; about 98 per cent of households have a television set and in winter the population aged five and over spend on average 20 hours a week watching programmes.

Other popular pursuits include: listening to the radio, records or tapes; reading; do-it-yourself (DIY; work done by amateur handy-men such as painting and decorating their homes); photography, needlework and many other hobbies; going out for a meal or for a drink to a public house (the 'pub' or 'local' is a traditional social centre for many people); gardening (a majority of British families have some garden or allotment despite the high proportion living in urban areas); open-air outings; games and sports (as both spectators and participants); dancing; going to social clubs[1] and leisure centres; cinema going (especially among young people); visits to buildings and museums; and social and voluntary work. The social activity with perhaps the largest participation is the visiting or entertaining of friends or relatives.

---

[1] These include clubs run by political groups; trade unions; church groups; social, cultural and academic groups; youth clubs and organisations; and groups of local business and professional people. The longer-established clubs organised on a national basis include the Working Men's Clubs and Institutes, the Townswomen's Guilds and the Women's Institutes.

2 Government

GENERAL SURVEY

The origins and traditions of the United Kingdom are to be found in each of its four component parts: England, Wales, Scotland and Northern Ireland. England was united as a kingdom a thousand years ago, and Wales formally became part of the kingdom in 1536. The thrones of England and Scotland were dynastically united in 1603, and in 1707 legislation passed in the two countries provided for the establishment of a single Parliament of Great Britain with supreme authority both in England and Wales and in Scotland. Ireland had had links with the kingdom of England since the thirteenth century, and in 1800 the creation of the United Kingdom was completed by a union joining the Irish Parliament to that of Great Britain. In 1922 Southern Ireland (now the Irish Republic) became a self-governing country. The six counties of Northern Ireland had in 1920 been given their own subordinate Parliament, and voted to remain within the United Kingdom.(Arrangements in Northern Ireland, where divisions between the Protestant majority and the Roman Catholic minority, deeply-rooted in history, are still an important factor, are described on p 54.)

The United Kingdom Parliament at Westminster in London—with an elected chamber comprising members from English, Scottish, Welsh and Northern Ireland constituencies—therefore represents people whose back-grounds and traditions vary considerably from one part of the country to another. It has ultimate authority for government and law-making, but administrative arrangements have developed in such a way as to take account of the particular needs of different areas.

Referenda under the Scotland and Wales Acts were held in 1979 to assess support for the elected assemblies with devolved powers which were to have been set up in Edinburgh and Cardiff. The results showed insufficient support (less than 40 per cent), and so the Acts were repealed.

Subsequently, ways are being considered by which the parliamentary administration of Scotland might be improved. The Government is holding talks with other political parties to find the best means of doing this.

Channel Islands and Isle of Man
The Channel Islands and the Isle of Man (which are Crown dependencies, and not part of the United Kingdom) have their own legislative assemblies and systems of local administration and of law, and their own courts. At the same time, they have a special relationship with the United Kingdom because of the antiquity of their connection with the Crown. The United Kingdom Government is responsible for their defence, their international relations and, ulti-mately, their good government. They have separate arrangements with the European Community which take into account their special relationship with the United Kingdom.

The Constitution
The United Kingdom constitution is formed partly by statute, partly by common law and partly by conventions, which have never been codified and are not directly enforceable in a court of law, but which, nevertheless, are regarded as rules of the constitution. Because the constitution is not contained

in any single document, and because it can be altered by the passing of an Act of Parliament or by general agreement to vary, abolish or create a convention, it can the more readily be adapted to changing political conditions and ideas.

The organs of government are readily distinguishable although their functions often intermingle and overlap. They are:

1. the legislature, the supreme authority in the realm (see p 24);
2. the executive, which consists of: (a) the Government—that is the Cabinet and other ministers of the Crown, who are responsible for initiating and directing national policy (see p 36); (b) government departments, most of them under the direct control of ministers and all staffed by civil servants, which are responsible for administration at the national level (see p 40); (c) local authorities, which administer and manage many services at the local level (see p 60); and (d) public corporations which may be responsible for the operation of particular nationalised industries or, for example, of a social or cultural service, and which are subject to ministerial control in varying degrees; and
3. the judiciary, which determines common law and interprets statutes, and is independent of both the legislature and the executive.

THE MONARCHY

The monarchy is the most ancient secular institution in the United Kingdom. Its continuity has been broken only once in over a thousand years; and, in spite of interruptions in the direct line of succession, the hereditary principle upon which it was founded has never been abandoned. The royal title in the United Kingdom is: 'Elizabeth the Second, by the Grace of God of the United Kingdom of Great Britain and Northern Ireland and of Her other Realms and Territories Queen, Head of the Commonwealth, Defender of the Faith'. The form of the royal title is varied for those other member States of the Commonwealth of which the Queen is head of State,[1] to suit the particular circumstances of each. (For a full list of members of the Commonwealth see p 77.)

The seat of the monarchy is in the United Kingdom. In the Channel Islands and the Isle of Man the Queen is represented by a Lieutenant-Governor. In the other member nations of the Commonwealth of which the Queen is head of State, her representative is the Governor-General, who is appointed by her on the advice of the ministers of the country concerned and is wholly independent of the United Kingdom Government. In the United Kingdom dependencies the Queen is usually represented by governors appointed by the Crown, with various executive and legislative powers, and responsible to the United Kingdom Government for the good government of the countries concerned.

Succession, Accession and Coronation

The title to the Crown derives partly from statute and partly from common law rules of descent. Lineal Protestant descendants of Princess Sophia (the Electress of Hanover, grand-daughter of James I of England and VI of Scotland) are alone eligible to succeed, and although succession is not bound to continue in its present line, it cannot now be altered other than by common consent of the member nations of the Commonwealth of which the Queen is head of State.

---

[1] The other Commonwealth countries of which the Queen is head of State are: Australia, Bahamas, Barbados, Canada, Fiji, Grenada, Jamaica, Mauritius, New Zealand, Papua New Guinea, Solomon Islands, Saint Lucia, Saint Vincent and the Grenadines, and Tuvalu.

Rules of descent provide that the sons of the Sovereign are in order of succession to the throne according to their seniority; if there are no sons, the daughters succeed in order of their seniority. When a daughter succeeds, she becomes Queen-Regnant and the powers of the Crown are vested in her as fully and effectively as though she were a king. By convention, the consort of a king takes the rank and style of her husband; the converse, however, does not apply and the constitution has never attached any special rank or privileges to the husband of the Queen-Regnant although in practice he fills an important role in the life of the nation.

There is no interregnum between the death of one Sovereign and the accession of another. Immediately on the death of his or her predecessor the new Sovereign is proclaimed at an Accession Council to which all members of the Privy Council are summoned. The Lords Spiritual and Temporal, the Lord Mayor, aldermen and other leading citizens of the City of London, and the High Commissioners in London of the member nations of the Commonwealth are also invited to attend.

The coronation of the Sovereign, by the Archbishop of Canterbury, follows the accession after an interval of possibly a year or more. The ceremony has remained much the same in substance for over a thousand years although the details have frequently been modified to conform with the customs of the time. The coronation service is held at Westminster Abbey in the presence of representatives of the Lords, the Commons and all the great public interests in the United Kingdom, of the Prime Ministers and leading citizens of the other Commonwealth countries and of representatives of foreign States.

Acts of Government

The Queen is the personification of the State. In law, she is the head of the executive, an integral part of the legislature, the head of the judiciary, the commander-in-chief of all the armed forces of the Crown and the temporal 'governor' of the established Church of England. In practice, as a result of a long evolutionary process during which the absolute power of the monarchy has been progressively reduced, the Queen acts on the advice of her ministers which she cannot constitutionally ignore. The United Kingdom is governed by Her Majesty's Government in the name of the Queen.

Within this framework, and in spite of a trend during the past hundred years towards assigning powers directly to ministers without any necessity for royal intervention, there are still important acts of government which require the participation of the Queen. These include the summoning, prorogation and dissolution of Parliament; giving royal assent to Bills passed by both Houses of Parliament; making appointments to all important State offices, including those of government ministers, judges, officers in the armed forces, governors, diplomats and all the leading positions in the established Church of England; conferring peerages, knighthoods and other honours[1]; and remitting all or part of the penalty imposed on a person convicted of a crime. An important function is the appointment of the Prime Minister. This is normally automatic, and the Queen must invite the leader of the political party commanding a majority in the House of Commons to form a government. If, however, no party has a majority, or if the majority party has no recognised leader, the Queen must select a Prime Minister, and can consult anyone she wishes. In international

---

[1] Although most honours are conferred by the Queen on the advice of the Prime Minister, a few are conferred on her personal selection—the Order of the Garter, the Order of the Thistle, the Order of Merit and the Royal Victorian Order.

The Royal Family

From the reign of Queen Victoria up to September 1980

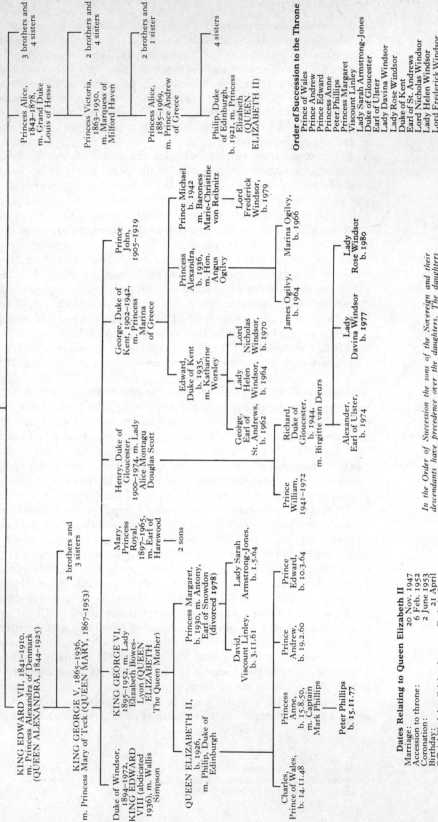

QUEEN VICTORIA, 1819–1901,
m. Prince Albert of Saxe-Coburg and Gotha (Prince Consort)

KING EDWARD VII, 1841–1910,
m. Princess Alexandra of Denmark
(QUEEN ALEXANDRA, 1844–1925)

KING GEORGE V, 1865–1936,
m. Princess Mary of Teck (QUEEN MARY, 1867–1953)

2 brothers and 3 sisters

Duke of Windsor, 1894–1972, KING EDWARD VIII (abdicated 1936), m. Wallis Simpson

KING GEORGE VI, 1895–1952, m. Lady Elizabeth Bowes-Lyon (QUEEN ELIZABETH 'The Queen Mother')

Mary, Princess Royal, 1897–1965, m. Earl of Harewood

2 sons

Henry, Duke of Gloucester, 1900–1974, m. Lady Alice Montagu Douglas Scott

George, Duke of Kent, 1902–1942, m. Princess Marina of Greece

Prince John, 1905–1919

QUEEN ELIZABETH II, b. 1926, m. Philip, Duke of Edinburgh

Princess Margaret, b. 1930, m. Antony, Earl of Snowdon (divorced 1978)

Prince William, 1941–1972

Richard, Duke of Gloucester, b. 1944, m. Birgitte van Deurs

Edward, Duke of Kent, b. 1935, m. Katharine Worsley

Princess Alexandra, b. 1936, m. Hon. Angus Ogilvy

Prince Michael b. 1942 m. Baroness Marie-Christine von Reibnitz

Charles, Prince of Wales, b. 14.11.48

Princess Anne, b. 15.8.50, m. Captain Mark Phillips

Prince Andrew, b. 19.2.60

Prince Edward, b. 10.3.64

David, Viscount Linley, b. 3.11.61

Lady Sarah Armstrong-Jones, b. 1.5.64

Alexander, Earl of Ulster, b. 1974

Lady Davina Windsor b. 1977

George, Earl of St. Andrews, b. 1962

Lady Helen Windsor, b. 1964

Lord Nicholas Windsor, b. 1970

James Ogilvy, b. 1964

Marina Ogilvy, b. 1966

Lord Frederick Windsor, b. 1979

Lady Rose Windsor b. 1980

Peter Phillips b. 15.11.77

Princess Alice, 1843–1878, m. Grand Duke Louis of Hesse

3 brothers and 4 sisters

Princess Victoria, 1863–1950, m. Marquess of Milford Haven

2 brothers and 4 sisters

Princess Alice, 1885–1969, m. Prince Andrew of Greece

2 brothers and 1 sister

Philip, Duke of Edinburgh, b. 1921, m. Princess Elizabeth (QUEEN ELIZABETH II)

4 sisters

Order of Succession to the Throne
Prince of Wales
Prince Andrew
Prince Edward
Princess Anne
Peter Phillips
Princess Margaret
Viscount Linley
Lady Sarah Armstrong-Jones
Duke of Gloucester
Earl of Ulster
Lady Davina Windsor
Lady Rose Windsor
Duke of Kent
Earl of St. Andrews
Lord Nicholas Windsor
Lady Helen Windsor
Lord Frederick Windsor
Princess Alexandra

In the Order of Succession the sons of the Sovereign and their descendants have precedence over the daughters. The daughters and their descendants have precedence over lateral lines.

Dates Relating to Queen Elizabeth II

Marriage:	20 Nov. 1947
Accession to throne:	6 Feb. 1952
Coronation:	2 June 1953
Birthday:	21 April
Official Birthday Celebration:	Early in June

affairs, the Queen as head of State has the power to declare war and make peace, to recognise foreign States and governments, to conclude treaties and to annexe or cede territory.

With rare exceptions (such as in the appointment of the Prime Minister) these and other acts involving the use of 'royal prerogative' powers are nowadays exercised by government ministers who are responsible to Parliament and can be questioned about a particular policy. The law does not require Parliament's prior authority before such powers can be exercised, but Parliament has the power to pass legislation to restrict or abolish a prerogative right.

Ministerial responsibility for the exercise of powers by the Crown does not, however, detract from the importance of the Queen's participation in the smooth working of government. She holds meetings of the Privy Council, gives audiences to her ministers and other holders of office at home and overseas, receives accounts of Cabinet decisions, reads dispatches and signs innumerable State papers; she must be informed and consulted on every aspect of the national life; and she must show complete impartiality.

Such is the significance attached to these royal functions that provision has been made for a regent to be appointed to fulfil them if the Sovereign is totally incapacitated (or is under the age of 18 years on accession to the throne). The regent would be the Queen's eldest son, the Prince of Wales, and thereafter those in succession to the throne who are of age. In the event of the Sovereign's partial incapacity or absence abroad, provision is made for the appointment of Counsellors of State (the Duke of Edinburgh, the four adult persons next in succession to the Crown, and the Queen Mother) to whom the Sovereign may delegate certain royal functions. Counsellors of State may not, however, dissolve Parliament (except on the express instructions of the Sovereign), or create peers.

Ceremonial and Royal Visits

Ceremonial has always been associated with British kings and queens, and, in spite of the changes that have taken place in the outlook of both the Sovereign and the people, many traditional customs and usages remain. Royal marriages and royal funerals are marked by public ceremony. The birthday of the Sovereign is officially celebrated early in June by Trooping the Colour on the Horse Guards Parade and is also celebrated as Commonwealth Day. State banquets take place when a foreign monarch or head of State visits the United Kingdom; investitures are held at Buckingham Palace; and royal processions add significance to such occasions as the opening of Parliament, when the Queen drives in state from Buckingham Palace. The Queen and other members of the royal family visit many parts of the United Kingdom every year, and their presence at scientific, artistic, industrial and charitable events of national importance encourages nationwide interest and publicity. The Queen pays State visits to foreign governments, accompanied by the Duke of Edinburgh, and undertakes lengthy tours in other countries of the Commonwealth. Other members of the royal family pay official visits overseas.

Royal Income and Expenditure

More than three-quarters of all expenditure arising from the official duties of the royal family is borne on the accounts of public departments—including, for example, the costs of the royal yacht, the Queen's Flight, travel by train and the upkeep of the royal palaces. Apart from this the Queen's public expenditure on staff and expenses incurred in carrying out offical duties as head of State is financed from the Civil List, approved by Parliament. Her private expenditure as Sovereign is met from the Privy Purse, which is supplied mainly from the revenues of the Duchy of Lancaster[1]; and her personal expenditure as a private individual from her own personal resources. Annual allowances approved by Parliament are made to certain other members of the royal family. No allowances are made to the Prince of Wales, who as Duke of Cornwall is entitled to the net revenue of the estate of the Duchy of Cornwall (he has voluntarily surrendered half the revenue to the nation). The Queen meets from her Privy Purse the official expenses of members of the royal family for whom Parliament has not provided.

PARLIAMENT

Parliament is the supreme legislative authority in the United Kingdom. The three elements of Parliament, the Queen, the House of Lords and the elected House of Commons, are outwardly separate; they are constituted on different principles; and they meet together only on occasions of symbolic significance such as the State opening of Parliament when the Commons are summoned by the Queen to the House of Lords. As a law-making organ of State, however, Parliament as a rule needs the concurrence of all its parts.

The Parliament at Westminster can legislate for the United Kingdom as a whole, for any of the constituent parts of the country separately, or for any combination of them. It can also legislate for the Channel Islands and the Isle of Man, which are Crown dependencies and not part of the United Kingdom, having subordinate legislatures which make laws on island affairs.[2]

Because it is not subject to the type of legal restraints imposed on the legislatures of countries with formal written constitutions, Parliament is free to legislate as it pleases: generally to make, unmake, or alter any law; to legalise past illegalities and make void and punishable what was lawful when done and thus reverse the decisions of the ordinary courts; and to destroy established conventions or turn a convention into binding law. It can prolong its own life beyond the normal period without consulting the electorate.

In practice, however, Parliament does not assert its supremacy in this way. Its members bear in mind the common law and have tended to act in accordance with precedent and tradition. Moreover, although the validity of an Act of Parliament that has been duly passed, legally promulgated and published by the proper authority cannot be disputed in the law courts, no Parliament would be likely to pass an Act which it knew would receive no public support. The system of party government helps to ensure that Parliament legislates with its responsibility to the electorate in mind.

As a member of the European Community, the United Kingdom recognises the various types of Community legislation, and sends 81 elected members to the European Parliament (see p 74).

The Functions of Parliament   The main functions of Parliament are (1) to pass laws regulating the life of the community, (2) to provide, by voting taxation, the means of carrying on the work of government; and (3) to scrutinise government policy and administra-

---

[1] The Duchy of Lancaster is an inheritance which, since 1399, has always been enjoyed by the reigning Sovereign; it is kept quite apart from his or her other possessions and is separately administered by the Chancellor of the Duchy.

[2] The legislatures of the Channel Islands (the States of Jersey and the States of Guernsey) and the Isle of Man (the Tynwald Court) consist of the Queen, the Privy Council and the local assemblies. It is the duty of the Home Secretary, as the member of the Privy Council primarily concerned with island affairs, to scrutinise each legislative measure before it is submitted to the Queen in Council.

tion, particularly proposals for expenditure. In discharging these three functions Parliament helps to bring the relevant facts and issues before the electorate. By custom, Parliament is also consulted before the ratification of all important international treaties and agreements, the making of treaties being, in theory at least, a royal prerogative exercised on the advice of the Government and not subject to parliamentary approval.

The Meeting of Parliament

A Parliament has a maximum duration of five years, but is often dissolved and a general election held before the end of this term. The maximum life has been prolonged by legislation in such rare circumstances as the two world wars. Dissolution is ordered by the Queen on the advice of the Prime Minister. A royal proclamation dissolves the existing Parliament, orders the issue of writs for an election, and announces the date on which the new Parliament is to meet (not less than 20 days after the dissolution).

The life of a Parliament is divided into sessions. Each usually lasts for one year—beginning and ending most often in October or November and interspersed with 'adjournments' at night, at weekends, at Christmas, Easter and the late (English) Spring Bank Holiday and during a long summer recess starting in late July or early August. The average number of 'sitting' days in a session is about 175 in the House of Commons and about 140 in the House of Lords. At the start of each session the Queen's speech to both Houses of Parliament outlines the Government's broad policies and proposed legislative programme. Each session is terminated by prorogation, a prerogative act which appoints the day of meeting in a new session. Parliament then 'stands prorogued' until the new session opens (on rare occasions Parliament has been dissolved without prorogation). A short speech is made on behalf of the Queen summarising Parliament's work during the past session. Whereas an adjournment does not affect uncompleted business, the effect of a prorogation is at once to terminate nearly all parliamentary business, so that all public Bills not completed in the session lapse, and must be reintroduced in the next unless they are to be abandoned.

The House of Lords

The House of Lords consists of the Lords Spiritual and the Lords Temporal. The Lords Spiritual are the Archbishops of Canterbury and York, the Bishops of London, Durham and Winchester, and 21 other bishops of the Church of England, according to their seniority as diocesan bishops. The Lords Temporal consist of (1) all hereditary peers and peeresses of England, Scotland, Great Britain and the United Kingdom who have not disclaimed their peerages under the Peerage Act 1963, (2) all life peers and peeresses created by the Crown under the Life Peerages Act 1958, and (3) those Lords of Appeal ('law lords') created life peers under the Appellate Jurisdiction Acts 1876 and 1887 (as amended) who are appointed to assist the House in its judicial duties. Hereditary peerages carry with them a right to sit in the House of Lords (subject to certain statutory disqualifications), provided the holder is 21 years of age or over, but anyone succeeding to a peerage may, within 12 months of succession, disclaim that peerage for his or her lifetime. Disclaimants lose their right to sit in the House of Lords but they gain the right to vote at parliamentary elections and to offer themselves for election to the House of Commons. Eighteen peers have so far disclaimed. No hereditary peerage has been conferred since 1965.

Not all peers with a right to sit in the House of Lords attend the sittings. Those who do not wish to attend may apply for leave of absence for the duration of a Parliament.

Peers who frequently attend the House of Lords (the average daily attendance is about 290) include elder statesmen and others who have spent their lives in public service. Lords receive no salary for their parliamentary work, but are entitled to recover expenses incurred in attending the House (except for judicial sittings) and certain travelling expenses.

The House of Lords is presided over by the Lord Chancellor, who takes his place on the woolsack as *ex officio* Speaker of the House. When the Lord Chancellor is absent, his place may be taken by a deputy speaker appointed by the Crown or a deputy chairman appointed by the House or, if neither a deputy speaker nor a deputy chairman is present, by a speaker chosen by the Lords present. The first of the deputy speakers is the Lord Chairman of Committees, who is appointed at the beginning of each session and takes the chair in all committees, unless the House decides otherwise. The Lord Chairman and the Principal Deputy Chairman of Committees are salaried officers of the House.

The permanent officers include the Clerk of the Parliaments, who is responsible for the records of proceedings including judgments and for the promulgation of Acts of Parliament; the other Clerks at the Table who with him and the other officers and officials of the House are collectively known as the Parliament Office; the Gentleman Usher of the Black Rod, who is also Serjeant-at-Arms in attendance upon the Lord Chancellor and who is responsible for security and for accommodation and services in the House of Lords' part of the Palace of Westminster, and the Yeoman Usher who is Deputy Serjeant-at-Arms and assists Black Rod in his duties.

The House of Commons

The House of Commons is a representative assembly elected by universal adult suffrage and consists of men and women (members of Parliament, 'MPs') from all sections of the community. There are 635 seats in the House of Commons (516 for England, 36 for Wales, 71 for Scotland, and 12 for Northern Ireland[1]).

General elections are held after a Parliament has been dissolved and a new one summoned by the Queen. If a vacancy occurs in the House as a result of the death or resignation[2] of an MP, or as a result of his elevation to the House of Lords, a by-election takes place. Members are paid an annual salary of £11,750 (to be increased to £13,150 in 1981) and an allowance for secretarial and research expenses. They also have a number of other allowances, including travel allowances, a supplement for London members and, for provincial members, subsistence allowances. (For ministers' salaries, see p 38.)

The chief officer of the House of Commons is the Speaker, who is elected by the members to preside over the House. Other parliamentary officers of the House are the Chairman of Ways and Means, and two deputy chairmen who act as Deputy Speakers; these officers are elected by the House on the nomination of the Government and, like the speaker, neither speak nor vote other than in their official capacity. The House is administered by a statutory Commission chaired by the Speaker.

Permanent officers of the House (that is, those who are not members of Parliament) include the Clerk of the House of Commons, who conducts the business of the House in the official department under his control and is the

---

[1] Under the House of Commons (Redistribution of Seats) Act 1979 the number of parliamentary constituencies in Northern Ireland is being increased from 12 to 17.
[2] An MP who wishes to resign from the House can do so only by using the technical device of applying for an office under the Crown (Bailiff of the Chiltern Hundreds or Steward of the Manor of Northstead), ancient offices which disqualify the holder from membership of the House but which carry no salary and have no responsibilities.

accounting officer for the two House of Commons Estimates, and the Serjeant-at-Arms, who waits upon the Speaker, carries out the orders of the House, is the official housekeeper of the Commons part of the building, and is responsible for its security.

Parliamentary Electoral System

For electoral purposes the United Kingdom is divided into geographical areas known as constituencies, each of which returns one member to the House of Commons. To ensure equitable representation, four permanent Boundary Commissions for England, Wales, Scotland and Northern Ireland make periodic reviews of constituencies and recommend any redistribution of seats that may seem necessary in the light of population movements or for some other reason.

Election to the House of Commons is decided by secret ballot. British subjects (including Commonwealth citizens) and citizens of the Irish Republic are entitled to vote provided they are aged 18 years or over, are resident in the United Kingdom, are registered in the annual register of electors, and are not subject to any disqualification. People not entitled to vote in a parliamentary election are members of the House of Lords, sentenced prisoners and those convicted within the previous five years of corrupt or illegal election practices. Service voters (that is, members of the armed forces and their spouses, Crown servants and staff of the British Council employed overseas, together with their wives and husbands if accompanying them) may also be registered for an address in a constituency, if they normally live there.

Each elector may cast one vote. Normally this is done in person at a polling station. Service voters resident abroad or merchant seamen may vote by proxy or, if in the United Kingdom at the time of the election, by post. Electors who are physically incapacitated or unable to vote in person, because of the nature of their employment, are also entitled to vote by post.

Voting is not compulsory; nearly 76 per cent of a total electorate of almost 41 million people voted in the general election of May 1979. The candidate who polls the most votes in a constituency is elected; an absolute majority (that is, more votes than those cast for all other candidates combined) is not required.

British subjects and citizens of the Irish Republic are entitled to stand and be elected as members of Parliament provided they are aged 21 years or over and are not subject to any disqualification. Those disqualified include, among others, undischarged bankrupts, clergy of the Church of England, Church of Scotland, Church of Ireland and Roman Catholic Church, peers, and certain people holding offices of profit under the Crown. The House of Commons Disqualification Act 1975 defines those who may not become members of Parliament. They include holders of judicial office, civil servants and some local government officers, members of the regular armed forces, members of the police forces and some members of public corporations and government commissions. A candidate's nomination for election must be supported by the signatures of a nominator, a seconder and eight assentors registered in the constituency. He or she does not require any party backing. A candidate is also required to deposit the sum of £150, which is forfeited if the candidate's votes do not exceed 12·5 per cent of the total of those validly cast in the election.

The maximum sum of money a candidate may spend on an election campaign is £1,750, plus 1½ pence for each elector in a borough constituency or 2 pence for each elector in a county constituency. A candidate may send free of postal charges an election address to each elector in the constituency. All other expenses of up to £100 must not exceed the statutory limit.

**The Party
System**

The party system, existing in one form or another since the seventeenth century, is an essential element in the working of the constitution.

The present system relies heavily upon the existence of organised political parties, each laying its own policies before the electorate. These parties are not registered or formally recognised in law, but in practice most candidates in constituency elections, and almost all winning candidates, belong to one of the main political parties, and the electorate indicates which of the different policies it would like to see put into effect.

The percentages of votes cast for the main political parties in the last general election held in May 1979 and the resulting distribution of seats in the House of Commons are given in Table 4.

TABLE 4: Percentages of Votes Cast, and Members Elected[a], in the May 1979
General Election

Party	% of Votes Cast	Party	Members Elected
Conservative	43·9	Conservative	339
Labour	36·9	Labour	268
Liberal	13·8	Liberal	11
Others	5·4	Scottish National	2
	——	Plaid Cymru (Welsh Nationalist)	2
	100·0	Official Unionist (Northern Ireland)	5
		Democratic Unionist (Northern Ireland)	3
		United Ulster Unionist	1
		Ulster Unionist	1
		Social Democratic and Labour (Northern Ireland)	1
		Independent (Northern Ireland)	1
		Speaker	1
			635

[a] In September 1980, the state of the parties (excluding the Speaker and his three deputies) was as follows: Conservative 337; Labour 267; Liberal 11; Scottish Nationalist 2; Plaid Cymru (Welsh Nationalist) 2; Official Unionist (Northern Ireland) 5; Democratic Unionist (Northern Ireland) 3; United Ulster Unionist 1; Ulster Progressive Unionist—elected as Ulster Unionist 1; Independent Socialist (Northern Ireland)—elected as Social Democratic and Labour 1; Independent (Northern Ireland) 1.

The party which wins most seats (although not necessarily the most votes) at a general election, or which has the support of a majority of members in the House of Commons, usually forms the Government. By tradition, the leader of the majority party is appointed Prime Minister by the Sovereign; and about 100 of its members in the House of Commons and the House of Lords receive ministerial appointments (including appointment to the Cabinet—see p 38) on the advice of the Prime Minister. The largest minority party becomes the official Opposition with its own leader and its own 'shadow Cabinet'; while the members of any other parties or any independents who have been elected may support or oppose the Government according to their party or their own view of the policy being debated at any given time. Leaders of the Government and Opposition sit on the front benches of the Commons with their supporters (the back-benchers) sitting behind them. Similar arrangements for the parties also apply in the House of Lords; however, Lords who do not wish to be associated with either the Government or the Opposition may sit on the cross benches of the Chamber.

The effectiveness of the party system in Parliament rests largely on the relationship between the Government and the opposition parties. Depending on the relative voting strengths of the parties in the House of Commons, the Opposition might seek to overthrow the Government by securing its defeat on a 'matter of confidence'. In general, however, its aims are to contribute to the formulation of policy and its expression in legislation by constructive criticism of the Government's approach; to oppose specific government proposals that it considers objectionable; to secure concessions on government Bills; and to increase support outside Parliament and enhance its chances of success in by-elections or at the next general election.

The detailed arrangements of government business are settled, under the direction of the Prime Minister and the Leaders of the two Houses, by the Chief Government Whips in consultation with the Chief Opposition Whips. The Chief Whips together constitute the 'usual channels' often referred to in each of the Houses when the question of the possibility of finding time for debating some particular issue is discussed. The direction of the business of the Houses is primarily the responsibility of the Leaders of the Houses and it is their duty to provide all reasonable facilities for the House to debate matters about which they are concerned.

Outside Parliament, party control is exercised by the national and local organisations. Inside Parliament, it is exercised by the Chief Whips and their assistants (chosen within the party) whose duties include keeping members informed of forthcoming parliamentary business, maintaining the voting strength of their parties by ensuring the attendance of members at important debates, and conveying upwards to the party leadership the opinions of their back-bench members. The Chief Government Whip in the House of Commons is Parliamentary Secretary to the Treasury; of the other Government Whips, three (one of whom is deputy Chief Whip) are officers of the Royal Household, five hold titular posts as Lords Commissioners of the Treasury and five are Assistant Whips. Salaries are likewise paid to the Chief Opposition Whips in both Houses and to two of the Assistant Whips for the Opposition in the Commons. The Government Whips in the Lords hold offices in the Royal Household and act as spokesmen for the Government in debates.

Annual financial assistance from public funds helps opposition parties in Parliament to carry out their business. It is limited to parties which had at least two members elected at the last general election or one member elected and a minimum of 150,000 votes cast. The formula is: £550 for every seat and £1·10 for every 200 votes, up to a maximum of £165,000.

Parliamentary Procedure

Parliamentary procedure is based on custom and precedent, partly formulated in standing orders governing details of practice in each House. The system of debate is much the same in the two Houses: the subject of every debate originates in the form of a motion (a proposal made by a member in order to elicit a decision from the House). When a motion has been moved and seconded, the Speaker proposes the question as the subject of debate. Members speak from wherever they have been sitting and not from a rostrum. Questions are decided by a vote, a simple majority being required to affirm or negative a question. The main difference between the two Houses is that in the Lords the office of Speaker carries with it no authority to check or curtail debate, such matters being decided by the general sense of the House, whereas in the Commons the Speaker has full authority to give effect, promptly and decisively, to the rules and orders of the House. The Speaker must guard against abuse of procedure or any infringement of minority rights, and has discretion to allow or disallow any closure motion (that is, a motion to end discussion so that the matter may be put to the vote). The Speaker has certain powers to check irrelevance and repetition in debate, and to save time in various other respects. In cases of grave disorder the House can be adjourned or the sitting suspended on the Speaker's own initiative. Voting in the House of Commons is under the direction of the Speaker whose duty it is to pronounce the final result. In the event of a tied vote the Speaker must give the casting vote, but he does so only in accordance with well-established conventions which preclude an expression of opinion on the merits of the question.

The procedure on voting in the House of Lords is similar to that in the House of Commons, except that the Speaker or chairman has an original, but no casting vote. The general principle is that Bills and subordinate legislation are allowed to proceed in the form before the House unless a majority votes to reject or amend them; on other motions the question is decided in the negative unless there is a majority in favour. When the House is sitting judicially (see pp 111 and 122) the judgment under appeal is not changed if the votes are equal.

The House of Commons has a public register of members' pecuniary interests. Members with a relevant pecuniary interest in a matter before the House, whether direct or indirect, must declare it when taking part in debate, though in order to operate as a disqualification from voting the interest must be direct, immediate and personal, and not merely of a general or remote character. In any other proceedings of the House or in transactions with other members or with ministers or civil servants, MPs must also disclose any relevant pecuniary interest or benefit.

All proceedings of both Houses are public, except on extremely rare occasions; the minutes (in the Commons called Votes and Proceedings and in the Lords, Minutes of Proceedings) and the speeches (The Official Report of Parliamentary Debates, *Hansard*) are published daily. The records of the Lords from 1497 and of the Commons from 1547, together with the parliamentary and political papers of certain past members of the Houses, are available to the public in the House of Lords Record Office. There are radio broadcasts of some of the proceedings of both Houses but no television transmissions.[1] A Parliamentary Sound Archive has been established.

Legislative Proceedings

The law undergoes constant reform in the courts as established principles are interpreted, clarified or reapplied to meet new circumstances, but substantial changes are the responsibility of Parliament and the Government through the normal legislative process.

Draft legislation takes the form of a parliamentary Bill. Most Bills are public Bills involving measures relating to public policy, but there are also private Bills which deal solely with matters of individual, corporate or local interest. Public Bills can be introduced either by a Government minister or by a private member of either House who does not hold office in the Government. Most public legislation is in practice drafted on behalf of ministers, and has the support of the Cabinet before being presented to Parliament.

Before a Government Bill is finally drafted, there is normally considerable consultation with, for instance, professional bodies, voluntary organisations and other agencies interested in the subject matter of the proposals, such as

---

[1] Debates on televising parliamentary proceedings have taken place on several occasions in recent years and in 1968 an internal television experiment took place in the Lords. In January 1980 the Commons voted to allow the introduction of a private member's Bill to permit the televising of proceedings, but it progressed no further.

major interest groups and 'pressure' groups which aim to promote a specific cause. Proposals for legislative changes are sometimes set out by the Government in 'White Papers' which may be debated in Parliament before the introduction of a Bill. From time to time consultative documents, sometimes called 'Green Papers', are published setting out for public discussion major ministerial proposals which are still at the formative stage.

Public Bills can be introduced in either House. As a rule, however, Government Bills likely to raise political controversy go through the Commons before the Lords, while those of an intricate but uncontroversial nature often pass through the Lords first. A Bill with a mainly financial purpose is nearly always introduced in the Commons, and a Bill involving taxation must be based on resolutions agreed to by that House, often after debate, before it can be introduced. If the main object of a Bill is to create a public charge, it can only be introduced by a government minister or, if brought from the Lords, be proceeded with in the Commons if taken up by a minister, which gives the Government considerable control over legislation.

At the beginning of each session private members of the Commons ballot for precedence in introducing a Bill on one of the Fridays specially allocated; the first 20 are successful. A private member may also present a Bill after question time (see p 34) on notice given, or seek leave to introduce a Bill under the 'ten minute rule' which allows two speeches, one in favour of and one against the measure, after which the House decides whether to allow the Bill to be brought in. Private members' Bills do not often proceed very far, but a few become law each session. If one secures a second reading, the Government usually introduces any necessary money resolution. Private members' Bills may be introduced in the House of Lords at any time, without notice, but the time that can be given to them in the Commons is strictly limited.

The process of passing a public Bill is similar in both Houses of Parliament. The Bill receives a formal first reading on introduction, it is printed, and after a while (between one day and several weeks depending on the nature of the Bill) is given a second reading after a debate on its general principles and merits. In the Commons a non-controversial Bill may be referred to a second reading committee to recommend whether it should be taken as read a second time. After a second reading in the Commons, a Bill is usually referred for detailed examination to a standing committee (see p 33). If the House so decides, the Bill may be referred to the whole House sitting in committee. The House may vote to limit the time devoted to examining a Bill by passing a timetable motion, commonly referred to as a 'guillotine'. In the Lords a Bill is considered by a committee of the whole House as a matter of course, unless the House takes the rare decision of referring it to a Public Bill Committee. The committee stage is followed by the report stage, during which previous amendments may be altered and new amendments incorporated. At the third reading a Bill is reviewed in its final form. In the Commons this stage is taken without a debate unless there is a motion in the name of six members that the question 'be not put forthwith'—a procedure frequently used.

After the third reading a Commons Bill is sent to the Lords where it goes through broadly the same stages. Similarly a Bill which starts in the Lords and is passed by that House is then sent to the Commons for all the stages there. Amendments made by the second House generally must be agreed by the first, or a compromise be reached, before a Bill can become law.

Most Government Bills introduced and passed in the Lords pass through the Commons without difficulty because of their non-controversial nature. However, should any non-governmental Lords Bill be unacceptable to the

Commons it would not generally become law because no debating time would be allotted to it. The Lords, on the other hand, cannot in general prevent a Bill insisted upon by the Commons from finally becoming law. In the normal course of events they either accept a Commons Bill without changes, or they amend and return it for consideration by the Commons, who frequently agree to the amendments made. In practice, the Lords pass without amendment such financial Bills as the Finance Bill, which authorises taxation, or Consolidated Fund or Appropriation Bills, which authorise national expenditure. A Bill that deals only with taxation or expenditure must become law within one month of being sent to the Lords, whether or not they have agreed to it, unless the Commons directs otherwise. If no agreement is reached between the two Houses on a non-financial Commons Bill (or an amendment to it) the Lords can in practice delay the Bill (with certain exceptions) for about 13 months. At the end of this time it becomes law in the form originally passed by the Commons. Bills to lengthen the life of a Parliament require the full assent of both Houses in the normal way. The limitations on the power of the Lords are based on the belief that the principal legislative function of the non-elected House nowadays is to act as a chamber of revision, complementing, not rivalling, the elected House.

When a Bill has passed through all its parliamentary stages, it is sent to the Queen for royal assent, after which it is part of the law of the land and known as an Act of Parliament. The royal assent has not been refused since 1707.

Private Bills, which can be promoted by people or organisations outside Parliament, go through substantially the same procedure as public Bills, but most of the work is done in committee, where proceedings follow a semi-judicial pattern: the promoter must prove the need for the powers or privileges he seeks, and objections on the part of the opposing interests are heard. Both parties may be legally represented.

Delegated Legislation

The system of delegated legislation, which is used to relieve pressure on parliamentary time, gives ministers and other authorities the power to regulate administrative details after a Bill has become an Act. In order to minimise the risk that powers thus conferred on the executive might supersede or weaken parliamentary government, they are normally delegated to the Queen in Council or to authorities directly responsible to Parliament, that is, to government ministers, government departments for which ministers are responsible, or to certain statutory organisations. Moreover, the Acts of Parliament by which particular powers are delegated normally provide for some measure of parliamentary control over legislation made in the exercise of these powers, for instance, by reserving to Parliament the right to affirm or annul the orders themselves. Certain Acts also require direct consultation with organisations which will be affected before rules and orders (in the form of statutory instruments) are made.

A joint committee of both Houses reports on the technical propriety of statutory instruments. In order to save time, the Commons also uses standing committees to consider the merits of instruments, with any decisions reserved to the House.

Parliamentary Committees
Committees of the Whole House

Either House may resolve itself into a committee (known as a committee of the whole house) to consider Bills in detail, clause by clause, after their second reading. A committee of the whole house is presided over by the Chairman of Ways and Means (the Chairman of Committees in the House of Lords) or a deputy chairman.

Standing
Committees

House of Commons standing committees include those which examine public Bills at the committee stage and, in certain cases, at the second reading and report stages; two Scottish standing committees; the Scottish Grand Committee; the Welsh Grand Committee; and the Northern Ireland standing committee. Ordinary standing committees have no distinctive names, being referred to simply as Standing Committee A, B, C, and so on, and are each appointed specially to consider a specific Bill. Each has between 16 and 50 members with the balance of the parties reflecting as far as possible that in the House as a whole. The Scottish Grand Committee, which comprises all 71 Scottish members and 10 to 15 others, considers the principles of Scottish Bills referred to it at second reading stage, the Scottish estimates and other matters relating exclusively to Scotland. The Welsh Grand Committee, with all 36 Welsh members and up to five others, considers Bills referred to it at second reading stage, and matters relating exclusively to Wales. The Northern Ireland committee considers matters relating specifically to the province. A standing committee on regional affairs comprising the 516 members from English constituencies considers matters relating to the English regions. The Lords equivalent to a standing committee, a Public Bill Committee, is rarely used.

Select
Committees

Select committees are generally set up, by either House, to help Parliament with the control of the executive by examining some aspect of administration and reporting to the House or to consider matters concerning the work of the House itself. They may be appointed as occasion demands, or for a session, or for the rest of the life of a Parliament. On rare occasions a parliamentary Bill is examined by a select committee (a procedure additional to the usual legislative process). Select committees are constituted in the Commons on a party basis, in approximate proportions to party strength in the House.

A new structure of select committees was introduced in the Commons in 1979 when committees dealing with specific topics (for example, nationalised industries and science and technology) were replaced by 12 new committees, each of which examines the work of one of the main government departments. Select committees on Scottish Affairs and on Welsh Affairs and a Liaison Committee to consider general matters relating to the work of select committees have also been established. Other committees include those on European Legislation, Public Accounts, Members' Interests and the Parliamentary Commissioner for Administration. The Committee of Selection and the Standing Orders Committee have duties relating to private Bills, and the Committee of Selection also chooses members to serve on standing and select committees.

In their scrutiny of administrative activity and government policies, the committees question ministers, senior civil servants and interested bodies and individuals. They bring before Parliament and the public generally, through their hearings and published reports, a body of fact and informed opinion on many important issues and they build up considerable expertise in their subjects of inquiry.

In the House of Lords, there are the Appeal and Appellate Committees in which the bulk of the House's judicial work is transacted. There are also committees on the European Communities (with seven sub-committees), Unemployment, Science and Technology, House of Lords Offices, Hybrid Instruments, Leave of Absence, Lords' Expenses, Personal Bills, Private Bills, Standing Orders, Privileges, Procedure, Selection and Sound Broadcasting.

Joint Committees   The two Houses may agree to set up joint select committees, and joint committees are also appointed in each session to deal with Consolidation Bills and delegated legislation.

Party Committees   In addition to the official committees of the two Houses there are several unofficial party organisations or committees. The Conservative and Unionist Members Committee, popularly known as the 1922 Committee, consists of the back-bench membership of the party. The Parliamentary Labour Party is a corporate body comprising all members of the party in both Houses; when the Labour Party is in office a liaison committee acts as a channel of communication between the Government and its back-benchers in both Houses; when the party is in opposition the Parliamentary Labour Party is organised under the direction of a Parliamentary Committee often referred to as the 'shadow Cabinet'.

Other Forms of Parliamentary Control   The effectiveness of parliamentary control of the Government is a subject of continuing discussion, both inside Parliament and in Britain generally. Control of the Government is exercised finally by the ability of the House of Commons to force the Government to resign by passing a resolution of 'no confidence' or by rejecting a proposal which the Government considers so vital to its policy that it has made it a 'matter of confidence' or, ultimately, by refusing to vote the money required for the public service. In addition to the system of close scrutiny by select committees (see p 33) the House of Commons offers a number of opportunities for a searching examination of government policy by both the Opposition and the Government's own back-benchers. These include:

1. Question time, which is an hour of parliamentary time on Monday, Tuesday, Wednesday and Thursday during which ministers, in rotation, answer questions put to them on matters for which they are responsible. Parliamentary questions are one means of eliciting information about the Government's intentions, as well as a way of airing, and possibly securing redress of, grievances brought to members' notice by constituents.

2. The right of members to use motions for the adjournment of the House to open discussions on constituency cases or matters of public concern. There is a half-hour adjournment period at the end of the business of the day; and immediately before the adjournment for each recess (Christmas, Easter, spring and summer) a day is spent discussing matters raised by private members. Moreover, a member wishing to discuss a 'specific and important matter that should have urgent consideration' may, at the end of question time, ask leave to move the adjournment of the House. If the Speaker accepts the terms of the motion, the MP asks the House for leave for the motion to be put forward. Leave can be given unanimously, or it can be given if 40 or more MPs support the motion, or if fewer than 40 but more than ten support it and the House (on a vote) is in favour. Once leave has been given, the matter is debated for three hours, usually on the following day.

3. The 29 'supply' days each session, which were formerly used to discuss details of proposed government expenditure, and which are nowadays time for the Opposition to choose subjects for debate. (Scrutiny by small committees has been found more apt for detailed expenditure proposals.)

Procedural opportunities for criticism of the Government also arise during the debate on the Queen's speech at the beginning of a session, during debates or motions of censure for which the Government gives up part of its own time, and during debates on the Government's legislative proposals.

Opportunities for criticism of the Government are also provided in the House of Lords at daily question time, during debates on specific motions and in 'unstarred' (that is, debatable) questions at the end of the day's business.

The involvement of Parliament, and more particularly the House of Commons, in the management of the revenues of the State and payments for the public service is described in Chapter 18, Finance.

The arrangements made in Parliament to keep the two Houses informed on European Community developments, and to enable them to scrutinise and debate Community policies and proposals include two select committees: a House of Commons committee on European Legislation and a House of Lords committee, with similar, but broader, terms of reference, on the European communities. In addition Ministers make regular statements about Community business.

Parliamentary Commissioner for Administration
The Parliamentary Commissioner for Administration (the 'Parliamentary Ombudsman') is an independent statutory officer whose function is to investigate complaints of maladministration when asked to do so by MPs on behalf of members of the public. Powers of investigation extend to administrative actions by central government departments but not to policy decisions (which are the concern of the Government and can be questioned in Parliament) nor to matters affecting relations with other countries. Complaints by British citizens arising from dealings with British posts overseas are open to investigation in some circumstances. The Commissioner has access to all departmental papers and reports the findings to the MP who presented the complaint. The Commissioner reports annually to Parliament and may submit other reports, for example, of individual investigations.

A select committee of the House of Commons makes recommendations over the Commissioner's work but does not review individual cases.

Parliamentary Privilege
Each House of Parliament enjoys certain rights and immunities designed to protect it from unnecessary obstruction in carrying out its duties. Those rights apply collectively to each House and individually to each member.

For the Commons the Speaker formally claims 'their ancient and undoubted rights and privileges' at the beginning of each Parliament. These include freedom of speech; freedom from arrest in civil actions; exemption from serving on juries, attending as witnesses or serving as sheriffs; and the right of access to the Crown, which is a collective privilege of the House. Further privileges include the right of the House to control its own proceedings (so that it is able, for instance, to exclude strangers if it wishes); the right to pronounce upon legal disqualifications for membership and to declare a seat vacant on such grounds; and the right to penalise those who commit a breach of its privileges.

The privileges of the House of Lords include: freedom of speech; freedom of access to the Sovereign for each peer individually; and the right to commit for contempt. These privileges are not formally claimed by the Speaker as in the House of Commons; they exist independently.

THE PRIVY COUNCIL

Until the eighteenth century, the Sovereign in Council, or Privy Council, was the chief source of executive power in the State. As the system of Cabinet government developed, however, the Privy Council became less prominent. Many of its powers were transferred to the Cabinet as an inner committee of the Privy Council, and much of its work was handed over to newly created government departments, some of which were originally committees of the Privy Council. Nowadays the main function of the Privy Council is to advise the Queen to approve Orders in Council. These are of two kinds, differing fundamentally in constitutional principle: those made under prerogative powers, such as Orders approving the grant of royal charters of incorporation; and those made under statutory powers, which are the highest form of delegated legislation. It is an accepted principle that members of the Privy Council attending meetings at which Orders in Council are made do not thereby become personally responsible for the policy upon which the orders are based; this rests with the minister responsible for the subject matter of the order in question, whether or not he or she was present at the meeting.

The Privy Council also advises the Crown on the issue of royal proclamations, some of the most important of which relate to prerogative acts (such as summoning or dissolving Parliament) of the same validity as Acts of Parliament. The Privy Council's own statutory responsibilities, which are independent of the powers of the Sovereign in Council, include powers of supervision over the registering bodies for the medical and allied professions.

Apart from Cabinet Ministers, who must be Privy Counsellors and are sworn of the Council on first assuming office, membership of the Privy Council (which is retained for life) is accorded by the Sovereign on the recommendation of the Prime Minister to certain eminent persons in independent monarchical countries of the Commonwealth. There are about 360 Privy Counsellors. A full Privy Council is summoned only on the death of the Sovereign or when the Sovereign announces his or her intention to marry.

Committees of the Privy Council

There are a number of advisory Privy Council committees whose meetings differ from those of the Privy Council itself in that the Sovereign cannot constitutionally be present. These may be prerogative committees, such as those dealing with legislative matters submitted by the legislatures of the Channel Islands and Isle of Man and with applications for charters of incorporation; or they may be provided for by statute as are those for the universities of Oxford and Cambridge and the Scottish universities.

The Judicial Committee of the Privy Council is the final court of appeal from the courts of the United Kingdom dependencies, courts of independent members of the Commonwealth which have not elected to discontinue the appeal, courts of the Channel Islands and the Isle of Man, and certain other courts, some professional and disciplinary committees and church sources.

The administrative work of the Privy Council committees is carried out in the Privy Council Office under the Lord President of the Council, a senior Cabinet minister.

HER MAJESTY'S GOVERNMENT

Her Majesty's Government is the body of ministers responsible for the administration of national affairs.

The Prime Minister is appointed by the Queen, and all other ministers are appointed by the Queen on the recommendation of the Prime Minister.

The majority of ministers are members of the Commons. However, the Government must be fully represented by ministers in the Lords as it requires spokesmen of standing to expound its policy and justify its actions to that House. The Lord Chancellor is always a member of the House of Lords.

Composition

The composition of the Government is subject to variation from time to time, both in the number of ministers and in the titles of some offices. The creation of a paid ministerial office with entirely new functions, the abolition of an office, the transfer of functions from one minister to another, or a change in the designation of a minister may be effected by Order in Council. Ministers may be classified as follows:

Prime Minister

The Prime Minister is also First Lord of the Treasury and Minister for the Civil Service. The head of the Government became known as the Prime Minister during the eighteenth century. The unique position of authority enjoyed by the holder of this office derives from the ability to command a majority in Parliament and from the power to submit a personal choice of ministers to the Queen and to obtain their resignation or dismissal individually. By modern convention, the Prime Minister always sits in the House of Commons.

The Prime Minister informs the Queen of the general business of the Government; presides over the Cabinet; and is responsible for the allocation of functions among ministers.

The Prime Minister's other responsibilities include making recommendations to the Queen for the appointment of Church of England archbishops, bishops and deans and the incumbents of some 200 Crown livings, as well as for appointments to high judicial offices, such as the Lord Chief Justice, Lords of Appeal in Ordinary, and Lord Justices of Appeal. They also include advising the Queen on appointments of Privy Counsellors, Lords-Lieutenant and certain civil appointments, such as Lord High Commissioner of the General Assembly of the Church of Scotland, Poet Laureate, Constable of the Tower, and some university appointments which are in the gift of the Crown. The Prime Minister makes similar recommendations for appointments to various public boards and institutions, such as the British Broadcasting Corporation, as well as to various royal and statutory commissions. Recommendations are likewise made to the Queen for the award of many civil honours and distinctions and of Civil List pensions (awarded to people who have achieved eminence in science and the arts and who are in some financial need). The Prime Minister also selects the trustees of certain national museums and institutions.

Departmental Ministers

Departmental ministers are in charge of government departments. The holders of these offices, who are usually in the Cabinet, are known as 'Secretary of State' or 'Minister', or they may have a special title, as in the case of the Chancellor of the Exchequer (who, as Second Lord, is the ministerial head of the Treasury and has overall responsibility for its work).

Non-Departmental Ministers

Non-departmental ministers include the holders of various traditional offices—the Lord President of the Council, the Chancellor of the Duchy of Lancaster, the Lord Privy Seal, the Paymaster General—and from time to time Ministers without Portfolio. These ministers may have few or no departmental duties and are thus available to perform any special duties which the Prime Minister may wish to entrust to them. The Chancellor of the Duchy of Lancaster, for example, has ministerial responsibility for the arts, and the Paymaster General is responsible for co-ordinating the presentation of information about Government policies.

Lord Chancellor and Law Officers   The Lord Chancellor holds a special position, being a Minister of the Crown with departmental functions and also head of the judiciary in England and Wales. The four Law Officers of the Crown are: for England and Wales, the Attorney General and the Solicitor General; for Scotland, the Lord Advocate and the Solicitor General for Scotland.

Ministers of State   Ministers of State are usually appointed to work with ministers in charge of government departments. Although the departmental minister is ultimately responsible for the department, Ministers of State may be responsible to him or her for specific functions and sometimes their titles reflect these particular functions. More than one Minister of State may be appointed to a particular department. It is possible for a Minister of State to be given a seat in the Cabinet and paid accordingly.

Junior Ministers   Junior ministers generally have the title of Parliamentary Secretary or, where the senior minister is a Secretary of State, Parliamentary Under Secretary of State. They share in parliamentary debates, answering parliamentary questions, and assisting in departmental duties. In certain cases, however, they may be given responsibility, directly under the departmental minister, for specific aspects of the department's work. The Parliamentary Secretary to the Treasury and other Lords Commissioners of the Treasury are in a different category as Government Whips (see p. 29).

Ministerial Salaries   The salaries of ministers in the House of Commons range[1] from £12,500 a year for junior ministers and £16,250 to £19,300 for more senior ministers to £23,500 for Cabinet ministers. The Prime Minister and the Lord Chancellor also receive £23,500. From June 1981 salaries will rise to £14,250 for junior ministers; to £18,650 to £21,900 for more senior ministers, and to £26,250 for the Prime Minister, Lord Chancellor and Cabinet ministers.

Ministers in the House of Commons, including the Prime Minister, also have parliamentary salaries of £6,930 a year (to be increased to £7,670 in 1981) in recognition of their constituency responsibilities and are entitled to claim the other allowances paid to all members of the House.

The Cabinet   The Cabinet is composed of about 20 ministers personally chosen by the Prime Minister and may include the holders of departmental and non-departmental offices. Its origins can be traced back to the informal conferences which the Sovereign held with leading ministers, independently of the Privy Council, during the seventeenth century. After the Sovereign's withdrawal from an active role in politics in the eighteenth century, and the development of organised political parties stimulated by successive extensions of the franchise from 1832 onwards, the Cabinet assumed its modern form.

The functions of the Cabinet are: the final determination of the policy to be submitted to Parliament; the supreme control of the national executive in accordance with the policy agreed by Parliament; and the continuous co-ordination of government departments. The exercise of these functions is vitally affected by the fact that the Cabinet is a group of party representatives, depending upon the support of a majority in the House of Commons.

---

[1] The Leader of the Opposition in the House of Commons receives an annual salary for that post, as well as a parliamentary salary; in the House of Lords the Leader of the Opposition receives an annual salary.

e Humber Bridge

th the longest single span in the world of
10 m (4,626 ft), the bridge, which is
aring completion, will link the ports of
imsby and Hull, reducing the road
irney time by $1\frac{1}{2}$ hours

Computer Services

The 12 m (39 ft) aerial dish, being erected at the Rutherford and Appleton Laboratories in southern England, will transmit and receive signals from the Infra-Red Astronomical Satellite after its launch in 1981. In a joint project with the United States and the Netherlands, Britain will be responsible for the ground operations systems and for the 'software' in the form of commands relayed to the satellite and stored in its computer.

computer terminal, claimed to be the
smallest and lightest in the world and to
contain 'software' at least two years ahead
of its rivals. Its main feature is that it
enables people travelling on business to
communicate with a central computer.

Robot

A robot welder, with a memory that can
store up to 64 different welding tasks, has a
control console using the latest
microprocessor technology.

Infra-red Telescope

The United Kingdom Infra-red Telescope
(front), the world's largest, erected at high
altitude in Hawaii, is operated by the Royal
Observatory, Edinburgh. Because of new
design features it combines the largest
telescope aperture with the smallest support
structure and housing on Mauna Kea.

Cabinet Meetings   The Cabinet meets in private and its proceedings are strictly confidential. Its members are bound by their oath as Privy Counsellors not to disclose information about its proceedings. The Official Secrets Acts forbid the publication of Cabinet as well as of other State papers (although after they have been in existence for 30 years they may be made available for inspection in the Public Record Office) and a resigning minister wishing to make a statement involving disclosure of Cabinet discussions should first obtain the permission of the Queen through the Prime Minister.

Normally the Cabinet meets for a few hours once or twice a week during parliamentary sittings, and rather less often when Parliament is not sitting. Additional meetings may be called by the Prime Minister at any time if a matter urgently requiring discussion should arise. To keep the amount of work coming before the Cabinet within manageable limits, a great deal of work is carried on through the committee system, which involves the reference of any issue either to a standing Cabinet committee or to an *ad hoc* committee composed of the ministers primarily concerned. The committee then considers the matter in detail and either disposes of it or reports upon it to the Cabinet with recommendations for action. The present Cabinet has four standing committees: a defence and overseas policy committee and an economic strategy committee both under the chairmanship of the Prime Minister; a home and social affairs committee under the chairmanship of the Home Secretary; and a legislation committee under the chairmanship of the Lord Chancellor. Sub-committees of the standing committees may be established. Membership and terms of reference of all Cabinet committees is confidential.

Ministers not in the Cabinet may attend its meetings for discussion of matters affecting their departments; they may also be members of Cabinet committees. The Secretary of the Cabinet and senior officials of the Cabinet Office also attend meetings of the Cabinet and its committees as appropriate.

Ministerial   The term 'ministerial responsibility' refers both to the collective responsibility
Responsibility   which ministers share for government policy and actions and to ministers' individual responsibility to Parliament for their departments' work.

The doctrine of collective responsibility, which was fully accepted by the middle of the nineteenth century, means that the Cabinet is bound to act unanimously even when Cabinet Ministers do not hold identical views on a given subject. Consequently it means that the policy of departmental ministers must be consistent with the policy of the Government as a whole. In principle, once the Government's policy on a matter has been decided, each minister is expected to support it, unless he or she chooses to resign. On rare occasions, ministers have been allowed free votes in Parliament on government policies involving important issues of principle. The individual responsibility of a minister for the work of his or her department means that, as political head of that department, he or she is answerable for all its acts and omissions and must bear the consequences of any defect of administration, any injustice to an individual or any aspect of policy which may be criticised in Parliament, whether personally responsible or not. Since the majority of ministers are members of the House of Commons, they are available to answer questions and to defend themselves against criticism in person. Departmental ministers in the House of Lords are represented in the Commons by someone qualified to speak on their behalf, usually a Minister of State or a Parliamentary Secretary.

Departmental ministers normally decide all matters within their responsibility, although on important political matters they usually consult their colleagues collectively, through the Cabinet or a Cabinet committee. Any decision by a departmental minister binds the Government as a whole.

The responsibility of ministers for their departments is an effective way of keeping government under public control, for the knowledge that any departmental action may be reported to and examined in Parliament discourages the taking of arbitrary and ill-considered decisions.

On assuming office ministers must resign directorships in private and public companies. In all other respects they must order their affairs in such a way that there is no conflict between their public duties and their private interests.

GOVERNMENT DEPARTMENTS

Government departments are the main instruments for giving effect to government policy when Parliament has passed the necessary legislation. They may, and frequently do, work with and through local authorities, statutory boards, and government-sponsored organisations operating under various degrees of government control.

A change of government does not necessarily affect the number or general functions of government departments, although a radical change in policy may be accompanied by some organisational change.

The work of some departments (for instance, the Ministry of Defence) covers the United Kingdom as a whole. Other departments (like the Department of Employment) cover England, Wales, and Scotland, but not Northern Ireland. Others, such as the Department of the Environment, are mainly concerned with affairs in England. There are separate departments for Scotland, Northern Ireland and Wales.

A department is usually headed by a minister. Certain departments in which questions of policy do not normally arise are headed by a permanent official, and a minister with other duties is responsible for them to Parliament. For instance, the minister in charge of the Civil Service Department is responsible for the Central Office of Information, Her Majesty's Stationery Office, and the Department of the Government Actuary; and Treasury ministers are responsible for the Customs and Excise, the Inland Revenue, the Department for National Savings and a number of small departments including the Treasury Solicitor's Department, the Royal Mint, and the National Debt Office. Generally, departments receive their funds directly out of money provided by Parliament and are staffed by the Civil Service.

Internal Organisation

Departments differ in size and in the volume, type and complexity of their work. Since each department makes its own arrangements for discharging its duties, there are variations in internal organisation. Most departments, however, have certain features in common: the minister of a major department is likely to have at the head of his or her officials a permanent secretary, sometimes assisted by one or more second permanent secretaries, and also one or more deputy secretaries, and a varying number of under secretaries and assistant secretaries. Usually major departments also have a principal finance officer and a principal personnel and organisation officer. Many also have their own legal advisers or solicitors, economists and statisticians and their own information divisions. The Government Statistical Service, which includes the Central Statistical Office (CSO), the Business Statistics Office (BSO), the Office of Population Censuses and Surveys and the statistics divisions of the major departments, provides a service of statistical information and advice.

Each department compiles and publishes statistics relating to its own policy area. Information about individual industries is published by the BSO in *Business Monitors.*

Some departments, such as the Department of Trade and the Central Office of Information, maintain a regional organisation, and some which have direct contact with the public throughout the country, for example, the Department of Employment, also have local offices.

Non-Departmental Public Bodies

A number of bodies with a role in the process of government are neither government departments nor part of a department. They are popularly described as 'quangos' (often taken to stand for 'quasi-autonomous non-governmental organisations', although there is no precise definition of the term). There are three kinds: executive bodies, advisory bodies and tribunals. Executive bodies (commonly called fringe bodies because of their functions on the fringes of central government) generally employ staff and spend money on their own account; advisory bodies and tribunals do not normally employ staff or spend money themselves, but their expenses are paid by government departments concerned. Many of the more important executive bodies are mentioned in this Handbook; a note on advisory bodies is set out below; and the position of tribunals is dealt with on p 124.

As a result of a review of non-departmental public bodies undertaken in 1979 by the Government, some 240 are being abolished.

Advisory Bodies

Many government departments are assisted by advisory councils or committees which undertake research and collect information, mainly to give ministers access to informed opinion before coming to a decision involving a legislative or executive act. In some cases there is a statutory obligation on a minister to consult a standing committee, but usually advisory bodies are appointed at the discretion of the minister concerned because he or she feels the need for their advice.

The membership of the advisory councils and committees varies according to the nature of the work involved, and may include civil servants and representatives of varying interests and professions—for instance, industrialists, trade unionists, university and industrial scientists, educationists, lawyers and local government councillors and officers.

In addition to these standing advisory bodies, there are committees frequently set up by the Government to examine and make recommendations on specific matters. For certain important inquiries Royal Commissions, whose members are chosen for their wide experience and diverse knowledge, may be appointed (by royal warrant). Royal Commissions examine written and oral evidence from government departments and interested organisations and individuals, and on this evidence submit recommendations. The Government may accept the recommendations in whole or in part, or may decide to take no further action or to delay action. Inquiries may also be undertaken by departmental committees, appointed by the head of the appropriate department.

Distribution of Functions

The following pages provide an outline of the principal functions of the main government departments. They are arranged in alphabetical order, except for the Cabinet Office, the Civil Service Department, and the Treasury (which, in view of their central positions, are placed first) and the Scottish and Northern Ireland departments (which are grouped at the end of the section). Further information on the work of departments is given in later chapters under the relevant subject headings.

The Cabinet Office

The Cabinet Office, headed by the Secretary of the Cabinet, under the direction of the Prime Minister, comprises the Cabinet Secretariat, the Central Policy Review Staff, the Central Statistical Office and the Historical Section.

The Cabinet Secretariat serves ministers collectively in the conduct of Cabinet business. It operates as an instrument in the co-ordination of policy at the highest level. Functions of the office include circulating the memoranda and other documents required for Cabinet or Cabinet committee business, preparing agenda for meetings of the Cabinet and its committees, recording their discussions and circulating the minutes, keeping in touch with the progress of action on decisions, and safeguarding the security of documents.

The Central Policy Review Staff (the 'Think Tank') advises ministers collectively on major issues of policy.

The Central Statistical Office is concerned with the preparation and interpretation of the statistics necessary to support economic and social policies and management. It is directly responsible for the central economic aggregates such as the national accounts, balance of payments, financial statistics and measures of output and it prepares a wide range of statistical publications. It co-ordinates the statistical work of other departments.

The Historical Section of the Cabinet Office is in the process of completing the official histories of the second world war, and is responsible for the preparation of official histories of certain peacetime events.

The Civil Service Department

The Civil Service Department is responsible for the management of the Civil Service. The Department is under the control of the Prime Minister as Minister for the Civil Service; a senior minister, the Lord President of the Council, is in charge of the Department on behalf of the Minister for the Civil Service and is assisted by a Minister of State. The Department's Permanent Secretary, its most senior civil servant, is the official head of the Home Civil Service.

The Department is also responsible for personnel management in the Civil Service, which includes policy and central arrangements for recruitment, training (including the Civil Service College), promotion, general career management, catering, welfare and retirement. Further responsibilities include advising the Prime Minister on the allocation of functions and responsibilities between ministers, making recommendations to the Prime Minister on senior appointments and advising on public appointments made by ministers generally. The Department is responsible for the overall efficiency of the Civil Service, taking the initiative in introducing new management techniques, scrutinising departments' methods of operation and controlling Civil Service manpower and related administrative expenses. In addition, the Department is responsible for negotiating the pay, pensions and conditions of service in the Civil Service, and for co-ordinating pay and pensions policies in the public service as a whole. The Department also seeks to maintain a system of industrial relations for the Civil Service that promotes the efficient discharge of public business. The Central Computer and Telecommunications Agency within the Department provides a centre of expertise in the economic purchase and effective use of computers in government.

The Civil Service Commission

The Civil Service Commission, which is responsible for recruitment to the Civil Service, is linked to the Civil Service Department. In matters concerned with recruitment policy, the commissioners are responsible to ministers in the normal way, but in the selection of individuals for appointment they act under Order in Council and are completely independent.

Parliamentary Counsel Office

The Office of the Parliamentary Counsel is responsible for the drafting of all Government Bills, except Bills or provisions of Bills related exclusively to Scotland, which are handled by the Lord Advocate's Department. The Office advises departments on questions of parliamentary procedure; and attends sittings (and committees) of both Houses as required. In addition the Parliamentary Counsel draft subordinate legislation when specially instructed, and advise the Government on legal, parliamentary and constitutional questions falling within their special experience.

The Treasury

Nominally the heads of the Treasury are the Lords Commissioners: the First Lord of the Treasury (always the Prime Minister), the Chancellor of the Exchequer and five junior Lords. In practice, the Lords Commissioners never meet as a board and their responsibilities are carried by the Chancellor of the Exchequer assisted by the Chief Secretary to the Treasury, the Financial Secretary and two Ministers of State. The Parliamentary Secretary to the Treasury is the Chief Government Whip in the House of Commons.

The Treasury is the government department primarily responsible for the development of Britain's overall economic strategy. Its Public Services Sector is responsible for controlling aggregate public expenditure and for most of the individual public expenditure programmes; the Domestic Economy Sector is concerned with fiscal and monetary policies, and with the Treasury's contribution to industrial policies, including control of public expenditure on industry and agriculture; the Overseas Finance Sector is responsible for balance of payments policies, the management of Britain's foreign currency reserves, international monetary questions, financial relations with other countries and the aid programme; and the Chief Economic Adviser's Sector is responsible for the preparation of short-term and medium-term economic forecasts and for specialist advice on broad economic policies.

The Ministry of Agriculture, Fisheries and Food

The Ministry of Agriculture, Fisheries and Food, which is directed by the Minister of Agriculture, Fisheries and Food (assisted by two Ministers of State and a Parliamentary Secretary), is responsible for administering government policy for agriculture, horticulture and fishing in England and for many food matters in the United Kingdom. Some of the Ministry's responsibilities for animal health extend to Great Britain. In association with the other agricultural departments in the United Kingdom and the Intervention Board for Agricultural Produce, it is responsible for the administration of the European Community common agricultural and fisheries policies and for various national support schemes. It administers schemes for the control and eradication of animal and plant diseases and for assistance to capital investment in farm and horticultural businesses and land drainage; it exercises responsibilities relating to research and development. The Ministry sponsors the food and drink manufacturing industries and the food and drink distributive trades. It is concerned with the supply and quality of food, food compositional standards, food hygiene and the labelling and advertising of food, and it has certain responsibilities for ensuring that public health standards are met in the manufacture, preparation and distribution of basic foods.

The Intervention Board for Agricultural Produce

An executive department under the direction and control of ministers responsible for agriculture, the Intervention Board for Agricultural Produce is responsible for implementing within the United Kingdom the market support arrangements and certain other aspects of the European Community's Common Agricultural Policy provided for under the guarantee section of the

European Agricultural Guidance and Guarantee Fund. In consultation with the Foreign and Commonwealth Office Overseas Development Administration, the Board is responsible for organising the supply of cereals for developing countries under the Food Aid Convention 1971, and for administering occasional Community donations of other commodities to developing countries and areas of national disasters.

Office of Arts and Libraries

The Office of Arts and Libraries is the responsibility of the Chancellor of the Duchy of Lancaster and deals with policy and financial support for the arts and for libraries and museums. Government support for activities in these areas is given mainly through independent bodies, for example, the Arts Council and the British Film Institute (see chapter 21, Promotion of the Arts). They also include the British Library, the National Heritage Memorial Fund, and the British Museum and other national museums and galleries. The governing bodies of these institutions are appointed mainly by the Prime Minister and the Chancellor of the Duchy of Lancaster and are responsible for making the necessary artistic and professional judgments and for allocating funds for particular purposes.

The Board of Customs and Excise

The primary work of the Board of Customs and Excise is to collect and administer the customs and excise duties, including value added tax, imposed from time to time in the annual Finance Acts or by other legislation, and to advise the Chancellor of the Exchequer on any matters connected with them. The Board is also responsible for preventing and detecting evasion of the revenue laws.

The Board undertakes, for other departments, a wide range of non-revenue agency work, for instance, the enforcement of prohibitions and restrictions on the import and export of certain classes of goods, and the compilation of United Kingdom overseas trade statistics from customs import and export documents. Parliamentary responsibility for the Board's work is exercised by Treasury ministers.

The Ministry of Defence

The Ministry of Defence is the government department responsible for defence policy and for the control and administration of the three armed services—Navy, Army and Air Force (including the procurement of defence equipment). The Secretary of State for Defence, assisted by a Minister of State, is in charge of the Department. Three Parliamentary Under Secretaries of State are responsible for the three armed services.

The Department of Education and Science

The Department of Education and Science is responsible for the general promotion of education in England; for the Government's relations with universities in Great Britain; and for fostering civil science both in Britain and internationally. The Department is directed by a Secretary of State, who is assisted by a Minister of State and two Parliamentary Under Secretaries of State. Matters relating to the development of school and post-school education for which the Department has responsibility include the broad allocation of resources for education, the capital programmes for building new schools and other institutions, the supply, training and superannuation of teachers, and the basic standards of education. The Department co-operates with the local education authorities which provide and run the schools and colleges in their areas. Its relations with the universities are conducted through the University Grants Committee. Responsibilities for civil science are discharged mainly through five research councils: the Agricultural Research Council, the Medical Research Council, the Natural Environment Research Council, the Science Research Council, and the Social Science Research Council. On questions of scientific policy an advisory board for the research councils advises the Secretary of State.

An important part of the Department is Her Majesty's Inspectorate which is responsible for inspecting and reporting on educational establishments and reporting to and advising the Secretary of State and the Department on the performance of the education service. Inspectors' duties are not confined to schools: they cover the whole range of education except the universities and private establishments and further education.

The Department of Employment

The Department of Employment has responsibility for manpower policies in Great Britain, either directly or through statutory agencies, and for the formulation of labour legislation. It is also responsible for monitoring labour market trends, including pay, and for producing statistics on them and on retail prices (from which the rate of inflation is calculated). The Department is responsible for the payment of unemployment benefit through its local offices; for the issue of work permits to workers from overseas; and for the Race Relations Employment Advisory Service. The Secretary of State for Employment is assisted by a Minister of State and two Parliamentary Under Secretaries of State.

The Department of Energy

The Department of Energy is concerned with the development of government policies for the supply and use of all forms of energy. It discharges functions connected with the nationalised coal and gas industries in Great Britain and the electricity industry in England and Wales; is responsible for the United Kingdom Atomic Energy Authority; and is the sponsoring department for the nuclear power and oil industries including the British National Oil Corporation. It is also responsible for the development policy for offshore oil and gas resources in the British sector of the continental shelf; and it sponsors, through the Offshore Supplies Office in Glasgow, the suppliers of equipment to the offshore operators. The Department also represents Britain in international discussions on energy policy, including relations and co-operation with oil-producing countries. It is the sponsoring and co-ordinating body for energy conservation policy, and also operates financial assistance schemes for energy surveys and technological demonstration projects. The Department encourages the development of new sources of energy, with assistance from the Energy Technology Support Unit at Harwell, Oxfordshire. The Secretary of State for Energy is assisted by a Minister of State and two Parliamentary Under Secretaries of State.

The Department of the Environment

The Department of the Environment is responsible in England for a wide range of functions relating to the physical environment in which people live and work. The Department is responsible for urban affairs and inner city renewal; new towns; local government; regional affairs; the finance and policy of the housing programme; the construction industries; planning, development control and land; special responsibilities for sport and recreation; the control of pollution; water and sewerage; minerals; countryside affairs; and the Property Services Agency (which provides nearly all government common services relating to land, property, building and furnishings).

The Department is also concerned with the conservation of historic towns, buildings and ancient monuments, and research into planning matters, building and construction, environmental pollution and resources.

The Secretary of State for the Environment is assisted by two Ministers of

State (one for Housing and Construction and the other for Local Government and Environmental Affairs) and four Parliamentary Under Secretaries of State, one of whom has special responsibility for sport and recreation.

Export Credits Guarantee Department
The Export Credits Guarantee Department, which is a separate government department within the responsibility of the Secretary of State for Trade, offers two main facilities to British exporters. It insures exporters against the risk of not being paid for goods and services (whether through the default or insolvency of the buyer or through other causes such as exchange difficulties in the buyer's country), and provides access to bank finance for exports, often at favourable rates of interest. In addition the Department provides support for 'buyer credits' (loans made direct to overseas buyers for capital goods contracts enabling the supplier to be paid on cash terms); insurance against the political risks of new overseas investment for up to 15 years; partial protection for large capital goods contracts against an unexpectedly high rise in costs; and support for the issue of performance bonds.

The Foreign and Commonwealth Office
The Foreign and Commonwealth Office provides, mainly through diplomatic missions, the means of communication between the British Government and other governments and international governmental organisations for the discussion and negotiation of all matters, including economic issues, falling within the field of international relations. In particular the Department is responsible for alerting the British Government to the implications of developments overseas; for protecting British interests overseas, including commercial interests; for protecting British citizens abroad; and for explaining British policies to, and wherever possible cultivating friendly relations with, governments and peoples overseas. The Department is also responsible for the discharge of British responsibilities in the Associated States (mainly for defence and external affairs) and dependent territories. In the dependent territories, each of which has its own internal administration, the British Government is finally responsible for good government and for the relations between these territories and other countries.

The Department is headed by the Secretary of State for Foreign and Commonwealth Affairs, who is assisted by the Lord Privy Seal and four Ministers of State (one of whom has responsibility for overseas development—see below) and a Parliamentary Under Secretary of State.

The Overseas Development Administration
Overseas development matters are the responsibility of the Secretary of State for Foreign and Commonwealth Affairs. The Overseas Development Administration is responsible for Britain's policy of financial aid and technical co-operation in developing countries. It is concerned with the aid programme as a whole and with its detailed composition. The provision of financial aid includes both grants and loans (the latter on concessional terms) and support for multilateral aid agencies, such as the IBRD (World Bank); technical co-operation comprises the supply of British experts and equipment, training of overseas personnel, and support of research and advisory services.

The Department of Health and Social Security
The Department of Health and Social Security, headed by the Secretary of State for Social Services, is responsible in England for the administration of the National Health Service; for the social services provided by local authorities for the elderly and handicapped, socially deprived families, and children in care; and for certain aspects of public health, including hygiene. Throughout Great Britain it is responsible for the collection of social security

contributions and the payment of benefits. The Department is concerned in making reciprocal health and social security arrangements with other countries and in administering European Community social security regulations for immigrant workers. It also represents the United Kingdom in the World Health Organisation.

The Department is also responsible for paying supplementary benefits and family income supplement, for resettlement centres, and for assessing the means of people applying for legal aid. The Department also has responsibility for pensions and welfare services (including in some cases the provision of medical and surgical treatment) for war pensioners in the United Kingdom, the Channel Islands and the Isle of Man, and, through its various agencies, for United Kingdom war pensioners living in other countries. Within the Department, the Social Security Advisory Committee, which replaced the National Insurance Advisory Committee and the Supplementary Benefit Commissions of Great Britain and Northern Ireland in 1980, provides advice and assistance for the Secretary of State on the major part of the social security system, while the Industrial Injuries Advisory Council, the Attendance Allowance Board and the Occupational Pensions Board advise on their highly specialised, often technical areas.

The Secretary of State for Social Services is assisted by two Ministers of State (the Minister for Health and the Minister for Social Security, who also has special responsibility for the disabled) and two Parliamentary Under Secretaries of State.

The Home Office

The Home Office deals with those internal affairs in England and Wales not assigned to other government departments. The Secretary of State is the means of communication between the Crown and the public, and between the United Kingdom Government and the Governments of the Channel Islands and the Isle of Man. The minister exercises certain prerogative powers of the Crown, of which the most important are the prerogative of mercy and the maintenance of the Queen's Peace. The Home Office is also concerned with: the administration of justice; criminal law; the treatment of offenders, including probation and the prison service; certain public safety matters; the police, fire and emergency services; immigration and nationality; community relations; co-ordination of government action in relation to voluntary social services. Race relations and sex discrimination policy and broad questions of national broadcasting policy are also Home Office matters.

Other responsibilities include: addresses and petitions to the Queen, preparation of patents of nobility for peers, and formal proceedings for the granting of honours; requests for the extradition of criminals; scrutiny of local authority by-laws; granting of licences for scientific experiments on animals; exhumation and removal of bodies; firearms; dangerous drugs; general policy on laws relating to liquor licensing; gaming and lotteries; charitable collections; and theatre and cinema licensing. The Secretary of State is assisted by two Ministers of State and a Parliamentary Under Secretary of State.

The Department of Industry

The Department of Industry, under a Secretary of State, is responsible for policy in relation to industry including policy towards small firms. It is responsible for regional industrial policy and for financial assistance to industry other than through the tax system, though some of its functions in these areas relate only to England. The Department sponsors the general manufacturing industries as well as British Aerospace; British Shipbuilders, the British Steel Corporation, the Post Office, Cable and Wireless Ltd and the National

Enterprise Board. It is responsible for the operation of the Government's research establishments, and for the Business Statistics Office.

The Department's regional offices also serve the Departments of Trade and Energy.

The Secretary of State is assisted by two Ministers of State and two Parliamentary Under Secretaries of State.

The Central Office of Information

The Central Office of Information (COI), a common service department, produces information and publicity material, and supplies publicity services required by other government departments (which are responsible for the policies expressed). In the United Kingdom it conducts press, television, radio and poster advertising; produces booklets, leaflets, films, radio and television material, exhibitions, photographs and other visual material; and distributes departmental press notices. For the Foreign and Commonwealth Office it supplies British information posts overseas with press, radio and television material, publications and reference services (including this official handbook), films, exhibitions, photographs, and display and reading-room material. The COI provides exhibition services (except for trade and cultural exhibitions); and organises visits (other than those sponsored by the British Council and the British Overseas Trade Board) for people officially invited to Britain. It also provides services for London-based correspondents of the overseas news media and training facilities for information officers of overseas governments. There are nine regional information offices in England providing services for the home departments and assisting the overseas services by supplying reports on developments within their regions and by arranging visits for overseas visitors; similar services are provided on a mutually agreed basis by the information staffs of the Scottish, Welsh and Northern Ireland Offices.

The Board of Inland Revenue

The Board of Inland Revenue administers the laws relating to income tax, corporation tax, capital gains tax, stamp duty, capital transfer tax, petroleum revenue tax, development land tax and certain other direct taxes, and advises the Chancellor of the Exchequer on any matters connected with them. It is also responsible for the valuation of land and buildings for such purposes as compensation for compulsory purchase and, in England and Wales, local rates (a form of local property taxation).

The Law Officers' Department

The Law Officers of the Crown for England and Wales (the Attorney General and the Solicitor General) appear on behalf of the Crown in important civil and criminal proceedings and before international tribunals such as the International Court of Justice at The Hague and the European Commission and Court of Human Rights at Strasbourg. The Attorney General is the senior legal adviser to the Government and has the ultimate responsibility for the enforcement of the criminal law; his consent is necessary before proceedings for a number of criminal offences can be undertaken and he superintends the work of the Director of Public Prosecutions. Legal proceedings for the enforcement of public rights and on behalf of the interests of charity are conducted in the name of the Attorney General, who also directs the work of the Queen's Proctor, an officer with duties connected with the operation of the divorce laws.

The Attorney General is also spokesman for the Lord Chancellor in the House of Commons on matters affecting the administration of justice. The Solicitor General is subject to the authority of the Attorney General, with the same rights and duties. The Law Officers, who are leading barristers, are always members of the House of Commons.

The Lord Chancellor's Office

The Chancellorship is a legislative, judicial and executive office held by an eminent ex-member of the judiciary or of the Bar and carrying Cabinet rank.

In addition to functions as Speaker of the House of Lords and Custodian of the Great Seal, the Lord Chancellor may sit judicially as a member of the Appellate Committee of the House of Lords or of the Judicial Committee of the Privy Council.

The Lord Chancellor is also the minister primarily responsible for the administration of the courts and of the law. The Home Secretary has important responsibilities for the criminal law but the Lord Chancellor appoints magistrates and recommends to the Crown most other appointments to the judiciary in England, Wales and Northern Ireland. Responsibility for the courts and for their administrative staff is exercised through six regional (or circuit) offices and their sub-offices.

The Lord Chancellor is responsible for court procedure and for law reform, including appointing the members of the Law Commission, and presenting the Commission's reports to Parliament.

The Lord Chancellor appoints the chairmen of certain administrative tribunals in England and Wales, and (with the Secretary of State for Scotland) the members of the Council on Tribunals: he is also responsible for the administration of the Judge Advocate General's Department,[1] the Department of the Official Solicitor[2] and the Public Record Office (which preserves, and provides access to, the national archives).

Ordnance Survey

The Ordnance Survey is responsible for the surveying and mapping of Great Britain (Northern Ireland has its own Ordnance Survey). This includes geodetic surveys and associated scientific work, topographic surveys and the production of maps at appropriate scales from these surveys. The Department also undertakes a considerable amount of agency work for other departments, particularly the Ministry of Defence, for the Institute of Geological Sciences and for the Land Registry. Parliamentary responsibility for the Ordnance Survey is exercised by ministers of the Department of the Environment.

The Paymaster General's Office

The Paymaster General's Office acts generally as a banker for government departments other than the Boards of Inland Revenue and Customs and Excise, for which separate arrangements exist. Money granted by Parliament is transferred (in whatever sums may be required from day to day) from the Exchequer account to the account of the Paymaster General at the Bank of England. Most departmental payments are made by means of payable orders drawn on the Paymaster General's Office; their recipients obtain payments through the commercial banks, whose accounts at the Bank of England are in turn reimbursed by the Paymaster General's Office. The Department is also responsible for the regular payment of many public service pensions.

---

[1] The Judge Advocate General's Department advises the Secretary of State for Defence and the Defence Council on legal matters arising out of the administration of military law, and reviews the proceedings of army and air force courts martial.
[2] The Official Solicitor is concerned with the interests of minors and people with a mental disability involved in proceedings in the High Court, who would otherwise not be represented. In addition the Official Solicitor protects the interests of people committed to prison for contempt of court, acts as Receiver for people with a mental disability and as Judicial Trustee in complex and disputed trusts.

The Office of Population Censuses and Surveys

The Office of Population Censuses and Surveys (OPCS) is the office of th Registrar General for England and Wales. It is responsible for administerin, the Marriage Acts and local registration of births, marriages and deaths estimating and projecting national, regional and local populations and th movement of people within Britain and between Britain and overseas; compil ing statistics of diseases, injuries and deaths, and other aspects of health servic information; taking the Census of Population and processing, analysing an(reporting the resulting statistics; and conducting surveys on a wide range o subjects for other government departments.

The Department of the Procurator General and Treasury Solicitor

The Treasury Solicitor provides a common legal service for a large number o government departments in England and Wales. The duties of the Departmen include instructing Parliamentary Counsel on Bills and drafting subordinat legislation, representing other departments in court, and giving general advic on the interpretation and application of the law. The Department undertakes considerable amount of conveyancing connected with the transfer of property administers the estates of people dying intestate and without known relative and deals with the outstanding property and rights of dissolved companies The Statutory Publications Office is staffed and controlled by the Treasur Solicitor, who reports annually on its work to the Statute Law Committee (body appointed by the Lord Chancellor from among the judiciary and lega profession in Great Britain).

Some government departments are wholly dependent on the Treasur Solicitor for their legal work; some have their own legal staffs for a proportior of the work and draw on the Treasury Solicitor for special advice and, often for litigation and conveyancing; others, whose administrative work is based or or deals with a code of specialised law or involves a great deal of legal work have their own independent legal sections.

The Treasury Solicitor is also the Queen's Proctor (an officer with certair duties relating to the divorce laws).

Her Majesty's Stationery Office

Her Majesty's Stationery Office (HMSO) is the publisher for Parliament anc the Government. The Controller is the Queen's Printer of Acts of Parliamen and is responsible for the copyright of all British government documents Official publications are sold by government bookshops in London, Edin burgh, Cardiff, Belfast, Manchester, Bristol and Birmingham, and througI agents and booksellers overseas. HMSO is the United Kingdom agent fo publications of the European Community and other principal internationa organisations.

HMSO provides a wide range of procurement services for Parliament anc the Government in the areas of printing and office supplies. It also operates its own printing presses and binderies, the latter concentrating on conservatior work for the national archives.

The Department is managed as a commercial body on the basis of its relationships with its customers and its borrowing from the National Loans Fund.

The Department of Trade

The Department of Trade is responsible, under a Secretary of State, for commercial policy and relations with overseas countries. It promotes British commercial interests overseas, negotiates trade and commercial matters, and administers British protective tariffs. It sponsors the work of the British Overseas Trade Board in export services and government support for overseas trade fairs and provides an information service to industry largely through its eight regional offices. It is responsible for consumer affairs and competition policy; companies legislation, supervision of the insurance industry, the insolvency service and for patent, trade mark and copyright matters. Other responsibilities include civil aviation, marine and shipping policy, tourism, the hotel and travel industries, the newspaper, printing, publishing and film industries, and the distributive and service trades. The Secretary of State is assisted by two Ministers of State (one of whom is Minister for Consumer Affairs) and two Parliamentary Under Secretaries of State.

The Department of Transport

The Department of Transport, headed by a Minister who is assisted by a Parliamentary Secretary, is responsible in England for the main transport industries, including railways, buses, freight and ports. It is also responsible for the planning and construction of motorways and trunk roads, although decisions arising from independent inspectors' reports on public inquiries into roads are shared with the Department of the Environment. Further responsibilities include local transport, road and vehicle safety, and vehicle and driver licensing.

The Welsh Office

The Secretary of State for Wales, a Cabinet minister, has full responsibility in Wales for ministerial functions relating to health and personal social services, housing, local government, education (except universities), town and country planning, new towns, water and sewerage, roads, agriculture, forestry, tourism, national parks, ancient monuments and historic buildings, the careers service and the work in Wales of the Manpower Services Commission. The Secretary of State has certain responsibilities relating to the National Library and the National Museum; the Wales Tourist Board and the Sports Council for Wales, and shared responsibility for the administration of urban grants to areas of acute social deprivation. The Secretary of State, who is assisted by two Parliamentary Under Secretaries of State, has direct ministerial responsibility in Wales for selective financial assistance to industry, as well as a general responsibility for economic development. The Welsh Development Agency and the Development Board for Rural Wales, which are responsible to the Secretary of State, also have important industrial, environmental and (in the case of the Board) social functions.

The Welsh Office maintains close and continuous contacts with the government departments mainly concerned with economic and industrial affairs. The main Welsh Office is in Cardiff, with branches throughout Wales and a small ministerial office in London.

SCOTLAND

Scotland has its own system of law and a wide measure of administrative autonomy. The Secretary of State for Scotland, a Cabinet minister, has responsibility in Scotland (with some exceptions) both for formulating and carrying out policy relating to agriculture and fisheries, education, law and order, local government and environmental services, social work, health, housing, roads and certain aspects of shipping and road transport services.

The Secretary of State also has a major and expanding role in the planning and development of the Scottish economy, and important functions related to industrial development, with responsibility for selective financial assistance to industry, for the Scottish Development Agency, and for the work of the Manpower Services Commission and the careers service. Moreover, the Secretary of State plays a full part in the Government's determination of energy policy, particularly in relation to responsibility for the electricity supply industry in Scotland.

The Secretary of State is responsible for legal services in Scotland, and other important functions are exercised by the two Scottish Law Officers: the Lord Advocate and the Solicitor General for Scotland. On many domestic matters, the distinctively Scottish features and the different conditions and needs of the country and its people are reflected in separate legislation relating wholly to Scotland, or else in sections of special application to Scotland only inserted in Acts which otherwise apply to the United Kingdom generally. The Secretary of State is also responsible for a range of other functions from fire services to sport and tourism. A Minister of State and three Parliamentary Under Secretaries of State assist the Secretary of State.

The United Kingdom Government's administrative functions arising from these responsibilities are carried out principally by five Scottish departments supported by Central Services, based in Edinburgh (although with some staff dispersed over Scotland), known collectively as the Scottish Office. The Scottish Office Management Group, under the chairmanship of the Permanent Under-Secretary of State, with a membership consisting of the head of each of the departments and the Deputy Secretary, Central Services, advises the Secretary of State, particularly on questions such as the allocation of resources and forward planning, with which more than one of the departments are concerned.

United Kingdom government departments with significant Scottish responsibilities have offices in Scotland with delegated powers and work closely with the Scottish Office.

The Department of Agriculture and Fisheries for Scotland

The Department of Agriculture and Fisheries for Scotland is responsible for promoting the agriculture and fishing industries in Scotland. For agriculture this includes taking part in European Community negotiations on agricultural policy, providing technical and financial help to farmers, supervising educational, advisory and research services, administering a variety of schemes for the improvement of land, farm stock and crops, developing crofting and managing a large area of agricultural land which is in public ownership. Its duties for fisheries include participating in international arrangements for conservation and other aspects of fishing and in the European Community negotiations on fisheries policy, providing financial support for the fishing industry, assistance for fishery harbours, scientific research and the protection of Scottish fisheries by the Department's fleet of fishery protection vessels.

The Scottish Development Department

The Scottish Development Department is concerned with a number of key services affecting the physical development of Scotland, such as town and country planning, housing, roads, water supplies and sewerage, coast protection, flood prevention, building standards and the prevention of river and air pollution (most of which are administered by local authorities). The Department is also responsible for general policy relating to local government organisation and for ancient monuments and historic buildings; certain transport functions including oversight of the Scottish Transport Group; and assistance for shipping services, ferry services, pier work, and air services in the Highlands and Islands.

The Scottish Economic Planning Department

The Scottish Economic Planning Department is responsible for industrial and economic development including the Scottish aspects of regional and industrial policies in relation to both the United Kingdom and the European Community, and the economic aspects of North Sea oil and gas development; selective assistance to industry; oversight of the Scottish Development

Agency; manpower policy, including employment and unemployment, training and retraining and the careers service; the Highlands and Islands Development Board and the Scottish Tourist Board; electricity; and new towns. The Department also acts as agent in Scotland for certain of the services of the Departments of Trade and Industry.

The Scottish Education Department

The Scottish Education Department is responsible for industrial and public education in Scotland in all its forms (except universities). Through its Social Work Services Group the Department has a responsibility for the guidance of local authorities in their provision and development of social work services. It is also concerned with sport, including the financing of the Scottish Sports Council, with the development of the arts, and with administering the National Galleries of Scotland, the Royal Scottish Museum (including the Scottish United Services Museum), the National Museum of Antiquities of Scotland, and the National Library of Scotland.

The Scottish Home and Health Department

The Scottish Home and Health Department is responsible for the central administration of functions relating to law and order, including the police service, criminal justice (other than the conduct of prosecutions), legal aid and the administration of penal institutions. It is also responsible for administering the National Health Service in Scotland, for legislation relating to public service superannuation schemes in Scotland and for administering the teachers' and National Health Service superannuation schemes. The Home and Health Department is the central authority in Scotland for the fire service, for certain home defence and emergency services, and for legislation concerning shops, theatres, cinemas, licensed premises and land tenure matters.

Central Services

Central Services provides a series of services to the other five departments. They include the Finance Divisions which, in addition to providing a common finance service, are responsible for developing and administering local government finance policy. They also include the Office of the Solicitor to the Secretary of State; the Inquiry Reporters Unit; Liaison Division in London; the Scottish Information Office; the Central Statistical Unit; and the Establishment and related divisions which provide supporting services such as personnel management, manpower control, computer telecommunications, library and office services.

Other Administrative Departments

In addition to the main departments, there are a number of other Scottish departments, all of which work in varying degrees under the direction of the Secretary of State. These include the Department of the Registrar-General for Scotland (the General Register Office); the Scottish Record Office; and the Department of the Registers of Scotland. There are also Scottish branches of the Great Britain and United Kingdom departments under the direction of controllers, who are responsible for ensuring that the policy and procedure of their departments are carried out in Scotland in accordance with Scottish conditions and needs.

The Scottish Law Officers

The Law Officers of the Crown for Scotland (the Lord Advocate and the Solicitor General for Scotland) are the chief legal advisers to the Government on Scottish questions and the principal representatives of the Crown for litigation in Scotland. The Lord Advocate is also closely concerned with questions of legal policy and administration and is responsible for instituting and directing all prosecutions on indictment in Scotland, and for controlling summary prosecutions in the Sheriff and District Courts, which are conducted by officials of the Procurator Fiscal Service. In some of this work the Lord Advocate is assisted by the Lord Advocate's Department and the Scottish Courts Administration. The members of the Lord Advocate's Department also act as legal advisers on Scottish questions to certain government departments which have no Scottish legal adviser of their own. The work relating to prosecutions is centred in the Crown Office in Edinburgh.

The Parliamentary Draftsmen for Scotland, incorporated in the Lord Advocate's Department, are responsible to the minister concerned and to the Law Officers for the drafting of government Bills affecting the law of Scotland.

The Scottish Courts Administration

The Scottish Courts Administration has a general responsibility to the Secretary of State for the organisation, administration and staffing of the courts and court offices, and is responsible to the Lord Advocate for certain functions in the field of law, including the programme of the Scottish Law Commission, proposals for law reform and questions involving private international law, internal conventions and associated problems, the jurisdiction and procedure of the Scottish courts, and enforcement of judgments.

NORTHERN IRELAND

The Government of Ireland Act 1920 enacted a constitution which, while preserving the supreme authority of the United Kingdom Parliament and reserving certain matters to that Parliament, provided Northern Ireland with its own legislature and executive to deal with domestic 'transferred' matters. This structure remained in force until 1972 when, following several years of sectarian violence and terrorism in Northern Ireland, the Northern Ireland Government resigned and a period of direct rule was introduced, with executive powers under the control of a Secretary of State for Northern Ireland. In 1973 a new constitution for the Province provided, among other things, for the devolution of powers to a legislative assembly and a 'power-sharing' executive with responsibility for the devolved services (such as agriculture, commerce, education, health and the environment). Responsibility for law and order, electoral matters and business of national importance such as foreign policy, defence and most aspects of taxation remained with the United Kingdom Government and Parliament. These arrangements came into force in January 1974, but following widespread opposition in Northern Ireland the Executive resigned and the Assembly was prorogued in May 1974. In July 1974 the Northern Ireland Act was passed, providing for the election of a Constitutional Convention to consider what arrangements for the government of Northern Ireland would be likely to command most widespread acceptance throughout the community. The Act provided for an interim period (defined as one year from the passing of the Act) during which the United Kingdom Government, through the Secretary of State for Northern Ireland, should continue to be responsible to the United Kingdom Parliament for the devolved services.

The Northern Ireland Assembly was finally dissolved at the end of March 1975, and elections to the Constitutional Convention and its first meeting took place in May of that year. In March 1976, the Convention was dissolved, having failed to reach agreement on the central issue of a system of government which would attract the widespread acceptance of the community. Direct rule as provided for in the Northern Ireland Act has since been extended for further periods of a year and Northern Ireland departments continue to discharge their functions under the direction and control of the Secretary of State for Northern Ireland. The Government's aim is to restore peace and security to the Province and to promote social and economic welfare. It is also seeking an acceptable way of restoring to the people of Northern Ireland more control over their own affairs and has published proposals for the future government of the Province (see Bibliography). These envisage a substantial transfer of power to a new Northern Ireland Assembly and Executive and set out two broad options for participation by representatives of the minority community.

The Northern Ireland Office

The Northern Ireland Office is the department of the Secretary of State for Northern Ireland who, assisted by two Ministers of State and three Parliamentary Under Secretaries of State, has overall responsibility, and is answerable to Parliament, for the government of Northern Ireland. Through this Office the Secretary of State has responsibility for constitutional developments, law and order and security, and electoral matters.

Northern Ireland Departments

Department of Agriculture

The Northern Ireland departments are subject to the direction and control of the Secretary of State. Their principal functions are listed below.

The Department of Agriculture is responsible for the development of Northern Ireland's agricultural, forestry and fishing industries. Its functions also include the collection of agricultural census data, the compilation of statistics, the provision of extensive advisory services to farmers, and the promotion of agricultural research, education and training. The Department acts as agent of the Ministry of Agriculture, Fisheries and Food in agricultural support and the implementation of the European Community's Common Agricultural Policy.

Department of the Civil Service

The Department of the Civil Service is responsible for the general management and control of the Northern Ireland Civil Service.

Department of Commerce

The Department of Commerce is concerned with the development of Northern Ireland's industry and commerce, and with the administration of schemes of assistance to industry including liaison with the Local Enterprise Development Unit and Northern Ireland Development Agency; trade promotion including supplies to the offshore oil industry sector; energy supply and conservation; development of tourism; harbours (other than fishery harbours); safety in mines and quarries; mineral development; consumer protection (including weights and measures); registration of companies; societies, credit unions and trade unions; control of insurance companies and unit trusts; industrial science and technology promotion.

Department of Education

The Department of Education is responsible for central policy, co-ordination, legislation and financial control of the education and library service. It is concerned not only with education and learning but with recreation, culture, and entertainment. The Department is responsible for the development of primary, secondary and further education, including higher education, community and adult education, special education, oversight of the five area education and library boards, teacher training, teachers' salaries and superannuation, examinations, the arts and libraries, youth services, sport and recreation and community services and facilities.

Department of the Environment

The Department of the Environment has direct responsibility for the construction and maintenance of all roads, the provision of water supplies and sewerage services and for planning and planning compensation. In addition it exercises certain controls over housing and local government and has responsibility for public health, public transport, road traffic management, motor taxation, historic monuments and buildings.

Department of
Finance

The Department of Finance's responsibilities include the control of the expenditure of the Northern Ireland departments, liaison with the United Kingdom Treasury and the Northern Ireland Office on financial matters, and economic and social research and statistics.

The Department also has responsibility for: rating policy and the collection of rates; borrowing; loan advances; charities; the provision and maintenance of public buildings; building regulations and liaison with the construction industry; Ordnance Survey; valuation; Public Record Office; the registration of births, marriages and deaths; Registry of Deeds; the registration of title of land; miscellaneous licensing; the registration of clubs; and Ulster Savings.

Department of
Health and Social
Services

The Department of Health and Social Services is responsible for social security and, through four Health and Social Services Boards and the Central Services Agency, for personal and public health services and for personal social services (including child care and adoption).

Department of
Manpower
Services

The Department of Manpower Services has responsibility for the administration of government policy in relation to the employment and training of labour. It operates Jobmarkets, employment service and careers offices; administers a comprehensive training programme; operates grant schemes to encourage training and employment; compiles statistics on employment and unemployment and undertakes research into employment matters. It provides a factory inspectorate and deals with industrial relations and the rehabilitation and employment of the disabled.

It is also responsible for sponsorship of the direct labour organisation of Enterprise Ulster and has functions in relation to the Industry Training Boards, Northern Ireland Training Executive, Fair Employment Agency, the Equal Opportunities Commission, the Labour Relations Agency and the Health and Safety Agency.

THE CIVIL SERVICE

The Civil Service is concerned with the conduct of the whole range of government activities as they affect the community. Civil servants' work extends from the formulation of policy proposals for ministers to the management of the machinery of Government and the carrying out of the day-to-day duties that public administration demands.

Civil Servants are servants of the Crown. They are responsible to the minister in whose department they work for the execution of the minister's policies. Ministers alone are answerable to Parliament for their policies and the actions of their staff. A change of minister, whether due to ministerial changes within the administration or to the advent of a Government of a different political complexion, does not involve a change of staff. (Ministers sometimes appoint special policy advisers from outside the Civil Service; the advisers are paid from public funds, but their appointments come to an end when the Government term of office finishes.) Selection to the Service is by open competition supervised by a formally independent body; the system of promotion within the Service is by merit.

Including part-time staff (two part-time officers being reckoned as equivalent to one full-time), there are about 700,200 civil servants (over 40 per cent of them women), roughly 320,000 of whom are engaged in the provision of public services, such as paying sickness benefits and pensions, collecting taxes and contributions, running employment services, staffing prisons, and providing services to industry and agriculture. About 240,000 are employed in the Ministry of Defence, including the Royal Ordnance factories and Royal Dockyards. The rest are about equally divided between: central administrative and policy duties; service-wide support services, such as accommodation, printing and information; and largely financially self-supporting services, for instance those provided by the Department for National Savings and the Royal Mint.

Three-quarters of civil servants work outside London. As part of its policy of reducing the claims of the public sector on the country's resources the Government is making significant cuts in Civil Service manpower. Between May 1979 and July 1980 numbers were reduced from 732,000 to 700,200; a further reduction to 630,000 by 1984 is planned.

The total number includes about 157,000 'industrial' civil servants, mainly manual workers in government industrial establishments, whose pay and conditions of service are on the whole separately administered from those of 'non-industrial' civil servants.

Structure

The structure of the Home Civil Service is designed to allow for a flexible deployment of staff so that talent can be used to the best advantage, with higher posts open to people of outstanding ability, whatever their specialist background or original method of entry into the Service. Although work requiring specialist skill is always done by appropriately qualified individuals, personnel management policies are designed to ensure that people with the necessary qualities gain suitable wide experience to fit them for higher posts.

At the top levels of the Civil Service, where staff are predominantly concerned with higher management and policy, there is an open and unified structure, comprising three grades—permanent secretary, deputy secretary and under secretary. With very few exceptions, staff at this level share the same pay and grading system whatever their background and duties.

At other levels the structure is based on a system of occupational groups, which are the basic groupings of staff for the purposes of pay, recruitment and personnel management, and categories which consist of one or more occupational groups having a common pay and grading pattern.

Categories include the General Category (covering the Administration, Economist, Statistician, Information Officer and Librarian groups), the Science Category, the Professional and Technology Category (including architects, surveyors, electrical and mechanical engineers, graphics officers and marine services staff), and the Training, Legal, Police, Secretarial, Data Processing, Research Officer, Social Security, Physical Security and Museum Categories. Together these 12 categories account for some 75 per cent of non-industrial staff.

The Diplomatic Service

The Diplomatic Service, a separate service of the Crown, provides the staff for service in the Foreign and Commonwealth Office and at United Kingdom diplomatic missions and consular posts in foreign and in independent Commonwealth countries. Its functions include advising on policy, negotiating with overseas governments and conducting business in international organisations; promoting British exports and trade generally, administering aid, presenting ideas, policies and objectives to the people of overseas countries;

and protecting British interests abroad. Nearly a third are employed on export promotion, a quarter on consular work, and the remainder are divided between political, economic, information and cultural work.

The Service has its own grade structure, linked for salary purposes with that of the Home Civil Service, and conditions of work are in many ways comparable while taking into account the special demands of the Service, particularly of postings overseas. The Service also has secretarial, communications and security officer branches. Members of the Home Civil Service and the armed forces, and individuals from the private sector, may serve in the Foreign and Commonwealth Office and at overseas posts on loan or attachment. A closer working relationship between the Diplomatic Service and the Home Civil Service is planned.

The Northern Ireland Civil Service

Northern Ireland has its own Civil Service which, subject to regional differences, is modelled on its counterpart in Great Britain, recruitment being effected through its own Civil Service Commission. Interchange of staff between the two Civil Services occurs to a minor extent only, and is a matter for departmental agreement in individual cases.

Public Services of Overseas Dependent Territories

Britain's dependent territories fill vacancies in their public services by the appointment of suitably qualified local candidates wherever possible; but when vacancies cannot be filled by this means the Foreign and Commonwealth Office, the Overseas Development Administration and the Crown Agents for Oversea Governments and Administrations are generally asked to recruit other candidates, principally from the United Kingdom. Hong Kong has its own Government office in London with responsibility for recruiting to the Hong Kong public service.

Recruitment and Training

Recruitment to the Home Civil Service and the Diplomatic Service is the responsibility of the Civil Service Commission which, in conjunction with departments, ensures that staff are selected solely on merit through fair and open competition. The selection of junior staff such as those engaged in clerical and manual work, is undertaken almost entirely by departments. The Commission, however, is responsible for issuing the 'certificate of qualification' necessary for permanent appointment. The appointment of a successful candidate is made by the department concerned.

For the Administration Group, the central part of the Home Civil Service, entry is at three levels relating broadly to the academic achievements of: an honours degree; GCE Advanced level; and GCE Ordinary level. The selection procedure for the highest of these levels (the Administration Trainee entry) comprises qualifying tests, followed by tests and interviews at the Civil Service Selection Board and an interview by the Final Selection Board. For the next level (the Executive Officer entry) selection involves qualifying tests for those possessing the necessary academic qualifications, followed by an interview. For the lower level (the clerical entry) selection is normally by interview of those holding the prescribed educational qualifications.

Entry to the professional and technical grades usually requires appropriate qualifications, and selection is on the basis of past record and by interview.

In all except the smallest government departments there are full-time training officers and tutors whose task is to help identify the training needs of the staff and to organise training by the most appropriate methods (for example, formal courses or self-instruction) to provide for their varying requirements. The Civil Service College provides that training which is most efficiently undertaken centrally, and considerable use is made of external institutions.

Civil servants under the age of 18 may continue their education by attending appropriate courses usually for one day a week ('day release' schemes). Adult staff are assisted financially to undertake, mainly in their own time, private studies leading to recognised educational or professional qualifications in approved subjects. There are also opportunities for civil servants in mid-career to obtain fellowships or to go on sabbatical leave to undertake research in areas of interest to themselves and their departments.

Promotion and Conditions of Service

All new entrants undergo a period of probation (varying according to grade, with extensions in certain instances). Promotions are made partly through centrally conducted competitions and partly by the departments themselves. Normally promotion is from grade to grade, but arrangements exist for accelerated promotion for staff who show exceptional promise. Promotions or appointments to deputy secretary-level posts and above and all transfers between departments at these levels are approved by the Prime Minister, advised by the official head of the Home Civil Service.

Civil Servants are encouraged to join the trade union which represents the grade to which they belong. The National Whitley Council, consisting of senior officials (called the Official Side) and representatives of the unions (known as the Trade Union Side) exists to discuss all matters affecting conditions of service of staff and to provide a forum for consultation. Whitley committees exist in all government departments. Pay negotiations are conducted directly with the individual unions or with the Trade Union Side representing all the unions.

Political and Private Activities

Civil servants are required to serve loyally the Government of the day, regardless of its political composition. In order therefore to maintain civil servants' reputation for political impartiality, some restrictions are placed on freedom to participate in political activities. No civil servant may be a member of Parliament, or (with certain exceptions corresponding to the 'politically free' group shown below) be adopted as parliamentary candidate.

Civil Service rules place staff in one of three groups for the purpose of political activities: (1) the 'politically free' group, consisting of industrial and non-office grades, who are free to engage in any political activity including standing for Parliament (although they would have to resign from the Service if elected); (2) the 'politically restricted' group, consisting of all staff above Executive Officer level, together with those Executive Officers and certain related grades such as Information Officers, who are debarred from national political activities but may apply for permission to take part in local political activities; and (3) the 'intermediate' group, comprising all other staff—mainly clerical and typing grades—who may apply for permission to take part in national or local political activity apart from adoption as a parliamentary candidate.

Where required, permission is granted to the maximum extent consistent with the reputation of the Civil Service for political impartiality and the avoidance of any conflict with official duties. It is granted subject to a code of discretion requiring moderation and the avoidance of embarrassment to ministers. An independent committee of inquiry, set up by the Government to review the Civil Service rules governing political activities, has reported in favour of retaining the general framework of these rules in order to maintain the principle of Civil Service political impartiality, and has recommended some changes which would transfer a substantial number of staff from the 'restricted' to the 'intermediate' group, establish standard criteria against which applications for permission could be judged, and provide an appeal body for staff who are refused permission. These recommendations are the subject of consultations.

All civil servants have the right to register their private political opinions by voting, for instance, at general or local authority elections. They may also engage in any private activities they wish, provided there is no conflict with official duties, nor with the provisions of the official secrets or prevention of corruption legislation. However, since civil servants must not use their official position to further private interests, they are subject to certain restrictions in commerce and business: for instance they may not hold private interests in public contracts nor use official information in writing, broadcasting or lecturing without the approval of their department.

Security

As a general rule the political views of civil servants are not a matter of official concern. However, no one whose loyalty is in doubt may be employed on work the nature of which is vital to the security of the State. For this reason certain posts are not open to anyone who is known to be a member of a Communist or Fascist organisation, or associated with such an organisation in a way that raises legitimate doubts about his or her reliability, or to anyone whose reliability may be in doubt for any other reason.

Each department is responsible for its own internal security, advised as necessary by the Security Service. The Security Commission, if requested to do so by the Prime Minister after consultation with the Leader of the Opposition, may investigate any report on breaches of security in the public service and advise whether any change in security procedure is necessary or desirable.

LOCAL GOVERNMENT

A wide range of public services is provided by local authorities throughout the United Kingdom, democratically elected in the areas for which they are responsible. The gradual expansion of local authority services, particularly in the period between the late 1940s and mid-1970s, has inevitably led to a steady rise in local government expenditure and in its support from central funds. In recent years central government has sought to check this growth as part of a general policy of reducing public expenditure, and at local level sections of the electorate have protested at having to meet the considerable annual increases in 'rates' (local property taxes—see p 66). Since taking office, the Government has emphasised the need to achieve substantial reductions in public expenditure in order to redress the balance between the public and private sectors of the national economy and has asked local authorities to reduce their expenditure in line with reductions being made in its own spending. Local authorities have also been asked to follow the example of central government and to reappraise urgently their staff recruitment and manpower requirements.

The specific powers and duties of local authorities are conferred on them by Act of Parliament, or by measures made under the authority of an Act. The actual administration, and the exercise of discretion within statutory limits, are the responsibility of the local authority. In the case of certain services, however, government ministers have powers, defined in the relevant Acts, to secure a measure of national uniformity in the standard of a service provided, to safeguard public health, or to protect the rights of individual citizens. For some services the minister concerned has wide powers of supervision; for others there are strictly limited powers.

Legislation before Parliament would introduce important changes in the relationship between central and local government. It includes proposals for removing a substantial number of central government controls over local government; for increasing the accountability of local authorities; for introducing in England and Wales a new system of financing local government; and for controlling local authorities' capital expenditure.

The main links between local authorities and the central Government are: in England, the Department of the Environment; in Scotland, the Scottish Development Department; in Wales, the Welsh Office; and in Northern Ireland, the Department of the Environment for Northern Ireland.

Principal Types of Local Authority

The main pattern of local government organisation in England and Wales (outside Greater London) is a division of the country into 53 large county authorities, within which there are 369 smaller district authorities. Both types of authority have independent, locally elected councils, and have separate functions to perform. County authorities normally provide the large-scale local government services, while the districts are responsible for the more local ones (see pp 63–4). However, in six of the English counties, which are heavily populated and known as 'metropolitan' counties, responsibility for some large-scale services rests with the district authorities. In England populations in the non-metropolitan counties range from 289,800 to about 1·5 million (the Isle of Wight with a population of about 115,000 is an exception), and in the metropolitan counties from 1·3 to 2·7 million. District authorities within metropolitan counties have populations of between 162,600 and 1 million: other districts have average populations of between 75,000 and 100,000 although many fall outside this range. The local government system in Wales closely resembles that in non-metropolitan areas of England. Populations in the counties range from 106,000 to 537,900 and the districts have populations of between 20,700 and 278,400. English parish councils or meetings serve as focuses for local opinion as bodies with limited powers of local interest. In Wales community councils have similar functions.

Greater London—an administrative area of about 1,580 sq km (610 sq miles) and a population of some 7 million—is administered by the Greater London Council, the councils of 32 London boroughs (with populations ranging from 135,700 to 320,500) and the Corporation of the City of London (the historic centre with a resident population of 5,500).

On the mainland of Scotland local government is on a two-tier basis: nine regions are divided into 53 districts, each area having its own elected council. There are three virtually all-purpose authorities for Orkney, Shetland and the Western Isles. Provision is made for local community councils to be formed. These councils have no statutory functions and are not local authorities.

The pattern of local authorities, and of their electoral arrangements, is kept up to date by Boundary Commissions for England, Wales and Scotland.

In Northern Ireland there are 26 district councils which are responsible for local environmental and certain other services. Statutory bodies and local offices, responsible to central departments, administer major services such as roads, water, education, health, and housing. Populations of the districts range from 13,000 to over 350,000.

Election of Councils

Local authority councils consist of a number of elected unpaid councillors presided over by a chairman. They can claim a flat-rate attendance allowance for performing council business; they are also entitled to travelling and subsistence allowances. Parish and community councillors cannot claim expenses for duties within their own areas.

In England, Wales and Northern Ireland each council annually elects a chairman and vice-chairman. Some districts have the ceremonial title of borough, or city, both granted by royal authority (except in Northern Ireland where they are granted by the Secretary of State). In boroughs and cities the chairman is normally known as the Mayor (in the City of London and certain other large cities, he or she is known as the Lord Mayor). In Scottish regions and islands areas the chairman is called the convener and the chairman of the district councils of each of the four cities is called the Lord Provost. No general title is laid down for the chairmen of the other district councils, but some are known as conveners, while others continue to use the old title of 'provost'.

The normal term of office for a councillor elected to any form of local government is usually four years. In England and Wales county council elections took place in 1977 and will be held every fourth year thereafter. Metropolitan district elections are held for a third of the seats in each year when there is no county council election. Non-metropolitan district councils may adopt the same procedure or opt for whole council elections; the latter took place in 1979 and will be held again every fourth year. In London elections to the Greater London Council were held in 1977 and elections to the London borough councils in 1978; elections will be held every fourth year. In Scotland elections for the regions and islands areas took place in 1978, and will be held again in 1982. Elections for the districts were held in 1977, again in 1980 and thereafter will take place every four years. Elections for the district councils in Northern Ireland took place in 1977 and will be held every fourth year thereafter.

Any person (including a member of the House of Lords) is entitled to vote at a local government election in Great Britain provided that he or she is aged 18 years or over, is a British subject or a citizen of the Irish Republic, is not subject to any legal incapacity and is registered as a local government elector for the area for which the election is held. A person qualifies for registration as a local government elector if, on the qualifying date for the register (compiled annually), he or she is resident in the council area. In Northern Ireland there are slightly different residence requirements.

A candidate for election as councillor—man or woman—normally stands as a representative of one of the national political parties, as a member of an association representing some local interest, or as an independent. Candidates must be British subjects or citizens of the Irish Republic and aged 21 or over. In addition they must be registered as a local government elector in the area of the local authority to which they seek election; or have resided or occupied (as owner or tenant) land or other premises in that area during the whole of the 12 months preceding the day on which they are nominated as candidates or, in that 12 months, have had their principal or only place of work there. Candidates are also subject to a number of statutory disqualifications designed to ensure that unsuitable people do not offer themselves for election.

Local authority areas are generally divided into electoral areas for local council elections. Administrative counties in England and Wales are divided into electoral divisions returning one or more councillors. Districts in England, Wales and Northern Ireland are divided into electoral 'wards'. In Scotland in the regions and islands areas the electoral areas are called electoral divisions, each returning a single member; the districts are divided into wards, similarly returning a single member. For parish or community council elections in England and Wales, each parish or community, or ward of a parish or community (or, in some cases, a combination of parishes or communities) forms an electoral area which returns one or more members. For elections to the Greater London Council, Greater London is divided into electoral divisions, each returning one councillor.

Voting takes place at polling stations arranged by the returning officer concerned, and under the supervision of a presiding officer appointed for the purpose. The procedure for local government voting in Great Britain is similar to that for parliamentary elections, although facilities for postal voting are more restricted. There is no postal voting for parish or community council elections. Each elector has one vote for each seat contested in the electoral area: he or she need not record every vote, but must not give more than one vote for each candidate. In Northern Ireland local government elections are held on the basis of proportional representation and electoral wards are grouped into district electoral areas. Facilities for postal voting are available.

Functions and Services

The functions of local authorities are far reaching. Some are framed primarily as duties on an authority, others are purely permissive.

Broadly speaking, functions in England and Wales are divided between county and district councils on the basis that county councils are responsible for matters requiring planning and administration over wide areas or requiring the support of substantial resources. Within the metropolitan areas district councils are responsible for functions needing substantial resources because they have populations large enough to give such support. District councils as a whole administer functions of more local significance. In London the division of functions is slightly different.

In England county councils are generally responsible for strategic planning, transportation planning, highways, traffic regulation, consumer protection, refuse disposal, police and the fire service. Education, libraries and the personal social services are functions of county councils in non-metropolitan areas and of district councils in metropolitan areas. All district councils are responsible, for instance, for environmental health, housing, decisions on most planning applications, and refuse collection. They may also provide off-street car parks subject to the consent of the county council. Powers to operate some functions—such as the provision of museums, art galleries and parks—are available at both levels; arrangements depend on local agreement.

In Greater London the London boroughs and the Corporation of the City of London are responsible for the same range of functions as district councils in metropolitan areas (with the addition of consumer protection). The Greater London Council (GLC) deals only with those services which by their nature require unified administration and control over the whole area. In the inner London area education is administered by the Inner London Education Authority, an autonomous committee of the GLC. Responsibility for highways in London is divided according to the type of road: the main strategic road network is a matter for the GLC, while the London boroughs look after the other roads. The boroughs have prime responsibility for the provision of housing. The GLC, which has maintained a substantial stock of housing, has relinquished its role as a primary housing authority (by transferring its housing stock to the boroughs and surrounding districts and by offering tenants the chance to buy their own homes) to concentrate on its strategic role focusing attention on areas of particular housing need. London's police force (see p 105) is directly responsible to the Home Secretary.

In Wales the division of functions between county and district councils is much the same as that between county and district councils in non-metropolitan areas of England. The main differences are that Welsh district councils are responsible for refuse disposal as well as collection; they may, subject to the consent of the county council, provide on-street as well as off-street car parking facilities; and they may, exceptionally, be responsible for library facilities.

Local authorities in England and Wales may arrange for most of their functions to be carried out on their behalf by another local authority. The exceptions to this general rule are functions relating to education, police, the personal social services and national parks.

In Scotland the regional and district authorities discharge local government functions in a way broadly similar to that of authorities in England and Wales. Orkney, Shetland and the Western Isles, because of their isolation from the mainland, have single, virtually all-purpose authorities.

In Northern Ireland, local environmental and certain other services are administered by the district councils, but responsibility for planning, roads, water supply and sewerage services is exercised in each district by a local office of the Department of the Environment for Northern Ireland working closely with the district council and its staff. Area boards, responsible to central departments, administer locally education, public libraries and the health and personal social services. The Northern Ireland Housing Executive, responsible to the Department of the Environment, administers housing.

Internal Organisation of Local Authorities

Local authorities are free to a very considerable extent to make their own internal arrangements for discharging their responsibilities. Most councils use the committee system, whereby questions of policy and principle are decided in full council, and committees are appointed to administer the various services. Parish and community councils in England and Wales are often able to do their work efficiently in full session although they appoint committees from time to time as necessary. Some councils have established policy advisory or co-ordinating committees with powers to originate policy, subject to the approval of the full council. The powers and duties of local authority committees (which may be advisory or executive) are usually laid down in the appointing council's standing orders.

A council is free to delegate all its powers to committees, except its powers in connection with raising loans, levying rates (see p 66), or making financial demands on other authorities liable to contribute; these are legally reserved to the council as a whole.

Local authorities can make arrangements among themselves for the discharge of their functions. These include co-operation through joint committees, joint teams and the loan of staff. One authority may discharge functions for another, and may also supply others with a range of goods and services.

The public and the press are admitted to all meetings of a council (and of committees) but may be excluded while a particular item is considered if the council (or committee) decides that publicity for that matter would be prejudicial to the public interest.

Officers and Employees

The execution of council policy rests with salaried officers and employees, of whom there may be tens of thousands in the larger authorities. Over 2 million people are employed by local authorities in Great Britain. These include administrative, professional and technical staff, teachers and manual workers.

Although a few appointments, such as chief education and fire officers and the director of social services, must by law be made by all the authorities responsible for the functions concerned, councils are individually responsible within national policy requirements for determining the size and composition of their work forces and the way they should be used. An authority must not, however, employ one of its own councillors. In Northern Ireland, each council must by law appoint a clerk of the council as its chief officer.

As a general rule, employees are of three kinds: heads of departments or chief officers, whose duties are mainly of an administrative and managerial kind; officers employed in an administrative, professional, clerical or technical capacity; and manual workers who are employed to do the physical work for which the council is responsible. Senior staff appointments are usually made on the recommendation of the committee or committees particularly concerned; most junior appointments are made by heads of departments, who are also responsible for engaging manual workers. Appointments and engagements always conform to the council's set establishment, and committees are informed of any appointments which they have not made themselves.

Pay and conditions of service for local authority staff are within the jurisdiction of the employing council, although there are recommended scales.

Local Government Finance

Local authority expenditure in the United Kingdom (on both current and capital accounts) was about £24,000 million in 1979. A clear distinction is made between capital and current expenditure. Capital expenditure (just under a quarter of the total) is financed partly from the current account surplus (about half), partly from borrowing (two-fifths) and the remainder from grants and other incomes. Housing, the major element, accounted for over half the total in 1979. Current expenditure by local authorities accounts for just over a quarter of total current account spending by central and local government. The education service represents over a third of this expenditure, followed by the police, personal social services, roads (including lighting), public health and debt interest. Current expenditure is financed mainly from central government grants (about three-fifths) and from local rates paid by occupiers of land and buildings (about one-third). Each local authority is responsible for its own finance, although in a few cases several authorities combine to provide a specialist service which it would be uneconomic for each to provide on its own.

Government Grants

Government 'rate support grants' to local authorities are paid in aid of revenues generally. Grants are also paid towards the cost of specific services—either towards current expenditure, such as on the police, or towards capital expenditure, such as on the acquisition and clearance of derelict land. (In Wales and Scotland approved schemes for acquiring and clearing derelict land are financed by the Welsh and Scottish Development Agencies.) Annual subsidies are paid for local authority housing.

Grants are also made towards the cost of rate rebates for people with low incomes.

Hitherto rate support grants were distributed among authorities in three parts: the 'needs' element, designed to give most help to authorities whose spending needs were greatest; the 'resources' element, used to supplement the rate income of authorities whose rateable value per head of population fell below a standard figure, prescribed for each year; and the 'domestic' element, which compensated authorities for loss of rate income from reductions in rate poundage which they were required to give to householders. The formula for distributing the 'needs' element was subject to annual variations.

The Government has proposed a new system for the distribution of rate support grant to local authorities in England and Wales, to take effect from 1981–82. This would consist of a single block grant in place of the needs and resources elements of the present grant, while ceilings would be prescribed for the level of total local authority capital expenditure. Authorities would receive annual capital amounts for housing, education, social services, transport and other services as they do at present, but would be free to determine their own spending priorities by the transfer of resources between spending allocations. One of the effects of the new rate support grant system would be to ensure that high-spending local authorities do not pre-empt even larger shares of government money, reducing the amount available to those which observe national financial guidelines.

In Scotland the system for the distribution of rate support grant is under review; local authority capital expenditure has been subject to direct control since 1975, which has been administered since 1977 in conjunction with a financial planning system.

In Northern Ireland district councils receive certain specific grants (for example, for the acquisition of open space) and grants to compensate them for loss of rate income arising from the partial derating of industrial premises. In addition, councils whose rating resources are below a standard level receive a resources grant to bring them up to that level.

Rates

Rates are local taxes paid by the occupiers of land and property (with certain exceptions, see below) to meet part of the cost of local services. Each occupier's payment is calculated annually by the rating authority by multiplying the rateable value of a property (broadly equivalent to its annual rental value) by the rate poundage—an amount per £ of rateable value fixed by the authority according to its projected financial needs. In England and Wales rateable values are assessed periodically by the Board of Inland Revenue (see p 48). The last general revaluation of all property was in 1973. Disputes about rating assessments are heard by local valuation courts, and on appeal by the Lands Tribunal. Public undertakings have their rates determined separately. Crown property is not rateable but payments are made, based on values assessed by the Treasury Valuer, in lieu of rates.

In Scotland valuation is carried out by assessors appointed by the regional and islands councils but independent of them. The last general revaluation was in 1978. Appeals are heard by the valuation appeal committees of each valuation area and thereafter by the Lands Valuation Appeal Court of the Court of Session.

In Northern Ireland valuations are carried out by the Valuation Officer of the Department of Finance. There is a right of appeal. The present valuations came into force in 1976.

Responsibility for levying and collecting rates in England and Wales lies with the district councils and London borough councils. Each county council (and the Greater London Council) determines the rate required to meet its estimated expenditure, and district councils (and London borough councils) include this element in the rate they levy. Householders benefit from domestic rate relief and those with lower incomes may also qualify for rate rebates; both reliefs are financed by government grants. Rates may be paid by instalments, normally in ten one-monthly payments. Rating relief is available in certain circumstances on premises adapted for the use of the disabled. Agricultural land and buildings (apart from living accommodation) and places of religious worship are exempted from rate payments. Charities pay half the full rate on premises occupied for charitable purposes and may be given further relief by rating authorities, who can also reduce or remit the rates for a wide range of non-profit-making bodies.

Rates may be levied on empty properties at any percentage up to the full amount and in the case of empty commercial property a rating surcharge may be payable.

In Scotland every authority determines a rate for its own services, but the collection of rates and the administration of rating is the responsibility of regional and island councils. Industrial (including freight transport) premises in Scotland are rated at a half of the net annual value and the right to pay rates in instalments extends to all ratepayers. There is empty property rating in Scotland but no empty property surcharge.

In Northern Ireland there are two rates: one set by the district councils and one set by the Department of Finance. Both are collected by the Department and the appropriate part paid over to the respective councils. Industrial (including freight transport) premises are rated at a quarter of net annual value and the degree of charitable exemption is decided by the Valuation Office. Empty properties are not rated.

Loans

Loans may be raised by local authorities to finance capital expenditure under general powers. For items of expenditure in key sectors (such as education, housing and roads) local authorities in England and Wales must seek central government approval before raising loans. For other capital expenditure, each authority receives an annual loan authorisation within which it determines the sums to borrow and the projects to undertake. The GLC applies annually for parliamentary sanction to raise the money needed for capital expenditure while the City of London has ancient charter powers to cover its borrowings. In Northern Ireland long-term borrowing by district councils is subject to central approval; in Scotland central approval is given to capital expenditure, not to loans.

Local authorities may raise long-term loans by means of private mortgages, issuing stock upon the Stock Exchange and bonds which may or may not be quoted on the Stock Exchange. Local authorities also have right of access to the Public Works Loan Board, financed by the Exchequer, or, in Northern Ireland, to the Government Loans Fund, for long-term borrowing to finance a proportion of their reckonable capital payments, and may borrow temporarily for a limited proportion of their current outstanding loan debt.

Control of Finance

Internal control of finance is normally exercised on behalf of the council concerned by a finance committee, whose function it is to keep the financial policy of the council under constant review. (There is no statutory requirement for local authorities to appoint a finance committee, but they have to make proper arrangements for the administration of their financial affairs.) Local authorities must have their accounts audited. Those in England and Wales can choose between the district auditor (appointed by the Secretary of State for the Environment) and an approved private auditor.

In Scotland the auditing of accounts is the responsibility of the independent Commission for Local Authority Accounts in Scotland appointed by the Secretary of State for Scotland, and in Northern Ireland it is carried out by independent local government auditors appointed by the Department of the Environment.

**Local
Government
Complaints
System**

A complaints system for local government in England, Wales and Scotland involves independent statutory Commissions for Local Administration comprising local commissioners (local government Ombudsmen). The English Commission consists of three local commissioners and the Welsh and Scottish commissions have one each. All commissioners are responsible in their particular area for investigating citizens' complaints of maladministration by local authorities. The commissioners help local authority councillors to protect the interests of constituents.

In Northern Ireland a Commissioner for Complaints deals with complaints alleging injustices suffered as a result of maladministration by district councils and certain other public bodies.

THE FIRE SERVICES

Every part of Britain is covered by a local fire service, which is subject to a measure of central control. The cost is borne by local authorities. Northern Ireland has its own service responsible to the Northern Ireland Department of the Environment.

Each of Britain's 64 fire authorities must by law make provision for firefighting, and in particular maintain a brigade of sufficient strength to meet all normal requirements (in some parts of Scotland, authorities combine to provide fire cover). Other fire-fighting organisations are maintained, for instance, by the Army and Air Force Departments of the Ministry of Defence; by the Department of Industry at certain establishments; and by some large industrial and commercial concerns.

The Home Secretary and the Secretary of State for Scotland have central responsibility in England and Wales and in Scotland respectively. Central control is directed mainly towards ensuring the operational efficiency of brigades. Ministers have statutory powers to make regulations on appointments and promotions, standards of training and equipment, pensions, and disciplinary matters. Their approval is also required for reductions in the strengths of fire brigades. Each minister is advised by a Central Fire Brigades Advisory Council, consisting of officers of the respective home departments, representatives of local authorities and of the associations representing members of fire brigades and other people with special qualifications, appointed by the minister concerned. Inspectorates of fire services advise on operational and technical matters. Most fire brigades include part-time personnel to augment and support the full-time strength in return for a retaining fee and call-out and attendance fee. Volunteer members (who receive no payment) undertake to attend a fire if called upon. Fire authorities also employ people for duties in controls communications and mobilising and staff duties. There are about 39,000 full-time and 17,000 part-time operational members of fire brigades in Britain.

Every fire authority must buy the appliances and equipment necessary to meet all normal fire-fighting requirements in its area. Certain equipment is standardised so that there is complete interchangeability when a fire is attended by brigades from more than one area. The principal types of fire-fighting appliances are bought by fire authorities to requirement specifications approved by the Home Office and the Scottish Home and Health Department on the advice of the Central Fire Brigades Advisory Councils. These specifications ensure that minimum standards are maintained, and allow sufficient freedom of design to meet special circumstances and encourage further developments.

Each fire authority must appoint a Chief Fire Officer (Firemaster in Scotland) for its brigade.

Central control is exercised by the Chief Fire Officer from brigade headquarters. Divisional officers in charge of the geographical divisions into which most brigade areas are divided are responsible for mobilising forces to deal with outbreaks of fire. Constant communication is maintained between divisional and brigade headquarters and, if a fire should be beyond the capabilities of a division, help is sent from one or more neighbouring divisions, or even from another fire authority. Under mutual help arrangements the nearest available force is sent to a fire, regardless of area boundaries.

Fire Prevention

Fire authorities are concerned in some way with fire precautions in most buildings used by the public and have major responsibility in enforcing legislation concerning fire precautions. They must also make efficient arrangements for giving advice on fire prevention, restricting the spread of fires, and means of escape. Courses in fire prevention are held at the Fire Service Technical College for fire brigade officers. In addition to their enforcement and advisory duties, brigades are also involved in education and publicity to promote fire safety, particularly in the home. The Government is advised on prevention by the Joint Fire Prevention Committee of the Central Fire Brigades Advisory Councils, representing the fire service and central and local authorities.

Research

Research into health hazards to firemen, fire brigade organisation and fire-fighting equipment is conducted by the Home Office with the help of the fire service under the auspices of the Joint Committee on Fire Research of the Central Fire Brigades Advisory Councils. Individual research projects are undertaken by the Home Office Scientific Advisory Branch or, under contract to the Home Office, by other government agencies, notably the Fire Research Station, which is part of the Building Research Establishment of the Department of the Environment, or by private consultants. The Fire Research Station is the main organisation studying and investigating technical aspects of fire.

Special Services

Fire authorities can use their brigades and equipment for purposes other than fire-fighting, and they are used, free of charge, in a variety of emergencies (such as rail, road and aircraft accidents, collapse of buildings, flooding of premises, leakage of harmful gas or liquids and the rescue of people or animals from dangerous situations). Brigades are also used by prior arrangement for such purposes as emptying swimming pools and filling water tanks.

Fire Losses

The direct cost of damage to buildings and goods destroyed by fires in Britain in 1979 amounted to an estimated £355·3 million (consequential losses from the interruption of business are not included in this total). Experience indicates that most fires involving heavy losses occur at night; and fires are more likely to start in storage areas than in production departments. Industries which suffer most severely include engineering and electrical firms, textiles, food, drink and tobacco, warehousing, chemical and allied industries, paper, printing and publishing firms, and retailing. About 1,000 people, particularly young children and the elderly, die in fires every year (most of them at home) and a further 8,000 suffer injuries. Among the chief causes of death are ignition of clothing by heaters and open fires, and fires started by smoking cigarettes in bed.

3 Overseas Relations

Britain has varied and world-wide overseas relations. It has diplomatic relations with some 150 countries, and with about 20 of these has special treaty relations providing for common security arrangements, principally through the North Atlantic Treaty Organisation (NATO). Commercial matters form a major component of relations with other countries, and Britain is a world financial centre. It has considerable overseas investments and extensive trade relations, reflecting its dependence on imports for nearly half its food and more than half of its raw material requirements and the relatively high proportion of its gross national product accounted for by exports (over a third); for details of trade and payments, see Chapter 19. British development assistance is provided to over 130 countries.

Since 1945 Britain has placed itself in a number of common decision-making structures or consultative processes with other nations with a view to achieving common solutions to shared problems—a recognition that, in an increasingly inter-dependent world, the attainment of overseas objectives and the ability to exert influence in support of them can best be provided for through international co-operation on a regional or global basis. As a result, Britain is now a member of some 120 international organisations ranging from the world-wide United Nations concerned with problems of world peace, international economic co-operation and social issues to regionally based and technically orientated bodies. In particular, Britain is a member of the European Community whose policies it helps to determine, and is increasingly co-ordinating its overseas policies through the Community's political co-operation mechanism (see p 74). As a member of the Commonwealth, Britain is a part of a representative cross-section of the international community, which has evolved from the former British Empire (since 1945 Britain has progressively, and largely peacefully, dismantled its Empire and prepared some 40 countries for independence) and whose 44 members share a common language, common technical standards, similar systems of law and close professional, academic, and commercial links.

Britain has strong ties, also, with the United States, including a common language and many common political and cultural traditions.

A long involvement in world affairs has given Britain both a vital interest and a firm belief in the maintenance of international order governed by respect for a generally accepted system of law. As a permanent member of the United Nations Security Council it makes support for the United Nations a central feature of its foreign policy.

Administration The responsibilities of most government departments have a significant overseas dimension, but overall conduct of Britain's overseas relations is the responsibility of the Secretary of State for Foreign and Commonwealth Affairs acting through the Foreign and Commonwealth Office and some 200 British missions overseas. The latter comprise embassies and high commissions in nearly 130 countries, together with subordinate consulates general and consulates, and missions at eight multilateral organisations. These posts, like the

Foreign and Commonwealth Office, are staffed by members of the Diplomatic Service (see p 57), together with locally engaged staff. About a third of these are employed on political and economic work, nearly a quarter on export promotion and other commercial matters, a fifth on consular and immigration work, and the remainder on aid administration, information and cultural work, and communications and other support activities. Other government departments which have a primary concern with overseas relations include the Ministry of Defence, the Department of Trade, the Treasury and the Overseas Development Administration which is part of the Foreign and Commonwealth Office, but the involvement of most departments has increased in recent years with the growing dependence of domestic economic policy on international decisions and with Britain's membership of the European Community.

Where questions of overseas policy involve matters within the responsibility of other departments, the Foreign and Commonwealth Office formulates policy in consultation with the departments concerned. The balance of responsibilities is a matter of constant adjustment, and the department with the predominant functional interest, even though it may be primarily domestic, takes the lead. This is particularly so in policy concerning the European Community and international monetary matters. In the case of policy towards the Community, the Foreign and Commonwealth Office exercises its co-ordinating role at official level through the machinery of the Cabinet Office.

A number of other official and unofficial bodies are also involved in the administration of overseas relations. These include the British Overseas Trade Board and the Export Credits Guarantee Department which provide export services for British industry; the Crown Agents for Oversea Governments and Administrations which helps to arrange purchases from British aid funds and appointments under technical co-operation programmes; and the British Council (see below), the Inter-University Council for Higher Education Overseas and the Technical Education and Training Organisation for Overseas Countries[1] which, between them, are responsible for administering the bulk of Britain's educational assistance programme (see pp 89–90).

The British Council

The purposes of the British Council, founded in 1934, are defined in its Royal Charter as the promotion of a wider knowledge of Britain and the English language abroad and the development of closer cultural relations between Britain and other countries. (For an outline of Britain's international scientific relations see pp 394–6). The activities of the Council, which has staff in over 80 countries, include the teaching of English and the recruitment of British teachers for posts overseas, administering the Government's technical co-operation training programme; fostering personal contacts overseas and in Britain between British and overseas people, especially in the educational, professional and scientific areas; running, or helping to maintain, libraries of British books and periodicals overseas and providing information through touring exhibitions and bibliographical services; and presenting overseas the best of British arts. In Britain, the Council is concerned mainly with arranging programmes for professional visitors and with the placing, administration and welfare of overseas students. A basic principle is that the Council's work should be of benefit both to Britain and to the receiving country.

About 80 per cent of the Council's budget in 1980–81, a total of some £113 million, is provided by the Foreign and Commonwealth Office (including

---

[1] This body will cease to exist after March 1981 when its functions will be transferred mainly to the British Council but also to the Overseas Development Administration.

funds from the Overseas Development Administration) and on its behalf the Council is responsible for the implementation of more than 30 cultural agreements between Britain and other countries. Overseas it acts as education adviser to Britain's diplomatic missions and is responsible for educational assistance in developing countries in which it is represented. Increasingly, the Council is undertaking education projects paid for by overseas clients and is providing English classes abroad; these activities are expected to provide about 15 per cent (some £18·5 million) of its income in 1980–81.

MEMBERSHIP OF THE EUROPEAN COMMUNITY

Britain, together with the Irish Republic and Denmark, joined the original six countries—Belgium, France, the Federal Republic of Germany, Italy, Luxembourg and the Netherlands—in the European Community on 1 January 1973.[1] In a national referendum in 1975, British membership of the Community was endorsed, after renegotiation of the terms of membership. Britain plays a full and positive part in all Community activities seeking actively with its partners to develop the Community in the interests of all its members.

The European Community consists of three communities set up by separate treaties—the European Coal and Steel Community, the European Economic Community and the European Atomic Energy Community.

The European Coal and Steel Community
The European Coal and Steel Community (ECSC), set up in 1952, established a common market for coal and steel and formed the model for the 'community' approach to economic integration. It is designed to ensure an orderly supply of coal and steel to member countries, to promote the rational expansion and modernisation of production and to provide better conditions of employment and living for the employees in the industries. The ECSC is financed mainly by a levy on production and provides funds for capital investment, research and other programmes as well as loans to help create new jobs where coal seams are being exhausted or where restructuring of the steel industry is taking place. Grants are also made to assist redundant coal and steel workers until they find new employment, or while they are undergoing retraining.

The European Economic Community
The European Economic Community (EEC) was created by the Treaty of Rome signed by the six countries in 1957. It aims to promote a continuous and balanced economic expansion by establishing a common market and progressively approximating the member states' economic policies. The preamble to the Treaty includes among the basic objectives of the EEC the laying of the foundations of an ever closer union among the peoples of Europe, the improvement of their living and working conditions, the progressive abolition of restrictions on trade, and the development of the prosperity of overseas countries. The initial steps towards the attainment of these objectives have been the abolition of internal tariffs and other barriers to trade and the establishment of a common customs tariff, the development of a common policy for agriculture, and the introduction of measures to establish the free movement of labour, capital and services. At the same time, provision has been made for the overseas countries which have special links with the member countries to have preferential treatment in aid and the development of trade.

---

[1] Greece becomes the Community's tenth member in January 1981 (see p 75).

The European Atomic Energy Community

The European Atomic Energy Community (Euratom) was set up by a second treaty signed in Rome in 1957, which provided for the co-ordinated development of members' atomic energy industries and of their other peaceful nuclear activities. Euratom has worked to develop a co-ordinated research programme (for power production, industrial and medical purposes) to ensure the dissemination of technical information, to facilitate the co-ordination of investment in the nuclear field, to ensure an adequate supply of nuclear ores and fuels, and to develop wider commercial outlets. Since 1959, there has been a common market for all nuclear materials, while the Community has established common nuclear legislation and a common control system for nuclear materials to prevent their diversion to purposes other than those declared.

Britain's Accession

The Treaty of Accession was signed by the applicant countries and the original member states in January 1972. Britain thereby became a party to the two treaties of Rome establishing the EEC and Euratom, adjusted as necessary to take account of enlargement. Accession to the ECSC was effected by a decision of the Council of Ministers. The European Communities Act 1972 made the legislative changes necessary for Britain to comply with the obligations entailed by membership of the Community and to exercise the rights of membership.

In 1977, following a transitional period during which tariffs on trade in industrial products between Britain and the original six members were progressively reduced, the internal tariffs were abolished and the phased introduction of the common customs tariff on British imports from countries neither members of the Community, nor having any special arrangements with it, was completed. Britain had also adopted, progressively, the Community system of agricultural support under the Common Agricultural Policy. The Treaty of Accession provided for a slightly longer period of adjustment (which ended in December 1979) with regard to payments to the Community budget. Other provisions included those relating to participation in the Community's institutions and to its relations with Commonwealth and other countries.

Community Institutions

The separate institutions established by the treaties for each of the three communities were merged in 1967. Each state has one representative on the Council of Ministers; in the other institutions Britain's representation is in line with that of the other large member states (France, the Federal Republic of Germany, and Italy). English is one of the Community's official languages.

The Council of Ministers is the principal decision-making body for all major community questions, member states being represented on it by foreign ministers or by other ministers as appropriate to the subject under discussion. The presidency of the Council changes at six-monthly intervals. Britain will next hold the presidency in the last six months of 1981. Most Council decisions are taken on the basis of a proposal by the Commission (see below). Some issues may be decided by majority, or qualified majority, with votes weighted according to provisions in the Treaty of Accession. Where very important interests of member states are involved, however, the Council's practice is to proceed only on the basis of unanimity. The Committee of Permanent Representatives (COREPER), composed of the member States' ambassadors to the Community, assists the Council by preparing its meetings and co-ordinating the work of other subordinate bodies and working groups.

The Commission is responsible for formulating detailed policy proposals for submission to the Council of Ministers, for promoting the Community interest and attempting to reconcile national viewpoints and for implementing the provisions of the treaties and Community measures. Delegated to it are some limited powers of decision relating mainly to the detailed administration of agriculture. It is composed of 13 commissioners (14 from 1981) nominated by the member governments; two are from Britain. The President of the Commission is appointed for a two-year renewable term as the Commission's representative and is responsible for its general administration. Each of the other commissioners is responsible for one or more of the main Community activities. The Commission is pledged to act independently of national or sectional interests and to formulate its proposals and administer policy in the interests of the Community as a whole. Its proposals are made only after extensive consultation with officials of the national governments and with producers, trade unions, employers' associations and many others.

The Court of Justice interprets and adjudicates on the meaning of the treaties and of any measures taken by the Council of Ministers and Commission under them, hears complaints and appeals brought by or against Community institutions, member states or individuals and gives preliminary rulings on questions referred to it by courts in the member states. As a court of final appeal, its procedure in such cases is broadly similar to that of the highest courts in member states; its rulings are binding on member countries, Community institutions and individuals. The Court consists of nine judges (ten from 1981), assisted by four advocates-general who make reasoned submissions concerning cases brought before the Court to help it in its interpretation and application of Community law.

The elected European Parliament is composed of 410 members, 81 elected from Britain, who sit according to party affiliation and not nationality. In 1981 Greece will send 24 members to the Parliament. The first direct elections to the Parliament, which was formerly a nominated body, were held in June 1979, and elections will subsequently be held every five years. The Parliament is consulted on and debates all major policy issues of the Community. Members may question the Council of Ministers and Commission, and have the power on a two-thirds majority to dismiss the Commission. The Parliament also has the power to reject in its entirety the Community's draft annual budget as presented by the Commission and approved by the Council. A formal conciliation procedure has been adopted for use in the event of disagreement between the Parliament and the Council of Ministers on matters with major budgetary or financial implications.

The European Court of Auditors, set up in 1977, examines all Community revenue and expenditure to ensure that it has been legally received and spent and to ensure sound financial management. It draws up an annual report, and may also submit observations on specific questions at the request of the Community institutions.

The Economic and Social Committee is a consultative body representing a cross-section of economic interests. Its members—representing employers' organisations, trade unions and other interests—are consulted by the Council of Ministers and the Commission during the formulation of policy. Britain is entitled to send 24 members out of a total of 144 (156 from 1981).

In addition to, and separately from, the institutions operating within the Community framework established by treaty, the member states have set up political co-operation machinery for the consideration of important problems of foreign policy. Britain attaches considerable importance to Community co-operation in this area. Community foreign ministers meet in this framework several times a year. Close contact is maintained with Community institutions when appropriate, and decisions are taken by consensus.

The Community's heads of State or of Government meet at least three times a year as the European Council. Established in 1974, the Council operates outside the treaty framework and may consider both Community matters and those arising in the context of political co-operation. As the highest decision making body in the Community, it discusses issues unresolved in the Council of Ministers as well as the general problems facing the Community, and lays down guidelines and an overall political direction for future work.

Community policies are implemented by regulations, which are legally binding and directly applicable in all member countries; directives, which are binding, as to the result to be achieved, on those member states to which they are addressed but allow national authorities to decide on the means of implementation; decisions, which are binding on those to whom they are addressed (for example, member states, firms, or individuals); and recommendations and opinions, which have no binding force. The Council can also indicate a general policy direction through resolutions.

Enlargement

Greece will become the tenth member state in January 1981, and a further enlargement of the Community is planned. Negotiations with Portugal and Spain are continuing and it is hoped they will join in 1983. Britain strongly supports this enlargement as a means of strengthening democracy in Europe.

Community Policies[1]

External Relations

The member Governments of the Community discuss a wide range of foreign policy issues and, where possible, reach common positions. At the General Assembly of the United Nations their policies are closely co-ordinated, and they have voted together on a large number of issues. They adopted a common strategy at the 1975 Helsinki Conference on Security and Co-operation in Europe (see p 81–2) and have since co-sponsored a number of proposals to improve the implementation of the Conference's Final Act. They have issued a number of statements on the Middle East, including a declaration in June 1980 setting out their views on the conditions necessary for a comprehensive settlement of the Arab-Israeli conflict. Other issues to which considerable attention has been given include human rights issues throughout the world, and southern Africa, where the Nine have adopted a code of conduct on employment practices for member states' companies operating in South Africa, and supported efforts to promote internationally acceptable solutions to the problems of Namibia and Rhodesia (now Zimbabwe). The Community has also endorsed a British proposal for a neutral Afghanistan with a view to defusing the serious situation which has followed the Soviet Union's invasion of that country.

On international trade matters the Community adopted a common negotiating position in the latest round of the General Agreements on Tariffs and Trade (GATT, see p 372) multilateral trade negotiations concluded in 1979. Commercial co-operation agreements have been concluded with a large number of countries in the Mediterranean area, the South Asian subcontinent, Latin America and other areas and with the Association of South East Asian Nations. Dialogues covering trade and other matters have taken place with regional groupings of Latin American and Arab countries.

The Community has also improved progressively its generalised scheme of preferences, which covers manufactures and semi-manufactures exported by developing countries, with the aim in particular of benefiting the poorest developing countries (see p 374).

---

[1] Some details of Community policies as they affect British domestic affairs will be found in the appropriate chapters.

The most recent convention governing aid, trade and co-operation between the Community and 58 developing countries in Africa, the Caribbean and the Pacific (ACP), the second Lomé Convention, came into operation in 1980. This provides for increased aid and European Investment Bank lending of about £3,345 million, industrial and agricultural co-operation, an extension of the scheme designed to stabilise the commodity export earnings of the ACP countries, assistance for ACP mineral producers whose production and income suffer from temporary disruptions beyond their control, and duty-free access to the Community of ACP countries' exports of all industrial and most agricultural goods, including improved access for exports such as rum and beef. All British dependent territories (with the exception of Bermuda, Gibraltar and Hong Kong), together with the overseas countries and territories of other Community members, are formally linked with the Community as a whole under conditions similar to those in the Lomé Convention.

Britain has played a leading part in urging the Community to adopt a new aid and development policy based on the criterion of need and applicable on a world-wide basis, thereby encompassing those developing countries (many of which are among the world's poorest) not covered by the Lomé Convention or having any other special relationship with the Community. Although it is still small, the aid programme for these non-associated states has grown steadily since 1976 and Britain supports its further expansion.

The Community has contributed to the North-South dialogue (see pp 90–1) and is providing $385 million (of which Britain's share is $115 million) to the $1,000 million special action aid programme agreed upon in 1977 at the Conference on International Economic Co-operation.

Internal Policies   All member countries contribute to a common budget which provides funds for specific Community policies. The budget is largely financed by an 'own resources' system of levies on agricultural imports, customs duties and a proportion, not exceeding 1 per cent, of the proceeds of the value added tax collected on an agreed range of goods and services.

In recent years Britain's budgetary contributions have been out of balance, resulting in its being one of the largest net contributors to the budget despite its relatively low gross domestic product per head. This problem was foreseen during the accession negotiations, and Britain was given an assurance that, if unacceptable situations arose, the very survival of the Community would demand that the institutions find equitable solutions. In 1980 the Community agreed on proposals providing for more equitable net budgetary contributions by Britain for the years 1980 and 1981. At the same time it agreed to review by 1982 the pattern of Community expenditure and the operation of the budget with a view to preventing the recurrence of such 'unacceptable situations' to any Community member. If this is not achieved by 1982, there will be similar restrictions on the level of Britain's contribution in 1982 as provided for in 1980 and 1981. In Britain's view, the Common Agricultural Policy (see chapter 15) absorbs too large a share of the budget in comparison with other sectors such as industrial, regional, social and urban policies. (Expenditure on the Policy accounts for 70 per cent of the total budget, while regional and social policies take only about 4 per cent each, aid to developing countries 3 per cent, and projects concerned with research, energy, industry and transport 2·5 per cent.) This situation, Britain believes, is detrimental to the fundamental objective of the Community, which is to strengthen the economies of the member states and, by reducing regional differences, to ensure their harmonious development.

The European Monetary System (see p 208) was established in 1979 with the aim of promoting monetary stability in Europe. Although Britain does not participate in the exchange rate mechanism of the scheme, it is taking part in other aspects such as the development of the new European currency unit and of the European Monetary Fund.

The European Social Fund finances schemes for the training and retraining of young people, migrant workers, workers in the textile and clothing industries, the handicapped and workers leaving agriculture. The European Regional Development Fund (see p 229) provides grants for industrial and infrastructure projects in the less developed or industrially declining regions of the Community with the aim of reducing existing imbalances or preenting the creation of new imbalances. Britain has received substantial grants from the two Funds, together with other grants and loans from the European Coal and Steel Community, the European Investment Bank (see p 230) and the European Agricultural Guidance and Guarantee Fund (see p 292).

Other areas of action include industrial policy, where the Community has taken an active role in safeguarding the interests of the steel industry, energy, environment and transport policy.

THE COMMONWEALTH

Britain is a member of the Commonwealth, a voluntary association of 44 independent states with a combined population of some 1,000 million, about a quarter of the world total. Britain participates fully in all activities of the Commonwealth and values it as a means of consulting and co-operating with peoples of widely differing cultures, thereby contributing to the promotion of international understanding and world peace.

Commonwealth members are a representative cross-section of mankind in all stages of political and economic development. Their peoples are drawn from practically all the world's main races and from all continents. As some of its members are very rich and others very poor, the Commonwealth acts as a bridge between rich and poor nations.

The member states are Australia, the Bahamas, Bangladesh, Barbados, Botswana, Britain, Canada, Cyprus, Dominica, Fiji, The Gambia, Ghana, Grenada, Guyana, India, Jamaica, Kenya, Kiribati, Lesotho, Malawi, Malaysia, Malta, Mauritius, Nauru, New Zealand, Nigeria, Papua New Guinea, Saint Lucia, Saint Vincent and the Grenadines, Seychelles, Sierra Leone, Singapore, Solomon Islands, Sri Lanka, Swaziland, Tanzania, Tonga, Trinidad and Tobago, Tuvalu, Uganda, Vanuatu, Western Samoa, Zambia and Zimbabwe. Nauru, Saint Vincent and the Grenadines, and Tuvalu are special members which are entitled to take part in all functional Commonwealth meetings and activities but not meetings of heads of Government. The Queen is recognised as head of the Commonwealth; she is also head of State in 15 countries, the remainder having their own monarchs or presidents.

The origin of the Commonwealth lies in the gradual granting of self-government to the older-established British colonies (later known as the Dominions) in Australia, Canada, New Zealand and South Africa[1] where European settlement had occurred on a large scale. During the last half of the nineteenth century and the first quarter of the twentieth, restrictions on the independence of the Dominions were gradually relaxed and their

---

[1] South Africa ceased to be a member of the Commonwealth in 1961.

fully-independent status in relation to Britain was legally formulated in the Statute of Westminster of 1931.

The main expansion in Commonwealth membership took place after the second world war following Britain's decision to guide its dependent territories towards self-government and independence. This process began in 1947 with the independence of India and Pakistan,[1] and in 1957 Ghana became the first British African territory to become independent. By the end of the 1960s nearly all the British dependencies in Africa had gained their independence as had many territories in the Caribbean and in Asia. The most recent Commonwealth members (1980) are Zimbabwe and Vanuatu.

Consultation

As a member of the Commonwealth, Britain participates in a system of mutual consultation and co-operation. The Commonwealth does not formulate central policies on, say, economic or foreign affairs. Nevertheless the extent of the consultation and co-operation, which is considerable, is not only of benefit to member countries but also contributes to international understanding.

Consultation takes place through diplomatic representatives known as High Commissioners, meetings of heads of Government, specialised conferences of other ministers and officials, and discussions at international conferences and the United Nations. Trade and cultural exhibitions and conferences of professional and unofficial medical, cultural, educational and economic organisations are other ways in which frequent contacts are made.

Heads of Government usually meet every two years, most recently in Lusaka in 1979. The next meeting will be held in Melbourne in 1981. Proceedings are normally in private thereby facilitating a frank, free and informal exchange of views. On international affairs no formal decisions are taken and no attempt is made to formulate specifically Commonwealth policies, although, on occasion, common views on matters of major international concern are formulated and reflected in the communiqués issued at the end of the meetings.

One of the most important Commonwealth activities is consultation and co-operation in economic affairs. Finance ministers meet annually to discuss world economic problems, these meetings being held on the eve of those of the International Monetary Fund and the World Bank. In recent years ministers have paid particular attention to the problems of development and the establishment of a fairer international economic order. Other ministerial meetings include the regular Commonwealth Education, Commonwealth Law Ministers' and Commonwealth Medical Conferences, last held in 1980.

The Commonwealth Secretariat

The Commonwealth Secretariat provides the central organisation for consultation and co-operation among member states. Established in London in 1965, headed by a Secretary-General appointed by the heads of Government, and financed by member governments, the Secretariat is responsible to Commonwealth Governments collectively.

As the main agency for multilateral communication between Governments, the Secretariat promotes consultation, disseminates information on matters of common concern, and organises meetings and conferences, including those of heads of Government and of ministers. It co-ordinates many Commonwealth activities, its main areas of operation being international affairs, economic affairs, education, information, legal matters, medical and scientific affairs, youth activities, and applied studies in government. It also administers the Commonwealth Fund for Technical Co-operation.

---

[1] Pakistan left the Commonwealth in 1972.

Because of its neutral position the Secretariat has been able to make its good offices available in cases of dispute, and has carried out, on request, special assignments requiring demonstrable impartiality.

Commonwealth Fund for Technical Co-operation Britain plays an active part in the work of the Commonwealth Fund for Technical Co-operation established within the Commonwealth Secretariat to provide technical co-operation for economic and social development in Commonwealth developing countries. The Fund is financed by contributions from both developed and developing states, Britain contributing about a third of its expenditure (Canada is the other major contributor). In 1980–81 the Fund's resources will amount to some £12 million.

The Fund provides experts to undertake advisory assignments or fill specific posts and uses consultancy firms to make studies for governments. Its education and training programme is of particular help in raising levels of technical and vocational skill, and makes wide use of training facilities within developing member countries for the benefit of other developing countries. It has a special programme to help countries develop their exports, another on food production and rural development and a small technical assistance group to give advice in key areas. An industrial development unit is the main executive agency of the Commonwealth Action Programme of Industrial Co-operation established in 1979.

Other Technical Co-operation Expenditure by Britain on technical co-operation with Commonwealth developing countries in 1979 was £91 million, the greater part being spent on financing staff for service for Commonwealth Governments (£48 million) and in financing training places in Britain for people from Commonwealth countries (£19 million); volunteers are also sent from Britain to serve overseas. Other technical help includes sending consultants to carry out feasibility surveys, the supply of training and research equipment, and making available the advisory services of British scientific and technical institutions.

Britain is a major contributor to the Commonwealth Scholarship and Fellowship Plan, a system of awards for people of high intellectual promise to study in Commonwealth countries other than their own, and provides 650 awards annually out of a total of over 1,000 within the scheme. Under the Aid for the Commonwealth Teaching of Science Scheme, Britain sends out experts to serve in curriculum development units, institutes of education and the inspectorates of ministries of education.

British financial aid to Commonwealth developing countries totalled £342 million in 1979 and included investment finance from the Commonwealth Development Corporation (see p 89).

Other Organisations A large number of organisations are concerned with the Commonwealth. The Commonwealth Institute, financed largely by the British Government, promotes knowledge about the Commonwealth through films, library services, lecture tours by members of the staff and study conferences for students; its headquarters in London has a permanent public exhibition depicting the life of member states, each country financing its own stand. The Commonwealth Foundation, financed by member Governments, administers a fund for increasing co-operation between professional organisations; it has assisted in the creation of 21 Commonwealth-wide professional associations, helped in the creation and growth of many national ones, and has created some 14 multidisciplinary professional centres. The Royal Commonwealth Society, which is over 100 years old, is a centre for the study and discussion of Commonwealth affairs, its library in London having one of the world's largest collections on the Commonwealth. The Society has branches, affiliated organisations and representatives in many countries.

In keeping with the fact that the Commonwealth is an association of peoples as well as Governments, many unofficial organisations, professional bodies and voluntary societies provide machinery for co-operation. Professional bodies include associations of architects, doctors, engineers, lawyers, librarians, magistrates, museum curators, nurses, pharmacists, planners, surveyors, and veterinary surgeons. Other organisations include the Commonwealth Parliamentary Association which organises an annual conference of parliamentarians, the Commonwealth Press Union, the Commonwealth Broadcasting Association, the Commonwealth Youth Exchange Council, the Commonwealth Games Federation, and the Commonwealth Arts Association.

DEPENDENCIES AND ASSOCIATED STATES

There are 13 remaining British dependent territories: Belize, Bermuda, British Antarctic Territory, British Indian Ocean Territory, British Virgin Islands, Cayman Islands, Falkland Islands and Dependencies, Gibraltar, Hong Kong, Montserrat, Pitcairn Island, St. Helena and Dependencies and the Turks and Caicos Islands. British policy is to give independence to those territories that want it, and not to force it on those which do not.

The population of the dependencies is about 5·25 million, ranging from Hong Kong with about 5 million people to Pitcairn Island with fewer than 100. Apart from Hong Kong, only Belize has a population of more than 100,000. Few of the dependencies are rich in natural resources, and some are scattered groups of islands. There are no permanent inhabitants in the British Antarctic Territory or British Indian Ocean Territory.

Most dependencies have considerable self-government with their own legislature and civil service. Britain is generally responsible, through a Governor, for defence, internal security and foreign affairs.

Some territories are on the way to independence: the Turks and Caicos Islands, for example, are expected to become self-governing in late 1980 with independence following in 1982. There are particular problems associated with Belize, the Falkland Islands and Gibraltar which are the subject of territorial claims by neighbouring states—Guatemala, Argentina and Spain respectively. In all three cases Britain refuses to accept that British sovereignty is in doubt. In Belize British policy, supported by the United Nations, is to bring the territory to secure independence as soon as possible. Britain has pointed out that Belize would be independent now had it not been for the Guatemalan claim. Fresh British proposals for a settlement were made to Guatemala in 1978 but were rejected. In both the Falkland Islands and Gibraltar the inhabitants wish to retain the link with Britain, and the Government is pledged not to support any transfer of sovereignty against their wishes.

Two territories in the Caribbean—St Kitts-Nevis-Anguilla, and Antigua, which have a combined population of some 140,000—are known as Associated States, a status providing for complete control of internal affairs with Britain retaining responsibility for external relations and defence. This arrangement originally covered six territories but four—Dominica, Grenada, Saint Lucia, and Saint Vincent and the Grenadines—have since become independent.

Associated statehood is entirely voluntary and can be terminated at any time by either party. Unlike dependencies, Associated States can proceed to independence without the consent or assistance of the British Government. Legislation to this effect has to be approved by a two-thirds majority in the territory's legislature and by a two-thirds majority in a referendum. Alternatively the

British Government can end the associated status through an Order in Council, the procedure followed at the request of all those which have become independent. Britain considers it right to take such action at an Associated State's request provided that it is satisfied that the majority of the people want independence and that the proposed independence constitution makes proper provision for the preservation of fundamental rights and freedoms.

INTERNATIONAL PEACE AND SECURITY

One of Britain's foremost foreign policy concerns is to protect its territorial integrity and political independence, as well as the interests of its remaining dependencies and Associated States and of its allies. The attainment of these objectives is seen as depending on an effective national security policy, in which defence is coupled with strenuous efforts towards removing or alleviating the causes of international tension, and widening and strengthening international arms control and disarmament measures.

British defence policy (see Chapter 4) is based on the North Atlantic Treaty Organisation (NATO)[1] which member countries regard as their guarantor of security, freedom and well-being, and as an important contribution to international peace and stability. All the members share a belief in democracy, human rights, justice and social progress. Britain makes a major contribution, devoting to NATO the greatest proportion of its defence effort and concentrating this in areas where it can best support NATO's security objectives.

NATO's twin aims are defence and détente. It pursues a strategy of deterrence, designed to convince any potential aggressor that the use of force, or the threat of it, carries risks far outweighing any likely advantage. In recent years NATO has placed increasing emphasis upon complementing its defensive capability with efforts to negotiate arms control and disarmament agreements with a view to maintaining the balance of security at a lower level of risk. In late 1979 it put forward a new package of proposals on arms control and disarmament designed to improve mutual security and co-operation in Europe.

The Soviet Union's invasion and subsequent occupation of Afghanistan has seriously damaged détente, but NATO has reaffirmed its attachment to it and its willingness to work for the improvement of East–West relations. At the same time it has reminded the Soviet Union that détente cannot be pursued in one region of the world regardless of developments in another and called on it to take positive action, including the withdrawal of its troops from Afghanistan to live up to the peaceful intentions it professes, and thereby restore the mutual confidence necessary for a co-operative East–West relationship.

Outside Europe, Britain is committed to joint consultation with Australia, New Zealand, Malaysia and Singapore under the Five Power Defence arrangement. It is also responsible for the security of its overseas dependencies and Associated States, and supports the UN peace-keeping efforts.

Détente Britain seeks genuine improvements in East–West relations based on undiminished security. It takes an active part in arms control and disarmament negotiations (see pp 82–3), and in the process initiated by the 1975 Helsinki Conference on Security and Co-operation in Europe. It attaches great import-

---

[1] NATO's 15 member countries are Belgium, Britain, Canada, Denmark, France, the Federal Republic of Germany, Greece, Iceland, Italy, Luxembourg, the Netherlands, Norway, Portugal, Turkey and the United States. Neither France nor Greece participates fully in NATO's integrated military structure.

ance to the full and balanced implementation by all participants of the provisions of the Conference's Final Act for increased stability in Europe and improved co-operation between the 35 European and North American signatory states (The Final Act is a charter and code of conduct of behaviour for what the participants hope will in time become a more normal and open relationship between both Governments and people in East and West. It includes undertakings about security, human rights, and co-operation in economic humanitarian and other matters.) Britain participated fully in the 1977-78 Belgrade follow-up meeting at which there was a thorough exchange of views on the implementation of the Final Act. It has since taken part in the various expert-level meetings agreed at Belgrade and is actively involved in preparations for the second follow-up meeting in Madrid in November 1980.

Together with France, the United States and the Soviet Union, Britain is a signatory to the Quadripartite Agreement on Berlin which came into force in 1972. The Agreement reaffirms the four countries' rights and responsibilities in Berlin, and provides for greatly improved travel and communications facilities between Berlin and both the Federal Republic of Germany and the German Democratic Republic, and for the maintenance and development of the ties between West Berlin and the Federal Republic.

Arms Control and Disarmament

Britain has played a prominent part in all the major multilateral disarmament negotiations, and has become party to all the treaties concluded as their result (It is a depository government for most of these agreements.) At the United Nations Special Session on Disarmament in 1978, Britain reaffirmed its commitment to work for progress through multilateral, balanced and verifiable arms control and disarmament agreements. It participates in the Committee on Disarmament (as it did in the Committee's predecessor, the Conference of the Committee on Disarmament) and in the arms control and disarmament work of the United Nations.

One of the world's nuclear-weapon states, Britain is committed to negotiating in good faith to halt the nuclear arms race and to move towards nuclear disarmament. It is engaged in negotiations with the Soviet Union and the United States for a comprehensive nuclear test ban treaty, which, in the British view, would curb the development of new types of nuclear weapons. Britain regards the widest international adherence to the treaty as an important objective; meanwhile, it adheres to the Partial Test Ban Treaty (which bans nuclear tests in the atmosphere, in outer space and under water), having been, with the Soviet Union and the United States, one of the first three signatories in 1963.

Britain fully supported the United States in its efforts to conclude an agreement with the Soviet Union in the second set of the strategic arms limitation talks (SALT II), and favours the eventual ratification of the agreement reached in June 1979 which is designed to establish parity in strategic nuclear weapons and enhance stability.

Britain believes it is possible to improve international access to the benefits of the peaceful uses of nuclear energy while minimising the risk of the spread of nuclear weapons technology, and has played a leading part in strengthening the regime of non-proliferation through the International Atomic Energy Agency and other organisations. A party to the 1968 Non-Proliferation Treaty (which is designed to curb the nuclear arms race and to provide an assurance, through international safeguards, that civil nuclear activities of non-nuclear-weapon states will not be diverted to making such weapons), Britain has undertaken not to use nuclear weapons against non-nuclear-weapon states which have internationally binding commitments not to manufacture or acquire nuclear explosive devices (except in the case of an attack on British interests by such a state in association with a nuclear-weapon state). Britain reaffirmed its full support for the Treaty at the Treaty's review conference in 1980.

The establishment of nuclear-weapon-free zones in different parts of the world can contribute to non-proliferation and regional security, and Britain supports proposals for such zones wherever possible. It was the first nuclear-weapon state to ratify the protocols to the 1967 Treaty for the Prohibition of Nuclear Weapons in Latin America (the Treaty of Tlatelolco).

As a result of a British initiative, another category of weapons of mass destruction, biological weapons, is the subject of the 1972 Convention on Prohibition of the Development, Production and Stockpiling of Bacteriological (Biological) and Toxin Weapons and on their Destruction. Britain took an active part in a conference in March 1980 which reviewed the operation of the Convention. Britain has also encouraged efforts to agree on a ban on chemical weapons, and in 1976 put forward a draft convention on the prohibition of their development, production and stock-piling; this has served as a focus of discussion in the Committee on Disarmament. Britain believes also that new scientific discoveries should not be used to create totally new weapons of mass destruction. In this context, it feels that the best approach is for the Committee on Disarmament to keep under review the question of the development of such weapons and to consider the desirability of formulating agreements with regard to them as and when they are identified.

On conventional weapons, which are still the main component of most countries' national armouries, Britain has argued for international discussions on ways to halt the world-wide build-up. In particular it believes in the value of regional agreements as a means of facilitating this. In the talks on Mutual and Balanced Force Reductions, Britain, together with its NATO allies, is working for an agreement with the Warsaw Pact participants which would contribute to a more stable relationship and to the strengthening of peace and security in Europe.[1] The NATO position is based on the principle that the outcome should be one of approximate parity between NATO and Warsaw Pact forces in central Europe. Britain has also proposed at the United Nations regional 'confidence-building' measures, such as notification of military movements and exchanges of observers, in areas of potential tension.

At a United Nations conference on 'inhumane' weapons, Britain has proposed a convention regulating the use of landmines and booby-traps, and has supported proposals for bans or restrictions on other weapons deemed likely to cause unnecessary suffering or to be indiscriminate in their effects.

Britain is concerned about the rising scale of military expenditure in the world, and has made proposals at the United Nations for a multilateral, balanced and verifiable reduction of military budgets. It is also playing a leading part in the United Nations study on the relationship between disarmament and development.

BRITAIN AND THE UNITED NATIONS

Support for the United Nations (UN) and the purposes and principles of its Charter has been a cornerstone of British policy since 1945. In particular,

---

[1] All NATO countries (except France, Iceland and Portugal) and all Warsaw Pact countries (Bulgaria, Czechoslovakia, the German Democratic Republic, Hungary, Poland, Romania and the Soviet Union) take part in the talks.

Britain is concerned that the United Nations should be able to act effectively as an agency for crisis anticipation, peace-keeping and peace-making; as a forum for the discussion of major world issues; and as an instrument for development and for providing a wide variety of specialised and technical services. Britain also sees a strong and effective United Nations as the best framework for pursuing and achieving many of its foreign policy objectives—the resolution of disputes, an ordered North-South dialogue, disarmament and arms control, the protection of human rights, the promotion of the rule of law—designed to contribute both to its own wellbeing and security and to the development of a more harmonious international community.

The United Nations has in recent years had a growing role as the central institution for the discussion of world issues. In addition to those of peace and war, these include arms control and disarmament, disaster relief, the sea-bed, action against terrorism, the world environment, energy, development and world resources. While in some cases there are specialised institutions, usually UN agencies, for dealing with these issues, in many others, including most of those referred to above, discussion takes place mainly in the United Nations itself. Britain plays an active and positive role in these debates.

Keeping the Peace

The maintenance of international peace and security, the primary purpose envisaged for the United Nations at the time of its establishment, remains one of the world's greatest problems. Britain supports the view that the United Nations, as the only forum in which the whole international community is represented, has the right and duty to be involved in disputes which threaten peace and stability whether on a regional or world scale. In concert with other members, it has worked to strengthen and make more effective the machinery of the Security Council, the organ with primary responsibility for security matters, for preventing and settling disputes. As a permanent member of the Security Council, Britain has a particular interest in and responsibility for questions of international peace and security, and plays an active role in the Council's work.

Another British concern is that the United Nations should have the capacity to play an effective peace-keeping role. Britain currently supplies the largest national contingent to the UN Force in Cyprus, together with logistic support for the entire force, and provides some logistic support for the UN Interim Force in Lebanon.

Human Rights

Britain has supported the UN's Universal Declaration of Human Rights since its adoption by the General Assembly in 1948. While not legally binding, the Declaration has inspired many other international instruments designed to secure the observance of its provisions. These include the two international covenants adopted by the General Assembly in 1966 which do impose legal obligations on those who ratify them—the Covenant on Economic, Social and Cultural Rights and the Covenant on Civil and Political Rights. Both came into force, and were ratified by Britain, in 1976. Britain has accepted Article 41 of the Covenant on Civil and Political Rights recognising the competence of the UN Human Rights Committee (set up to supervise the Covenant's implementation) to receive and consider state-to-state complaints.

Britain is also a party to a number of more specific conventions aimed at implementing particular rights contained in the Universal Declaration, including those on the elimination of racial discrimination, on the rights of women, the status of refugees and stateless persons and slavery.

Britain recognises, however, that the adoption of conventions and covenants in itself is insufficient to secure the protection of human rights, and believes it is necessary to develop effective procedures to ensure the implementation of standards which such arrangements contain. Britain also believes that UN member states, through their voluntary acceptance of the Universal Declaration and the international covenants, have demonstrated that abuses of human rights wherever they occur are the legitimate subject of international concern; and that a consistent policy on the part of a member government in breach of these obligations is a proper matter for UN discussion.

Overall responsibility within the United Nations for human rights activities lies with the Economic and Social Council. The bodies directly concerned are the Commission on Human Rights, its Sub-Commission on Prevention of Discrimination and Protection of Minorities, and the Commission on the Status of Women. Britain is represented on all these bodies and plays an active part in their work.

Economic and Social Affairs

The Charter states that 'the promotion of the economic and social advancement of all peoples' is one of the principal aims of the United Nations, and it is estimated that some 90 per cent of the organisation's efforts, in terms of resources and personnel, are now employed to this end. With the growing concern for and assistance to meet the problems of development, the main emphasis in this work has become increasingly the provision of operational programmes of direct assistance for member states. The UN system is now the largest single source of technical assistance for developing countries, as well as providing considerable emergency and relief aid and assistance for refugees. (The provision of capital assistance has been generally confined to the World Bank group and regional development banks whose operations are generally considered separately from those of the rest of the UN system.)

Successive British governments have affirmed their support for the functional and developmental work of the United Nations and have continued to increase the amount of funds made available to the UN system for assisting developing countries. Britain is the seventh largest contributor to the UN's regular budget, providing some £10·1 million, 4·5 per cent of the total, in 1979. In addition, it contributed about £3·8 million to the World Health Organisation, £2·5 million to the International Labour Organisation, £2·5 million to the Food and Agriculture Organisation and £3 million to the UN Educational, Scientific and Cultural Organisation. Britain provides a considerably larger proportion of the UN's voluntary funds, donating some £65·2 million in 1979, including £28·5 million for the UN Development Programme, £4·4 million for the UN Relief and Works Agency for Palestinian Refugees, £5·3 million for the UN Children's Fund, £2 million for the UN Fund for Population Activities, about £8·9 million for the UN High Commissioner for Refugees, and £6 million for the World Food Programme.

Britain plays an active role in the deliberations of the governing bodies of the various agencies and programmes, especially with a view to encouraging the deployment of resources towards the poorest countries and the poorest communities in the developing world. It also seeks to ensure that the institutions make the most efficient use of the development resources placed at their disposal, and to promote improvements in the co-ordination, control and effectiveness of the system, especially in order to avoid unnecessary duplication and overlapping of responsibilities.

The United Nations is central to the North-South dialogue, not only through the involvement of its agencies in development and other international economic problems, but also as the forum within which the dialogue is reviewed. In the General Assembly's Committee of the Whole, set up in 1978 to monitor developments in the dialogue, and at its special session on global economic issues in 1980, Britain played an active role in the discussions on a new international development strategy for the 1980s, believing that this should reflect the interdependent nature of the world economy and be addressed to the responsibilities of all governments, irrespective of their level of development and of their social and economic system (see p 88).

OTHER INTERNATIONAL ORGANISATIONS

Britain is an active member of a number of other international organisations including those concerned with the management of the world economy and which, therefore, have an important role to play in the North-South dialogue (see p 90). It is a founder member of the International Monetary Fund established in 1944 (along with the World Bank—see p 90) as the principal administrator of the international financial system and as a source of credit for member states facing balance of payments problems, and has welcomed the creation by the Fund of facilities to provide special assistance to developing countries experiencing financial or trading difficulties. It is a strong supporter of efforts under the General Agreement on Tariffs and Trade to liberalise further and promote the growth of world trade, and to improve the developing countries' participation in it (see pp 91 and 372).

Britain is also a member of the Organisation for Economic Co-operation and Development (OECD), an instrument for inter-governmental co-operation among 24 industrialised countries on matters relating to economic and social policy. Its aims are to promote policies designed to achieve the highest sustainable economic growth and employment, and a rising living standard, in member countries while maintaining financial stability, and thus to contribute to the development of the world economy; to contribute to sound economic expansion in member as well as non-member countries in economic development; and to contribute to the expansion of world trade on a multilateral non-discriminatory basis in accordance with international obligations.

Other organisations to which Britain belongs or extends support are more restricted in their operations and include the regional development banks in Africa, the Americas and Asia and specialist technical, agricultural and medical institutions.

With 20 other nations Britain is a member of the Council of Europe which aims to provide the widest possible European forum for the discussion of current political, economic, social and scientific issues with a view to achieving a greater unity between its members. Membership is open to any European state which is a parliamentary democracy and accepts the principles of the rule of law and the protection of human rights. The Council was responsible for the adoption in 1950 of the European Convention on Human Rights, to which Britain is a party.

DEVELOPMENT CO-OPERATION

The basic objective of Britain's aid programme, which is the responsibility of the Overseas Development Administration, is to help developing countries efforts to raise their living standards. This involves assistance in the broadest sense (from the provision of finance for the purchase of capital goods to expert advice and training) to supplement developing countries' own programmes for generating economic growth and social development. Aid is provided either bilaterally on a government-to-government basis or multilaterally through contributions to international development agencies.

Recent British aid policy has focused on reducing absolute poverty in the developing world, reflecting a recognition that the poorest countries find it most difficult to generate investment funds domestically or attract external private flows. The emphasis in the aid programme, therefore, has been on the poorest countries and on the poorest communities within these countries. While developmental objectives will continue to be at the basis of British aid policy, greater weight will in future be given to political, commercial and industrial considerations in the deployment of aid resources. Britain's ability to support development overseas is dependent on the state of its own economy; the aid programme will be used increasingly in ways which are to the mutual benefit of both the developing countries and Britain.

In addition to the official aid programme, private investment in developing countries is encouraged by the provision of government insurance to private investors by the Export Credits Guarantee Department, and was further facilitated by the abolition of exchange controls in 1979. An important contribution is also made by the work of private voluntary organisations.

Official Flows Since 1945 total official aid disbursements have amounted to about £7,731 million. The average gross annual disbursement over the four years 1976–79 was about £705 million. In 1979 official aid flows totalled some £941 million, of which £876 million represented official development assistance[1] and £65 million other official flows. Of the overall total, bilateral aid accounted for £685 million including technical co-operation funds of £185 million; assistance provided through multilateral agencies was £256 million. Repayments of capital and payments of interest on loans made previously came to £73 million and £47 million respectively.

The strategy for the Second UN Development Decade, adopted in 1970, recommended that each developed country should progressively increase its official development assistance to the developing countries and exert its best efforts to contribute a minimum net amount of 0·7 per cent of its gross national product (GNP) annually. Britain has accepted this in principle without commitment to a target date, progress being dependent on Britain's own economy and other calls on resources. In 1979, net disbursements of official development assistance (see Table 5) amounted to £804 million, 0·43 per cent of GNP (the net official flow figure was £867 million, 0·46 per cent of GNP). On a new alternative basis,[2] Britain's net official development assistance in 1979 amounted to £974 million, 0·52 per cent of GNP. (The average for all donor members of the OECD's Development Assistance Committee was 0·34 per cent of GNP.) Total net financial flows from Britain to the developing countries (that is, including private and official flows) amounted to £5,288 million in 1979, some 2·8 per cent of GNP and well above the UN target of 1 per cent of GNP.

---

[1] Official development assistance, the international basis for reporting on aid performances, is defined as official flows for development purposes with a grant (concessional) element of 25 per cent or more.
[2] On this basis, which is designed to allow stricter comparability with other donor countries, contributions to multilateral agencies made by means of promissory notes deposited in banks are taken to represent flows as soon as they are deposited instead of when the agency draws upon them. This is a technical change in reporting only and does not represent a real increase in aid flows.

The international development strategy for the 1980s agreed at a special session of the General Assembly in late 1980 (see p 86) envisages the eventual adoption of a 1 per cent of GNP target for official development assistance by developed countries, including those with centrally planned economies, and a speeding up of progress towards the 0·7 per cent target. It also urges greatly increased aid for the poorest countries and that this should be provided mainly in grants, a policy already adopted by Britain (see below).

Bilateral Aid

Historically, Britain's aid programme began as part of the discharge of its responsibilities towards dependent territories, and the main emphasis remains on the Commonwealth which includes among its members some of the world's poorest countries. In 1979 £434 million (68 per cent) of bilateral aid went to Commonwealth countries. Of this, £26 million went to Britain's remaining dependencies, which are a first charge on the aid programme, and £3 million to the Associated States.

In regional terms, most British aid goes to Asia, which in 1979 received £283 million (44 per cent) of the bilateral programme, followed by Africa (£220 million), Latin America and the Caribbean (£42 million) and Oceania (£29 million). The country receiving the largest amount was India with £153 million. Other major recipients included Pakistan, Bangladesh, Malawi, Kenya, Zambia and Tanzania.

In line with the policy of concentrating aid on the poorest countries, £361 million (57 per cent) of bilateral aid went to countries with a 1978 per capita income of $320 or less.

TABLE 5: Official Development Assistance to Developing Countries 1976–79

£ million

	1976	1977	1978	1979
Bilateral	381·1	375·8	496·8	619·5
Commonwealth countries (including dependent territories)	304·3	251·0	367·5	419·3
Grants	*163·9*	*151·2*	*235·7*	*266·3*
Technical co-operation (grants)	*94·9*	*60·1*	*74·9*	*91·3*
Loans	*45·5*	*39·7*	*57·0*	*61·7*
Other countries	76·8	123·5	129·3	200·2
Grants	*21·7*	*30·1*	*31·9*	*79·8*
Technical co-operation (grants)	*32·5*	*66·5*	*78·3*	*94·2*
Loans	*22·6*	*27·0*	*19·0*	*26·2*
Contributions to multilateral agencies	141·1	205·9	187·8	256·0
Total	522·9	581·7	684·7	875·5
Total net of amortisation (as used for calculation of the 0·7 per cent target)	462·4	523·7	631·6	804·0
Interest receipts	38·4	37·8	37·3	39·3

Source: *British Aid Statistics*
Differences between totals and the sum of their constituent parts are due to rounding.

Financial Aid

Bilateral financial aid in 1979 totalled £454 million; over 72 per cent was in grants and the rest in concessionary loans. Budgetary aid, over £11 million in 1979, is provided in the form of grants. Development aid can be in grant or loan form, but the greater part is provided in grants following a decision to provide aid to the poorest developing countries (which include India, Bangladesh, Sr

Lanka and many African countries) in grant form only. The terms of development loans have been progressively relaxed since 1958. In 1979 loan commitments, excluding investments by the Commonwealth Development Corporation (see below) totalled £39 million. Where loans bear interest it is at fixed concessionary rates ranging from 2 per cent to 6 per cent, and both kinds of loan carry from three to seven years' grace periods, during which repayments of capital are not made. Of all loans committed in 1979 the average maturity was 25 years. Britain has more than fulfilled the 1972 and 1978 recommendations of the Development Assistance Committee of the Organisation for Economic Co-operation and Development on easing the terms of financial aid. In 1978 Britain announced its intention of removing the burden of past aid loans (retrospective terms adjustment) worth £900 million to 17 of the poorest countries.

Loans and grants are normally tied to the purchase of goods, equipment and services from Britain, although there may be an element for local costs and a foreign content in contracts financed from tied aid in appropriate cases. New loan commitments can be untied, if the recipient agrees, to the extent that goods can be purchased either from the poorest developing countries or from Britain.

An important role in development assistance is played by Britain's Commonwealth Development Corporation, set up in 1948 to assist the economic development of the then dependent territories. Subsequent legislation extended its area of operations to independent Commonwealth countries and, with British Government approval, to other countries. By the end of 1979 some £313 million had been invested out of a total commitment of £449 million. Of the latter £10 million was in East Asia and the Pacific, £62 million in the Caribbean and virtually all of the remainder in Africa. Commitments approved in 1979 totalled over £83 million, of which nearly 90 per cent went to the poorest countries and 60 per cent to renewable natural resources projects.

Technical Co-operation

Technical co-operation, the transfer of specialised knowledge and skills from country to country, is complementary to financial aid, the availability of such expertise often being a precondition of a successful programme of financial aid or investment. Expenditure on it has increased in recent years and was £185 million, 29 per cent of bilateral aid, in 1979. Of this, £79 million was for the provision of expert personnel, including volunteers, £34 million for students and trainees in Britain and overseas, £11 million for research services and projects, £19 million for consultancy services, and £42 million in support of various British institutions, including the British Council, and for the provision of equipment and supplies.

During 1979, there were 7,463 people financed by Britain (other than volunteers) working in developing countries, of whom some 3,478 were engaged in the field of education, 1,337 in public works and communications, 1,064 in public administration, 981 in agriculture and allied fields, 522 in health services, and 136 in industrial posts. In addition, under the British Volunteer Programme there were 1,302 volunteers, mainly graduates or otherwise qualified, working in developing countries, the majority of them teaching. Recruitment, training and placing overseas is undertaken by four voluntary bodies: Catholic Institute for International Relations, International Voluntary Service, United Nations Association International Service and Voluntary Service Overseas; 90 per cent of the organisations' costs are met by the British Government.

Britain receives large numbers of students and trainees from developing countries. Over 16,000 were financed in Britain in 1979 under regional programmes of technical co-operation, by awards under the Commonwealth Scholarships and Fellowship Plan, and under British Council schemes.

To support practical development activity overseas, the Government maintains four specialist scientific organisations (the Directorate of Overseas Surveys, the Land Resources Development Centre, the Tropical Products Institute and the Centre for Overseas Pest Research) and provides support for many others. The latter includes overseas units/divisions of the government financed Transport and Road Research Laboratory, the Building Research Establishment, the Hydraulics Research Station and the Institute of Geological Sciences. These organisations provide specialist information and advice and experts for service overseas, and undertake field and laboratory research investigations.

Multilateral Aid

Britain is the second largest subscriber (after the United States) to the World Bank group of institutions—the International Bank for Reconstruction and Development, the International Development Association (IDA) and the International Finance Corporation. The British commitment to the IDA's Fifth Replenishment (for 1977 to 1980) was £474 million, and its proposed commitment to the Sixth Replenishment (for 1980 to 1983) is £555 million. Britain has contributed or has agreed to contribute, to the Asian Development Bank, the Inter-American Development Bank, the Caribbean Development Bank and the African Development Fund. Britain's contribution to the United Nations Development Programme for 1979 was £28·5 million, and it is the largest source for expertise and fellowships provided under the Programme. In addition there is a major British contribution to other UN agencies and programmes and an increasing proportion of British development assistance is now channelled through the European Community's aid programme.

Voluntary Agencies

Voluntary agencies provided some £27 million for their work in developing countries in 1979. The funds were spent mainly on agriculture, health and nutrition, and education projects and on emergency relief operations. The Government co-operates with the agencies in various ways, especially in immediate post-disaster relief and rehabilitation operations and through its Joint Funding Scheme. Under this Scheme, the Government meets half the cost of selected development projects undertaken by the agencies and aimed at helping the poorest. Such projects include community health, non-formal education, the improvement of food supplies, agricultural training, water supply and irrigation. Expenditure on the Scheme in 1979 was over £1·5 million.

Voluntary agencies' work on behalf of refugees overseas also receives government support. The Government finances about half the annual budget of the United Kingdom Standing Conference on Refugees, a consultative body for agencies engaged in assisting refugees, and in 1977 introduced a scheme for financing voluntary agency projects for refugees overseas. Some £166,500 had been spent under the scheme by the end of March 1980, the projects being concerned mainly with improving the health and general well-being of the refugees. Some, however, were development projects.

THE NORTH-SOUTH DIALOGUE

The North-South dialogue, which embraces questions of development, transfer of resources, raw materials, trade and international monetary issues, is being conducted between the industrialised nations and the developing countries with a view to evolving a more equitable balance in the world's economy. Britain attaches importance to securing progress in the dialogue, and, in its approach to the discussions involved, works in close association with its partners in the European Community. At the Venice economic summit meeting in June 1980, Britain and six other major Western industrialised nations welcomed the recent Report of the Independent Commission on International Development Issues (the Brandt Report), and promised to consider its recommendations carefully.

As a Community member state Britain contributed significantly to the work of the Conference on International Economic Co-operation.[1] The Conference did not achieve complete success but reached a considerable degree of agreement particularly on development issues (see p 76).

A major development in aid policy in 1978 was the commitment by major donor countries, at a ministerial meeting of the Trade and Development Board of the UN Conference on Trade and Development (UNCTAD), to adjust the terms of past bilateral aid to bring them into line with prevailing more relaxed terms—known as retrospective or retroactive terms adjustment—or to take equivalent measures. It was following this that Britain decided to relieve 17 of the poorest countries of debt repayments worth some £900 million to the end of the century, thus placing past aid to these countries on the same grant-only basis as present assistance programmes (see p 89).

In the commodities field, Britain took the initiative at the Commonwealth Heads of Government Meeting in 1975 in giving impetus to the establishment of price stabilisation arrangements on a commodity-by-commodity basis. This took shape in the programme of work on individual international commodity agreements initiated by the Resolution on the Integrated Programme for Commodities (IPC) adopted by UNCTAD in 1976; the Resolution also called for a Common Fund to help finance the agreements. In the subsequent negotiations on the Common Fund and on individual commodities, Britain has played an active part within the European Community and consumer countries generally in the search for appropriate solutions. The first agreement concluded under the IPC was reached in October 1979. A final agreement for the establishment of the Common Fund was concluded in June 1980.

In 1964 Britain was the first major developed country to support the idea of extending tariff preferences on a non-reciprocal and non-discriminatory basis to all developing countries. It therefore strongly supported the objectives of the latest round of multilateral trade negotiations. Set out in the 1973 Tokyo Declaration (see p 76), these were the further liberalisation of world trade through the progressive dismantling of tariff and non-tariff barriers, and within this, the provision of special and more favourable treatment for the developing countries where possible.

Since its entry into the European Community, Britain has adopted the Community's trade arrangements, which are among the most liberal applied by industrial nations, and has played a significant role in determining their nature. In particular it took a major part in the negotiations for the first Lomé Convention (see p 76), not only with a view to safeguarding the trading interests of Commonwealth developing countries, but also to ensure that

[1] The Conference on International Economic Co-operation met in Paris from December 1975 to June 1977 and was, while it continued, the focal point of the North-South dialogue. It was attended by representatives of eight western industrial countries (including the European Community as a single entity), known as the 'Group of Eight'; and seven members of the Organisation of Petroleum Exporting Countries and 12 other developing countries, who made up the 'Group of 19'. Discussions have since reverted to the United Nations and its constituent bodies.

reciprocal preferences would not be demanded from the developing countries as had been the case with previous Community arrangements. Britain also contributed to the successful conclusion of the second Lomé Convention in October 1979 (see p 76). In addition, Britain has supported improvements to the Community's Generalised System of Preferences scheme (see p 373), especially with regard to more liberal access into the Community for imports of manufactured and processed agricultural products and in its application to the poorest developed countries, particularly those in South Asia. Before entering the Community, Britain secured a commitment to expand and reinforce Community trade relations with the Commonwealth countries of Asia, and this has led to the conclusion of commercial co-operation agreements with India, Sri Lanka and Bangladesh.

4 Defence

POLICY

For over thirty years Britain's defence policy has been based on the continued strength of the North Atlantic Treaty Organisation (NATO—see also pp 81) whose collective defence provides each of its members with far greater security than any could achieve alone. Britain is fully committed to NATO, and with the greater part of its military forces assigned to the North Atlantic Alliance makes a major contribution to the full range of deterrent capabilities, both conventional and nuclear, required to maintain its defences.

Britain is participating fully in the NATO Long Term Defence Programme which is a major undertaking adopted by the Alliance in 1978 in order to maintain its defence and deterrent posture in the face of the continuing build-up in Warsaw Pact military strength. It is also taking an active part in the programme agreed in 1979 for the modernisation of NATO's long-range theatre nuclear forces (see p 95). In the 'Eurogroup' Britain and ten other European members are working to improve the effectiveness of their contribution to the Alliance and to achieve better co-ordination, thereby making the best possible use of the available resources. The sub-groups of the Eurogroup concentrate on specific areas of co-operation, such as training or logistics.

The Alliance complements its defence preparations with efforts to reduce tension and achieve a more just and lasting peaceful order in Europe through such measures as arms control and disarmament agreements, and Britain plays a major part in these efforts (see pp 81–3). In recent years, Britain has withdrawn from its commitments outside NATO wherever this has been consistent with its fundamental military and political obligations (see p 81). However, in support of these, and with a view to playing a full part in firm collective responses by the West to threats to its world-wide interests, it is taking steps to improve its capability to operate effectively outside NATO without diminishing its central commitment to the Alliance.

PLANNING AND CONTROL

Supreme responsibility for national defence rests with the Government as a whole, which is responsible to Parliament. The formulation of defence policy is the responsibility of the Secretary of State for Defence who is assisted by a Minister of State, and by three Under-Secretaries of State—for the Navy, Army and Air Force respectively. They, together with the Chief of the Defence Staff, the three Service Chiefs of Staff, the Permanent Under-Secretary of State for Defence, the Vice-Chief of Defence Staff (Personnel and Logistics), the Chief Scientific Adviser and the Chief of Defence Procurement, form the Defence Council, which deals with major aspects of defence policy. The Chiefs of Staff Committee is responsible for giving professional advice on strategy and operations, and on the military implications of defence policy. The day-to-day management of the three Services is the responsibility of the Admiralty, Army and Air Force Boards of the Defence Council.

Expenditure   The defence estimate for 1980–81 totals £10,785 million. This is about 3·5 per cent more in real terms than in 1979–80, and thus exceeds the NATO aim of an annual increase in each member's defence spending of around 3 per cent in real terms. Planned defence expenditure for the three years from 1981–82 also fully accords with this aim. Of the 1980–81 total, £4,527 million (42 per cent) is for personnel (pay, allowances, pensions), £4,336 million (41 per cent) is for equipment, and £1,922 million (18 per cent) is for buildings and miscellaneous stores and services). Using the NATO definition of defence expenditure, British defence spending in 1980–81 will account for 5·1 per cent of gross domestic product at market prices. This proportion is 40 per cent greater than the average for NATO's European members.

Functional analysis of defence expenditure 1980-81

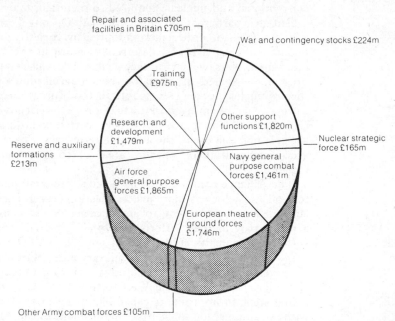

Total £10,785 million
(including miscellaneous expenditure and receipts totalling £27 million)

DEPLOYMENT

NATO Strategy   The NATO strategy of flexible response, together with the principle of forward defence, is based on the premise that peace and stability can only be maintained if a potential aggressor is convinced that it would lose far more than it could ever hope to gain by the use of force. The strategy is designed to enable NATO to respond to aggression at a variety of levels, being flexible enough to allow the appropriate degree of effective military action to be taken. It requires the possession of a wide range of mobile and well-equipped conventional forces, and of theatre nuclear and strategic nuclear capabilities which are sufficiently closely linked together to provide a chain of options from which to choose the appropriate method of countering aggression.

Britain's NATO Contribution

Britain makes a major contribution to the forces required by NATO's present strategy. The British Polaris strategic force (to be replaced by a Trident force in the 1990s) represents a unique European contribution to NATO's nuclear deterrent, providing a second and independent centre of strategic nuclear decision-making within the Alliance. Britain's theatre nuclear systems are also committed to NATO, and it has agreed to provide bases for 160 of the 464 ground-launched cruise missiles which, with 108 Pershing II missiles, will be deployed in Europe under a programme agreed in 1979 to modernise NATO's long-range theatre nuclear forces.

The Royal Navy is the largest NATO navy in Western Europe, and virtually all ships of frigate size and above are earmarked for assignment in an emergency to NATO. It also contributes to NATO's Standing Naval Force Atlantic, Standing Naval Force Channel, and the Naval On Call Force Mediterranean. The British Army of the Rhine (BAOR) and Royal Air Force (RAF) Germany are deployed in the Federal Republic of Germany. (Britain also maintains a Field Force in Berlin, but this is not committed to NATO.) The main combat element of BAOR is First (British) Corps which comprises four armoured divisions, an artillery division, and an infantry formation. Its peacetime strength of around 55,000 would be more than doubled on mobilisation by reinforcements and reserves from Britain (see pp 99–100) and up to 70 per cent of the British Army would be deployed in Central Europe in wartime. Virtually all the RAF's combat and combat support aircraft are assigned to NATO. RAF Germany is a tactical air force with 12 squadrons (one of helicopters) equipped for strike/attack, reconnaissance, close support and air-defence roles. In addition, combat units based in Britain are part of NATO's mobile reinforcement capability. These include the ground elements of the United Kingdom Mobile Force, the British contribution to the Allied Command Europe Mobile Force (Land) and three squadrons of 22 Special Air Service Regiment. RAF Strike Command provides forces for strike/attack, reconnaissance, close support, air defence and maritime patrol and anti-submarine warfare, together with transport forces and air elements for the United Kingdom Mobile Force and Allied Command Europe Mobile Force (Air).

Forces from all three Services are also stationed at Gibraltar, the position of which at the western entry to the Mediterranean makes it an important asset and base for NATO.

Outside NATO

In the Mediterranean, British forces are deployed in Cyprus to meet Britain's commitment to the United Nations Force (to which Britain provides the largest component) and to provide for the security of the Sovereign Base Areas. In Hong Kong, units of all three Services provide a garrison for external defence, and a Gurkha battalion is stationed in Brunei. A Royal Marines detachment is maintained in the Falkland Islands; and in the Caribbean, units of the Army and the RAF provide a garrison for the external defence of Belize, and a Royal Navy warship is deployed as the Belize guardship.

Northern Ireland

At home a major task of the armed forces since 1969 has been to assist the civil authorities in Northern Ireland in the maintenance of law and order, and they have operated to counter the terrorist activities of extremist organisations.

THE ARMED FORCES

Personnel

Britain's armed forces excluding non-United Kingdom personnel totalled about 319,400 on 1 January 1980, 71,900 in the Royal Navy and Royal Marines, 159,100 in the Army and 88,400 in the Royal Air Force. The forecast total for 1 April 1981 is 323,300. The armed forces consist entirely of personnel serving on a voluntary basis. To help to improve force strengths and overcome shortages of skilled personnel, service conditions are being improved. In particular, pay has been restored to the levels comparable to those in civilian life, and the Government has undertaken to maintain it at these levels in future. The average number of civilian staff expected to be employed by the Ministry of Defence during 1980–81 is 255,500.

The Women's Royal Naval Service, the Women's Royal Army Corps, and the Women's Royal Air Force (which have a combined strength of some 12,700) are integral parts of the armed forces, and servicewomen serve alongside servicemen in Britain and overseas, mainly in support roles. Their importance is expected to increase in coming years, and the possibility of women bearing arms for self-defence and, perhaps, base defence is being considered. Nursing services are provided by Queen Alexandra's Royal Naval Nursing Service, Queen Alexandra's Royal Army Nursing Corps and Princess Mary's Royal Air Force Nursing Service.

Engagements

Engagements available to non-commissioned ranks range from three to 22 years, with a wide freedom of choice on the length and terms of service. Recruits to non-commissioned ranks are committed for only a minimum period of service (about three years, excluding training) and, subject to that minimum, may leave at any time at 18 months' notice. Discharge may also be granted on compassionate grounds, by purchase, or on grounds of conscience (appeals for the last being assessed by an independent committee). Commissions may be granted for short, medium and long terms. In all three Services there are opportunities for promotion from the ranks. Direct entry to commissioned ranks is on the basis of educational and other qualifications. All three Services have schemes for university cadetships.

Training

Entrants to non-commissioned ranks are given basic training, supplemented by further and specialist training during the course of their careers. Young servicemen and women are encouraged to study for educational qualifications, and extensive facilities exist for this. Trade and technical training, though primarily designed for Service purposes, leads to nationally recognised qualifications for a about half the total number of service personnel.

Service technical training is highly valued in industry, which is a significant advantage on return to civilian life. To assist resettlement the Services provide an advisory service, familiarisation attachments to civilian organisations, and opportunity and assistance to study for suitable civilian qualifications. There are also opportunities for short- and longer-term retraining both before and after discharge from the Services.

Entrants to commissioned ranks receive initial training at the Britannia Royal Naval College, Dartmouth, the Royal Military Academy, Sandhurst, the Royal Air Force College, Cranwell, or similar institutions. This is followed by specialist training, often including degree courses at university or Service establishments.

Staff training is provided by the Royal Naval College, Greenwich, the Army Staff College at Camberley, and the Royal Air Force Staff College at Bracknell.

Functional analysis of defence personnel 1980-81

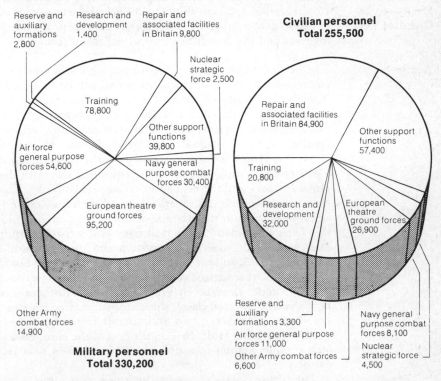

Reserve and auxiliary formations 2,800

Research and development 1,400

Repair and associated facilities in Britain 9,800

Nuclear strategic force 2,500

Training 78,800

Other support functions 39,800

Air force general purpose forces 54,600

Navy general purpose combat forces 30,400

European theatre ground forces 95,200

Other Army combat forces 14,900

Military personnel Total 330,200

Civilian personnel Total 255,500

Repair and associated facilities in Britain 84,900

Other support functions 57,400

Training 20,800

Research and development 32,000

European theatre ground forces 26,900

Reserve and auxiliary formations 3,300

Air force general purpose forces 11,000

Other Army combat forces 6,600

Navy general purpose combat forces 8,100

Nuclear strategic force 4,500

Note: These are average strengths and include locally enlisted personnel, but exclude Ministry of Defence civilians employed in the Royal Ordnance Factories, and Department of Environment staff employed on defence work.

The National Defence College at Latimer is designed to fit selected mid-career officers of all three Services for key posts that contribute to formulation of defence policy in the Ministry of Defence and on international staffs. Specially selected senior officers and civilian officials from Britain, the Commonwealth, NATO and other countries attend the Royal College of Defence Studies in London, which provides the wider background necessary for those destined to fill higher appointments.

Considerable operational training is carried out through joint-Service and inter-allied exercises. All three Services provide training for the armed forces of allied and Commonwealth countries and for many other countries.

COMBAT FORCES Combat forces are functionally divided into the nuclear strategic force, Royal Navy general purpose combat forces, European theatre ground forces, other Army combat forces and Royal Air Force general purpose forces.

Strategic Nuclear Force The British contribution to NATO's strategic deterrent comprises the Royal Navy's force of four Polaris nuclear submarines—*Resolution, Repulse, Renown,* and *Revenge.* Each can remain on underwater patrol for long periods and is equipped with 16 Polaris missiles, armed with nuclear warheads. A £1,000 million programme called 'Chevaline', designed to maintain the effectiveness of the force until its replacement in the early 1990s by a force of four or five nuclear submarines equipped with Trident missiles, is nearing completion.

**Royal Navy
General
Purpose
Combat Forces**

Britain's maritime forces are concentrated in the Eastern Atlantic and English Channel, where they provide the majority of forces readily available to NATO. However, they retain an ability to be deployed world-wide in defence and allied or national interests. Nearer home they provide protection for Britain's fishing interests and the North Sea oil and gas installations.

Equipment

The first of a new class of anti-submarine warfare carrier, HMS *Invincible*, entered service in 1980, and another two will be deployed by the mid-1980s. Their primary task will be to act as command ships for anti-submarine warfare forces. They will deploy the Sea King anti-submarine helicopter, and carry the Sea Dart missile system and Sea Harrier maritime vertical short-take-off and landing (V/STOL) aircraft for area air defence and anti-surface ship operations. Sea Kings are also embarked on the anti-submarine warfare carriers HMS *Hermes* (which is soon to be equipped also with the Sea Harrier) and HMS *Bulwark* and the helicopter cruiser HMS *Blake*. There are five County class guided-missile destroyers all armed with Seaslug and Seacat surface-to-air missiles and four with the Exocet surface-to-surface guided-missile system, the Type 82 guided-missile destroyer HMS *Bristol* (equipped with the Sea Dart area air defence missile system and the Ikara anti-submarine guided weapon system), and seven of the new class of Type 42 Sea Dart guided-missile destroyers. Other surface vessels include 49 general purpose frigates (comprising 26 Leander class, seven Tribal class, eight Rothesay class and eight of the new Type 21 Amazon class), three anti-submarine frigates (including the first two Type 22 frigates), two anti-aircraft frigates, 37 mine counter-measure vessels (including HMS *Brecon*, the first of the Hunt class of glass-reinforced-plastic mine counter-measure vessels) and seven new Island class offshore patrol vessels.

The frigate classes are variously armed with automatic guns, surface-to-air missile systems, underwater detection and anti-submarine weapons. Most have the Wasp helicopter embarked, which is being replaced, where appropriate, by the Anglo-French Lynx.

Exocet missile systems are being installed in some Leander class and Type 21 frigates, giving these vessels a better surface-to-surface capability, and in the Type 22 frigates, which also have the Seawolf surface-to-air missile system. Some Leander class frigates are also equipped with the Ikara anti-submarine weapon. Eleven nuclear-fleet submarines are in service, and these will be joined by another, the last of the Swiftsure class, in late 1980; and there are 16 conventional patrol submarines. There is also an amphibious capability comprising the two assault ships HMS *Fearless* and HMS *Intrepid* and the Royal Marines Commando Forces, supported by HMS *Hermes* and HMS *Bulwark* which retain a secondary role as commando ships.

Ships under construction include HMS *Illustrious*, and HMS *Ark Royal*, the second and third of the anti-submarine warfare carriers and four Type 22 frigates. In addition, work is in hand on three of the new Trafalgar class nuclear-fleet submarines, seven Type 42 Sea Dart destroyers, and eight Hunt class mine counter-measure vessels.

**European
Theatre
Ground Forces**

The European theatre ground forces consist of BAOR, and the forces stationed in Britain, the main elements of which have primary roles in support of the North Atlantic Alliance (see p 81).

**Other Army
Combat Forces**

Other Army combat forces comprise land forces stationed overseas to meet treaty commitments to Commonwealth and other countries (see p 95).

Equipment   Armoured regiments are equipped with the Chieftain main battle tank; Challenger, a new main battle tank fitted with Chobham armour, will enter service in the mid-1980s. A new series of tracked combat reconnaissance vehicles is in service, including Scorpion and Scimitar, mounting respectively a 76 mm and a 30 mm gun, Striker, carrying the Swingfire anti-tank missile, and Sultan, a command vehicle. The primary tracked armoured personnel carrier used by mechanised infantry battalions is the FV432, which is to be replaced by the MCV80 beginning in the mid-1980s. Entering service with the infantry is the crew-portable Milan medium-range anti-tank guided weapon system (all BAOR's mechanised infantry units will be equipped with it by the end of 1980) and the TOW long-range anti-tank guided weapon is to be fitted to the Lynx helicopter. Artillery units are equipped with the Abbot 105 mm self-propelled gun, 155 mm and 175 mm self-propelled guns, the 105 mm light gun and Field Artillery Computer Equipment (FACE). The FH70 155 mm field howitzer has begun to enter service. Tactical nuclear support is provided by the Lance missile system. Air defence is provided by the Rapier low-level surface-to-air missile system and the Blowpipe man-portable very-low-level missile.

Royal Air Force General Purpose Forces   The Royal Air Force general purpose forces consist of aircraft for air defence, strike/attack, reconnaissance, ground support, airborne early warning, maritime patrol and anti-submarine warfare, transport and in-flight refuelling, communications and the RAF Regiment field squadrons in the anti-aircraft and ground defence roles.

Equipment   Phantom and Lightning aircraft, together with Rapier and Bloodhound surface-to-air missiles, are employed in air defence. Radar warning is provided by Shackleton airborne early warning aircraft (to be replaced in the 1980s by specially equipped Nimrods which will form part of NATO's integrated airborne early warning force) and by the ground radars and control and reporting centres of the United Kingdom Air Defence Ground Environment system. Jaguars, Buccaneers and Vulcans operate in the strike/attack role; Jaguars, Canberras and Vulcans are employed for reconnaissance; Jaguars and the Harrier V/STOL aircraft provide ground support (with the Harrier also having a tactical reconnaissance capability); and Nimrods are used for long-range maritime patrol and anti-submarine warfare and for offshore surveillance and fishery protection duty. The Tornado multi-role combat aircraft will replace the Vulcan, Buccaneer, Canberra, Phantom and Lightning aircraft in their respective roles during the 1980s. The first version, the GR1, entered service in the strike/attack role in 1980.

The VC10 provides strategic transport and the Hercules (which also has a strategic capability) is used for tactical transport over medium ranges. For short-range tasks, the Wessex and Puma helicopters are used, while for search and rescue operations Wessex, Whirlwind and Sea King helicopters are used in Britain. Victor tankers are used for in-flight refuelling, which gives added range and flexibility to combat aircraft.

RESERVE FORCES   Reserve and auxiliary forces are an integral part of the armed forces. Apart from their essential military role—to supplement the regular forces in time of war or emergency with trained personnel able immediately to take their places in the Services either as formed units or as individual reinforcements—they form an important link between the Services and the civil community. Some of their members have a reserve liability following a period of regular service (regular reserve); others are volunteer men and women who devote their spare time to training for the roles they would undertake in war or an emergency. The latter include the Territorial Army (TA) whose role is to reinforce the ground forces committed to NATO and to assist in maintaining a secure home base in the United Kingdom, the Royal Naval Reserve, the Royal Marines Reserve, the Royal Auxiliary Air Force Regiment and the Royal Air Force Volunteer Reserve. There is also the Ulster Defence Regiment which is a locally-recruited and largely part-time force designed to support the regular forces in Northern Ireland. On 1 January 1980 regular reserves totalled 187,900, and volunteer reserves and auxiliary forces 75,600. Cadet forces, which make a significant contribution to recruitment to the regular forces, totalled 137,600.

CIVIL DEFENCE

Civil defence arrangements, are principally based on the extended and adapted use of existing public services operated by nationalised industries, local authorities, the police and government departments. Supplementary effort from volunteers and voluntary organisations would be brought in in time of crisis. Recent policy has aimed at improving the preparedness of local government to meet a war emergency. Since there is common ground between such planning and that required for a major peace-time emergency or national disaster a closer relationship in local planning for the different emergencies of peace and war has also been sought.

Following a review of existing arrangements in 1980, an additional £45 million is to be spent on civil defence in the years to 1983–84, by when annual expenditure will total £45 million. This will be used to improve the quality of central and local government planning; increase training opportunities arranged by the Home Office on staff college lines at the Home Defence College, Easingwold; help local authorities to plan for better community involvement in civil defence; and improve the emergency system for de-centralised government control and communications. Improvements will also be made in the communications, equipment and administrative facilities of the United Kingdom Warning and Monitoring Organisation. This includes the civilian Royal Observer Corps, which is organised to provide public warning of an attack, of the location and strength of nuclear explosions, and of the distribution and level of radioactive fall-out.

DEFENCE PROCUREMENT

Responsibility for the procurement (that is, research, development and production) of defence equipment lies with the Procurement Executive within the Ministry of Defence. The Executive is responsible for liaising between the Service users and the machinery for procurement, and co-ordination with industry in the formulation of programmes; this ensures a cost-effective approach.

Research and Development

Most research is undertaken by the Ministry of Defence's research and development establishments, but the Ministry also sponsors a substantial amount of research by industry and the universities. The Ministry's establishments have a very wide technological capability, which has civil as well as military applications: for example, support is given to civil aerospace projects and advanced aero-engines. On the development side, the establishments collaborate closely with the Ministry's contractors by monitoring their progress, and by assisting in testing programmes and in solving particular technical problems.

Modern defence equipment is becoming ever more complex, and its development requires a high initial investment; the cost of British equipment research and development in 1980–81 is estimated at over £1,490 million. The search for a more efficient use of resources has focused attention on the opportunities presented by Allied collaboration for sharing the cost of research and the development of equipment. This is one of the principal aims of the NATO Conference of National Armaments Directors in which Britain plays a full part. In some cases, the outright purchase of foreign equipment is the most economical solution. Nevertheless, the importance of maintaining a sound national industrial base for defence procurement is recognised, and there is close consultation between government and industry both in the National Defence Industries Council and through other specialised machinery.

Collaboration between Britain and its European allies is extensive, and is expected to increase, particularly through the work of the European Programme Group which consists of all NATO's European members except Iceland. The Group promotes opportunities for co-operation in defence equipment procurement among its members and so contributes to greater co-operation throughout the Alliance. Successful joint projects include the Anglo-French Jaguar aircraft, the Martel air-to-surface missile, the Lynx, Puma and Gazelle helicopters and the Anglo-Belgian family of armoured combat reconnaissance vehicles. With the Federal Republic of Germany and Italy, Britain is co-operating in the production and development of the Tornado multi-role combat aircraft and of medium artillery equipment, the FH70 and SP70. Britain also favours increased transatlantic co-operation, and, with other European countries, is collaborating with the United States in the procurement of a multiple launch rocket system, and discussing with it the possible joint development of a new generation of air-to-air missiles. Equipment collaboration also facilitates joint logistic support and training arrangements, like those taking place among the five European countries which have agreed to purchase the Lance surface-to-surface missile system from the United States.

National Projects A considerable number of projects, covering all the main equipment areas, are under development. They include an air defence variant of the Tornado; a light man-portable anti-armour weapon; a sea-skimming anti-ship missile (Sea Eagle) to replace the Martel; and a lightweight torpedo (Sting Ray) equipped with advanced homing devices for anti-submarine warfare. An airborne early warning (AEW) version of the Nimrod is being developed, equipped with an advanced AEW radar, which will complement the AEW force which other NATO countries are planning to procure.

Production Following the development of defence equipment, either nationally or in co-operation with allies, production is usually undertaken by private industry on a contract basis or by the Royal Ordnance Factories and Royal Dockyards. Production may also be undertaken on a collaborative basis. The Defence Sales Organisation provides support, assistance and advice to British industry and the Royal Ordnance Factories in promoting the sales of defence equipment overseas. In 1980–81 sales of British defence equipment and associated services are expected to amount to some £1,200 million.

5 Justice and the Law

THE LAW

Although the United Kingdom is a unitary State, it does not have a single body of law. England and Wales, Scotland and Northern Ireland each have their own legal systems and law courts. There is substantial similarity on many points, but considerable differences remain in law and in organisation and practice. In Northern Ireland procedure closely resembles that of England and Wales but there are often differences in enacted law. However, a large volume of modern legislation applies throughout the United Kingdom.

A feature common to the legal systems of the United Kingdom is the distinction made between the criminal law and the civil law. The criminal law is concerned with wrongful acts harmful to the community while civil law is concerned with the rights, duties and obligations of individual members of society among themselves.

The main sources of law are legislation, common law and European Community law. Legislation consists of Acts of Parliament, orders (rules and regulations made by ministers under the authority of an Act of Parliament) and by-laws made by local government or other authorities exercising powers conferred by Parliament. Common law, the ancient law of the land deduced from custom and interpreted in court cases by the judges, has never been precisely defined or codified but forms the basis of the law except when it has been superseded by legislation.

European Community law (see p 75) is confined mainly to economic and social matters; in certain circumstances it takes precedence over domestic law. It is normally applied by the domestic courts, but the most authoritative rulings are given by the European Court of Justice (see p 74).

CRIMINAL JUSTICE

Four distinct stages are involved in the British system of criminal justice: the enactment of criminal legislation which defines prohibited acts, establishes criminal courts and provides for the treatment of offenders; the prevention of crime and the enforcement of the law—largely matters for the police service; the determination by the courts of the guilt or innocence of people accused of crimes, and the selection of appropriate sentences for the guilty; and the treatment of convicted offenders.

A Royal Commission is examining the powers and duties of the police in England and Wales, the rights and duties of suspects and accused people, and the process of and responsibility for the prosecution of criminal offences. A similar review conducted by a departmental committee in Scotland made recommendations which are under consideration by Parliament.

In spite of plans to reduce public expenditure generally over the period ending 1983–84, expenditure on the programme for law and order will increase to reflect the priority given by the Government to these services.

The Criminal Law

The criminal law, like the law generally, undergoes constant reform in the courts as established principles are interpreted, clarified or refashioned to meet new circumstances. Substantial changes are the responsibility of Parliament. In practice most legislation affecting the criminal law is government-sponsored, but there is often consultation between government departments and bodies representing the legal profession, the police and the probation and prison services. The views of voluntary bodies are also considered.

Crime Statistics

Chief constables in England and Wales have a duty to supply statistics relating to offences, offenders, criminal proceedings and the state of crime in their areas. Crime statistics are published annually by the Home Office and further information about crime trends (as well as about police matters) is contained in the annual reports of Her Majesty's Chief Inspector of Constabulary and (for London) the Commissioner of Police of the Metropolis. Similar arrangements operate in Scotland and Northern Ireland.

The differences in the legal systems of the United Kingdom make it impractical to analyse in detail trends in criminality for the country as a whole. In considering trends it has to be remembered that the number of offences recorded by the police does not cover all offences committed since some offences go undiscovered and others are not reported to the police. Nevertheless it is clear that, as in western Europe generally, there has been an upsurge in crime since the early 1950s.

Table 6 shows the rate of indictable offences (the more serious offences) recorded by the police in 1978 (the latest year for which figures are available) in England and Wales.

TABLE 6: Indictable Offences Recorded by the Police, per 100,000 Population (England and Wales) 1978

Offence Group	1978
Homicide	1
Violence against the person (excluding homicide)	176
Sexual offences	46
Burglary	1,152
Robbery	27
Theft and handling stolen goods	2,934
Fraud and forgery	249
Criminal damage	624
Other offences	7
TOTAL	5,216

Source: *Home Office*

The number of serious offences recorded by the police in England and Wales in 1979 was 2,537,000, as against 2,561,000 for 1978. Recorded offences of robbery decreased by 5 per cent in 1979, burglary and fraud and forgery by 3 per cent, and sexual offences and theft and handling of stolen goods, by 2 per cent. Offences of violence against the person increased by 9 per cent, and criminal damage, by 5 per cent. The number of serious offences cleared up by the police in 1979 was 981,000 (41 per cent of the total recorded) compared with 998,000 (39 per cent) in 1978.

Criminological Research

A wide range of research into criminal and social policies is carried out by the Home Office Research Unit and by the research branch of the Scottish Home and Health Department. Results are published in learned journals, in the

Home Office Research Studies series, in the Research Bulletin (available from the Research Unit) and in the Scottish Office Social Research Studies series. Research is also carried out in university departments, much of it financed by the Government. The principal university criminological research establishment is the Institute of Criminology at Cambridge.

Criminal Injuries Compensation Scheme

The Criminal Injuries Compensation Scheme provides *ex gratia* compensation to victims of violent crimes including victims of violence within the family and to people hurt as a result of attempting to arrest offenders and prevent offences. It is administered by a board consisting of legally qualified members appointed by the Home Secretary and the Secretary of State for Scotland after consultation with the Lord Chancellor. Compensation, which is assessed on the basis of common law damages and usually takes the form of a lump sum payment, has totalled over £63 million since the Scheme began.

In Northern Ireland there is separate, statutory provision in certain circumstances for compensation from public funds for criminal injuries caused to people and also for malicious damage to property. Compensation for property damage includes losses of profits arising from the damage.

Measures to Combat Terrorism

Various temporary measures to deal with terrorism in connection with Northern Ireland have affected some aspects of the British criminal justice system. Wide-ranging emergency powers in Great Britain and Northern Ireland, contained in legislation, include: the right to search, arrest and detain suspected terrorists; the proscription of organisations engaged in terrorism connected with Northern Ireland affairs and occurring in the United Kingdom; and the exclusion from Great Britain and Northern Ireland of people involved in terrorism. There is also a system of controls at ports on passengers travelling between Great Britain and Ireland.

Trials in Northern Ireland criminal courts of terrorist offences are heard by a judge without a jury to obviate the danger of intimidation of jurors.

The emergency laws are temporary and must be reviewed periodically; they have also been subject to independent examination. Although they confer special powers on the appropriate Secretary of State, they have been used sparingly. No one can be imprisoned for political beliefs; all prisoners except those awaiting trial have been found guilty in court of criminal offences.

The security forces in Northern Ireland are subject to the law and can be prosecuted for criminal offences. Procedures for handling complaints against the police involve two independent elements: the Director of Public Prosecutions where allegations of criminal conduct are made; and the Police Complaints Board for Northern Ireland where complaints relate only to disciplinary offences.

The Criminal Jurisdiction Act 1975 creates extra-territorial offences under Northern Ireland law so that it is possible to try in the province a person accused of certain offences committed in the Irish Republic. It also enables evidence to be obtained in Northern Ireland for the trial of offences in the Irish Republic. Reciprocal legislation is in force in the Irish Republic.

THE POLICE SERVICE

Crime prevention and crime investigation, preserving the peace and bringing offenders to trial are primarily the concern of the police service. British police action in enforcing the law rests mainly upon common consent, for there are only a small number of officers in relation to the population (roughly one officer to 425 people). Officers do not normally carry firearms (their only weapon is a truncheon) and there are strict limitations on police powers.

Forces

There are 43 police forces in England and Wales, eight in Scotland and one (the Royal Ulster Constabulary) in Northern Ireland. Each is responsible for law enforcement in its area, but there is constant co-operation among them.

Outside London most counties (regions or islands in Scotland) have their own police forces, though in the interests of efficiency several have combined forces. In London, the Metropolitan Police Force, with headquarters at New Scotland Yard, is responsible for an area within a radius of about 24 kilometres (15 miles) from the centre, but excluding the City of London, where there is a separate force. The strength of the regular police force in Great Britain is almost 128,000 (including nearly 9,800 policewomen); in Northern Ireland the strength is about 6,800 (arrangements are being made to increase this to 7,500). The size of individual police forces depends on the area and population served. The strength of the Metropolitan Police Force is over 22,800.

In addition to the regular police forces, constabularies are maintained by the British Railways Board, the United Kingdom Atomic Energy Authority, the Ministry of Defence and a few other public bodies. Considerable numbers of people are employed by commercial security organisations which are subject to the ordinary law of the land.

Police Authorities and Chief Constables

Each of the regular police forces is maintained by a police authority, a committee consisting of local councillors and, in England and Wales, magistrates. The police authority for the Metropolitan Police Force is the Home Secretary. In Northern Ireland the police authority is appointed by the Secretary of State.

The primary duty of the police authority is to provide an adequate and efficient police force for its area. Its functions, some of which are subject to ministerial approval, include appointing the chief constable, deputy chief constable and assistant chief constables and, if necessary, calling on them to retire; fixing the maximum permitted strength of the force; and providing buildings and equipment. In the Metropolitan Police area the commissioner of police and his immediate subordinates are appointed on the recommendation of the Home Secretary.

Chief constables are responsible for the direction and control of police forces and for the appointment, promotion and discipline of all ranks below assistant chief constable. They are generally answerable to the police authorities on matters of efficiency, and must submit a written report every year.

Central Authorities

The Home Secretary, and the Secretaries of State for Scotland and Northern Ireland are concerned with the organisation, administration and operation of the police service. They approve the appointment of chief constables, and may require a police authority to retire a chief constable in the interests of efficiency, call for a report from a chief constable on any matters relating to the policing of his area, or institute a local inquiry. They also have the power to make regulations covering such matters as police ranks; qualifications for appointment, promotion and retirement; discipline; hours of duty, leave, pay and allowances; and uniform. Some of these regulations are first negotiable on the Police Negotiating Board, which has an independent chairman and representatives of the police authorities, police staff associations and the home departments. Matters of a non-negotiable kind are discussed by the Police Advisory Boards, together with any general questions affecting the police service. Other regulations are discussed on representative advisory bodies, together with any general questions affecting the police service.

All police forces in Great Britain (except the Metropolitan Police for which the Home Secretary is directly responsible) are subject to inspection. Inspectors of constabulary carry out, under Her Majesty's Inspector of Constabulary and Her Majesty's Chief Inspector of Constabulary for Scotland, a formal annual inspection of the forces in their regions, inquiring into efficiency and reporting to the Home Secretary or the Secretary of State for Scotland. Annual reports are published, covering the whole range of police matters. The inspectors also maintain close touch with forces for which they are responsible, and have various advisory functions.

In Northern Ireland periodic inspections of the Royal Ulster Constabulary are made by Her Majesty's Inspector of Constabulary.

Finance

The police authorities are financed by central and local government. The central government's contribution, which is a half of approved expenditure (a third in the City of London), is conditional on the Home Secretary or the Secretary of State for Scotland being satisfied that a force is being efficiently administered and maintained.

Officers and Ancillary Staff

In general, entry to the regular police force is open to men and women between the ages of $18\frac{1}{2}$ and 30. A chief constable may approve the appointment of especially suitable older men and women.

The standard police ranks in England, Scotland and Wales (except in the Metropolitan Police and City of London Police areas) are: chief constable, assistant chief constable, chief superintendent, superintendent, chief inspector, inspector, sergeant and constable. The chief officer in the Metropolitan Police area (the Commissioner of Police of the Metropolis) is assisted by a deputy commissioner and four assistant commissioners. Next in rank are deputy assistant commissioners, and then commanders; from chief superintendent the ranks are the same as in the regions. In the City of London the ranks are the same as in the regions except that the chief officer is the Commissioner of Police and the second in command is an assistant commissioner. Police ranks in Northern Ireland are similar to those in the rest of the United Kingdom.

Cadet training is designed to prepare young people between 16 and $18\frac{1}{2}$ years of age for a police service career. Cadets have no police powers but, in addition to their educational studies and physical training, they are instructed in elementary police work.

In order to release as many uniformed police officers as possible for operational duties, police authorities employ some 25,500 civilians on administrative and technical duties.

Traffic wardens (of whom there are over 4,800) discharge specified duties normally undertaken by the police. They may be authorised to issue fixed penalty notices for some minor traffic offences[1]; to man police car pounds (except in Scotland and Northern Ireland); to enforce some aspects of the vehicle excise laws; and to obtain the names and addresses of people thought to have committed certain types of traffic offence. They may also be employed to direct traffic, to act as parking attendants at street parking places, and as school-crossing patrols. Wardens are under the control of the chief constable.

Each force has an attachment of special constables who volunteer to perform

---

[1] A fixed penalty notice gives the recipient the option of paying a specified sum to the clerk of the appropriate court instead of having his case tried in the ordinary way. A government review of some aspects of traffic law, including the issue of fixed penalties, is in progress.

police duties without pay in their spare time. In England and Wales they act as auxiliaries to the regular force when required. In Scotland they are used only in emergencies although they may be assigned to duty for training. In Northern Ireland there is a part-time and full-time reserve which is paid.

Status and Duties

A police officer in Britain is an independent holder of an appointment under the Crown, an agent of the law of the land, not of the police authority nor of the Government, and may be sued or prosecuted for any wrongful act committed in carrying out police duties. Strict procedures, normally including an independent element, govern the way in which complaints against police officers are handled.

Members of the police service may not belong to a trade union nor may they withdraw their labour in furtherance of a trade dispute. All ranks, however, have their own staff associations which can make representations to ministers or to police authorities on matters of interest or concern to their members.

Police work ranges from the protection of people and property, road or street patrolling and traffic control to crime prevention, criminal investigation and the arrest of offenders. In urban areas, particularly, police officers often have to deal with social problems and they can bring in other social agencies and expert help. In England and Wales they also prosecute accused people and may decide whether or not to grant bail before the court proceedings (see p 108).

The main departments in all forces are the uniform department, criminal investigation department, traffic department and specialised departments, including river or marine police, mounted police, and dog handlers.

Common Services

A number of common services are provided by the central government departments and by arrangements made between forces. The most important of these are: training services; a Forensic Science Service in England and Wales (the Metropolitan Police maintains its own laboratory); telecommunications services which supply and maintain police radio equipment; and central and provincial criminal records which are available to all forces. Regional crime squad teams of experienced detectives from several forces investigate major crimes involving inquiries in more than one police area. The Scottish Crime Squad assists forces in the investigation and prevention of crime.

Certain special services such as liaison with the International Criminal Police Organisation (Interpol) are provided for other British forces by the Metropolitan Police Force. The services of the Force are available, on request, to help any other police force in England and Wales in criminal investigation, as are the services of the Fraud Squad, which is run jointly by the Metropolitan Police and the City of London Police for investigating company frauds.

Research into technical services is organised in separate units within the Home Office Police Department: the Forensic Science Service and a Central Research Establishment staffed by scientists; and a Directorate of Telecommunications with one section of engineers engaged solely on research and development. The Police Scientific Development Branch is staffed by scientists and technicians assisted by police officers seconded from the Police Research Services Unit; both the Branch and the Unit are concerned with operational research into police methods and the development of equipment for police forces.

In all aspects of police work the use of scientific aids is widespread. A national police computer has been developed to rationalise the keeping of records and so speed up the dissemination of information.

Powers of Arrest

In England and Wales arrest may be made either on a warrant issued by a magistrate or without a warrant. An arrested person is entitled to ask the police to notify a named person, such as a relative or a solicitor, about his (or her) arrest. The police may delay notification if they think it necessary in the interests of the investigation, the prevention of crime or the apprehension of offenders. When a person has been arrested the police may question him or her while in custody, so long as he or she has not been charged with the offence and has been informed that he or she may be prosecuted for it. Evidence of answers given to such questions is, in principle, admissible in any subsequent proceedings against the person concerned, provided it has been given voluntarily.

Guidance to the police on the manner in which they may question those arrested is contained in the Judges' Rules and Administrative Directions to the Police; although these do not have the force of law, the police must comply with them.

The Judges' Rules also require the police to caution an arrested person before charging him or her. Once a person has been charged with an offence, the police may not put any further questions, except in exceptional circumstances, to prevent or minimise harm or loss to some other person or to the public or to clear up an ambiguity in a previous answer or statement.

If the police decide not to charge the arrested person (for example, because of insufficient evidence to justify prosecution) he or she may be released immediately. Alternatively, the police may decide to release the person and proceed by way of summons, or to issue a caution (reprimand). If the police need to make further inquiries they may release the arrested person on bail to return to the police station, where he or she may be charged on re-appearance.

Anyone arrested without a warrant must be released by the police on bail if he or she cannot be brought before a magistrates' court within 24 hours, unless the alleged offence is serious. If detained in custody, the defendant must be brought before a magistrates' court as soon as practicable. On appearance before a magistrates' court, a defendant charged with an imprisonable offence may be refused bail in certain specified circumstances only, the most important of these being that there are substantial grounds for believing that he or she might abscond, commit further offences or otherwise interfere with the course of justice. If bail is refused by the magistrates, the defendant can apply to a judge of the High Court and, if committed to the Crown Court, may apply for bail to that court. In 1979 nearly 80 per cent of people committed for trial by magistrates were given bail.

A person detained in custody who thinks that the grounds for detention are unlawful[1] may apply for a writ of habeas corpus against the person who detained him or her, this person being required to appear before the court on the day named to justify the detention. An application for this writ is normally made to a divisional court of the High Court either by the person detained or by someone acting on his or her behalf. Similar procedures apply in Northern Ireland.

In Scotland the police have powers of arrest similar to those of the police in England and Wales. In Scotland, however, an arrest must be accompanied by a criminal charge, and there is little scope for questioning an arrested person. Although the Judges' Rules do not apply, an arrested person must be cautioned

---

[1] Detention is lawful in pursuance of criminal justice, for contempt of court or of either House of Parliament and when expressly authorised by Parliament. It is also lawful in certain circumstances in the case of people found to be mentally disordered.

before being charged. Thereafter only voluntary statements made by the arrested person are used in evidence at the trial and the court will reject any statements he or she made unless satisfied that they have been fairly obtained. Anyone arrested must be brought before a court with the least possible delay. Where a prosecution on indictment is intended, the accused is brought before a judge for judicial examination and may then be committed for trial or for further examination. Eight days may elapse between commitment for further examination and commitment for trial.

People in custody in Scotland, other than those charged with murder or treason, may be freed on bail by the sheriff or, if the offence is within the jurisdiction of a summary court other than the sheriff court, that court or the police may grant bail. Even in the case of murder or treason, bail may be granted at the discretion of the Lord Advocate or the High Court of Justiciary. There is a right of appeal to the High Court by the accused person against the refusal of bail, by the prosecutor against the granting of bail, or by either party against the amount fixed. The writ of habeas corpus does not apply in Scotland, but the High Court of Justiciary has power to release anyone unlawfully detained and trials must be brought to a conclusion within 110 days of commital to custody.

CRIMINAL COURTS

Prosecution

The decision to prosecute normally rests, in England and Wales, with the police and in Scotland with public prosecutors. In Northern Ireland there is a Director of Public Prosecutions (see p 110). In England and Wales (and very exceptionally in Scotland) a private person may institute criminal proceedings. Police have powers to issue cautions (warnings in Scotland) instead of prosecuting, especially in the case of young people.

England and Wales

In England and Wales some offences can only be prosecuted by, or with the consent of, the Attorney General, or the Director of Public Prosecutions, who acts under the superintendence of the Attorney General. These offences include crimes such as bribery and corruption of officials, and the use and possession of explosives. Where the consent of the Attorney General is required, the Director in practice prosecutes the case.

The Director always prosecutes crimes such as treason and murder. The police must report to the Director's office a further list of offences, including serious offences against the person, sedition, criminal offences by police officers, and offences relating to obscene or indecent publications. The Director does not necessarily prosecute all such cases referred but may do so in any that appear to be important or where intervention is thought to be necessary; otherwise proceedings are conducted by solicitors employed by the police. The Director also considers whether proceedings should be taken in cases reported by government departments, and advises the police and others concerned with administration of the criminal law.

When cases go for trial, barristers in private practice are instructed to appear on the Director's behalf; at the Central Criminal Court in London, these are drawn from a panel of 'Treasury Counsel' appointed by the Attorney General.

Scotland

The prosecution process in Scotland is different from that in the rest of the United Kingdom. The Lord Advocate (see p 126) is responsible for the prosecution of all crimes but delegates most of the work to the Solicitor General (see p 126), to ten advocates depute and to procurators fiscal. The permanent adviser to the Lord Advocate on prosecution matters is the Crown Agent who is head of the procurator fiscal service and is assisted by a staff of civil servants known as the Crown Office. Prosecutions in the High Court of Justiciary are prepared by the Crown Office while crimes tried before the sheriff and district courts are prosecuted by the procurators fiscal who are lawyers and full-time civil servants. The police investigate offences known to them and report to the procurator fiscal who decides whether or not to prosecute, subject to the discretion and control of the Crown Office.

Northern Ireland The Director of Public Prosecutions for Northern Ireland, who is responsible to the Attorney General, prosecutes all offences tried on indictment, and may do so in summary cases of a serious nature. Other summary offences are prosecuted by the police.

Courts in England and Wales Magistrates' courts deal with about 98 per cent of criminal cases in England and Wales, and conduct preliminary investigations into the more serious offences. The Crown Court, situated in a number of towns and cities, takes all criminal work above the level of magistrates' courts and trials are held before a jury.

Magistrates' courts hear and determine charges against people accused of 'summary offences', that is those that can be legally disposed of by magistrates sitting without a jury. There are some 700 courts and some 23,000 magistrates ('justices of the peace', JPs) who are advised on points of law and procedure by a clerk to the justices (or an assistant) who is normally legally qualified and is also in charge of the court's administrative arrangements. Each court normally consists of a bench of three unpaid lay magistrates whose function is to ascertain the facts of a case and apply the law to them. Magistrates are appointed by the Lord Chancellor.

In inner London and some other large urban areas where work is heavy and continuous there are also professional 'stipendiary' magistrates who are full-time, salaried and legally qualified. They usually preside alone.

Magistrates must as a rule sit in open court, but when they make preliminary inquiries into a more serious case to see whether there is sufficient evidence to justify committal for trial in the Crown Court the proceedings must not be reported in the press at the time except at the defendant's request, unless the person is discharged by the magistrates.

Magistrates cannot usually impose a sentence of more than six months' imprisonment or a fine exceeding £1,000. If an offence carries a higher maximum penalty, they may commit the offender for sentence at the Crown Court if they consider their own power inadequate.

Cases involving people under the age of 17 are heard in juvenile courts. These are specially constituted magistrates' courts which sit either in a different room or building from other courts, or at a different time; only limited publicity is allowed. If a young person under the age of 17 is charged jointly with someone of 17 or over, the case is heard in the ordinary magistrates' court. If the young person is found guilty, that court may remit the case to a juvenile court, unless it wishes to dispose of the case by penalty.

The Crown Court is responsible for trials of the more serious cases, the sentencing of offenders committed for sentence by magistrates' courts, and appeals from magistrates' courts. It has about 90 centres and is presided over by High Court judges, full-time 'circuit judges' and part-time recorders. All contested trials in the court take place before a jury. A High Court judge sits alone for the most serious cases. A circuit judge or recorder sits with between two and four magistrates for appeals and committals for sentence from magistrates' courts and may sit with magistrates to try the less important cases.

The Crown Court may impose a fine of any amount on a convicted offender and, within the maximum penalty determined for the offence by Parliament, any other custodial or non-custodial penalty.

In 1979 the Crown Court tried 68,581 people; 41,000 pleaded guilty to at least one charge and 25,150 not guilty to all charges. About one half of the defendants pleading not guilty to all counts were acquitted.

Appeals

A person convicted by a magistrates' court may appeal to the Crown Court against the sentence imposed and, if he or she has contested his or her guilt, against the conviction itself. Where the appeal is on a point of law, either the prosecutor or the defendant may appeal from the magistrates' court to the High Court, which sits in London and some regional centres (see pp 121–2). Appeals from the Crown Court, either against conviction or against sentence, are usually made to the Court of Appeal (Criminal Division). A further appeal from the Court of Appeal to the House of Lords can be brought if the court certifies that a point of law of general public importance is involved and it appears to the court or the House of Lords that the point is one that ought to be considered by the House. A prosecutor or defendant may appeal to the House of Lords from a decision of the High Court in a criminal case.

The Attorney General may seek the opinion of the Court of Appeal on a point of law which has arisen in a case where a person tried on indictment is acquitted; the court has power to refer the point to the House of Lords if necessary. The acquittal in the original case is not affected, nor is the identity of the acquitted person revealed without his or her consent.

Scotland

There are three criminal courts: the High Court of Justiciary, the sheriff court and the district court. The High Court tries serious crimes such as murder, treason and rape while the sheriff court is concerned with less serious offences and the district court with minor offences.

Criminal cases are heard either under solemn procedure, when proceedings are taken on indictment and the judge sits with a jury of 15 members, or under summary procedure, when the judge sits without a jury. All cases in the High Court of Justiciary and the more serious ones in the sheriff courts are tried by a judge and jury. Proceedings are taken under summary procedure in the less serious cases in the sheriff courts, and in all cases in the district courts.

A government committee is considering the effect on the criminal courts and the prosecution system of the volume of minor offences dealt with by summary prosecution and whether some other process could be devised to deal with such offences while maintaining safeguards for accused people.

District courts are the administrative responsibility of the district and islands local government authorities. The judges are lay justices of the peace including up to one-quarter of the membership of district and islands authorities who may be nominated as *ex officio* justices. In Glasgow there are three stipendiary magistrates who are full-time salaried lawyers.

Scotland is divided into six sheriffdoms which are further divided into sheriff court districts, each of which, depending on size, has a sheriff or sheriffs, who are the judges of the court.

The High Court of Justiciary is Scotland's supreme criminal court. It is both a trial court and an appeal court. Any one of the following judges is entitled to try cases in the High Court: the Lord Justice General (the head of the court), the Lord Justice Clerk (the judge next in seniority) or one of the Lord Commissioners of Justiciary who preside at sessions of the court in other towns. The main seat of the court is in Edinburgh where all appeals are heard.

Appeals

All appeals are dealt with by the High Court of Justiciary. In both solemn and summary procedure, an appeal may be brought against conviction, or sentence, or both. The High Court cannot order a retrial if it sets aside a conviction. Appeals are heard by three or more judges; there is no further appeal to the House of Lords.

Children's Hearings

Children under 16 years (and in some cases young people between 16 and 18) who have committed an offence or are considered in need of compulsory care may be brought before an informal children's hearing comprising three members of the local community (see p 119).

Northern Ireland

The structure of the courts in Northern Ireland is broadly similar to that of England and Wales. The day-to-day work of dealing summarily with minor local cases is carried out by magistrates' courts presided over by a full-time resident magistrate appointed from the legal profession by the Queen, on the recommendation of the Lord Chancellor. Young offenders under 17 years and young people under 17 who need care, protection and control are dealt with by juvenile courts consisting of the resident magistrate and two lay members (at least one of whom must be a woman) specially qualified to deal with juveniles. Appeals from magistrates' courts are dealt with by the county court.

The Crown Court in Northern Ireland deals with all trials on indictment of criminal cases. It is divided into four circuits and is served by High Court and county court judges. Proceedings in the Crown Court are heard before a single judge, and all contested cases, other than those involving scheduled offences under emergency legislation, take place before a jury.

Appeals

Appeals from the Crown Court, either against conviction or sentence, rest with the Northern Ireland Court of Appeal. Procedures for a further appeal to the House of Lords are similar to those in operation in England and Wales.

Trial

All criminal trials in the United Kingdom take the form of a contest between the prosecution and the defence. Since the criminal law presumes the innocence of an accused person until guilt has been proved, the prosecution is not granted any advantage, apparent or real, over the defence. A defendant has the right to employ a legal adviser and in certain circumstances may be granted legal aid wholly or partly from public funds. If remanded in custody, the person may be visited in prison by a legal adviser to ensure that a defence is properly prepared. In England, Wales and Northern Ireland during the preparation of the case, the prosecution usually informs the defence of any relevant documents which it is not proposed to put in evidence and discloses them if asked to do so. The prosecution should also inform the defence of any witnesses whose evidence may help the accused and whom the prosecution does not propose to call. The defence or prosecution may suggest that the mental state of the defendant renders him or her unfit to be tried. If the jury decides that the defendant is unfit, he or she is admitted to a hospital specified by the Home Secretary in England and Wales, and in Northern Ireland to one specified by a health and social services board.

Criminal trials in the United Kingdom are normally held in open court and the rules of evidence (which are concerned with the proof of facts) are rigorously applied. If evidence is admitted in contravention of the law, a conviction can be quashed on appeal.

During the trial the defendant has the right to hear and subsequently to cross-examine (normally through his or her lawyer) all the witnesses for the prosecution; to call his or her own witnesses who, if they will not attend voluntarily may be legally compelled to attend; and to address the court either in person or through a lawyer, the defence having the right to the last speech at the trial. Moreover, the defendant cannot be questioned without consenting to be sworn as a witness in his or her own defence. When he or she does testify, cross-examination about character or other conduct may be made only in exceptional circumstances and generally the prosecution may not introduce evidence of such matters. Although confessions made in the course of previous judicial proceedings are admissible as evidence if they have been made on oath, no confessions made in any other circumstances are admitted unless it can be proved that they were made voluntarily.

The Jury

In jury trials the judge determines questions of law, sums up the evidence for the benefit of the jury, and discharges the accused or passes sentence. Only the jury decides whether the defendant is guilty or not guilty. If the jury cannot reach a unanimous verdict, the judge may direct it to bring in a majority verdict provided that, in the normal jury of 12 people, there are not more than two dissentients. If the jury returns a verdict of 'not guilty', the prosecution has no right of appeal against the verdict and the defendant cannot be tried again for the same offence. From a verdict of 'guilty' the defendant has a right of appeal to the appropriate court.

A jury is completely independent of the judiciary. Once members are sworn in, they are protected from interference of any kind. Both the prosecution and the defence can object to particular jurors. In England, Wales and Northern Ireland people whose names appear on the electoral register are liable for jury service and their names are chosen at random; in Scotland, where the minimum age for jurors is 21, not all those on the register are eligible to serve as the minimum voting age is 18.

Scotland

At summary trials in Scotland accused people are asked to plead to the charge at the first calling of the case and, if they plead guilty, the court may dispose of the case. Where the plea is 'not guilty', the court may proceed to trial at once or, more usually, may appoint a later date.

In trials on indictment, the 'pleading' proceedings take place in the sheriff court, where the accused person is called upon to plead guilty or not guilty. If the plea is not guilty, the case is continued to the 'trial' proceedings in the appropriate court. If the plea is guilty, and the case is to be dealt with in the sheriff court, the sheriff may dispose of it at once. If it is a High Court case, it is continued to the 'trial' proceedings in the High Court of Justiciary.

The trial proceedings are held at least nine days after the pleading proceedings, either before the sheriff or the High Court, with a jury of 15. Evidence is presented without opening speeches, and there are closing speeches for the prosecution and for the defence, followed by the judge's charge to the jury. The jury may return a verdict of 'not guilty' or 'not proven', both of which result in acquittal, or it may find the accused 'guilty', in which case the court proceeds to deliver sentence. The verdict may be reached by a simple majority. With a few minor exceptions, no person may be convicted without the evidence of at least two witnesses, or corroboration of one witness by facts and circumstances which clearly implicate the accused in the crime.

SPECIAL COURTS
Coroners'
Courts

Most of the work of coroners' courts involves the investigation of violent and unnatural deaths or sudden deaths where the cause is unknown. Cases may be brought before the local coroner (a senior lawyer or doctor appointed by local government) by doctors, the police, various public authorities or members of the public, and it is the coroner's duty to hold an inquiry into how, when and where the deceased died. If the death is a sudden one of which the cause is unknown, the coroner need not hold an inquest in court, but may order a post-mortem examination to determine cause of death. Where there is reason to believe that the deceased died a violent or unnatural death or died in prison or in other specified circumstances the coroner must hold an inquest.

In Scotland the office of coroner does not exist. The local procurator fiscal inquires privately into all sudden and suspicious deaths in his district and may report the findings to the Crown Agent.

Coroners in Northern Ireland are mostly senior lawyers and are appointed by the Lord Chancellor; the work of their courts is similar to that of coroners' courts in England and Wales.

Courts Martial Courts martial have jurisdiction over serving members of the armed forces and in certain circumstances over their dependants and other civilians who accompany them overseas. The courts do not deal with certain serious offences if committed in the United Kingdom, such as treason, murder, manslaughter, and rape; these are dealt with in the ordinary courts.

TREATMENT OF OFFENDERS While custodial treatment is an important part of British penal practice, it is only one of several ways of dealing with people who break the law.

Sentencing The criminal courts' discretion in selecting the most appropriate sentence for an offender is modified by statutory provisions designed to ensure that prison sentences are kept to a minimum. In England, Wales and Northern Ireland a person who has not previously served a custodial sentence of a particular kind may not be sentenced to custodial treatment of that kind unless he or she is legally represented or has chosen not to be, and unless the court is satisfied that no other sentence will suffice. In England and Wales, extended sentences longer than the normal maximum term may be imposed on persistent offenders. In the case of murder there is a mandatory penalty of life imprisonment. This is the maximum penalty for a number of serious offences such as robbery, rape, arson and manslaughter. Although the death penalty may still, in theory, be imposed for certain offences, such as treason, it has in practice fallen into disuse for offences committed in peace-time.

In Scotland, unless the sentence is limited by statute, the maximum penalty is determined by the status of the court trying the accused. In trials on indictment, the High Court may impose a sentence of imprisonment for any term up to life, and the Sheriff Court any term up to two years. In summary cases, the sheriff may impose up to six months' imprisonment.

Non-Custodial Treatment Non-custodial treatment includes fines; probation; absolute or (in England, Wales and Northern Ireland) conditional discharge for up to three years (one year in Northern Ireland)—a discharge being made when the court considers there is no need to impose punishment on a convicted person; and 'binding over' where the offender is required to pledge money, with or without sureties, to keep the peace and be of good behaviour.

In England and Wales, offenders aged 17 or over convicted of imprisonable offences can, with their consent, be given community service orders. The court may order between 40 and 240 hours' unpaid service to be completed within 12 months. Examples of work done include decorating the houses of old or disabled people and building adventure playgrounds for children. Community service schemes have begun in Scotland and Northern Ireland.

The sentence imposed on an offender in England, Wales and Northern Ireland may also, with his or her consent, be deferred for up to six months to enable a court to arrive at the most appropriate sentence, taking into account conduct after some expected change in circumstances.

The courts may order a convicted offender to pay compensation for any personal injury, loss or damage resulting from an offence. In cases where the loss amounts to £15,000 or more they may make a criminal bankruptcy order against an offender. In Scotland a committee has reported to the Secretary of State and the Lord Advocate on the potential role of the criminal court in ordering reparation by the offender to the victim.

In England, Wales and Northern Ireland a judge is free to pass a suspended sentence of not more than two years. The sentence is not served by the offender unless he or she is convicted of a further offence punishable with imprisonment; in that event the suspended sentence normally takes effect and another sentence may be imposed for the new offence. An offender receiving a suspended sentence of more than six months may be placed under the supervision of a probation officer for all or part of the period. The Criminal Law Act 1977 provided the courts in England and Wales with power, when passing a sentence of between six months' and two years' imprisonment, to order that part should be served and the rest held in suspense, the suspended part being not less than one quarter nor more than three quarters of the whole. This provision has not yet, however, been brought into force.

In certain circumstances courts may order forfeiture of property involved in the commission of crime. An offender convicted of a serious crime may be disqualified from driving if a motor vehicle was used in its commission.

In most circumstances, after a rehabilitation period of from six months to ten years depending on the nature of the sentence imposed, a person convicted of a criminal offence need not disclose it, and the offence will not be held against him or her. This does not apply to those who have received a prison sentence of more than 2½ years.

Probation

Probation is designed to secure the rehabilitation of an offender, who continues to live an ordinary life under the supervision of a probation officer whose duty is to advise, assist and befriend the probationer. Before making a probation order (which lasts between six months and three years), the court must explain its effects and make sure that the probationer understands that failure to comply with its requirements will make him or her liable to be dealt with again for the original offence. An order can be made only if the offender is aged 17 years or over and has given his or her consent. The order usually requires the probationer to keep in regular touch with the probation officer, to be of good behaviour and lead a responsible life. In Northern Ireland an order can be made for anyone over the age of criminal responsibility (10 years), but consent is required where the offender is aged 14 or over. It may also require the offender to live in a specified place (such as an approved hostel), or in certain circumstances, receive psychiatric treatment.

In England and Wales the probation service is administered locally by probation and after-care committees consisting of local magistrates and co-opted members with legal and specialist interests. In Northern Ireland it is administered by the Northern Ireland Office. Probation officers are usually members of small teams, although each has a large measure of independence in his or her casework with an offender.

Probation and after-care committees may, with the approval of the Home Secretary, provide and maintain day training centres (which offenders may be required to attend for up to 60 days), bail hostels, probation hostels and other establishments for use in the rehabilitation of offenders. The service is also responsible for administering the community service scheme.

In England, Wales and Northern Ireland, the services of probation and after-care officers are available to every criminal court. In Scotland, offenders subject to probation orders or to after-care supervision are supervised by specially approved local authority social workers.

Prisons

Although the courts have made proportionately less use of prison as a penalty for criminal activity, there has been an increase in the prison population as a result of the rise in crime. In 1979 the daily average number of people in prisons, borstals, and detention centres was about 42,200 in England and Wales and 4,580 in Scotland; there are 115 prison service establishments and the size of the prison service in 1979 was 22,300. Policies announced in 1980, based on the report of a committee of inquiry, include the continuation of efforts to reduce the prison population and plans to increase the building programme, the reorganisation of prison service administration, and the appointment of a Chief Inspector of Prisons, separate from the Prison Department.

Prisons to which offenders may be committed directly by a court are known as 'local prisons'; all are closed establishments. Other prisons, which may be open or closed, receive prisoners on transfer from local prisons (open prisons do not have physical barriers to prevent escape). Sentenced prisoners are classified into four groups for the purposes of security. There are separate prisons for women.

People awaiting trial are entitled to privileges not granted to convicted prisoners and, as far as practicable, are separated from convicted prisoners. Prisoners under 21 are separated from older prisoners.

Many British prisons were built during the nineteenth century and are unsatisfactory by modern standards. Overcrowding is also a problem. However, a number of new prisons have been built in the past few years, and existing establishments are being redeveloped and modernised.

Remission of Sentence and Parole

All prisoners in Great Britain serving a determinate sentence of more than one month, except those sentenced to imprisonment for life, are allowed remission of one-third of their sentence provided that this does not reduce the sentence to less than 31 days (in Scotland, 30 days). Remission may be forfeited for serious misconduct in prison. Prisoners serving fixed sentences of more than 18 months become eligible for consideration for release on parole after serving one-third of their sentence or 12 months, whichever expires later.

The parole licence remains in force until the date on which the prisoner would have been released but for the parole. It prescribes the conditions with which the offender must comply when on parole. About 8·8 per cent of prisoners granted parole in England and Wales in 1979 were recalled to prison.

Prisoners serving life sentences are also eligible for release on licence, after consideration by the Home Secretary or the Secretary of State for Scotland who consults the judiciary, and on the recommendation of the Parole Board. Those released in this way remain on licence for the rest of their lives and are subject to recall at any time should the circumstances warrant.

In Northern Ireland, where there is no parole scheme, prisoners receive one-half remission on determinate sentences, provided that remission does not reduce the sentence to below 31 days. For those serving over a year, a court can order all or part of the outstanding balance of the remitted period to be served in the event of reconviction in the remitted period for an imprisonable offence, in addition to any penalty imposed for a further offence.

Prison Industries   Prison industries aim both to give inmates work experience which will assist them when released and to secure an economic return which will reduce the cost of the prison system to public funds. The main industries are clothing and textile manufacture, engineering, woodwork, laundering, electro-mechanical production, farming and horticulture. Most production caters for internal needs and for other public services but a considerable volume is for the commercial market. A few prisoners are employed outside prison. Small payments are made to inmates for the work they do; in some prisons, incentive schemes provide an opportunity for higher earnings on the basis of output and skill.

Education   Education for those in custody is financed by the prison service and provided by the local education authorities. Every prison department establishment in England and Wales has an education officer assisted by a team of full-time and part-time teachers. Education is compulsory, full-time, for young offenders below school leaving age and part-time for those between 16 and 21. For all older offenders it is voluntary. Some prisoners study for public examinations (including those of the Open University). Within the resources available there is teaching in recreational and leisure pursuits. Vocational training is provided directly by the prison service. Similar opportunities for education and vocational training are available in Northern Ireland prisons.

Physical education is voluntary but offenders under 21 have to attend a certain number of classes. Many establishments lack the proper facilities, although there have been recent improvements.

Medical Services   The prison medical service has a general responsibility for the physical and mental health of all those in custody. Each establishment has accommodation for sick people and there are some larger prison hospitals (some with up to 100 beds) to which patients can be transferred if necessary. Four prisons have surgical units and patients can also be transferred to hospitals within the National Health Service. Psychiatric care is available to all prisoners who need it and there is one specialist psychiatric prison.

Psychological Services   The work of psychologists varies from place to place but includes evaluating treatment programmes, studying management practices, contributing to the management and treatment programmes of individuals and groups, taking part in advisory and training work with prison staff and making assessments for treatment or allocation purposes.

Privileges and Discipline   All prisoners have a general entitlement to write and receive letters and to be visited by their relatives at regular intervals. Privileges include a personal radio, books, periodicals and newspapers, and the right to make purchases from the canteen with money earned in prison. Depending on the facilities available, prisoners may be granted the further privileges of dining and recreation in association and watching television in the evening.

Breaches of discipline are dealt with by the prison governor, or by the board of visitors (visiting committee in Scotland), who have power to order, among other penalties, forfeiture of remission and forfeiture of privileges. Boards of visitors (and visiting committees) consist of lay people, two of whom must be magistrates.

Welfare

The welfare of prisoners is the general concern of all the prison staff. Much of this work is the responsibility of probation officers (in Scotland social workers) stationed in prisons who help prisoners in their relations with individuals and agencies outside and make plans for after-care on release. Prisoners may also receive visits from specially appointed prison visitors whose work is voluntary.

Chaplains give spiritual help and advice to inmates and are increasingly involved in management decisions affecting their needs and quality of life. A chaplain of the Church of England (in Scotland of the Church of Scotland, and in Northern Ireland of the Church of Ireland and of the Presbyterian Church), a Roman Catholic priest and a Methodist minister are appointed to every prison. Ministers of other denominations are appointed or called in as needed.

Discharge

All prisons in England and Wales arrange pre-release preparations for prisoners. Those serving sentences of four years or more are considered for outside employment for a period before release. If selected, work is found outside the prison for about the last six months of sentence; during the period prisoners may live in a separate part of the prison or in a hostel outside. Normal wages are paid so that they can resume support for their families. In Scotland pre-release arrangements differ from these in some respects.

Periods of home leave may be granted in the last nine months of sentence to those serving two years or more to assist resettlement.

After-care

The aim of after-care, run by the probation and after-care service, is to assist offenders on return to society by offering them the help of skilled case workers. Compulsory supervision by probation officers is given to most offenders under 21 when released, adult offenders released on parole, and those released on licence from a sentence of life imprisonment. A voluntary system is offered to the remainder. After-care is also provided by a number of voluntary societies, most of which are members of the National Association for the Care and Resettlement of Offenders. Hostels and other forms of accommodation are provided, often with some financial help from the Home Office.

Children in Trouble

England and Wales

In England and Wales no child under ten years can be held guilty of an offence. A child aged ten to 16 years who is alleged to have committed an offence may be the subject of criminal proceedings or of 'care' proceedings, both of which are normally held before juvenile courts (see p 110).

In care proceedings the fact that a child is found guilty of an offence is not in itself sufficient justification for the making of an order; the court must also consider the child to be in need of care or control which he or she is unlikely to receive unless an order is made. In criminal proceedings a court may make a care order without having to consider whether the child is in need of care or control; this applies to a child found guilty of an offence (other than homicide) punishable in the case of an adult by imprisonment.

A number of orders are available to courts in both care and criminal proceedings. A care order commits the child to the care of the local authority, which becomes responsible for deciding where the child should be accommodated, whether, for example, with foster parents or in a community home (see p 142). The Government is reviewing this procedure, and intends to give the courts powers to make a residential care order in criminal proceedings. The authority must review each care order every six months and consider whether an application should be made to the court to have the order ended; the order normally expires when the child reaches 18 or 19. For children who are too severely disturbed or disruptive to be treated in other child care homes, 'youth treatment centres' are provided by the Department of Health and Social Security.

Under a supervision order (usually valid for three years or less) a child normally remains at home under the supervision of a local authority social worker or a probation officer, but may be required to live with a specified person or to comply with specified directions of his or her supervisor. The child may have to undergo 'intermediate treatment', a compromise between measures involving complete removal from home and those which do not, and consisting of participation, under a supervisor, in a variety of constructive and remedial activities through a short residential course or, more usually, attendance at a day or evening centre. An intermediate treatment fund, administered by the Rainer Foundation with the help of government finance, has been set up to give grants to individuals, groups or organisations willing to provide intermediate treatment facilities.

A court may also make an order requiring a parent or guardian to agree to take proper care of the child and to exercise proper control over him or her; such an order may only be made with the consent of the parent or guardian. In care proceedings, the court may order a stay in hospital in accordance with the mental health legislation.

The courts may also order payments of compensation, or impose fines or grant a conditional or absolute discharge. Offenders, both male and female, may be ordered to spend a total of up to 24 hours of their spare time on Saturdays at an attendance centre (up to three hours on any one occasion). The centres which provide physical training and instruction in handicrafts or some other practical subject are for those found guilty of offences for which older people could be sent to prison. Boys aged 14 to 16 may be sent to a junior detention centre, where the regime is similar to that in senior detention centres (see p 120). Boys and girls aged 15 or 16 may be committed to the Crown Court for a sentence of borstal training. In the case of a very serious crime, the Crown Court may order detention in a place approved by the Home Secretary.

Scotland

In Scotland the age of criminal responsibility is eight years but prosecution of children in the criminal courts is rare and can take place only on the instructions of the Lord Advocate; court proceedings usually apply only to very serious offences such as murder or assault. Instead children under 16 years who have committed an offence or need care and protection may be brought before an informal children's hearing which decides the most appropriate measures of care and treatment (see p 142). An official 'reporter' decides whether a child should come before a hearing. If the grounds for referral are not accepted by the child and parents, the case goes to the sheriff court (sitting in its civil capacity) for proof. It can then come back to the hearing. The sheriff also decides appeals against a decision of a children's hearing.

Northern Ireland

The age of criminal responsibility in Northern Ireland is ten. Children aged 16 and under charged with committing a criminal offence may be brought before a juvenile court. If the child is found guilty of an offence punishable by imprisonment if committed by an adult, he or she may be sent to a training school, placed in the care of a 'fit person', possibly the area Health and Social Services Board or under supervision. Alternatively the court can order a period of attendance at an attendance centre or a remand home, or impose a fine or compensation. A conditional or absolute discharge is also possible. Whatever other order it makes, a juvenile court can also make an order requiring parents ensure the child's good behaviour. Young people aged 16 or over may be given a sentence of borstal training. Children brought before the courts in need of care and protection may be placed in care locally. The law relating to young offenders and the care of children is under review.

Young Adult Offenders

Offenders aged 17 to 20 years (16 to 21 years in Scotland) are recognised as a category distinct from child and adult offenders. The main non-custodial measures are generally the same as those used in dealing with adults. In England and Wales the custodial sentences available are: detention in a detention centre (males only), borstal training or imprisonment and, in Northern Ireland, detention in a young offenders' centre. Some 11 senior detention centres provide a means of treating young male offenders (age 17–21) for whom a long period of residential training away from home does not seem necessary or justified by the offence, but who need to be taught respect for the law through some form of custody. The normal period of detention is three months but there is power to award up to six months. Life in a centre demands high standards of discipline. Training comprises a normal working week of 40 hours, including an hour each day of physical training, with considerable attention paid to education. After discharge, offenders are supervised for up to a year. A pilot project involving more rigorous regimes is in progress at one junior and one senior detention centre in England.

Borstal training is remedial and educational, based on personal training by carefully selected staff. Emphasis is placed on vocational training in skilled trades. There is much freedom of movement and many borstals are open establishments. Offenders are placed as near their homes as possible in order to maintain their ties with the local community. Borstals are available for offenders aged 15 to 20 years (16 to 20 years in Northern Ireland). Courts rarely order borstal training unless they have already tried fines, probation or detention centre training, perhaps all three. The training period usually ranges from six months to two years and is followed by supervision in the community.

A person under 17 years cannot be sent to prison in England and Wales, and no court may pass a sentence of imprisonment on an offender aged 17 to 20 years unless satisfied that no other penalty is appropriate. A court cannot impose a sentence of between six months and three years unless the offender has already served a term of borstal training or at least six months' imprisonment. Sentences of up to two years may be ordered by a court to be suspended. Prisoners under the age of 21 at the time of sentence are classified as 'young prisoners', and generally serve their sentences separately from older prisoners unless they are reclassified as adults and treated as such in an adult prison. In Scotland no offender under 21 years may be sent to prison. A single sentence of detention is available for young offenders. This is served in a detention centre if the sentence is between 28 days and 4 months, and in a young offenders' institute if otherwise. Remission of part of the sentence for good conduct, release on parole, and supervision in the community after release are available. In Northern Ireland, no offender under 21 who has been sentenced to three years or less may be sent to prison. Where borstal is not suitable, detention in a young offenders' centre may be ordered for those aged 17 and over, and, exceptionally, for 16 year olds.

Custodial sentences for young adult offenders in England and Wales are under review. The Government has announced its intention of amending the legislation which limits the courts' power to sentence young offenders.

CIVIL JUSTICE

The Civil Law

The main sub-divisions of the civil law of England, Wales and Northern Ireland are: family law, the law of property, the law of contract and the law of torts (covering injuries suffered by one person at the hands of another irrespective of any contract between them and including concepts such as negligence, defamation and trespass). Other branches of the civil law include constitutional and administrative law (particularly concerned with the use of executive power), industrial law, maritime law and ecclesiastical law. Scottish civil law has its own, often analogous, branches.

CIVIL COURTS
England and
Wales

The limited civil jurisdiction of magistrates' courts extends to matrimonial proceedings for custody and maintenance orders, adoption orders and affiliation and guardianship orders. The courts also have jurisdiction concerning nuisances under the Public Health Acts and the recovery of rates. Committees of magistrates license public houses, betting shops and clubs.

The jurisdiction of the 300 or so county courts covers actions founded upon contract and tort (with minor exceptions) where the amount claimed is not more than £2,000; trust and mortgage cases, where the amount does not exceed £15,000; and actions for the recovery of land where the net annual value for rating does not exceed £2,000. Cases outside these limits may be tried in the county court by consent of the parties, or may in certain circumstances be transferred from the High Court to the county court.

Other matters dealt with by the county courts include hire purchase, the Rent Acts, landlord and tenant and adoption cases. In addition, undefended divorce cases are heard and determined in county courts designated as divorce county courts (defended cases are transferred to the High Court) and outside London bankruptcies are dealt with in certain county courts. The courts also deal with complaints of race and sex discrimination in education and the provision of goods, facilities, services and premises (see p 152). Where small claims are concerned (especially those for less than £200 involving consumers), there are special facilities for arbitration and simplified procedures.

All judges of the Supreme Court (comprising the Court of Appeal, the Crown Court and the High Court) and all circuit judges and recorders have power to sit in the county courts, but each court has one or more circuit judges assigned to it by the Lord Chancellor, and the regular sittings of the court are mostly taken by them. The judge normally sits alone, although on the request of a party the court may, in exceptional cases, order a trial with a jury.

The High Court of Justice is divided into the Chancery Division, the Queen's Bench Division and the Family Division. Its jurisdiction, which is both original and appellate and covers all civil and some criminal cases, is vested in all its divisions. In general, particular types of work are assigned to a particular division. The Family Division, for instance, is concerned with all jurisdiction affecting the family, including that relating to adoption and guardianship of children. The Chancery Division deals with the interpretation of wills and the administration of estates. (Its work is under review.) Maritime and commercial law is the responsibility of admiralty and commercial courts of the Queen's Bench Division.

There are 75 High Court judges, each of whom is attached to one division on appointment but may be transferred to any other division while in office. The Lord Chancellor is president of the Chancery Division, the administration of which is the responsibility of the senior judge known as the Vice-Chancellor. The Queen's Bench Division is presided over by the Lord Chief Justice of England, who ranks next to the Lord Chancellor in the legal hierarchy, and the Family Division is headed by the President. Outside London (where the High Court sits at the Royal Courts of Justice) sittings are held at 23 Crown Court centres.

For the hearing of cases at first instance, High Court judges sit alone. Appellate jurisdiction in civil matters from inferior courts is exercised by courts of two (or sometimes three) judges, or by single judges of the appropriate division, nominated by the Lord Chancellor.

Appeals

Appeals in matrimonial, adoption and guardianship proceedings heard by magistrates' courts go to a divisional court of the Family Division of the High Court. Affiliation appeals are heard by the Crown Court, as are appeals from decisions of the licensing committees of magistrates. Appeals from the High Court and the county courts are heard in the Court of Appeal (Civil Division) and may go on to the House of Lords, the final court of appeal in civil cases.

The *ex officio* members of the Court of Appeal are the Lord Chancellor, the Lord Chief Justice, the President of the Family Division and the Master of the Rolls; the ordinary members are 18 Lords Justices of Appeal.

The judges in the House of Lords are the nine Lords of Appeal in Ordinary, who must have a quorum of three, but usually sit as a group of five, and sometimes even of seven. Lay peers do not attend the hearing of appeals (which normally take place in a committee room and not in the legislative chamber), but peers who hold or have held high judicial office may also sit. The president of the House in its judicial capacity is the Lord Chancellor, and proceedings take the form of the normal proceedings of the House; judgments are given in the form of speeches to a motion, and the decision is in the form of a vote.

Scotland

The main civil courts are the sheriff courts and the Court of Session.

The civil jurisdiction of the sheriff court extends to most kinds of action and is normally unlimited by the value of the case. Much of the work is done by the sheriff, against whose decisions an appeal may be made to the sheriff-principal or directly to the Court of Session.

The Court of Session sits only in Edinburgh, and subject to a few exceptions has jurisdiction to deal with all kinds of action. The main exception is an action exclusive to the sheriff court, namely one where the value claimed is less than £500. The Court of Session has sole jurisdiction in divorce and certain other actions. The court is divided into two parts: the Outer House, a court of first instance, and the Inner House, which is mainly an appeal court. The Inner House is divided into two divisions of equal status, each consisting of four judges—the first division being presided over by the Lord President and the second division by the Lord Justice Clerk. Appeals to the Inner House may be made from the Outer House and from the sheriff court. From the Inner House an appeal may go to the House of Lords. The judges of the Court of Session are the same as those of the High Court of Justiciary. The Lord President of the Court holds the office of Lord Justice General in the High Court (see p 111).

The Scottish Land Court

The Scottish Land Court is a special court whose jurisdiction relates to agricultural tenancies and similar matters. It consists of a judge (ranking equally with the judges of the Court of Session) and four laymen who are specialists in agriculture.

Northern Ireland

Minor civil cases in Northern Ireland where the amount in dispute is less than £2,000 are dealt with in county courts, though magistrates' courts also deal with certain classes of minor civil cases. The superior civil law court is the High Court of Justice from which an appeal may be made to the Court of Appeal. These two courts, together with the Crown Court, comprise the Supreme Court of Judicature of Northern Ireland and their practice and procedure are similar to those in the corresponding English courts. The House of Lords is the final civil appeal court.

Civil Proceedings

In England and Wales civil proceedings are instituted by the aggrieved person; no preliminary inquiry on the authenticity of the grievance is required. An action in a magistrates' court is begun by a complaint on which the court may serve the defendant with a summons. This contains details of the complaint and the date on which it will be heard by the court. The parties and any witnesses give their evidence at the court hearing. Domestic proceedings are heard by not more than three lay justices including, where practicable, a woman justice; members of the public are not allowed to be present. The court may make an order containing provision for the custody and supervision of children, as well as for maintenance payments for spouses and children. Actions in the High Court are usually begun by a writ of summons served on the defendant by the plaintiff, notifying the defendant that the plaintiff has a claim and stating its nature. If the defendant intends to contest the claim he or she informs the court. Documents setting out the precise question in dispute (the pleadings) are then delivered to the court. County court proceedings are initiated by a 'request' served on the defendant by the court; subsequent procedure is simpler than in the High Court.

A decree of divorce must be pronounced in open court, but a special procedure extending to most undefended cases dispenses with the need to give evidence in court and permits written evidence to be considered by the registrar.

Civil proceedings, because they are a private matter, can usually be abandoned or compromised at any time without the court's permission, the parties to a dispute being able to settle their differences through their solicitors before the actual trial is reached. Actions that are brought to court are usually tried by a judge without a jury, except in cases involving claims for defamation, false imprisonment, or malicious prosecution, when either party may insist on trial by jury, or in a case of fraud, when the person against whom fraud is alleged may claim this right. The jury decides questions of fact and damages awarded to the injured party; majority verdicts may be accepted.

Judgments in civil cases are enforceable through the authority of the court. Most are for sums of money and may be enforced, in cases of default, by seizure of the debtor's goods or by attachment of earnings (a court order requiring an employer to make periodic payments to the court by deduction from the debtor's wages). Other judgments can take the form of an injunction restraining someone from performing an illegal act. Refusal to obey a judgment ordering the defendant to do something or to refrain from doing something may result in imprisonment for contempt of court. Arrest under an order of committal may be effected only on a warrant of the court.

The general rule is that the costs of the action (barristers' fees, solicitors' charges, court fees and other payments) are within the discretion of the court.

Normally, the court orders them to be paid by the party losing the action, but in the case of family law maintenance proceedings a magistrates' court has discretion, whatever its judgment, to order either party to pay the whole or part of the other's costs.

In Scotland proceedings in the Court of Session or ordinary actions (of a value exceeding £500) in the sheriff court are initiated by serving the defender with a summons (an initial writ in the sheriff court). In Court of Session actions the next step is the publication of the action in the court lists.

A defender who intends to contest the action must inform the court; if he or she does not appear, the court grants a decree in absence in favour of the pursuer. In ordinary actions in the sheriff court the defender is simply required to enter appearance within a certain number of days after service of the initial writ, and this is followed by a formal appearance in court by the parties to the dispute or their solicitors.

In summary causes (actions normally of a value less than £500) in the sheriff court the procedure is less formal. The statement of claim is incorporated in the summons (a printed form obtained from the sheriff clerk). The procedure is designed to enable most actions to be carried through without the parties involved having to appear in court. Normally they (or their representatives) need appear only when an action is defended. Proceedings in Northern Ireland are similar to those in England and Wales.

Restrictive Practices Court The Restrictive Practices Court is a specialised United Kingdom court which deals with monopolies and restrictive trade practices. It comprises five judges and up to ten other people with experience and expertise in industry, commerce or public life.

Administrative Tribunals Administrative tribunals consist of persons or bodies exercising judicial functions outside the ordinary hierarchy of the courts. As a rule, they are set up under statutory powers which also govern their constitution, functions and procedure. Their composition and procedures vary greatly. Compared with the courts, they are regarded as less expensive, less formal and more accessible; they also have expert knowledge of their particular subjects. The expansion of the tribunal system is comparatively recent, most tribunals having been set up since 1945. Independently of the executive, tribunals decide the rights and obligations of private citizens towards each other or towards a government department or other public authority. A number of important tribunals (notably the rent and the industrial tribunals) decide disputes between private citizens. Some (such as those concerned with social security) resolve claims by private citizens against public authorities. A further group (including tax tribunals) decide disputed claims by public authorities against private citizens, and still others decide issues in dispute which do not directly affect financial rights or liabilities, such as entitlement to licences or the right to enter the United Kingdom, or issues of personal liberty, for example, those decided by mental health review tribunals. Tribunals usually consist of an uneven number of people so that a majority decision can be reached; some consist of one person sitting alone. Members are normally appointed by the minister concerned with the subject but other authorities (for instance, the Lord Chancellor) have the power of appointment in appropriate cases. The Lord Chancellor (or the Lord President of the Court of Session in Scotland) makes appointments in most cases where a lawyer chairman or member is required. Members usually hold office for a specified period.

There are also tribunals which enforce professional discipline (for example of doctors and solicitors) but these are entirely different in constitution from the statutory tribunals and have no jurisdiction over the general public.

Appeals on a point of law from all the more important tribunals may be made in England and Wales to the High Court, in Scotland to the Court of Session and in Northern Ireland to the Court of Appeal. An appeal may also be made to a specially constituted appeal tribunal, to a minister of the Crown or to an independent referee. The Employment Appeal Tribunal, which hears appeals on questions of law from decisions of industrial tribunals (see p 338), has High Court and Court of Session status. The Council on Tribunals (appointed jointly by the Lord Chancellor and the Lord Advocate) exercises general supervision over tribunals, advising on draft rules of procedure, monitoring their activities and reporting on particular matters; those peculiar to Scotland are dealt with by the Scottish Committee of the Council.

ADMINISTRATION OF THE LAW

GOVERNMENT RESPONSI-BILITIES

The United Kingdom judiciary is entirely independent of the Government and is not subject to ministerial direction or control. There is no minister of justice. Responsibility for the administration of justice rests with the Lord Chancellor, the Home Secretary and the Secretaries of State for Scotland and Northern Ireland. Also concerned is the Prime Minister who recommends the highest judicial appointments to the Crown.

England and Wales

The Lord Chancellor is the head of the judiciary (and sometimes sits as a judge in the House of Lords); he is concerned with court procedure, is responsible for the administration of all courts other than magistrates' courts, appoints magistrates, and has general responsibility for the legal aid and advice scheme. He is also responsible for the administration of civil law reform.

The Home Secretary is concerned with the criminal law (including law reform), the police service, prisons and the probation and after-care service. A general supervision over magistrates' courts is also held with some specific responsibilities (such as approving the appointment of justices' clerks). On matters relating to crime prevention and the treatment of offenders, the Home Secretary is advised by the Advisory Council on the Penal System. Prison policy and the administration of custodial centres are functions of the Home Office Prison Department, and the Home Secretary appoints to each centre a board of visitors representing the local community to investigate and advise on the state of prison premises, administration and treatment of inmates. The boards have certain disciplinary powers in relation to serious breaches of discipline and they hear applications or complaints from inmates. The Home Secretary is advised by a special Parole Board on the release of prisoners on licence.

Responsibility for the treatment of offenders under the age of 17 is shared between the Home Office and the Department of Health and Social Security.

The Home Secretary is also responsible for advising the Queen on the exercise of the royal prerogative of mercy to grant a free pardon to a person convicted of a crime or to cancel all or part of a penalty imposed on an offender by a court.

The Secretary of State for the Environment is responsible for providing accommodation for all the superior courts in England and Wales, except the Central Criminal Court, which is the responsibility of the City of London.

The Attorney General and the Solicitor General (the Law Officers of the Crown for England and Wales) are the Government's principal advisers on

English law, and represent the Crown in appropriate domestic and international cases. They are senior barristers, elected members of the House of Commons and hold ministerial posts. The Attorney General is also Attorney General for Northern Ireland.

As well as exercising various civil law functions, the Attorney General has final responsibility for enforcing the criminal law; the Director of Public Prosecutions (see p 109) is subject to the Attorney General's superintendence. The Attorney General is concerned with instituting and prosecuting certain types of criminal proceedings, but must exercise an independent discretion, and must not be influenced by government colleagues. The Solicitor General is, in effect, the deputy of the Attorney General.

Scotland

The Secretary of State for Scotland recommends the appointment of all judges other than the most senior ones, appoints the staff of the High Court of Justiciary and the Court of Session and is responsible for the composition staffing and organisation of the sheriff courts. District courts are staffed and administered by the district and islands local authorities. The Secretary of State is also responsible for crime prevention, and the police and the penal system, and is advised on parole matters by the Parole Board for Scotland.

The Lord Advocate and the Solicitor General for Scotland are the chief legal advisers to the Government on Scottish questions and the principal representatives of the Crown for the purposes of litigation in Scotland. The Lord Advocate is closely concerned with questions of legal policy and administration and is also responsible for the Scottish parliamentary draftsmen, and for the public prosecution of all major crimes (see p 109).

Northern Ireland

In Northern Ireland the judiciary is appointed by the Queen on the advice of the Lord Chancellor. The administration of all courts is the responsibility of the Lord Chancellor, while the Northern Ireland Office, under the Secretary of State, deals with the police and the penal system.

THE PERSONNEL OF THE LAW

The courts of the United Kingdom are the Queen's Courts since the Crown is the historic source of all judicial power. The Queen, acting on the advice of ministers, is responsible for all appointments to the judiciary.

Judges

Full-time judges do not engage in politics, except for the Lord Chancellor, who is head of the judiciary, speaker of the House of Lords and a Cabinet minister. With the exception of lay magistrates, judges are normally appointed from practising barristers (advocates in Scotland) or solicitors. Lay magistrates in England and Wales need no legal qualifications but on appointment they undergo a period of basic training, to give them sufficient knowledge of the law, including the rules of evidence, and to enable them to understand the nature and purpose of sentencing. A special committee advises the Lord Chancellor on training policies. The Scottish district court justices of the peace likewise need no legal qualifications, and the Secretary of State for Scotland is responsible for training. In Northern Ireland lay magistrates serving on juvenile courts undertake training courses; resident magistrates are drawn from practising solicitors or barristers. In certain circumstances (for instance in cases of misconduct or proven incapacity) judges of the inferior courts in England, Wales and Northern Ireland may be removed from their positions by the Lord Chancellor, and in Scotland, by the Secretary of State on a report by the Lord President of the Court of Session and the Lord Justice Clerk.

In order to safeguard and perpetuate the independence of the judiciary from the executive, superior judges in England and Wales and Northern Ireland (other than the Lord Chancellor who, as a Cabinet minister, changes with the Government) are subject to a power of removal only by the Sovereign on an address presented by both Houses of Parliament; in Scotland there is no statutory provision for removing of judges of the Court of Session or High Court of Justiciary from office and it is probable that special legislation would be needed to secure such a dismissal.

The Legal Profession

The legal profession is divided into two branches: barristers (advocates in Scotland) and solicitors. Barristers are known collectively as the 'Bar', and collectively and individually as 'counsel'. Solicitors undertake legal business for lay clients, while barristers advise on legal problems submitted through solicitors and present cases in the higher courts; certain functions, however, are common to both. Although people are free to conduct their own cases, most people prefer to be legally represented in the more serious court cases.

A Royal Commission reported in 1979 on the provision of legal services in England, Wales and Northern Ireland. A similar Commission, inquiring into legal services in Scotland, reported in May 1980 (see Bibliography).

In England and Wales every barrister and every student wishing to become a barrister must be a member of one of the four Inns of Court (Lincoln's Inn, Inner Temple, Middle Temple and Gray's Inn). To become a student member of an Inn, an entrant must normally have a law degree from a United Kingdom university or polytechnic. People with other degrees and 'mature' students may also be accepted, but they must pass a diploma in law. All students must pass the professional examinations run by the Council of Legal Education. After training, a student can be called to the Bar, but may not practise independently until a year's pupillage with an established barrister has been completed. The governing body of the profession is the Senate of the Inns of Court and the Bar. The Bar Council (composed of members of the Senate elected by the Bar) maintains the standards and independence of the profession and improves its services.

A prospective solicitor in England and Wales must be considered suitable by the Council of the Law Society (the professional organisation of solicitors) and must enter into 'articles of clerkship' with a practising solicitor of not less than five years' standing before beginning a professional career. The term of articles lasts from two to four years, depending on the educational qualifications of the student. An articled clerk must pass the necessary examinations prescribed by the Law Society and, with very few exceptions, is required to attend a course of studies at a recognised law school. Once qualified, a solicitor may become a member of the Law Society.

In Scotland prospective advocates and solicitors undergo similar training. While the respective professional organisations—the Faculty of Advocates and the Law Society of Scotland—have their own professional examinations, candidates usually obtain exemption from them by including the necessary subjects in a law degree of a Scottish university. The prospective advocate must, thereafter, undergo a period of training (either of 21 months or of 12 months depending on whether or not exemption from nine months' training has been granted) in a solicitor's office, followed by about nine months' pupillage with a practising advocate. The prospective solicitor must serve an apprenticeship of two years in a solicitor's office before beginning a professional career.

In Northern Ireland most students wishing to become solicitors or barristers must, after attaining a law degree, undertake a period of study at the Institute of Professional Legal Studies for one year before being eligible to practise. Barristers are members of the Inn of Court of Northern Ireland; there is also a General Council of the Bar of Northern Ireland. The professional organisation for solicitors is the Incorporated Law Society of Northern Ireland.

LEGAL AID, ADVICE AND ASSISTANCE

Assistance from funds provided by the State is available to a person requiring help in meeting the cost of legal advice and representation in court proceedings. The State is entitled to be reimbursed from contributions which assisted people may have to pay according to their means and costs, and from money or property recovered from legally aided people's opponents in litigation, or awarded by the court.

Advice and Assistance

Where court proceedings are not involved, people with moderate means can obtain help from a solicitor on any legal matter either free or subject to a contribution. This includes giving advice, writing letters, drafting wills and obtaining opinions from a barrister. A solicitor may act for a client until costs and expenses reach a total of £25 (£55 for divorce or judicial separation cases), but authority must be obtained for this limit to be exceeded. The legal advice and assistance scheme is also used for representation by a solicitor in certain civil proceedings in magistrates' courts. A person seeking help must give the solicitor brief details about income and savings. The income limit laid down by the scheme is reviewed at least once a year.

Law Centres

In a number of deprived urban areas law centres provide free legal advice to people of limited means who might not otherwise obtain it. All law centres, which are voluntary organisations financed from various sources, including government grants, have at least one full-time salaried lawyer and many employ community workers. Most centres devote the largest proportion of their time to tenant-landlord disputes and other housing problems. Free legal advice is also available in many Citizens Advice Bureaux, consumer and housing advice centres and in specialist advice centres run by various voluntary organisations.

Aid in Civil Proceedings

Legal aid for civil proceedings is available to people whose disposable incomes and capital fall below certain prescribed amounts, but a contribution is payable according to the level of the applicant's income; if that is below a prescribed amount, legal aid is given free. As in the case of legal advice and assistance, the qualifying income limits are reviewed at least once a year.

An applicant for legal aid must also show reasonable grounds for taking or defending the proceedings. If the application is successful the case is then conducted in the ordinary way, except that no money passes between the assisted person and the solicitor—payments being made in and out of the legal aid fund. The costs of an action which an assisted litigant loses against an unassisted opponent may also, subject to certain conditions and if the court so orders, be met out of the fund. Solicitors and counsel must review the case at each stage to see that it is not being pursued unreasonably at public expense. Legal aid is not generally available in cases where redress is sought for alleged defamation or for representation in most proceedings in administrative tribunals.

The civil legal aid schemes are run by the Law Society, the Law Society of Scotland and the Incorporated Law Society of Northern Ireland, under the general guidance respectively of the Lord Chancellor, the Secretary of State for Scotland and the Secretary of State for Northern Ireland.

Aid in Criminal Proceedings

In criminal proceedings in England and Wales a legal aid order may be made by the court concerned if it appears to be in the interests of justice and if a defendant needs financial help in meeting the costs of the proceedings. An order must be made when a person is committed for trial on a charge of murder or where the prosecutor appeals or applies for leave to appeal from the Court of Appeal (Criminal Division) or the Court Martial Appeal Court to the House of Lords. No person who is unrepresented can be given a custodial sentence for the first time unless given the opportunity to apply for legal aid.

Voluntary duty solicitor schemes at many magistrates' courts provide 'standby' help for unrepresented defendants.

The criminal legal aid scheme in England and Wales is administered by the courts, under the overall responsibility of the Lord Chancellor.

The arrangements for aid in criminal proceedings in Scotland and Northern Ireland are broadly similar, but in Scotland there is a statutory duty solicitor scheme for accused people in custody in sheriff, and district, court cases and the 'interests of justice' test applies only in summary cases.

LAW REFORM

The duty of keeping the law under review to ensure that it meets the needs of modern society lies in England and Wales with the Law Reform Committee, the Criminal Law Revision Committee and the Law Commission, and in Scotland with the Scottish Law Commission. The Law Reform Committee and the Criminal Law Revision Committee are standing committees of judges and distinguished practising and academic lawyers, appointed respectively by the Lord Chancellor and the Home Secretary, to examine aspects of the civil and criminal law referred to them by the appropriate minister. The Criminal Law Revision Committee has produced 14 reports; of the 12 recommending legislation, ten have been wholly or partly enacted.

The Law Commission is a permanent body consisting of five lawyers of high standing, responsible for scrutinising the law with a view to its systematic development and reform, including the possibility of codification, elimination of anomalies, repeal of obsolete and unnecessary enactments, and reduction of the number of separate enactments. It reports to the Lord Chancellor. The Scottish Law Commission, whose constitution and functions are similar to those of the English body, reports to the Lord Advocate. The work of the two commissions has produced changes in many areas of the law, the repeal of some 950 obsolete Acts and the pruning of the contents of nearly 1,400 others.

The Law Commission is also concerned with the reform in Northern Ireland of those branches of the law which were outside the scope of the powers of the former Parliament of Northern Ireland. Other aspects of law reform in Northern Ireland are dealt with by the Office of Law Reform.

6 Social Welfare

The British social welfare system comprises the National Health Service, the personal social services and social security. Education is described in Chapter 7, and housing in Chapter 9. The National Health Service provides a comprehensive range of medical services which are available to all residents, irrespective of means. The local authority personal social services and voluntary organisations provide advice and help to elderly people, disabled people and children in need of care. The social security system is designed to secure a basic standard of living for people in financial need by providing income during periods of inability to earn, help for families and compensation for disablement.

Joint finance and planning between health and local authorities aims to prevent overlapping of services and to encourage the development of community services. In deciding their priorities, some local authorities attach greater importance than others to the personal social services and to the various categories of people in need of help, with the result that provision can vary from area to area.

Central government is responsible directly for the National Health Service, administered by health authorities and boards acting as its agents, and for the social security system. It has an indirect responsibility for the personal social services administered by local government authorities.

Spending on social welfare in 1979 was: health £8,863 million (5·4 per cent of gross domestic product), personal social services £1,733 million (1 per cent), and social security £18,497 million (11·3 per cent). In spite of plans to reduce public expenditure in the period to 1983–84, and to effect economies in local authority services, social welfare spending will increase. Social security is by far the largest public expenditure programme.

NATIONAL HEALTH SERVICE

The National Health Service (NHS) is based upon the principle that there should be a comprehensive range of publicly provided services designed to promote improvement in the health of the people and in the prevention, diagnosis and treatment of illness. All taxpayers, employers and employees contribute to its cost so that those members of the community who do not require health care help to pay for those who do. At the time of use there may be moderate charges (as for prescriptions and spectacles—though not for children and people with low incomes) or none at all (for example for hospital care). Some 60 per cent of NHS expenditure goes on children, the elderly, the disabled, and the mentally ill and handicapped.

Visitors to Britain are not entitled to use the NHS except where reciprocal health agreements with their countries apply (see p 138). They may be allowed free NHS treatment in certain emergencies. Visitors are expected to pay if the purpose of their visit is to seek treatment.

How far the improvements in the nation's health over the past 30 years or so are attributable to the NHS is impossible to determine, but some changes have been aided by the planning and provision of a national system of care; the advances in maternal and child care, for example, the use of vaccines for the benefit of all sections of the community, the more efficient use of acute hospital services (for surgery, gynaecology and childbirth), and the establishment of primary health care teams and health centres. Like health care systems in other countries, the National Health Service has its problems, however. They range from regional disparities in health provision to shortages of resources and industrial relations difficulties. An additional problem is the high cost of technologically advanced equipment required for diagnosis and treatment and of such advanced surgery as heart transplantation.

The Government has announced its intention of improving the use of available resources within the National Health Service and of simplifying its organisation by removing the area health authority tier of its administrative structure in England by April 1983. Proposals for simplifying administration in Scotland and Wales have also been made. It also believes that there is a bigger place for private medicine and that this should be facilitated and encouraged. The Royal Commission on the National Health Service which reported in 1979 (see Bibliography) recommended a greater emphasis in the role of preventive medicine, measures to simplify the administration of the Service, changes in internal financing methods, and a review of national arrangements for negotiating pay and settling disputes.

ADMINISTRATION The health ministers—the Secretary of State for Social Services in England and the Secretaries of State for Scotland, Wales and Northern Ireland—are responsible for all aspects of the health services in their respective areas. Within each of the four parts of the country the health departments (the Department of Health and Social Security in England, the Scottish Home and Health Department, the Welsh Office and the Department of Health and Social Services in Northern Ireland) are responsible for strategic planning. Area health authorities in England and Wales and health boards in Scotland are responsible for planning and operational control of all health services in their area. In England, because of its greater size and population, a tier of regional authorities is responsible for regional planning and certain services best administered on a regional basis (for example, research and major capital building work).

There are 14 regional health authorities and 90 area health authorities in England, 8 area health authorities in Wales, 15 health boards in Scotland and 4 health and social services boards in Northern Ireland. The authorities and boards, which consist of unpaid, part-time members are statutory agencies of central government and co-operate closely with local authorities responsible for social work, environmental health, education and other services. In general the areas covered by area health authorities and health boards correspond with those of the major local authorities. Health and local authorities in England, Wales and Scotland co-operate by means of joint planning arrangements and joint consultative committees.

In Northern Ireland the four health and social services boards act as agents for the Department of Health and Social Services, spanning both health and personal social services.

The area authorities and health boards can determine the pattern of services best suited to their areas but have to take account of national priorities. In most areas the day-to-day running of services is carried out by management teams in districts which usually contain a district general hospital and have a population of between 200,000 and 500,000, though some are considerably larger (in

Scotland, Wales and Northern Ireland they may be much smaller). In Scotland a Common Services Agency organises certain central services; there are similar agencies in Wales and Northern Ireland.

There is statutory provision for professional advisory committees at national, regional and area level; the authorities have a duty to consult them. There are also such advisory bodies as the Committee on Vaccination and Immunisation, the Scottish Health Service Planning Council in Scotland and the Health and Social Services Council in Northern Ireland. The Health Advisory Service for England and Wales reports to the Secretaries of State on conditions in hospitals and the community health service. The Scottish Hospital Advisory Service reports to health boards and to the Secretary of State.

Public representation in the Service for England and Wales is provided by community health councils. These consist of about 20 to 30 members, half of them appointed by local government councils and the rest mainly on the nomination of voluntary bodies interested in local health services. They have access to the area health authority, the right to secure information and the right to visit hospitals. In Scotland local health councils have been set up by the health boards to represent the interests of the public. District committees exercise this function in Northern Ireland.

Health Service Commissioners   Legislation provides for the appointment of three Health Service Commissioners (for England, Scotland and Wales) to investigate complaints from members of the public about the health service. All three posts are held by the Parliamentary Commissioner for Administration (see p 35), whose health service jurisdiction covers the failure of a health authority to carry out its statutory duties, a failure in a service provided, or maladministration causing injustice or hardship. Complaints can only be considered if they are first sent to the relevant health authority; sufficient time must be given for the authorities to investigate the problem and reply to the complainant. Matters outside the Commissioner's jurisdiction include action taken solely in the exercise of clinical judgment and the action of family practitioners (see p 133).

The Commissioner reports annually to ministers who lay the reports before Parliament; and also publishes at regular intervals full texts of selected investigations without, however, naming individuals or institutions.

In Northern Ireland the Commissioner for Complaints (see p 68) investigates complaints concerning the health service, but not the actions of medical practitioners or the professions supplementary to medicine.

Finance   About 87 per cent of the cost of the health services is paid for through general taxation; the rest is met from the National Health Service contribution paid with the national insurance contribution and from the charges towards the cost of certain items such as drugs prescribed by a family doctor, dental treatment and spectacles. Legislation has been passed which gives health authorities powers to raise funds from voluntary sources.

The charges for medical prescriptions do not apply to children under 16 years, expectant and nursing mothers, women aged 60 and over and men aged 65 and over, patients suffering from certain medical conditions, war and Service disablement pensioners (for treatment of their disability), and families with very low incomes, including those receiving supplementary benefits and family income supplement. About two-thirds of prescription items are supplied free of charge. Charges for dental treatment do not apply to clinical examination only, or to people under 21 (with the exception that young people between 16 and 21 who have left school pay for dentures), pregnant women or those who have had a baby within the last year. Children's spectacles are free. Certain low income groups are exempt from dental and optical charges.

A limited amount of hospital accommodation may be made available at a small charge for patients wanting privacy as long as the accommodation is not needed on medical grounds for non-paying patients.

Provision is also made at certain hospitals for patients to be treated as private patients on payment of the whole cost of their accommodation and treatment.

Hospital medical staffs are salaried and can be employed full-time or part-time. Part-time hospital doctors can accept private patients. General medical practitioners are self-employed, paid by a system of fees and allowances designed to reflect responsibilities, work load and practice expenses.

Dentists providing treatment in their own surgeries are paid on a prescribed scale of fees according to the treatment they have carried out. Pharmacists dispensing on their own premises are paid on the ingredient cost of the prescriptions they dispense. Ophthalmic medical practitioners and ophthalmic opticians taking part in the general ophthalmic service receive approved fees for each sight test made; opticians who dispense spectacles are paid according to the number and type of pairs supplied.

PRIMARY HEALTH CARE

Primary health care is in the hands of doctors, dentists, opticians and pharmacists working within the Service as independent practitioners, and district nurses, midwives and health visitors employed by the health authorities; a wide range of other services is also available including the school health service, social services and chiropody service.

Family Practitioner Services

The family practitioner services are those given to patients by doctors, dentists, opticians and pharmacists of their own choice. They are administered in England and Wales by family practitioner committees established by the health authorities, in Scotland by the health boards and in Northern Ireland by the Central Services Agency on behalf of the health and social services boards.

There are nearly 27,000 family doctors under contract to the National Health Service. A doctor may not normally have more than 3,500 patients; the average in Great Britain is about 2,300 and in Northern Ireland 2,100. Access to most other parts of the health service is obtained through the family doctor.

There are 920 ophthalmic medical practitioners and over 7,200 ophthalmic and dispensing opticians engaged in the general ophthalmic services which provide for the testing of sight and supply of spectacles. Patients requiring treatment are dealt with through the hospital eye service.

There are over 14,300 dentists taking part in the health service.

About 11,000 retail pharmacies under contract to the National Health Service are responsible for dispensing prescriptions.

District Nurses, Midwives and Health Visitors

District nurses give skilled nursing care to people at home or elsewhere outside hospital; they also play an important role in preventive care and health education. Although almost all babies are born in hospital, there is a domiciliary service for mothers having their babies at home, with midwives and family doctors caring for mothers and babies after birth. Midwives also assist births in hospital. Health visitors are concerned with the health of the household as a whole and offer an advisory service for families including those with young children and elderly people; they undertake health teaching, assist in preventing ill-health, and work closely with family doctors, district nurses and social workers.

Group Practices and Health Centres

Family doctors often work as members of primary health care teams with health visitors, district nurses, and sometimes midwives or social workers. About four-fifths are in partnership or group practices. About a fifth of the doctors in Great Britain and just over a half in Northern Ireland work in modern and well-equipped health centres built and maintained by the health authorities. At health centres, child health services can be provided as well as facilities for health education, family planning, speech therapy, chiropody, assessment of hearing, physiotherapy and remedial exercises. Dental, pharmaceutical and ophthalmic services, hospital out-patient services and supporting social work services may also be provided.

HOSPITALS AND SPECIALIST SERVICES

The hospital and specialist services include district general hospitals with treatment and diagnostic facilities for in-patients, day-patients and out-patients, hospital maternity departments, infectious disease units, psychiatric and geriatric facilities, rehabilitation facilities, convalescent homes and all forms of specialised treatment. A number of specialist hospitals for mentally ill, mentally handicapped and elderly people are also provided.

Hospitals

A large proportion of the hospitals in the National Health Service were built in the nineteenth century; some trace their origins to much earlier charitable foundations, such as the famous St. Thomas' and St. Bartholomew's hospitals in London. Much has been done to improve and extend existing hospitals, some of which are housed in inconvenient buildings, and many new hospitals have been or are being opened. The most recent development in hospital design is the 'nucleus' hospital of some 300 beds which will make a more intensive use of space and facilities; it can be used either as the first stage of a new hospital or as an extension of an existing hospital. Building work on the first nucleus hospital began in 1978 and the design is now being used widely.

The policy of recent Governments has been to concentrate acute facilities in large district general hospitals, and to limit the role of the small hospital in acute medicine while expanding its role in the care of the long-stay patient, particularly the elderly (although in Scotland more of the smaller hospitals have been retained for acute medicine). The Government has reviewed this policy which, it considers, involves the construction of excessively large hospitals and the risk of hospital services becoming too remote from the local communities that they serve. Consultations are taking place on changing the emphasis in hospital building policy to provide smaller hospitals in local communities. There are 2,625 National Health Service hospitals with about 474,000 beds and a nursing and midwifery staff of over 440,000 (whole time equivalent). There are over 40,000 medical staff including over 13,450 consultants.

Rehabilitation

Rehabilitation is an important part of medical care beginning at the onset of illness or injury and aimed at helping people to live as normally as possible. It is especially important for elderly, disabled and mentally-ill people who need such help to become self-sufficient. Facilities are provided in most hospitals and at special centres. The work is carried out by teams of doctors, nurses, physiotherapists, remedial gymnasts, occupational therapists, speech therapists and social workers. The hospital departments work closely with the Disablement Resettlement Service of the Manpower Services Commission (the Department of Manpower Services in Northern Ireland).

Medical services may include the provision, free of charge, of artificial limbs and eyes, hearing aids, surgical supports, wheelchairs, and other appliances.

Equipment for the Disabled

A fold-away tricycle, steered and powered by handlebars that rotate like the pedals of a bicycle, can be dismantled in seconds and carried in the boot of a car.

A completely safe battery-powered 'go-kart' for physically handicapped children from four years to teenage is controlled by a light-action joystick.

Equipment for the Disabled

'Invashrew', the five-seater invalid car conceived and built by boys of Shrewsbury School, Shropshire. It can be driven from a wheelchair, and can carry another disabled person and three additional passengers.

A new vacuum forming machine, developed by the Biomedical Research Unit, Queen Mary's Hospital, Roehampton, enables artificial limbs to be provided in one day compared with up to two or three months by other methods.

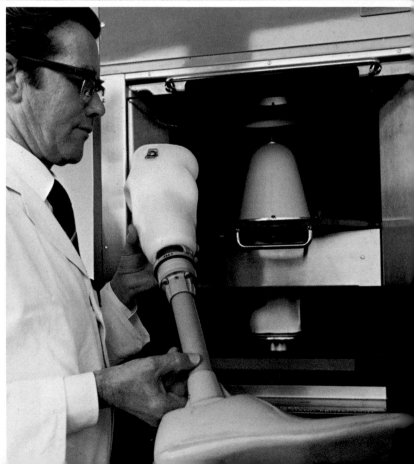

A close-circuit television system that magnifies objects placed beneath a camera lens as an aid for the partially sighted.

An audible aid to guide blind athletes has been developed by the founder of the charity Research into Child Blindness. The inexpensive, completely portable, system emits a high or low bleep which is transmitted to the earpiece worn by the athlete.

Equipment for the Disabled

A typewriter for the disabled, called 'Popstar' needs no special installation. It can be used with hand- or finger-controlled joystick, a suck/blow unit, or pressure pads for the hand, elbow or foot. The equipment has sockets for other electrical appliances such as a radio or door release.

'Splink' for the deaf and speech handicapped has a microprocessor-controlled keyboard with basic words and phrases, linked to an ordinary television set.

Very severely physically handicapped patients may be issued with electrical control equipment which enables them to operate devices such as alarm bells, radio and television, a telephone, and heating. Nursing aids for the handicapped at home can be borrowed.

Social workers, home helps and occupational therapists are available to hospital patients who, due to their illness, have difficulties on returning to their homes.

Hospices

Some 50 hospices provide care for the dying either directly in residential homes or through the provision of nursing and other assistance in the patient's own home. About ten are administered entirely by the National Health Service; the remainder, most of which receive support from public funds, are run by independent charitable organisations. Control of symptoms and psychological support for patients and their families form the central features of hospice care. The hospice movement, which is worldwide, originated in Britain.

Drug Dependence

Treatment for narcotic drug dependence is provided mostly on an out-patient basis in the drug treatment units provided by the National Health Service, although some addicts have a period of in-patient treatment when necessary. Following legislation in 1968, only doctors licensed by the Home Secretary are allowed to prescribe heroin and cocaine for the treatment of drug addiction. (In Northern Ireland licensing is the responsibility of the Department of Health and Social Services.) These doctors work mainly in National Health Service treatment centres. Doctors who are not licensed can no longer prescribe these drugs except for the relief of pain due to organic disease or injury. All doctors must notify the Home Secretary of any patient they consider to be addicted to certain controlled drugs (in Northern Ireland the chief medical officer of the health department).

In addition to hospital-based facilities there are a number of non-statutory agencies which work with and complement the Health Service provision. In 1978 an experimental short-stay residential unit for unstable young multiple drug users was established with substantial financial support from the Department of Health and Social Security.

Rehabilitation facilities are less commonly available and are mainly provided by voluntary organisations, some of which receive financial help from local authorities. Social work help is given by the probation service and local social services departments.

The Advisory Council on the Misuse of Drugs, set up under the Misuse of Drugs Act 1971, advises ministers on a wide range of matters associated with the prevention and treatment of drug abuse and connected social problems.

Alcoholism

Treatment and rehabilitation for alcoholics is provided by the National Health Service, social services and voluntary organisations. Treatment includes in-patient and out-patient services in general hospitals, psychiatric units and hospitals and in 34 specialised alcoholism treatment units. Primary care teams (general practitioners, nurses and social workers) play an important part.

Parents and Children

Special preventive health services, including free dental care, are available for expectant and nursing mothers and young children. A feature of the services is the education of parents before and after the birth by means of talks, discussion groups, demonstrations and classes. Pre-school-age children receive regular medical examinations and are tested for vision, hearing, speech and language deficiencies so that any handicap can be identified. Family planning advice and help is provided at many clinics, and welfare foods (dried milk and vitamins) are distributed from them.

Sick children are treated at home or in hospital as in-patients, day-patients or out-patients. If admission to hospital is necessary, the Government encourages health authorities to accommodate them in children's departments under the care of consultant paediatricians and specially trained nurses.

The school health service, which is part of the National Health Service, organises health surveillance of school children including medical inspection and dental inspection and treatment where appropriate. The staff of the school health service work closely with local education authorities in the medical assessment of handicapped children thought to need special attention.

Child guidance and child psychiatric services provide help and advice for children with psychological or emotional problems.

Family Planning

Free family planning facilities are available to everyone through family planning clinics, hospitals and a domiciliary service. Most family doctors provide a similar service for women only.

Abortion

Under the Abortion Act 1967 termination of a pregnancy may take place if two registered doctors think that its continuance would involve a greater risk to the life of the pregnant woman (or injury to her physical or mental health or that of any existing children in the family) than if the pregnancy were ended. Termination may also be allowed if the two doctors think that there is a substantial risk of the child being born with severe physical or mental abnormalities. Abortions may be carried out in National Health Service hospitals or in private premises officially approved for the purpose. Just over half the 119,000 legal abortions to women resident in England and Wales in 1979 were performed in private hospitals and clinics. The Act does not apply in Northern Ireland.

Blood Transfusion

The blood transfusion service has about 2 million voluntary unpaid donors. There are 19 regional transfusion centres in Britain recruiting donors and organising donor sessions in towns and villages, factories and offices, and in establishments maintained by the armed forces. Donors must be between the ages of 18 and 65. The centres are also responsible for blood grouping and testing, maintaining blood banks, providing a consultant service to hospitals, teaching in medical schools, and instructing doctors, nurses and technicians. Four laboratories prepare blood products and undertake research.

Ambulance Services

Where necessary on medical grounds, free transport by ambulance is provided by the health authorities. The work of the ambulance service falls into two categories: emergency work dealing with sudden illness, urgent maternity cases, and accidents of all kinds; and non-urgent work providing transport for people needing out-patient treatment at hospitals, clinics and day hospitals. Because of increasing demands on the ambulance service its role and structure are under review.

The London Ambulance Service is probably the largest of its kind in the world, catering for 7 million residents and non-residents in an area of 1,580 sq km (610 sq miles). It uses over 1,000 vehicles at 76 ambulance stations and has a staff of over 2,600. On an average day it receives 1,700 emergency calls (over one call every minute) and carries out 9,000 non-urgent patient journeys.

In some areas the ambulance service for non-urgent cases is augmented by volunteers using their own cars. In Scotland an air ambulance service is available in the islands and in the remoter parts of the mainland.

HEALTH EDUCATION

In England, Wales and Northern Ireland health education is promoted by the Health Education Council which assists in the development of programmes of health education with the health authorities, professional organisations, voluntary bodies and industry. Health education services in Scotland are organised by the Scottish Health Education Group, which is part of the Common Services Agency. Major themes of publicity campaigns are family planning, health in pregnancy, correct diet and exercise, and the dangers of cigarette smoking and excessive consumption of alcohol. Although expenditure for health education is met largely from central government funds, the Health Education Council is free to determine its own priorities and programme.

Within the Health Service, medical officers advise health authorities on health education, and specialist officers have executive responsibility.

SAFETY OF MEDICINES

Under the Medicines Act 1968, which came into force in 1971 and applies to the whole of the United Kingdom, the health and agriculture ministers are responsible for licensing the manufacture, marketing and importation of medicines for human and veterinary use. The Medicines Commission advises the ministers on policy regarding medicines and a Committee on Safety of Medicines advises the health ministers on the safety, efficacy and quality of new medicines and monitors adverse drug reactions. The Committee on Dental and Surgical Materials gives advice on products not appropriate to the Committee on Safety of Medicines or the Veterinary Products Committee. A review of medicines on the market is being undertaken, the health ministers being advised by the Committee on the Review of Medicines. The Act also controls the advertising, labelling, packaging, distribution, sale and supply of medicines.

THE HEALTH PROFESSIONS

Only people whose names are on the medical and dental registers may practise as doctors and dentists in the National Health Service. University medical and dental schools are responsible for teaching medical students; the National Health Service provides hospital clinical facilities for their training. Registration as a doctor requires five or six years' training in medical school and hospital, with an additional year's experience in a hospital; for a dentist, four or more years' training at a dental school is required. The governing body of the medical profession is the General Medical Council and that of the dentists is the General Dental Council. The main professional associations are the British Medical Association and the British Dental Association.

The minimum period of hospital training required to qualify for registration as a nurse is normally three years. Training may be in general, sick children's, mental or mental subnormality nursing. An enrolled nurse takes a two-year course. The examining bodies of the nursing profession in England and Wales and in Scotland are the general nursing councils. Midwives in England and Wales and in Scotland must have the certificate of the appropriate Midwives Board. The examining body for nurses and midwives in Northern Ireland is the Northern Ireland Council of Nurses and Midwives. Pupil midwives are usually registered general nurses or sick children's nurses; for them the training period is one year and for other registered and enrolled nurses 18 months. The Royal College of Nursing and the Royal College of Midwives are the professional bodies for nurses and midwives. Health visitors are registered general nurses with midwifery or approved obstetric experience who have undergone at least the first part of the midwifery course or obstetric nursing before taking a year's course in health visiting, promoted by the Council for the Education and Training of Health Visitors. District nurses are state registered or state enrolled nurses, the majority of whom have undertaken additional training. Arrangements are being made to establish a United Kingdom Central Council for Nursing, Midwifery and Health Visiting which will assume responsibility for regulating these professions.

Pharmacists in general practice and in hospital must be registered by the Pharmaceutical Society of Great Britain, which is the professional body for pharmacy; in Northern Ireland the register is maintained by the Department of Health and Social Services on behalf of the Pharmaceutical Society of Northern Ireland. A three-year degree course approved by the Pharmaceutical Society followed by a year's approved training are necessary before registration. The majority of medicines can be sold or dispensed only by, or under the supervision of, a registered pharmacist.

The General Optical Council regulates the professions of ophthalmic optician and dispensing optician; only registered ophthalmic opticians (or registered medical practitioners) may test sight. Training of ophthalmic opticians takes four years including a year of practical experience under supervision. Dispensing opticians may take a two-year full-time course with a year's practical experience or a part-time day-release course while employed with an optician.

State registration may be obtained by chiropodists, dietitians, medical laboratory scientific officers, occupational therapists, orthoptists, physiotherapists, radiographers and remedial gymnasts. The governing bodies are eight boards, corresponding to the eight professions, under the general supervision of the Council for Professions Supplementary to Medicine. Professional training lasting two to four years is needed to qualify for registration. Only members of those professions who are state registered may be employed in the National Health Service and some other public services.

Dental therapists (who have undergone a two-year training course) and dental hygienists (who have undergone a training course of about a year) may carry out some simple dental work under the direction of a registered dentist.

HEALTH ARRANGEMENTS WITH OTHER COUNTRIES

Britain has special health arrangements with other member states of the European Community under which most United Kingdom nationals are entitled to receive necessary treatment during visits to another Community country. There are also arrangements to cover people who go to work or live in other Community countries. In addition there are reciprocal arrangements with some other countries under which medical treatment is available.

PRIVATE MEDICAL TREATMENT

People who wish to do so are free to make arrangements for private medical care, though the scale of private practice in relation to the NHS is small. In 1979 there were some 2,800 private paybeds in NHS hospitals and in England some 2 per cent of acute hospital beds were in private hospitals and nursing homes. It is estimated that about half of those receiving acute treatment in NHS pay beds or private hospitals are covered by provident schemes which make provision for private health care in return for annual subscriptions. In 1978 there were some 1·12 million subscribers to such schemes of whom 869,000 were members of group schemes. Subscriptions often cover more than one person and a total of 2·39 million were covered.

Private practice is also undertaken by family doctors and dentists who are free to accept as much private work as they wish, subject to their NHS obligations. For the majority of doctors, however, income from private patients represents a small part of their income, though private work by dentists is more substantial.

It is the policy of the Government to encourage the private sector to meet a larger share of the nation's health needs and an Act passed in 1980 repealed earlier legislation designed to phase out private facilities within the National Health Service, so facilitating a wider use of private medical care. The Government believes that an expansion of private care will benefit the service by relieving pressure on it.

ENVIRONMENTAL HEALTH

Environmental health officers employed by local authorities are responsible for the control of air pollution, noise, food hygiene and quality, the inspection of offices, the investigation of unfit housing, and in some instances for refuse collection. Doctors who specialise in community medicine and are employed by the health authorities advise local authorities on the medical aspects of environmental health. They may also assist the water authorities responsible for water supply and sewerage. Environmental health officers are also stationed at ports and airports where they carry out a range of duties concerned with shipping, inspection of imported foods and disease control.

In Northern Ireland district councils are responsible for noise control, collection and disposal of refuse, clean air, and food composition, labelling and hygiene.

Safety of Food

It is illegal to sell food which is injurious to health, unfit for human consumption, or not of the nature, substance or quality demanded by the buyer. In England and Wales the composition, labelling and description of food are the concern of food and drugs authorities (county councils, London borough councils and the City of London Corporation) while food hygiene and the safety and fitness of food are the concern of district councils, London borough councils and port health authorities. Premises where food or drink is prepared, handled, stored or sold must conform to certain hygiene standards. Environmental health officers may take for analysis or for bacteriological or other examination samples of any food on sale for human consumption. There are special regulations controlling the safety of particular foods such as milk, meat and ice-cream. The Department of Health and Social Security, the Ministry of Agriculture, Fisheries and Food and the Welsh Office are the central departments responsible for giving advice and making regulations. Expert committees of these departments review food regulations.

In Scotland regional and islands councils are responsible for food standards and labelling, and district and islands councils for food hygiene. District councils in Northern Ireland are responsible for food hygiene, food standards and labelling.

CONTROL OF INFECTIOUS DISEASES

The health authorities have general responsibility for the prevention of disease and co-operate with the local authority environmental health services. The area health authorities and health boards carry out programmes of vaccination and immunisation against diphtheria, measles, rubella (females only), poliomyelitis, tetanus, tuberculosis and whooping cough. Although vaccination is voluntary, the Government encourages parents to obtain protection for their children from these diseases.

Community physicians are responsible for the prevention and control of infectious diseases and are supported by the Public Health Laboratory Service which provides a network of bacteriological and virological laboratories throughout England and Wales which conduct research and assist in the diagnosis, prevention and control of epidemic diseases. Its largest establishment is the Central Public Health Laboratory at Colindale, in north-west

London, which includes the National Collection of Type Cultures, the Food Hygiene Laboratory, and reference laboratories specialising in the identification of infective micro-organisms. In addition it has a surveillance centre, which investigates and monitors human communicable diseases. In Scotland bacteriological work is done mainly in hospital laboratories. In Northern Ireland a central public health laboratory shares the bacteriological work with hospital laboratories.

PERSONAL SOCIAL SERVICES

Responsibility for personal social services rests with the social services authorities (local authority social services departments in England and Wales, social work departments in Scotland and health and social services boards in Northern Ireland). Many of their services are directed towards the same groups of people needing health services, for example, elderly or disabled people. Other groups helped include young families with social problems, children deprived of a normal home life, the mentally ill or handicapped and young offenders. Close co-operation is maintained between local authority social services departments and health authorities. In Scotland local authorities also undertake duties similar to those of the separate probation and after-care service in England and Wales (see p 115).

Much of the care given to the elderly and disabled is provided in the community itself, by their families, self-help groups and through the voluntary movement. The statutory sector offers the special skilled care needed in particular services. The Government recognises the importance of the contribution made by the voluntary organisations, especially when economies are being made in public expenditure.

Advice on health and personal social services for children in England and Wales is given by the Children's Committee.

The Handicapped

Social services authorities have a duty to provide social services for disabled people. They are required to establish the number of disabled people in their area and to publicise services. A wide range of facilities may be available including advice on personal and social problems arising from disability, assistance in overcoming the effects of disability, adaptations to people's homes (such as fitting ramps, ground floor toilets and grab rails) and various aids to daily living. In certain circumstances a telephone or a television set may be installed. Other facilities include social and occupational clubs, residential homes and the organisation of outings and holidays. In addition some authorities make arrangements for the teaching of handicrafts and other occupations. Voluntary organisations also provide services for disabled people.

Help available from other sources includes social security, medical treatment, special education, employment and training services and specially designed housing and means of access to public buildings.

The Elderly

Services for elderly people are provided by statutory and voluntary bodies to help them to live at home whenever possible. These may include the advice and help of social workers, domestic help, delivery of cooked meals, sitters-in, night attendants and laundry services as well as day centres, clubs and recreational workshops. In many areas 'good neighbour' and friendly visiting services are arranged by the local authority or a voluntary organisation. Social services authorities also provide residential accommodation for the elderly and infirm and have powers to register homes run by voluntary organisations or privately. The newer homes usually have accommodation for some 30–50 residents. About 2,600 homes for elderly people are provided by local authorities in England which house about 1·5 per cent of the population over the age of 65. There are similar homes in Scotland, Wales and Northern Ireland.

Local authorities, as part of their responsibility for public housing, build flats specially designed for elderly people; some of these blocks have resident wardens. Housing associations also build this type of accommodation.

The Mentally Ill and the Mentally Handicapped

Social services authorities must make arrangements for helping the mentally ill or mentally handicapped in the community, and for prevention and after-care services. Recent developments in the treatment of mental illness, which enable patients either to be treated at home or to be discharged from hospital more quickly provided support is available in the community, are adding to demands for these services and particularly for social work support. Arrangements include training centres for the mentally handicapped, day centres for the mentally ill, as well as social centres and a variety of residential care for the mentally ill and mentally handicapped of all ages. Social workers help patients and their families to deal with social problems arising from mental illness or handicap and can arrange compulsory admission (on a medical recommendation) of mentally disordered people to hospital in certain circumstances.

Help to Families

Social services authorities, through their own social workers or a voluntary organisation, make available help and advice to families facing special problems. The home help service provides practical assistance at home for sick and disabled people, elderly people and expectant mothers.

Some authorities make direct provision for the special needs of unmarried mothers and their babies, but most contribute to the cost of work done by voluntary organisations and other bodies.

Child Care

Day care facilities for children under five are provided by local authorities, voluntary agencies and privately. In allocating places in day nurseries and other facilities they themselves provide, local authorities give priority to children with special social or health needs for day care. They also register, and provide support and advice services for, childminders, private day nurseries and play-groups operating in their area.

The authorities have a duty to offer advice, guidance and assistance to families in difficulties in order to promote the welfare of children. The aim is to intervene at an early stage to reduce the need to receive children into care or bring them before a juvenile court.

The recognition, prevention and management of cases of child abuse are the concern of many authorities, agencies and professions, and area review committees have been established throughout the country to provide a forum for the discussion and co-ordination of all those involved and to draw up policies and procedures for handling these cases.

Authorities must receive into their care any child under the age of 17 who has no parent or guardian or who has been abandoned or whose parents are unable to provide for him or her if they are satisfied that such intervention is in the interests of the child. The child remains in care until the age of 18 unless discharged to the care of parents, other relatives or friends before that time. In certain circumstances the local authority may pass a resolution assuming the rights and duties of one or both parents. The parents must be notified and if they give notice of objection the continuance of the resolution will depend upon its being upheld by a court of law. When taking a decision on a child in care, the authorities have to give first consideration to the need to safeguard and promote the welfare of the child. Where children are in care, efforts are made to work with their families in order, where appropriate, to enable the children to return home.

Children in England and Wales may be brought before a juvenile court if they are neglected or ill-treated, exposed to moral danger, are beyond the control of parents, not attending school or (if ten years or over) have committed an offence other than homicide. At the same time it must be shown that the children are in need of care or control which they are unlikely to receive unless a care or other relevant order is made by the court. Local authorities are responsible for undertaking inquiries through social workers, consultation with parents, schools and the police. Children may be committed to the care of a local authority under a care order if the juvenile court is satisfied that they are in need of care or control. As an alternative the court may make a supervision order for a period of up to three years. Supervision is carried out by a social worker or a probation officer.

In Northern Ireland the court may send children to a training school (see p 119), commit them to the care of a fit person (which may include a health and social services board), or make a supervision order. The law relating to children has been reviewed and it is intended in future to form a distinction between the young offenders and children in need of care and protection.

In Scotland children in trouble (see p 119) or in need may be brought before a children's hearing which can impose a supervision requirement on a child if it thinks that compulsory measures of care are appropriate. Under these requirements most children are allowed to remain at home under the supervision of a social worker but some may be sent to a residential establishment while under supervision. Supervision requirements are reviewed at intervals of not more than one year until terminated by a children's hearing.

When practicable, children in care are boarded out with foster parents, who receive an allowance to cover the cost of maintenance. If foster homes are not considered appropriate or cannot be found, the children may be placed in children's homes, voluntary homes or other suitable residential accommodation. Community homes for children in care in England and Wales comprise local authority and some voluntary children's homes and include community homes with education on the premises which provide long-term care usually for the more difficult children. In Scotland local authorities are responsible for placing children in their care either in foster homes, in local authority or voluntary homes, or in residential schools. In Northern Ireland there are residential homes for children in the care of the health and social services boards; training schools and remand homes are administered separately.

Regulations regarding conduct of community homes and registered voluntary homes and the boarding out of children in care are made by central government.

Voluntary Organisations

Voluntary organisations, many of which were pioneers in child care, continue to play a major part in providing accommodation for children both in the care of local authorities and voluntary organisations. Some children's homes run by voluntary organisations which are not within the community homes system are registered with central government.

Voluntary bodies concerned with the welfare of children in their own homes include local family casework agencies and the Family Service Units. The National Society for the Prevention of Cruelty to Children and its Scottish counterpart maintain inspectors and visitors to investigate reported cruelty or neglect.

Adoption   Adoption of children is strictly regulated by legislation and some 10,870 adoption orders were made in England and Wales in 1979, 1,144 in Scotland and 359 in Northern Ireland; the Registrars General keep confidential registers of adopted children. Local authorities have the power to act as adoption agencies and eventually will be obliged to offer such a service. Voluntary adoption societies (some 60 societies in Britain arrange adoptions) must be registered with their local authority.

Adoptions of minors under the laws of some European and Commonwealth countries are recognised but this does not confer British citizenship on the adopted person.

Social Workers   The effective operation of the social services is largely dependent upon the availability of professionally qualified social workers trained in the methods of social work. Training courses in social work are provided by universities, polytechnics and colleges of further education; their length depends upon previous educational qualifications and can extend from one to four years. The Central Council for Education and Training in Social Work recognises social work courses and offers advice to people considering entry to the profession.

Professional social workers (including those working in the National Health Service) are employed by social service departments or local authorities. Others work in voluntary organisations or in the probation service (see p 115). Not all social workers employed by social service departments or local authorities are professionally qualified, but efforts are being made to increase the number of trained personnel.

SOCIAL SECURITY

National insurance, industrial injuries benefits, child benefit, family income supplement, supplementary benefits, and war pensions constitute a comprehensive system of social security. The payment of many benefits depends on prior payments to the national insurance scheme, while others are available without contribution conditions. The former are paid from the national insurance fund which consists of contributions from employed people and their employers, self-employed people and the Government. Non-contributory benefits are financed from general taxation revenue.

The social security programme accounts for about a quarter of all public expenditure. It has grown, in real terms, by £7,000 million since 1970 and now costs the equivalent of nearly £1,000 a year for every household. Part of the increase has been due to the rising numbers of the elderly, and part to the growth in unemployment; much, however, has been due to real improvement in the level of benefits, and new benefits and increased family support.

The Department of Health and Social Security administers the services in Great Britain; in Northern Ireland they are administered by the Department of Health and Social Services. Pensions and welfare services for war pensioners and their dependants are the responsibility of the Department of Health and Social Security throughout the United Kingdom. Appeals relating to claims for the various benefits are decided by independent tribunals.

The Government is examining and changing a number of aspects of the social security system, both to make it more comprehensible and to reduce the rate of growth of its cost to public funds. A new Social Security Advisory

Committee is to be established to bring together in one body advice on the national insurance, supplementary benefit, child benefit and family income supplement schemes. The Committee will replace the former Supplementary Benefits Commission, the separate Supplementary Benefits Commission for Northern Ireland and the National Insurance Advisory Committee. It is also intended to change the basis on which the annual increases for longer-term benefits are made; to reduce the amount of supplementary benefit payable to strikers' families; and to take further steps to ensure that social security payments go only to those for whom they are intended. It is proposed to reduce from 1981 and to end, from the beginning of 1982, the earning-related supplements paid with certain benefits and to introduce measures to help particular groups in need to meet rising fuel costs. Consultations are taking place on proposals to make employers responsible for sick pay during the early weeks of sickness and the industrial injuries scheme is under review.

CONTRIBUTIONS

Employees and Employers

Class 1 contributions are related to earnings and cover the employee for retirement pension, sickness and invalidity benefits, unemployment benefit, maternity benefits, widows' benefits, death grant and child's special allowance. Earnings-related supplement to sickness and unemployment benefit and maternity allowance and earnings-related addition to widows' allowance are also covered (although these are being phased out—see above). Industrial injuries benefits, although non-contributory, are payable from the national insurance fund. Additional payments are made for dependants.

The contribution paid by the employee varies; if he or she is not a member of a 'contracted-out' occupational pension scheme run by his or her employers (see p 145), the contribution is 6·75 per cent of earnings up to £165 a week (the upper earnings limit) provided that these earnings are at least £23 (the lower earnings limit). The employer pays 10·2 per cent of the same earnings range. If the employee is a member of a 'contracted-out' occupational pension scheme, a lower Class 1 contribution is payable, namely 6·75 per cent of earnings up to the lower earnings limit and 4·25 per cent of earnings between the two limits; the employer's contribution is 13·7 per cent and 5·7 per cent respectively. Contributions are collected through the 'Pay As You Earn' income tax system. The employer also pays to the Exchequer a national insurance surcharge of 3·5 per cent of the earnings range for each employee (see p 356). These rates may be revised from year to year.

Self-employed People

Self-employed people pay a flat-rate Class 2 contribution of £2·50 a week and a Class 4 contribution amounting to 5 per cent of net profits or gains between £2,650 and £8,300 a year. Self-employed contributors receive basic retirement pension (see below) and the same benefits as employees with the exception of unemployment benefit, earnings-related supplements (although this is being phased out), and industrial injuries benefits.

Married Women and Widows

Certain married women and widows retain the right to pay Class 1 contributions at the reduced rate of 2 per cent when employed and to pay no Class 2 contributions when self-employed. This right is being phased out and is retained, subject to certain conditions, only by those entitled to it at 5 April 1978. Reduced contributions do not count for the purposes of benefit. The employer's contribution is not affected.

Voluntary Contributions

Voluntary Class 3 contributions of £2·40 are payable by people wanting to safeguard rights to some benefits. Class 3 (and Class 2) contributions are paid by stamping a national insurance card or by direct debit of a bank or National Girobank account.

Exemptions

Some people do not have to pay contributions. Employees who continue working after pensionable age (60 for women and 65 for men) do not pay contributions though the employer remains liable. People earning less than the lower earnings limit are not liable for contributions, neither are their employers. Self-employed people with earnings below £1,250 a year may apply for exemption and those over pensionable age are excused payment of contributions.

BENEFITS

For most of the benefits there are two contribution conditions. First, before benefit can be paid at all, certain contributions have to be paid; secondly, the full rate of benefit cannot be paid unless contributions have been paid or credited up to a specific level over a specified period. There are special rules to help a widow not entitled to a widow's pension at widowhood or when her children have grown up, to qualify for sickness, unemployment or maternity benefit in the period before she can have established or re-established herself in insurance through her own contributions; there are also provisions to help a divorced woman who was not paying contributions during her marriage. The main benefits (payable weekly) are summarised below. The rates quoted are those effective from November 1980; allowances for children are paid in addition to child benefit.

Since 1975 benefits such as retirement pension have been increased annually in line with percentage movements in retail prices or average earnings, whichever was the greater; short-term benefits such as sickness benefit have been linked with movements in retail prices. From November 1980 the uprating of benefits will be linked with percentage increases in retail prices.

Retirement Pension

A state retirement pension is payable to women at the age of 60 and to men at the age of 65. People who are still working five years after the minimum pension age are eligible to receive the pension. The weekly rate of basic pension is £27·15 for men and women qualifying on their own contributions and £16·30 for a married woman qualifying on her husband's contributions. In 1978 the new state pension scheme came into operation and will mature fully after 20 years of contributions; the retirement pension will consist of the basic pension plus an additional (earnings-related) pension. The additional pension will be 1·25 per cent of earnings between the earnings limits (see p 144) for each year of contributions up to a maximum of 20 years.

Employers are free to 'contract-out' their employees from the state scheme for additional pension and provide their own occupational pension in its place provided that the latter is at least as good as the state additional pension. The State remains responsible for the basic pension. Lower national insurance contributions are payable if contracting-out takes place.

Rights to basic pension are safeguarded for mothers who are away from work looking after children or for people giving up work to care for severely disabled relatives. Women contributors receive the same pension as men with the same earnings.

A small pension may also be payable to those people who contributed to the state graduated pension scheme which operated between 1961 and 1975. Since 1978 graduated pension has also been protected against inflation.

In real terms the value of the basic retirement pension for a married couple has more than doubled since 1948.

A non-contributory retirement pension of £16·30 for a man, single woman or widow and £9·80 for a married woman (including an age addition of 25p) is payable to people over the age of 80 who have not qualified for a contributory pension or who qualified for one at a lower rate than the non-contributory pension. The age addition is also paid to all other pensioners aged over 80.

Mothers and Children

Maternity Benefits

A maternity grant of £25 is payable for each living child born and for a still-born child if the pregnancy lasts for at least 28 weeks. Maternity allowance is £20·65 a week and is payable normally from 11 weeks before the expected week of confinement until the end of the sixth week following the birth. Mothers who have paid full Class 1 or Class 2 contributions while they were working may qualify for maternity allowance even if they gave up work some time previously. An earnings-related supplement may also be payable, although this is being phased out. From 1982 the maternity grant will become non-contributory.

Child Benefit

The non-contributory child benefit is the main social security benefit for children. The rate is £4·75 for each child; an additional £3 is payable to certain people bringing up children alone for the first or only child in the family. Child benefit, which is tax free and is normally paid to the mother, is payable for children up to the age of 16 and for those up to the age of 19 if they continue in full-time education; benefit is not payable if the young person is taking a degree, teacher training or any other advanced course or if the education is sponsored by an employer or the Manpower Services Commission, or in Northern Ireland, by a body such as the Department of Manpower Services or an Industrial Training Board. Benefit is payable in addition to the allowance for children paid to recipients of social security benefits.

Child's Special Allowance

A contributory child's special allowance of £7·50 a week for each child is payable to a mother on the death of a former husband if the marriage was dissolved or annulled and he was contributing to the support of the children.

Guardian's Allowance

A non-contributory guardian's allowance is a weekly payment of £7·50 for an orphaned child payable to a person who is entitled to child benefit for that child. In certain circumstances it can be paid on the death of only one parent. One of the dead parents must have satisfied a residence condition.

Other Benefits

Additions for children are payable with widows', sickness, unemployment and other benefits.

Widows

A widow's allowance is payable for the first 26 weeks of widowhood at the rate of £38 plus £7·50 for each child. An earnings-related addition earned by the late husband's Class 1 contributions may also be payable, although this is being discontinued. After this a widowed mother receives a basic widowed mother's allowance of £27·15 plus £7·50 for each child. Widow's pension is payable to a widow who is 40 years or over when her husband dies or when her entitlement to widowed mother's allowance ends; the rates payable range from £8·15 for widows of 40 to £27·15 for widows of 50 or over.

The widow's pension and widowed mother's allowance consists of a basic pension and an additional pension earned by the late husband's contributions. If the widow is aged between 40 and 50 when widowed (or when her children have grown up), additional pension is reduced like the basic pension. Payment continues until the widow remarries or begins drawing retirement pension.

A man whose wife dies when both are over pension age inherits his wife's pension rights just as a widow inherits her husband's rights.

Industrial
Injuries

There are also benefits for widows under the industrial injuries scheme. A pension of £38 is payable for the first 26 weeks of widowhood. A widow may also receive an earnings-related addition if sufficient Class 1 contributions have been paid by her late husband on earnings in excess of the lower earnings limit in the relevant tax year (although this is being phased out). Thereafter, she can receive a pension of £27·70 a week if she was aged 50 at the date of her husband's death, or has dependent children or fulfils certain other conditions; otherwise, she receives £8·15 a week. If she was living apart from her husband, a pension is payable only if she was receiving or entitled to receive at least 25p a week for her maintenance from him.

In addition allowances are paid for children within the child benefit age limits. For widows the rate is £7·50 a week for each child.

Certain other dependants, such as parents and other relatives, may be entitled to pensions, allowances or gratuities.

Sick and Disabled People

There is a large variety of benefits for people unable to work because of sickness or disablement.

Sickness Benefit

Contributory sickness benefit of £20·65 a week is payable for up to 28 weeks. There are allowances of £12·75 for a wife or other adult dependant and £1·25 for each child in addition to child benefit. An earnings-related supplement, which is being phased out, may be payable for up to six months but the total of flat-rate benefit (including increases for dependants) and supplement cannot exceed 85 per cent of the reckonable weekly earnings on which the supplement is based. Where the flat-rate benefit alone exceeds this it is payable in full.

Invalidity
Pension and
Allowance

Invalidity pension of £26 plus £15·60 for a wife and £7·50 for a child, is payable when sickness benefit ends if the beneficiary is still incapable of work. Invalidity allowance (ranging from £1·75 to £5·45 according to age) is paid with the pension to those people who become sick more than five years before retirement age. Invalidity pension consists of a basic pension and an earnings-related pension calculated in the same way as that for retirement pension.

Industrial
Injuries Benefits

Various benefits are payable for injury or disablement caused by an accident at work or a prescribed disease.

Injury benefit for an adult is £23·40 a week plus £12·75 for an adult dependant and £1·25 for each child, in addition to child benefit. It is paid when the employed earner is incapable of work and payment can continue for a maximum of 26 weeks beginning on the date of the accident or development of the disease. A person entitled to sickness benefit who draws injury benefit instead, also receives any earnings-related supplement to which he or she is entitled subject to the 85 per cent limit on total benefit.

When injury benefit ends disablement benefit may be paid if, as the result of the industrial accident or prescribed disease, there is a loss of physical or mental faculty. The amount depends on the extent of the disablement as assessed by a medical board; it varies from £44·30 a week for 100 per cent disablement to £8·90 for 20 per cent disablement, but for disablement of less than 20 per cent a gratuity is normally paid.

In certain circumstances disablement benefit may be supplemented as follows: unemployability supplement at the weekly rate of £26; invalidity allowance according to age (see above); constant attendance allowance of up to £17·70 a week normally, or up to £35·40 in exceptionally severe cases; an allowance of £17·70 a week payable in addition to constant attendance allowance in certain cases of exceptionally severe disablement; a special hardship allowance of up to £17·70 for a person who is unfit to return to his or her regular job or to do work of an equivalent standard; and hospital treatment allowance which raises the disablement benefit to that for a 100 per cent assessment during hospital treatment for the industrial injury. Increases of disablement benefit for dependants may be payable with unemployability supplement. There are benefits for widows and their children (see p 146).

Other Benefits   An attendance allowance of £21·65 may be payable to severely disabled people requiring a great deal of attention by day and at night. A lower rate of £14·45 may be paid to those who need help either by day or at night. A non-contributory invalidity pension of £16·30 is payable to people of working age unable to work and not qualifying for the national insurance invalidity pension; it is also payable to disabled housewives incapable of work and unable to perform their normal household tasks.

A weekly invalid care allowance of £16·30 may be payable to certain categories of people (aged between 16 and pension age) who cannot go out to work because they are caring for a severely disabled relative receiving an attendance allowance.

Physically disabled people unable or virtually unable to walk may be entitled to a mobility allowance of £14·50 a week to help pay their transport costs. People aged between 5 and 65 are eligible to claim the allowance. Those who establish an entitlement before the age of 65 may keep the allowance until the age of 75. An independent organisation called Motability assists those disabled drivers and disabled passengers wanting to use their mobility allowance to obtain a vehicle.

Unemployment Benefit   Unemployment benefit at the same rate as sickness benefit (see p 147) is payable for up to 312 days (not counting Sundays) in any one spell of unemployment. Periods of unemployment benefit which are 6 weeks or less apart and periods of unemployment benefit which are more than 6 weeks apart but which are linked by periods of sickness benefit, maternity allowance or training allowance count as one period. Earnings-related supplement, which is being phased out, may be payable on the same basis as that for sickness benefit. Generally speaking anyone claiming unemployment benefit has to be registered for employment at a local office of the Manpower Services Commission (in Northern Ireland the Department of Manpower Services) which helps people to find jobs.

Death Grant   A death grant is payable on the death of a contributor or a contributor's near relative. It is normally £30 for an adult and a smaller sum for a child.

SUPPLEMENTARY BENEFITS   The supplementary benefits scheme provides a safety net of support for the poorest people, covering more than 3 million beneficiaries at any one time.

Any person aged 16 or over who is not in full-time work and who does not have enough money to live on may be entitled to benefit. It is not normally awarded to people attending school or for their own needs to people involved in industrial disputes (dependants of strikers are covered, however, but under new legislation assessments for benefit assume that strikers are providing £12 a week themselves, either in trade union strike pay or from some other source).

In Northern Ireland a residence condition must also be satisfied. The benefit takes the form of a supplementary allowance for people under the minimum retirement age, and a supplementary pension for those over. The benefit is the amount by which a person's needs exceed his or her available resources, both being defined by rules approved by Parliament. The calculation of needs is based on different amounts for single people and family groups (for blind people there is a special addition) with, in each case, an addition for rent. A higher long-term scale is used for people over pensionable age and for people under pension age who have received supplementary benefit for more than a year without having to register for work. Additions can be made for requirements such as a special diet or extra heating. Certain needy groups receive the heating addition automatically. A single payment may be made to meet an exceptional need. When resources are calculated, most social security benefits are taken into account in full. Part of most other income including part-time earnings, disablement benefit and war widow's pension is ignored, as is the capital value of an owner-occupied house or other capital resources of less than £1,250 (this is being increased to £2,000).

The payment of a supplementary allowance to an able-bodied person of working age may be conditional on registering for work at an unemployment benefit office of the Department of Employment or, in Northern Ireland, the Department of Manpower Services.

The Department of Health and Social Security has a duty to influence people without a settled way of living to lead a more normal life. It provides temporary accommodation for them in 23 reception centres, one of which is administered by a local authority on its behalf. For men who have been unemployed for long periods and who are receiving supplementary allowances, there are 17 re-establishment centres, three of which have residential accommodation, where they are given help to fit them again for work. These provisions do not apply in Northern Ireland.

FAMILY INCOME SUPPLEMENT

Family income supplement is a cash benefit for families with small incomes where the head of the family is in full-time work and where there is at least one dependent child. It is payable when the gross weekly income of a family falls below a prescribed amount, fixed at £67 a week where there is one child plus £7 for each additional child. The weekly rate of the supplement is half the difference between the family's income and the prescribed amount up to a maximum of £17 for a one-child family and this is increased by £1·50 for each additional child. The supplement includes a special addition to help with the cost of heating.

Families receiving the supplement are automatically entitled to a number of other benefits including free school meals, milk and vitamins for expectant mothers and for children under school age, exemption from prescription charges and National Health Service charges for dental treatment and glasses.

A similar, but independent, scheme is run in Northern Ireland.

WAR PENSIONS AND RELATED SERVICES

The war pensions scheme is administered throughout the United Kingdom by the Department of Health and Social Security. Pensions are payable to people disabled as a result of service in the armed forces or from injuries received in the merchant navy or civil service during war-time or to civilians injured by enemy action.

The current basic pension for 100 per cent disablement for a private soldier is £44·30 a week, but the amount varies according to rank and to the degree of disablement. An allowance for dependants is paid in addition to the basic pension. There is a wide range of supplementary allowances, the main ones being for unemployability (£28·80 a week), constant attendance (from £8·85 to £35·40 a week), comforts (£3·85 to £7·70 a week), and lowered standard of occupation (up to £17·70 a week). An age allowance (from £3·10 to £9·60 a week) is payable to disabled pensioners who are aged 65 or over and whose assessment is 40 per cent or more.

Pensions are also paid to war widows and war orphans. The standard rate of pension for widows of private soldiers is £35·30 a week, with additional allowances for their children and, in certain cases, a rent allowance (up to £13·40 a week). There is an additional allowance of £3·45 for widows aged 65 which is increased to £6·90 at the age of 70. Parents or other relatives who were dependent on a person whose death resulted from service in the Forces may receive pensions if they are in financial need.

The Department of Health and Social Security maintains a welfare service for war pensioners, war widows and war orphans. It works closely with many voluntary and ex-Service organisations who give financial aid and personal help to disabled ex-Service men and women and their families.

TAXATION

Social security benefits, other than child, maternity, unemployment, sickness, invalidity, injury or disablement benefit, are included in the taxable income on which income tax is assessed (although some short-term benefits are to be taxed from 1982). On the other hand various income tax reliefs and exemptions are allowed on account of age or liability for the support of dependants. Supplementary benefit, family income supplement, attendance allowances and war disability pensions including supplementary allowances, war widows' pensions and allowances are not taxable.

OTHER WELFARE BENEFITS

In addition to payments provided under the social security legislation, there are a number of other benefits for which people with low incomes may be eligible. These include legal aid and assistance (see p 128), rent rebates and allowances (see p 193), rate rebates (see p 66), exemption from health service charges (see p 132) and free school meals (see p 162).

EUROPEAN COMMUNITY

As part of the Community's efforts to promote the free movement of labour, there are regulations providing for equality of treatment and the protection of social security rights for employed people taking up a job in another member state. The regulations also cover retirement pensioners and other beneficiaries who have been employed, as well as dependants. Benefits affected include child benefit and those for sickness and maternity, unemployment, retirement, invalidity, accidents at work and occupational diseases.

VOLUNTARY SERVICES

There is a long tradition of voluntary service to the community and the partnership between the voluntary and statutory agencies is encouraged. It has been estimated that about 5 million people take part in some voluntary work during the course of a year. Central and local government make grants to voluntary agencies and public authorities plan and carry out their duties taking account of the work of voluntary organisations. Many services are provided for by both local authorities and voluntary agencies, for example, residential care for elderly, disabled, mentally ill and mentally handicapped people and for children. At the same time, however, voluntary provision and community self-help enable local authorities to continue the trend towards community rather than institutional care for elderly, mentally ill and mentally handicapped people. The Government is maintaining the real value of its grants to national voluntary bodies, and financing some experimental work at local level. Tax changes in the financial years 1980–81 and 1981–82 are designed to help the voluntary movement to secure a larger flow of funds.

Co-ordination of government interests in voluntary social service throughout Britain is the responsibility of the Home Office Voluntary Services Unit.

Many voluntary organisations are registered charities, and in England and Wales the Charity Commission, a government agency, gives free advice to trustees of charities, making schemes to modify their purposes or facilitate their administration when necessary. It maintains central and local registers of charities which are open to public inspection, and it investigates and checks abuses, though it has no power to act in the administration of a charity.

Voluntary Organisations

There are thousands of voluntary organisations ranging from national bodies to small individual local groups. Most are members of larger associations or are represented on local or national co-ordinating councils or committees. Some are chiefly concerned with giving personal service, others in the formation of public opinion and exchange of information. Some carry out both functions. They may be staffed by both professional and voluntary workers.

The main voluntary body in England which aims to provide central links between voluntary organisations and official bodies is the National Council for Voluntary Organisations which acts as a resource and development agency for the voluntary sector. It works to extend the involvement of voluntary organisations in dealing with social issues, to protect the interests and independence of voluntary agencies, and to provide them with a range of advice, information and other services. There are also the Scottish Council of Social Service, the Council of Social Service for Wales and the Northern Ireland Council of Social Service, which perform similar functions.

Specialist voluntary organisations concerned with personal and family problems include the family casework agencies like the Family Welfare Association, Family Service Units, and the National Society for the Prevention of Cruelty to Children; marriage guidance centres affiliated to the National Marriage Guidance Council; the National Council of Voluntary Child Care Organisations; the National Council for One Parent Families; Child Poverty Action Group and the Claimants' Union, both of which provide expert advice on social security benefits; and the Samaritans, who help the lonely, the depressed and the suicidal.

Community service of many kinds is given by young people; this is often channelled through national and local organisations such as Community Service Volunteers, Task Force, Scouts and Girl Guides.

Voluntary service to the sick and disabled is given by—among others— the British Red Cross Society, St John Ambulance, the Women's Royal Voluntary Service and the Leagues of Hospital Friends. Societies which help people with particular disabilities and difficulties include the Royal National Institute for the Blind, the Royal National Institute for the Deaf, MIND (National Association for Mental Health), the National Society for Mentally Handicapped Children, the Spastics Society, Alcoholics Anonymous, Age Concern, Help the Aged and their equivalents in Scotland and Northern Ireland.

National organisations whose work is specifically religious in inspiration include the Salvation Army, the Church Army, Toc H, the Committee on Social Service of the Church of Scotland, the Church of England Children's Society, the Church of England Council for Social Aid, the Young Men's

Christian Association, the Young Women's Christian Association, the Catholic Marriage Advisory Council and the Jewish Welfare Board.

A wide range of voluntary personal service is given by the Women's Royal Voluntary Service, which brings 'meals on wheels' to housebound invalids and old people, provides flatlets and residential clubs for the elderly, helps with family problems and assists in hospitals and clinics, and work in emergencies.

Some 825 Citizens Advice Bureaux give explanation and advice to citizens who are in doubt about their rights or who do not know about the State or voluntary services available. There are law centres (see p 128) and housing advisory centres in some areas.

The Volunteer Centre   The Volunteer Centre is a national voluntary organisation and a centre for information and research on voluntary work, established with the aid of a government grant. There are many local volunteer bureaux.

EQUAL OPPORTUNITIES FOR WOMEN

The Sex Discrimination Act 1975, makes discrimination between men and women unlawful in employment, education, training and the provision of housing, goods, facilities and services. Discriminatory advertisements which breach the Act are also unlawful. The Act applies to both direct and indirect sex discrimination: direct discrimination is treating one person less favourably than another on the grounds of his or her sex; indirect discrimination is applying a condition or requirement which, though apparently neutral, in effect acts significantly to the disadvantage of one sex and cannot be justified on its merits. Northern Ireland has similar legislation.

Under the Equal Pay Act 1970 (and corresponding legislation in Northern Ireland), women are entitled to equal pay with men when doing work that is the same or broadly similar or work which has been given an equal value under a job evaluation scheme.

The Equal Opportunities Commission was established to enforce both Acts and promote equal opportunities between the sexes. There is a separate commission in Northern Ireland.

Preventing Sex Discrimination   Employers must not discriminate against a man or woman because of his or her sex. This applies to recruitment, promotion, the provision of benefits, dismissals and training. It is also unlawful for employers to discriminate against a person on grounds of marriage. There are a limited number of exceptions including employment in private households and employment in jobs where a person's sex is a 'genuine occupational qualification', such as acting. Employers of not more than five people are exempt from the Act.

Co-educational schools, colleges and universities may not discriminate in the provision of facilities or in their admissions. Single-sex establishments are permissible, however, and there are arrangements for such institutions to move gradually towards co-education if they wish.

It is unlawful to discriminate against a man or a woman in the sale or letting of land, houses, flats and business premises. The law applies equally to public and private housing, furnished and unfurnished. The Act does not apply to lettings in a small dwelling occupied by the landlord or a near relative.

Discrimination is also unlawful in the provision of goods, facilities and services. For example, banks, building societies or finance companies must not refuse to give credit, mortgages or loans to women on terms that would be applied to men. Exceptions include services provided in certain special care establishments such as hospitals; places used for religious purposes where religious susceptibilities would be offended; places where it is necessary to preserve decency or privacy; competitive sports in which for reasons of physique women would be at a disadvantage; and life insurance and similar matters where risk is assessed on reliable actuarial or other data.

It is unlawful to publish or place advertisements which contravene the Sex Discrimination Act whether for jobs, goods, facilities or services.

Complaints Complaints of discrimination may be brought before the county courts in England and Wales or the sheriff courts in Scotland, except for complaints concerning employment, which are dealt with by industrial tribunals (see p 338). Complaints concerning State educational establishments must first be made to the relevant Secretary of State before they can be brought before a court. Only the Equal Opportunities Commission is responsible for handling complaints about discriminatory advertisements and can bring proceedings in matters concerning advertising. Where necessary, legal advice or assistance, or legal aid if the case is taken to court, are available for complainants with low incomes (see p 128). Legal aid is not available for industrial tribunal cases but applicants can receive advice and assistance.

Equal Opportunities Commission The Equal Opportunities Commission was established to enforce the Sex Discrimination Act and the Equal Pay Act. Its aims are to eliminate sex discrimination and to promote equal opportunities. The Commission advises people of their rights under both Acts, and in certain circumstances, may give financial help or assist individuals to prepare and conduct a case before a court or tribunal. It may also attempt to secure a settlement. The Commission has power to conduct formal investigations and, if satisfied that practices are unlawful, can issue non-discrimination notices requiring discriminatory practices to stop. For certain formal investigations, the Commission has the power to require a person to give information and to attend hearings to give evidence. In addition it keeps the workings of the Sex Discrimination and Equal Pay Acts under review and may submit proposals for amending them to the Home Secretary and the Secretary of State for Employment respectively.

RACE RELATIONS

After the 1950s considerable numbers of people entered Britain from Commonwealth countries in the West Indies, Asia and Africa to settle and take up employment, and they make an important contribution to the economy and the public services. In 1978 the population of New Commonwealth[1] and Pakistani ethnic origin was estimated at some 1·9 million (about 3·5 per cent of the total population) of whom some 40 per cent were born in Britain. Nearly three-quarters live in the south-east and the west Midlands. Although, as Commonwealth citizens, they have full political and civic rights, many suffer from social and economic disadvantages. This can be partly attributed to the fact that many initially lack the skills needed in an industrial society and occupy low-status jobs in poor environments of the older towns. Unemployment is relatively high among young people in some ethnic minority communities. Another factor, the extent of which is difficult to determine, is that of racial discrimination.

---

[1] All Commonwealth countries except Canada, Australia and New Zealand and including, therefore, people from Cyprus, Malta and Gibraltar.

The difficulties experienced by residents of the older inner city areas are being alleviated by continuous social programmes which benefit the whole community and others which are directed at areas of special social need. Additional teachers have been appointed to schools with ethnic minorities and government grants are available to local authorities with substantial ethnic minority groups towards the salaries of extra staff, such as interpreters, health visitors and helpers in schools and community homes. Language teaching is recognised to be of prime importance in schools and schemes arranged for adults include classes at their place of work and language groups run by voluntary organisations. The welfare of ethnic minorities and good relations between minorities and the local community are promoted by community relations councils and other voluntary bodies. In recognition of the special problems and tensions that can arise between the police and ethnic minorities, police community liaison work is seen as having particular importance. Policies for promoting equality of opportunity among ethnic minorities are pursued against a background of legislation designed to protect them from discrimination.

Race Relations Act

The Race Relations Act 1976 makes discrimination unlawful on grounds of colour, race or ethnic or national origin in the provision of goods, facilities and services, in employment, training and related matters, in education, in housing and in advertising. It strengthened legislation passed in 1968 which, in turn, widened the scope of the first race relations legislation enacted in 1965.

The 1976 Act brought the law against racial discrimination into line with that against sex discrimination (see above), and gave complainants direct access to civil courts and, in the case of employment complaints, to industrial tribunals. Complaints concerning educational establishments are made first to the appropriate education minister. The remedies available from the courts are damages, a declaration of rights or an injunction. Industrial tribunals are also able to declare the rights of parties, make recommendations or award compensation. Legal aid (see p 128) is available to complainants with low incomes.

The 1976 Act also strengthened the criminal law on incitement to racial hatred. A prosecution made under the Act may only be brought in England and Wales by, or with the consent of, the Attorney General.

Commission for Racial Equality

The Commission for Racial Equality works towards the elimination of discrimination and to promote equality of opportunity and good relations between different racial groups. It has powers to investigate unlawful discriminatory practices and to issue non-discrimination notices, enforceable in the courts, requiring that such practices should cease. The Commission has sole responsibility for those contraventions of the 1976 Act which do not result in a particular person being discriminated against, for example, discriminatory advertisements and instructions; it may also assist individuals with their complaints. It has an important educational role and has power to issue codes of practice in employment.

The Commission supports and co-ordinates the work of some 110 local community relations councils operating in areas with significant minority groups; their purpose is to promote harmonious community relations. It makes grants towards the salaries of community relations officers and towards special projects which help to improve community relations or to assist members of the ethnic minorities. Particular encouragement is given to self-help schemes run by members of the minority communities.

7 Education

British education aims to develop fully the abilities of individuals, both young and old, for their own benefit and that of society as a whole. The aim has assumed a new importance in an age of rapid technological change. Compulsory schooling for children takes place between the ages of 5 and 16, although some provision is made for those under 5, and many pupils remain at school beyond the minimum leaving age. Post-school education (mainly at universities, polytechnics and further education colleges) is organised flexibly to provide a wide range of opportunities for academic and vocational education and continuing study throughout life.

For many years British education has been characterised by change, and much of the post-1945 period has also been marked by growth: large increases in the number of pupils, the expansion of higher educational opportunities, and increased expenditure. Although the process of change continues, recent years have seen increasing reassessment and consolidation as well as a number of other significant developments, including the beginning of a substantial drop in the number of school children following a fall in the birth rate, a slowing down in the demand for higher education, and the need, because of economic circumstances, to reduce public expenditure. The number of primary school children has already fallen sharply, and the decline in numbers is about to affect secondary schools. It has led to a reduced demand for new teachers (although there is still a need for more teachers of certain specialised subjects) and the teacher training system has been reorganised to cope with the new situation while retaining flexibility for future expansion.

Policies

The Government's education policies have been formulated to increase parental choice and involvement in school organisation, to allow local authorities to organise publicly maintained schools according to local needs and to take up places for pupils at independent schools where appropriate, and to assist children from less well-off homes to benefit from attendance at certain non-maintained schools. Proposals are being developed in England and Wales for national agreement on a framework for the school curriculum, and for the replacement of the dual system of examinations taken at about the age of 16 by a single examination. Other proposals include the improvement of special educational facilities for handicapped children, and the provision of better vocational education and training for the 16-to-18 age group. It is recognised that co-operation between education and industry can help the young to acquire the skills necessary to allow Britain to maintain its position as one of the world's leading exporters of manufactured goods. Many organisations already work to improve contacts between educational institutions and industry, and further links are being encouraged, especially locally. A four-year programme to give schools and colleges a better understanding of micro-electronics is being planned to serve as a means of equipping young people with the skills they need to exploit the economic potential of this technology.

About 80 per cent of education expenditure is incurred by local authorities, to which grants are made by central government in support of services, with the authorities planning their own spending according to local needs and circumstances. Support for the universities and certain other higher education institutions, and grants to students, account for most of the direct expenditure by central government. Spending on education (some £9,542 million in 1979, 5·8 per cent of the gross domestic product) amounts to more than 11 per cent of all public expenditure, but a reduction is planned in the years to 1983–84 taking into account the declining number of school children and considerable savings in the provision of school meals and milk. In spite of cuts in expenditure, government policy is to maintain and improve the quality of education.

Administration Educational responsibilities are devolved in varying degrees to ministers of the four countries of Britain. The Secretary of State for Education and Science is responsible for all aspects of education in England, and for the Government's relations with and support for universities throughout Great Britain. (He is also responsible for civil science, p 44.) The Secretaries of State for Wales, Scotland and Northern Ireland have full responsibility in their respective countries for non-university education; they are consulted about (but do not carry formal responsibility for) education in universities and civil science.

Administration of publicly provided schools and further education is decentralised. Responsibilities are divided between the central government departments (the Department of Education and Science, the Welsh Office, the Scottish Education Department, and the Department of Education for Northern Ireland), local education authorities (education and library boards in Northern Ireland), and various voluntary organisations. The relationship between these bodies is based on consultation and co-operation.

Local education authorities are responsible for the provision of school education and most post-school education outside the universities, and provide grants to students proceeding to higher education (including universities). They employ the teachers and other staff, provide and maintain the buildings, supply equipment and materials and decide local policy. In Scotland the central institutions which provide most vocational further education to degree level, and colleges of education which provide teacher training, are administered by independent governing bodies. Three of the central institutions are financed by the Department of Agriculture and Fisheries for Scotland; all the remaining central institutions and all the colleges of education are financed directly by the Scottish Education Department which also pays grants to students on advanced courses. In Northern Ireland the Ulster Polytechnic (an institution of higher education) is likewise administered by an independent board of governors and is financed directly by the Department of Education for Northern Ireland. Colleges of education are controlled by the Department or voluntary agencies.

Universities are autonomous, with governing bodies appointed according to the terms of individual charters or statutory provisions. The Government exercises its responsibilities in relation to the universities and provides financial help to them through the University Grants Committee (see p 163).

SCHOOLS Parents are required by law to see that their children receive efficient full-time education, at school or elsewhere, between the ages of 5 and 16.

Over 11 million children attend Britain's 38,500 schools. Most receive free education financed from public funds, but a small proportion (very roughly 6 per cent) attend schools wholly independent of public financial support.

Boys and girls are taught together in most primary schools and in an increasing number of secondary schools. Over 80 per cent of pupils in maintained secondary schools in England and Wales and over 50 per cent in Northern Ireland attend mixed schools. In Scotland nearly all secondary schools are mixed. Most independent schools for younger children are co-educational, but the majority providing secondary education are single-sex.

Management

Schools supported from public funds are of two main kinds in England and Wales: county schools and voluntary schools. County schools are provided and maintained by local education authorities wholly out of public funds. Voluntary schools have mostly been established by religious denominations; they are wholly maintained from public funds but the governors of some types of voluntary school contribute to capital costs. Nearly a third of the 30,400 schools maintained by local education authorities in England and Wales are voluntary schools: of the remainder some 5,760 are Church of England, 2,640 are Roman Catholic, and 330 belong to other groups and religious denominations. Each publicly maintained school has a governing body, which includes governors appointed by the local education authority. The Education Act 1980 provides for the wider representation of parents and teachers on school governing bodies: it is proposed that all schools should have at least two parent and two teacher governors normally elected by parents and teachers. In Scotland most of the schools supported from public funds are provided by education authorities and are known as public schools (in England this term is used for a type of independent school, see p 158).

In Northern Ireland there are two main categories of school: voluntary schools which are mainly under Roman Catholic management receiving grants of up to 85 per cent of capital costs and up to 100 per cent of running costs; and controlled schools owned and managed by the area education and library boards and having all their expenditure met from public funds. Government policy is to encourage integration between Protestant and Roman Catholic school education where there is a local desire for it, but it is not the intention to enforce integrated education against the wishes of local communities.

Fees

In England and Wales no fees are charged to parents of children attending maintained schools, and books and equipment are free. In Scotland, education authorities may charge fees where this can be done without prejudice to the adequate provision of free school education (although no authorities make use of this power). In Northern Ireland no fees are charged to parents of children attending grant-aided schools, with the exception of grammar schools, where a small proportion of pupils are admitted on a fee-paying basis.

Nursery and Primary Schools

Successive Governments have expanded nursery education within the constraints of limited resources, and by 1979 the number of children in nursery schools or nursery classes in England had risen to over 210,000. In addition about 218,000 children under five were attending infants' classes in primary schools. This means that over half of four-year-olds and almost a fifth of three-year-olds were receiving education in publicly-maintained schools. In addition many children attend informal pre-school playgroups organised by parents and voluntary bodies.

Compulsory education begins at five when children in England and Wales go to infant schools or departments; at seven they go on to junior schools or departments. The usual age of transfer from primary to secondary schools is 11 in England, Wales and Northern Ireland but a number of local authorities in England have established 'first' schools for pupils aged 5 to 8 or 10 and 'middle' schools covering various age ranges between 9 and 14. In Scotland, the primary schools take children from 5 to 12, normally having infant classes for children under 7, although in a few areas there are separate infant schools.

Secondary Schools

The publicly maintained system of education aims to give all children an education suited to their particular abilities. Over 85 per cent of the maintained secondary school population in England and Wales attend some 3,600 comprehensive schools which take pupils without reference to ability or aptitude and provide a wide range of secondary education for all or most of the children of a district. They can be organised in a number of ways including schools that take the full secondary school age-range from 11 to 18; middle schools whose pupils move on to senior comprehensive schools at 12, 13 or 14, leaving at 16 or 18; and schools with an age-range of 11 or 12 to 16 combined with a sixth-form or 'tertiary' college for pupils over 16. Most other children receive secondary education in 'grammar' and 'secondary modern' schools to which they are allocated after selection procedures at the age of 11; in 1979 there were 261 grammar schools in England and Wales and 547 secondary modern schools. Under the Education Act 1980 the compulsion on local education authorities to reorganise their schools on comprehensive lines has been removed.

Under the same Act parents' wishes must be taken into account as fully as possible in the choice of schools for their children, and they must receive full information about the schools available and have open to them an effective channel of appeal at a local level. The Act also provides for the establishment of an assisted-places scheme devised to help (by means of a system of fees remission related to parental income) children of high ability from less well-off homes to attend independent schools belonging to the scheme. The scheme will operate in England and Wales from 1981.

Scottish secondary education is almost completely organised according to the comprehensive principle and almost all pupils in education authority secondary schools are in schools with a non-selective intake. The majority of schools are six-year comprehensive schools. Because of local circumstances there are some comprehensive schools at which courses may extend to four years or less; pupils may transfer at the end of their second or fourth years to a six-year comprehensive school. Consultations are taking place about involving parents in the choice of their children's schools and there are plans to establish an assisted-places scheme similar to that in England and Wales. Northern Ireland secondary education is organised largely along selective lines.

Independent Schools

Independent schools receive no grants from public funds but all are open to inspection and must register with the appropriate government education department which has power to require them to remedy any objectionable features in their premises, accommodation or instruction and to exclude any person regarded as unsuitable to teach in or to be the proprietor of a school. In default, the appropriate Secretary of State can, in effect, close a school, but schools have a right of appeal to an independent tribunal against any of the requirements. There are about 2,400 registered independent schools.

Independent schools cater for pupils of all ages. The largest and most important of them are the public schools,[1] which accept pupils at about 12 or 13

---

[1] 'Public schools' are usually taken to mean those schools in membership of the Headmasters' Conference, the Governing Bodies Association or the Governing Bodies of Girls' Schools Association. They should not be confused with the State-supported public schools in Scotland.

years of age usually on the basis of a fairly demanding examination. There are about 460 public schools in England and Wales, most of them single-sex (about half of them for girls) and at least partly boarding; but there are some co-educational schools, and certain boys' schools have recently begun to admit girls direct to their senior forms. Combined tuition and boarding fees in the public schools are on average £2,600 a year, but some of this may be remitted for children winning competitive scholarships. Local education authorities in England and Wales may assist with the payment of fees for children at independent and other non-maintained schools. A number of preparatory schools prepare children for entry to the public schools.

Special Education

There are some 2,000 separate special schools (both day and boarding) for several categories of disability: the blind, partially sighted, deaf, partially hearing, delicate, educationally subnormal (mentally handicapped in Scotland), epileptic, maladjusted, physically handicapped, autistic and those suffering from speech defects. There is no separate category for the delicate in Scotland.

For a number of years the general trend has been increasingly to provide special educational treatment in ordinary schools where this is in the educational interest of the particular child and the nature of his or her disability permits. Legislation yet to be brought into effect in England and Wales provides for such children to be educated in such schools whenever practicable and compatible with efficient teaching. There are a number of new arrangements whereby varying degrees of integration are being achieved between special schools and ordinary primary and secondary schools.

In 1978 the Warnock Committee report (see Bibliography) recommended that the concept of special education appropriate to defined categories of bodily or mental handicap should be replaced by the broader notion of the special educational needs of individual children. This would cover not only children with physical or mental disabilities but also those with emotional or behavioural disorders and those with significant learning difficulties. The Government proposes to introduce a new framework for special education substantially along the lines recommended in the report.

Teachers

Teachers in publicly maintained schools are appointed by local education authorities or school governing bodies. There are more than 500,000 teachers (including the full-time equivalent of part-time teachers) in publicly maintained and assisted schools in Britain and the pupil/teacher ratio is about 18 to 1. Teachers must hold qualifications approved by the appropriate education department. Their salaries are determined by nationally negotiated scales, taking account of qualifications, responsibilities and experience.

The Curriculum

In England and Wales the secular curriculum in maintained schools is the responsibility of the local education authority, or, in the case of secondary schools, of the schools' governors. In practice, responsibility is largely devolved upon head teachers and their staff. In Wales, the Welsh language is taught and is used as either the main or secondary medium of teaching in some schools. Her Majesty's Inspectors of Schools are responsible to the Secretary of State for Education and Science and the Secretary of State for Wales for the inspection of all schools, including independent schools. They review and report on the content and value of the education provided and advise local education authorities, schools and the Government. Local education authorities also employ inspectors or advisers to guide them on maintained schools. Institutions concerned with the education and training of teachers are additional sources of advice. Curriculum materials and further guidance and encouragement for school-based research and development are available to teachers through the Schools Council for Curriculum and Examinations. The Council, an independent body representative of all concerned with education, acts as an advisory body and sponsors and carries out research and development work on curricula, teaching methods and examinations in primary and secondary schools. The Schools Committee for Wales carries out similar activities. In many cases there are Teachers' Centres (some 500 in England and Wales) at which teachers meet for curriculum development work, discussion and in-service training.

In Scotland the function of Her Majesty's Inspectors is in general the same as in England and Wales; the content and balance of the curriculum is kept under continuous review by the Consultative Committee on the Curriculum. Provision is made, where appropriate, for the teaching of Gaelic. Northern Ireland has a Schools Curriculum Committee which works in close liaison with the Schools Council; the Inspectorate of the Department of Education helps and advises teachers and inspects and evaluates the work of all schools.

The content, balance and breadth of the school curriculum, and the extent to which it meets national needs by preparing pupils for working life, has been the subject of continuing public interest in recent years. Following the review of local authority arrangements for the school curriculum in England and Wales the subjects considered as essential to every pupil's education were set out in the consultative document *A Framework for the School Curriculum* (see Bibliography). A final version, after further discussion, will contain guidance for local education authorities and schools. In Scotland consideration is being given to similar proposals for a core of essential subjects in secondary schools.

Religious Education in Schools

In England and Wales by law all children in county or voluntary schools receive religious instruction and take part in a daily corporate act of worship unless their parents choose otherwise. In county schools, and sometimes in voluntary schools, religious instruction of a non-denominational character is given which may include the study of comparative religions. In all kinds of voluntary schools there is opportunity for denominational instruction. In Scotland, subject to safeguards for the individual conscience, religious instruction must be given, but the content is determined by education authorities and by the schools themselves. Roman Catholic children generally have their own schools. In controlled schools in Northern Ireland clergy have a right of access which may be used for denominational instruction; in voluntary schools corporate worship and religious education are controlled by the management authorities.

Educational Standards

There is a general concern that there should be a coherent and soundly-based means of assessing pupils, schools, and the educational system as a whole.

The Assessment of Performance Unit of the Department of Education and Science, which promotes the development of methods for assessing and monitoring the performance of children at school, has commissioned research teams to develop tests suitable for national monitoring of English language, mathematics and science at the end of the primary stage of education and again at the age of 15. The first national survey of mathematics performance of pupils aged 11 has been completed and the Unit is undertaking surveys in mathematics at 15-plus and in English language and science at both primary and secondary level. It is also looking into the possibility of monitoring performance in foreign languages and other subjects. The Unit is also devising tests to set national standards in reading, writing, and arithmetic.

Educational Aids

In the majority of schools, teachers and pupils make use of a range of educational aids to assist the processes of teaching and learning. In addition to printed resources, these also include audio-visual aids of every kind which may be commercially made or produced in a resource centre, either within the school or in one serving all the schools in a local education authority's area. Educational broadcasting is of major importance. Almost all schools can receive radio and television programmes. Flexibility in use is increased when these are recorded; most educational radio programmes are used in this way as are an increasing number of educational television programmes. In addition the British Broadcasting Corporation produces a large number of radiovision programmes which, in effect, are low cost tape/slide units. Teachers' notes and pupils' pamphlets accompany many broadcast series. Each year more than 500 hours of school radio and 600 hours of school television are transmitted by the BBC and the independent broadcasting companies.

The Council for Educational Technology for the United Kingdom and the Educational Foundation for Visual Aids, among their other functions, offer advice on the use of audio-visual aids. In Scotland this function is undertaken by the Scottish Council for Educational Technology.

Computers are increasingly used to assist learning, to plan timetables, and in the management of courses.

Secondary School Examinations

There is no national school-leaving examination in England and Wales, but secondary school pupils may attempt examinations, in various subjects, leading to the Certificate of Secondary Education (CSE) or the General Certificate of Education (GCE). Both the CSE and the GCE Ordinary ('O') level are designed for pupils completing five years of secondary schooling and are normally taken at the age of 16. The GCE Advanced ('A') level is normally taken after a further two years' study. The CSE is controlled by 14 regional examining boards while the GCE examinations are conducted by eight independent examining boards, most of them connected with a university. Entries for GCE examinations are accepted from candidates at further education establishments and from candidates entering privately.

The highest grade in the CSE is widely accepted as being of the same standard as at least grade C at GCE 'O' level and these are the qualifying grades for entry to further education and training. The 'A' level examination is the standard for entrance to higher education, university and to many forms of professional training. The examination system has been widely discussed for some years by the Government, the Schools Council and others. The Government has proposed that the present system should be simplified by replacing the 'O' level and CSE with a single examination, and is reviewing suggestions for the introduction of an additional examination, the Certificate of Extended Education (CEE), to be taken after a one-year course by those who stay on in full-time education after 16 but for whom 'A' levels are not suitable.

In Scotland examinations are conducted by the Scottish Certificate of Education Examination Board. School pupils in the fourth year of secondary courses sit an examination at 16 years for the Ordinary grade of the Scottish Certificate of Education, and pupils in the fifth or sixth year are presented for the Higher grade. Passes at the Higher grade are the basis for entry to university or professional training. For those who have completed their main studies at the Higher grade but wish to continue their studies in particular subjects there is a Certificate of Sixth Year Studies. Proposals have been made for the development of courses and examinations suitable for less able pupils who do not take, or achieve a low grade, in the 'O' grade examination as well as courses more challenging than 'O' grade for particularly able pupils. These are expected to be introduced from 1986.

In Northern Ireland candidates may take the Northern Ireland General Certificate of Education or the Northern Ireland Certificate of Secondary Education, which are equivalent to those examinations in England and Wales.

The International Baccalaureate, which is offered to sixth formers by several educational institutions in Britain, leads either to a diploma, or to separate subject certificates, the latter being recognised for admission to higher education in Britain and many other countries.

Health and Welfare of School Children

Physical education, including organised games, is part of the curriculum of all schools. Those receiving financial assistance from public funds must have the use of a playing field, and most secondary schools have a gymnasium.

The Department of Health and Social Security is responsible for the medical inspection of school children and for advice and treatment of specific medical and dental problems associated with children of school age.

In keeping with the Government's policy of reducing the level of spending in the non-educational section of the education budget, the statutory duty on education authorities to provide school meals and milk has been relaxed. Local education authorities are given discretion to decide what milk, meals or other refreshment to provide at their schools, and what charges to make. Provision has to be made free of charge, however, for pupils from families receiving certain social security benefits. Those local authorities providing milk for school children at a reduced price are eligible for a European Community subsidy. Under certain conditions the authorities must provide free school transport, and they have discretionary powers to assist financially in the provision of transport for pupils between their home and school.

School Building

Local education authorities and voluntary bodies (in Scotland education authorities) are responsible, under the general supervision of the central departments, for providing the schools and other buildings needed for public education in their areas. The central departments determine the maximum size of the authorities' individual programmes in the light of national priorities; they also offer guidance to authorities in various ways.

Since 1945 an extensive school building programme has been carried out resulting in the completion of about 16,500 new schools in Britain, together with extensions, alterations and remodelling of existing schools; over 9 million new places have been provided.

Government grants are normally available to help with the costs of building new voluntary aided schools and with alterations and external repairs to existing aided schools.

The school building programme has provided for new ideas and methods in design and construction. Industrialised building techniques have been widely adopted. New schools are designed to be light, airy and colourful as well as to have enough teaching area and space for auxiliary activities and outdoor games.

POST-SCHOOL EDUCATION

Education for those who have left school is organised very flexibly. It is available to everyone above school-leaving age, is provided at all levels and may be part-time or full-time, vocational or non-vocational.

More than a third of young people receive some form of post-school education, compared with a fifth in 1965. Many courses lead to recognised qualifications, varying from degrees and professional qualifications through technician level to qualifications similar to those obtained before leaving school. Further education is a broad term usually taken to refer to all post-school education outside the universities. Higher education (postgraduate, first-degree and similar level work) is provided at universities and on advanced courses at polytechnics and other establishments of higher and further education. Adults of every age make extensive use of facilities for the educational and cultural leisure activities included under the term 'adult education'.

Institutions   The principal institutions of post-school education are the 45 universities (see p 164); the 30 polytechnics in England and Wales and the 14 Scottish central institutions; the Ulster Polytechnic in Northern Ireland; and well over 800 other colleges which are maintained or assisted from public funds, some of which provide a very wide range of courses, while others concentrate on particular subjects. All these institutions offer courses leading to recognised qualifications, while their premises as well as school and other premises are often also used for adult education.

Apart from the universities, most establishments of post-school education are maintained and administered by the local education authorities. However, the Scottish central institutions, the Scottish colleges of education and the Ulster Polytechnic do not come under the control of the education authorities, but are managed by independent governing bodies, representing the authorities and other appropriate interests.

In addition, there are many independent specialist establishments, such as secretarial colleges, correspondence colleges and colleges teaching English as a foreign language; a number of voluntary bodies and private undertakings providing cultural and general education, sometimes with financial or other assistance from local education authorities; and a large number of other education and training schemes run by public or private organisations.

Finance   Most establishments for post-school education are either maintained or assisted from public funds. Where industrial training is provided by a college, the charges are the responsibility of the employer, and broadly reflect the economic cost of provision.

Although largely dependent on public funds, the universities are guaranteed as autonomous institutions by a special financial arrangement. The University Grants Committee is appointed by the Secretary of State for Education and Science to advise on State aid to the universities; its members are drawn from the academic and business worlds. This body acts as a link and buffer between the Government from which it receives a block grant and the universities to which it allocates this grant. So, although the Government is responsible for financing over 90 per cent of universities' expenditure (universities or colleges within universities may have their own investments, endowments and budgets), it does not control their work or teaching. The Open University (see p 165) is financed directly by the Department of Education and Science; in Northern Ireland government grants are made direct to the universities by the Department of Education.

Students   Some 845,000 students take full-time and sandwich courses (courses where substantial periods of full-time study alternate with periods of supervised experience on a relevant job) at universities and major establishments of further education in Britain (1977–78 figures). Of these about 288,000 are at universities while another 233,000 follow advanced courses outside universities, at colleges of further and higher education, polytechnics and Scottish central institutions. More than 324,000 take non-advanced courses, most of them studying for recognised vocational or educational qualifications.

Additionally, there are over 3·3 million part-time students, over 600,000 of whom are released by their employers for further education during working hours. Many of the remainder take part in adult education classes (see p 167).

Student Grants   Many full-time students are helped by awards from public funds. These awards are mandatory for most students taking first-degree and other comparable courses who qualify under national rules. (Grants for other courses may be given at the discretion of a local education authority.) They are assessed to cover tuition fees and a maintenance grant, but where parents can afford to contribute towards the cost this is taken into account. In England and Wales these awards are made by local education authorities up to first-degree level; in Scotland by the Scottish Education Department; and in Northern Ireland by the Department of Education for Northern Ireland. Grants for postgraduate study and research are offered by the education departments and the research councils. In all, about 90 per cent of students on full-time and sandwich advanced courses receive help from public funds. Some scholarships are available from endowments and from particular industries or companies.

Higher Education   Following rapid expansion during the last two decades higher education is moving into a period of consolidation. Some 8 per cent of 18-year-olds enter courses of higher education. About 522,000 full-time and sandwich course students and about 246,000 part-time students follow courses at a variety of institutions.

The expansion was achieved by creating new universities; by developing a number of colleges into universities; and by establishing 30 polytechnics also specialising in advanced work. Colleges of education specialising in teacher training also experienced rapid expansion but, more recently, because of the fall in pupil numbers, some of these have been closed while many have been amalgamated with other colleges leading, in some cases, to the development of institutes or colleges of higher education providing a range of courses.

The number of students taking full-time and sandwich courses (excluding teacher training) is evenly divided between science-based and arts-based courses; although this is not a matter for explicit government policy, it has been the subject of much public discussion.

Universities   There are 45 universities in Britain, including the Open University, compared with 17 in 1945.

The English universities are: Aston (Birmingham), Bath, Birmingham, Bradford, Bristol, Brunel (London), Cambridge, City (London), Durham, East Anglia, Essex, Exeter, Hull, Keele, Kent at Canterbury, Lancaster, Leeds, Leicester, Liverpool, London, Loughborough, Manchester, Newcastle upon Tyne, Nottingham, Oxford, Reading, Salford, Sheffield, Southampton, Surrey, Sussex, Warwick, and York. The London Graduate School of Business Studies and the Manchester Business School also have university status. The federated University of Wales includes five university colleges, the Welsh National School of Medicine, and the University of Wales Institute of Science and Technology. The Scottish universities are: Aberdeen, Dundee, Edinburgh, Glasgow, Heriot-Watt (Edinburgh), St. Andrews, Stirling, and

Strathclyde (Glasgow). In Northern Ireland there are the Queen's University of Belfast, and the New University of Ulster in Coleraine.

The universities of Oxford and Cambridge date from the twelfth and thirteenth centuries, and the Scottish universities of St. Andrews, Glasgow, Aberdeen and Edinburgh from the fifteenth and sixteenth centuries. All the other universities were founded in the nineteenth or twentieth centuries.

Admission to universities is by examination or by selection. Prospective candidates for nearly all the universities apply for places through the Universities Central Council on Admissions. The only students to apply directly are applicants to the Open University and British candidates who apply only to the universities of Glasgow, Aberdeen and Strathclyde.

Most students at universities are undergraduates: in 1978–79 there were about 288,000 full-time university students in Britain, including over 49,000 postgraduates. Just under a half lived in colleges and halls of residence, over one-third were in privately rented accommodation, and the remainder lived at home. There were about 32,700 full-time university teachers paid wholly from university funds. The ratio of staff to students was about one to nine, one of the most favourable in the world.

Except at the Open University, first-degree courses are mainly full-time and usually last three or four years, though medical and veterinary courses usually require five or six. In spite of the extension of facilities for obtaining a degree in other ways the majority of students on full-time first-degree courses are at universities (the non-university sector offers a variety of other higher-education courses besides degrees).

Actual degree titles vary according to the practice of each university; in England and Wales the most common titles for a first degree are Bachelor of Arts (BA) or Bachelor of Science (BSc) and for a second degree Master of Arts (MA), Master of Science (MSc), Doctor of Philosophy (PhD); while in Scotland Master is occasionally used for a first degree in arts subjects. On the other hand, uniformity of standards between universities is promoted by the practice of employing outside examiners for all university examinations, and the general pattern of teaching (a combination of lectures, small group seminars or tutorials with practical classes where necessary) is fairly similar throughout Britain.

In addition to the universities, there is the University College at Buckingham which opened in 1976 and which receives no assistance from public funds. It does not yet award degrees, but its Licence has been accepted as the equivalent of a degree by relevant professional bodies and by other universities for admission to postgraduate studies.

The Open University

The Open University is a non-residential university which provides part-time degrees and other courses, using a combination of television and radio broadcasts, correspondence courses and summer schools, together with a network of viewing and listening centres. No formal academic qualifications are required to register for these courses, but the standards of its degrees are the same as those of other universities. The university's first degree, the BA (Open), is a general degree awarded on a system of credits for each course completed; the average amount of study needed for a full course is estimated at 12 to 14 hours a week. The first courses began in 1971, and in 1980 some 65,000 undergraduate and over 20,000 associate students were following courses. About 5,400 people a year obtain degrees from the Open University—about 1 in 16 of the total for Britain. The university has advised many other countries on the setting-up of similar institutions.

Teacher Training

In order to teach in a maintained school in England and Wales all new entrants to teaching must generally have taken a recognised course of teacher training. Courses are offered by most universities and by a number of polytechnics and other institutions of higher education. The most usual route to a teaching qualification for non-graduates is by way of a three- or four-year course leading to the Bachelor of Education degree; graduates qualify by taking a one-year postgraduate Certificate of Education course.

In response to the change in demand for newly trained teachers, caused by restrictions on public expenditure and the decline in the size of the school population, the number of training places planned for 1981 has been considerably cut. However, because of a shortage of qualified teachers of mathematics, science, craft, design and technology and business studies, special financial arrangements are being offered to encourage suitably qualified mature people to undertake one-year training courses to enter the profession.

In Scotland all teachers in education authority and grant-aided schools must be registered with the General Teaching Council for Scotland and all teachers of academic subjects in secondary schools must be graduates. Training capacity has also been reduced in response to demographic trends but is being maintained in the colleges of education established for this purpose. Courses lead to the award of a Teaching Qualification (Primary Education or Secondary Education). Graduates and holders of specialist diplomas take a one-year course; courses in practical and aesthetic subjects for non-graduates extend to two, three or four years. Most Scottish colleges of education also offer four-year courses leading to the degree of Bachelor of Education.

In Northern Ireland teacher training takes place in the two university education departments, three colleges of education, the Ulster Polytechnic and one technical college. The principal courses are the certificate (three years of study) and the Bachelor of Education (four years) but there are also one-year courses for graduates or holders of other appropriate qualifications.

Increased importance is being given to the continued professional training of practising teachers, and local authorities, universities and colleges provide a variety of in-service courses.

Other Advanced Courses

In 1978–79 about 388,000 students, including part-time students, were taking advanced courses other than in universities in a wide variety of subjects, including architecture, art and design, catering, engineering, natural sciences, social work, business and management studies and teacher training. An increasing proportion of the students were taking courses leading to the awards of the Council for National Academic Awards (CNAA). The Council awards degrees and other academic qualifications, comparable in standard with those granted by universities, to students who successfully complete approved courses of study in establishments which do not award their own degrees. The courses range from science and technology to the arts, social studies, business studies and law, but the proportion of technological, business or other broadly vocational courses is much higher than in universities.

In England and Wales a major contribution to higher education provision is being made by 30 major national institutions named polytechnics. These provide all types of courses (full-time, sandwich and part-time) on a wide range of subjects at all levels, though the trend is towards a concentration on advanced work. In Scotland similar provision is made in 14 central institutions and a few further education colleges managed by education authorities, though there is a tendency for the Scottish establishments to specialise in particular subjects to a greater extent than the English polytechnics. In

Northern Ireland such higher education provision is concentrated within the Ulster Polytechnic.

The institutes and colleges of higher education, formed as the result of the integration of teacher training with the rest of higher education, account for a significant proportion of higher education students, and other further education colleges run some, usually specialised, higher education courses.

Vocational Courses

The British education systems offer facilities for obtaining all types of vocational education and training, to both school leavers and adults, and are notable for providing alternative routes to higher qualifications for those who were unable to continue full-time education after leaving school.

Many broadly vocational educational courses are available at the polytechnics and the 800 or so further and higher education colleges. Some university courses have always had close links with certain industries and professions and these links have grown.

There is a wide variety of courses for people in various trades and occupations, leading to nationally recognised qualifications at the end of courses of up to five years. At technician level the Technician Education Council (TEC) has responsibility for developing a unified system of courses in England, Wales and Northern Ireland and courses leading to TEC certificates and diplomas and higher certificates and diplomas are replacing those formerly available. (TEC higher diplomas approach the standard of a pass degree.) A similar council has been established in Scotland.

Many further education colleges offer courses in shorthand, typing, bookkeeping, and office studies. More advanced business studies are generally available in polytechnics and some other colleges. The further education sector makes a major contribution to management education at all levels (for example, courses for the postgraduate Diploma in Management Studies for those with experience of the work are run by about 75 colleges) and this work in England and Wales is co-ordinated by 12 regional management centres.

Much business education is related to the specialised examination requirements of various professional bodies, and courses leading to them are provided in many colleges, although numbers of candidates seeking such qualifications do so through correspondence courses. There is a Business Education Council with the same functions as the Technician Education Council (see above) in relation to courses of business education. In Scotland, similar courses lead to the Scottish National Certificate, the Scottish Higher National Certificate and the Scottish National Diploma in Business Studies, awarded by the Scottish Business Education Council.

Adult Education

There is increasing recognition that school and even immediately post-school education cannot provide for everyone's needs throughout life, and growing emphasis is put on opportunities for adults to take up both vocational and general education and training. 'Adult education' is a broad term, ranging from the development of the special skills required by rapid change in industry and technology to 'self-fulfilment' through a very wide range of courses. An important element is remedial, allowing people to make up for opportunities missed at school; the adult literacy campaign and programmes to help members of minority ethnic groups are particular examples. Courses are provided by local education authorities, residential colleges, extra-mural departments of universities, the Open University and various other bodies including a number of voluntary organisations. In England and Wales an Advisory Council for

Adult and Continuing Education aims to promote the effective use of resources and consider future policies and priorities; in Scotland a similar function is performed by the Scottish Council for Community Education.

A major part of adult education is financed by local education authorities and provided mainly in their establishments, including schools used for adult evening classes and in some cases in 'community schools' which provide educational, social and cultural opportunities for the wider community. Most courses are part time. In addition local authorities maintain or aid most of the short-term residential colleges or centres (45 in England and Wales) which provide courses lasting between a weekend and a fortnight. Many courses are practical, but there are widespread opportunities for academic study.

Long-term residential colleges (seven in England and Wales, one in Scotland), grant-aided by central government departments, provide courses of one or two years. They aim to provide a liberal education without academic entry tests. Most students admitted are entitled to full maintenance grants.

University extra-mural departments and the Workers' Educational Association (WEA), the largest recognised voluntary body, provide extended part-time courses of more academic studies, though recently the number of short courses organised for special (including vocational) interests has increased. Often the WEA provides the organisation and the universities the tutors.

Many other organisations, national and local, provide many kinds of education and training. Several, such as the National Federation of Women's Institutes and the National Council of Young Men's Christian Associations, receive government grants; others are commercially or privately financed. Some are open to the public as a whole, others to a particular group, such as the disabled or the unemployed, or the employees or members of an organisation.

The National Institute of Adult Education provides a national centre of information, research and publication for adult education, as well as a channel of co-operation and consultation for the many interested organisations in England and Wales. It is mainly financed by contributions from local education authorities and assisted by a grant from the Department of Education and Science. The Institute has a government-funded adult literacy and basic skills unit which covers proficiency in areas such as numeracy and communication, as well as literacy, without which people are impeded in applying or being considered for employment. The Institute's counterpart in Scotland is the Scottish Institute of Adult Education.

Teaching Methods

The general pattern of teaching and learning on full-time courses at universities and colleges remains a mixture of lectures, prescribed or suggested reading, seminars or tutorials, exercises and tests, and, where appropriate, practical work. Modern educational aids, including computers, language laboratories, radio and television for both teaching and research, are widely available at most universities, polytechnics and colleges.

Radio and television programmes, both specifically educational and general, are important media for continuing education and are often linked to a range of supplementary publications, courses and activities. BBC radio study programmes are transmitted in half-hour sessions late at night on weekdays and in a four-hour session on Sunday afternoons. Educational television programmes are shown on Saturday and Sunday mornings, during the day on weekdays with some early and late evening transmissions. Both the BBC and independent television provide programmes which range from basic education and progressive vocational training to domestic, social and craft skills. The BBC also works with the Open University (see p 165), producing and broadcasting radio and television programmes as part of the courses.

EDUCATIONAL
RESEARCH

Research into the theory and practice of education and the organisation of educational services is supported financially by the central government education departments, local education authorities, philanthropic organisations, universities and teachers' associations. Some research is also sponsored at further education institutions and by a few independent organisations. The Schools Council and the Social Science Research Council are important channels for government support.

The major institute undertaking research in education, outside the universities, is the National Foundation for Educational Research in England and Wales, an autonomous body which derives its income mainly from funds received from research projects and from corporate members, including local education authorities, teachers' organisations and universities. It receives an annual grant from the Department of Education and Science. There are also the Scottish Council for Research in Education and the Northern Ireland Council for Educational Research.

EDUCATIONAL
LINKS OVERSEAS

The interchange of ideas and the movement of people between different countries is an important part of education. School children, students, teachers and experts come to Britain from overseas to study and British people work and train overseas. Many opportunities for such movement are the result of international co-operation at government level within the European Community and within the Commonwealth and of educational schemes, courses and professional contacts organised by official and voluntary organisations in Britain. The British aid programme also encourages links between educational institutions in Britain and in developing countries.

British membership of the European Community is creating closer ties with other countries. Both in schools and in the colleges and universities there has been an expansion of interest in European studies and languages. Post-to-post exchange of teachers have been encouraged and exchanges take place between school children and students within the Community. Britain has adhered to the Statute of the European Schools (nine of which have been established throughout the Community including one at Culham, Oxfordshire) to provide school education for children of people employed in Community institutions.

Three aspects of education being given particular attention within the Community are foreign language learning, the language and other educational needs of migrants and their children, and the relationship between education and working life. In addition, studies are being made of policies of admission to higher education in member countries.

Educational
Exchanges

The promotion of cultural and educational relations with other countries is a major concern of the British Council (see p 71), which plays an important part in the management of the British aid programme to education. It recruits teachers for work overseas, organises short visits overseas by British experts and encourages cultural exchange visits. The Council is also responsible for a variety of schemes to promote academic interchange including the Academic Links Scheme between universities and higher education institutions in Britain and Europe; the Commonwealth University Interchange Scheme; the Academic Interchange with Europe Scheme; the Young Research Workers Interchange Scheme; and a number of schemes to encourage exchange between Britain and individual countries overseas.

The Central Bureau for Educational Visits and Exchanges is an independent foundation financed by the Government which has considerable experience over the whole range of educational travel and exchange. It is responsible, with the League for the Exchange of Commonwealth Teachers, for the schemes for the exchange and interchange of teachers with a number of foreign and Commonwealth countries; and for the linking of British schools and local education authorities and their overseas counterparts. The resulting visits and exchanges have been largely related to the teaching of modern languages, but other areas of the curriculum have been involved. The Bureau's publications include a series of annual guides on visits to other countries for students and teachers and a journal published each term, called *Educational Exchange*.

The Inter-University Council for Higher Education Overseas, funded from the official aid programme, encourages co-operation between universities in developing countries and in Britain. It assists with staff recruitment, secondment of staff from British universities, inter-departmental/faculty link schemes, local staff development, short-term teaching and advisory visits and general consultative services.

The Association of Commonwealth Universities promotes co-operation between 222 member universities in 28 Commonwealth countries. It organises meetings of various kinds; provides information (see Bibliography) and academic appointments services; administers the Commonwealth Scholarship and Fellowship Plan in Britain; and generally promotes the movement of academic and administrative staff and of students from one country to another.

The Commonwealth Education Liaison Committee supplements normal direct dealings on education between the countries of the Commonwealth. The United Kingdom Council for Overseas Student Affairs is an independent body serving overseas students and organisations and individuals concerned in student affairs.

Overseas Students in Britain

Students come to Britain from countries throughout the world to study at universities or other educational institutions or for professional training. In the academic year 1978–79 there were about 86,500 students in publicly maintained institutions, some 36,800 at univerisities and about 49,700 at further education establishments. In addition, others (around 38,000 in 1977–78) were training as nurses, for the law, banking and accountancy, for industry or services. About 43 per cent of all overseas students were from the Commonwealth and 79 per cent from developing countries.

Many of those who come to Britain do so for advanced training. Of the 50,000 students enrolled for full-time postgraduate study or research at British universities in 1978, 38 per cent came from overseas. Of those working for a master's degree 46 per cent came from overseas and of those working for a doctorate 35 per cent. British universities, polytechnics and other further education establishments have built up their reputation overseas by providing tuition of the highest standards, maintaining low staff to student ratios, and adopting courses and qualifications to meet present-day and possible future needs. First degree courses tend to be shorter in Britain than overseas (three years is the average length).

The majority of overseas students pay their own fees and expenses or hold awards from their own governments. In addition, over 5,700 overseas students were fully supported in 1979 under British technical co-operation with developing countries. From the academic year 1980–81 new students from overseas in higher and further education have to meet the full cost of their tuition, but students from other member countries of the European

Community are charged the lower level tuition fees that apply to British students. There is, however, a scheme to provide financial help for overseas research students of high ability to attend universities.

A range of public and private scholarships and fellowships are available to students from overseas (and to British students who want to study overseas). Among the best known are the British Council Scholarships, the Commonwealth Scholarship and Fellowship Plan, the Marshall Scholarships and the independently funded Rhodes Scholarships, and the Churchill Scholarships for men and women in all walks of life. Many British universities and colleges offer scholarships for which graduates of any nationality are eligible. (The British Council and the Association of Commonwealth Universities are involved in the selection of British students for awards offered by many overseas countries.) The Atlantic College at St. Donat's, south Wales (one of the colleges of the United World Colleges), provides two-year residential courses for overseas students prior to their entering university.

The Teaching of English

The continuing increase in interest in English as a foreign language is reflected in the growth of the number of private language schools and the greater proportion of these recognised as efficient after inspection by the Department of Education and Science in collaboration with the British Council. Much of this demand is for English needed for specific educational or vocational purposes. At the same time the British Council has greatly expanded the volume of its own teaching of English overseas by opening new centres in many countries and extending existing ones. Publications and other material relating to English language teaching have also increased in number and are now a large component in publishers' lists and constitute a major export.

The BBC's English by Radio and Television Service provides a worldwide facility for the individual learner in his or her own home.

THE YOUTH SERVICE

The aim of the youth service is to promote the social and informal education of young people by offering them opportunities in their leisure time to mix socially and to develop and enlarge their range of interests. The service is provided by a partnership between public authorities and a large variety of voluntary organisations. Membership of groups is voluntary and there is no attempt to create anything in the nature of a national youth movement.

State Involvement

The youth service forms part of the education system. Government education departments formulate broad policy objectives for the service and encourage their achievement through financial assistance and advice. They assist national and local voluntary youth organisations through grants towards administrative and building costs. The Scottish Education Department is advised by the Scottish Council for Community Education while in Northern Ireland the advisory body is the Youth Committee for Northern Ireland.

Local education authorities (education and library boards in Northern Ireland) are responsible for local administration of the youth service. Authorities provide and run their own youth clubs and centres (some of which are residential) which may be purpose-built or associated with schools. They also assist local voluntary youth groups by lending premises and equipment and by contributing to their capital and running costs. Many authorities have appointed youth committees on which official and voluntary bodies are represented, and employ youth organisers to co-ordinate youth work and to arrange in-service training. In Scotland these committees and organisers are normally concerned with services for both young people and adults.

Voluntary Organisations

Although there are many local education authority youth clubs and centres, national voluntary organisations still promote the largest share of youth activities through local groups which raise most of their day-to-day running expenses by their own efforts. These have an estimated combined membership of over 6 million. They vary greatly in character, some concentrating on social and recreational pursuits, others on educational or religious activities. Most of the national organisations in England are members of the National Council of Voluntary Youth Services, a consultative body which takes action in the name of its member bodies. The Council has 65 national organisations and 47 local co-ordinating bodies as members. In Scotland, Wales and Northern Ireland there are similar representative bodies.

Among the largest of the voluntary youth organisations in membership of the National Council are the Scout and Girl Guides Associations (with about 542,000 and 859,000 members), the National Association of Youth Clubs (about 500,000), the National Association of Boys' Clubs (some 162,000) and the Youth Hostels Association (about 293,000). The three pre-service organisations (the Combined Cadet Force, Army Cadet Force and Air Training Corps) are observer members. They are financially assisted by the Ministry of Defence and combine social, educational and physical development with training for possible entry to the armed forces.

Training of Youth Workers

There are some 3,000 full-time youth workers in Britain and these are supported by many thousands of part-time workers, many of them unpaid. Part-time workers usually have no professional qualification in youth work but some have allied qualifications, for instance as teachers, and a large number attend short courses and conferences on youth work. Qualified school teachers are recognised as qualified youth workers.

In England and Wales, there is a basic two-year training for youth and community workers. Provided at certain universities and higher education colleges, the course leads to the status of a qualified youth and community worker. In addition a number of colleges of higher education provide a study of youth work as a principal or subsidiary subject within teacher-training courses. In Scotland one- and three-year courses are provided at certain colleges of education and in Northern Ireland courses are provided by the Ulster Polytechnic.

Other Organisations Concerned with Young People

The Duke of Edinburgh's Award Scheme, which operates through bodies such as local authorities, schools, youth organisations and industrial firms, is a challenge for young people from Britain and other Commonwealth countries to reach certain standards in leisure-time activities with the voluntary assistance of adults. The scheme celebrates its 25th anniversary in 1981.

A substantial sum of money is awarded by the many grant-giving foundations and trusts each year for activities involving young people.

The Royal Jubilee Trusts, formed in 1978 from King George's Jubilee Trust (started in 1935 at the time of the Silver Jubilee of King George V) and the Queen's Silver Jubilee Trust (which arose from the 1977 Queen's Silver Jubilee Appeal) exist to support work involving young people aged 8 to 18 (King George's Jubilee Trust) and young people up to the age of 25 involved in community service work (the Queen's Silver Jubilee Trust). King George's

Jubilee Trust has distributed over £3·75 million since 1935 and the Queen's Silver Jubilee Trust over £4·38 million since May 1978.

Community Service by Young People

Thousands of young people voluntarily take part in community service designed to assist those in need, including the elderly and the disabled. Organisations providing opportunities for community service such as International Voluntary Service, Task Force and Community Service Volunteers receive grants from the Government. Many schools also organise community service activities as part of the curriculum.

The Community Projects Foundation is an independent body which advises interested organisations in England and Wales on methods of involving young people in providing service to the community. The Foundation is grant-aided by the Government and employs teams of young people who are available on request to assist such bodies as local authorities, voluntary organisations and hospital boards in promoting voluntary service.

8 Planning and the Environment

By comprehensive land-use planning and development control Britain has had considerable success in resolving the conflicting demands of industry, commerce, housing, transport, agriculture and recreation and in reducing environmental pollution. There is no 'national plan' for urban and land development, but there is a statutory system of land-use planning applying over the whole country and to virtually every kind of development, and there are laws dealing specifically with environmental health and the control of pollution. All development requires local 'planning permission', and applications for permission are dealt with in the light of development plans which set out strategies for each area on such matters as housing, transport, industry and open land. The underlying approach is to identify people's needs and possible ways of meeting them, and there is a growing move away from narrow land-use allocation towards broader strategic planning recognising the community's social and economic goals. Throughout Britain voluntary organisations, too, take an active interest in planning, conversation and the control of pollution.

The system of land-use planning in Great Britain involves a centralised structure under the Secretaries of State for the Environment, Wales and Scotland, and compulsory planning duties for local planning authorities. The Department of the Environment brings together the major responsibilities in England for land-use planning, housing and construction, countryside policy and environmental protection. The Welsh Office and the Scottish Development Department have broadly equivalent responsibilities. Large-scale planning in England and Wales is primarily the responsibility of the county councils and the Greater London Council while district councils and the councils of the London boroughs and the City of London are responsible for most local plans and development control, the main housing functions and many other environmental health matters. In Scotland, planning functions are undertaken by regional and district councils whose responsibilities are divided on a basis broadly similar to that in England and Wales. In the more rural regions and the islands, all planning responsibilities are carried out by the regional and islands councils respectively. In Northern Ireland the Department of the Environment for Northern Ireland is responsible for planning matters through its local offices which work closely with the district councils. The councils have local environmental health responsibilities.

Special provisions, in addition to the general town and country planning measures, control the location of major industry (see p 226). General problems of industrial development are dealt with jointly by a number of government departments, but each development scheme, as a rule, requires the local planning authority's consent. Financial incentives from the Government encourage the location of industry in particular areas.

Development Plans and Development Control

The development plan system in England and Wales involves 'structure' and 'local' plans. Structure plans are prepared by county planning authorities and require ministerial approval. They set out broad policies for the development and other use of land (including measures for the improvement of the physical environment and traffic management) and indicate 'action areas' where comprehensive development or improvement is expected to start within a specified period. Local plans, which have to conform generally with the structure plan, contain detailed proposals including plans for 'action areas' and are normally prepared by district councils, though sometimes by county councils. Local plans are adopted by the planning authorities without being subject to ministerial approval unless the Secretary of State calls in a plan for his own decision. All plans are under continuous review and may be altered from time to time. Scotland has a similar system which can also include the production of a regional report by regional and island authorities, outlining their broad priorities and policies. In Northern Ireland there is a single-tier system; plans are prepared by the Department of the Environment for Northern Ireland.

Members of the public and interested organisations are given an opportunity to express their views on the planning of their areas during the formative stages of the structure and local plans. The local planning authorities must ensure adequate publicity for matters proposed for inclusion in the plans; representations may be made about them to the authorities. These opportunities for public participation are additional to provisions for objecting to prepared plans. In the case of structure plans the Secretary of State holds an examination in public of matters on which he requires more information in order to reach a decision. In the case of local plans objectors have a right to be heard, and a public local inquiry is normally held by the planning authorities.

Where specific proposals for development differ substantially from the intentions of a development plan, they must be publicised locally. Other schemes affecting a large number of people are usually advertised by the local planning authority and applications seeking permission for certain types of development must also be advertised. The applicant has a right of appeal to the appropriate Secretary of State if planning permission is refused or granted subject to conditions. Most appeals are transferred for decision to inspectors (in Scotland reporters) appointed by the Secretary of State.

The Secretary of State can direct that a planning application be referred to him for decision. This power is exercised sparingly and usually only in respect of proposals of national or regional importance. The applicant has the right to be heard by a person appointed by the Secretary of State and a public inquiry is normally held for this purpose. In the case of development schemes of national or regional importance or of a technical or scientific nature, and if an ordinary inquiry is inadequate for the purpose, the ministers responsible may decide to set up planning inquiry commissions to carry out investigations and hold inquiries locally. Where highway development is proposed, the government minister concerned can hold such inquiries as he considers appropriate.

Similar provision is made in Northern Ireland for public participation in the planning process and for the hearing of objections. There is a right of appeal to an independent Planning Appeals Commission.

Regional Planning

For many administrative purposes England is divided into eight regions: Northern, Yorkshire and Humberside, East Midlands, East Anglia, South East, South West, West Midlands and North West. Each has a regional board consisting of civil servants who are normally the senior representatives in the regional offices of government departments. The chairmen of the boards are the regional directors of the Departments of the Environment and Transport. The main task of the boards is to provide for the co-ordination of inter-departmental activities; they also keep in touch with bodies such as local authorities and the regional councils of the Trades Union Congress and the Confederation of British Industry.

Scotland has an Economic Council chaired by the Secretary of State for Scotland which provides a forum for discussion of all aspects of Scottish economic development; members are appointed by the Secretary of State in a personal capacity. There is also a Scottish Economic Planning Board. In Wales there is an Economic Planning Board with a role similar to that of the regional boards in England. The Northern Ireland Economic Council, an independent body appointed by the Secretary of State for Northern Ireland, provides the Government with advice on all aspects of economic policy in the Province. It represents trade unions, employers' organisations and independent interests.

New Towns

Since 1946, 32 new towns have been designated and they represent one of the most successful achievements of recent British planning. Of these, most of which had as a nucleus an existing town or village, 21 are in England, 2 in Wales, 5 in Scotland and 4 in Northern Ireland. The policy behind their creation was mainly one of encouraging the gradual dispersal of industry and population from congested cities to new areas, planned in advance to become self-contained towns with services and amenities within convenient distance of the whole community.

A government review of the new towns policy, undertaken against a background of substantial reductions in population forecasts and a need to pay more attention to the regeneration of declining inner city areas (see p 177), has led to a reduction in the long-term target populations of some towns. The momentum of new town development is to be substantially maintained, however, over the next few years.

The planning and growth of each new town is supervised by a government-appointed development corporation which is given general powers to acquire, by compulsory purchase if necessary, land or property needed for the provision of houses, factories and other buildings and for roads and essential services.

In England four of the new towns have been substantially completed and the development corporations dissolved. Target dates for the dissolution of a further eight new towns development corporations by the early 1980s have been announced. In Wales responsibility for one of the two new towns has been taken over by the Development Board for Rural Wales. In Northern Ireland, development of the new towns has been incorporated in a new District Towns Strategy which is the responsibility of the Department of the Environment for Northern Ireland.

The capital cost is advanced from public funds and is repayable over 60 years. Parliament has approved a fund to provide for advances to the development corporations, which, for Great Britain, stands at £3,250 million (net of repayments). The Government plans substantial disposals of the completed assets of the new towns in order to release resources for investment and to reduce the involvement of the public sector.

The new towns have a total population of over 2 million. Young people form a somewhat higher proportion than in the population of the country as a whole. Several of the more developed towns are becoming regional centres and, as the populations grow large enough to give the necessary support, offices, hotels and department stores, as well as art centres and full entertainment and recreational facilities, are gradually being provided.

The new towns programme has included the expansion of large existing towns such as Northampton, Peterborough and Warrington; this has the advantage, among others, that many facilities are already available.

Town development (or 'expanding town') schemes involve the transfer of people and industry from overcrowded areas to existing towns suitable for expansion; these are arranged directly between the local authorities of the towns concerned. Most of the towns expanded under these schemes (for example, Aylesbury, Basingstoke, Swindon and Thetford) are well established and are providing homes, jobs and amenities for people from large cities.

Inner City Policies

Revitalising the inner areas of many towns and cities presents one of the most important challenges to modern British planning. Past policies have produced many successes (most of the slums have been replaced, much old housing has been improved and the clean air legislation has enhanced the general environment and public health) but some of the problems associated with poor housing have still to be overcome. In many areas they have been joined by problems of high unemployment, decay and dereliction and unbalanced population structures with relatively high proportions of the elderly and the disadvantaged. The extent of these problems varies from place to place, and the inter-relationship between them is complex. Government policy is not to seek a universal solution but to work out for each city the package of measures that is most likely to improve conditions and to encourage, as far as possible, local voluntary action.

Greater resources and priority have been given to the inner city areas. The Inner Urban Areas Act 1978 gave powers to selected inner city local authorities to support the creation of new employment opportunities and to improve the environment of industrial areas. The urban aid programme has been increased from a 1977–78 level in England and Wales of under £30 million a year to £206 million a year in 1980–81 (in Scotland from about £6 million a year to £20 million a year by 1980–81). The programme traditionally complemented the work of major social programmes by providing extra facilities which would otherwise not have been available, such as day nurseries, centres for the elderly and language classes for immigrants, but has been recast so as to cover industrial, commercial, environmental and recreational provision as well. The urban programme represents only a small part of the central assistance to urban, and other, local authorities. The main contribution is through the annual 'rate support' grant, transport supplementary grant (in England and Wales only), housing subsidy and other programmes. The Government also approved some £64 million for a special programme of inner city construction work between 1977 and 1980.

In certain places, special schemes are in operation. A co-ordinated 'partnership' approach has been adopted in seven English areas whereby central and local government work together to tackle places where the problems are greatest. Each partnership has a three-year action programme rolled forward annually, which is based on the needs of the area and its particular priorities. Partnerships receive allocations of urban programme resources ranging from £8 million to £25 million a year. To meet the particular problems and opportunities of the London docklands and the Merseyside dock area the Government has set up urban development corporations, modelled on the new town development corporations. Elsewhere in England 15 areas have been identified where the problems are on a slightly smaller scale but still merit special attention. These areas prepare their own inner city programmes and like the partnerships receive special allocations of urban programme resources. Additional resources are also made available to a further 14 English and five Welsh districts designated under the Inner Urban Areas Act.

In Scotland a major urban renewal exercise in Glasgow to regenerate the city's east end is organised on somewhat similar lines to the partnership areas in England, and a further eight Scottish districts have been designated under the Inner Urban Areas Act. In Northern Ireland a special effort is being made to tackle Belfast's inner city problems.

The Government proposes to establish seven 'enterprise zones' (in London's Docklands, Swansea, Manchester, Liverpool, Newcastle upon Tyne, Clydebank and Belfast) to bring new life to areas of urban decay. Each zone, to be designated initially for ten years, will cover up to 200 hectares (500 acres) and will be granted concessions and exemptions on rates, taxation, planning procedures and certain standard governmental requirements. Additional zones will be designated later.

Historic Buildings and Areas

Lists of buildings of special architectural or historic interest are compiled, as required by the planning Acts, by the Secretary of State for the Environment and the Secretaries of State for Scotland and Wales; over 300,000 buildings are already listed. It is an offence to demolish or alter the character of any listed building without special consent from the local planning authority or the appropriate Secretary of State; where consent is given to demolish a building, the Royal Commission on Historical Monuments (for England) and similar bodies for Scotland and Wales have an opportunity to make a photographic record of the building. Emergency 'building preservation notices' can be served by the local planning authority to protect buildings not yet listed.

The respective Secretaries of State (on the recommendation of the appropriate Historic Buildings Council) can make grants and loans for the repair or maintenance of buildings (or groups of buildings) of outstanding interest, and local authorities can make grants and loans for any building of architectural or historic interest even if it is not listed. The Architectural Heritage Fund, voluntary contributions to which are matched by the Government, provides loans for local historic buildings trusts.

Local planning authorities have designated for special protection over 4,800 'conservation areas' of particular architectural or historic interest. Grants and loans are available for works for the preservation or enhancement of outstanding conservation areas.

The Secretaries of State for the Environment, Scotland and Wales are responsible for the maintenance of royal parks and palaces and for the protection of ancient monuments of which about 800 are in their care. The Ancient Monument Boards recommend which monuments are considered to be of national importance and therefore worthy of preservation.

In Northern Ireland the Department of the Environment for Northern Ireland is responsible for the protection of historic monuments, of which 149 are in their care. The Department, acting on the advice of the Historic Buildings Council, is also responsible for the listing of buildings of special architectural or historic interest, for the designation of conservation areas, and for the payment of grants.

Tree Preservation

The local planning authorities have power to protect trees and woodlands in the interest of amenity by means of tree preservation orders. When granting planning permission for development, a local planning authority must, where appropriate, impose conditions to secure the preservation or planting of trees.

Landowners are generally required to replace 'preserved' trees which die or are removed or destroyed in contravention of a preservation order.

Green Belts

In order to restrict the further sprawl of large built-up areas, to prevent adjacent towns merging into one another, and in some cases to preserve the character of a town and the amenities of the countryside, 'green belts' (areas where it is intended that the land should be left open and free from building development and where people can seek recreation) have been established or proposed on the fringes of certain urban areas. Much of London's green belt, for example, is agricultural land or woodland, some of which is used for recreation. There are also areas specifically for recreational use, such as country parks, public open spaces, playing fields and golf courses.

The Coast

The maritime local planning authorities are responsible for planning land use at the coast providing, for example, recreational facilities and amenities for holidaymakers and local residents; at the same time they attempt to safeguard and enhance the coast's natural attractions and preserve coastal areas of scientific interest.

A comprehensive study of the coastline of England and Wales, undertaken by the Countryside Commission (see p 180) in 1966–70, recommended that certain stretches of undeveloped coast of particular scenic beauty should be treated as heritage coast. There is a practical programme aimed at the designation of 42 such coasts which together would cover over 1,300 kilometres (808 miles), some 40 per cent of the undeveloped coastline. Jointly with local authorities, the Commission has defined 34 of these coasts so far, protecting just over 1,000 kilometres (621 miles).

In 1965 the National Trust (see p 188) launched its Enterprise Neptune campaign to raise funds for the nation to acquire stretches of coastline of great natural beauty and recreational value. More than £4 million has been raised so far and as a result the Trust has under its protection 644 kilometres (400 miles) of coastline in England and Wales. Some 127 kilometres (79 miles) of coast in Scotland are protected by conservation agreements with the National Trust for Scotland. In Northern Ireland 56 kilometres (35 miles) of coast and coastal path have been acquired.

In exceptional cases economic arguments override conservation; development associated with North Sea oil and gas is occurring on remote and unspoiled coastal areas in Scotland, for instance, but planning guidelines drawn up by the Scottish Development Department aim to ensure that oil-related activities are sited so as to make the best use of existing labour and infrastructure and to minimise the effect on the coastline. Provision has also been made for funds to be set aside for the restoration of sites once there is no further need for them.

The protection of the coastline against erosion, for which the Department of the Environment, the Welsh Office and the Scottish Office are centrally responsible in Great Britain, presents difficult engineering problems and heavy costs for the maritime local authorities. All coast protection schemes drawn up by the authorities under the Coast Protection Act 1949 are investigated by government engineering staff. Substantial grants from central funds (up to a maximum of 79 per cent) may be made to the authorities. Protection against sea flooding where there is no question of erosion is the primary responsibility of the water authorities (see pp 283 and 294). To help to prevent the pollution of the sea and coastline, international conventions restrict the discharge of oil into the sea (see p 185).

Outdoor Advertising

The display of outdoor advertisements is controlled by planning legislation. General consents have been issued for certain classes of advertisement but these can be withdrawn in particular cases where there is a serious threat to amenity or public safety. Consent for advertisements outside these classes must be sought from the local planning authority. Rural areas and urban areas requiring special protection can be designated as areas of special control which impose more restrictive standards.

Countryside Commissions

Two Countryside Commissions (one for England and Wales, the other for Scotland) are responsible for encouraging and promoting measures to conserve and enhance the natural beauty and amenity of the countryside and for encouraging the development of facilities for open-air recreation in the countryside. These include the provision by local authorities (sometimes in association with other bodies) and private individuals of country parks and picnic sites often within easy reach of towns; the provision or improvement of recreational paths; the establishment of transit caravan and camping sites; the encouragement of amenity tree-planting schemes; and the increased use of reservoirs, canals and other waterways for bathing, sailing and other activities. Some 150 country parks and 200 picnic sites have been recognised in England and Wales by the Countryside Commission. In Scotland a large number of local authority schemes for the provision of a variety of countryside facilities have been approved for grant aid. The Commissions may undertake research projects and experimental schemes, working in consultation with local authorities and such bodies as the Nature Conservancy Council (see p 182) and the Sports Councils (see p 428). In England and Wales, the Countryside Commission may give financial assistance to public bodies and individuals carrying out countryside recreation and amenity projects. Attention is increasingly being given to small-scale amenity tree-planting and to techniques of countryside management to supplement the statutory planning controls.

National Parks, Areas of Outstanding Natural Beauty

The Countryside Commission (for England and Wales) is empowered to designate, for confirmation by the appropriate minister, national parks and 'areas of outstanding natural beauty'; to define heritage coasts in conjunction with local authorities (see p 179); and to make proposals for the creation of long-distance footpaths and bridleways. Ten national parks have been established: Northumberland, the Lake District, the Yorkshire Dales, the North York Moors and the Peak District in northern England; Snowdonia, the Pembrokeshire Coast and the Brecon Beacons in Wales; Exmoor and Dartmoor in south-west England. They cover some 13,600 sq km (5,250 square miles), or 9 per cent of the area of England and Wales. Administration is the responsibility of special committees or planning boards which carry out all or most of the planning functions. Some 33 areas of outstanding natural beauty have been designated, covering some 14,500 sq km (5,600 square miles).

The land in these designated areas generally remains privately owned, but agreements or orders to secure additional public access may be made by local authorities. Steps are taken to preserve and enhance the landscape's natural beauty by high standards of development control, and by positive measures, for which grants are available, such as tree planting and preservation, and the removal of eyesores. In the national parks, other measures for the benefit of the public include the provision of car parks, camping and caravan areas, and information centres. All national parks and some other designated areas have warden services. Most local authority expenditure on national parks is met by central government grants. Some 2,528 km (1,580 miles) of long-distance footpaths and bridleways have been approved. Large stretches of these paths are already public rights of way.

In Northern Ireland the Ulster Countryside Committee advises on the preservation of amenities and the designation of areas of outstanding natural beauty. Eight areas of outstanding natural beauty have been designated and six areas are being managed as country parks and one as a regional park.

In Scotland there are no national parks as such, but there are 40 'national scenic areas' where certain kinds of development are subject to consultation with and advice from the Countryside Commission for Scotland, and the Secretary of State for Scotland, in the event of a disagreement.

Forest Parks The Forestry Commission (see p 301) has formed, and opened to the public, seven forest parks in some of the finest country in Great Britain: Argyll, Galloway, Glen More and the Queen Elizabeth Forest Park in Scotland; the Forest of Dean and the Wye valley woods on the borders of England and Wales; Snowdonia in Wales; and the Border Forest Park on the borders of England and Scotland. They cover some 243,000 hectares (600,000 acres), and camping and other recreational facilities are provided in all of them. The historic New Forest, in Hampshire, although not a forest park, is also open to the public. The Forestry Commission and Hampshire County Council jointly manage the Queen Elizabeth Country Park in Hampshire. In addition the Forestry Commission welcomes the public to much of the land under its management. In Northern Ireland, the Department of Agriculture has established six forest parks (Tollymore, Castlewellan, Gortin Glen, Drum Manor, Gosford and Glenariff) and there are also forest scenic drives and many recreational facilities in these and other forests.

Local Footpaths and Open Country County councils in England and Wales are required to prepare definitive maps showing all public rights of way, which must be kept free of obstruction. If a path is not shown on the map, a private citizen may claim that it is a public right of way if it has been used and regarded as such without hindrance for at least 20 years. Public footpaths are maintained by local authorities who must also provide signposts and supervise landowners' duties to repair stiles and gates. Local authorities in Great Britain can create paths, close existing paths no longer needed for public use and divert paths to secure either a shorter route or the efficient use of land. Local planning authorities can also convert minor roads into footpaths or bridleways to improve the amenities of their area.

There is no automatic right of public access to open country, although many landowners permit such access more or less freely. Local planning authorities can secure access by means of agreements with landowners; if agreements cannot be obtained, authorities may acquire land or make orders for public access. Similar powers cover Scotland, while the introduction of comparable legislation is under consideration in Northern Ireland.

Common land, a large proportion of which is open to the public, totals an estimated 600,000 hectares (1·5 million acres) in England and Wales. (There is no common land in Scotland or Northern Ireland.) This land is usually privately owned, but people other than the owner have various rights on or over it, for example, of pasture for farm animals. Commons are protected by law and cannot be built on or enclosed without the consent of the Secretaries of State for the Environment or Wales. The Commons Registration Act 1965 provided for the registration of all commons and village greens. Under the Countryside Act 1968 local authorities can provide facilities for enjoyment on any common land to which the public has access.

Nature Conservation

The official body responsible for nature conservation in Great Britain is the Nature Conservancy Council which has the functions of establishing, maintaining and managing nature reserves, advising ministers, providing general information and advice, and commissioning or supporting research. There are some 167 national nature reserves covering 132,600 hectares (327,700 acres). Some 3,700 sites of special scientific interest have been scheduled because of their flora, fauna or geological or physiographical features.

About 8,000 hectares (20,000 acres) of Forestry Commission land are managed as areas in which nature conservation is the main object. Local authorities have declared more than 60 nature reserves, and voluntary organisations, which play an important part in protecting wildlife, have established nearly 1,100 reserves.

In Northern Ireland the Nature Reserves Committee advises the Department of the Environment for Northern Ireland on the designation of nature reserves and areas of scientific interest; there are 34 and 46 respectively.

Land Reclamation

Derelict land, often concentrated in places associated with nineteenth century industrial development, presents special problems to planners. It includes mineral waste tips, old mineral workings, obsolete industrial buildings and disused railways and docks. In England most derelict land reclamation is undertaken, with the help of central government grant, by local authorities, who have the power to acquire derelict land and bring it back into use or improve its appearance. Mainly as a result of government encouragement, local authorities have shown an increasing interest in reclaiming derelict land, and greater emphasis is being placed on grant assistance for the reclamation of derelict land in urban areas for industrial and other development. There are proposals to extend the scope and flexibility of the grant scheme to promote this new emphasis.

In Scotland and Wales responsibility for derelict land reclamation rests with the respective development agencies, who may acquire land and reclaim it themselves, employ local authorities as their agents (in Scotland) or make grants to local authorities for the purpose (in Wales). In Northern Ireland grants are paid to landowners who restore or improve derelict sites.

To prevent new dereliction, planning controls require that when permission is given for mineral working various measures must be taken to minimise the disturbance caused by the work and to secure whatever restoration is practicable, either progressively or when working ceases. The use of land for disposal of waste materials is also subject to conditions restricting height or requiring treatment on completion.

CONTROL OF POLLUTION

Government measures to control environmental pollution, in which industry and voluntary organisations co-operate, are long established, and are seen as complementary to the planning system and the various measures to conserve amenities and the country's heritage.

The Control of Pollution Act 1974, which applies to England, Scotland and Wales provides a comprehensive framework to tackle pollution problems. It extends a wide range of new powers and duties to local and water authorities, increases their powers to deal with controlled wastes, air and water pollution and noise, and contains important provisions on the release of information to the public on environmental conditions. In particular, the provisions dealing with waste on land institute a new system for the comprehensive planning of waste disposal operations so as to ensure that disposal is carried out to satisfactory standards and that the best use is made of waste materials. The Act also increases the penalties for a large number of pollution offences. The provisions relating to noise and air pollution are fully in force, as are a substantial number of those relating to waste on land, but most of the part which deals with water pollution has not yet been brought into effect. Similar legislation applies in Northern Ireland.

Administration Responsibility for the control of pollution is shared by various central government departments, local and water authorities and statutory agencies. Industry co-operates with these authorities and voluntary organisations help to focus public interest on the process of control. An independent standing Royal Commission on Environmental Pollution advises the Government on national and international matters concerning the pollution of the environment, on the adequacy of research and on the future possibilities of danger to the environment. In England and Wales the Secretary of State for the Environment has a co-ordinating role concerning pollution matters as a whole, exercised through a Central Directorate on Environmental Pollution within his department, while an independent Standing Commission on Energy and the Environment provides the Government with advice on the inter-action of energy policies and the environment.

Specific responsibilities of the Department of the Environment in England include air pollution control, fresh water pollution control, waste disposal, control of civil radioactive wastes (jointly with the Ministry of Agriculture, Fisheries and Food), of oil and chemicals on beaches and of noise other than aircraft noise, traffic noise and noise at work. Most of these responsibilities in Scotland are exercised by the Scottish Development Department, in Wales by the Welsh Office and in Northern Ireland by the Department of the Environment for Northern Ireland.

The Department of Trade is responsible for the control of oil pollution at sea (other than from offshore operations) and its clearance, and for the control of aircraft noise. The Department of Transport is responsible for policies for the control of traffic noise. The Department of Energy is responsible for the control of pollution arising from the exploration for, and exploitation of oil. The Ministry of Agriculture, Fisheries and Food, the Department of Agriculture and Fisheries for Scotland, the Northern Ireland Departments of Agriculture and the Environment (together with the Health and Safety Executive) are responsible for the control of agricultural chemicals such as pesticides, for the protection of fisheries from pollution and for the prevention of food contamination. The protection of the health of employees at work (see p 341) is the responsibility of the Department of Employment and is controlled by the Factory Inspectorate which forms part of the Health and Safety Executive; in Northern Ireland it is the responsibility of the Department of Manpower Services. Other departments such as the Department of Education and Science, the Department of Health and Social Security and the Scottish Home and Health Department have an interest in health aspects of pollution control.

Local authorities are responsible for matters such as collection and disposal of domestic wastes; control of air pollution from domestic and certain industrial premises and noise abatement measures. Sewerage and sewage treatment and disposal are the responsibilities of water authorities in England and Wales, of local authorities in Scotland and of the Department of the Environment in

Northern Ireland. The regional water authorities in England, the Welsh Water Authority, the river purification boards and islands councils in Scotland and the Department of the Environment for Northern Ireland are responsible for control of water pollution.

The European Community has adopted a Community Environment Programme as a result of which a number of measures for Community action are being developed.

The Land

The main risks of land pollution lie in the indiscriminate dumping of waste materials on land, careless disposal of pesticides and chemicals, fall-out of materials from the atmosphere and the deposition of materials from floodwater. The application of sewage sludge on farms, too, involves risks as well as benefits to the land.

The Control of Pollution Act laid a duty on waste disposal authorities (county councils and the Greater London Council in England, for example) to ensure that there were adequate arrangements to dispose of controlled wastes and to draw up and revise periodically a waste disposal plan. It also established a licensing system for all waste disposal sites, treatment plants and storage facilities receiving controlled wastes. In addition it provided for a more intensive control system for certain specially hazardous or difficult wastes.

The Pesticides Safety Precautions Scheme (PSPS) is a scheme through which pesticides are cleared for safety before being marketed. Clearance is not given unless the Government, advised by the Advisory Committee on Pesticides, is satisfied that a product can be used without risk to people, livestock and domestic animals, and with minimum harm to wildlife, provided recommended precautions are taken. The scheme has been extended to include certain non-agricultural uses of pesticides. The British Agrochemical Supply Industry Scheme, an independent registration scheme for distributors of crop protection products, ensures that distributors sell only products which have been cleared through the PSPS.

Under the Litter Act 1958 it was made an offence to leave litter on land in the open air to which the public have free access. The Dangerous Litter Act 1971 increased the maximum fine from £10 to £100. Under the Refuse Disposal (Amenity) Act 1978 the deliberate dumping of rubbish carries a similar maximum fine with the possibility of a £200 fine and three months' imprisonment for subsequent offences.

Recycling and Materials Reclamation

The Government encourages the reclamation and recycling of waste materials wherever this is practicable and economic in order to reduce imports and waste disposal costs and to help to conserve natural resources. Industry already makes considerable use of reclaimed waste material such as metals, paper and textiles. Local authorities collect about 200,000 tonnes of waste paper annually and about 100,000 tonnes of ferrous scrap. Waste disposal authorities are required under the Control of Pollution Act to take full account of opportunities for waste reclamation in drawing up their waste disposal plans. Voluntary organisations also organise collections of waste material.

The Government has set up a Waste Management Advisory Council and launched a National Anti-Waste Programme to co-ordinate policy and promote opportunities for reclamation and recycling through education and advice. Extensive Government-supported research and development in this area is in progress. The Department of the Environment is providing financial and technical help to South Yorkshire and Tyne and Wear County Councils for full-scale prototype plants for the mechanical sorting of household refuse. The two plants, at Doncaster and Byker, are in operation. In addition Britain participates in discussion on waste reclamation and recycling in the European Community, the OECD and the Economic Commission for Europe.

Water Pollution

There has been a steady and significant improvement in water quality: the level of pollution in the tidal Thames, for example, has been reduced to a quarter of the 1950s' level and some 97 different kinds of fish have been identified there since 1964. Discharges of polluting matter into rivers, lakes, estuaries and some coastal waters are controlled by law. The Control of Pollution Act 1974 contains a number of provisions which, when implemented, will considerably strengthen existing legislation; for example, it will extend control to all inland water (including specific underground waters) and all coastal waters within the three-mile limit.

More than 90 per cent of the British population is provided with main drainage, and public authority sewage treatment works serve over four-fifths of the population—a very high proportion by international standards.

Marine Pollution

Control of marine pollution from ships is based largely on international conventions drawn up under the auspices of the Inter-Governmental Maritime Consultative Organisation, a United Nations agency with headquarters in London, and implemented for British ships by domestic legislation. The Prevention of Oil Pollution Act 1971, which gave effect to the International Convention for the Prevention of the Pollution of the Sea by Oil 1954, as amended in 1962 and 1969, makes it an offence for ships of any nationality to discharge any oil into British territorial waters and for British registered ships to discharge persistent oil anywhere at sea, except in accordance with very stringent regulations. Further amendments to the convention, made in 1971 but not yet in force, relate to the design of tankers and are aimed at reducing the volume of oil that could escape in the event of an accident. The International Convention for the Prevention of Pollution from Ships 1973 (as modified by the 1978 Protocol) will, when in force, replace the 1954 convention by more stringent requirements and will eventually regulate pollution by chemicals, sewage and garbage as well as by oil.

The Department of Trade has developed a nationwide organisation using the resources of its Coastguard and Marine Survey Services, to deal with oil spills at sea which threaten to cause coastal pollution or are likely to endanger wildlife. If necessary, action is taken to clear the oil by using low toxicity dispersant and spraying equipment. Central government and local authorities have contingency plans under review for dealing with oil and chemical pollution of beaches and in inshore waters. Following several oil tanker disasters off the coasts of Britain and France in 1978, the Government increased expenditure on contingency arrangements. This included the setting up in 1979 of a Marine Pollution Control Unit within the Department to co-ordinate contingency arrangements and take charge of operations to deal with pollution at sea.

The development of the offshore oil industry has brought an increased risk of oil pollution in the North Sea. Offshore operators are required to ensure that oil does not escape into the sea and are also expected to have contingency plans for dealing with oil spills. Not all traces of oil can be removed from water separated from crude oil before its discharge from production platforms into the sea, and these discharges from offshore installations are normally granted exemption from the 1971 Act subject to strict controls laid down by the Department of Energy. The Department of the Environment, the Welsh

Office, the Scottish Development Department and the Northern Ireland Department of the Environment have powers to grant exemptions subject to similar controls for discharges from land-based sources.

The loading of wastes for dumping at sea by means of vehicles, ships, aircraft, hovercraft, marine platforms and conveyor belts is controlled by the Ministry of Agriculture, Fisheries and Food, the Welsh Office, the Department of Agriculture and Fisheries for Scotland and the Northern Ireland Department of the Environment through the Dumping at Sea Act 1974 which gave statutory backing to the voluntary arrangements which had operated for several years. A licence has to be obtained for the permanent deposit of any substance or article into tidal waters and the sea. Dumping at sea is permitted on the basis of the scientific criteria set out in the annexes to the Oslo Convention (International Convention for the Prevention of Marine Pollution by Dumping from Ships and Aircraft 1972) and the London Convention on the Prevention of Marine Pollution by Dumping Wastes and Other Matter 1972. The 1974 Act does not however control discharges of liquid effluent from pipelines, which will be covered by the Control of Pollution Act, nor discharges incidental to or derived from the normal operation of a ship, aircraft, vehicle, hovercraft or marine structure.

Clean Air

Responsibility for clean air rests primarily with local authorities. Under the provisions of the Clean Air Acts 1956 and 1968 they may declare 'smoke control areas' within which the emission of smoke from chimneys constitutes an offence. About two-thirds of the premises in the conurbations are now covered by smoke control orders. Emissions from most industrial premises are also subject to the control of local authorities under the Clean Air Acts. The emission of dark smoke from any trade or industrial premises or from the chimney of any building is in general prohibited, and new furnaces must be capable as far as practicable of smokeless operation. The height of the chimney serving a new furnace must generally be approved by the local authority, and approved grit and dust arrestment plant has to be installed. Regulations have been made which prescribe specific limits to the quantities of grit and dust which may be emitted from certain furnaces. Industrial premises that give rise to particularly offensive or dangerous emissions are, in England and Wales, under the control of the Alkali and Clean Air Inspectorate of the Health and Safety Executive. The Inspectorate requires the best practicable means to be used to prevent or abate emissions. Similar legislation and controls apply in Northern Ireland. Controls are also in force on emissions from motor vehicles, such as the maximum permitted lead content of petrol which was reduced from 0·84 grammes per litre in 1973 to 0·45 grammes per litre at the beginning of 1978 (and is to be reduced further to 0·40 grammes from 1 January 1981).

Notable progress has been made towards the achievement of cleaner air and a better environment, especially in the last 20 years or so. Total emissions and average concentration of smoke in the air have fallen by nearly 80 per cent since 1960. The domestic smoke control programme has been particularly important in achieving this result. London no longer experiences the dense smoke-laden 'smogs' of the 1950s and in central London winter sunshine has been increasing since the 1940s when average hours a day were about 40 per cent less than at Kew in outer London; the levels are now virtually the same. Similar improvement has been achieved in other cities including Glasgow and Sheffield. Control measures have reduced urban ground-level concentrations of sulphur dioxide in Britain by 40 per cent in the last ten years.

Noise

The control of noise is enforced by local authorities who inspect their areas for noise nuisances and deal with them. The Control of Pollution Act 1974 (and similar legislation in Northern Ireland) provides authorities with the power to control environmental noise from commercial, industrial or domestic premises. It also enables them to set up 'noise abatement zones' within which they can require levels of noise from scheduled buildings to be held constant or reduced, and within which these noise levels may not be increased without their permission. The Act contains special provisions to control noise from construction and demolition sites.

Transport is one of the main offenders in noise pollution, and control measures are aimed at reducing noise at source, through requirements that aircraft and motor vehicles be quieter, and by protecting people from its effects. The Motor Vehicles (Construction and Use) Regulations 1978 set out the permissible noise levels for various classes of vehicles when new and when in use, and further reduction of those levels is under consideration.

Under the Land Compensation Act 1973 compensation is payable for loss in property values caused by physical factors including noise arising from the use of new or improved public works such as roads and airports. The Act also enables highway authorities to carry out or make grants for insulation of homes subject to specified levels of increased noise caused by new or improved roads. Noise insulation may also be provided where construction work for new roads is likely seriously to affect nearby homes.

Noise emission levels of most aircraft on the United Kingdom Register of Civil Aircraft are regulated in accordance with standards agreed by the International Civil Aviation Organisation (ICAO). Subsonic jets acquired by British operators after September 1978 must already meet the noise certification criteria agreed by ICAO, and all those on the United Kingdom Register will have to do so from 1 January 1986. Various operational restrictions have been introduced to reduce noise disturbance further, and people living in the worst affected areas round a number of airports may be eligible for noise insulation grants.

Radioactivity

In Britain radiation resulting from industrial and other processes represents only a small fraction of that to which the population is exposed from the natural environment. Nevertheless, that fraction is subject to stringent control because of possible effects on health or longer-term genetic effects. Under the Radioactive Substances Act 1960 users of radioactive materials other than those subject to licence under the Nuclear Installations Act (see below) must be registered by the appropriate department, and authorisation is also required for the disposal of radioactive waste, with exemption for very minor uses and disposals. The Health and Safety Executive, through its Nuclear Installations Inspectorate, is the authority concerned with the granting of nuclear site licences for commercial nuclear installations. No such installation may be constructed or operated without a licence granted by the Executive.

The Government is carrying out a review of the existing arrangements for the control of radioactive waste. Various methods are used for disposing of it. Most low-level solid waste is buried; intermediate-level solid waste is mostly stored, with some disposed of at sea; and highly radioactive liquid waste is stored in tanks while research proceeds on methods of disposal.

The National Radiological Protection Board established under the Radiological Protection Act 1970 provides an authoritative point of reference on radiological protection and represents British interests internationally.

The Radioactive Waste Management Advisory Committee advises Government ministers about policies for the management of civil radioactive wastes, including the waste management implications of nuclear policy, of the design of nuclear systems, and of research and development; and the environmental aspects of the handling and treatment of wastes.

VOLUNTARY ORGANISATIONS

Voluntary organisations are particularly active in ensuring that proposed changes in the use of land take full account of the interests of the public and considerations of amenity. The National Trust for Places of Historic Interest or Natural Beauty (for England, Wales and Northern Ireland), founded in 1895, is the largest private landowner in Britain and has 990,000 members. For the benefit of the public it owns 180,000 hectares (445,000 acres) of land and protects from harmful development a further 30,000 hectares (74,000 acres). It owns 240 historic buildings and large stretches of coastline. Properties in Scotland covering some 33,200 hectares (82,000 acres) are protected by the National Trust for Scotland, an independent body founded in 1931, which has over 91,000 members.

The Town and Country Planning Association, founded in 1899, seeks to improve the qualities of land use and planning and operates a planning aid service for local amenity groups; while the Royal Town Planning Institute encourages high standards in town planning. The Civic Trust, established in 1957, encourages the protection and improvement of the environment, and high standards in architecture and planning and has been closely associated with the drafting of conservation legislation. It supports and advises over 1,250 local amenity societies. Associate trusts are linked with the Civic Trust in the north-east and north-west of England, Scotland and Wales.

Other voluntary societies concerned with amenity in town and country include: the Council for the Protection of Rural England, the Council for the Protection of Rural Wales, the Association for the Protection of Rural Scotland and the Ulster Society for the Preservation of the Countryside; the National Association for Environmental Education; the Keep Britain Tidy Group; the Commons, Open Spaces and Footpaths Preservation Society and the Scottish Rights of Way Society; the Ramblers' Association; the Society for the Protection of Ancient Buildings and the Ancient Monuments Society; the Georgian Group and the Scottish Georgian Society; the Saltire Society (which encourages the preservation of the architectural heritage in Scotland) and the Ulster Architectural Heritage Society; the Victorian Society; the Pilgrim Trust; the Council for British Archaeology; the Historic Churches Preservation Trust; the Council for National Parks; the Prince of Wales's Committee (which promotes environmental improvements in Wales); the Inland Waterways Association; Friends of the Earth; the Conservation Society; the Noise Abatement Society; and the National Society for Clean Air.

Among a large number of voluntary bodies concerned with nature conservation are the Society for the Promotion of Nature Conservation, the Royal Society for the Protection of Birds and the Scottish Wildlife Trust.

The Council for Environmental Conservation, comprising many of the main voluntary organisations, acts as a liaison body and is concerned with broader questions of amenity than those covered by individual societies.

9 Housing

There has been a significant general improvement in housing conditions during the last 30 years. In national terms the supply of housing and the demand are in better balance, and needs and problems have become increasingly specific and local. The emphasis of public sector housing policy is being shifted from new building to modernisation, improvement and making better use of the existing stock. In the private sector encouragement of home ownership and of the rented sector are central policy aims. The Housing Act 1980 reflects this in providing a tenants' charter for public sector tenants, with the right for many to buy their homes, a new system of shorthold tenancies, a more effective improvement and repair grant system and a more flexible subsidy system.

Since 1978–79, when a system of local housing strategies and investment programmes was introduced, local authorities have been able, in consultation with other bodies concerned, to plan their housing investment in the light of a comprehensive assessment of local housing needs. From 1980–81 capital allocations under this system are to be given in a single block within which local authorities will be free to decide their own priorities for housing investment.

Public expenditure provision for housing stood at nearly £5,400 million in 1979–80, but the figure is likely to decline in subsequent years in line with government expenditure plans.

Housing Characteristics

There are over 21 million dwellings, houses being much more common than flats (the ratio is roughly four to one). Nationally the number of dwellings is slightly larger than the number of households, but there continue to be shortages in certain areas and, because of changing social habits, the houses available are not always of the type in demand.

More than two families in every five live in a post-1945 home, but there remain a large number of old dwellings, some of which have been kept in good repair and modernised, but many others of which (particularly in the centres of cities) are unsatisfactory by modern standards.

Throughout this century pressure on housing accommodation has been increased more by the rapid rise in the number of separate households than by the increase in the population. While the number of people has increased by about two-fifths, the number of households has more than doubled. Families are smaller, there has been a substantial reduction in the sharing of homes by different generations of the same family and there has been an increase in the number of one-person households. The *National Dwelling and Housing Survey* (results only for England so far; see Bibliography) showed a fall, from 800,000 to 500,000, in the number of households sharing a dwelling between 1971 and 1977–78, a halving, from 2·8 million to 1·4 million, in the number of households without exclusive use of at least one of the basic amenities, such as a bath, and a fall of two-thirds, from 219,000 to 73,000, in the number of overcrowded households.

Over half of all dwellings are owned by their occupiers, nearly a third are rented from public housing authorities, and most of the remainder are rented from private landlords. There are variations, however, in the distribution of tenure between different parts of the country; in Scotland more than half the dwellings are rented from public authorities. Private rented accommodation is generally more common in the central parts of large towns, while owner-occupation is more frequent in outer suburbs and in country areas.

New house construction is undertaken, on a roughly equal scale, by both public and private sectors, and in addition about 10 per cent of new building is carried out by voluntary housing associations and societies. Public authorities provide dwellings mainly for renting while private interests build mainly for sale to owner-occupiers. There is very little building of private dwellings to rent (see p 192), although there are provisions in the Housing Act 1980 designed to encourage new building for private letting by such bodies as building societies, pension funds and insurance companies.

Administration Responsibility for formulating housing policy and supervising the housing programme in Great Britain is borne by the Secretary of State for the Environment in England and by the Secretaries of State for Scotland and Wales. (For Northern Ireland see p 194.)

Most of the public housing is provided by 459 local housing authorities, which are responsible for ensuring that the supply of housing in their areas is adequate. The authorities are: in England and Wales (outside London) the district councils; in London, the Greater London Council, the London borough councils and the Common Council of the City of London; and in Scotland, the district and islands councils. Other public housing authorities are the new town authorities, the Scottish Special Housing Association which supplements building by local authorities in Scotland, and the Development Board for Rural Wales. Subsidies are made available to the authorities to assist them with housing costs, and guidance is given on design and layout.

The construction or structural alteration of housing in both the public and private sectors is subject to the Building Regulations in England (except inner London) and Wales. The regulations, which are made by the Secretary of State for the Environment, have the force of law. They are enforced by the local authorities and are made primarily for the health and safety of people in and around the buildings, although they also include requirements for the conservation of energy. Different systems with the same aims are operated in inner London, Scotland and Northern Ireland.

Local authorities are involved in many other aspects of housing policy, such as the payment of house renovation grants and the implementation of housing renewal programmes. Many have established housing advisory centres to provide information on most aspects of housing.

Research and Development Research into building materials and techniques, as well as into the social, economic and design aspects of housing, is undertaken within the Department of the Environment. It is carried out by the Building Research Establishment of the Department's research directorate as well as by the directorates of economics, statistics and housing development. The Research and Development Group of the Scottish Development Department also undertakes research. Sponsored work is carried out by academic institutes, consultancies, market research firms and the Office of Population Censuses and Surveys, and local authorities may also have housing research programmes. Advice on ways of increasing quality, productivity and efficiency in house-building is provided by the National Building Agency.

**Home
Ownership**

The number of people owning their own homes has more than doubled in the last 20 years, and the 11 million owner-occupied dwellings in Britain account for over half of the total housing stock.

Mortgage Loans

Loans to enable people to buy their own homes are available from various sources, including building societies, insurance companies, industrial and provident societies, local authorities and banks.

Building societies (see also p 364) are by far the largest sources of such funds, their share of the market being about 80 per cent. They do not build houses themselves but lend money upon security by way of a mortgage on the home bought for owner-occupation. They usually advance up to 80 per cent of their valuation of a property but it is possible to borrow up to 100 per cent with the help of an appropriate insurance guarantee. Loans are normally repayable over periods of 20 or 25 years (up to 30 or 35 years in certain circumstances) by equal monthly instalments to cover capital and interest. The average price in Britain of all houses bought with a building society mortgage at the end of 1979 was about £24,100. In 1979 the societies advanced nearly £8,860 million.

Owner-occupiers are entitled to tax relief on their mortgage interest payments arising on up to £25,000 of their mortgages (on one house only) and in 1979–80 this totalled about £1,450 million. An alternative form of assistance is the option mortgage scheme, designed to help those with smaller incomes. It allows the borrower to receive, instead of tax relief, a subsidy which has the effect of reducing the rate of interest on the loan. Assistance under this scheme in Great Britain totalled £190 million in 1979–80. There is an associated guarantee scheme under which mortgage loans of up to 100 per cent of the valuation of a house (not exceeding £14,000) may be made to option borrowers. Other ways of helping people with lower incomes to become owner-occupiers include schemes operated by a number of local authorities which allow those buying homes for the first time, subject to certain conditions, to defer part of the mortgage payments that would normally be due in the early years until later in the mortgage term; and shared ownership schemes, under which the occupant purchases a part share of his or her home, paying rent on the remaining share.

From 1 December 1980 first-time home buyers who have saved for two years under the new homeloan scheme (set up under the Home Purchase Assistance and Housing Corporation Guarantee Act 1978) and are buying a home in the lower-price range, may qualify for a loan of £600, interest free for up to five years, and a tax-free cash bonus of up to £110.

*Building
Standards*

For building in the private sector the National House Building Council sets standards and enforces them by inspection and certification. Almost all new private houses are covered by the Council's insurance scheme which provides ten-year protection against major structural defects. Two-year protection is also given against faulty workmanship. Most lenders will not grant mortgages on a new house unless it is covered by a Council certificate.

**Public Sector
Housing**

Public housing authorities own nearly seven million houses and flats. The number of homes owned by each authority varies widely, several of the larger authorities having a stock of well over 100,000.

Local authorities meet the capital costs of new house construction and of modernisation of their existing stock by raising loans on the open market or by borrowing from the Public Works Loan Board. Current expenditure, including maintenance and management costs and loan interest and repayments, is met from rents, supplemented by subsidies from the Government and, where required to balance housing revenue accounts, from the rates. Local authorities are required to charge their tenants reasonable rents (which keep a balance between the interests of tenants and ratepayers). Subsidies for public housing in Great Britain during 1979–80 are expected to total some £2,500 million (including rent rebates payable to poorer tenants to assist in meeting rents of accommodation suited to their needs). Supplementary subsidies assist local authorities with slum clearance.

Most building is undertaken by private firms under contract although a number of authorities employ direct labour to build houses. Some authorities work in consortia to make the best use of experience and technical information, and to initiate research and development projects.

Sheltered accommodation (with an alarm system and resident warden) is provided for elderly people who need this degree of support. Increasing importance is also being placed on the housing needs of physically handi-capped people, and a small but growing proportion of the new housing stock is suitable for them. Also receiving attention are the needs of other 'disadvantaged' groups such as one-parent families, those who have suffered from mental illness, and victims of violence within the family.

Public housing is built to high standards, which include mandatory space and heating requirements. In England and Wales, for example, some 98·3 per cent of the new houses built for local authorities in 1978 had central heating and the average floor area of houses to accommodate five people was 89 square metres (958 square feet).

Local authorities have a statutory duty to ensure that accommodation (not necessarily an authority house) is available for homeless people who have dependent children or are vulnerable on grounds such as age or disability.

The Housing Act 1980 establishes a charter for public-sector tenants, giving them statutory rights such as security of tenure, provision for succession by a resident relative to the tenancy on death, rights of subletting and taking in lodgers, and reimbursement for improvements made by the tenant. With certain exceptions, public sector tenants of at least three years' standing can buy the freehold of their house, or a long lease of their flat, at a discount on the market price of from 33 per cent to 50 per cent, depending on the length of their occupation. The discount must be repaid in part or in full if the property is resold within five years. Tenants also have the right to be given a mortgage by the local authority to effect the purchase. Similar provisions for Scotland are contained in the Tenants' Rights etc (Scotland) Act 1980.

Privately Rented Housing

During the last quarter of a century there has been a steady decline in the number of rented dwellings available from private landlords (including tied accommodation)—from over 50 per cent of the housing stock to about 12 per cent (2·6 million). Major factors have been the increased demand for owner-occupation, the greater availability of public rented housing, and the operation of rent restriction. Privately rented dwellings form a high proportion of the older housing, most landlords being individuals with limited holdings; some rented housing is provided by larger property owners, including property companies.

Most privately rented dwellings are subject to rent restriction. Tenants have a wide degree of security of tenure, and may not be evicted without a court order. Harassment of residential occupiers is a criminal offence. To increase the availability of privately rented property the Government has introduced in the Housing Act 1980 and in the Tenants' Rights etc (Scotland) Act 1980 a new system of 'shorthold' lettings, under which tenants have security of tenure at a fair rent for an agreed period of between one and five years, but not for life; existing regulated lettings are not affected by the new legislation. Tenants with incomes up to average levels are eligible for assistance with their rent under a national scheme of rent allowances which is operated by local authorities and financed mainly by government subsidies.

There are two forms of rent restriction: regulation and the fixing of a reasonable rent by a rent tribunal. In a regulated tenancy a 'fair rent' is fixed by independent rent officers, at the request of the landlord, the tenant, or both; if the rent officer's decision is objected to by the landlord or the tenant, it is referred to a rent assessment committee. Once fixed, the rent is registered and not normally reviewed for at least two years. The other form of rent restriction applies to tenants with resident landlords and tenants of a few other types of furnished accommodation who may refer their tenancy agreements to a rent tribunal for determination of a reasonable rent. Tribunals may grant tenants security of tenure for up to six months with a possibility of further periods.

Housing Associations

Housing associations extend the choice of housing (which for most people is between owner-occupying or renting from a public authority or a private landlord) by providing an increasing amount of accommodation available for rent through new building or the rehabilitation of older property. The associations normally cater for people who would otherwise look to a local authority for a home. In addition to normal family housing, they provide particularly for the special needs of elderly, disabled and single people.

Since the early 1960s the Government has encouraged the growth of these non-profit-making associations which between them own nearly 340,000 dwellings. Rented housing schemes carried out by housing associations qualify for a government grant but only if the association is registered with the Housing Corporation, a statutory body set up by the Government. Some 2,800 associations are registered with the Corporation. Rented dwellings owned by housing associations come within the fair rent and rent allowance arrangements and many housing association tenants have rights under the tenants' charter in the Housing Act 1980 (see p 192).

Alternative forms of tenure on local authority estates and within the housing association sector are being encouraged in order to give occupiers a greater stake in the ownership or management of their homes. The Housing Corporation is engaged in a pilot programme including co-ownership and community leasehold schemes.

Improving Older Houses

Modernisation and conversion of sub-standard housing, with the help of grants from public funds, has increasingly been encouraged as an alternative to clearing and rebuilding and as a way of preserving established communities and of making more economic use of resources.

Renovation grants paid to householders to improve over 1·4 million homes were paid in Great Britain between 1967 and 1979. A further 1·2 million public sector homes were also improved in this period.

There are four types of renovation grant: improvement grants, for carrying out improvements to a high standard or for conversion into flats; intermediate grants, for the provision of standard amenities and associated repairs; repair grants; and special grants (not available in Scotland) for providing standard amenities, repairs and means of escape from fire in houses which are in multiple occupation.

Declaring 'general improvement areas' and 'housing action areas' enables local authorities in England and Wales to tackle the improvement of whole areas of older housing systematically. General improvement areas (of which there are about 1,300) consist of fundamentally sound houses and a stable population. Housing action areas (about 440) are characterised by particularly poor housing and bad physical conditions combined with social stress. Local authorities have special powers to bring about an improvement in living conditions for the benefit of residents within a five-year period. In both types of area government financial aid for environmental improvement is available to local authorities. Grants to householders may range up to 75 per cent, and in certain cases (such as hardship) up to 90 per cent.

An 'improvement-for-sale' scheme has also been introduced; the Government makes contributions towards any loss a local authority may make in buying, improving and selling rundown or neglected housing.

In Scotland, the term 'general improvement area' is not used; 'housing action area' powers are available for areas in which at least half the houses fail to meet prescribed physical standards and there is no time limit on the period within which improvement must be carried out. Outside housing action areas in Scotland local authorities have power to require the improvement of houses below the statutory tolerable standard, or lacking a bathroom, by improvement orders and grants payable at 75 per cent of eligible costs.

Slum Clearance

In urban areas of Britain slum clearance and redevelopment have been major features of housing policy. Since the mid-1950s about 3½ million people have been rehoused in England and Wales as a result of slum clearance programmes. Clearance of large areas of 'irredeemable' slums is now almost at an end and greater emphasis is placed on renewal and modernisation wherever possible. Local authorities receive special financial assistance from the Government.

Housing authorities are obliged to see that other accommodation exists, or can be provided by them, for people displaced by slum clearance. Owners of land compulsorily acquired during slum clearance programmes receive as compensation either the full market value or, if the land consists of unfit houses, a sum based on the value of the cleared site; additional payments are, however, made to most owner-occupiers of unfit houses to bring their compensation up to market value.

Redevelopment of the slums has presented many problems. Most of the areas were seriously overcrowded; but while they usually lacked social facilities they had the advantage of already being provided with the basic utilities, jobs were usually available in the vicinity and town centre facilities were not far away. The aim in carrying out slum clearance was thus to house as many people as possible on the cleared sites. This was most easily achieved if fairly large areas were cleared and high-rise flats built. The results in many areas are now seen as less than satisfactory in spite of the high standard of many of the homes themselves. The main criticisms of multi-storey flats are that they are inhuman in scale and unsuitable for families with young children because of the lack of convenient play space. The need to build to a reasonably high density in inner city areas still exists, but is now being met by carefully grouped low-rise blocks, including individual houses wherever possible.

Northern Ireland

The Northern Ireland Department of the Environment is responsible for housing policy in Northern Ireland. The Northern Ireland Housing Executive, with a stock of some 190,000 dwellings, is responsible for the provision and management of public authority housing and for dealing with unfit dwellings whether publicly or privately owned.

Northern Ireland has a major problem of unfit and derelict housing, especially in Belfast, and the situation has been made worse by civil disturbance. Housing policy is therefore directed towards maintaining and improving the existing dwelling stock and mounting a major attack on housing problems in Belfast. The concept of housing action areas has been developed to facilitate concerted action in designated areas and a five-year programme for the rehabilitation of Belfast began in 1977. Action has also been taken to stimulate the voluntary housing movement and with the encouragement of the Department in conjunction with the Northern Ireland Federation of Housing Associations, registered housing associations are undertaking a large programme of schemes for groups such as the elderly and disabled and are also playing a significant part in the rehabilitation of older dwellings, especially in Belfast.

In the private rented sector the Rent (Northern Ireland) Order 1978 replaced earlier legislation with a single statute designed to safeguard tenants' rights while providing landlords with sufficient rental income to maintain their property in good condition. Under the Order landlords are empowered to increase the rents of certain properties meeting a specified standard of physical condition to a level comparable with those charged by the Northern Ireland Housing Executive. Policy for the private sector is under review.

Another trend in housing policy is the attempt to widen housing options available to families, particularly those who wish to own their own homes. The Option Mortgage Scheme is in operation and the Home Loan Scheme for first-time buyers has been extended to Northern Ireland. The concept of shared ownership (see p 191) is being developed in the public sector by the Northern Ireland Housing Executive and in the private sector by the Northern Ireland Co-Ownership Housing Association. In line with government policy, the Northern Ireland Housing Executive has offered its dwellings (with the exception of flats, maisonettes and sheltered dwellings) for sale to sitting tenants.

10 The Churches

Everyone in Britain has the right of religious freedom (in teaching, worship and observance) without interference from the community or the State. Churches and religious societies may own property, conduct schools, and propagate their beliefs in speech and writing. There is no religious or denominational bar to the holding of public office.

Clergy of the established churches of England and Scotland work in services administered by the State, such as the armed forces, national hospitals and prisons, and are paid a salary by the State. Clergy of other denominations are also appointed. Voluntary schools provided by any religious denomination may be wholly or partly maintained from public funds.

There is no precise or uniform information about the number of church adherents since no inquiries are normally made about religious beliefs in censuses or other official returns, and each church adopts its own criteria in counting its members. Membership figures in this chapter are therefore approximate.

The Church of England

The established Church of England's relationship with the State is one of mutual obligation—privileges accorded to the Church balanced by certain duties which it must fulfil. The Sovereign must always be a member of the Church, and promises to uphold it; Church of England archbishops, bishops and deans are appointed by the Sovereign on the advice of the Prime Minister; all clergy take an oath of allegiance to the Crown. The Church can regulate its own worship. The two archbishops (of Canterbury and York), the bishops of London, Durham and Winchester, and 21 other bishops (according to their seniority as diocesan bishops) sit in the House of Lords. Clergy of the Church (together with those of the Church of Scotland, the Church of Ireland and the Roman Catholic Church) are not allowed to sit in the House of Commons.

The Church has two provinces: Canterbury, comprising 29 dioceses, and York, 14 dioceses. The dioceses are divided into parishes, of which there are some 13,860. The Archbishop of Canterbury is 'Primate of All England', and the Archbishop of York 'Primate of England'. Of the population born and resident in the two provinces (roughly 46 million), about 58 per cent are baptised into the Church and some 19 per cent are confirmed members.

The central governing body, the General Synod, has both spiritual authority and legislative and administrative powers; and bishops, clergy and lay members are involved in decisions. Certain important issues must be referred for the approval of the dioceses before being decided by the Synod. Lay members are associated with church government in the parishes through the ancient office of churchwarden and the modern parochial church councils.

The General Synod is the centre of an administrative system dealing with such matters as education, mission, inter-church relations, social questions, recruitment and training for the ministry, church work at home and overseas and the care of church buildings, particularly those of historic and architectural interest. The Synod is also concerned with church schools; church colleges of education; theological colleges; and establishments for training women in pastoral work.

The Church has its own courts whose jurisdiction today extends only to matters of purely ecclesiastical concern.

Church finance is administered locally by the parishes and the dioceses, with contributions to a central fund for the maintenance of central services, including capital expenditure on training and theological colleges and grants for training candidates for ordination. The State makes no direct financial contribution to church expenses. The Church's endowment income is mainly administered by the Church Commissioners, the body largely responsible for the payment of clergy stipends and pensions.

The Anglican Communion

The Anglican Communion comprises 25 autonomous provinces in Britain and overseas and three regional councils overseas with a total membership of about 67 million. In the British Isles, there are four provinces: the Church of England (established), the Church in Wales, the Episcopal Church in Scotland, and the Church of Ireland.

Every ten years the Lambeth Conference meets for unofficial consultation among all Anglican bishops (the last meeting was in 1978): presided over by the Archbishop of Canterbury, it has no executive authority, but enjoys great prestige, and its findings on doctrine, discipline, relations with other communions, and attitudes to political and social questions are widely studied. The Anglican Consultative Council—an assembly of laymen and clergy as well as bishops which meets every two or three years—is designed to provide consultations within the Anglican Communion and to serve as an instrument of common action. The Council last met in 1979.

The Church of Scotland

The Church of Scotland has a presbyterian form of government. Its status as the national church derives from the Treaty of Union 1707 and the Church of Scotland Act 1921 which confirmed its complete freedom in all spiritual matters. It appoints its own officers, and its decisions on questions of doctrine and discipline are not subject to parliamentary discussion or modification.

All ministers have equal status, each of some 1,870 churches being governed locally by the Kirk Session, consisting of the minister and the elected elders of the Church; above the Kirk Session is the Court of the Presbytery, then the Court of the Synod, and finally the General Assembly, consisting of elected ministers and elders, which meets annually under the presidency of an elected moderator who serves for one year. The Sovereign is represented at the General Assembly by the Lord High Commissioner. The adult communicant membership of the Church of Scotland is estimated at over 970,000.

The Free Churches

The phrase 'Free Churches' is commonly used to describe the 'nonconformist' churches of England and Wales (which dissent from certain practices of the established church and, generally speaking, have distinctive convictions regarding organisation and worship) and Protestant churches in other parts of Britain (apart from the established Church of Scotland). Certain other churches and religious associations have links with the main Free Churches.

The Methodist Church, the largest of the Free Churches with nearly 517,000 adult full members, originated in the eighteenth century following the evangelical revival by John Wesley, and is based on a 1932 union of most of the separate Methodist Churches. The Methodist Churches which did not join the union include the Independent Methodists (5,000 members) and the Wesleyan Reform Union (with some 4,000 members).

The Baptists are nearly all grouped in associations of churches, most of which belong to the Baptist Union of Great Britain and Ireland (formed in 1813), with a total membership of about 178,000; in addition there are separate Baptist Unions for Scotland, Wales and Ireland and other Baptist churches.

The United Reformed Church, with some 157,000 members, was formed in 1972 when the Congregational Church in England and Wales (the oldest community of dissenters in Britain) and the Presbyterian Church of England merged—the first transdenominational union of churches in Britain since the Reformation in the sixteenth century.

Among the other Free Churches are the Presbyterian Church in Ireland (with some 132,000 regular communicants in Northern Ireland); the Presbyterian (or Calvinistic Methodist) Church of Wales, which arose from the revivalist movement led in 1735 by Howell Harris and now numbers about 87,000; the Union of Welsh Independents; the Free Church of Scotland; the United Free Church of Scotland; the Free Presbyterian Church of Scotland; the Reformed Presbyterian Church of Scotland; the Reformed Presbyterian Church of Ireland; and the Non-Subscribing Presbyterian Church of Ireland.

Other Protestant denominations include: the Unitarian and Free Christian Churches; the Churches of Christ (known also in the United States of America as Disciples of Christ), which have been an organised community in Britain since early in the nineteenth century; the British Province of the Moravian Church, which is an international missionary church; the Free Church of England (or Reformed Episcopal Church), which was formed in 1844 as a direct result of the Oxford Movement; and the Congregational Federation, formed from Congregational churches which did not enter the United Reformed Church.

The Religious Society of Friends (Quakers), with about 19,000 members in Britain and over 440 places for worship, came into being in the middle of the seventeenth century under the leadership of George Fox and works for peace and the relief of suffering in many parts of the world.

The Salvation Army, founded in Britain in 1865, has since spread to 82 other countries and has a strength of about 2·5 million. Within Britain it has some 100,000 active members operating from more than 1,000 centres of worship. Believing in a very practical expression of Christian concern, the Salvation Army has 200 centres to help people in need.

There are also a number of other religious organisations with churches or assemblies in Britain, including the Church of Jesus Christ of Latter-Day Saints (the Mormon Church); and the Christian Scientists with some 262 branch churches and societies in the British Isles.

The Roman Catholic Church

The Roman Catholic hierarchy in England and Wales, which became temporarily extinct during the sixteenth century, was restored in 1850; the Scottish hierarchy became extinct in the early seventeenth century and was restored in 1878. There are now six Roman Catholic provinces in Great Britain, each under an archbishop, 26 episcopal dioceses, and some 3,000 parishes. In Northern Ireland, there are nine dioceses, some of which have territory partly in the Irish Republic. It is estimated that there are some 5 million adherents (including children) to the Roman Catholic faith in the whole of Britain.

The Roman Catholic Church attaches great importance to the education of its children and requires its members to try to bring up their children in the Catholic faith. Many schools for Catholic children are staffed by members of the religious orders who also undertake other social work such as nursing, child care, and the conduct of homes for old people.

Jewry

Jews first settled in England at the time of the Norman conquest, but the community in Britain dates from 1656; consisting of some 400,000 people, including both Sephardi (originally from Spain and Portugal) and Ashkenazi (from Germany and Eastern Europe), it has become one of the largest groups of Jews in Europe. The community is divided into two schools of thought—the Orthodox, to which about 80 per cent of practising Jews belong; and the Reform, which originated in 1840 and was followed in 1901 by the Liberal Jewish movement. The Chief Rabbi is the head of the largest group (Ashkenazi) within Orthodox Jewry; the Haham is the head of the Sephardi group. Jewish congregations in Britain number about 300. Jewish denominational schools are attended by about one in four Jewish children.

Other Religious Communities

Immigrants to Britain from Commonwealth and foreign countries have established centres of worship, especially in London, for their own communities. Among the Christian communities represented are Orthodox, Lutheran and Reformed Churches of various European countries and the Armenian Church.

The principal non-Christian communities in Britain, apart from the Jews, are the Muslims, Buddhists, Hindus and Sikhs. For the many Muslims in Britain there are mosques or Islamic centres in London, Birmingham, Manchester, Cardiff, Glasgow and in many other large cities. The community's headquarters are at the London Central Mosque and Islamic Cultural Centre.

The Buddhist Society, with headquarters in London and centres in most large towns and many universities, publishes and makes known the principles of Buddhism and encourages their study and practice. It adheres to no one school of Buddhism. There are other centres for Buddhism, and also centres of eastern philosophy and religion among immigrant communities.

Co-operation among the Churches

The British Council of Churches, with representatives or observers from all the main Christian churches in the British Isles, facilitates common action and seeks to further Christian unity. It works through five divisions: Christian Aid (which has a separate constitution); Conference for World Mission; Ecumenical Affairs; Community Affairs; and International Affairs.

The Free Church Federal Council (which has a concordat with the British Council of Churches) comprises most of the Free Churches in England and Wales. It promotes unity and joint action among the Free Churches and is a channel for communication with central and local government.

The permanent Anglican-Roman Catholic Commission explores points of possible unity between the two communions.

The Anglican and the main Free Churches in the British Isles also participate in the World Council of Churches (of which the British Council of Churches is an associated national council) which links together some 300 churches in over 80 countries for co-operation and the study of common problems. The Council of Christians and Jews works for better understanding among members of the two religions and deals with problems in the social field. The British Broadcasting Corporation has also established a committee for Relations with People of Other Faiths.

The Sharing of Church Buildings Act 1969 enables agreements to be made by two or more churches for the sharing of church buildings.

11 · The National Economy

Britain exports a larger part of its production of goods and services than any other industrial nation of comparable size—about one-third of gross domestic product, a higher proportion than in the Federal Republic of Germany or France and considerably higher than in the United States or Japan. Manufacturing industry accounts for 28 per cent of total domestic output and services[1] for 62 per cent.

Britain ranks fifth in world trade (after the United States, the Federal Republic of Germany, Japan and France), and accounts for 5·5 per cent of total world trade. It takes around 7 per cent of the world's exports of primary products (excluding food) and has provided about 9 per cent of the main manufacturing countries' exports of manufactured goods in each of the last seven years. It is one of the world's largest importers of agricultural products, raw materials and semi-manufactures, and is among the largest exporters of aerospace products, motor vehicles, electrical equipment, finished textiles, and most types of machinery. It is also a growing oil exporter.

The economy is largely based on private enterprise, but has some major State-owned (nationalised) industries and some enterprises with both private and state participation (see p 222).

With the discovery and exploitation of North Sea oil and gas, Britain achieved virtual self-sufficiency in oil and gas in 1980 with substantial benefits to the balance of payments through the reduction of oil imports. Other economic effects of the offshore oil industry include the revenues accruing through taxation, the new jobs created, and the stimulus provided for the development and sales of highly specialised equipment and services.

A high level of agricultural productivity enables Britain to provide just over half the food it needs from its own soil, although only 2·6 per cent of the employed labour force is engaged in agriculture—a lower proportion than in any other major industrial country.

Britain earns overseas currency by exports of (mainly) manufactured goods and by invisible transactions—in overseas investment, travel, civil aviation, shipping, and financial and other services. It accounts for almost 9 per cent of world invisible receipts (excluding government transactions) and is second only to the United States in its invisible surplus.

The significant contribution made to export earnings by invisibles is in large measure a reflection of Britain's position as a major financial centre. Its banks, insurance underwriters and brokers and other financial institutions provide worldwide financial services. The City of London contains perhaps the most comprehensive and advanced capital market in the world.

ECONOMIC DEVELOPMENT

Earlier History As a result of the Industrial Revolution during the eighteenth and nineteenth centuries (when a series of inventions led to a complete change in the character

---

[1] Services in this context cover transport, communications, distributive trades, insurance, banking, finance and business services, ownership of dwellings, public administration and defence, public health and education, and other services.

of production), Britain emerged as the first great industrial nation and as a pioneer of new methods in transport, communications and technology. It occupied the leading position as world manufacturer, merchant, carrier, banker and investor, and its fast-growing economy supported a rapidly increasing population. In the period from 1870 to 1890 British industry had a clear though declining lead over that of other countries. Between 1890 and 1914, industrial competition from Europe and North America grew, but its effects on Britain's export industries, particularly cotton textiles and coal, were offset by a number of factors including the rise in world trade and the returns on Britain's large overseas investments.

Following the first world war Britain's older industries met increasing competition, for example, in coal and iron and steel from other European countries and in textiles from some eastern countries where labour was cheaper. The difficulties were increased by the world economic depression which began in 1929 and the associated attempts by many countries to reduce imports. The result in Britain, as in many other countries, was heavy unemployment. After 1932 levels of production and employment rose. The decade saw a strong expansion in the vehicles, electrical, chemical and aircraft industries, while the construction of 3 million houses brought about a large growth in the building and ancillary industries.

The Second World War and After

During the second world war (1939–45) rapid and far-reaching re-orientation of the economy towards the war effort was secured by central planning. The Government involvement in the economy which this implied has remained, in a modified form, a feature of the British economic system.

In spite of generous aid from the United States and Canada, the war made heavy inroads on British domestic capital through shipping losses, bomb damage, and arrears of industrial maintenance and replacements. Large quantities of overseas investments were sold, new external debts were accumulated, and exports were greatly reduced.

After the war rationing and other controls were relaxed gradually as civil production expanded and trade recovered. The period after 1945 was one of rising production and, until 1970, a low level of unemployment (generally 2·5 per cent or lower); but economic growth, which averaged 2 to 3 per cent up to 1971, was slower than in most other western European countries. There were also certain persistent economic problems, particularly the periodic difficulties with the balance of payments. In spite of the contribution from invisibles, there were substantial deficits on current account in a number of years.

In the 1960s successive governments sought to deal with these problems in a number of ways, sometimes restraining the growth in home demand and implementing policies designed to hold down rises in incomes and prices. Following the devaluation of sterling in 1967, from $2·80 to $2·40=£1, exports recovered, leading to a substantial surplus on visible trade and a record current account surplus in 1971.

Recent Developments

In 1973, the economy achieved an annual growth rate of about 7 per cent. However, with, among other things, general inflation and the abrupt increase in the prices of commodities in 1972 and 1973, particularly of oil in late 1973, the world economy entered a phase of recession. At the same time, the very large balance of payments surpluses of the oil-producing countries following the rise in oil prices gave rise to a corresponding deficit for the oil-importing countries collectively, which could not quickly be eliminated. Although some recovery from this recession was evident from about 1976, it proved to be weak, especially in Britain.

The rate of price inflation accelerated in almost all countries in 1979, with crude oil prices almost doubling over the year. Output in the industrial countries was, however, relatively buoyant although unemployment began to rise again. World trade in manufactures grew by around 5 per cent, slightly faster than in 1978 but well below the pre-1973 trend of 10 per cent annually. Industrial countries as a whole moved into balance of payments deficit.

The British economy grew slowly in 1979. Gross domestic product (output measure) rose by 1·7 per cent in real terms compared with an annual average rate of growth of 1 per cent over the period 1973–78 and 3 per cent from 1963 to 1973. The North Sea oil and gas sector was responsible for about half of the growth in gross domestic product in 1979, production rising by more than 40 per cent, following a four-fold increase over the period 1976–78. In 1979 the value of oil and gas sales from the UK Continental Shelf (at contract prices) plus identifiable balance of payments current account items (net) is estimated to have amounted to £4,300 million.

Real disposable incomes increased substantially in Britain in 1979 as gross earnings rose faster than prices and income tax was reduced. Real personal disposable income was 6 per cent higher in 1979 than in 1978. Consumers' spending rose in real terms by 4 per cent over the same period.

Total fixed investment fell by 1·4 per cent in 1979 in real terms, with reduced investment in the North Sea oil and gas industries and in dwellings. Investment by the distributive and service industries (after adjusting for leasing) rose by 4·4 per cent in 1979, the fourth successive year of growth. Manufacturing investment, including leased assets, rose by 2·7 per cent. The growth in leasing has been a recent development.

The volume of exports of goods increased by about 4 per cent in 1979, compared with some 3 per cent in 1978. Within the 1979 total, exports of fuels increased by 33 per cent, but exports of manufactures were virtually unchanged. The volume of imports grew by 10 per cent in the year but, within this, imports of manufactures rose by 15 per cent, particularly consumer products and especially passenger motor cars, reflecting the fact that much of the rise in consumer demand was met by imports.

The slow fall in unemployment over the previous two years ended towards the close of 1979 and during the first half of 1980 the level of unemployment increased.

Retail prices rose by an average of 16 per cent a year between 1973 and 1978. The rate of increase, which dipped temporarily from 1977, began to accelerate in 1979 as earlier favourable movements in commodity prices ended and as accelerating wage costs were reflected in prices. By September 1980 the retail prices index was 15·9 per cent higher than a year earlier. The tax and price index, which takes account of changes in both prices and direct taxation, was 17·3 per cent higher than a year earlier.

Economic Policy

The Government elected in May 1979 has identified the long-term weaknesses of the British economy as high inflation, slow growth and poor industrial performance. As the beginning of a medium-term policy to reverse the decline, the Budget strategy announced in June 1979 was to curb inflation by firm fiscal and monetary policies and to improve the supply side of the economy by removing obstacles and allowing market forces to work. To strengthen incentives the burden of taxation was partly shifted from direct to indirect taxation.

In November 1979 the Government announced a series of measures which underlined its determination to secure monetary control. These included raising the Bank of England minimum lending rate to 17 per cent (reduced to 16 per cent in July 1980).

A four-year financial strategy covering expenditure, taxation and the money supply was announced in the March 1980 Budget. The Government's first priority remains to reduce the rate of inflation by means of a steady reduction in the rate of monetary growth, supported by cuts in public spending and borrowing and a continuing strengthening of the supply side of the economy by tax and other incentives and improved efficiency. The strategy shows growth of sterling M3 (money in circulation and UK residents' sterling bank deposits) falling from 7–11 per cent in 1980–81 to about 6 per cent in 1983–84. In order to achieve this without intolerably high interest rates, public sector borrowing is to be reduced from 4·75 per cent of GDP in 1979–80 to 1·5 per cent in 1983–84. The volume of public spending is to be progressively reduced to a level in 1983–84 about 4 per cent lower than in 1979–80. Planned spending in 1980–81 will be reduced by over 0·5 per cent in real terms. Spending on defence, law and order, health and social security will rise over the period; the main reductions in expenditure will be in the industry, energy and employment programmes, housing and education. The reduction in the net contribution to the European Community budget, negotiated in mid-1980, will bring about a further saving.

ECONOMIC MANAGEMENT

The Government's policies are carried out by the main departments with economic responsibilities on a national scale: the Treasury, the Departments of Trade, Industry, Employment, Energy, the Environment, and Transport and the Ministry of Agriculture, Fisheries and Food. Other specialist bodies advise on specific aspects of economic policy and include the National Economic Development Council, which brings together representatives of government, management and trade unions under the chairmanship of the Prime Minister, the Office of Fair Trading, a government agency concerned with the conduct of trade and industry (see p 231) and the Monopolies and Mergers Commission (see p 231).

On matters of major public policy such as the broad economic strategy, and on the economic problems it faces, the Government makes known its purposes, and keeps in touch with developments throughout the economy, by means of informal and continuous links with the chief industrial, financial, labour and other interests. Final responsibility for the broad lines of economic policy rests with the Cabinet. For regional economic planning see Chapter 8.

Public Enterprise

In Britain's mixed economy, direct State intervention in industry and commerce (as well as in social, cultural and other affairs) has often been effected through special public corporations set up, usually by statute, to deal with a particular activity. Though not part of a government department, the corporations are under varying degrees of public control. The Government is reducing the extent of State-ownership of industry by selling off some assets, increasing competition and providing opportunities for employees to participate where appropriate. Shares are to be sold in British Aerospace and (eventually) British Airways, changing their status to limited liability companies.

The major nationalised industries are the National Coal Board, British Gas, the electricity industry and the British National Oil Corporation; the British Steel Corporation, British Aerospace and British Shipbuilders; the Post

Office; British Rail, the National Freight Corporation, the National Bus Company and British Airways. These industries and services, which employ about 8 per cent of all employees, are described in their relevant sections. The public sector employs about 30 per cent of the working population.

NATIONAL INCOME AND EXPENDITURE

The following sections sketch briefly the structure and disposal of Britain's national income in recent years.

Output

In 1979 Britain's gross national product at factor cost (the measure of the total value of goods and services produced at home and net income from abroad) is estimated to have amounted to nearly £164,000 million. After allowing for price changes, the increase over the ten years since 1969 was 21 per cent.

Just under 30 per cent of total output can be attributed to manufacturing industry, rather less than a decade ago. Expanding industry groups in recent years have been mining and quarrying (reflecting the contribution of North Sea oil and gas), and services including insurance, banking and finance and health and education.

TABLE 7: Gross Domestic Product by Industry[a] *(at current prices)*

	1969		1974		1979	
	£m.	per cent	£m.	per cent	£m.	per cent
Agriculture, forestry and fishing	1,198	3·0	2,078	2·8	3,792	2·3
Mining and quarrying	614	1·6	1,076	1·5	7,807	4·8
Manufacturing	13,094	33·0	21,601	29·0	45,582	27·9
Construction	2,704	6·8	5,996	8·1	10,237	6·3
Gas, electricity and water	1,387	3·5	2,277	3·1	4,752	2·9
Transport	2,493	6·3	4,360	5·9	9,491	5·8
Communications	925	2·3	2,129	2·9	4,307	2·6
Distributive trades	4,213	10·6	7,754	10·4	17,146	10·5
Insurance, banking and finance (including real estate)	2,710	6·8	6,232	8·4	14,891	9·1
Ownership of dwellings	2,080	5·2	4,609	6·2	9,837	6·0
Public administration and defence	2,635	6·7	5,472	7·4	11,752	7·2
Public health and educational services	2,093	5·3	4,838	6·5	11,030	6·7
Other services	5,082	12·8	9,326	12·5	22,267	13·6
Adjustment for financial services	1,245	3·1	3,542	4·8	7,809	4·8
Residual error	350	0·9	208	0·3	1,435	0·9
Gross domestic product at factor cost	39,633	100·0	74,414	100·0	163,647	100·0
Net property income from abroad	498		1,428		289	
Gross national product at factor cost	40,131		75,842		163,936	

Source: *National Income and Expenditure 1980 Edition*
[a] Before provision for depreciation but after deducting stock appreciation.
[b] Differences between totals and the sums of their component parts are due to rounding.

**Use of
Resources**

Table 8 shows the distribution of total supplies of goods and services in 1969, 1974 and 1979 at 1975 market prices. Among the main trends since 1969 is a rise in the proportion devoted to exports.

TABLE 8: Distribution of Total Supplies of Goods and Services (*at 1975 market prices*)

	1969		1974		1979	
	£m.	per cent	£m.	per cent	£m.	per cent
Consumers' expenditure	56,313	48·8	64,881	47·6	70,816	47·2
General government final consumption*a*	18,829	16·3	21,761	16·0	24,334	16·2
Gross domestic capital formation	19,973	17·3	22,044	16·2	22,116	14·7
*Private sector*b	10,390		11,641		13,761	
*Public sector*b	8,586		8,975		6,745	
Exports of goods and services	20,387	17·7	27,695	20·3	32,896	21·9
Total final expenditure	115,383	100·0	136,381	100·0	150,162	100·0

Source: *National Income and Expenditure 1980 Edition*
a Current expenditure on goods and services plus non-trading capital consumption.
b Excluding value of physical change in stocks and work in progress (£1,610 million in total in 1979).
Differences between totals and the sums of their component parts are due to rounding. The discrepancy for 1969 is particularly large owing to the method used to rebase at 1975 prices.

**Personal
Income and
Consumers'
Expenditure**

Personal incomes before tax at current prices rose rapidly and fairly steadily from £39,240 million in 1969 to £166,470 million in 1979. Real personal disposable income was 6 per cent higher in 1979 than in 1978.

Consumers' expenditure amounted to 69 per cent of total pre-tax income in 1979 compared with 74 per cent in 1969. The difference is accounted for by a sharp rise in the personal savings ratio.

Sources of Income   Income from employment in 1979 totalled £113,930 million and accounted for about 68 per cent of total personal income. The three other main sources of personal income were self-employment (9 per cent), income from rent, dividends and interest (10 per cent), and grants from general government (13 per cent).

The combined effect of all taxation and transfer payments and benefits in kind is to redistribute income on more egalitarian lines. According to studies by the Central Statistical Office, the effect is broadly to raise the share of the poorest fifth of households from about 1 per cent of total original income to about 9 per cent of all final income. This group contains 12 per cent of the population and consists mainly of retired people, dependent on State pensions. The share of the richest fifth falls from about 44 per cent to about 36 per cent.

*Consumers'
Expenditure*

A rise in the volume of consumers' spending has been accompanied, in Britain as in other advanced industrial countries, by changes in its pattern.

Table 9 shows the amounts and proportions of consumers' expenditure at current prices in 1969 and 1979. Over this period the proportions spent on food, tobacco, and clothing and footwear fell while the proportions spent on alcoholic drink, housing and cars and motorcycles rose. At constant (1975) prices consumers' expenditure increased by 4 per cent between 1978 and 1979.

Personal income and expenditure 1979 (at current prices)

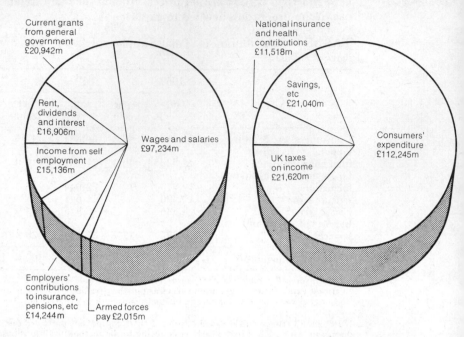

Current grants from general government £20,942m

National insurance and health contributions £11,518m

Rent, dividends and interest £16,906m

Income from self employment £15,136m

Savings, etc £21,040m

Wages and salaries £97,234m

UK taxes on income £21,620m

Consumers' expenditure £112,245m

Employers' contributions to insurance, pensions, etc £14,244m

Armed forces pay £2,015m

Income (before tax)   **Expenditure**

Note: Figures are estimates (rounded to nearest million) and exclude items under £375 million.

TABLE 9: Changes in Pattern of Consumers' Spending (*at current prices*)

	1969		1979	
	£m.	per cent	£m.	per cent
Food (household expenditure)	6,019	20·6	20,505	17·9
Alcoholic drink	2,029	6·9	8,873	7·7
Tobacco	1,694	5·8	4,279	3·7
Housing (rent, rates, repairs, etc.)	3,679	12·6	16,501	14·4
Fuel and light	1,430	4·9	5,327	4·6
Clothing and footwear	2,505	8·6	8,876	7·7
Cars and motorcycles	809	2·8	4,728	4·1
Other durable goods	1,254	4·3	5,583	4·9
Running costs of motor vehicles	1,616	5·5	6,917	6·0
Other travel expenditure	932	3·2	3,795	3·3
Catering (meals and accommodation)	1,427	4·9	6,253	5·4
Other goods	2,787	9·5	12,075	10·5
Other services	3,041	10·4	12,197	10·6
Other items[a]	11	—	−1,104	−1·0
TOTAL	29,233	100·0	114,805	100·0

Source: *National Income and Expenditure 1980 Edition*
[a] Consumers' expenditure abroad, less expenditure by foreign tourists in Britain, plus income in kind not included elsewhere.

Current Expenditure of General Government

Current expenditure on goods and services by the central Government and local authorities rose by about 29 per cent at 1975 market prices over the period 1969 to 1979 when it amounted to almost 23 per cent of the gross domestic product (at current prices). The main cause of this increase was the growth over the period of the social services, especially education and the National Health Service. In the same period defence accounted for a declining share of general government expenditure on goods and services (22 per cent in 1978 and 1979 compared with 32 per cent in 1968 and 48 per cent in 1953).

In addition to their expenditure on goods and services, public authorities transfer large sums to other sectors, mainly the personal sector, by way of national insurance and other social security benefits, grants, and interest and subsidies (see pp 145 and 191). The Government also makes grants to local authorities to finance about 60 per cent of their current expenditure.

Investment

Gross domestic fixed capital formation (total fixed investment) represents about 20 per cent of the gross domestic product at factor cost. The total value of fixed assets in Britain, valued at constant replacement cost, is estimated to have increased by 37 per cent between 1969 and 1979 when their current replacement value, net of depreciation, was some £605,400 million, of which about two-thirds was accounted for by buildings and one-third by plant and machinery, and vehicles.

Within the total of gross domestic fixed capital formation in 1979 (£20,506 million compared with a peak of £21,195 million in 1973 at constant 1975 prices) private sector investment accounted for 67 per cent (58 per cent in 1973), general government for 16 per cent (27 per cent) and public corporations for 17 per cent (15 per cent). The approximate shares of industry groups in total fixed investment in 1979 were (1973 figures in brackets): manufacturing, 20 per cent (16 per cent), gas, electricity and water, 5 per cent (5 per cent), petroleum and natural gas 6 per cent (1 per cent), transport and communications, 9 per cent (13 per cent), distributive trades, 7 per cent (6 per cent), dwellings, 17 per cent (19 per cent), social and other public services, 10 per cent (16 per cent), and other industries, 26 per cent (22 per cent). There is a marked cyclical pattern in the flow of investment by manufacturing industry; it was at a peak in 1970 and 1974, fell in 1975 and 1976 but increased in 1977, 1978 and 1979. Among the trends in recent years has been the increase in investment in North Sea oil and gas equipment which reached a peak in 1976.

THE EXTERNAL POSITION

Overseas Trade and Payments

A broad picture of Britain's trade in the 1970s shows a strong trade balance in the early part of the period which deteriorated considerably in 1973 and 1974 after sharp increases in oil and other commodity prices. Some of the pressure was offset by falls in the sterling exchange rate following floating of the pound in 1972 (see p 208) and export volume increased by 30 per cent between 1973 and 1979, with a surplus on the current account in 1978. However, a large deterioration in visible trade occurred in 1979. The contribution from oil continued to increase but there was a substantial fall in the surplus on manufactured goods. (A major factor in this decline was the worsening international competitiveness of British goods caused by the failure of the sterling exchange rate to adjust in line with relative inflation rates.) A fall in the invisibles surplus was caused mainly by sharp increases in the profits of overseas oil companies in Britain, higher contributions to the European Community budget and higher aid payments. There was a surplus on the capital account in 1979, a net identified inflow of £1,170 million representing a balance between the substantial capital outflows following abolition of exchange controls during the year and inflows resulting from a marked change in the attractiveness of sterling. For details of overseas trade and payments see Chapter 19.

Exchange Rates and External Debt

In 1971, a general international realignment of exchange rates was agreed at a meeting held in the Smithsonian Institute in Washington, in which all the main currencies were in effect revalued against the dollar. (The rates of exchange fixed in that agreement are called Smithsonian parities.) As part of this realignment, the sterling rate for the dollar moved up by just over 8½ per cent, the new middle rate being $2·60571 compared with the old par value of $2·40. In June 1972 sterling was allowed to float. Subsequent movements were broadly downwards to a low level in 1976, after which, helped by the positive economic implications of Britain's energy prospects, the pressure on the pound in the foreign exchange markets was generally upwards. Since 1979 sterling has been among the stronger currencies, reflecting the market's favourable assessment of Britain's position as an oil producer at a time of rising oil prices and its relatively high interest rates. At the beginning of September 1980 the effective rate was 76·5 (December 1971 = 100) and the market rate £1 = $2·42.

Britain incurred large overseas debts to finance balance of payments deficits in the years 1973–76. In consequence total official foreign borrowing outstanding rose to $25,200 million by the end of 1977 (compared with some $5,000 million at the end of 1972, largely accounted for by long-term post-war debts). By the end of 1977, however, the improvement in the external position enabled policy to be directed towards reducing the total debt outstanding and the concentration of debt due to be repaid in 1979–84. This has been done by a combination of early repayments of debt and taking out new borrowing to refinance existing debt due to mature during the period. During 1979 the Government and the public sector made net debt repayments of $2,100 million. Further early repayments to the IMF in early 1979 effectively extinguished Britain's debt to the IMF, apart from the oil facility of some $1,200 million which was drawn in 1976 and is being repaid in 16 equal instalments over the period 1979–83.

The reserves are officially revalued at the end of March each year to bring their published value more closely in line with their market worth by valuing non-dollar reserves on a market-related basis. Revaluation increased the value of the reserves to $27,000 million at the end of March 1980. At the end of September 1980 the reserves stood at $27,637 million.

The European Community established a European Monetary System in March 1979 aimed at the creation of a zone of monetary stability in Europe. It consists of an exchange rate mechanism, a monetary unit known as the European Currency Unit (ECU—based on a basket of national currencies including sterling, its value being recalculated daily) and enlarged Community short- and medium-term credit facilities. The member states of the European Community are also committed to the establishment of a European Monetary Fund as part of this system. Britain has participated in the system from the outset although not in the exchange rate arrangements and has deposited 20 per cent of its gold and dollar reserve with the European Monetary Co-operation Fund in exchange for European Currency Units. The Government intends that Britain should join the exchange rate mechanism when conditions permit. Its first and overriding priority is to gain control of domestic monetary conditions and to reduce the rate of inflation to nearer the Community average.

International Monetary Developments

A second set of amendments to the Articles of Agreement of the International Monetary Fund (IMF) entered into force on 1 April 1978. (The first amendments were made in 1969 when the Special Drawing Right—SDR—was established.) They bring the articles up to date and provide for necessary flexibility. The amendments were drawn up under the guidance of the Interim Committee, which succeeded the Committee of Twenty in 1974.

Members undertake a general obligation to collaborate with the IMF and with other members in order to ensure orderly exchange arrangements and to promote a stable system of exchange rates. Under the new provisions the Fund will be able to determine that, in accordance with specified criteria, international economic conditions permit the introduction of a system based on stable but adjustable par values. Each member will then be able, though not bound, to establish a par value. The amendments provided for a gradual reduction in the role of gold in the international monetary system. The function of gold as the unit of value of the SDR has been eliminated, the official price has been abolished and members are free to deal in gold in the market and among themselves without reference to any official price, and obligatory payments in gold by members to the Fund and by the Fund to members have been abrogated. The IMF's gold holdings have been reduced; one-sixth has been returned to members, and a further sixth has been auctioned, the major proportion of the proceeds from the auctions being disbursed through a trust fund, set up to provide medium-term balance of payments support to the poorest developing countries. Changes have been made in the role of the SDR in order to enhance its status as an international reserve asset. The amendment also provides for changes in the organisation of the Fund and in its financial operations (see also below).

The IMF set up borrowing arrangements (known as the oil facility) in 1974 and on a larger and more liberal scale in 1975, through which countries were able to draw on funds lent mainly by the oil-producers. The facility was fully drawn and creditors will be repaid by 1983.

An extended facility for medium-term assistance to members with special balance of payments problems caused by structural economic changes was also introduced in 1974. A supplementary financing facility entered into force in 1979, to provide financial assistance to members whose payments imbalances were large in relation to their economies and to their quotas in the Fund.

The entry into force of the Second Amendment of the IMF's articles in 1978 enabled the implementation of increases under the Sixth General Review of Quotas. As a result, total Fund quotas were raised from SDR 29,000 million to SDR 39,000 million.

12 The Framework of Industry

The production industries (mining and quarrying, manufacturing, construction, and gas, electricity and water), together with the distributive trades and transport and communications, account for some 61 per cent of Britain's gross domestic product (see Table 7 on p 204) and for about 54 per cent of total employment. Financial and business services, professional and scientific services (excluding public health and education services) and the various service trades (such as catering, entertainment, and personal and household services) contribute a further 23 per cent of gross domestic product.

This chapter describes some of the general features of industrial activity, such as the forms of enterprise and trends in production, productivity and investment, and the geographical distribution of industry. It also describes government measures to stimulate or, where necessary, regulate industrial activity. The chapters following cover the main areas of industrial and commercial activity.

ORGANISATION AND PRODUCTION

Structure   The forms of industrial organisation and the pattern of ownership and control are varied. Personal, corporate (including co-operative) and public sector enterprise all assume a number of different forms, and all are important in the economy.

Excluding farmers, there were about 1·8 million personal enterprises (professional persons and other sole traders and partnerships) in Britain in 1979, generating domestic income of about £15,270 million. The domestic income of public sector enterprise (see pp 203 and 222) amounted to some £5,580 million, excluding income from rent and non-trading income. Corporate enterprise (see p 233) comprises industrial, commercial and financial companies and certain other financial institutions. Within this sector the domestic income of industrial and commercial enterprises amounted to £28,660 million in 1979, excluding income from rent and non-trading income. Companies may be either public or private (see p 233). Most of Britain's large firms are public companies, while the great majority of private companies are small. There were 16,283 public companies at the end of 1979 and 720,323 private companies.

Most manufacturing (with the exceptions of steel, aerospace and shipbuilding) is in the hands of private enterprise, as are the construction and distributive and other service industries.

Most of the energy, transport and communications industries are in public sector ownership.

The largest organisations in terms of employees in 1979 were public sector corporations such as the Post Office (411,000) and the National Coal Board (300,000) and companies such as BL, formerly British Leyland, (192,000), General Electric Company (191,000), BAT Industries (153,000) and Imperial Chemical Industries (151,000). The largest companies in terms of capital employed (net assets) were British Petroleum (£8,400 million) and Shell

Transport and Trading (£5,600 million). Altogether more than 90 companies registered in Britain each had net assets over £250 million; in terms of annual sales four of the top 20 industrial groups in Europe were British.

Where profitable operation has become dependent on concentration and economies of scale, regrouping has taken place. In some sectors a small number of big companies and their subsidiaries are responsible for a great proportion of total production. Examples are oil refining, non-ferrous metal smelting, motor vehicles and aircraft, heavy electrical engineering, electronics, machine tools, brewing, textiles, basic chemicals, tobacco and magazine publishing. Shares in these companies are, however, usually distributed among many holders or are held by insurance companies or pension funds representing a broad cross-section of the community, and it is rare for a few holders to have a controlling interest other than in the case of private companies. (See also p 231.)

Alongside these large organisations the many hundreds of thousands of small firms play an essential part in the economy. The Government has taken a number of measures to encourage existing small businesses and promote the development of new ones (see p 228).

Production Industrial production was severely affected by the world recession in industry in 1980, after rising between 1975 and 1979 (see Table 10). Mining and quarrying output rose sharply up to 1979 owing to increased production of North Sea oil and gas. Manufacturing output grew more gradually (see also Table 14, p 236). In general, production industries are described in this book on the basis of information up to the end of 1979.

TABLE 10: Index of Output 1974–79 (1975=100)

Industry Group	1974	1975	1976	1977	1978	1979
Production Industries						
Mining and quarrying	89·9	100	125·8	187·7	232·5	294·7
Manufacturing	106·6	100	101·4	103·0	103·8	104·1
Construction	105·8	100	98·6	98·3	105·0	102·1
Gas, electricity, water	99·2	100	102·9	107·1	110·2	116·7
Total production industries	105·2	100	102·0	106·0	109·8	112·6
Transport and communications	101·6	100	99·4	102·5	105·7	110·0
Distributive trades	103·3	100	100·8	98·9	103·5	105·9

Source: *Monthly Digest of Statistics*

Productivity The improvement of productivity, which by international standards has shown a relatively slow rate of growth in Britain, is recognised as being of prime importance for the economy. Productivity, as measured by output per head, increased by 18 per cent in all production industries between 1975 and 1979 (see Table 11). In manufacturing the increase was 9·7 per cent and in mining and quarrying (including North Sea oil and gas activity) 207 per cent. Both the long-term and the short-term growth of productivity are influenced by such factors as the rate of capital investment, management, advances in products, machinery processes and methods of work, sales promotion and labour. Over the last decade the size of the labour force employed in industry has fallen steadily.

The improvement of productivity rests primarily with the management and the workforce in individual enterprises. The Department of Industry provides support by assisting the introduction of advanced machinery and techniques into industry, providing technical advisory services and sponsoring the Computer-Aided Design Centre and the National Computing Centre. It is concerned directly with research into such factors as production engineering and communication networks. The Department of Employment advises firms on manpower utilisation, job satisfaction and industrial relations. Many educational establishments also provide advice and assistance.

Within industry, employers' organisations often provide technical assistance and support schemes of vocational education and training, as do many trade unions. The British Council of Productivity Associations is one of many bodies, both public and private, concerned with various aspects of productivity. The Council provides information and advisory services to industry through a national network of 28 local associations.

TABLE 11: Index of Output per head 1974–79 (1975=100)

	Total employed labour force	Gross domestic product per head	All production industries		Manufacturing industries	
			Employ-ment	Output per head	Employ-ment	Output per head
1974	100·6	101·4	104·1	101·6	104·7	102·6
1975	100	100	100	100	100	100
1976	99·4	102·8	97·5	105·1	96·9	105·4
1977	99·6	105·2	97·2	109·7	97·1	107·1
1978	99·9	108·0	96·7	114·0	96·4	108·2
1979	100·2	109·3	95·9	117·6	95·1	109·7

Source: *Monthly Digest of Statistics*

Investment

Productivity is particularly dependent on the quantity and efficiency of the capital assets which the labour force has at its disposal. Details of investment in the period 1974–79 are contained in Table 12 (see also p 235). The figures do not include expenditure on the leasing of assets, a practice which grew rapidly in the 1970s (see p 352).

TABLE 12: Gross Domestic Fixed Capital Formation 1974–79 (1975 prices)
£ million

	Mining and quarrying[a]	Manu-facturing	Gas, electricity and water	Transport and communica-tions	Distributive trades
1974	870	3,782	1,197	2,437	1,191
1975	1,570	3,522	1,263	2,204	1,034
1976	2,091	3,326	1,217	2,024	989
1977	1,976	3,510	1,055	2,054	1,160
1978	1,935	3,773	1,013	1,928	1,210
1979	1,666	3,873	984	1,798	1,388

Source: *National Income and Expenditure 1980 Edition*
[a] Including extraction of petroleum and natural gas.

Part of the investment in plant and machinery is associated with the introduction of new techniques and equipment. The progress of automation (see below) is changing the pattern and organisation of many industries and has brought substantial increases in production and efficiency. Much investment, however, still consists of replacements, additions and improvements of a more traditional kind. Industrial technologies of plant maintenance, materials handling, lubrication and corrosion protection, well developed in Britain, make possible large savings in costs.

Automation

In Britain, as in other industrialised countries, automation has been steadily extended to a wide range of industrial and commercial activities. Extensive use of automation is to be found across the whole range of production industries, including metal manufacture, the petroleum and chemical industries, engineering, food, drink and tobacco manufacture, printing and publishing, and power transmission; and in service industries such as transport, posts and telecommunications, retailing, wholesale distribution and business and financial services.

The growth of digital measurement and control techniques, including the use of computers, has greatly extended the range for automatic operations; it is now possible for an entire production process to be controlled automatically, and for information to be provided rapidly for managerial, commercial and technical purposes. Britain has many advanced applications of computer control in operation in both the public and private sectors of industry, and is among the world's leading nations in the provision of 'software' services and systems (that is, the preparation of instructions for computer operations and related services).

The scope of electronic controls has been extended still further by the development of micro-electronics, and in particular the microprocessor, a term commonly used to refer to a miniature wafer or 'chip' (usually of silicon) about 5mm (0·2 inches) square, on which are placed electronic circuits equivalent to those found in the central processing unit of a computer. The importance of this development has been widely recognised in Britain, partly through government initiatives, including a microprocessor awareness campaign aimed at industrialists and trade unions. In addition financial support has been provided for the micro-electronics industry, and for applications of micro-electronics. British companies are also improving the performance of operations which are already automated by developing more comprehensive and powerful control systems.

Industrial Association

Voluntary associations are formed by private enterprises for a number of different purposes, including the provision of common services, the exchange of information and representation of their members' point of view; the regulation of trading practices; and negotiation with trade unions on wages and conditions of work. These associations cover, with varying completeness, most of British industry. Trade associations, concerned mainly with representation to the Government, the provision of common services and the regulation of trading practices, are normally composed of firms manufacturing (and/or retailing) a particular product or group of products. Employers' organisations which deal with employment matters usually consist of firms engaged in the same type of operation or manufacturing process. In an industrial sector concerned wholly with an allied group of products, one association may undertake all the functions. The national employers' organisations are usually concerned with negotiation of wages and conditions of work (see p 337).

The central body representing British business and industry nationally is the Confederation of British Industry (CBI), recognised by the Government as a channel for consultation between government departments and representatives of both the private and the public sector employers as a whole. The CBI represents directly and indirectly more than 300,000 companies through parent companies, subsidiaries, employers' organisations, trade and commercial associations and the majority of the nationalised industries. For its members it acts as an advisory and consultative body providing them with information and statistics, ascertaining their collective views and representing them nationally to the Government and the public and also internationally (see p 338). CBI representatives sit on the National Economic Development Council, the Manpower Services Commission, the Health and Safety Commission, the Advisory, Conciliation and Arbitration Service and other official advisory committees and voluntary bodies concerned with matters affecting industry.

In matters of common concern the CBI often acts jointly with the chambers of commerce. These are open to all kinds of producers and traders and exist to promote the interests of local, regional and national industry and commerce. Most chambers provide export facilities, including the sponsorship of outward trade missions and visits. The Association of British Chambers of Commerce is the co-ordinating body to which about 85 local chambers are affiliated, together with 21 British Chambers of Commerce operating in Europe and elsewhere. The chambers operating in Britain have a membership of about 53,000 firms. In Scotland there is an additional central organisation, the Association of Scottish Chambers of Commerce, and in Northern Ireland the Northern Ireland Chamber of Commerce and Industry, to which local chambers are affiliated. Other voluntary associations include industrial development associations for particular areas or regions, which are sponsored by local authorities, trade associations and individual firms. Four of these bodies (the North of England Development Council, the North West Industrial Development Association, the Yorkshire and Humberside Development Association and the Devon and Cornwall Development Bureau) receive government grants, while the Scottish Council (Development and Industry) is funded by its constituent members without government grant and the Development Corporation for Wales receives grants from the Welsh Development Agency.

Management Education

In Britain, as elsewhere, it is recognised that managers require special skills and training. The British Institute of Management (BIM), which is playing an increasingly representative role for the management and administrative professions, provides a wide range of information services and has a particular interest in management education and training. The Institute of Directors also provides information and other services to directors of all types of company. The Industrial Society, whose membership includes trade unions as well as employers and their associations, works to promote better use of human resources; it advises members and conducts conferences and courses.

A large proportion of management education is provided by polytechnics and many of the colleges of further education throughout Britain; 12 regional centres of management education have been established in England and Wales through the association of polytechnics and colleges which have high reputations for management studies (see also p 167). Universities also make an important contribution, especially the full-time postgraduate programmes at the business schools of London and Manchester Universities. Training courses for higher management are offered by several colleges including the Administrative Staff College, Henley-on-Thames, and Ashridge College of Management, Berkhamsted. The Council of Industry for Management Education, jointly sponsored by the CBI, the BIM and the Foundation for Management Education, works to foster the development of business and management education. Many firms provide general management courses for senior executives or systems of informal training. There are also a number of bodies concerned with specialised branches of management, for example, the Institute of Personnel Management, the Institution of Industrial Managers, the Institute of Administrative Management, the Institute of Supervisory Management, the Institute of Marketing, the Institute of Chartered Secretaries and Administrators and the Institute of Purchasing and Supply.

The large number of professional people working as management consultants indicates the concern for improved management performance in Britain. Such consultancy services are being increasingly used by overseas clients. (Industrial training and education below management level are summarised on pp 331 and 167.)

Design

Design is an important factor in improving the quality and competitiveness of manufactured goods. Improvement of the design of British goods is the concern of the government-sponsored Design Council and its separate Scottish Committee, while the Computer-Aided Design Centre (see p 388) also provides assistance to individual firms.

At the Council's Design Centres in London and Glasgow there are permanent displays of well-designed modern British goods, together with special exhibitions illustrating new design developments. There is a third, smaller showroom in Cardiff. All the products displayed are chosen from the Council's Design Index, a record of some 7,000 current British products, chosen by independent committees for their high standards of design, safety and performance. The Council's services include advice on design matters, the organisation of product displays at overseas trade fairs, conferences and seminars on design, help for design education and the publication of a range of material. It provides annual awards for manufacturers of consumer and engineering products and for medical equipment and motor vehicles.

Other bodies concerned with industrial design include the Royal Society of Arts (see p 393), the Society of Industrial Artists and Designers, which is the representative professional body in Great Britain of industrial designers, and the Design and Industries Association, a voluntary association of industrial companies, designers, and others interested in the promotion of good design in industry. The Crafts Council, the British Crafts Centre, and the Scottish Craft Centre are grant-aided and work to improve craft design by, for example, organising regular exhibitions and other events (see also p 408).

Industrial Property

There is a substantial body of legislation designed to secure the rights of the originators of inventions relating to manufacture, new industrial designs and trade marks. These matters are administered respectively by the Patent Office, the Design Registry and the Trade Marks Registry, while governmental responsibility is exercised by the Department of Trade. It is also open to British residents to apply for protection under international agreements such as the European Patent Convention and the Patent Co-operation Treaty, both of which came into effect in 1978. International protection for patents, designs and trade marks is available under the International Convention for the Protection of Industrial Property.

Standards

The British Standards Institution (BSI) is a voluntary non-profit-making body incorporated by Royal Charter, funded in part by sale of standards, by subscription and by government grant. It prepares and promulgates standards which, variously, specify dimensions, performance and safety criteria, testing methods and codes of practice for a large range of products and processes in most fields of production. Voluntary acceptance of such standards by manufacturers, buyers and sellers reduces unnecessary variety and simplifies the specification of requirements. BSI is governed by an executive board which includes representatives of the main organisations of employers and workers, professional institutions, consumers and the larger government departments.

The British Calibration Service (BCS) was established in 1966 in response to the growth in demand for industrial calibration services, which was beginning to exceed the capacity of the National Physical Laboratory (NPL, see p 388), Britain's national calibration authority. The BCS, which is a service of the NPL, is an organisation of over 80 laboratories, located in industry, universities and government establishments which offers 'authenticated calibrations traceable to national standards', a phrase which means that measurements are made within a known and approved uncertainty and with instruments which are calibrated directly by the NPL or against secondary standards which are themselves calibrated by NPL. BCS laboratories issue calibration certificates for electrical, mechanical, flow, optical, pressure, thermal and time interval measurements; the range covers those essential to quality, efficiency and safety in manufacturing and process industries. The BCS has provided a model which several other countries have followed. As a complement to the BCS, a national testing laboratory accreditation scheme is to be set up in 1981 which will provide official recognition of the competence of laboratories to undertake defined types of test.

Location

The following is a summary of how British industry is distributed through the eight standard regions of England and Wales, Scotland and Northern Ireland.

South East Region

London is Britain's capital and main communication centre, and is one of the world's most important financial and tourist centres. Lying at the head of ocean navigation on the Thames estuary it is one of the world's largest cities and largest ports, though much deep-sea-going traffic has moved down-river to Tilbury docks. It is the main centre in Britain of printing and the manufacture of ladies' clothing, materials for the arts, precision instruments, jewellery, and many other specialised products. Small firms predominate in many of these industries and the average size of manufacturing firms (particularly in the central area) is well below the national average. London is also important, especially in its outer ring, for light engineering, chemicals and consumer goods and has some heavy engineering plants and a number of leading research establishments. There has been in recent years, however, a considerable drop in employment and population. The regeneration of the dockland areas is one of a number of projects being implemented to attract new industry.

Towards the periphery of Greater London and in the surrounding Outer Metropolitan Area, industry, particularly the electronics and consumer goods industries, has expanded greatly; some of the largest aircraft plants are in these areas, for example at Weybridge and Hatfield, as well as two of the four main motor vehicle manufacturers at Dagenham, Luton and Dunstable. There are other major motor vehicle manufacturing plants at Cowley, Oxford, some 50 miles north-west of London. High technology industries are well represented in Berkshire and Hertfordshire, and Chelmsford is an important centre for the electronics industry. Along the lower Thames and Medway estuaries there are large oil refineries as well as some smaller shipyards, engineering works and major concentrations of the paper and pulp and cement industries. There are centres of manufacturing industry at Crawley, Basingstoke, Slough and Reading, in the Medway towns and the Aldershot–Farnborough area. Heathrow and Gatwick airports are of major importance and are large employers.

A great part of the Channel coast eastwards from Southampton consists of built-up areas, many of which are partly residential areas for people working in London. Holiday resorts fringe the coast. Portsmouth is a naval port with some shipbuilding and general manufacturing. Southampton is one of Britain's leading ports for both passengers and freight; its industries include ship repairing, oil refining, cable-making, electronics and synthetic rubber. Dover, Folkestone and Newhaven are ferry ports. Brighton, apart from being an important holiday, residential and conference centre, is a university town and has important manufacturing plant.

South West   Though famous for its tourism, leisure industries and agriculture, the southwest of England has a busy manufacturing sector. Bristol is the region's administrative and commercial centre, and the largest industrial city, having tobacco, packaging materials, printing, aerospace, chocolate, chemicals and non-ferrous metal manufactures as well as a wide range of engineering, electronic and other industries. There are extensive modern docks, including the Royal Portbury Dock and Avonmouth. Fast rail and road links connect Bristol with other major commercial and industrial centres.

Plymouth, with the naval dockyard and electrical and other industries, is an important manufacturing centre. The towns of Gloucester, Poole, Christchurch, Cheltenham and Bath are major producers of machinery, instrumentation and other engineering products. Swindon has vehicle, electrical and electronic engineering, and has recently attracted a number of major service industries. Helicopters and leather are produced at Yeovil and chemical and engineering products are made at Taunton and Bridgwater. Clothing and other textile products and footwear are made at several centres. In the Camborne, Redruth, Falmouth and St. Austell areas of Cornwall there is china clay and tin mining, machinery manufacture, and other forms of engineering.

East Anglia   Although the smallest of the regions East Anglia has been rapidly growing in terms of both population and employment. A major contribution to this growth was made by a scheme under which nine towns absorbed an overspill of population and industry from London. The area is one of the most productive agricultural regions in the world and this has provided a firm base for the growth of the food processing industry, which is concerned mainly with canning, and more recently freezing local produce. Cambridge is a major centre of research-based industry; Ipswich and Peterborough are noted for diesel engines, agricultural machinery and engineering generally and Norwich for footwear and food manufacture. Cambridge, Ipswich and Norwich have become increasingly important as centres for service industries. The east coast ports of Great Yarmouth and Lowestoft are important bases for companies associated with natural gas exploitation in the North Sea.

West Midlands   This is the only landlocked region and it has a greater dependency on manufacturing industry than any other region. However, more than three-quarters of the land is still used for agriculture and includes some areas of great natural beauty, particularly in the south and west. The National Agricultural Centre is based at Stoneleigh, Warwickshire. The main concentration of industry is in the West Midlands metropolitan county which includes the districts of Birmingham, Coventry, Dudley, Sandwell, Solihull, Walsall and Wolver-hampton. The economy is largely dependent upon the metal-using industries and in particular on motor vehicle manufacture. Other notable industries are mechanical and electrical engineering, machine tools, castings, tubes, locks, jewellery, domestic metalware and rubber manufactures. The metropolitan county also contains the National Exhibition Centre, which is one of the largest and most modern exhibition complexes in the world.

In north Staffordshire, a smaller conurbation centred upon Stoke-on-Trent is the centre of the British pottery and china industry and the region's major coalmining area. Other industries are rubber and electrical products. Coal-mining is also important in the Cannock Chase and north Warwickshire areas.

Other important centres include Stafford, with heavy electrical and other engineering; Worcester, mechanical engineering and pottery; Burton-on-Trent, brewing and rubber; Kidderminster, carpets; and Rugby, electrical engineering. Stratford-upon-Avon, the birthplace of William Shakespeare, is an international tourist centre.

The two major new towns, Telford and Redditch, have large metal-based industries.

East Midlands Although some major industries are heavily concentrated in the East Midlands (over 60 per cent of Britain's hosiery and knitwear, 40 per cent of its footwear and more than 20 per cent of its coal) industry is well diversified. North Nottinghamshire and Derbyshire are traditional coalmining areas where pro-ductivity rates are high. In the northern part of the region engineering is also important. In Nottingham a high proportion of employment is in pharmaceut-icals, electronics, tobacco and bicycle manufacture. Nottingham lace is famous throughout the world, but textiles and clothing are of more importance. Derby is primarily an engineering town with aero-engines, rail rolling stock, boilers and castings among a wide range of engineering products. The production of man-made fibres is also of considerable importance. Agriculture is significant in Lincolnshire as well as food processing and engineering, much of which produces agricultural and constructional equipment. Lincoln has a substantial engineering industry. Engineering is also a major industry in Leicester, much of it supplying other local industries such as textiles and footwear. Electrical engineering is of especial importance in Loughborough. Northamptonshire is famous for high-quality footwear. In recent years light engineering, much of it related to the electronics industry, has expanded considerably.

North West The North West comprises the metropolitan counties of Greater Manchester and Merseyside and the counties of Lancashire and Cheshire. The Depart-ment of Industry's administration of this region extends also into parts of Cumbria and Derbyshire. The region is one of the most highly industrialised in Britain. Manchester is Britain's second most important commercial and financial centre. It is one of the chief centres for electrical and heavy engineer-ing and for the production of a wide range of goods including computers, electronic equipment, petrochemicals, clothing, dye-stuffs and pharmaceuti-cals. Manchester's traditional role as the centre for the Lancashire textile industry is only a small part of its present-day activities.

The textile towns, while adapting to the decline of traditional textiles and to increasing use of man-made fibres and moving into new textile products, such as carpets, have for the most part seen engineering outgrow the textile indus-try. The largest towns, Bolton, Stockport, Oldham, Blackburn, Preston, Rochdale, Burnley, Wigan and Bury, are diversified with such industries as paper-making, textile and electrical machinery, light engineering and consumer durables, plastics, foods, chemicals, nuclear process plant, electronics, aircraft and heavy commercial vehicles.

The Manchester Ship Canal, which carries a substantial volume of export traffic, links Manchester and Merseyside. It passes through Warrington, with its new town, Widnes, Runcorn, also a new town, with the chemical industry, and Ellesmere Port with its oil refinery installations, before reaching the Mersey estuary. St. Helens to the north of the canal, has become the world's leading centre of the flat glass industry. Liverpool, with its modernised dock system, is one of Britain's leading seaports and, after London, the largest centre for processing and converting imported foodstuffs and raw materials (grain milling, oils, fats and tobacco, sugar refining and rubber products). Much of economic activity in Merseyside is still centred on its port, but its industrial strength has moved from older industries closely related to the port to the newer industries including motor vehicles, electrical and electronic engineering, industrial plant and machinery and chemicals.

To the north of this industrial belt lie Southport, Blackpool and Lancaster with light industries and seaside tourist trade, and to the south, the Cheshire plain with agriculture, while a variety of industries such as salt, chemicals, motor vehicles, pharmaceuticals and rail engineering are located among the smaller towns.

The region contains some of Britain's most fertile farmland. The large tourist industry has the attractions of the coast, historic towns such as Chester, and the four National Parks on or near its boundaries.

Manchester airport with its international and inter-continental services is second in England only to the London airports. Liverpool also has a busy airport. The region has a highly developed rail system and one of the most advanced motorway networks in Britain, providing fast access to London and the rest of the country, and to continental Europe through the east coast ports, as well as throughout the region itself.

Yorkshire and Humberside

Though some parts of Yorkshire and Humberside are heavily industrialised, more than four-fifths of the region is open country, forming one of Britain's major agricultural areas.

The region's industrial structure is diverse. About 70 per cent of Britain's worsted and woollen industry is located in West Yorkshire. Bradford is the commercial centre of the wool trade. In addition there are strong sectors of engineering, printing and carpets. The metropolitan district of Leeds is an important commercial centre and also has a variety of industries including men's clothing and various engineering industries. In the south, the steel centre based on Sheffield and Rotherham is noted for the manufacture of high quality steels, tools and cutlery. Yorkshire's coalfields are particularly important and production is to be extended to the Selby area, where major new reserves have been discovered. Doncaster, with tractor and wire rope manufacturing, and Barnsley are the largest towns on the coalfield where dependence on steel and coal has been reduced by the introduction of new industries in and around the major towns.

North Yorkshire is mainly agricultural but York, a leading tourist attraction, is also noted for chocolate and confectionery manufacture. It is an important railway centre, and has substantial railway workshops, besides being the home of the National Railway Museum.

Kingston upon Hull is the principal industrial town in Humberside, which is a major centre for maritime trade with ports at Grimsby, Immingham and

Goole in addition to Hull. Besides being fishing ports, Hull and Grimsby contain specialised food processing and cold storage facilities. The Humber ports are strategically situated for direct access to Western Europe, while the Humber Bridge (see p 303) will improve domestic communications. The British Steel Corporation has a large steel plant at Scunthorpe. Also in south Humberside are chemical, fertiliser, oil refining, and food processing plants. The north bank of the Humber contains a large proportion of Britain's caravan manufacturing industry.

Northern

The greater part of this region (the metropolitan county of Tyne and Wear and the counties of Northumberland, Durham, Cleveland and Cumbria) is an area of mountains, lakes and moorland. The tourist industry, already strong in the Lake District, is developing in other areas. Industrial activity and the bulk of the population is concentrated in the eastern coastal strip stretching from the coalfields north of the River Tyne southwards to the River Tees, and to a lesser extent, on the western coastal strip of Cumbria.

The region is relatively more dependent than other parts of England on the long-established heavy industries, notably coalmining, iron and steel manufacture, shipbuilding and ship-repairing and chemicals (the complex of chemical plants on both banks of the Tees is probably the most extensive in Europe). Major investment at Teesside has increased steelmaking capacity to nearly 5 million tonnes a year. New industries, however, with a broader technological base, have been attracted to the region and the industrial structure is becoming more diversified. Manufacture of electrical plant is a major industry.

Other industries include electric components, plastics, domestic appliances, pharmaceuticals, machine tools, ropes, paint, glass, clothing and scientific instruments as well as mining machinery, rolling mill plant and earth-moving equipment. An aluminium smelter is operating on the Northumberland coast. Atomic energy is important, with two nuclear power stations and other installations in Cumbria, and a further nuclear power station at an advanced stage of construction at Hartlepool. Considerable investment is taking place in the coalmining industry to exploit large coal reserves below the sea bed off the Northumberland and Durham coasts and to boost open-cast coal production. The region is also involved in the North Sea oil programme. The new oil terminal at Teesside has a potential capacity of one million barrels a day of North Sea oil. A major new reservoir at Kielder will, when completed, provide water supplies for industry on Tyneside and Teesside.

Wales

Some two-thirds of the population (which totals 2·8 million) live in industrial south Wales. This area has a diverse range of modern manufacturing industries, including mechanical and electrical engineering, motor vehicles components, plastics, chemicals and textiles. Though coalmining has declined substantially, the south Wales coalfield still produces virtually all Britain's anthracite and much of its steam and other specialised coals. Steel, the other traditional industry of south Wales, is less dominant in employment terms than formerly but still supplies all of Britain's tinplate and much of its sheet steel. Cardiff, Newport and Swansea are the largest urban centres and with Barry and Port Talbot, are also the major ports of the region. This latter has one of the largest steel-making plants in Britain and a deep water harbour for importing iron ore. Milford Haven is one of the finest natural deep water harbours in the world and has developed as Britain's major oil-importing port with four oil refineries and a link with a fifth at Llandarcy.

The other main industrial area is in north-east Wales. Coalmining has now contracted in importance but steel finishing, chemicals, man-made fibres and aircraft construction remain significant sources of employment despite some shedding of labour in recent years. A range of new lighter industry has been introduced in the post-war years, particularly around Wrexham. The remainder of Wales is predominantly rural with agriculture, forestry and tourism the traditional basis of the economy, but here too manufacturing firms have been introduced in many towns, and one or two very large scale undertakings such as an aluminium plant at Holyhead, Anglesey, have been established.

Scotland

About three-quarters of Scotland's population of 5·2 million and most of the industrial activity is concentrated in the central lowlands between the Firth of Clyde and the Firth of Forth. The principal cities in this area are Glasgow, a major industrial and commercial centre, and Edinburgh, Scotland's capital, an administrative, financial and cultural centre. There is a wide variety of manufacturing industries. Clydeside, which includes Glasgow, is a major shipbuilding and marine engineering centre; it produces a great variety of general engineering products, which include platform modules, pumps and other products for the offshore oil and gas industries.

Clydeside is also an important centre for food, drink and tobacco manufactures, carpets and printing and publishing. The steel industry, sited mainly in Central Strathclyde, has been substantially modernised. There are important coalmining works in the Strathclyde, Central, Lothian and Fife regions. The computer and electronics equipment industry is strongly represented in Strathclyde, Fife and Dundee, as well as in Edinburgh, where this and other modern industries are expanding alongside the traditional engineering, printing and publishing and brewing industries. Large-scale plants producing cars in Linwood, near Paisley, and commercial vehicles in West Lothian and the Scotstoun district of Glasgow, are well established, while heavy earth-moving equipment and tracked vehicles are produced in Uddingston and Airdrie. The chemical industry is concentrated in Ayrshire and at Grangemouth, where there is also a major oil refinery. The Firth of Clyde provides central Scotland with valuable deep water facilities.

North-east Scotland is now the centre of the offshore oil industry and a wide variety of oil-related projects have been established. Aberdeen, one of two main industrial cities outside the central belt, has additionally become the chief servicing and administrative centre for the oil industry. In June 1978 between 60,000 and 70,000 people were employed in Scotland as a whole in work directly or indirectly related to oil and the total has risen since then. However, the older industries in the north-east (whisky distilling, paper manufacture and food and fish processing) continue to flourish.

Elsewhere outside the central belt there is considerable industrial concentration in and around Dundee, where the traditional manufacture, jute, has been supplemented by office machinery, clocks and watches, tyres and electronic products. Numerous smaller towns outside the central lowlands have also attracted light industry in recent years.

Much of the rest of Scotland is mountainous and therefore sparsely populated. In the Highlands and Islands, the main industries include high quality tweed and knitwear, papermaking and aluminium smelting and there are significant resources of hydro-electric power. Nuclear power is also generated. The development of North Sea oil has led to very substantial oil-related activities including oil platform production yards. The oil terminal at Sullom Voe, Shetland, which became operational in 1978, is the largest in Europe. In the Borders and south-west of Scotland, the wool, cloth and knitwear industries are important, together with food processing and chemicals manufacture. Tourism is important throughout Scotland and there are extensive holiday and recreational facilities.

Northern Ireland Although the area of Northern Ireland is relatively small there is substantial and growing industrialisation, particularly in and around Belfast, the capital city, and Londonderry. Britain's largest single shipyard is in Belfast; other well-established activities include the manufacture of aircraft, textile machinery and a wide range of other engineering products, tobacco and clothing. Northern Ireland has also long been an important centre for textiles; the textile industry is extensively diversified and Northern Ireland is an important area for man-made fibre production, providing a substantial portion of Britain's output. There has also been extensive development in vehicle components, oil-well equipment, electronic instruments, telecommunication equipment, carpets and synthetic rubber.

THE GOVERNMENT AND INDUSTRY

The chief aim of the industrial policy of the Government elected in 1979 is to encourage industrial enterprise and initiative in a flexible and competitive market economy. Steps have been taken to reduce the extent of state ownership (see p 203), a review of industrial subsidies has been carried out (see p 226) and industrial investment agencies in the public sector have been encouraged to secure private sector participation in their projects. Competition policy (see p 231) has been strengthened in order to create a climate in which commerce can flourish. The Government also aims to stimulate the development of small businesses (see p 228) by reducing the administrative burdens laid on them and through taxation and other policies.

The departments chiefly responsible for the Government's relations with industry are the Department of Industry (responsible for manufacturing and for industrial research and design), the Department of Energy, the Department of Trade (aviation, shipping, tourism, printing and publishing and the distributive and service industries), the Department of Transport (inland transport), the Department of the Environment (construction and water supply), and the appropriate departments of the Scottish, Welsh and Northern Ireland Offices.

The Government also has close relations with industry through the National Economic Development Council (see p 203), subcommittees of which bring together representatives of the Government, the Bank of England, the nationalised industries, managements and trade unions to make recommendations on certain industrial sectors and on various aspects of industry.

Official recognition of outstanding industrial performance is conferred by the Queen's Awards for Export and Technology which are made annually to firms in all sectors of industry (including services) on the advice of a committee composed of businessmen, trade union representatives and civil servants.

Public Enterprise Direct state participation in industry is mainly effected through public corporations sponsored by government departments and responsible for particular sectors of industrial activity. Such corporations are responsible for most of Britain's energy and transport sectors and for several within manufacturing their activities are described in the relevant chapters.

The managing boards and staffs of the nationalised industries are not generally civil servants and although accountable to Parliament for their actions in a variety of ways, it is they and not the ministers of the sponsoring departments who are responsible for management.

The extent to which the responsible minister has power over the working of the boards which have been set up to run the nationalised industries varies from industry to industry, but two features are common to almost all of them. First, the minister appoints (and may dismiss) the chairman and members of each board, and, secondly, has power to give general directions as to how the industry should be run, but does not interfere in day-to-day management. It is usually also laid down that the board shall give to the minister any information, statistics and financial accounts which may be required. In practice, as the responsible minister is kept fully informed and major policy decisions are reached in consultation, there is very seldom occasion for a general directive to be issued. Indeed, the Government's policy is to keep ministerial intervention to a minimum and to encourage the nationalised industries to behave as far as possible as commercial enterprises.

The minister also has financial powers and responsibilities. The usual statutory requirement is that the board is required to conduct its business so that receipts at least balance outgoings over a period. However, financial targets have been agreed by the Government for certain industries and targets for the remaining industries are to be set as soon as possible. The main form of target, usually set for three to five years, is a real return before interest on average net assets employed. Finance for capital expenditure which cannot be found from internal sources is provided mainly by interest-bearing loans from the Exchequer. Other sources of finance include grants and Public Dividend Capital on which dividends are paid to the Government.

It is usual for the minister responsible for each nationalised industry to be required by statute to take steps to see that the interests of the industry's customers are protected. This is done for certain of the industries (see p 233) by the establishment of representative consumers' councils to consider complaints and suggestions, and to advise the board or the minister on the changes they think desirable.

Government policy towards the nationalised industries is subject to the approval of Parliament. Opportunities for parliamentary discussion are afforded by debates, including debates on their annual reports and accounts, and by answers to parliamentary questions, which, in principle, are admissible only if concerned with policy rather than details of administration. Provision is also made for the examination of the affairs of the nationalised industries within the parliamentary committee system.

Regional Development

Economic imbalance between different parts of the country is due partly to the steady decline over the years of older industries, such as steel-making and shipbuilding, causing a high level of unemployment in certain regions and such adverse factors as poor amenities, derelict buildings and land and net outward migration. In addition, the newer and expanding industries have tended to develop mostly in the Midlands and the South East, and unemployment has remained a persistent problem in Scotland, Wales, Northern Ireland and some parts of England, particularly the North and Merseyside. The ending of regional imbalance has been an objective of successive Governments. Financial and other aid to areas of high unemployment began in the 1930s and has been expanded considerably over the years.

Assisted Areas

In parts of Great Britain designated as 'assisted areas' incentives are offered by the Government to encourage industrial development and the growth of office

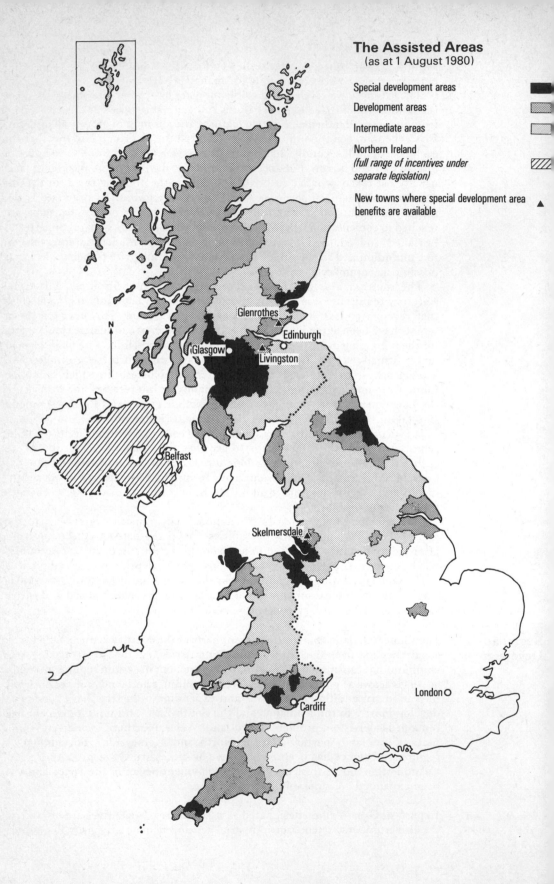

The Assisted Areas
(as at 1 August 1980)

Special development areas

Development areas

Intermediate areas

Northern Ireland
*(full range of incentives under
separate legislation)*

New towns where special development area
benefits are available

Glenrothes

Edinburgh

Glasgow

Livingston

Belfast

Skelmersdale

London

Cardiff

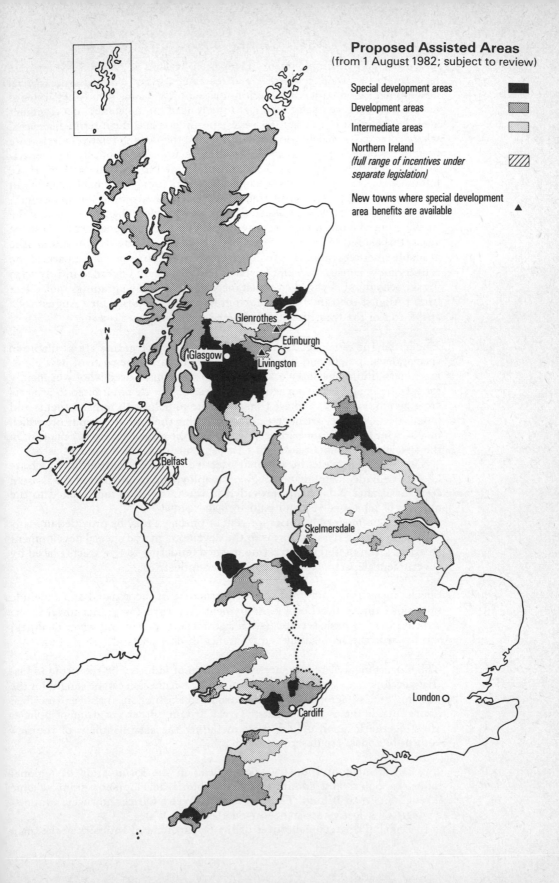

Proposed Assisted Areas
(from 1 August 1982; subject to review)

Special development areas

Development areas

Intermediate areas

Northern Ireland
(full range of incentives under separate legislation)

New towns where special development area benefits are available ▲

N

Glenrothes
Edinburgh
Glasgow
Livingston

Belfast

Skelmersdale

London

Cardiff

and other service employment. (Northern Ireland is covered by separate legislation; see p 227.) There are three categories of assisted area: special development areas, where the economic situation and consistently high rates of unemployment give rise to the most urgent need for assistance; development areas with similar but rather less severe problems; and the intermediate area, where some assistance is necessary but where the need is relatively less acute than in the other types of area. Following a review carried out by the Department of Industry in 1979 the Government decided to continue with an active but more selective policy, at the same time maintaining reasonable stability in the framework of regional investment incentives and avoiding abrupt changes. At the time of the review the assisted areas covered more than 40 per cent of the working population; it was proposed that, over a transitional period of three years, this should be reduced to about 25 per cent in order to concentrate the available resources more effectively on them, and to treat different parts of the country more consistently and fairly. A few areas were upgraded in July 1979 to take account of changed circumstances. The first downgradings took effect from 1 August 1980 and further downgradings are proposed for 1 August 1982 at the end of the transitional period (see maps on pp 224–225).

Incentives for Industry

Under the Industry Act 1972 regional development grants are available in special development and development areas towards the costs of new plant, machinery, buildings and works provided on premises used wholly or mainly for specified manufacturing activities. These grants are not limited to projects creating employment, and are thus available to help with improvements and modernisation. They are not treated as reducing the capital expenditure which qualifies for tax allowances. For new projects the rate of grant is 22 per cent in the special development areas and 15 per cent in the development areas.

The Act also provides for regional selective assistance for projects which are likely to provide, maintain or safeguard employment in any part of the assisted area. Assistance is normally provided in the form of a grant related to the number of jobs involved and paid in instalments.

In addition modern factories for rent or purchase may be provided in many parts of the assisted areas. Firms in the development and special development areas are given preferential treatment when tendering for contracts placed by government departments and nationalised industries.

Infrastructure

Special measures to improve the infrastructure in the assisted areas include provisions under the Local Employment Act 1972 for grants towards the improvement of basic services (such as transport, power and water facilities) and towards the acquisition and clearance of derelict land (see p 182).

Controls on Industrial Location

The Government also influences the location of industry by requiring industrial development certificates before planning permission can be sought for the building of new factories (or for extensions to existing ones) above prescribed limits outside the assisted areas of Great Britain. Other government policies affecting the location of industry, including the establishment of the new enterprise zones, are described on p 178.

Administrative Arrangements

The Department of Industry takes a lead in the formulation of regional industrial policy and administers the regional development grant scheme throughout Great Britain. The Scottish and Welsh Offices however, administer regional selective assistance in Scotland and Wales.

In England the regional offices of the Department of Industry in the main assisted areas (the North, North West and Yorkshire and Humberside offices) deal with applications for regional selective assistance where projects costs are less than £10 million, and can authorise grants of up to £2 million without reference to the Department's headquarters. The delegated powers of the South West, East Midlands and West Midlands offices are less extensive but enable them to deal with most applications they receive. The Secretary of State for Industry has access to advice from the Industrial Development Advisory Board, a statutory body composed of prominent members of the industrial and financial community, which makes recommendations on industrial opportunities and on applications for selective financial assistance. Non-statutory industrial development boards have also been established for the North, North West, South West and Yorkshire and Humberside regions. The English Industrial Estates Corporation is responsible for government factories and those built in partnership with the private sector in the English assisted areas.

In Scotland and Wales, day-to-day work is carried out by the Scottish Economic Planning Department and by the Industry Department of the Welsh Office. Statutory Scottish and Welsh Industrial Development Advisory Boards advise the respective Secretaries of State for Scotland and Wales. The Scottish and Welsh Development Agencies (see p 228) are responsible for the provision of factories for rent or purchase and are also concerned with the reclamation of derelict land.

Northern Ireland Under separate legislation (the Industries Development Acts 1966 and 1971, as amended in 1976) the Northern Ireland Department of Commerce offers a full range of incentives comparable to those available in the assisted areas of Great Britain.

All firms establishing factories in Northern Ireland, without regard to the number of jobs created, are eligible for capital grants at the rate of 30 per cent of the cost of new buildings, machinery and equipment; for grants towards training and free use of government training services; for grants towards the cost of transferring key workers; and for the derating of industrial buildings by 75 per cent. The capital grants, like regional development grants in Great Britain, are not treated as reducing the capital expenditure which qualifies for tax allowances. Projects which are especially attractive because of the number of jobs created can obtain special benefits which include industrial development grants of up to 50 per cent of the cost of new buildings, machinery and equipment (as an alternative to capital grants); contributions towards setting-up costs; modern factories for rent or purchase; and loans, loan guarantees and interest relief grants.

Industrial development certificates (see p 226) are not required in Northern Ireland.

Grants of up to 50 per cent are available for research and development projects up to a maximum of £250,000 for any one project.

Assistance is also available to firms in the service sector which have a genuine choice of location within Britain and which create additional net employment. Projects serving primarily local needs are not assisted. The forms of aid available to the manufacturing sector may also be offered to service sector projects. The Northern Ireland Development Agency may also assist financially with industrial development projects.

Encouragement of Investment While the Government encourages the private sector to generate its own funds for investment in industry, there is a national system of official incentives for industrial development. Under the Finance Act 1972 incentives to encourage capital expenditure in plant and machinery take the form of a system of free depreciation enabling the whole of such expenditure to be written off against profits for tax purposes in the year in which it is incurred; there is in addition a 54 per cent initial allowance on new industrial buildings and structures and an annual writing down allowance of 4 per cent thereafter. Corporation tax relief on the inflationary increase in the value of stocks is also allowed (see p 354).

Direct financial assistance, in the form of grants and loans, is available in a number of ways. In addition to regional development assistance (see above), aid may be provided throughout Britain under the Industry Acts 1972 and 1975 where it is judged to be in the national interest. High technology developments in industry are eligible for support under the Science and Technology Act 1965. Direct investment from overseas is also encouraged, and overseas firms are offered the same facilities and incentives as those applying to British-owned companies. Official aid for exporters is also available (see p 375).

Industrial Promotion Agencies
Certain Government agencies promote areas of Britain to investors. In Scotland this is done by the Scottish Development Agency, and in Wales by the Welsh Development Agency. Both agencies may also provide investment funds and promote new ventures (although they are expected to encourage maximum private sector participation in their projects), and they have responsibilities relating to factory building, land reclamation (see p 226) and small firms (see below). In Northern Ireland the Northern Ireland Development Agency has a similar role, although other agencies are responsible for factory building, land reclamation and small firms.

The National Enterprise Board (NEB) is a public corporation which acts as a state holding company and has certain limited investment functions. Under revised guidelines issued in 1980 the NEB has an investment role in certain defined circumstances in relation to: companies in which it already has an interest; companies engaged in the development of, or exploitation of, advanced technologies; companies carrying on an industrial undertaking which is wholly or mainly in the assisted areas in England; and loans of up to £50,000 to small firms. The NEB, also, must have regard to the need to attract private investment.

Small Firms
The Department of Industry has a separate division which is the focal point for the formation of policy towards small firms. In association with the Scottish and Welsh Offices, the division administers a chain of small firms centres throughout Great Britain which provide an information and counselling service for small businessmen. Other government measures to assist small firms include tax concessions (see p 354) and experimental schemes to provide premises and new sources of venture capital.

Assistance for small firms is also provided by the development agencies and the NEB and by the agencies for rural industry (see below). In Northern Ireland the Local Enterprise Development Unit, established to promote the development of smaller industries, provides grants, loans, premises and management advice to new and expanding companies.

Rural Industries
Encouragement for the development of rural industries in England is provided under the aegis of the Development Commission set up in 1909. Through the agency of the Council for Small Industries in Rural Areas (CoSIRA), the commission provides managerial and technical advice, training facilities and a credit service to small manufacturing and service industries in rural areas.

Loans and advice are also provided for small tourism enterprises in the rural parts of the development areas and in the Commission's special investment areas. In addition the Commission provides factory premises in rural areas and lends support for pioneering and experimental schemes bearing on the rural economy, for voluntary bodies aiming to enrich social and cultural life in the countryside, and for surveys and other work in rural areas.

In Scotland and Wales these services are provided by the Scottish and Welsh Development Agencies. Separate bodies, however, cater for particular rural areas. In Scotland the Highlands and Islands Development Board, set up by Act of Parliament in 1965, provides assistance to the Highland region, and surrounding islands, and to parts of the Strathclyde region. It provides grants and loans to industrial and commercial enterprises, builds factories, and has powers to acquire land and set up businesses. The Development Board for Rural Wales has the general function of promoting and undertaking measures for economic and social development in the county of Powys and the districts of Meirionnydd and Ceredigion. It has a particular responsibility for new towns in those areas and can acquire land, carry out building and provide basic services. Within its area the board owns and manages government estates and factories and also acts as agent for the Welsh Development Agency in the provision of investment finance for small firms.

Tourism

Government support and assistance for the tourist industry is provided under the Development of Tourism Act 1969. The Act established four grant-aided statutory bodies—the British Tourist Authority, which is responsible for the overseas promotion of tourism to Great Britain and has a general responsibility for tourism within Great Britain, and the English, Scottish and Wales Tourist Boards which are responsible for promoting tourism in their respective countries within Great Britain and for encouraging and assisting the development and improvement of accommodation and of facilities and amenities for tourists. Each national board administers a scheme of financial assistance for selected tourist projects in the assisted areas. In Scotland the Highlands and Islands Development Board also assists the tourist industry. It is the Government's policy to encourage the industry in areas which could benefit from it, particularly in the assisted areas, thus relieving congestion in the more popular tourist centres. The Northern Ireland Tourist Board, established under separate legislation, has a function broadly similar to that of other British tourist boards except that financial assistance to tourism projects is only available from Northern Ireland Department of Commerce.

European Community Regional Policy and Aid

European Community regional policy has two major aims—the reduction of existing regional imbalances and the prevention of new imbalances arising from the adoption of Community policies. Although the principal responsibility for helping depressed areas remains with the national authorities concerned, the Community may complement schemes through aid from a number of sources.

European Regional Development Fund

The Regional Development Fund is the principal European Community instrument for regional development and assists regions affected by industrial change, structural under-employment and an over-reliance on agriculture. The fund offers support for public works contributing to the improvement of the regional infrastructure, for example, the building of new roads, ports or industrial estates, and also for the development of tourism. The rate of grant is usually between 10 and 30 per cent of the investment incurred by public

authorities, but may increase to 40 per cent for projects of particular importance to the region concerned.

The fund also offers support for investments in industrial, handicraft or
service activities which benefit from national regional aids and which create or
maintain at least ten jobs. The fund contribution may be up to 50 per cent of
the regional aids paid to an approved project provided that this does not exceed
20 per cent of the fixed investment costs and subject to a cost-per-job limit. In
the case of services and handicrafts this 20 per cent can be exceeded provided
that the contribution does not exceed 50 per cent of the national aid or a
cost-per-job allowance.

Britain's share of the fund in the period 1975–79 was £413 million. In 1979
the fund was given authority to finance specific measures to assist in the
implementation of European Community policies in other fields or to offset
any adverse regional consequences these may have. There is an allocation of 5
per cent of the total fund for these purposes.

*European
Investment Bank*

The European Investment Bank (EIB) is a self-governing institution set up by
the Treaty of Rome with member states of the European Community subscribing to its capital. The Bank's aims are to help to stimulate development in less
favoured regions, to modernise or convert industries, to help to create new
activities and to offset structural difficulties affecting certain sectors. The Bank
also serves projects of common interest to several member states or the European Community as a whole, for example, by reducing dependence on
imported energy sources or improving communications between member
states. It can lend up to 50 per cent of the fixed capital costs of projects. Loans
are normally for seven to ten years at fixed interest rates and are made in
mixtures of foreign currencies, mainly dollars and deutschemarks.

*European Coal
and Steel
Community*

The European Coal and Steel Community (ECSC) makes loans to companies
in the coal and steel industries, and for projects in any industry which contributes to the redeployment of redundant coal and steel workers. Non-repayable
aid may be available for workers who have been made redundant. The aid
consists of the payment of tide-over and re-settlement allowances to workers
and financing the retraining of workers having to change their employment.
The ECSC can lend up to 50 per cent of the fixed capital costs of projects.
Loans are normally for eight years at fixed interest rates and are made in a
mixture of dollars and deutschemarks.

*Exchange Risk
Guarantee
Scheme*

Exchange risk cover may be available on EIB and certain ECSC loans to
private sector borrowers in the assisted areas and Northern Ireland, provided
the projects concerned meet the criteria for regional selective assistance. Under
the scheme the British borrower takes on only a sterling liability; the Government carries the exchange risk in return for an annual premium on the
outstanding balance of the loan.

COMPETITION POLICY AND CONSUMER PROTECTION

A major feature of the Government's economic policy is the stimulation of
competition and the control of practices which are restrictive or anti-
competitive. Linked to this policy is the encouragement of fair trading, with
the particular aim of helping consumers and safeguarding their rights. The
Minister of State for Consumer Affairs, who is answerable to the Secretary of
State for Trade, has special responsibilities for competition policy and con-

sumer affairs (although certain matters, such as safety of foodstuffs and road vehicles, are the concern of other departments).

The Office of Fair Trading, a government agency headed by the Director General of Fair Trading, is concerned with the conduct of trade and industry in Britain.

Competition Policy

Competition policy has led to the development of machinery for scrutinising and regulating monopolies, mergers, anti-competitive practices and restrictive trade practices and of powers to regulate any structural changes or anti-competitive practices which operate against the public interest. The Director General of Fair Trading administers the Fair Trading Act 1973, which regulates monopolies and mergers, the Restrictive Trade Practices Act 1976, which regulates restrictive trading agreements and the Competition Act 1980, which regulates anti-competitive practices.

Monopolies and Mergers

The Secretary of State for Trade and the Director General of Fair Trading can refer monopolies for investigation by the Monopolies and Mergers Commission. The legislation defines a monopoly as a situation where at least a quarter of a particular kind of goods or service is supplied by or to a single person, or two or more people acting in a common manner. Local monopolies and arrangements which prevent, restrict or distort competition, and monopolies in public sector industries can also be referred to the Commission. If the Commission finds that a monopoly operates against the public interest, the Secretary of State for Trade has powers to make orders and otherwise to remedy or prevent the harm which the Commission considers may exist. It is more usual, however, for the Director General to be asked to negotiate undertakings to remedy the adverse effects identified by the Commission.

Proposals for a merger (defined as occurring when two or more enterprises are brought under common ownership or control) may be referred to the Commission by the Secretary of State for Trade if it would result in or intensify a monopoly or if the total value of gross assets taken over exceeds £15 million. If the Commission finds that a merger or proposed merger may be expected to operate against the public interest, the Secretary of State can prevent it from taking place or, if it has already taken place, require it to be reversed. There are special provisions relating to newspaper and certain other mergers.

Anti-competitive Practices

The Competition Act 1980 strengthens the powers of the Director General and the Monopolies and Mergers Commission to deal with practices, other than registrable restrictive agreements (see p 232), which are anti-competitive. Subject to certain exemptions, the Director General can investigate any practice carried out by a business (whether in the public or private sector) which may restrict, distort or prevent competition in the production, supply or acquisition of goods or services in Britain. If an anti-competitive practice is found, the Director General can suggest that it be referred to the Monopolies and Mergers Commission to establish whether it operates against the public interest. As an alternative the Director General can accept an undertaking from the business responsible for the practice. On an adverse finding by the Commission, the Secretary of State has powers to take remedial action. The Act also empowers the Secretary of State to refer to the Commission any question on the efficiency and costs of, the service provided by, or the possible abuse of a monopoly situation by particular named bodies in the public sector.

Restrictive Trade Practices

Under the Restrictive Trade Practices Act 1976 restrictive trading agreements have to be registered with the Director General of Fair Trading. Broadly, an agreement is registrable if two or more parties to it engaged in business in Britain in the supply of goods or services accept some limitation on their freedom to make their own decisions about matters such as prices or conditions of sale. Failure to register an agreement means that the restrictions are void and the parties are liable to legal proceedings. Having placed an agreement on the register, the Director General has the duty of referring it to the Restrictive Practices Court and the Court must declare the restrictions in it contrary to the public interest unless the parties can satisfy the Court by reference to criteria laid down in the Act that this is not the case. Restrictions declared contrary to the public interest are void and the Court can order the parties not to give effect to them or make any similar agreement. In practice, however, many agreements do not need to be referred to the Court because, for example, the parties choose to give up the restrictions rather than go to Court, or the Secretary of State accepts the Director General's advice that the restrictions are not significant enough to warrant reference to the Court.

European Community

The objective of the competition policy of the European Community is to promote free and fair competition in trade between member countries. The Community's rules of competition, which are set out in the Treaty of Rome, apply to industrial and commercial practices likely to affect trade and prevent, restrict or distort competition in the Community. Agreements which fall within the rules must be notified to the European Commission, which has its own Competition Department; the Commission has powers to exempt agreements which, though restrictive of competition between member countries, benefit the Community in defined ways.

Consumer Protection

The Fair Trading Act 1973 provides machinery (headed by the Director General of Fair Trading) for the continuous review of consumer affairs, for action to deal with both trading practices which unfairly affect consumers' interests and persistent offenders under existing law, and for the negotiation of self-regulatory codes of practice to raise trading standards.

The consumer's interests with regard to the purity of foods, the description and performance of goods, and pricing information are safeguarded by the Food and Drugs Acts 1955 and 1956, the Trades Descriptions Acts 1968 and 1972, the Unfair Contract Terms Act 1977 and the Sale of Goods Act 1979. The marking and accuracy of quantities are regulated by the Weights and Measures Acts 1963 and 1979, the latter introducing a system of average weights for certain pre-packed goods. The other major area of legislation is concerned with the prevention of the sale of dangerous or harmful consumer goods. The principal laws here are the Consumer Protection Acts 1961 and 1971, and the Consumer Safety Act 1978, which empower the Government to make regulations to ensure the safety of any class of goods and to prohibit the supply of any goods which are deemed to be unsafe.

Provision of consumer information and advice is an important function of those in local and central Government, and of several independent organisations concerned with consumer protection. The local outlets are the Citizens Advice Bureaux (see p 152) and in some areas Consumer Advice Centres.

The independent, non-statutory National Consumer Council (and associated councils for Scotland, Wales and Northern Ireland), which also receives government finance, ensures that the consumer's view is made known to those in Government and industry whose decisions affect consumers.

Consumer councils for the energy and rail nationalised industries and for the Post Office investigate questions of concern to the consumer, while some trade associations in industry and commerce have established codes of practice designed to protect the consumer. In addition several private organisations work to further consumer interests. The largest is the Consumers' Association, funded by the subscriptions of its membership of over 600,000. The Association conducts an extensive programme of comparative testing of goods and investigation of services; its views and test reports are published in its monthly magazine *Which?* or its satellite publications. The Association also provides an advice service on subscription. Consultancy work on European legislation is undertaken by the Association for the Department of Trade. Local consumer groups, many belonging to the National Federation of Consumer Groups, also promote consumers' interests and provide information and advice.

The European Community's consumer programme covers a number of important topics, such as health and safety, protection of the consumer's economic interests when purchasing goods and services, promotion of consumer education and strengthening the representation of consumers. The views of British organisations interested in consumer affairs are represented at community level by the European Community Group (UK).

COMPANY LAW

The formation and conduct of private sector corporations is regulated by the Companies Acts (notably that of 1948, as amended). 'Incorporation' means registering an enterprise with an official registrar of companies, with related obligations such as the capital structure of a company, the rights and duties of its directors and members, and the preparation of accounts. Nearly all corporate businesses are 'limited liability' companies, which means that each company is a legal entity distinct from its members, who are not as such liable for its debts. Their liability is limited to contributing an amount related to their shareholding. (In unincorporated businesses, such as sole proprietorships or partnerships, by contrast, individuals are personally liable for any debts a business may incur.)

The European Community is pursuing a programme for the harmonisation of company law among member states. In accordance with the programme the Companies Act 1980 provides for new arrangements for the classification and registration of companies and their capital structure and distribution of profits and assets. The Act sets out new criteria for public companies (hitherto defined only as those not meeting one or other of the tests for private companies) and defines private companies as those which are not public. It continues to be the case that private companies may not offer shares to the public. Following a review by the Government, the Act also lays down rules concerning the conduct of company directors, and makes illegal share dealings that depend upon certain privileged kinds of information.

Certain specialised types of private sector organisation such as banks, building societies and insurance companies are subject to additional or alternative statutory regulation.

13 Manufacturing and Service Industries

Manufacturing plays a vital role in the economy. It accounts for some 26 per cent of gross domestic product; about 29 per cent of the employed labour force is engaged in manufacturing; and around 77 per cent of visible exports consists of manufactured or semi-manufactured goods.

The manufacturing industries are described by sector in this chapter, together with the construction industry and the distributive and service industries.

MANUFACTURING

Most manufacturing is carried out by private enterprise. Though the greater parts of the iron and steel, shipbuilding and aerospace industries are in public ownership, it is the Government's general policy to reduce the extent of state ownership of industry. Products from the state-controlled sector also include locomotives and rolling-stock built in the workshops of British Railways, military equipment and supplies made in establishments of the defence services, and fissile materials and radioactive isotopes. The Government also has shareholdings in a number of companies, including British Petroleum Ltd., Harland and Wolff Ltd., Rolls-Royce Ltd. and Short Brothers Ltd. Shareholdings in some companies, including BL Ltd., are held for the Government by the National Enterprise Board.

The most recent complete analysis of the size distribution of establishments and enterprises in manufacturing industry, and of the degree of concentration, is contained in the *Report on the Census of Production 1977*. This shows that some 69 per cent (74,852) of the 108,028 establishments in manufacturing industry had fewer than 20 employees each and accounted for 7 per cent of total employment; 30,721 establishments had between 20 and 499 employees and accounted for some 39 per cent of the total labour force; 1,846 establishments, each with between 500 and 1,499 employees, were responsible for 21 per cent of employment; and one-third was in the hands of the 608 establishments each with 1,500 or more employees. About 57 per cent of the largest establishments were in the engineering, and metal and vehicle manufacturing industries. An enterprise, as defined in the census, normally consists of either a single establishment or of two or more establishments under common ownership. In the private sector of British manufacturing industry in 1977 37 per cent of all employment was accounted for by the largest 100 enterprises.

Output and Investment

The figures for manufacturing output in Tables 13 and 14 show the relative size of the sectors of manufacturing and their growth rates. Expansion up to 1979 was evident in those industries using advanced technologies such as electronics, instrument engineering, most sectors of the chemical industry and paper, printing and publishing. A major stimulus has been provided by the various needs of the offshore oil and gas industries. In other long-established industries (for example, shipbuilding and marine engineering and electrical engineering) extensive re-organisation, re-equipment and modernisation are being undertaken to meet changing economic conditions. Production during 1980 was increasingly affected by the world-wide industrial recession.

TABLE 13: Manufacturing Industry: Net Output 1976–78[a]

Industry Group	£ million			Percentage of total	per head £		
	1976	1977	1978	1978	1976	1977	1978
Food, drink and tobacco	5,829	6,576	7,542	13·0	7,655	8,626	10,179
Coal and petroleum products	906	1,142	859	1·5	25,753	33,375	25,279
Chemicals and allied industries	4,377	5,169	5,602	9·6	10,842	12,723	13,971
Metal manufacture	2,904	2,899	3,321	5·7	6,177	6,227	7,319
Mechanical engineering	5,442	6,480	7,681	13·2	5,934	7,011	8,338
Instrument engineering	773	935	1,116	1·9	5,021	5,981	7,095
Electrical engineering	3,928	4,392	5,251	9·0	5,562	6,250	7,403
Shipbuilding and marine engineering	754	874	877	1·5	4,223	5,045	4,973
Vehicles	4,226	5,167	5,761	9·9	5,504	6,636	7,523
Metal goods not elsewhere specified	2,730	3,136	3,615	6·2	5,239	6,001	7,038
Textiles	2,344	2,463	2,825	4·9	4,526	4,895	5,745
Leather, leather goods and fur	186	197	227	0·4	4,397	4,868	5,838
Clothing and footwear	1,216	1,390	1,629	2·8	2,990	3,509	4,152
Bricks, pottery, glass, cement, etc.	1,833	2,107	2,378	4·1	7,091	8,078	9,199
Timber, furniture, etc.	1,465	1,610	1,910	3·3	5,426	6,100	7,275
Paper, printing and publishing	3,552	4,093	4,954	8·5	6,433	7,491	9,120
Other manufacturing industries	1,965	2,233	2,556	4·4	5,744	6,492	7,414
All manufacturing industries	44,434	50,862	58,106	100·0	6,083	6,986	8,064

Source: *Business Statistics Office*
[a] 1978 results are provisional
Differences between totals and the sums of their constituent parts are due to rounding.

Investment in manufacturing tends to reflect the level of demand in the economy as a whole, with some time lag between the start of an increase in output and the implementation of investment plans. There is thus a marked cyclical pattern in the flow of investment by manufacturing industry, and since 1965 there have been three discernible cycles.

Total manufacturing investment in 1979 at current prices was £6,583 million, apportioned as follows: food, drink and tobacco £906 million, coal and petroleum products £286 million, chemicals £1,172 million, metal manufacture £504 million, engineering, shipbuilding and metal goods £1,427 million, vehicles £855 million, textiles, leather and clothing £353 million, paper, printing and publishing £450 million and other manufacturing industries £630 million. Analysed by type of asset, investment was divided into £987 million for new building work, £473 million for vehicles and £5,123 million for plant and machinery. The growing practice of leasing rather than purchasing new equipment is estimated to have contributed an extra £750 million to manufacturing investment in 1979.

In the tables in the following sections, relating to the main sectors of manufacturing industry, employment statistics are for June 1979 and are based on figures supplied by the Department of Employment and the Northern Ireland Department of Manpower Services. Sales figures are compiled by the Department of Industry from returns made by firms in industry. Export figures come from *Business Monitor MQ10: Overseas Trade Analysed in Terms of Industries.* Unless otherwise stated, export and manufacturers' sales figures include parts. (The tables contain a selection of leading activities within each sector and are not comprehensive.) Figures in the text are for 1979.

TABLE 14: Index of Manufacturing Production 1974–79 (1975=100)

Industry Group	1974	1975	1976	1977	1978	1979
Food, drink and tobacco	102·5	100	102·7	104·0	106·2	107·4
Coal and petroleum products	115·9	100	105·7	102·7	101·4	105·3
Chemical industries	109·5	100	112·0	115·9	117·0	119·0
Metal manufacture	114·5	100	103·9	103·5	102·5	103·7
Mechanical engineering	101·3	100	95·1	94·0	92·4	91·6
Instrument engineering	98·7	100	96·6	98·7	105·4	108·4
Electrical engineering	104·5	100	98·5	102·7	108·1	113·6
Shipbuilding and marine engineering	98·9	100	96·5	93·5	86·4	78·1
Vehicles	108·9	100	99·2	102·1	100·1	97·0
Metal goods not elsewhere specified	109·1	100	99·0	103·8	102·2	98·3
Textiles	105·9	100	103·0	100·9	99·3	96·6
Leather, leather goods and fur	98·7	100	102·3	97·1	97·0	91·6
Clothing and footwear	100·2	100	97·1	103·2	105·4	106·5
Bricks, pottery, glass, cement, etc.	107·2	100	100·7	99·7	101·6	101·2
Timber, furniture, etc.	102·7	100	103·4	96·9	101·4	103·4
Paper, printing and publishing	115·5	100	102·5	106·9	109·2	112·1
Other manufacturing	106·8	100	108·7	114·7	118·0	117·7

Source: *Monthly Digest of Statistics*

METAL MANUFACTURE

1979	Employment '000s	Manufacturers' Sales £ million	Exports £ million
iron and steel products	258	5,806	1,212
iron castings	74	1,231	54
non-ferrous metals	112	3,236	906

Iron and Steel   Most of the early developments in iron and steel production originated in Britain, today the world's eighth largest steel-producing nation. The Iron and Steel Act 1967 brought together into public ownership 14 major steel companies and created the British Steel Corporation (BSC). In recent years BSC has produced about 82 per cent of Britain's crude steel and is the largest steel undertaking in Europe. It employs some 166,000 people, of whom 138,000 are involved in iron and steel manufacturing and 28,000 in other activities, such as chemicals and overseas consultancy. The remaining (private sector) companies are represented by the British Independent Steel Producers' Association whose members employ some 60,000 people and account for over a third of the value of the industry's turnover. The private sector is particularly strong in the manufacture of alloy and stainless steels and of finished products for the engineering industry. The main steel producing areas are Yorkshire and Humberside (32 per cent of crude steel output in 1979), Wales (32 per cent), the Northern region (15 per cent), Scotland (8 per cent) and the West Midlands (5 per cent).

About 75 per cent of British steel producers' deliveries of finished steel products are used by home industry and the remainder for direct export, the major markets for which are the rest of the European Community and the United States. A large part of the steel used by industry in Britain is also subsequently exported as part of other finished products.

BSC has invested heavily in modernising its production capacity in recent years. With the ending of steel-making at Shotton (north Wales), the obsolete open hearth process has been entirely replaced by basic oxygen steel-making (for bulk production) and the electric arc process (for more specialised tasks). Bulk steel-making is concentrated at five main sites (Port Talbot and Llanwern in south Wales, Ravenscraig near Glasgow, Redcar/Lackenby in Cleveland and Scunthorpe, south Humberside) which have a good access to deep water for imports of raw materials. Because of a marked fall in demand for steel, BSC has had to accelerate the closure of its older steelworks and reduce capacity at some of the more modern works.

Iron and Steel Castings

The castings industry plays an important role in meeting the needs of manufacturers for essential components for products sold both in Britain and abroad. Its main customers are the vehicle, mechanical engineering and building and construction industries. The larger mechanised foundries are dominant, but many smaller craft foundries meet needs for specialised and low-volume castings. Output (by volume) has been falling and the industry has been progressively changing. While some foundries have been closing, many others have been investing in new melting equipment, moulding equipment and processes, and process and quality control equipment, both to meet demands for castings of higher quality and strength and to improve working and environmental conditions. The British Cast Iron Research Association and the Steel Casting Research and Trade Association conduct much of the research and development in the industry.

Non-ferrous Metals

Britain's non-ferrous metal processing and fabricating industry is one of the largest in Europe. Its major products are aluminium (both virgin and secondary metal), secondary refined copper, lead and primary zinc. Tin mining in Cornwall supplies about 25 per cent of Britain's tin requirements (see p 283) but otherwise British metal smelting and refining industries are based on imported ores and concentrates except for substantial secondary production from scrap metal. Britain is also a major producer of the newer specialised metals including uranium, zirconium and beryllium for the nuclear energy industry, niobium for aircraft production and selenium, silicon, germanium and tantalum for electronic apparatus. Titanium and titanium alloys are also produced and used in aircraft production, power generation and North Sea oil production, where their lightness, resistance to stress, flexibility and resistance to oxidisation are especially valued. Nearly half the industry is situated in the Midlands. Other centres include south Wales, London, Tyneside and Avonmouth, where a zinc smelter of some 100,000 tonnes capacity operates. Three large-scale aluminium smelters provide 85 per cent of Britain's requirements for primary aluminium. The large non-ferrous metals fabricating industry uses large quantities of imported refined metals such as copper, lead, zinc and aluminium. A wide range of semi-manufactures is produced in these metals and their alloys, and, particularly in aluminium, firms are engaged in smelting, casting and fabrication by rolling, extrusion and drawing; advanced techniques of powder metallurgy and pressure die-castings are also employed. In recent years considerable progress has been made in the development of 'superplastic' alloys, which are more ductile and elastic than conventional alloys.

Scientific and technological research for the industry is conducted by the Warren Spring Laboratory of the Department of Industry and by the British Non-Ferrous (BNF) Metals Technology Centre.

The main products exported, including alloys and semi-finished products, are copper, nickel, aluminium, lead, tin and zinc. Exports of aluminium and aluminium alloys reached £244 million in 1979 while exports in the same year of copper, brass and other copper alloys reached £217 million. Exports of silver, platinum and other metals of the platinum group totalled nearly £397 million in 1979. The major export markets for the whole industry are the United States and the Federal Republic of Germany.

MECHANICAL ENGINEERING

1979	Employment '000s	Manufacturers' Sales £ million	Exports £ million
metal-working machine tools	64	797	345
industrial plant and steelwork	154	2,036	605
industrial engines	27	471	312
pumps, valves and compressors	83	1,222	482
textile machinery	25	295	216
construction and earth-moving equipment	42	950	734
mechanical handling equipment	60	1,129	371
agricultural machinery (except tractors)	28	298	134
office machinery	23	149	149

The mechanical engineering industry comprises a group of industries manufacturing all types of machinery, machine tools, industrial engines, mechanical handling equipment, construction equipment and industrial plant. About half the industry's production is for the home market. The major customers for the heavy equipment sectors are the nationalised fuel industries, the chemical industry and the British Steel Corporation. A wide range of equipment is supplied to the building and construction industry. Demand for other types of equipment comes from all the production industries in Britain.

Machine Tools   Britain was the birthplace of the machine tool industry and produces a very wide range of machine tools. Almost all machine tools produced are purchased by engineering, vehicles and metal goods industries.

The most important types of metal cutting machine tools are milling, grinding and turning machines. There is an increasing demand for automatic control and Britain is an important producer of numerically controlled machine tools, including machining centres. The largest export markets for the industry in 1979 were the rest of the European Community, the United States and Poland. The Machine Tool Trades Association represents most of the industry and is responsible for the international machine tool exhibition held in Britain every four years, the next being due in 1984. The Machine Tool Industry Research Association carries out research into design and performance of tools and into production methods, with which the Production Engineering Research Association is also concerned.

Manufacturing Plant and Machinery

British industry manufactures almost every type of industrial (including process) plant and steelwork (for nuclear power station construction see Chapter 14). Of particular importance are fabricated products such as pressure vessels, heat exchangers and storage tanks for chemical and oil refining (process) plant, steam-raising boilers (including those of high capacity for power stations), sintering plant, metallurgical furnaces and plant, lime and cement kilns, nuclear reactors, water and sewage treatment plant and fabricated steelwork for bridges, buildings and industrial installations. The industrial plant industry comprises both equipment manufacturers and contractors responsible for the design, engineering, construction and commissioning of complete plants for process industries. British manufacturers have contributed to major advances in process technology and British contractors are carrying out major plant projects in many overseas countries. Gas turbines for industrial application, in particular for power generation in the fuel industries, are another important section of the industry, where exports have done well in recent years. Three large firms are pre-eminent in the manufacture of industrial engines, including those derived from aero-engines. Industrial pumps, valves and compressors are vital components in many industrial processes, particularly in the chemicals, oil and electric power industries: over half the production of all types of such equipment is exported. The fluid power industry makes oil hydraulic and pneumatic equipment for operating machinery and construction and other equipment. There are many new areas where these powerful and flexible systems may be used.

Machines and accessories for the manufacture and processing of yarns and fabrics from all types of natural and man-made fibres are produced by the textile machinery industry in Britain, which is noted for the range, scale and versatility of its operations. British inventions have remained the foundation of many textile processes in use internationally and progress has been made in applying automated techniques (including the use of micro-electronics) in the industry. In 1979 75 per cent of the industry's total sales were to export markets. Research and development is carried out by the large firms and the four research associations connected with the textile industry.

Machinery for food and drink preparation, processing and sterilisation is another important sector. Refrigerating machinery (excluding domestic equipment) is used for food and drink processing, but the industry also covers plant for ships and vehicles and equipment for conserving drinks, food and ice-cream for the distributive and catering industries.

Construction and Mining Equipment

Almost the whole range of plant required by the construction industry is produced, including excavating, earth-moving and road-making equipment, pile drivers and quarry crushing and screening plant. Overseas sales of construction equipment and mining machinery and equipment, including coal cutting and coal face loading machinery, are substantial. Mechanical handling equipment is used not only for construction and related activities but throughout industry generally. It extends from individual units and accessories to complete operating systems, the main products being cranes and bridge transporters, lifts, escalators, conveyors, elevators, hoists and certain special powered trucks. Electronic control and completely automatic handling systems are also available.

Agricultural Machinery

Britain produces a wide range of equipment for general and special use, including many special purpose machines such as fruit harvesters and improved root harvesters (for tractors see p 243). Mechanisation is extensively used in the arable farming and dairy farming sectors. Much of the new machinery is designed for use in a variety of conditions to meet the needs of overseas farmers. A large-scale annual exhibition of the industry's products is the Royal Smithfield Show and Agricultural Machinery Exhibition held in London in December. The main trade association for the industry is the Agricultural Engineers Association.

Office Machinery

The industry covers a wide range of products including duplicators, photo-copiers, typewriters, word processors, microfilm, dictation and mail-room equipment, and accounting machines and cash registers. A large proportion of the industry is owned by multi-national companies, and is likely to continue to be so, as the rapidly advancing technologies involved require a heavy commit-ment to research and development. In particular, the incorporation of micro-electronics into office products is rapidly increasing. The industry is strong in microfilm readers/printers, duplicators and office offset litho and rapid high volume photocopiers.

Other Machinery

The other major products of the mechanical engineering industry include printing, bookbinding and paper goods machinery, space heating, ventilating and air-conditioning equipment, packaging and bottling machinery, hand tools, garden tools, portable power tools and miscellaneous non-electrical machinery, such as boot- and shoe-making machinery, laundry equipment, automatic vending machines, plastic working machinery and other types of specialised equipment.

General Mechanical Engineering

Alongside the firms manufacturing the products of the mechanical engineering industry are enterprises which supply parts and components and undertake general sub-contracting, fabricating and repair work. Particularly important is the production of ball, roller, needle and other bearings, about 25 per cent of which is for the motor vehicle industry, and of other components, such as industrial fasteners, precision fasteners and chains, gears and drop-forgings.

INSTRUMENT ENGINEERING

1979	Employment '000s	Manufacturers' Sales £ million	Exports £ million
scientific and industrial instruments	99	1,266	573
photographic equipment	11	274	301
watches and clocks	12	99	68
surgical instruments and appliances	28	280	149

Instrument engineering is a particularly important sector of the engineering industry. Electronic techniques are widely used, particularly in the industrial instrument sector, which comprises industrial and process measuring and control instruments and equipment, optical instruments, electrical measuring and testing instruments, analytical instruments and a diverse group of others. The chemicals, power, petroleum and iron and steel industries account for about 80 per cent of process control applications, the largest sector of the industry and one which is expanding. Major advances have been made in automatic testing equipment and analytical instruments for medical diagnosis and pollution control. The industry is served mainly by five trade associations—the Scientific Instrument Manufacturers Association, the Control and Automation Manufacturers Association, the British Industrial Measuring and Control Apparatus Manufacturers Association, the Electronic Engineering Association and the British Photographic Manufacturers Association. The Sira Institute Ltd. conducts research on behalf of the industry and operates an information service for member firms.

Photographic equipment includes photographic and cinematographic cameras, projectors and document copying machines. Other sectors of the instrument industry are concerned with watches, clocks and time recorders and with surgical instruments and appliances and related products.

ELECTRICAL AND ELECTRONIC ENGINEERING

1979	Employment '000s	Manufacturers' Sales £ million	Exports £ million
electrical machinery	134	1,580	745
insulated wires and cables	43	769	150
electrical domestic appliances	63	894	179
electronic equipment:			
telecommunications	67	681	111
components	129	1,282	660
consumer goods	47	720	178
computers	48	1,008	835
capital goods	96	1,360	404

The electrical engineering industry is engaged in the manufacture and installation of a wide variety of equipment, including all types of power generation, transmission and distribution equipment, motors, telecommunications and broadcasting equipment and domestic electrical appliances. The electronics industry, which makes a vital contribution to the efficiency of many branches of the country's economy, has become one of the most important sectors of British industry.

Leading representative organisations are the British Electrical and Allied Manufacturers' Association, the Association of Manufacturers of Domestic Appliances and the Electronic Engineering Association, a member of the Conference of the Electronics Industry which brings together the six principal trade associations for the electronics industry. Research is carried out by ERA Technology Ltd. (formerly the Electrical Research Association).

Electrical Engineering

The main product categories are power equipment (generators, turbines, motors, converters, transformers and rectifiers) and switchgear, starting and control gear.

The industry produces cables and wires for the distribution of electric power, for telecommunication networks and other purposes; its products include submarine cables and cables insulated by a great variety of materials. Optical fibres (hair-thin strands of pure glass) have been developed, which have much greater capacity than the copper wiring used in telecommunications networks. Four major groups are responsible for more than half the industry's output and for a large proportion of the world's submarine cable requirements.

A few large firms also dominate the market for other electrical goods, including domestic appliances. Domestic equipment includes heating and cooking equipment, washing machines and dryers, refrigerators, vacuum cleaners, irons and electric kettles. Other major sectors are electrical equipment for motor vehicles and aircraft, electric lamps and light fittings, and batteries and accumulators.

Electronic Equipment

The British electronics industry is one of the largest and most comprehensive in the world and British scientists and companies have made important contributions to electronics technology. Because the applications of electronics technology are continuing to multiply rapidly, an exact definition of the industry must be arbitrary, but the sectors included are radar and navigational aids, telecommunications equipment, security systems, components, consumer goods, computers and communication and other capital equipment, as well as electronic process control and industrial instrumentation (see p 240).

The dependence of the telecommunications industry on electronic techniques is increasing as new switching systems are introduced (see p 323). The main products are switching and transmission equipment for telephone, telex and telegraph systems and subscribers' apparatus such as telephones, private automatic branch exchanges, teleprinters and facsimile systems. The Post Office is the main customer in the home market, which is largely supplied by four companies, and carries out research and development work in co-operation with companies.

The components sector manufactures a wide range of both active and passive electronic components. In addition to a comprehensive indigenous industry, a number of large United States companies are manufacturing components in Britain. The sector meets requirements for components in Britain, and is also very active in international trade. The manufacture of integrated circuits (in which many components are fabricated within a tiny chip of semi-conductor material, see also p 213) is an area of particularly rapid change. Britain is improving its position in the manufacture of advanced components.

The major consumer goods produced are radio and television sets, music centres and high-fidelity audio equipment. In the audio field, British manufacturers have a reputation for high-quality goods but are less strong in the mass market. Equipment is also being manufactured for reception of Britain's 'Prestel' and 'teletext' services (see pp 324 and 426).

In the computer sector, an extensive range of computer systems, central processors and peripheral equipment, from large computers for large-scale data processing and scientific work to mini- and micro-computers for use in control and automation systems and for home and office use, are produced. Essential to the sector is the 'software' industry, in which Britain is especially strong, which produces programs and associated services and complements the hardware industry, enabling the systems manufacturers to provide complete solutions to meet the requirements of users.

An expanding sector of the industry is that which covers the manufacture of radio communication equipment, radar and radio navigational aids for ships and aircraft, alarms and signalling equipment, public broadcasting equipment and other capital goods. British equipment is used extensively overseas, for defence, civil aviation, shipping, health, educational and other purposes.

An important advance in medical diagnosis has been the computerised tomography X-ray scanner, which was developed in Britain. This has made a world-wide impact by providing images of sections of brain or whole body on living subjects.

VEHICLES, AIRCRAFT AND SHIPS

1979	Employment '000s	Manufacturers' Sales £ million	Exports £ million
cars and commercial vehicles	473	8,303	3,127
wheeled tractors	34	973	702
motor cycles and pedal cycles	13	130	80
railway vehicles and equipment	44	309	126
aerospace	206	2,526	1,041
shipbuilding and marine engineering	175	1,015	363

Motor Vehicles

The motor vehicle industry comprises the manufacture of cars and commercial vehicles, caravans and trailers, and parts and components. Output of cars and commercial vehicles is dominated by four large groups: BL Ltd., in which there is a majority public shareholding, Ford, Vauxhall and Talbot (formerly Chrysler UK), which account for over 99 per cent of car production and some 97 per cent of commercial vehicle output; the remainder is in the hands of smaller, specialist producers of cars, heavy commercial vehicles, buses and coaches. There has traditionally been a substantial positive balance of trade in the industry, though in 1979 surpluses of £239 million on commercial vehicles and £684 million on parts and accessories were offset by a deficit of £1,757 million on cars.

The principal trade association for the industry is the Society of Motor Manufacturers and Traders which holds a biennial motor industry show at the National Exhibition Centre, Birmingham.

Wheeled Tractors

Agricultural tractors account for the bulk of wheeled tractors produced; Britain is the third largest producer of four-wheeled agricultural tractors in the world and a leading exporter. Production is dominated by three large firms, with two others responsible for most of the remainder.

Motor and Pedal Cycles

Though in recent years the motor cycle industry has contracted and the domestic market is largely supplied by imports, the market for pedal cycles has doubled in the last decade and is mainly supplied by British firms. TI Raleigh is the largest maker and exporter of bicycles in the world.

Railway Equipment

British Rail's requirements of locomotives and rolling stock are largely met by its own workshops; it also supplies equipment and provides consultancy services to many overseas countries. There is also a large private sector, which builds trains for London Transport and rapid-transit networks, as well as railway equipment for home and export markets (including components, traction and control gear, signalling, heating and ventilation systems and track equipment), undertakes electrification and other major works overseas and provides overseas consultancy services.

Aerospace

Britain's aerospace industry is one of the largest and most comprehensive in Western Europe and the Western world. The products of the industry include civil and military aircraft, helicopters, aero-engines, guided weapons, hovercraft and space vehicles, supported by a comprehensive range of aircraft and airfield equipment and systems.

British Aerospace (BAe), a public corporation, and the publicly-owned companies Short Brothers and Rolls-Royce are responsible for the greater part of aircraft, guided weapon and aero-engine manufacture in Britain. BAe, in which the British Aircraft Corporation, Hawker Siddeley Aviation, Hawker Siddeley Dynamics and Scottish Aviation were vested in 1977, is the largest British aircraft and guided weapons manufacturer. The British Aerospace Act 1980 provides for the whole of BAe's business to be vested in a successor company to be called British Aerospace Limited and the Government intends that shares in the company should subsequently be offered for sale, subject to a limitation on the proportion of foreign ownership. Rolls-Royce is responsible for almost the entire output of aero-engines in Britain; it is one of the world's three leading aero-engine manufacturers and over 10,000 of the world's civil and military aircraft are powered by Rolls-Royce engines.

The private sector is composed of a number of aircraft companies, including Westland Aircraft and its subsidiary, Westland Helicopters (which specialises in helicopter design and manufacture and, in addition, performs a wide range of aviation equipment work) and all of the aviation equipment sector.

Production of BAe includes such civil aircraft as the HS748 feederliner and the HS125 business jet, while the new BAe 146 feederjet and Jetstream 31 transport aircraft are expected to be in service by 1982. BAe is a full partner in the European consortium Airbus Industrie; it is continuing to manufacture the wings for the A300 Airbus and is designing and manufacturing the wings for the A310 derivative. Military aircraft include the unique Harrier vertical/short take-off and landing aircraft (which has achieved substantial sales to the United States), the Hawk advanced trainer, the Anglo-French Jaguar tactical fighter/operational trainer and the Tornado multi-role combat aircraft, which is a collaborative venture by Britain, the Federal Republic of Germany and Italy.

BAe is also a major producer of guided weapons including a number which have been sold overseas, in particular the Rapier ground-to-air missile. Collaborative guided weapon projects between Britain and its NATO partners are becoming increasingly important.

Short Brothers, which is based in Belfast, produces the Skyvan, the SD 330 commuter airliner, airframe components and missiles. Westland Helicopters manufacture the successful Sea King and are the British partners in the Anglo-French collaborative programmes on the Puma Gazelle and Lynx helicopters, which are being produced for the armed forces of a number of countries besides Britain and France.

Rolls-Royce aero-engines in production include the collaboratively-produced RB199 for the Tornado, the RB211 civil engine and its more powerful derivative the RB211–524, the Pegasus vectored-thrust engine for the Harrier and the Gem helicopter engine. More advanced versions of the RB211–524 are under development, as is another RB211 derivative, RB211–535, which will be the launch engine for the new Boeing 757 airliner. Industrial versions of aero-engines such as the RB211 and the Olympus (developed for Concorde) are being produced for use in oil and gas transmission and as stand-by power generators. Versions for marine use, in particular of the Olympus and the Tyne, are being used to power a new generation of warships for the Royal Navy and many overseas navies.

The aviation equipment manufacturers provide a wide range of systems essential to the design of engines and aircraft, including engine and flight controls, electrical generation, mechanical and hydraulic power systems, cabin furnishings and flight deck information displays, which are sold both in domestic and overseas markets. They also supply equipment for ground operation including that needed for radar and air traffic control, ground power suppliers and flight simulators, to airports and airlines throughout the world.

The space sector's main effort is directed towards the programmes of the European Space Agency (ESA, see p 396), although sales of sub-systems are made world-wide. The Ariel VI satellite, still in operation (see p 396) was built for the Science Research Council. Through the ESA, BAe's Dynamics Group has acted as prime contractor for the OTS experimental communications satellite and the GEOS scientific satellites. Manufacture of the operational European Communications Satellites (ECS) for the European telecommunications satellite organisation EUTELSAT, and the maritime satellites (MARECS) expected to be used operationally by the International Maritime Satellite Organisation (INMARSAT) is in hand. Ground stations have been constructed for the Post Office (see p 324).

The industry is thus extensively involved in the manufacture of space systems and in scientific research in other European collaborative programmes. It carries out an extensive programme of research and development on airframes, aero-engines and equipment, including avionics, while considerable research is also undertaken by universities and Government research establishments.

Aerospace production and exports, which are fairly evenly divided between aircraft, engines and equipment (including avionics), have made considerable progress over the past few years and now stand at record levels. The principal destinations for exports are the United States and countries with which Britain is involved in collaborative ventures such as France and the Federal Republic of Germany.

The main trade association for the industry is the Society of British Aerospace Companies which organises a major international air show at Farnborough, Hampshire, every two years. Major suppliers of avionics equipment are also members of the Electronic Engineering Association.

Shipbuilding and Marine Engineering

Britain has a long-established tradition of shipbuilding and accounts for about 4·8 per cent of world output of merchant shipping. Naval shipbuilding and the construction of vessels and structures connected with offshore oil production are important sectors of the industry. In merchant shipbuilding the SD14 general cargo series has been especially successful. Programmes of modernisation and reorganisation have taken place in most of the major shipyards, including the construction of several covered-berth ship 'factories'. British yards include some which are among the most modern and efficient in the world. Employment in the industry continues to contract, however, as a result of an over-capacity in world shipping.

Nineteen of the principal shipbuilding companies, five companies manufacturing slow-speed marine diesel engines and three training companies and their subsidiaries were taken into public ownership in 1977 under a public corporation, British Shipbuilders. Also in public ownership is the Belfast firm, Harland and Wolff, which is administered by the Northern Ireland Department of Commerce. The public sector accounts for 98 per cent of output in merchant shipbuilding, for all slow-speed marine diesel engines and for some 50 per cent of turnover in ship-repairing. The public sector also includes a number of companies engaged in general engineering work connected with the marine industries.

Following a review in 1979 of the prospects for the merchant shipbuilding activities of British Shipbuilders it was concluded that, given the world shipbuilding recession and the need for the corporation to achieve viability, further contraction within the industry would be inevitable.

A number of yards in the private sector build smaller vessels, including patrol boats, fishing and harbour craft, supply vessels, tugs, cargo ships, small tankers, ferries, pleasure boats and yachts.

About 35 per cent of the output of British yards is exported. Most private sector companies in the shipbuilding and ship-repairing industries are represented by the Shiprepairers and Shipbuilders Independent Association. Research into shipbuilding and marine engineering is undertaken by the British Ship Research Association.

METAL PRODUCTS

1979	Employment '000s	Manufacturers' Sales £ million	Exports £ million
engineers' small tools and gauges	61	612	133
cutlery (including razor blades)	12	143	64
hand tools and implements	18	204	93
bolts, nuts, screws, rivets, etc.	33	370	71
wire and wire manufactures	36	984	142
cans and metal boxes	30	734	54

A range of metal products other than those described in previous sections is produced by a group of industries made up of a very large number of firms. One of the main groups, in which small firms predominate, manufactures engineers' small tools and gauges, which include jigs and fixtures, press tools and moulds, hard metal-tipped tools and other metal cutting tools. Another group manufactures cutlery and tableware (including safety razors and blades). Although there are many small firms in the industry, seven relatively large concerns are responsible for over half of output.

A wide variety of domestic utensils, such as saucepans, buckets and dustbins, made mainly from aluminium and wrought steel, are produced by the hollow-ware industry, together with industrial hollow-ware, such as kegs, drums and barrels. The manufacture of hand tools, including files, saws, hammers, axes and spades, is a long-established industry. About half of its total production is for export. Jewellery, gold and silver-ware and the refining of precious metals is an industry in which British craftsmen are world famous; there are many small craft firms in all sectors, but five relatively large companies provide about 60 per cent of manufacturing capacity. The Royal Mint makes coins for some 70 overseas countries. Other main groups of metal goods are bolts, nuts, and screws, cans and metal boxes, metal furniture, metal windows, metallic closures, metal small-ware such as needles and pins, safes, locks and keys, domestic gas appliances and drop forgings.

CHEMICALS AND COAL AND PETROLEUM PRODUCTS

1979	Employment '000s	Manufacturers' Sales £ million	Exports £ million
general chemicals	138	5,331	2,515
pharmaceuticals	74	1,690	602
plastics and synthetics	52	2,170	793
fertilisers	12	621	58
dyestuffs and pigments	22	450	249
paint	27	797	119
toilet preparations, soap and detergents	41	1,374	317
coal and petroleum products	37	10,415	1,496

The chemicals industry is one of the most successful industries in Britain as well as being its third largest industrial sector, accounting for about 10 per cent of net manufacturing output. The industry is also the second largest in Europe and its exports of £5,212 million in 1979 (accounting for 16 per cent of British manufacturing exports) placed Britain among the top five chemical exporting nations. The industry is undertaking a considerable investment programme, despite continuing uncertainties over the price and availability of raw materials. The largest British chemicals group, Imperial Chemical Industries, is the fifth largest chemicals company in the world, accounting for some 25 per cent of production in Britain. A further 40 per cent is in the hands of 20 other large- and medium-sized companies. The industry is represented by the Chemical Industries Association. Research and development work is financed by the companies themselves. Western Europe is the major export market.

General Chemicals

About a quarter of the output of the general chemicals industry consists of a limited number of relatively simple inorganic chemicals, such as sulphuric acid and metallic and non-metallic oxides, serving as basic materials for industry. Substantial quantities of inorganic chemicals are used in the manufacture of fertilisers, detergents, paint, glass, metals and other products.

Organic chemicals include the heavy organics produced in bulk and the speciality intermediate products. About three-quarters of the output of organic chemicals is made up of petroleum-based chemicals. The most important products (by weight) are ethylene, propylene and benzene. The main uses of organic chemicals are in solvents, plastics and synthetic resins, synthetic rubber, man-made fibres and detergents, and as intermediate chemicals in the manufacture of many other products.

Outside the inorganic and organic sectors is a wide range of general chemicals formulated for specific uses. Radioisotopes are produced by The Radiochemical Centre Ltd.; over half the centre's production is for export.

Pharmaceuticals

Britain, whose scientists have discovered and developed many basic medicines and drugs, produces a complete range of pharmaceutical preparations. These include antibiotics, sulphonamides, anti-malarial drugs, anti-histamine products, anaesthetics, vaccine sera and naturally occurring drugs. Manufacturers in Britain are among the world's leading producers and exporters of preparations for the treatment of human and animal diseases. This sector is one of the major growth areas of the chemical industry.

Plastics and Synthetics

Many of the basic discoveries in plastics, including polyethylene, were made in Britain. Plastics manufacture has been a fast growing section of industry and one third of total production is exported. Expansion in recent years has mainly been in thermoplastic materials, of which the most important are polyethylene (used on coverings and packaging—notably for foodstuffs), polyvinyl chloride (known as PVC and used for a wide range of industrial purposes and consumer goods), polystyrene (a material used for toys, light mouldings and many consumer goods) and polypropylene (which can be fabricated as mouldings, films and fibres). A new group of plastics materials reinforced with carbon fibres is also in commercial production in Britain; they have up to three times the strength but are only 20 per cent of the weight of steel, and are being increasingly used in, for example, vehicle manufacture. Styrene-butadiene and polybutadiene rubbers used for tyres, high styrene rubbers for shoe soles and flooring, and nitrile rubbers for use where oil resistance is required, are also in large-scale production, together with neoprene rubber.

Fertilisers and Crop Protection

The development of chemical fertilisers owes much to the pioneer work of British scientists. Production is dominated by three firms, with a number of firms marketing compound fertilisers from the principal constituents—nitrogen, phosphorus and potassium—and is almost entirely for the domestic market. The use of ammonium nitrate, ammonium phosphate and urea is resulting in more concentrated fertilisers. Notable discoveries and developments by the British crop protection industry include the insecticidal property of BHC (benzene hexachloride), the first selective hormone weed-killer, MCPA, *Gramoxone*, a non-residual general herbicide, and Milstem, an organic fungicide which acts against mildew in various food crops. Herbicides are the largest category of sales of pesticides and allied products.

Paint

Britain is a major producer of paints, varnishes and allied products. In recent years many improved techniques have been introduced into the paint and varnish industry, including new ranges of synthetic resins and pigments, powder coatings, non-drip, quick-drying paints and paints needing only one application.

Toilet Preparations, Soap and Detergents

These industries include besides soap, detergents and toilet preparations, cosmetics and perfumes. Many of the firms in the toiletries industry are owned or financed by United States companies but there are a number of long-established British cosmetics, toiletries and soap manufacturers. Both sectors are significant exporters.

Other Chemical Products

There is a varied group of chemical products which account for about 10 per cent of the industry's net output. It includes formulated adhesives, printing ink, colours and dyestuffs, photographic chemical materials and floor and furniture polishes.

Coal and Petroleum Products

Refined mineral oil (see also p 267) is the largest product in this sector, together with medicinal paraffin, paraffin wax, petroleum jelly and other manufactures. Production of coke, other manufactured solid fuels, lubricating oils and greases is also included.

FOOD, DRINK AND TOBACCO

1979	Employment '000s	Manufacturers' Sales £ million	Exports £ million
bread, bakery products, biscuits, flour confectionery	147	2,116	92
chocolate and sugar confectionery	72	1,409	214
bacon curing, meat products, fish products	105	2,773	159
milk and milk products	62	3,110	227
drinks	131	5,027	902
tobacco	36	3,500	232
fruit and vegetable products	57	1,395	122

Although Britain is a net importer of foodstuffs, it is one of the world's leading manufacturers of food and drink products. The industry is one of the most important sectors in the economy, employing over 600,000 people and earning about £20,830 million in 1979. Exports in the same year totalled about £2,044 million.

Bakery products

About two-thirds of the bread in Britain is manufactured in large mechanised bakeries, most of which use a process (the 'Chorleywood' process) developed by the industry's principal research organisation, the Flour Milling and Baking Research Association, and now widely used in other countries. Two groups are predominant; Allied Bakeries and Rank Hovis McDougall. In smaller bakeries production of cakes and other flour confectionery is usually allied to bread production. Biscuits and related products are a major sector of the industry and have gained a world-wide reputation. Another sector is grain milling and the production of various specialised flours and meal.

Confectionery

The cocoa, chocolate and sugar confectionery industry is composed of a small number of very large manufacturers and many medium-sized and small firms. The three main manufacturers are Rowntree Mackintosh, Cadbury Schweppes and Mars. A substantial proportion of total world exports of chocolate and sugar confectionery are supplied by Britain.

Bacon Curing, Meat and Fish Products

The industry comprises the curing of bacon and ham, the canning and preserving of meat and fish, the manufacture of sausages and pies and the preparation of extracts and pastes. In addition to the output of quick-frozen fish, small quantities are also canned.

Fruit, Vegetable and Other Products

Fruit and vegetable products include canned, frozen and dried fruit and vegetables, jam, marmalade, pickles and sauces. Other products of the food processing industry include sugar, sugar preparations and honey, dairy products and eggs, vegetable and animal oils and fats, coffee, cocoa, tea and spices and cereal preparations.

Beverages

Of prime importance among the alcoholic beverages produced in Britain, and in the food and drink industry as a whole, is whisky. Scotch whisky accounts for almost all whisky production in Britain. About four-fifths of annual sales are to overseas buyers; the United States imports nearly a third of the distilled alcoholic beverages exported from Britain. The rest of the European Community and Japan are the other largest markets. Production of gin in Britain has risen steadily since the early 1950s. One company accounts for a large proportion of output. Some of the larger manufacturers also own distilleries abroad.

In the brewing and malting industry there are seven major brewery groups whose products are sold nationally, and about 80 smaller enterprises who mainly supply locally, or regionally, many of them because of a demand for traditionally brewed beers. Firms have introduced new production methods, including continuous brewing processes, and automated batch production plants are well established. The main raw materials used are malt, hops and some sugar. British malt, which is made almost entirely from home-grown barley, is used by brewers throughout the world. In recent years the popularity of lager has increased considerably.

Three major groups account for much of the cider and perry produced in Britain. The industry is based mainly in Devon, Somerset and Hereford and Worcester. Imported grape and fruit juices are used in the production of most of the made wine. A much smaller, though expanding viticultural industry produces wine from grapes grown in vineyards, mostly in southern England.

The soft drinks industry has expanded markedly in the last decade. There are some very large firms among about 20 producing brands which are marketed on a national scale, while other firms supply regional markets. There is some specialisation among firms in the production of various types, such as carbonated drinks, cola-based drinks, squashes and cordials, tonic waters and 'mixers', fruit juices and health drinks.

Tobacco

The British tobacco industry manufactures almost all the cigarettes and tobacco goods sold in Britain. It is made up of four major companies and a number of smaller ones, and specialises in the production of high-quality cigarettes made from flue-cured tobacco. Exports, mainly of cigarettes, are shipped to many overseas countries including Belgium, Saudi Arabia and the Netherlands. Britain imports raw tobacco in large amounts from the United States, India and Canada.

TEXTILES, CLOTHING AND FOOTWEAR

1979	Employment '000s	Manufacturers' Sales £ million	Exports £ million
man-made fibres	38	688	361
cotton ⎤ linen ⎦	91	1,249	491
wool	76	1,134	386
carpets	34	659	159
hosiery and knitwear	117	1,261	251
clothing	311	2,699	539
leather and leather goods	39	555	160
footwear	76	592	121

The historical branches of the industry, based on the natural fibres of cotton and wool, linen and jute, have retained their separate identities but the boundaries between them are becoming blurred with the increasing use of man-made fibres. The growth of man-made fibres has stimulated the development of new processes and new types of yarn and cloth and has strongly influenced the structure of the industry. A small number of large multi-fibre, multi-process groups have emerged, although in many sectors there is still a preponderance of small firms engaged in just one or two operations.

British textile firms manufacture a wide variety of goods, including lace, narrow fabrics and household textiles, such as blankets, sheets, towels, and tablecloths. Rope, twine, nets and netting are manufactured by the cordage industry, which is one of the largest in Europe. A recent development is the production of non-woven fabric by the melded process, which dispenses with the conventional weaving and knitting stages.

Research for the industry is provided by the Shirley Institute (cotton, silk, and man-made fibres), the Lambeg Industrial Research Association, WIRA (formerly the Wool Industries Research Association) and HATRA (formerly the Hosiery and Allied Trades Research Association). The Department of Industry sponsors research and development both for these research associations and also directly within the industry.

Man-made Fibres

Much of the early development of man-made fibres took place in Britain and continuing extensive research has produced a wide variety of types with their own special characteristics. The two main types are still those first developed—the cellulosic fibres, such as rayon, and the synthetic fibres, such as nylon and polyester, made wholly by chemical processes. Acrylic fibres, including *Courtelle* (a British discovery), *Acrilan* and *Orlon* are important products, as are the elastomeric or spandex fibres which have inherent properties of stretch and recovery, anti-static synthetic yarns embedded with carbon and various fire-resistant yarns. More recently there has been a greater use of the polyolefins (polypropylene and polyethylene) in the carpet and carpet backing and packaging fields and still more recently in household textiles and clothing. Output in the man-made fibre industry is concentrated in the hands of a few large firms.

Cotton

During the nineteenth century cotton was Britain's chief consumer goods industry and cotton piece goods its largest export. Low-cost competition has cut progressively into British markets and made necessary extensive reorganisation, modernisation and the introduction of new techniques. Production includes single and double cotton yarn, spun man-made fibre and mixture cloth. The largest markets for cotton fabrics in 1978 were the rest of the European Community, the United States, Finland, Togo, South Africa, Zaire and Australia.

Linen

The linen industry is centred in Northern Ireland, where the lighter types of fabrics for apparel, furnishings and household textiles are produced. The heavyweight canvas for sailcloth, tents, awnings and tarpaulins is mainly produced in Scotland.

Wool

The wool textile industry, the export sales of which are usually double the value of imports, is one of the largest in the world and includes the world's biggest wool textile company, Illingworth, Morris. There are two main branches, woollen and worsted. An increasing amount of man-made fibre is now blended with wool. West Yorkshire is the main producing area but Scotland and the west of England are also famous as specialised producers of high quality yarn and cloth. Large quantities of raw wool are scoured and cleaned in Britain to prepare it for spinning. Britain is also a growing exporter of raw wool. The largest markets for woollen and worsted fabrics are Japan, the United States and the rest of the European Community.

Carpets

Some 75 per cent of the output of the carpet and rug industry is made up of tufted carpets, in the production of which the pile, usually with a high man-made fibre content, is inserted into a pre-woven backing. Woven carpets, such as Axminster and Wilton, account for most of the remainder of sales. There is a higher wool content in woven types, although they too are making more use of man-made fibres. The high quality and variety of design make Britain the world's leading producer of woven carpets.

Jute

Jute products are manufactured in the Dundee area. Jute yarn and the man-made polypropylene yarn are used in the manufacturing of carpets, cordage and ropes and woven into fabrics for a wide range of applications in the packaging, upholstery, building and motor car industries. New uses for jute, for example, as a plastics reinforcement and for decorative wall coverings, are also being considered.

Hosiery and Knitwear

The hosiery and knitwear industry comprises more than 1,000 firms, situated mainly in the East Midlands and Scotland, of which most are small to medium in size. The industry produces fabrics, outerwear, underwear, tights, socks, stockings, gloves and accessories.

Clothing

The British clothing industry is one of the largest in Europe; it is highly labour intensive and dominated by small firms, with about 6,000 firms, accounting for only 4 per cent of Britain's total employment in manufacturing. The negotiation of the Multi-Fibre Arrangement of the General Agreement on Tariffs and Trade (see p 372) has encouraged investment and exports have risen somewhat since 1977, although import penetration has continued to increase. The Clothing Export Council, which represents a major part of the industry, co-ordinates its promotional activities.

Footwear

The British footwear industry is largely made up of small firms. After being severely affected by the recession and by increasing imports, the industry has more than half of the domestic market.

Leather

Leather tanning and leather goods manufacturing is another long-established industry in Britain. All types of leather (including heavy types for industrial use) and leather goods are produced. Collective research is carried out by the British Leather Manufacturers' Research Association.

BRICKS, CEMENT, POTTERY AND GLASS

1979	Employment '000s	Manufacturers' Sales £ million	Exports £ million
bricks, fireclay and refractory goods	40	607	98
cement	14	478	32
pottery	59	514	181
glass	68	967	186

Bricks, Fireclay and Refractory Goods

Firms in the industry manufacture such items as bricks, roofing tiles, chimney pots, fireclay ware and heat-resisting products, including furnace and kiln linings. Brickmaking is one of Britain's oldest industries, but most manufacture is now based on highly mechanised systems. One company, the London Brick Company, supplies about 40 per cent of total brick deliveries. Refractory goods include firebricks, silica bricks, magnesite bricks, chrome-magnesite bricks and alumina bricks.

Cement

The cement industry is chiefly concerned with the manufacture of Portland cement for the home market. Invented by Joseph Aspdin and patented in 1824, this material and the methods of its production have been the subject of continuous technical improvement and intensive research. One new variation, glass-reinforced cement composites, consists of ordinary Portland cement and sand combined with an alkali-resistant glass fibre. The capacity of the industry as a whole has been substantially expanded in recent years.

Pottery

The pottery industry, centred largely in Staffordshire, supplies almost all home needs for domestic and industrial pottery. It uses largely indigenous clay from Cornwall and Devon. There has been considerable re-equipment in the industry; kilns fired by gas or electricity have replaced all the coal-fired kilns and new decorating techniques and automatic and semi-automatic machinery such as automatic glazing machines, have been introduced. Domestic pottery including china, earthenware and stoneware, accounts for two-thirds of the industry's output; the other main divisions are glazed tiles, sanitary ware and electrical ware, and such specialised industrial products as acid-proof stone ware, porous ceramics and laboratory porcelain. Production of tableware is concentrated in two major groups. Britain is the world's principal manufac turer of fine bone china, much of which is exported; famous makes include *Wedgwood, Spode, Royal Worcester, Royal Doulton, Minton, Aynsley, Coalport* and *Royal Crown Derby*.

Glass

Britain's glass industry is one of the biggest in the world. Glass containers form the largest part of the industry; another major section is devoted to the manufacture of flat glass in its various forms, chiefly 'float' glass, a process developed in Britain and licensed to glassmakers throughout the world. The use of glass for internal decoration and as a finish for internal and external walls has greatly increased in recent years. Large quantities of safety glass are produced for the motor and other industries. Other products include tubular glass, mirrors, lamp and bulb glass, scientific and medical glassware, glass fibres, and all types of glass containers (mostly made automatically). A traditional product is hand-made lead crystal glassware of very high quality. Collective research is undertaken by the British Glass Industry Research Association, and much research work is also carried out by the Department of Ceramics, Glasses and Polymers of Sheffield University.

PAPER, PRINTING AND PUBLISHING

1979	Employment '000s	Manufacturers' Sales £ million	Exports £ million
paper and board	61	1,515	262
converted products	142	2,978	204
printing and publishing	342	3,604	403

Paper and Board Manufacture and Conversion

The British paper and board industry is one of the largest in Europe. The larger British groups hold considerable interests abroad, including pulp and paper producing mills in the United States, Canada, other parts of the Commonwealth and Europe. In recent years paper production has concentrated on printing and writing papers and boards and speciality grades. There has also been a significant trend towards waste-based packaging grades, in order to reduce the industry's reliance on imported woodpulp supplies. Domestically produced woodpulp represents only a small percentage of raw material supplies but the use of recycled waste paper is increasing; together they currently provide nearly 60 per cent of the industry's needs. The main types of paper and board produced are printing and writing papers and board, packaging board, household tissues and industrial and special purpose papers.

The packaging and converting industries manufacture a variety of converted products, including cardboard boxes, cartons, fibreboard packaging and business stationery products.

Printing and Publishing

The printing and publishing industries produce a wide range of products, including national and provincial newspapers, periodicals, books, business stationery and greeting cards. Mergers have led to the formation of large groups in the newspaper, magazine and book publishing sectors, but general printing, engraving, bookbinding and a large part of publishing remain essentially industries of small firms. Production processes include high-speed printing equipment, including electronic engraving, advanced processes of photographic reproduction and computer typesetting. Security printers (of, for example, banknotes and postage stamps) have a high reputation and are important exporters.

The most important overseas markets for printed matter are the United States, the Irish Republic and Australia.

OTHER
MANUFACTURING

1979	Employment '000s	Manufacturers' Sales £ million	Exports £ million
rubber and rubber manufactures	109	1,726	426
furniture (wooden), bedding, etc.	111	1,918	185
timber	91	1,429	69
plastics products, floorcoverings etc.	136	2,505	264
toys, games, sports equipment	42	541	198

Rubber

Tyres and tubes represent nearly half the output of the industry, but firms make a variety of other goods, the most important being vehicle components and accessories, conveyor belting, cables, hose, latex foam products and rubber footwear, gloves and clothing. Rubber is also used for inflatable life rafts, containers for fuel and other industrial liquids and seals for storage tanks and other products where there are problems of air exclusion and vapour suppression. One of the largest tyre groups in Europe, Dunlop-Pirelli Union, was formed in 1971 between Britain's leading rubber and tyre company and its Italian equivalent. Tyre manufacturers include several subsidiaries of United States and other overseas companies. The industry's consumption of rubber includes natural, synthetic and recycled rubber.

Furniture, Brushes and Timber

Numerous enterprises manufacture furniture in Britain (including domestic, office, school and other furniture) with a few large firms predominating. In recent years the industry has experienced an increase in demand from overseas. Exports have risen from £69 million in 1975 to £231 million in 1979. The industry comprises wooden, metal and plastic furniture, upholstery, bedding and soft furnishings. A Development Council for the industry has existed since 1949. Scientific research and technical and other information services are provided by the Furniture Industry Research Association.

The brush industry is located throughout Britain and includes highly mechanised establishments as well as small craft units.

Domestic production of timber has been steadily increasing but the timber industries are mainly dependent on imported supplies. A large proportion of timber sales are dependent on the construction industry. Chipboard is the fastest growing sector of the industry; other important sectors are hardwood and plywood.

Plastics Products

In addition to the plastics components and accessories supplied to many different industries, the plastics products industry manufactures a wide range of building materials, such as pipes, sheeting for roofs, sanitary ware, tanks and other products. It also supplies flexible foams, used in the vehicle, furniture and other industries; rigid foams; packaging products, including bottles, containers and bags; domestic and industrial hollow-ware; many kinds of household goods; vinyl and other floorcoverings; and leathercloth.

Toys, Games and Sports Equipment

The industry manufactures toys, games, sports equipment and children's carriages. There are about 600 toy and games makers in Britain but some 20 companies dominate the market. The greatest expansion has been in the field of craft and hobby kits, but electronic toys and games are becoming increasingly important. British diecast toys and model construction kits are well known overseas; more than a third of the output of toys and games is for export. France, the Federal Republic of Germany and the United States are the major markets for toys while the United States and the European Community are the main markets for sports equipment.

CONSTRUCTION

The construction industry, which accounted for about 6 per cent of gross domestic product in 1979, includes firms engaged on the design, construction, alteration, repair and maintenance of buildings, highways, airfields, drainage and sewerage systems, docks, harbours and canals, sea defence works, offshore structures, electrical wiring, heating and other installation work, and structural work connected with thermal and hydroelectric power stations and telecommunications. About 1·3 million people are employed in construction, accounting for nearly 6 per cent of total employment. There are also about 385,000 self-employed. About 19 per cent of construction workers are employed by public authorities. In 1979 repair and maintenance accounted for 36 per cent of the value of construction output in Great Britain.

Structure
Construction work is carried out both by private contractors and by public authorities which employ their own labour. In 1979 about 89 per cent of the work was done by private firms. Although there were about 63,000 firms employing two or more people 93 per cent of them employed fewer than 25.

Public authorities as a whole employed about 220,000 operatives but a very large proportion of these were engaged on repair and maintenance work for local authorities.

Some 46 per cent of operatives were occupied on building maintenance, valued at about £6,762 million annually. The total labour force includes about 68,000 trainees, training under the industry's apprenticeship schemes. The normal apprenticeship period is three years.

Some firms are vertically integrated, owning quarries and workshops, mechanised plant and standard builders' equipment; some undertake responsibility for projects from initial design to finished building. All but the smallest projects are generally carried out under professional direction, either by architects or, in the case of the more complicated civil engineering projects, by consulting engineers. The functions of the latter, acting on behalf of a client, embrace advice on the feasibility of projects, the drawing up of plans and the supervision of the construction work by the contractor.

The Property Services Agency (PSA), which is an integral part of the Department of the Environment (see p 45), is responsible for the construction programmes undertaken directly by the Government, including work for the armed forces both in Britain and overseas. In 1978–79 the PSA spent £577 million on design and construction. The Department of the Environment is responsible for the sponsorship of the construction industry. Among other things, this involves both formal and informal consultation with the industry. The Department is also responsible for co-ordinating research and development in construction throughout Government and seeks to influence techniques and methods within the industry.

Output
The value of the work done in Britain in 1979 amounted to £18,866 million of which £4,505 million represented new housing and £7,599 million other new work; repair and maintenance accounted for the remaining £6,762 million.

Housing
During 1979 a total of 220,900 dwellings were started in Great Britain. Starts in the public sector were 80,300 and those for private owners 140,600. In the

course of the same year 235,600 dwellings were completed, of which 101,200 were in the public sector and 134,500 in the private sector. Industrialised building methods employing prefabricated components are used in some of the work in both sectors.

The National Building Agency is an independent advisory body, managed by a board of directors appointed by the Secretaries of State for the Environment and for Scotland and Wales. Its main function is to encourage the adoption of advanced methods of building, and to provide technical advice and services to government departments, local authorities and other clients.

The Association of Building Centres represents the interests of the 12 building centres throughout Britain most of which provide both a comprehensive permanent exhibition and information services on building materials and products, building services and techniques.

Civil Engineering Projects

Among important construction projects in hand in Britain in 1980 were nuclear power stations (see p 277), hospitals, large-scale housing developments, and roads, tunnels and bridges, including the new bridge being built across the river Humber (see p 303), and the Thames Barrier which will form part of London's flood defences.

Overseas Construction

Total overseas earnings of all sectors of the construction industry in 1978–79 were estimated at about £2,700 million, some £130 million more than in the previous 12 months. British contractors earned £345 million from overseas customers and a further £65 million from overseas branches and subsidiaries. The related professions (consulting engineers, architects and surveyors) had earnings of £460 million, while exports of building materials, plant and machinery accounted for some £1,900 million.

In 1978–79 British construction firms carried out work overseas valued at £1,667 million, an increase of £80 million over the previous year. New contracts worth £1,299 million were won overseas in 1978–79.

The Government and the construction industry are represented on the Exports Standing Committee of the National Consultative Council for the Building and Civil Engineering Industries.

Research

Within the Department of the Environment, the Building Research Establishment (BRE) is concerned with all aspects of construction research. In addition, the Building Research Advisory Service of the BRE provides technical advice over a wide range of construction problems. An Agrément Board tests and certifies building products and methods.

The construction industry is served by several of the industrial research associations, while the major construction firms have research departments working on plant, materials and methods. Other bodies concerned with research include the universities and colleges of technology. The larger producers of primary building materials do some research into production methods and new developments.

SERVICE INDUSTRIES

There has been a steady rise in the proportion of employees in Britain working in the service industries and in June 1979 about 58·3 per cent of employees (13 million people) were engaged in this sector, compared with 50·8 per cent in 1969. The contribution of the various groups to gross domestic product can be seen in Table 7, p 204. The main areas of growth have been concentrated in the financial, professional and scientific services, hotels and catering, and the miscellaneous services sector, while employment in the distributive trades has changed little and in transport and communications it has declined.

In Great Britain there were about 2·7 million employees in the distributive trades in 1979, together with a large number of owners of businesses. The distributive trades accounted for about 10 per cent of Britain's national income in 1978, retailing contributing a little more than wholesaling. Closely connected with the distributive trades are those which offer a service directly to the public, such as the hotel and catering trades, garage and motor repair trades, laundries and dry cleaners, hairdressers and shoe repairers. Among the other services described elsewhere are education (see Chapter 7), national and local government services (see Chapter 2), transport and communications (see Chapter 16), services provided by financial institutions (see Chapter 18) and research and development services (see Chapter 20).

RETAIL TRADES Turnover of the retail trades has been growing gradually in real terms for many years. In 1979 retail sales were 44 per cent higher than in 1976, representing, however, only a 2 per cent increase in volume. In 1978 there were an estimated 235,000 businesses in the retail trade in Great Britain with a turnover of more than £10,000 (see Table 15); they had 350,000 outlets, of which about 59 per cent were accounted for by single-outlet retailers. Their turnover was nearly £45,000 million in 1978 when they invested £1,093 million. Over 2·4 million people (including a large number of part-time staff) were engaged in retailing in 1978. As the large multiple retailers (those with ten or more outlets) have grown in size and diversified their product ranges there has been a decline in the number of retail businesses and outlets, particularly of the small independent businesses.

The largest multiple retailers in the packaged grocery market are the retail co-operatives, followed by Tesco, Sainsbury, Asda, Fine Fare, Kwiksave and International Stores. Retail co-operative societies are voluntary organisations controlled by their members, membership being open to anyone paying a small deposit on a minimum share; at the end of 1979 the 216 retail societies had 10·4 million members and 9,800 retail outlets. Turnover in 1979 amounted to £3,400 million, 6·7 per cent of total retail trade. Retail co-operatives and the Co-operative Wholesale Society (see p 260) are members of the Co-operative Union as are a number of other co-operative bodies such as the Co-operative Bank. Tesco has some 530 stores and sales in 1979–80 were valued at some £1,602 million. Sainsbury has more than 200 outlets and the company's sales amounted to £1,227 million in 1979–80.

The leading specialist multiple stores are Marks and Spencer (with sales of £1,543 million in 1979–80), Boots, F. W. Woolworth, W. H. Smith and British Home Stores.

Department stores, which sell a very wide range of goods, account for about 5 per cent of retail turnover. The six largest groups are responsible for about 85 per cent of turnover with three of the groups, House of Fraser, Debenham and the John Lewis partnership, accounting for some 29, 19 and 14 per cent respectively.

There are a number of discount stores operating on the principle of selling most or all of their goods at a reduced price. Electrical goods, furniture, carpets and do-it-yourself supplies are some of the main items sold by discount stores.

Mail order is accounting for a growing proportion of retail sales and about 16

TABLE 15: Retail Trade in Great Britain 1978[a]

	Number of businesses	Number of outlets	Number of people engaged (thousand)	Turnover (£ million)
Single-outlet retailers	208,022	208,022	903	14,212
Small multiple retailers	25,538	67,933	368	6,515
Large multiple retailers (ten or more retail outlets)	1,225	74,083	1,153	23,928
of which, co-operative societies	*202*	*10,207*	*153*	*3,004*
Grocers and general food retailers	41,481	52,289	421	9,518
Other food retailers	46,440	67,908	307	5,198
Confectioners, tobacconists and newsagents	38,363	49,491	253	3,668
Clothing, footwear and textile retailers	33,903	60,263	315	4,389
Household goods retailers	36,832	56,358	306	6,489
Other non-food retailers	33,681	45,363	222	3,568
Mixed retail businesses	4,084	18,367	601	11,826
Total retail trade	234,785	350,038	2,424	44,656

Source: *British Business*

[a] Figures cover businesses above the threshold of value-added tax (£10,000 at that time). It is thought that in 1978 there were a further 20,000–25,000 retail businesses with turnover of between £5,000 and £10,000, and aggregate turnover of about 0·5 per cent of retail turnover.

Discrepancies between totals and the sums of their constituent parts are due to rounding.

million people regularly shop by post. In 1978 mail order sales totalled some £2,100 million, representing 5 per cent of retail sales and 8·7 per cent of retail sales excluding food shops. The leading items sold by mail order are clothing, footwear, furniture and floor coverings.

Trends

One of the most significant trends in retailing in recent years has been the increase in the proportion of turnover accounted for by large multiple retailers; they have 54 per cent of retail turnover. Other important trends have been the increase in very large self-service stores selling a wide variety of products, diversification by food multiples into selling a wider range of goods, the development of specially-designed shopping precincts and an even stronger emphasis on price competition.

Supermarkets, Superstores and Hypermarkets

There are supermarkets in most towns and cities in Britain. The main multiple grocery companies have been steadily increasing the size of their supermarkets and closing the smaller and less efficient ones. The trend to greater size has led to a growing number of superstores and hypermarkets, single-level, self-service stores offering a wider range of food and non-food merchandise and which have at least 2,500 square metres (26,900 square feet) and 5,000 square metres (53,800 square feet) respectively of selling space. They are designed primarily for shoppers with cars and substantial free car-parking space is usually provided. In Britain the first such store was opened in the mid-1960s and by March 1980 there were some 140 superstores and 36 hypermarkets, with a combined selling space of 682,500 square metres (7·3 million square feet), while planning permission for a further 71 superstores and 10 hypermarkets, with a combined selling space of 302,100 square metres (3·3 million square feet), had been granted. It is Government policy that these stores should be located within urban areas, preferably within shopping centres, where they are accessible to all shoppers including those without cars.

Shopping Centres Britain has a variety of new purpose-built shopping centres. Among the largest are those at Brent Cross in London, the Victoria Centre in Nottingham and the Eldon Square development in Newcastle upon Tyne, while the centre in Milton Keynes (Buckinghamshire) is one of the largest in Europe.

Diversification Many of the large multiple groups have diversified over the last few years to offer a much bigger range of goods than previously. This has been especially noticeable for the large food retailers, which often sell non-food products, such as beer, wines and spirits, clothing and household appliances, as well as packaged groceries. Another trend is that many superstores and large supermarkets offer fresh as well as packaged food, often with special counters or areas for fresh meat, fish, vegetables and bread baked on the premises.

Promotions Retailers are placing greater emphasis on price competition as a means of promoting sales, while trading stamps, which were an important method of sales promotion in the late 1960s and early 1970s, have become much less significant. With the growth of payments by credit card, many of the large retailers have issued their own credit cards for regular customers to use in their branches in an attempt to increase sales, particularly of high-value goods.

Operations Numerous improvements to speed up the flow of customers through supermarket check-outs include conveyor belts for goods being handled beside the tills, change-giving machines and special check-outs for customers with a small number of purchases. Store lay-outs have been improved, with wider aisles allowing more room for shoppers and their trolleys. Laser-scanning electronic check-outs are expected to have a major impact on retailing in the next few years. Under this system, the package of each item is marked with a special bar-code which is read by a low-power laser beam at the point of sale and the price is automatically retrieved from a central computer. The customer is given a receipt showing the price and identity of each item purchased, while the store's stock records are altered automatically. Substantial savings are expected from improved stock control and a reduction of individual price marking in stores. Key Markets introduced the first operational laser-scanning electronic check-out in Britain at Spalding (Lincolnshire) in 1979. Further systems were introduced early in 1980 by Sainsbury at Broadfield, near Crawley (West Sussex), and by International Stores at Folkestone (Kent).

WHOLESALE TRADES In 1974 (when the most recent wholesaling census was conducted) there were some 80,000 businesses engaged in wholesaling and dealing. Turnover (including sales to other wholesalers and dealers) amounted to £49,800 million and just over 1 million people were employed in this sector. The main areas in which wholesalers are dominant are groceries and provisions, petroleum products and ores and metals. A number of the large retailers carry out the functions of the wholesaler by having their own warehouses, and buying and distributive organisations.

Two large groups, Booker McConnell and Linfood, predominate in the wholesale food trade. London's wholesale markets play a significant part in the distribution of foodstuffs. Covent Garden is the main market for fruit and vegetables, Smithfield for meat and Billingsgate for fish.

The co-operative movement in Britain has its own wholesale organisation, the Co-operative Wholesale Society (CWS), to serve the needs of retail societies; its turnover was £1,659 million in 1979. Retail societies are encouraged to buy from the CWS, which supplies about two-thirds of their requirements.

'Cash and carry' wholesaling is becoming increasingly important. By bulk purchasing and limiting their expenditure on premises and credit and delivery facilities, these wholesalers can offer large discounts to their customers. There were some 650 'cash and carry' depots in Britain in 1979; total sales by the cash and carry members of the National Federation of Wholesale Grocers and Provision Merchants were estimated at about £1,625 million.

In the grocery trade there are a number of voluntary groups which have been formed by wholesalers with small retailers, whereby the retailers are encouraged by discounts and other incentives to buy as much as possible from the wholesaler. This has helped to preserve the existence of retail outlets for the wholesaler, and also the traditional 'corner shops' and village stores, of value to local communities, and has given small retailers the advantages of bulk buying and co-ordinated distribution.

SERVICES

Among the other services provided directly to the public, some of the financial services, notably building societies, have been increasing the number of branches in the High Street as their activities have expanded (see p 364). Business services which have been developing more rapidly in recent years include advertising, market research, public relations, consultancy, conference centres and employment agencies. Advertising expenditure rose by 16 per cent in 1979 to £2,129 million, according to the Advertising Association, of which advertising in the press accounted for 70 per cent, advertising on television for 22 per cent and advertising on commercial radio for 2·4 per cent. Advertising campaigns are planned mainly by advertising agencies (of which there are several hundred in Britain) and, in some cases, the agencies also provide marketing, consumer research and other services. Sales by the 28 member companies of the Association of Market Survey Organisations amounted to more than £50 million in 1979, when the total of market research commissioned was estimated at £85 million. There are a number of major conference and/or exhibition centres including the National Exhibition Centre at Birmingham, the Wembley Conference Centre in London, and the Brighton Centre. Conference centres under construction include an £83 million centre at the Barbican in London and a new centre at Harrogate (North Yorkshire).

The travel business is another growth sector, and some 2,000 travel agents with about 4,500 offices (about 90 per cent of the total) belong to the Association of British Travel Agents. Many travel agents are small businesses, but there are a few large firms (of which the biggest is Thomas Cook) with many High Street branches. A growing number of people are engaged in the professions; these include solicitors (of whom there are about 41,000 in practice in Britain) and estate agents (of whom there are an estimated 25,000 in Britain).

In June 1978 about 895,000 people were employed in the hotel and catering trades in Britain: 286,000 in hotels and other residential establishments; 173,000 in restaurants, cafes and snack bars; 256,000 in public houses; 109,000 in clubs; and 71,000 by catering contractors. A large number of self-employed people are also engaged in hotels and catering. There were about 12,500 licensed hotels in Great Britain in 1977 with a total turnover of £1,600 million. Hotels are concentrated in the main business centres, notably London, and in seaside and other holiday resorts. Many licensed hotels as well as most of the numerous guest houses are small, with fewer than 20 rooms, although there are also several large groups of hotels. The biggest is Trusthouse Forte Ltd, the world's largest hotel, catering and leisure company, which runs over 800 hotels including more than 200 in Britain. In 1977 there were over 9,000 licensed restaurants (with a total turnover of about £750 million) in Great Britain, and a further 31,000 unlicensed establishments (with a total turnover of more than £850 million) including snack bars, cafes, fish and chip shops and other establishments selling 'take-away' food. Britain has a very wide range of restaurants including a substantial number specialising in the dishes of other countries such as Chinese, Italian, Indian and Greek foods. 'Fast food' catering, in which establishments sell hot food such as hamburgers or chicken to be eaten either on the premises or elsewhere, is becoming increasingly significant. Take-away meals now account for more than one-third of all meals bought in restaurants and other catering establishments. There are about 56,000 'pubs' (public houses, which mainly sell beer, wines and spirits for consumption on the premises) in Great Britain, with a total turnover of more than £3,000 million in 1977.

In June 1978 some 469,000 people were employed in garages, petrol stations and by motor repairers and distributors in Britain. In spite of the continuing increase in the number of road vehicles, the number of petrol stations is declining and in 1979 there were some 26,500 (6 per cent fewer than in 1978), of which 31 per cent were owned by oil companies. Self-service stations are becoming increasingly important and in 1979 they accounted for 20 per cent of petrol stations and more than half of petrol sales in Britain.

Other services provided include hairdressing and manicure (94,000 employees in June 1978), laundries (55,000), dry cleaning, window cleaning, boot and shoe repair, antique dealing, photocopying, television rentals and funeral services.

14 Energy and Natural Resources

Britain has the largest energy resources of any country in the European Community. Minerals as a whole make an important contribution to the economy. The approximate value of minerals produced in 1978 was £7,282 million, of which coal accounted for 40 per cent, crude oil 39 per cent and natural gas 6 per cent. The value of mineral production was 30 per cent higher at constant prices than in 1970, virtually all of the increase being accounted for by oil and gas.

All minerals in Great Britain are privately owned, with the exception of gold, silver, oil and natural gas (which are owned by the Crown) and coal and some minerals associated with coal. On the United Kingdom Continental Shelf (UKCS) the right to exploit all minerals except coal is vested in the Crown. The exclusive right to extract coal, or license others to do so, both on land and under the sea, is vested in the National Coal Board. Normally, ownership of minerals runs with the ownership of the land surface but in some areas, particularly where mining has taken place, these rights have become separated. Mining and quarrying, apart from coal, are usually carried out by privately owned companies.

Water resources are normally sufficient for domestic and industrial requirements; supplies are obtained from surface sources such as mountain lakes and from underground sources by such means as wells and boreholes.

ENERGY

Four main primary sources of energy—petroleum, coal, natural gas and nuclear power—are used in Britain, together with some water power; secondary sources produced from these are electricity, coke and very small quantities of town gas. During 1980 Britain became self-sufficient in energy in net terms as a result of the continued growth in offshore oil production. Net self-sufficiency is likely to be maintained for a number of years. Coal and nuclear power are nevertheless likely to have an increasingly important role in Britain's primary energy supply particularly in the long term. Estimated operating reserves of coal, Britain's richest natural resource, are 6,000 million tonnes, sufficient to support present rates of extraction for 50 years, although total coal resources are many times higher. A major capital investment programme in the coal industry is in progress. Nuclear power provided about 13 per cent of electricity available through the public supply system in 1979 and the proportion will grow as further nuclear power stations now under construction, or planned, are brought into service.

Privately owned companies predominate in offshore oil and gas production and oil refining, while publicly owned bodies are responsible for most coal production, gas distribution, and electricity generation and distribution. The publicly owned fuel and power industries in Britain employ in total some 500,000 people, just over 2 per cent of the working population; their annual turnover is about £18,000 million and capital investment about £2,200 million. In Great Britain the Secretary of State for Energy is responsible for these industries, except for electricity in Scotland which is the responsibility of the Secretary of State for Scotland.

Energy Policy

The Government's energy strategy involves ensuring the security and availability of energy supplies, using oil and gas reserves at an optimum rate, developing competitive coal production, expanding the nuclear power programme, supporting research into renewable sources of energy and encouraging measures which result in lower energy consumption. Pricing that reflects the true long-term costs of energy supplies is also central to the Government's approach to energy policy, both to discourage the wasteful use of energy and to stimulate new methods of utilising and saving it.

Britain is actively engaged in international collaboration on energy questions, notably through its membership of the European Community and of the International Energy Agency (IEA, a body with 21 member countries attached to the Organisation for Economic Co-operation and Development). Since its establishment in 1974, the IEA has agreed a wide range of co-operative measures to achieve the objective of reducing member nations' dependence on imported oil. The rapid increase of North Sea oil production, together with the Government's policies on coal, nuclear power and energy conservation, has meant that, from being net oil importers of 41 million tonnes of oil in 1978, Britain has been able to accept, as a contribution to the European Community's response to the world economic summit in Tokyo in 1979, a target for 1985 of net exports of 5 million tonnes of oil. The Government also attaches considerable importance to the creation of a common understanding between energy producers and energy consumers.

ENERGY CONSUMPTION

In 1979 inland primary energy consumption amounted to 355·9 million tonnes of coal equivalent (see Table 16), 4·7 per cent more than in 1978, reflecting the very cold weather in the early part of the year. Petroleum accounted for 39·1 per cent of primary consumption, coal 36·4 per cent, natural gas 20 per cent, nuclear power 3·9 per cent and hydro-electric power 0·6 per cent. Energy consumption by final users in 1979 amounted to 61,701 million therms[1] on a 'heat supplied' basis. Industrial users consumed about 38 per cent, domestic users 27 per cent, transport 23 per cent, public services 6 per cent and agriculture 1 per cent.

TABLE 16: Inland Energy Consumption (in terms of primary sources)

million tonnes coal equivalent

	1969	1974	1977	1978	1979
Oil	139·6	152·5	136·6	139·3	139·0
Coal	164·1	117·9	122·7	119·9	129·6
Natural gas	9·4	52·9	62·8	65·1	71·3
Nuclear energy	10·7	12·1	14·3	13·4	13·8
Hydro-electric power	1·7	2·1	2·0	2·1	2·2
Total	325·5	337·5	338·4	339·8	355·9

Source: *Department of Energy*

ENERGY CONSERVATION

Energy conservation has a central place in the Government's energy strategy and rational pricing of energy, supported by the provision of conservation information to consumers, is a major part of energy conservation policy. The

---

[1] 1 therm = 105,506 kilojoules.

Secretary of State for Energy is advised by an independent Advisory Council on Energy Conservation, while studies on energy conservation and alternative sources of energy are undertaken by a number of organisations, notably the Energy Technology Support Unit of the Department of Energy and the National Engineering Laboratory of the Department of Industry.

Conservation Measures

Several schemes to assist industry and commerce to conserve energy are in operation, including assistance towards the cost of consultants' surveys, energy audits in selected industries and financial assistance for research, development and demonstration projects. Firms are encouraged to appoint energy managers (of whom there are some 5,000) to draw up and administer energy conservation measures in factories and offices. Many firms have achieved significant economies through measures such as better use of heating and lighting, improved operational and maintenance techniques, and the installation of draught-proofing and additional insulation. To improve insulation in houses, grants towards the installation of basic insulation in uninsulated roofs are available under the Homes Insulation Act 1978. Following discussions with the Government, the motor manufacturers are working towards a voluntary target of a 10 per cent improvement by 1985 in the average mileage per gallon achieved by new cars sold in Britain. Other conservation measures have included a maximum limit of 19° Centigrade on heating levels in commercial and industrial buildings; publication of official fuel consumption figures for new cars, so that potential purchasers can assess the petrol usage of different models; the production of teaching material, for primary schools, on energy and its efficient use; and a government publicity campaign to promote the efficient use of energy.

OFFSHORE OIL AND GAS

The total value of the substantial oil and gas reserves discovered in the United Kingdom Continental Shelf is estimated at about £300,000 million. It is one of the world's most attractive offshore areas for oil and gas, the average success rate for exploration drilling comparing very favourably with other offshore areas. Seismic prospecting began in the early 1960s and full-scale exploration activities in 1964. The total area covered by production licences is some 69,300 square kilometres (26,750 square miles) out of a total designated area of about 643,000 square kilometres (248,250 square miles), over which Britain has exercised its rights to explore and exploit the seabed and subsoil. A new round of offshore petroleum production licensing, the seventh, is being held in 1980.

Large-scale investment has been made in offshore exploration and development, amounting to over £15,000 million (at 1979 prices) so far, of which 92 per cent has been made by private sector industry. Investment in 1979 was estimated at about £2,000 million. By the end of 1979, 859 exploration or appraisal wells and 586 development wells had been drilled or begun; of these 49 and 107 respectively were drilled in 1979.

Offshore Supplies

The Department of Energy's Offshore Supplies Office seeks to ensure that British industry can compete effectively for orders for offshore equipment by helping firms to identify the needs of offshore operators, assisting operators to identify British suppliers of offshore equipment and services, and promoting new ventures to increase British involvement in the industry. British companies increased their share of the offshore market, worth £2,679 million in 1979, from between 25 and 30 per cent in 1973 to 79 per cent in 1979 and are increasingly involved in supplying other offshore markets.

OIL

During most of the twentieth century Britain has been almost wholly dependent for its oil supplies on imports, the only indigenous supplies coming from a small number of land-based oilfields. The discovery of oil offshore in the UKCS has transformed the position, however. The first discovery of oil in the UKCS was made in 1969 and the first oil was brought ashore in 1975. Britain is now producing about 1·6 million barrels (220,000 tonnes) a day. (For estimates of the growing economic benefits of North Sea oil revenues see p 202.)

North Sea
Fields

Fifteen fields in the UKCS are producing oil: Brent and Forties, two of the largest offshore oilfields in the world; Argyll; Auk; Beryl; Claymore; Dunlin; Heather; Montrose; Ninian; Piper; South Cormorant; Statfjord; Murchison; and Thistle. A further 11 fields are under development while more than 40 further significant finds that have been made may prove to be commercial after further appraisal. Production from most large fields is controlled from production platforms of either steel or concrete which have been built to withstand severe weather including gusts of wind of up to 257 km/h (160 mph) and waves of 30 metres (100 feet).

Britain's primary oil production, including condensates and petroleum gases, amounted to nearly 78 million tonnes in 1979 (see Table 17), over 40 per cent more than in 1978 and was equivalent to over four-fifths of Britain's oil requirements for energy and non-energy purposes and for international marine bunkers. Production is expected to continue to rise rapidly, reaching between 80 million and 85 million tonnes in 1980, and rising to between 90 million and 120 million tonnes in 1982. Remaining proven reserves of oil in the UKCS amount to nearly 1,200 million tonnes while the total remaining reserves of the UKCS could be as high as 4,200 million tonnes. The Government has announced that it is in the national interest to prolong high levels of UKCS oil production until the end of the twentieth century. This requires increased exploration, which the Government is encouraging, and the deferment of some oil production from the 1980s.

TABLE 17: Oil Statistics   *million tonnes*

	1969	1974	1977	1978	1979
Oil production[a]					
land	0·1	0·1	0·1	0·1	0·1
offshore	—	0·3	38·1	53·9	77·8
Refinery output	85·1	103·1	86·3	89·2	90·6
Deliveries of petroleum products for inland consumption	85·4	93·4	82·8	84·1	84·6
Exports (including re-exports): crude petroleum	0·6[b]	0·9	15·3	23·1	38·8
refined petroleum products and process oils	14·2[c]	15·3	15·2	14·3	14·4
Imports: crude petroleum	94·4[b]	110·8	68·6	65·5	57·9
refined petroleum products and process oils	20·7[c]	18·3	16·3	14·7	16·5

Sources: *Department of Energy* and *Board of Customs and Excise*
[a] Crude oil plus condensates and petroleum gases derived at onshore treatment plants.
[b] Includes process oils.   [c] Excludes process oils.

Structure of
the Oil
Industry

The two leading British oil companies are British Petroleum (BP) and Shell Transport and Trading, which are the two largest industrial companies in Britain in terms of turnover, and are the first and third largest in Europe respectively. Sales by BP (in which the Government has a 46 per cent stake)

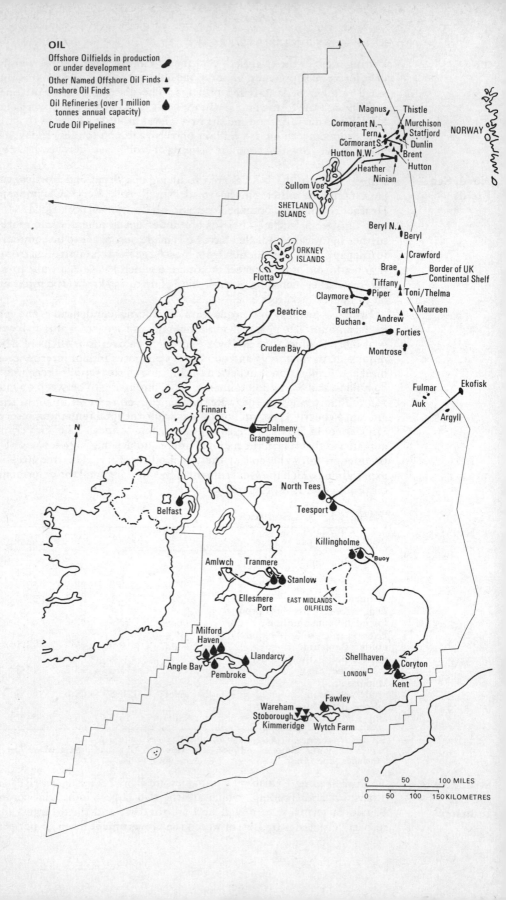

OIL

Offshore Oilfields in production or under development

Other Named Offshore Oil Finds ▲

Onshore Oil Finds ▼

Oil Refineries (over 1 million tonnes annual capacity) 🛢

Crude Oil Pipelines ━━━━

Magnus Thistle
Cormorant N. Murchison
Tern Statfjord
Cormorant S. Dunlin
Hutton N.W. Brent
Heather Hutton
Ninian

NORWAY

Sullom Voe

SHETLAND ISLANDS

Beryl N. ▲
Beryl

Crawford

Brae

ORKNEY ISLANDS

Border of UK Continental Shelf

Flotta

Tiffany
Claymore Piper Toni/Thelma
Tartan
Buchan Maureen
Beatrice Andrew

Cruden Bay Forties
Montrose

Ekofisk
Fulmar
Auk
Finnart Argyll

Dalmeny
Grangemouth

North Tees
Teesport

Belfast

Killingholme
Buoy

Amlwch Tranmere
Stanlow
Ellesmere Port

EAST MIDLANDS OILFIELDS

Milford Haven
Llandarcy
Angle Bay
Pembroke

Shellhaven Coryton
LONDON Kent

Fawley
Wareham
Stoborough Wytch Farm
Kimmeridge

N

0   50   100 MILES
0   50   100   150 KILOMETRES

averaged 3·7 million barrels a day of crude oil and petroleum products in 1979 and its gross income was £23,000 million. It has about 113,000 employees, of whom 38,700 are employed in Britain.

The British National Oil Corporation, a public corporation set up in 1976, is engaged in two main activities: as an oil trader on a large scale, mainly by virtue of its right, through participation agreements with other oil companies, to purchase 51 per cent of most of the oil produced on the UKCS; and as a substantial enterprise engaged in North Sea exploration, development and production. The Government has announced its intention to introduce private capital into BNOC's oil-producing business. The oil trading activities will remain as a wholly government-owned operation.

There are several other large oil companies operating in Britain or engaged in work on the UKCS. In addition, there are about 30 independent oil exploration companies with interests in North Sea developments.

Land-based Fields

Onshore production of crude oil in Britain is much less significant than offshore production, amounting in 1979 to about 120,000 tonnes. However, production is expected to grow substantially as output builds up from Britain's largest onshore field, at Wytch Farm (Dorset), which started production in 1979. Twelve other onshore fields are in operation, notably Bothamsall and Egmanton in Nottinghamshire, Gainsborough in Lincolnshire and Kimmeridge in Dorset.

Refineries

In 1980 the crude distillation capacity of Britain's oil refineries amounted to 132·9 million tonnes a year. All but three of the 20 refineries in operation have a distillation capacity of over 1 million tonnes a year and are shown on the map on p 266. Three have a crude distillation capacity of over 10 million tonnes a year: Fawley, near Southampton (17·3 million tonnes); Stanlow, in Cheshire (16·8 million tonnes); and Kent (10·4 million tonnes). Existing refineries are being adapted to the changing pattern of demand by the construction of new upgrading facilities which are leading to a higher output of motor spirit and naphtha at the expense of fuel oil.

Consumption

Deliveries of petroleum products for inland consumption (excluding refinery consumption) in 1979 totalled 84·6 million tonnes including 27·5 million tonnes of fuel oil, 19·9 million tonnes of gas and diesel oil (including derv fuel used in road vehicles), 18·7 million tonnes of motor spirit and 7·4 million tonnes of kerosene.

International Trade

The volume of imports of crude oil has been declining recently (see Table 17); in 1979 they were valued at over £3,670 million. The main sources were Saudi Arabia (which supplied about 24 per cent by value), Kuwait (18 per cent), Iraq (11 per cent) and Norway (7 per cent), while a further 9 per cent was imported via the Netherlands. The tonnage imported is expected to continue to decline, although heavy crude oil will still be imported for particular uses.

High quality premium oil from the UKCS is being exported and crude oil exports, which have risen considerably, accounted for 50 per cent of production in 1979. The value of exports of crude oil amounted to over £2,710 million, and more than £1,470 million of petroleum products were also exported. Most oil exports are sent to other countries in Western Europe.

Oil Pipelines

Oil pipelines brought ashore about 80 per cent of offshore oil in 1979. About 750 miles (1,200 kilometres) of submarine pipeline have been built to bring ashore oil from a number of North Sea oilfields (see map). Pipelines distribute crude oil to refineries from harbours, North Sea land terminals or offshore moorings capable of berthing very large tankers, for example, from Finnart to Grangemouth; from Angle Bay, Milford Haven, to Llandarcy; from Tranmere to Stanlow; from Amlwch (Gwynedd) to Stanlow; and from Cruden Bay to Grangemouth. Pipelines also carry refined products and petrochemical feedstocks to major marketing areas; for example, a 300-mile (480-kilometre) pipeline runs from Milford Haven to the Midlands and Manchester.

Research

Research into problems of petroleum technology is carried out mainly by the leading oil companies, which have also endowed research at the universities on a substantial scale. Research centres are situated at Sunbury-on-Thames (BP), Ellesmere Port in Cheshire and Woodstock in Kent (Shell), and Abingdon in Oxfordshire (Esso). Work in progress includes the evolution of new and improved fuels and lubricants, and the development of new uses for petroleum products and of new products based on petroleum, especially chemicals. The main Government research and development effort in offshore technology is undertaken by the Department of Energy with the advice of the Offshore Energy Technology Board (see p 386). In 1980–81 the Department of Energy expects to spend some £20 million in support of offshore technology.

GAS

Public supply of manufactured gas in Britain began in the early nineteenth century in Westminster in central London. For many years gas was produced from coal but during the 1960s, when growing supplies of oil were being imported, there was a switch to producing town gas from oil-based feedstocks. However, a more significant change began in the late 1960s following the first commercial natural gas discovery in the UKCS in 1965 and the start of offshore gas production in 1967. Supplies of offshore natural gas grew rapidly and natural gas has now replaced town gas as the source of gas for the public supply system in Great Britain. Originally used almost exclusively for lighting, gas is now primarily used for domestic cooking and heating and for industrial and commercial purposes.

Structure

The Gas Act 1948 brought the industry in Great Britain under public ownership and control in 1949. As a result of the change to natural gas necessitating more centralised control of production and transmission, the British Gas Corporation was set up in 1973 under the Gas Act 1972 to replace the Gas Council and area gas boards. The Corporation's powers in connection with its main duty of developing and maintaining an efficient, co-ordinated and economical system of gas supply and of satisfying reasonable demands for gas are: to search for and extract natural gas and any oil discovered in the course of searching for gas; to manufacture or acquire, transmit and distribute gas; to manufacture, supply, or sell by-products; and to manufacture, install, maintain or remove gas plant and fittings. It has about 104,400 employees.

Natural gas is not available in Northern Ireland and the industry there, which is controlled by nine municipal undertakings and four private sector companies, uses town gas produced from oil feedstocks. In 1979 the Government decided that the large-scale expenditure required for a natural gas pipeline from Great Britain to Northern Ireland could not be justified and that it could not subsidise the industry's operations. Accordingly, most of the gas undertakings have decided that they cannot continue a viable supply of piped gas and arrangements are in hand for a phased rundown of the industry.

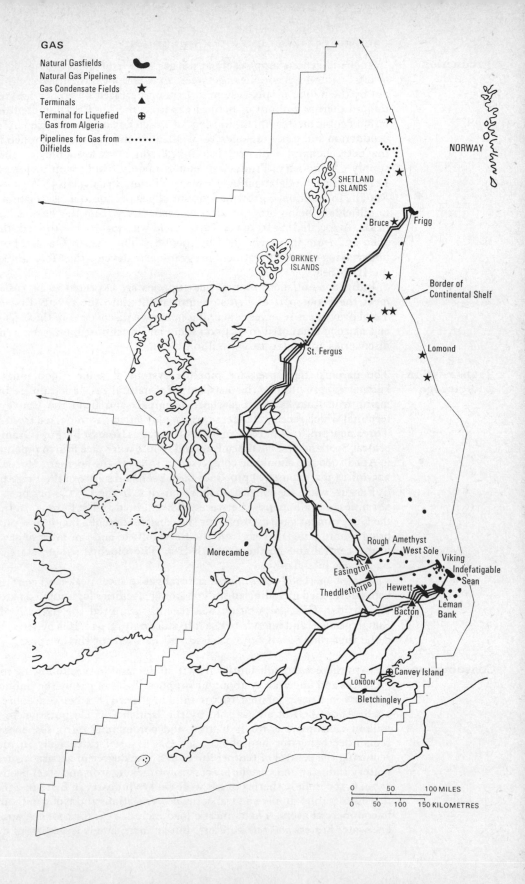

NORWAY

SHETLAND
ISLANDS

ORKNEY
ISLANDS

Bruce • ● Frigg

Border of
Continental Shelf

★ ★★

Lomond ★

★

St. Fergus

N

Rough Amethyst
West Sole
Viking
Easington Indefatigable
Sean
Morecambe
Theddlethorpe Hewett
Bacton Leman
Bank

⊕ Canvey Island
LONDON
Bletchingley

0   50   100 MILES

0   50   100   150 KILOMETRES

Production

In 1979 indigenous supplies of natural gas were equivalent to about 81 per cent of total natural gas supplies. Between 1974 and 1979 the quantity of gas sent out by the public supply system in Britain increased by 29 per cent to 17,315 million therms. Output of natural gas from the UKCS amounted to 39,228 million cubic metres (mcm) in 1979, of which 895 mcm were used for drilling, production and pumping operations offshore and 164 mcm supplied direct to the petrochemical industry, leaving 38,169 mcm available for the public supply gas industry. Production comes mainly from seven major gasfields: Leman Bank, Indefatigable, Hewett, Viking, Frigg (UK), West Sole and Rough. In addition, a growing amount of gas produced in association with oil in oilfields is being brought ashore, particularly from the Forties and Piper fields. Associated gas from the Tartan field will start to flow towards the end of 1980 and from the Brent field in 1980–81. The British Gas Corporation is undertaking a major investment programme to develop the Morecambe field in the Irish Sea.

Indigenous offshore natural gas supplies are expected to be sufficient to meet the major part of British requirements into the twenty-first century. Total proven gas reserves remaining in known discoveries in the UKCS at the end of 1979 amounted to 754,000 mcm and total possible reserves in known discoveries amounted to 1·5 million mcm.

Transmission and Storage

The national high pressure pipeline system of some 3,500 miles (5,600 kilometres) provides for the distribution of natural gas. It is supplied by feeder mains from four North Sea shore terminals and from the Canvey Island terminal which receives tankers carrying liquefied gas imported from Algeria. Three new pipelines have been built to carry gas from St Fergus (Grampian) to central Scotland and northern England, while work on a fourth pipeline began in April 1980 and should be completed in 1982. In the northern North Sea two 225-mile (362-kilometre) pipelines have been laid between the Frigg field and St Fergus, while the longest offshore pipeline in the UKCS has been laid for 281 miles (452 kilometres) between the Brent field and St Fergus. In June 1980 the Government gave approval for the construction of a major new pipeline to bring ashore associated gas from the Beryl oilfield and a number of other fields in the central and northern North Sea. The pipeline should start to bring ashore gas in 1984–85.

Various methods of storage of natural gas to meet peak load conditions are being developed including additional storage facilities for liquefied natural gas. The British Gas Corporation has recently acquired the partially depleted Rough gasfield and intends to use it to store natural gas. It is believed that this is the first time an offshore gasfield will be used for this purpose.

Consumption

In 1979 there was a substantial growth in demand for gas following increased oil prices and uncertainty about oil supplies. Sales of gas by the public supply industry in Britain totalled 16,591 million therms, 8·4 per cent more than in 1978. About half of all gas sold by the British Gas Corporation to its 15·3 million consumers is for industrial and commercial purposes, most of the remainder being for household use. Gas is used extensively in industries requiring the control of temperatures to a fine degree of accuracy such as the pottery industry and certain processes for making iron and steel products. In 1979, 6,160 million therms of gas were sold to industry in Britain, 239 million therms to public supply and transport power stations and 1,967 million therms to commercial users. The domestic load includes gas for cookers, space heaters, water heaters and refrigerators, but an increasingly large part of domestic demand is for gas for central heating. In 1979, 8,225 million therms were sold to domestic users, 13·3 per cent more than in 1978.

Operations

In 1979–80 the turnover of the British Gas Corporation and its subsidiary companies amounted to £3,513 million, of which sales of gas accounted for £2,977 million. After interest payments there was a profit of £426 million. Recently the Corporation has been wholly self-financing. It has repaid all its long-term debt to the Government and is depositing its cash surpluses with the National Loans Fund. The Corporation has a large investment programme, amounting to more than £4,000 million in the five years from 1980–81, for new production, transmission and storage facilities. Capital expenditure on projects to increase the availability of gas has been brought forward to help to meet the growth in demand.

Research

The British Gas Corporation conducts research at five research stations into all aspects of gas supply and use. Its total expenditure on research and development and on technical service and testing amounted to £36 million in 1979–80. Work on processes for the manufacture of substitute natural gas (SNG) from either oil or coal is one of the Corporation's main research projects and it has a 20-year programme, expected to cost some £300 million, to enable it to produce commercial quantities of SNG when this is required to augment supplies of natural gas. A demonstration coal gasification plant has been built at the Westfield Development Centre in Fife and a prototype plant to make SNG from oil is planned at Killingholme (Humberside) and should be in operation by 1982.

COAL

Coalmining in Britain can be traced back to the thirteenth century. It played a crucial part in the industrial revolution of the early nineteenth century and in its peak year, 1913, the industry produced 292 million tonnes of coal, exported 98 million tonnes and employed over a million workers. In 1947 the coal mines passed into public ownership by means of the Coal Industry Nationalisation Act 1946, which set up the National Coal Board (NCB) as a statutory corporation to manage the industry.

The National Coal Board

The NCB has, with limited exceptions, exclusive rights over the extraction of coal in Great Britain, but is empowered to license private operators to work small mines and opencast sites. It also has powers to work other minerals, where discoveries are made in the course of searching for, or working, coal; and to engage in certain petrochemical activities beneficial to the future of the coal industry. Retail sales remain largely in private hands, although the NCB makes bulk sales to large industrial consumers. Two holding companies, wholly owned by the NCB, run most of its non-mining activities. NCB (Ancillaries) Ltd's responsibilities include certain retail fuel distribution operations, computer services and engineering. NCB (Coal Products) Ltd is responsible for solid smokeless fuel manufacture and chemical and by-products plants.

At the end of March 1980 there were 219 NCB collieries in operation grouped into 12 areas, each controlled by a director responsible to the NCB. The main coal-bearing areas are shown on the map on p 272 and the main trends in the coal industry are shown in Table 18.

Production and Productivity

In 1979–80 output of 125·1 million tonnes comprised 109·3 million tonnes from the NCB's deep mines, 13·4 million tonnes from opencast mines and 2·4 million tonnes from licensed mines and other sources. Britain's coal industry

COAL

Coalfields

Potential Coalfields

0   20   40   60   80   100 MILES

0   20   40   60   80   100   120 KILOMETRES

N

Glasgow

Edinburgh

Newcastle upon Tyne

Durham

Carlisle

Workington

Leeds

Selby

Liverpool

Doncaster

Manchester

Sheffield

Nottingham

Birmingham

Swansea

Cardiff

Bristol

London

Dover

TABLE 18: Coal Statistics

year ended March

	Unit	1970	1975	1978	1979	1980
Output	million tonnes	152·5	128·6	122·6	121·5	125·1
of which, opencast	million tonnes	6·7	9·7	14·0	13·8	13·4
Output per manshift[a]:						
underground	tonnes	2·86	2·94	2·79	2·86	2·89
overall	tonnes	2·20	2·29	2·19	2·24	2·27
Inland consumption	million tonnes	161·7	127·2	121·6	122·5	128·3
Average labour force[a]	'000	305·1	246·0	240·5	234·9	232·5
Collieries in operation[a]	number	299	246	231	223	219

Source: *Department of Energy*
[a] NCB mines only.

remains the largest in Western Europe and is one of the world's most technologically advanced. Substantial progress has been made in techniques for mining coal. Developments are concentrated on the introduction of computerised automatic monitoring and remote control of machines, together with the installation of heavy-duty equipment, such as powered roof supports, power loaders and armoured flexible conveyors, capable of sustained high performance with minimum maintenance. Productivity in terms of output per manshift rose to 2·27 tonnes in 1979–80, 1·5 per cent more than in 1978–79.

Financial Structure

In 1979–80 the NCB's income was £3,863 million including sales of coal of £3,136 million. Although the NCB made a trading profit of £27·6 million, it recorded a net loss of £159·3 million after taking account of interest payments and other items. The NCB's borrowing limit is £3,400 million, with provision for an additional increase up to £4,200 million which is subject to parliamentary approval.

Capital Investment

Capital expenditure on collieries amounted to £617 million in 1979–80. The Board's Plan for Coal, a general strategy for the ten years to the mid-1980s, involves investment of £5,300 million at 1979 prices of which nearly half is expenditure on major new projects. NCB deep mines are expected to be producing 120 million tonnes a year by the mid-1980s, with about 42 million tonnes coming from new capacity created under the 'Plan for Coal' to replace that lost by exhaustion of old collieries. Some 43 major projects have already been completed and new coal mines have been opened at Kinsley and Royston, both near Barnsley, and at Betws (Dyfed). By far the largest NCB project is the new mining complex at Selby in North Yorkshire (which will be one of the world's most advanced deep mines) where production should start in 1982 and build up to the full rate of 10 million tonnes a year by 1987–88.

Although many good seams of coal have now been worked out due to the early development of the industry, total coal reserves in Britain are estimated at 190,000 million tonnes, of which about 45,000 million tonnes (sufficient for at least 300 years at present rates of consumption) are recoverable using existing mining technology. The NCB's national exploration programme is proving fresh reserves of economically workable coal at the rate of 500 million tonnes a year, four times the annual consumption of coal. A public inquiry has been held into the NCB's proposals to develop the North-east Leicestershire coalfield, which has recoverable reserves of 520 million tonnes. Other major new finds have been located at Park (Staffordshire), west of Coventry, under the Firth of Forth off Musselburgh (Lothian), at Margam (West Glamorgan), and in north Oxfordshire.

Consumption   In 1979–80 internal consumption of coal was 128·3 million tonnes of which 69 per cent went to power stations, 11 per cent to coke ovens and 8 per cent to domestic users. The proportion of coal used by the electricity supply industry compared with other fuels used for generation has increased, and NCB sales of coal to power stations reached a record 86·3 million tonnes in 1979–80.

Exports of coal in 1979–80 were 2·5 million tonnes, almost all of which went to Western European countries, while imports amounted to 5·1 million tonnes.

Research   In 1979–80 the NCB spent £41 million on research. It has two main research organisations: the Coal Research Establishment (CRE) at Stoke Orchard (Gloucestershire), concerned with the combustion and utilisation of coal; and the Mining Research and Development Establishment at Stanhope Bretby (Staffordshire), for work on mining methods and equipment, particularly improving the performance and reliability of existing equipment and developing systems for remote and automatic control. Two CRE processes are being developed for converting coal to liquid fuels and chemical feedstocks. Pilot plants are planned for construction at Point of Ayr (Clwyd).

Agreements to exchange technical information have been signed by the NCB with several countries. Britain is responsible through an NCB subsidiary for managing a programme of international coal research projects on behalf of the International Energy Agency. Five collaborative coal research projects, including a £17 million project to develop pressurised fluidised bed combustion (a method of steam-raising for power generation) are based in Britain.

ELECTRICITY   The first public supply of electricity in Britain was in 1881, at Godalming (Surrey). In 1948 all municipal and private undertakings in Great Britain were acquired under the Electricity Act 1947 and vested in the British Electricity Authority and 14 regional boards, except in the north of Scotland where they became the responsibility of the North of Scotland Hydro-Electric Board (NSHEB), which had been set up in 1943. Two subsequent Acts (1954 and 1957) effected a measure of decentralisation and established the present structure of public corporations. Electricity from the public supply system is available to virtually all premises in Britain, the only exceptions being very remote rural households.

Structure   The Electricity Council is the central co-ordinating body of the supply industry in England and Wales. It has a general responsibility for promoting the development and maintenance of an efficient, co-ordinated and economical system of electricity supply. Electricity is generated and transmitted by the Central Electricity Generating Board (CEGB), which is responsible for the operation and maintenance of power stations and the main transmission system (national grid). Twelve area electricity boards are responsible for distribution and for the retail sale of electricity. The chairman and two designated members of the CEGB, together with the chairman of the area electricity boards, are among the members of the board of the Electricity Council.

In Scotland two boards, the NSHEB and the South of Scotland Electricity Board (SSEB), generate, distribute and sell electricity. The boundary separating their areas runs from Dumbarton on the Firth of Clyde to Newburgh on the Firth of Tay (see map, p 276). Each board has a chairman and between four and eight members, one of whom is the chairman of the other board.

In Northern Ireland generation, transmission and distribution are carried out by the publicly owned Northern Ireland Electricity Service.

Operations

In 1979–80 the income of the electricity supply industry in England and Wales was £6,171 million and its profit after interest payments was £37 million. In Scotland the income of the SSEB and the NSHEB was £519 million and £203 million respectively and their profits were £0·1 million and £1·7 million. In 1979–80 the Northern Ireland Electricity Service's income totalled £193 million and it had a net deficit of £15·7 million. Annual capital investment amounts to £834 million in England and Wales, £107 million in Scotland and £54 million in Northern Ireland. The statutory limit to borrowings by the industry in England and Wales is £6,500 million, in Northern Ireland £650 million and in Scotland £1,500 million, with provision for a further increase up to £1,950 million. About 183,000 people are employed in the electricity supply industry in Britain.

Generation

Generation by the public supply electricity industry in Britain reached a record 279,482 gigawatt hours (GWh)[1] in 1979, 4·8 per cent more than in 1978. Conventional steam power stations provided 86 per cent of the total, nuclear stations 12 per cent and gas turbine, hydro-electric and diesel plant 2 per cent. Public supply power stations in Britain consumed 122 million tonnes of coal equivalent in 1979 of which coal accounted for 73 per cent and oil 15 per cent. The output capacity of the 222 generating stations of the electricity boards in Britain at the end of 1979 totalled 68,882 megawatts (MW) including 56,765 MW run by the CEGB, 8,060 MW by the SSEB, 2,094 MW by the NSHEB and 1,938 MW by the Northern Ireland Electricity Service. An analysis of electricity generation by and output capacity of the public supply system in Britain is given in Table 19.

Generation of electricity outside the public supply system is relatively small (20,509 GWh in 1979). The major sources outside the fuel industries are the chemical, engineering, paper, and iron and steel industries and the nuclear power plants of the United Kingdom Atomic Energy Authority (UKAEA) and British Nuclear Fuels Ltd (BNFL). In 1979 these nuclear plants supplied 3,182 GWh of electricity to the public supply system.

New large-scale power stations are based on units of 500 MW

TABLE 19: Generation by and Capacity of Public Supply Power Stations

	Electricity generated (GWh)				Output capacity at end of 1979 (MW)
	1969	1974	1978	1979	
Nuclear plant	25,271	29,395	33,339	34,604	5,527
Other steam plant	188,185	215,701	228,193	239,317	57,307
Gas turbines and oil engines	1,017	1,139	688	758	3,704
Pumped-storage plant	1,122	697	1,183	1,175	1,060
Other hydro-electric plant	2,807	3,534	3,388	3,628	1,284
Total	218,402	250,466	266,791	279,482	68,882
Electricity supplied (net)[a]	201,970	232,402	248,003	259,836	

Source: *Department of Energy*
[a] Electricity generated less electricity used at power stations (including electricity used for pumping at pumped-storage stations).

[1] One gigawatt hour = 1,000 megawatt hours = one million kilowatt hours.

ELECTRICITY

Conventional Power Stations
(1,000 MW and over) ■
Under construction □
Nuclear Power Stations ●
Under construction ○
Power-producing reactors of ◆
the UKAEA or BNFL
Hydro-Electric Power Stations ★
(over 45 MW capacity)
Pumped Storage Schemes △
Under construction △
Boundary of the SSEB ----
and NSHEB

0 20 40 60 80 100 MILE
0 20 40 60 80 100 120 KILOMETRES

Dounreay

Fasnakyle

Peterhead

Foyers

Errochty
Rannoch
Cruachan   Clunie
Lochay

Sloy
Inverkip   Longannet   Torness
Hunterston A   Cockenzie
Hunterston B

Chapelcross   Blyth B

Windscale   Hartlepool
Calder Hall

Heysham

Ferrybridge C   Drax
Eggborough   Thorpe Marsh
Fiddler's Ferry   West Burton A
Cottam
Wylfa   Ince B   High Marnham

Dinorwic
Ffestiniog
Trawsfynydd   Drakelow C   Ratcliffe-upon-Soar

Rheidol

Sizewell A

Tilbury   Bradwell
Didcot   W. Thurrock
Berkeley   B   Grain
Pembroke   Aberthaw B   Oldbury   Littlebrook D   Kingsnorth

Hinkley Pt. B   Dungeness B   Dungeness
Hinkley Pt. A   Fawley
Winfrith

and 660 MW. Station capacities have increased and there are 11 stations each with a capacity of 2,000 MW including Kingsnorth (Kent), Europe's largest mixed-fuel station burning either coal or oil, while Britain's largest power station is at Longannet (Fife), a 2,400 MW station with four cross-compound units. The larger units have a higher thermal efficiency (the ratio of the net electrical energy output to the heat energy input) than earlier units and their introduction, coupled with the closure of less efficient plant has resulted in a gradual rise in thermal efficiency, leading to substantial savings in fuel consumption. Average thermal efficiency of conventional steam stations in England and Wales rose from 20·91 per cent in 1947–48 to 31·68 per cent in 1979–80 when the CEGB's 20 most efficient stations had an average thermal efficiency of 33·74 per cent.

About 15,000 MW of plant are under construction including a 2,000 MW coal-fired extension to the Drax station (North Yorkshire) and five nuclear power stations (see below). Work is also in progress on the construction of a pumped-storage station at Dinorwic (Gwynedd), which will be the largest of its type in the world when completed in 1983 and will have an average generated output of 1,680 MW. (In pumped-storage schemes electricity generated in off-peak periods is used to pump water to high-level reservoirs from which it descends to drive turbines, rapidly providing a large supply of electricity at peak periods or to meet sudden increases in demand.) A further large-scale pumped-storage scheme is being considered by the NSHEB for construction at Craigroyston on Loch Lomond.

A new combined heat and power (CHP) station designed to sell heat normally discharged to the atmosphere as a by-product of electricity generation to neighbouring firms was opened at Hereford in March 1980. It is a 15 MW station with thermal efficiency of around 76 per cent. In April 1980 the Government announced the inauguration of a programme to test the feasibility of CHP and district heating in particular locations in Britain.

Nuclear Power

Britain has been developing nuclear power since 1956 when the world's first large-scale nuclear power station, at Calder Hall (Cumbria), began to supply electricity to the national grid. The Government believes that nuclear power has a vital role in helping to meet Britain's long-term energy requirements. Accordingly, it is supporting the electricity supply industry's plans to order at least one new nuclear power station a year between 1982 and 1991, representing a ten-year programme of some 15,000 MW.

Power Stations

There are 11 nuclear power stations in operation controlled by the electricity authorities, while a further five stations are controlled by the United Kingdom Atomic Energy Authority (see p 387) or British Nuclear Fuels Ltd. The UKAEA has three experimental or prototype stations which feed electricity into the national grid: the Advanced Gas-cooled Reactor (AGR) at Windscale, Cumbria (32 MW); the Steam Generating Heavy Water Reactor at Winfrith, Dorset (100 MW); and the Prototype Fast Reactor (PFR) at Dounreay, Highland (250 MW). BNFL operates the two original Magnox stations, both with a capacity of 198 MW, at Calder Hall and Chapelcross (Dumfries and Galloway).

Nuclear Power Programme

Under the first commercial programme, nine Magnox stations with a total gross capacity of about 4,000 MW were commissioned between 1962 and 1971. They range in size from Berkeley (Gloucestershire) with a capacity of 332 MW to the most recent, Wylfa (Gwynedd), which has a capacity of 990 MW. The second main programme was based on the AGR and the first two commercial AGRs, 1,320 MW stations at Hinkley Point B (Somerset) and Hunterston B (Strathclyde), began operating in 1976. Three AGRs (Dungeness B, Kent, 1,200 MW; Hartlepool, Cleveland, 1,320 MW; and Heysham, Lancashire, 1,320 MW) are under construction and the first units should be commissioned in 1981 or 1982. Initial work on two more AGRs, a 1,320 MW extension at Heysham and a 1,320 MW station at Torness (Lothian), has also started. It is intended that the next reactor order will be for a pressurised water reactor system (the main type in use overseas), subject to the necessary consents and safety clearances being obtained. Government policy on fast reactor development, including whether or not to proceed with a full-scale commercial demonstration fast reactor, is under review. Any decision to proceed would be subject to a full public inquiry.

British Nuclear Fuels Ltd　　BNFL provides nuclear fuel services covering the design and development of plant, procurement and processing of uranium, uranium enrichment, fuel element fabrication, transport and reprocessing of spent fuel, and the manufacture of specialised components and preparation of radioactive materials. All of BNFL's shares are held by the UKAEA on behalf of the Government. BNFL is organised into three divisions covering uranium enrichment, based at Capenhurst (Cheshire); fuel manufacture at Springfields (Lancashire); and reprocessing at Windscale (Cumbria) where uranium, plutonium and radioactive wastes are separated from irradiated fuel. BNFL's head office is at Risley (Cheshire). It is engaged on a large-scale investment programme costing about £2,500 million over the next ten years. This includes the refurbishing of facilities for storing and reprocessing spent fuel from Magnox power stations, the doubling of capacity of the centrifuge enrichment plant at Capenhurst, the construction of a new thermal oxide reprocessing plant (THORP) at Windscale which will deal with spent fuel from Britain's AGRs and will also reprocess spent fuel for a number of overseas customers, and the construction of a demonstration plant for vitrifying radioactive waste.

Transmission and Distribution　　The British system is the largest fully interconnected power network under unified control in the western world. By 31st March 1980 the main transmission lines of the CEGB totalled 14,123 circuit kilometres, of which 11,666 circuit kilometres were at 400,000 volts and the remainder at 275,000 volts. Primary distribution in England and Wales is at 132,000 volts, secondary distribution at 33,000 volts, tertiary at 11,000 volts or below and general low voltage distribution at 240 volts single phase. In Scotland there were 8,671 circuit kilometres of main transmission lines at the end of March 1980 of which 340 kilometres operated at 400,000 volts, 3,256 circuit kilometres at 275,000 volts and the remainder at 132,000 volts. Primary distribution in Scotland is at 33,000 volts. The national grid in England and Wales is divided into seven grid control areas and operations are co-ordinated by a National Control Centre in London. The grid in Scotland is operated from the control centres at Pitlochry (NSHEB) and at Kirkintilloch (SSEB).

Twin cross-Channel cables between Lydd and Boulogne are capable of transmitting up to 160 MW. Experience with this relatively low-capacity link demonstrated the benefits of the transfer of electricity between Britain and France. The CEGB and Electricité de France are proposing a 2,000 MW cable link between Folkestone and Sangatte (near Calais) to allow much larger quantities of electricity to be exchanged. The first 1,000 MW stage should be commissioned in 1984 and the second stage in 1985.

Consumption

Sales of electricity in 1979 amounted to 240,786 GWh. Industry took 39·4 per cent of the total, domestic users 37·2 per cent and commercial and other users the remainder. About one-fifth of domestic sales is for space heating, one-quarter for water heating and one-tenth for cooking. Electricity is used in industry mainly for motive power, melting, heating and lighting. The electricity industry supplies 23·1 million consumers of whom 20·4 million are in England and Wales, 1·6 million are supplied by the SSEB, 536,000 by the NSHEB and 522,000 by the Northern Ireland Electricity Service.

Research

The Electricity Council, in consultation with the Secretary of State for Energy, is responsible for drawing up a general programme of research comprising direct research carried out by the Council and electricity boards supported by co-operative research with selected industrial research associations and by research contracts placed with universities and other organisations. Much of the work is carried out in collaboration with the SSEB, the NSHEB and the Northern Ireland Electricity Service which contribute towards the cost of research (£66·2 million in 1979–80). Collaboration on research between the supply industry and the plant manufacturers is co-ordinated by the Power Engineering Research Steering Committee. The research establishments run by the CEGB comprise the Central Electricity Research Laboratories at Leatherhead (Surrey), the Berkeley Nuclear Laboratories in Gloucestershire and the Marchwood Engineering Laboratories on Southampton Water. Research on distribution technology and electricity utilisation is undertaken at the Electricity Council Research Centre at Capenhurst (Cheshire) and by the area boards.

RENEWABLE SOURCES OF ENERGY

Research is in progress on assessing the potential contribution of alternative sources of energy (sea-wave, wind and tidal power for electricity generation, and solar and geothermal energy for low-grade heat for domestic and industrial uses) and the ways in which they may be harnessed. Development in Britain is at an early stage and they are not expected to make a major contribution to energy supplies in the next few years, although they may have a more significant role in the long term as indigenous offshore oil and gas production declines. In principle, the most promising long-term renewable sources are wave power (because of Britain's long coastline and favourable geographical position) and solar heat.

The aim of the Government's wave power programme is to develop the most appropriate devices to full-scale prototypes for sea trials. Work is in progress on a number of types of wave energy devices and includes one-tenth scale trials, full-scale component development, test tank experiments and the study of problems common to all the devices. In 1977 a four-year government-funded programme of research and development on solar energy was inaugurated to identify its potential contribution and to stimulate the development of cost-effective solar technologies, particularly on water and space heating in houses (the areas of greatest potential return).

Research on geothermal energy involves collection of data in the areas considered to have the most suitable conditions and assessment of the markets for the relatively low-grade heat produced. The first exploratory borehole in Britain directed towards geothermal deposits was drilled near Southampton in 1979–80. The Department of Energy and an industrial consortium are working on a project to establish the technical and economic potential for generating electricity from wind power. A detailed design study for a large aerogenerator has been completed and the first stage in the construction of a 3·7 MW prototype, covering detailed design and component testing, is in progress. Studies have been made of a project for harnessing the tides in the Severn Estuary, one of the world's most suitable sites for tidal power, and the Government has set up an independent Severn Barrage Committee to assist in reaching a decision on whether to proceed with such a project. The Committee has found that such a project would be technically feasible.

NON-FUEL MINERALS

Although much of Britain's requirements of industrial raw materials is met by imports, non-fuel minerals produced in Britain make an important contribution to the economy. Output of non-fuel minerals in 1978 totalled 319 million tonnes, valued at £1,021 million. The total number of employees in the industry was 42,900 in 1978. The geographical locations of some of the more important minerals produced in Britain are shown on the maps on p 282.

Exploration

The exploration for and exploitation of indigenous mineral resources to meet the requirements of British industry are being encouraged by the Government to minimise dependence on imports. Under the Mineral Exploration and Investment Grants Act 1972 there is provision for financial assistance of up to 35 per cent of the cost of searching for mineral deposits in Great Britain and on the UKCS and evaluating them for commercial purposes. Minerals included in the scheme are the ores of non-ferrous metals, fluorspar, barium minerals and potash. By the end of March 1980, 57 companies had sought assistance totalling £5·9 million in respect of 186 exploration projects, mainly for non-ferrous metals. Work on 126 projects had been completed. A similar scheme was introduced in Northern Ireland in 1979.

The Institute of Geological Sciences is carrying out for the Department of Industry a programme aimed at identifying areas with the potential for economic extraction of minerals. It also has a programme for the Department of the Environment to assess resources of sand and gravel, and limestone.

Production

The tonnage extracted of some of the main non-fuel minerals produced in Britain is given in Table 20. In terms of value, production of sand and gravel was estimated at £298 million in 1978, limestone £228 million, igneous rock

TABLE 20: Output of Some of the Main Non-fuel Minerals

million tonnes

	1968	1973	1977	1978
Common sand and gravel	118·2	136·0	106·9	110·2
Special sands	4·9	6·8	6·3	6·2
Igneous rock	34·1	47·6	35·6	35·3
Limestone and dolomite	81·2	108·4	86·4	88·8
Chalk	19·0	22·2	16·3	16·7
Sandstone	13·4	16·8	12·2	13·4
Gypsum	2·9	3·8	3·2	3·2
Salt including salt in brine	7·8	8·5	8·2	7·3
Common clay and shale	37·7	33·7	23·5	25·5[a]
China clay, ball clay and potters' clay	3·5	4·2	4·4	4·2
Fireclay	2·0	1·8	1·5	1·4
Iron ore	13·9	7·1	3·7	4·2

Source: *United Kingdom Mineral Statistics 1979*
[a] Production in Great Britain.

£141 million, clays £110 million, sandstone £55 million, non-ferrous ores £38 million, chalk £22 million, gypsum and anhydrite £14 million, iron ore £12 million and fluorspar £10 million.

Britain is a major world producer of several important industrial minerals including china clay, ball clay, fuller's earth and gypsum, and also produces significant amounts of limestone, dolomite, chalk, fluorspar, potash (produced at Boulby in Cleveland), salt, industrial sands, fireclay, common clay and shale, barytes, talc and celestite, mostly for home consumption. Small amounts of diatomite, slate, calcspar, chert and flint, anhydrite and china stone are also produced. In 1978 the production of metal from non-ferrous ores totalled 10,700 tonnes including 4,600 tonnes of lead-in-ore (mostly from northern England). Output of tin-in-ore, mostly from Cornwall, was 3,200 tonnes, supplying 26 per cent of Britain's tin requirements. Small amounts of copper, zinc and silver were produced in association with the tin. The South Crofty tin mine near Camborne is one of the largest tin mines in the world. Britain's only tungsten mine, near Penrith (Cumbria), was reopened in 1977 and its capacity increased in 1978.

Production of sand, gravel and crushed rock (from limestone, igneous rock and sandstone) as aggregates for use in construction constitutes over half of Britain's output of non-fuel minerals. Britain is the world's second largest producer of marine-dredged sand and gravel (15·8 million tonnes in 1978).

WATER

Britain's water resources are normally sufficient for domestic and industrial requirements. Supplies are obtained partly from surface sources such as mountain lakes, streams impounded in upland gathering grounds and river intakes (one-third comes from rivers), and partly from underground sources by means of wells, adits and boreholes. Water consumption in Britain continues to increase and in 1978 amounted to about 18·3 million cubic metres a day (mcmd), comprising 17·6 mcmd of potable (drinkable) water and 0·7 mcmd of non-potable water. Average daily consumption per head was 329 litres.

In general, householders pay for their domestic water supply, sewerage and sewage disposal services through charges based on the rateable value of their property, whereas industrial users are charged for their water supply according to actual metered consumption.

England and Wales

Responsibility for promoting a national policy for water in England and Wales rests with the Secretaries of State for the Environment and for Wales and the Minister of Agriculture, Fisheries and Food who, under the Water Act 1973, are charged with responsibility for securing the conservation, augmentation, distribution and proper use of water resources and the provision of water supplies; the provision of sewerage and sewage disposal services; the restoration and maintenance of the wholesomeness of rivers and other inland waters; the use of inland waters for navigation and recreation; the provision of land drainage; and the protection and development of fisheries.

National Water Council

The National Water Council advises and assists ministers and water authorities. It consists of a chairman appointed by the Secretaries of State, the chairmen of the water authorities, and ten other members with special relevant knowledge, of whom eight are appointed by the Secretaries of State and two by the Minister of Agriculture, Fisheries and Food.

SOME MINERALS PRODUCED IN BRITAIN

Iron ore
Non-ferrous ores

Celestite
Gypsum, anhydrite
Fluorspar
Salt

Fireclay
Ball clay, potters' clay
China clay
Fuller's earth

Limestone
Chalk

The maps above are based on county or regional boundaries and not those for geological outcrops.

Water Authorities Nine regional water authorities in England and the Welsh Water Authority in Wales are responsible for the management of water services; the development of water resources; water distribution and supply; the prevention of pollution (see p 185); sewerage and sewage treatment; river management; land drainage; sea defences; recreation; and freshwater fisheries. Each water authority has a membership consisting of a chairman and several members appointed by the Secretary of State for the Environment (or, in the case of the Welsh Authority, by the Secretary of State for Wales), a few members appointed by the Minister of Agriculture, Fisheries and Food (for the English authorities only) and a small majority of members appointed by the county and district councils within the area of the authority. District councils usually act as agents of water authorities for the design, construction, operation and maintenance of public sewers in their areas.

Statutory Water Companies There are 29 statutory water supply companies, accounting for about one-quarter of total supplies, operating under the Water Act 1973. Special arrangements govern the relationship of statutory water companies to the water authorities.

Supplies Some 12,678 million cubic metres of water were abstracted in England and Wales in 1978. Public water supplies, reaching over 99 per cent of the population, accounted for 5,709 million cubic metres. The Central Electricity Generating Board took 4,496 million cubic metres, primarily for cooling in connection with electricity generation, other industry 2,375 million cubic metres and the remainder was used in agriculture. Water authorities' estimated revenue for 1980–81 is some £1,671 million.

Water authorities have powers to restrict consumption when there are severe water shortages. Under the Drought Act 1976, passed in the driest period of weather since records began to be kept in 1727, they can limit or prohibit the use of water and, if necessary, restrict domestic water supplies.

Scotland In Scotland responsibility for public water supply, sewerage and sewage disposal rests with the nine regional and three islands councils. Additionally the Central Scotland Water Development Board, established under the Water (Scotland) Act 1967, is primarily responsible for developing large water sources and supplying water in bulk to its five constituent member authorities, the regional councils in Central Scotland.

Scotland has a relative abundance of unpolluted water from upland sources. Over 98 per cent of the population has a public water supply. About 840 million cubic metres of water were abstracted in Scotland in 1979 for public water supplies. The Secretary of State for Scotland is responsible for the promotion of the conservation of water resources and the provision by water authorities of adequate water supplies, and also has a duty to promote the cleanliness of rivers and other inland waters and the tidal waters of Scotland.

Northern Ireland The Water Service of the Northern Ireland Department of the Environment is responsible for water supply and sewerage in Northern Ireland. The Department is also responsible for the conservation, cleanliness and planned development of Northern Ireland's water resources. Northern Ireland has abundant potential supplies of water for both domestic and industrial use. About 150 million gallons (682 million litres) of water a day are supplied to over 90 per cent of the population.

**Development
Projects**

Investment is taking place in projects intended to ensure that there is an adequate water supply to meet the expected rise in demand. Among the new reservoirs being built is the Kielder Reservoir in Northumberland, which will be one of the largest man-made reservoirs in Europe when completed towards the end of 1980. In 1979–80 capital expenditure on water supply, sewerage and sewage disposal amounted to £452 million in England and Wales, £82 million in Scotland and £26 million in Northern Ireland.

Research

The central research organisation for the water industry in Britain is the Water Research Centre at Henley-on-Thames (Oxfordshire). The Centre's laboratory at Stevenage (Hertfordshire) is concerned with water pollution including sewage and industrial waste water treatment, sludge treatment and disposal, flow measurement, estuarine pollution and the development of analytical methods and quality monitoring systems. Its laboratory at Medmenham (Buckinghamshire) deals with water resources, water treatment, health aspects of water quality, distribution and operational research.

Other research is conducted by the Hydraulics Research Station of the Department of the Environment at Wallingford (Oxfordshire), which predicts the performance of hydraulic civil engineering works and their effects on the environment; the Institute of Hydrology of the Natural Environment Research Council (NERC) at Wallingford, which studies the whole hydrological cycle; the Meteorological Office, which is concerned with rainfall; and the Institute of Geological Sciences, also part of the NERC, which is concerned with water resources.

15 Agriculture, Fisheries and Forestry

AGRICULTURE

Although Britain is a densely populated, industrialised country relying on imports for nearly half its food supply, agriculture remains one of its most important industries. It occupies 648,000 people or 2.6 per cent of the total civilian working population, provides about 2·4 per cent of the gross domestic product, and uses nearly 19 million of the 24 million hectares (47 million of the 60 million acres) of land. Exports in and related to the agricultural sector (including machinery and fertilisers) in 1979 amounted to nearly £3,743 million.

THE LAND AND ITS USES

The soils of the country are varied (see p 4). Land used for farming is usually divided into that suitable for cultivation (crops and grass) and rough grazing. In hill country the area of cultivated land is often small, but is usually supplemented by grazing on a comparatively large area of hill land.

There are 12 million hectares (30 million acres) under crops and grass. Cultivated land, rough grazing, woodland and other land on agricultural holdings together represent 78 per cent of the land area. The rest is mountain and forest, or put to urban and kindred uses. The area available for farming is gradually decreasing to meet the needs of housing, industry and road transport; so far, the loss has been offset by the increase in productivity on the land being farmed.

Size and Ownership of Farms

There are about 257,000 farming units in Britain. About half are very small units, mostly farmed part-time, and accounting for 10 per cent of the industry's total output. Some 30,000 large farm businesses (capable of employing four or more full-time workers), accounting for a little over 10 per cent of the number of holdings, produce about half of the industry's total output. There are about 45,000 medium-sized (two or three workers) and some 50,000 small full-time farm businesses.

Amalgamation of small farms into larger, more viable units has been encouraged by successive governments. The average size of full-time holdings is about 113 hectares (279 acres) of crops and grass and rough grazings.

In Great Britain about 65 per cent of the farms, and in Northern Ireland almost all farms, are owner-occupied.

Types of Farming

British agriculture is characterised by the preponderance of livestock farming. Three-fifths of the full-time farms in Britain are devoted mainly to dairying or beef cattle and sheep; one in six is a cropping farm and the remainder specialise in pigs, poultry or horticulture, or are mixed farms. The farms devoted primarily to arable crops are found mainly in the eastern parts of England and Scotland. Large-scale potato and vegetable production is undertaken in the Fens (in south Lincolnshire and Cambridgeshire), the alluvial areas around the rivers Thames and Humber and the peaty lands in south Lancashire. Early potatoes are an important crop in south-west Wales and south-west England.

Elsewhere, horticultural crops are widely dispersed amongst agricultural crops.

Dairying occurs widely, but there are concentrations in south-west Scotland, the western parts of England and south-west Wales, where the wetter climate encourages the growth of good grass. Sheep and cattle are reared in the hill and moorland areas of Scotland, Wales and northern and south-western England. Beef fattening takes place partly in better grassland areas and partly in yards on arable farms.

In Northern Ireland dairying is the main occupation on 42 per cent of the full-time farms, while a further 37 per cent concentrate on beef and sheep production. The remainder specialise in other products or are mixed farms.

Mechanisation Britain has one of the heaviest tractor densities in the world, with 435,000 tractors in 1979, or one to every 16 hectares (39 acres) of arable land. Power-take-off implements characterise arable farming; and some 57,600 combine harvesters were in use in 1979. A wide variety of machines for harvesting and preservation of grass are employed. Milking machines are installed on all except the smallest farms.

Over 90 per cent of farms have an electricity supply and accompanying equipment. Through machinery syndicates farmers have the use of expensive equipment whose capital cost is shared among members.

HOME FOOD SUPPLIES Britain produces 55 per cent of its total food requirements. Some 70 per cent of the country's supplies of indigenous-type foods (that is, foods grown commercially in significant quantities) are home grown. Home production of the principal foods is shown as a percentage by weight of total supplies (that is, output plus imports less exports) in Table 21.

TABLE 21: British Production as a Percentage of Total Supplies

Food product	1968–70 average	1979 (provisional)
Meat	72	82
Eggs	100	101
Milk for human consumption (as liquid)	100	100
Cheese	44	69
Butter	12	42
Sugar (as refined)	33	45
Wheat	44	74
Potatoes for human consumption	91	90

Source: Ministry of Agriculture, Fisheries and Food

AGRICULTURAL PRODUCTION Britain has a long tradition of efficient farming based on technological progress and research. Modern farming methods were first pioneered as early as the eighteenth century. The rapid growth of productivity in recent years is due largely to advisory services based on research, much of which is undertaken by the Government.

The expansion in production and in yields per hectare over the last decade despite falling manpower is summarised in Table 22. There has been a substantial growth in the number of beef cattle and a less marked increase in the number of dairy cattle, sheep, and poultry. Total cereal production has increased by almost a third. Potato yields are highly dependent on weather conditions, but in the past decade yields have tended to rise, so that the crop has usually continued to supply over 90 per cent of home demand, despite the reduced area. Increases in output of meat and milk have been associated with higher consumption of feedingstuffs, mostly from home resources. In 1979 some 4·6 million tonnes of concentrated feeds were imported; the level of imports depends, however, on the size of the home crop of cereals.

The index of agricultural net product at constant prices (1975 = 100), rose from 99 in 1969 to an estimated 114 in 1979. (The relatively low level in 1975, the base year, was due to unfavourable weather; the indices for the years 1971–74 ranged between 111 and 114.)

Crops
Cereals

Wheat is grown mainly in eastern and southern England. About half the crop is normally used for flour milling, the remainder mainly for animal feed.

Since 1960 the area under barley has increased by about 75 per cent. In recent years, between 15 and 23 per cent of the crop has been used for malting and distilling; most of the remainder is used as feed for livestock.

The universal use of combine harvesters has necessitated the installation of drying and storage facilities on many farms. Such equipment is also often used on a co-operative basis.

Fodder Crops

There has been a decline in the area of traditional fodder crops since 1960 because farmers have been able to provide winter feed more economically by increased grass production and improved methods of conservation. Apart from grass, the main fodder crops are field beans, maize and kale, principally used to supplement grass, hay and silage for winter feeding.

Sugar

Sugar from home-grown sugar beet provides about 45 per cent of requirements and is grown under contract to the British Sugar Corporation Ltd. Most of the other sugar used in Britain is refined from raw sugar imported from developing countries under the Lomé Convention (see p 76).

Potatoes

Harvesting of early potatoes starts at the end of May, and of main-crop varieties usually in September. Seed potato production is chiefly centred in Scotland and Northern Ireland; a substantial quantity is exported.

Hops

Hops, grown for the brewing industry, occupy only about 6,000 hectares (15,000 acres) but have a very high yield per hectare and value by weight.

Grassland

The British climate suits grassland farming. Grass supplies about 80 per cent of feed requirements of cattle and sheep (in terms of energy); its production has been enhanced over recent years by the development and application of new techniques, notably the increased use of fertilisers, new methods of grazing control, improved herbage conservation for winter feed and irrigation. Rough grazings are used for extensively-grazed sheep and cattle, producing young animals for fattening elsewhere.

Livestock

A number of specialised breeds of livestock have been developed over the centuries in Britain. Substantial sales of animals and semen are made to overseas buyers to replenish and improve their herds and flocks. In recent years farmers have introduced and developed a number of breeds of cattle and sheep from elsewhere in Europe.

Artificial insemination plays an important part in cattle breeding, most of the dairy cattle in England and Wales and a significant proportion in Scotland and Northern Ireland being bred in this way.

TABLE 22: Manpower, Land Use, Produce and Livestock

Item and Unit	Average 1968–70	1977	1978	1979	1979 imperial units
Manpower in Agriculture ('000)[a]	780	661	664	648	
Land Use ('000 hectares)					
Total crop and fallow	4,946	4,863	4,932	4,976	12,297[c]
Grass (excluding rough grazings)	7,294	7,127	7,070	7,047	17,413[c]
Rough grazings	6,966	6,400	6,375	6,328	15,637[c]
Other land on agricultural holdings	168[b]	451	467	478	1,181[c]
TOTAL	19,374	18,840	18,846	18,829	46,528[c]
Main crops					
Wheat: area ('000 hectares)	940	1,076	1,257	1,371	3,388[c]
harvest ('000 tonnes)	3,690	5,274	6,613	7,140[j]	7,027[d]
yield (tonnes per hectare)	3·92	4·90	5·26	5·21[j]	2·07[e]
Barley: area ('000 hectares)	2,352	2,400	2,348	2,343	5,790[c]
harvest ('000 tonnes)	8,155	10,531	9,848	9,550[j]	9,399[d]
yield (tonnes per hectare)	3·47	4·39	4·19	4·08[j]	1·62[e]
Oats: area ('000 hectares)	380	195	180	136	336[c]
harvest ('000 tonnes)	1,249	790	706	535[j]	527[d]
yield (tonnes per hectare)	3·28	4·06	3·92	3·96[j]	1·57[e]
Potatoes: area ('000 hectares)	266	232	214	203	502[c]
harvest ('000 tonnes)	6,857	6,621	7,331	6,485[j]	6,383[d]
yield (tonnes per hectare)	25·80	28·50	34·20	32·30	12·70
Sugar area ('000 hectares)	178	200	204	214	529[c]
beet: harvest[f] ('000 hectares)	888	949	1,022	1,154	1,136
yield (tonnes per hectare)[g]	4·98	4·74	5·01	5·41	2·15
Livestock ('000 head)					
Cattle and calves	12,369	13,854	13,625	13,543	
Sheep and lambs	26,896	28,104	29,686	29,860	
Pigs	7,753	7,736	7,708	7,844	
Poultry	132,467	134,286	137,329	134,700	
Livestock Products					
Milk (million litres)	12,115	14,595	15,274	15,364	3,380[h]
Eggs (million dozen)	1,233	1,156	1,188	1,175	—
Beef and veal ('000 tonnes)	949	1,032	1,048	1,034	1,018[d]
Mutton and lamb ('000 tonnes)	233	229	238	235	231[d]
Pigmeat ('000 tonnes)	888	903	877	933	918[d]
Poultry meat ('000 tonnes)	559	716	726	757	745[d]

Source: *Annual Review of Agriculture 1980* and Agriculture Departments
[a] In addition, the following numbers of wives or husbands of farmers were engaged in farm work; 74,000 in 1977, 73,000 in 1978, and 72,000 in 1979 (the figure for 1968–70 is not available).
[b] Estimate
[c] '000 acres.   [d] '000 tons.   [e] Tons per acre.
[f] Amount of sugar produced.
[g] Sugar produced per hectare harvested
[h] Million gallons.   [j] Provisional figures.
Differences between totals and the sums of their constituent parts are due to rounding.

Dairy Farming   In England, Scotland and Wales about half of the milk produced goes for liquid consumption and the remainder for manufacture, but in Northern Ireland the greater part of the milk is used for manufactured products. Average consumption of liquid milk per head in 1979 by domestic households in Great Britain was estimated at about 2·56 litres (4·5 pints) a week. The level of British consumption of fresh milk is half as high again as the average in the European Community.

Average yields per dairy cow have increased during the last decade by about a quarter and were some 4,635 litres (1,020 gallons) in 1979. Freedom from tuberculosis has reduced herd wastage, and a campaign to eradicate brucellosis is well advanced. Milk production has been stimulated by advances in grass-land management, new methods of grass conservation and programmes of controlled use of concentrated feedingstuffs.

The average size of dairy herds in 1979 was some 49 cows a herd, the largest in the European Community.

Beef Cattle

About two-thirds of home-fed beef production derives from the national dairy herd, in which the Friesian breed is predominant. While pure-bred Friesians make a substantial contribution to Britain's beef supplies, many other dairy cows are crossed with beef bulls for beef production.

The hill and upland areas are important in the production of store cattle which are moved to lowland pastures for fattening.

Sheep

Britain has a long tradition of sheep production, with more than 40 breeds and many crosses between these breeds. Research has provided vaccine and sera protection against nearly all the epidemic diseases.

In hill areas, where winters are usually severe, hardy native breeds are used for the rearing of lambs. Most of the lambs are transferred each autumn to lowland farms for fattening, while some ewes are taken to farms at intermediate altitudes for mating with rams of a larger and more rapidly maturing breed; then, the cross-bred female progeny pass on to the milder lowland conditions, where they are often crossed again with Down rams for fat lamb production. The hill breeds bring in hardiness, and the lowland sires fecundity and early maturity. Lamb production is the main source of income for sheep farmers but wool is also important, especially in hill areas.

Pigs

Pig production is carried on in most areas but is particularly important in eastern and southern England, north-east Scotland and Northern Ireland. There is an increasing concentration into specialist units and larger herds. Artificial insemination is available nationally. About a third of the pigmeat is used for bacon, a third for pork and a third for processing into sausages, pies and other products.

Poultry

The poultry industry has expanded rapidly, aided by improved husbandry and management techniques in intensive production units and by genetic improvements in stock. Some 85 per cent of the laying birds on farms are in flocks of 5,000 or more, while about 74 per cent of the broilers are in flocks of 50,000 or more. The average yield of eggs per bird is about 245 a year. Nearly all eggs and poultry meat consumed in Britain are home-produced.

Horticultural Industry

The horticultural industry produces a wide variety of fruit, vegetables and flowers, which are worth about 10 per cent of the total value of agricultural output; in 1979 their value was estimated at £783 million.

In 1979 the land on which these crops were grown amounted to nearly 295,000 hectares (729,000 acres), about 2·3 per cent of the land used for crops and grass. Fruit accounted for about 59,000 hectares (146,000 acres), vegetables grown in the open, excluding potatoes, for about 222,000 hectares (548,000 acres) and flowers, bulbs and nursery stock for about 11,000 hectares (27,000 acres). Crops under glass, plastic and in sheds, including mushrooms, occupied about 4,000 hectares (10,000 acres).

Horticultural crops are largely grown on specialised holdings, but some, particularly vegetables for processing, are produced on arable farms. Most horticultural enterprises are increasing output per unit area with the help of improved planting material, new techniques of cultivation and environmental control, and the widespread use of machinery.

Field Vegetables

Field vegetables account for some 44 per cent of the horticultural output and are widely spread over the country, with the most intensive concentrations in the Thames Valley and the Vale of Evesham and extensive production in the eastern counties. Some 15 per cent are destined for processing.

Fruit

Dessert apples are the most important fruit crop. Britain is one of the few countries which grow varieties of apples especially suitable for cooking; these are produced in England and Northern Ireland. Some high-quality pears are produced in the east and south-east of England. Cherries and plums are grown in Kent, and plums also in the Vale of Evesham and parts of East Anglia. Around Perth in Scotland is the world's largest concentration of raspberry plantations.

Strawberries are the most widely grown soft fruit, with early production in the south and west of England. Blackcurrants are also widely grown, mainly for the manufacture of soft drinks and of flavouring for confectionery. Other fruits include gooseberries, red and white currants, loganberries and blackberries.

Glasshouse Crops

Much of the glasshouse sector of the horticultural industry has been re-equipped since the mid-1960s with the aid of government grants. Widespread use is made of units with automatic control of heating and ventilation, semi-automatic control of watering and carbon-dioxide enrichment of the atmosphere. Tomatoes are the most important crop, and, together with lettuce and cucumbers, represent some 95 per cent of the total value of glasshouse vegetable output. Mushrooms are grown in specially constructed sheds in most parts of Britain, with concentrations in south-eastern and northern England.

Other Crops

Flowers and bulbs grown in the open occupied some 4,000 hectares (9,88c acres) in June 1979, and hardy nursery stock some 7,000 hectares (17,30c acres).

MARKETING AND CO-OPERATION

Agricultural products are marketed mainly through private traders, but also through producers' co-operatives and marketing boards. The boards are essentially producers' organisations with certain statutory powers to regulate the marketing of particular products. A scheme to establish a marketing board must be approved by Parliament and (except in the case of Northern Ireland boards) by a majority of the producers concerned. Most of the members of each board are elected by registered producers and a small minority of independent members are appointed by Agricultural Ministers. Various safeguards exist to protect the public interest generally, including the interests of individual producers and consumers. Most marketing boards either buy from all registered producers or control all contracts between producers and first buyers. This applies to the marketing boards for milk, wool and hops. The Potato Marketing Board, on the other hand, maintains only a broad control over marketing conditions, leaving producers free to deal individually with buyers. The Milk Marketing Boards are formally recognised as part of the European Community milk regime.

For certain other commodities there are broadly based organisations representing producer, distributor and independent interests. The object of the

Home-Grown Cereals Authority is to improve the marketing of home-grown cereals. It provides a market intelligence service and promotes research and development. It also acts as agent for the Intervention Board for Agricultural Produce (see p 43) with regard to cereals and oilseed rape.

The Meat and Livestock Commission's range of functions includes the promotion and improvement of many activities concerning livestock and livestock products in Great Britain. In Northern Ireland, the Livestock Marketing Commission promotes better organisation, development and marketing in the livestock and livestock products industry. The Eggs Authority has the general duty of improving the marketing of eggs.

Under the Common Agricultural Policy of the European Community (see p 292) a wide range of horticultural produce (both home-grown and imported) is subject to common quality standards.

Co-operation

Agricultural co-operatives are concerned with marketing, production, services, and with supply of farmers' requirements. There are, in addition, machinery syndicates.

The Government provides grants for co-operative production and marketing of agricultural and horticultural produce on the recommendation of the Central Council for Agricultural and Horticultural Co-operation, a statutory body for promotion and development of co-operation among farmers and growers throughout Britain.

FARM EXPENDITURE AND EARNINGS

The aggregate net farming income in 1979 is estimated at £1,193 million (excluding stock appreciation). Of the total farm output, estimated at £7,975 million in 1979, about two-thirds was in the form of livestock and livestock products.

Feedingstuffs amount to approximately one-third of agriculture's total cost, and wages and machinery (including depreciation) to about one-fifth each. In recent years agricultural workers' earnings have risen in real terms but the labour force has continued to decline because of increased mechanisation and larger farms. Labour productivity (defined as gross product per person engaged in agriculture) rose by about 3·5 per cent a year on average between 1969 and 1979.

Capital Requirements

It is estimated that £388 million was invested in buildings and works in 1979 and £687 million in plant, machinery and vehicles. Most of the capital for investment is generated from within the farm business. Banks are the main source of short- and medium-term credit. Mortgage loans form the chief source of long-term credit and are provided by specialised financial institutions (see p 293) and private sources.

Net Incomes

In 1978–79 the average net income (excluding stock appreciation of breeding livestock) for different types of full-time farm in England and Wales varied from about £30 per hectare (£12 per acre) on hill and upland sheep farms with large areas of rough grazing to £170 per hectare (£69 per acre) on specialist dairy farms with the exception of pig and poultry farms and horticultural holdings which are typically more intensive in their use of land.

THE ROLE OF THE GOVERNMENT AND THE LAW

Responsibility for carrying out the Government's agricultural policy is vested in the Minister of Agriculture, Fisheries and Food in England; and the respective Secretaries of State in Scotland, Wales and Northern Ireland. The day-to-day work is carried out by the Ministry of Agriculture, Fisheries and

Food, the Department of Agriculture and Fisheries for Scotland, the Welsh Office Agriculture Department, and the Northern Ireland Department of Agriculture.

Market arrangements under the Common Agricultural Policy (CAP) of the European Community are administered by the Intervention Board for Agricultural Produce, which is responsible to the Agricultural Ministers.

Price Support

Under the CAP, producers' returns for most of the main commodities are supported by a combination of charges on imports from outside the Community and internal support prices which are maintained by intervention buying when necessary. In addition, export refunds enable Community exporters to sell on world markets when world prices are below Community price levels. There is also provision for certain direct payments to producers, including beef premiums. CAP support price levels, as well as rates of levy and subsidy, are set in European currency units (see p 77) and are converted into the currencies of the member States at fixed rates of exchange (commonly called 'green rates') which do not vary automatically in line with changes in real exchange rates. The green rates can thus be out of line with the market rate of exchange between each currency and the European Currency Unit, giving rise to different real support price levels in the different member States. Monetary compensatory amounts, based on the percentage difference between the green and market rates of each currency, are applied to prevent distortions in trade. They operate as import subsidies and export levies for countries whose currencies' market rates are below the green rates, and as import levies and export subsidies in the opposite case.

The level of support prices under the CAP is reviewed by the Community each year. The Government is seeking significant improvements in the operation of the CAP; it believes that support prices should be set at levels which do not produce unwanted surpluses but offer security to reasonably efficient producers. The storage and disposal of the surpluses adds significantly to the Community's budget expenditure. The Government would particularly like to see the removal of the major structural surpluses of dairy products and sugar.

The Community's agricultural expenditure is channelled through the European Agricultural Guidance and Guarantee Fund. The Fund's guarantee section is used to finance market support arrangements, while the guidance section finances expenditure on structural reform (for example contributions to capital and production grants—see p 293). The CAP absorbs over 70 per cent of the Community's budget; most of this is attributable to the cost of storage and disposal of agricultural surpluses, particularly milk products.

Price Guarantees

Sheep producers receive guarantee payments if average weekly market prices fall below guaranteed levels. For sheepmeat, however, agreement was reached in May 1980 on the establishment of a Community regime providing in effect for the continuation in Britain of a deficiency payments system with a guaranteed return to producers financed by the Community. The regime which comes into force in October 1980 also provides for an annual quota for New Zealand lamb of 234,000 tons and the halving of the tariff on such lamb.

For wool and (except in Northern Ireland) for potatoes, the Government operates the guarantees through the appropriate marketing boards. The Potato Marketing Board may, with government agreement, undertake support buying of any surplus, re-selling as much as possible for stockfeed. In

Northern Ireland, the potato guarantee is operated by the Department of Agriculture.

Other Grants and Subsidies

In addition to market support under the CAP and the British guaranteed prices, producers receive support through certain capital and production grants, some of them based on Community decisions. The grants include, for example, those paid under the Farm and Horticulture Development Scheme (towards the implementation of farmers' development plans) and under the Farm Capital Grant Scheme and Horticulture Capital Grant Scheme (towards the cost of capital investment).

There is also a Payments to Outgoers Scheme designed to assist in the improvement of farm structure and a Milk Non-Marketing and Conversion Scheme under which grants are available to farmers who cease production of milk for sale, with advantageous rates if they convert to beef or sheep production. Special financial assistance is available under Community and national arrangements for farmers in less favoured (hill) areas. Community assistance may also be made available for improvements to facilities for the marketing and processing of agricultural products. There are also grants for co-operatives.

Cost of Support

Expenditure in 1979–80 on price guarantees, grants and subsidies and on CAP market regulation is estimated at about £333 million and £406 million respectively. An estimated £430 million was reimbursed from the Community.

Consultative Machinery

Each year the agricultural ministers review the economic condition and prospects of the industry in consultation with representatives of producers (the farmers' unions). In addition, there is continuing consultation with the farmers' unions and other interested organisations on developments in the CAP.

The National Economic Development Council (see p 203) has a committee for agriculture, comprising representatives of farmers, workers and landowners, as well as official and independent members.

Agricultural Credit

In England and Wales, mortgage loans for the purchase or improvement of agricultural land and buildings are available from the Agricultural Mortgage Corporation Ltd, a company which has some government financial backing but raises its funds on the London capital market. The Scottish Agricultural Securities Corporation Ltd fulfils a similar role in Scotland.

In any part of Britain, the Agricultural Credit Corporation Ltd may provide guarantees for bank loans. The Corporation may receive government help if necessary.

Agricultural Development and Advisory Service

In England and Wales scientific, technological and management advice and services are available through the Agricultural Development and Advisory Service (ADAS) which also helps to identify problems requiring investigation and research, suggests priorities for such work, and, where appropriate, contributes to possible solutions. ADAS provides free impartial advice to landowners, farmers and growers, but charges are made for certain services.

In Scotland the advisory service is provided by the three regional independent colleges of agriculture financed almost entirely by public funds.

Advisory work in Northern Ireland is under the direction of the Department of Agriculture. The resources of the agricultural colleges, the research centres and the specialist divisions of the Department are available to the advisory service.

Smallholdings and Crofts

Local authorities provide about 8,200 smallholdings in England and about 1,000 in Wales. In England about 750 lettable holdings are provided by the Ministry of Agriculture, Fisheries and Food. The Minister and local authorities may make loans of up to 75 per cent of required working capital to their smallholding tenants.

Land settlement in Scotland has always been carried out by the Government, which owns and maintains about 163,000 hectares (403,000 acres) of land settlement estates, comprising some 2,700 crofts and holdings.

Crofting

Within the crofting areas of Scotland (situated in Strathclyde, Highland, Western Isles, Orkney Islands and Shetland Islands) much of the land is held by crofters, tenants whose holdings are generally either rented at a cost of not more than £100 a year or have an area not exceeding 30 hectares (75 acres). Crofting is administered by the Crofters Commission, and benefits from government grants for land improvement and some other agricultural work.

Tenancy Legislation

A code of landlord-tenant relationships has been written into legislation in order to protect the respective interests of landlords and tenants and to eliminate uncertainty as to their rights and obligations. Rent is a matter for negotiation between landlord and tenant and may be varied by agreement or, failing agreement, by arbitration.

Most agricultural tenants have the right to contest a notice to quit, which then becomes inoperative unless the landlord obtains consent to its operation from an independent body (in England and Wales the Agricultural Land Tribunal and in Scotland the Scottish Land Court).

On termination of tenancy, the tenant is entitled to compensation in accordance with a special code.

There are provisions for succession of a close relative on the death of a tenant.

Safety at Work

The Agricultural Inspectorate of the Health and Safety Executive (see p 341) is responsible for the enforcement of the Health and Safety at Work etc Act 1974 and regulations relating to the health and safety of workers in agriculture. The regulations cover such matters as the guarding of field and stationary machinery, work places, the fitting of safety cabs to tractors, and the use of chemicals.

Arterial Drainage and Sea Defence

Ten regional water authorities are responsible for land drainage (including flood prevention) in England and Wales. Most of the funds needed by water authorities are obtained from local authorities, but the Government pays grants towards the cost of improvement schemes. In some low-lying areas where there are special local problems of land drainage, internal drainage boards carry out work for the special benefit and protection of their districts. The boards finance their work from drainage rates levied on owners and occupiers, and from government grants payable on improvement works.

Local authorities in England and Wales also have general land drainage powers and may receive government grants towards the cost of improvements.

In Scotland local authorities deal with coast protection and urban land flood prevention, while arterial drainage and agricultural land flood prevention are the owners' responsibility. Grants are available to owners or occupiers of agricultural land who carry out arterial drainage work.

In Northern Ireland the Department of Agriculture is the drainage authority.

New Cars

The Rolls-Royce Silver Spirit, with a 6,750 cc V-8 engine, has a completely restyled body, modern and aerodynamically efficient. The glass area has been increased by 30 per cent. The car incorporates a unique fully-automatic split level air conditioning system.

BL's Mini Metro is produced in five models, three powered by a four-cylinder 998 cc engine and two by a 1,275 cc version. It has more interior space than other hatchbacks, many new safety features, and is shown by fuel test figures to be the most economical car in Europe.

Technological Research at Universities

The British Submerged Cylinder, a model of which is undergoing tests at the University of Bristol, is the latest device being developed by British engineers as part of a system to extract power from the sea.

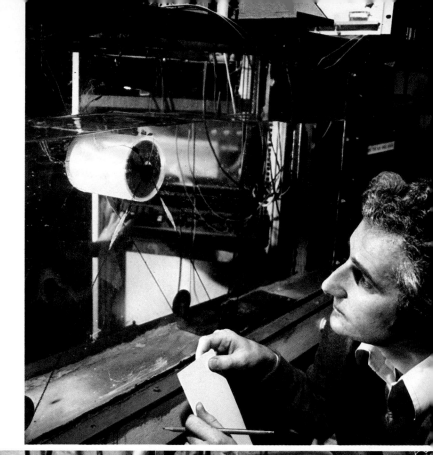

Researchers at the University of Newcastle have developed a diesel engine which reduces oil costs. An emulsifier is used to produce a mixture of water and oil which burns efficiently.

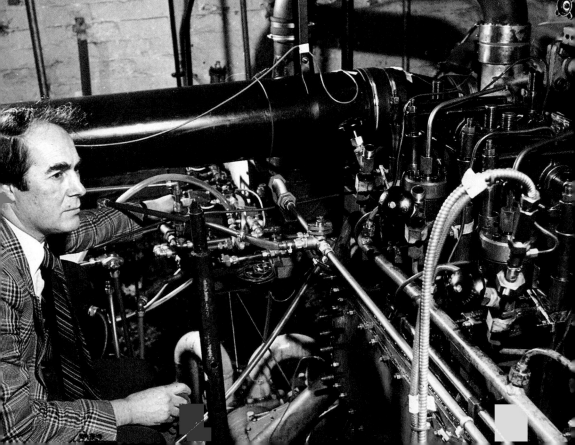

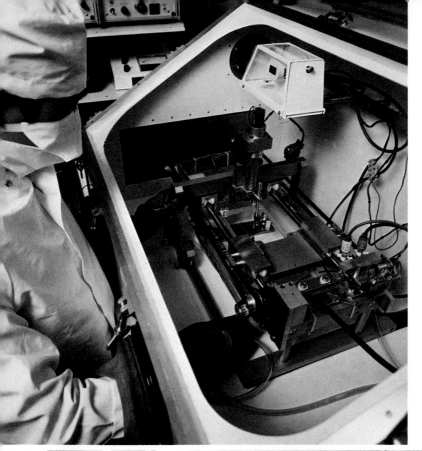

Scientists from the University of Durham have developed what is claimed to be the world's first 'organic transistor', more sensitive than traditional ones, using a product of coal-tar distillation.

The Department of Physics at the University of Lancaster has developed, for safer driving, a device called a self-oscillating mixer which can give drivers advance warning of stationary or slow moving vehicles ahead, to help to prevent collisions, especially in fog.

Aircraft

The Royal Air Force aerobatic team the 'Red Arrows'. The 'Hawk' aircraft, a ground-attack trainer, has a maximum speed of over Mach One at altitude.

The 'Optica', Britain's newest and most extraordinary aircraft, was designed to operate within the costs of a light aircraft yet provide the all-round characteristics of a helicopter.

**Animal
Welfare**

The Agriculture Ministers are responsible for government policy on the welfare of farm animals and livestock. It is an offence to cause unnecessary pain or distress to animals on the farm, and regulations provide, for example, for the daily inspection by the stock keeper of intensively farmed livestock and the equipment upon which they depend and for the control of certain operations such as the tail docking of cattle and pigs. Inspections by members of the State Veterinary Service (part of the Agricultural Development and Advisory Service) are carried out to monitor compliance with welfare provisions. Other regulations, enforced by local government authorities, make it an offence to cause injury or unnecessary suffering to farm animals in transit at markets.

The Farm Animal Welfare Council, set up in 1979, keeps under review the welfare of farm animals and those in transit, in pens and at markets and the place of slaughter, and advises the Agriculture Ministers in Great Britain. One of the objectives of the Advisory Committee on Animal Experiments, also set up in 1979, is the protection of animals against avoidable suffering.

**CONTROL OF
DISEASES AND
PESTS**

Animals

Responsibility for the Government's policy on animal health matters in Great Britain rests with the agricultural departments. Professional advice and action on the control of animal disease and the welfare of farm livestock is the responsibility of the State Veterinary Service. The day-to-day work of treating animal disease is the responsibility of the practising veterinary surgeon.

The Veterinary Service has extensive laboratory facilities, and there are 24 investigation centres in England and Wales, which perform work requiring specialist knowledge and give advice on disease problems to private practitioners. In Scotland the service is provided by three regional agricultural colleges.

Strict veterinary controls are exercised on the import of all animals, meat and meat products, live poultry and other captive birds, and poultry meat, so as to prevent the introduction of animal or poultry diseases.

Foot-and-mouth disease and swine fever have been eradicated by a slaughter policy applied to all infected animals and those exposed to infection. Swine vesicular disease is combated by a similar slaughter policy backed up by control of pig movements and of swill feeding. Rigorous measures have been taken to eradicate sheep scab which now appears to be under control. The incidence of bovine tuberculosis is now very low; cattle (except for certain categories) are tested at regular intervals, and reactors to the test are slaughtered; compensation is paid to the owners. Compulsory eradication of brucellosis on an area basis began in 1972. By March 1980 some 96 per cent of all herds in Great Britain were declared free of the disease, many areas being completely free. Newcastle disease (fowl pest) has declined to a low level because of a vaccination policy. As a result of these measures, Great Britain is free from many serious animal diseases. Non-farm animals are subject to import licence and six months' quarantine as a precaution against the introduction of rabies, and there are severe penalties for those breaking the law. There has been no case of rabies in Britain since 1970.

In Northern Ireland the legislation on the control of animal diseases is administered by the Department of Agriculture, which has its own veterinary service supplemented by a central veterinary laboratory. The Department's strict animal health control policies and the geographical situation have kept Northern Ireland free from the major animal diseases, including rabies and swine vesicular disease. A brucellosis eradication scheme has been successfully carried out and in 1971 Northern Ireland was declared brucellosis-free.

Plants
The plant health services, operated by the agricultural departments, are responsible for statutory controls designed to limit the spread of plant pests and diseases present in Britain and prevent the introduction of new ones from abroad. They also issue the health certificates required by other countries to accompany plant material imported from Britain. Certification schemes are operated to encourage the development of healthy, vigorous and true-to-type planting stocks. The Harpenden Laboratory in Hertfordshire, and the Agricultural Scientific Services Station, East Craigs, Edinburgh, provide advice on which these controls and schemes are based.

Pests and Storage
The central laboratories of the Agricultural Development and Advisory Service's Agricultural Science Service and the Agricultural Scientific Services of the Department of Agriculture and Fisheries for Scotland undertake research and provide advice on harmful mammals and birds and on insects, mites and moulds associated with grain and other stored food products.

Agricultural Chemicals
There are safeguards against the dangers which could arise from uncontrolled use of pesticides. Products must be cleared for safety under the Pesticides Safety Precautions Scheme (see p 184), and may be submitted through the Agricultural Chemicals Approval Scheme for efficacy approval.

Veterinary Medicinal Products
The Medicines Act 1968 provides through a system of licensing for the control of the manufacture, sale and supply of veterinary medicinal products. The licences are issued by the Agriculture Ministers, who are advised on safety, quality and efficacy by the Veterinary Products Committee. (For other provisions of the Act see p 137.)

RESEARCH AND DEVELOPMENT
An outline of the organisation of British agricultural research and development, including that carried out by the Agricultural Research Council and the universities, is given in chapter 20. The Ministry of Agriculture, Fisheries and Food carries out research and development at its own laboratories and on the 21 experimental husbandry farms and horticulture stations operated by the Agricultural Development and Advisory Service, and commissions work from the Agricultural Research Council, the Natural Environment Research Council and outside research organisations. The Department of Agriculture and Fisheries for Scotland carries out research and development at its own laboratories, and commissions the work of eight independent research organisations; the Department also commissions research and development work from the three colleges which provide the advisory service (see p 293). In England and Wales, research in agricultural economics is undertaken by 12 university departments of agricultural economics. In Scotland, agricultural economists are on the staff of the three regional agricultural colleges and the Department of Agriculture and Fisheries. At the University of Reading in England, the Centre for Agricultural Strategy provides an assessment of British agriculture with a view to developing long-term strategies.

In Northern Ireland the Department of Agriculture has eight research divisions concerned with the agricultural, veterinary and food sciences; their staff also teach at Queen's University, Belfast. Applied research also takes place at the three agricultural colleges.

Education and Training
Sixteen British universities provide degree and postgraduate courses in agriculture, horticulture, agricultural sciences or agricultural economics. The National College of Agricultural Engineering at Silsoe, Bedfordshire offers

degree and postgraduate courses. Sandwich courses leading to a Higher National Diploma are available at nine agricultural colleges in England and Wales and there are about 50 local authority and other agricultural colleges providing full-time and part-time courses on different aspects of agriculture, horticulture and related subjects. A centre for European agricultural studies is based at London University's Wye College at Ashford, Kent.

In Scotland the three agricultural colleges which have the advisory and development functions are also teaching establishments. They mainly provide sandwich courses leading to Higher and Ordinary National Diplomas, post-diploma courses and certain short courses, and are also associated with universities in the provision of degree-level education.

Local education authorities throughout Britain provide full-time and part-time courses for farmers, farm workers and horticulturists, as well as an advisory service for domestic producers.

In Great Britain the Agricultural Training Board provides a training advisory service, organises training courses and pays training grants. In Northern Ireland training courses are organised by the Department of Agriculture. Degree and postgraduate courses in veterinary medicine are provided at four universities in England and two universities in Scotland.

FISHERIES

With its long coastline and its maritime tradition, Britain is one of Europe's most important fishing nations. The fishing industry, which provides about 70 per cent of Britain's fish supplies, constitutes a small but important part of the national economy. Fishing is one of the main elements in the business of many major ports, and forms the basis of many communities around the coast.

The industry catches demersal fish (caught on or near the bottom of the sea), pelagic fish (caught nearer the surface) and shellfish. Demersal fish accounts for about 44 per cent (by weight) of the total catch, pelagic fish for over 48 per cent and shellfish for 8 per cent. The principal demersal fish (in terms of value) are cod, haddock, plaice and whiting. The most important pelagic species is mackerel. Shellfish include crustacea (such as lobsters and crabs) and molluscs (such as mussels and oysters).

Fishery Limits Since 1977 Britain's fishery limits have extended to 200 miles (or, where the distance between two countries' coasts is less than 400 miles, up to the line half-way between the two countries). This followed the European Community member States' agreement to adopt such limits jointly, after similar extensions, with resulting restrictions on Community vessels, had been announced by many maritime nations.

Community countries, and non-Community countries having temporary agreements with the Community, have the right to fish up to Britain's 12-mile limit. Designated Community countries may also fish in certain areas of Britain's 6 to 12 mile zone. The only non-Community country which may fish in this zone is Norway, which has very restricted rights in some areas off the Scottish coast. No foreign vessels may fish within Britain's 6-mile limit. All fishing within British fishery limits is subject to British conservation measures.

Common Fisheries Policy
External Regime

The Community has negotiated exchanges of fishing rights within member States' waters for reciprocal rights within the waters of several non-member countries. For 1980 reciprocal agreements were negotiated with Norway, the Faroe Islands, Sweden and Spain and non-reciprocal agreements with

Canada, Senegal and Guinea-Bissau. Quotas were also established in United States and international waters in the north-west Atlantic.

Internal Regime   With the extension of fishery limits to 200 miles, it became necessary to revise the Community fisheries' internal regime to allow for controlled Community fishing in the greatly extended area. Britain has a particularly strong interest in such control, since about 60 per cent of the total catch within the new limits is taken in British waters, while the loss of fishing opportunities in distant waters (such as Iceland) has reduced the British industry's total catch more than that of other Community States. As a result Britain is looking for adequate access arrangements and a fair share of the quotas proposed for the fish stocks around Britain's coasts and in other countries' waters. Community members aim to reach agreement on a revised common fisheries policy by the end of 1980.

There is also a need for effective and enforceable conservation measures within the waters of member States. The Government is continuing to work towards a common fisheries policy which meets these needs. However, in the absence of an agreed Community policy, it has introduced a number of conservation measures where these have proved necessary. In September 1980 a series of measures on fish conservation was agreed by Community fisheries ministers.

In January 1980 the Community reached agreement on total allowable catches for 1980 and on the introduction of a system for recording and reporting catches.

Marketing and Structural Policy   The Community's fishing industry is also subject to a common organisation of the market and to a common structural policy which has not yet been fully developed. The organisation of the market aims at assisting in the adaptation of supplies to marketing requirements, while ensuring, as far as possible, a reasonable return to producers, by means of the establishment of a grading and price system, and rules on competition. Provision is also made for the protection of the Community market against disruption by imports from non-member countries. The responsibility for market organisation is placed largely in the hands of the industry itself through producers' organisations. Intra-Community fish trade is tariff-free and there is a common external tariff.

The structural policy aims at promoting the rational development of the fishing industry and at ensuring an equitable standard of living for those dependent on fishing. In pursuit of these aims it envisages common measures for financing structural improvement, but to date little progress has been made towards agreeing these measures.

Fishing Ports   The principal fishing ports in England and Wales are Brixham, Falmouth, Fleetwood, Grimsby, Hull, Lowestoft, Milford Haven, Newlyn, North Shields and Plymouth. In Scotland the chief ports are Aberdeen, Ayr, Fraserburgh, Lerwick, Mallaig, Peterhead, Stornaway and Ullapool. In Northern Ireland the main fishing ports are Ardglass, Kilkeel and Portavogie.

Employment   In 1979 there were some 16,600 fishermen in regular employment and about 5,300 occasionally employed; about 46 per cent of the former and 23 per cent of the latter were based on Scottish ports. In Northern Ireland there are about 700 full-time fishermen and about 300 part-time. It is estimated that for every fisherman there are between three and five jobs in associated trades.

Fishing is an important source of employment and income in certain areas, in many of which unemployment is well above the national average. Maintenance of fishing opportunities, through conservation of stocks and through the preservation of British fishermen's access to their traditional grounds, is thus vital to Britain.

The Fishing Fleet

At the end of 1979 the deep-sea fleet comprised some 270 vessels; of these, distant-water trawlers, which operate mainly from Hull and Grimsby, numbered 58. They are about 43 metres (140 feet) and over in length and are of two types, the older, traditional side trawlers, which can only preserve their catches on ice, and modern stern freezer/factory trawlers (31 in number). Traditionally all have fished in the north-east Arctic and still do within the constraints of quota agreements which have reduced activity. Some side trawlers have been diverted to home waters hitherto fished by smaller vessels. Stern trawlers also fish the north-east Arctic but have recently been successful in mackerel fishing, mainly off south-west England. Middle-water trawlers between about 34 and 43 metres in length (110–140 feet) have also had to diversify their activity into northern North Sea grounds consequent upon reduced quota allocations off the Faroes. The inshore group consists of some 2,000 vessels of over 12 metres (40 feet) and about 5,000 smaller vessels.

Supplies

In 1979, landings of all types of fish (excluding salmon and trout) by British fishing vessels totalled 838,000 tonnes valued at £254 million. Cod accounted for 29 per cent of the total value of demersal and pelagic fish landed haddock (17 per cent), mackerel (17 per cent), and plaice (8 per cent) were the other most important sources of earnings to the industry.

Increasing attention is being paid to fish and shellfish farming and the farming of some species of sea fish is being developed.

Experiments are being carried out in the catching and processing, for human consumption and fish meal (for animal feed), of previously under-exploited species of fish (for example, blue whiting and horse mackerel) of which large stocks are known to exist in the sea adjacent to the British Isles.

In 1980, the Government provided over £1·4 million to help to finance exploratory voyages aimed at assessing the commercial potential of under-exploited fish stocks and methods of fishing.

Home production of fish meal in 1979 was about 50,000 tonnes. Fish oil production was about 10,000 tonnes.

Imports of all fresh, frozen, cured and canned fish and shellfish totalled 311,000 tonnes valued at £318 million. Imports of fish meal amounted to 255,000 tonnes, worth £55 million, and those of fish oils to 215,000 tonnes, worth £48 million. Exports and re-exports of fish and fish products amounted to 442,000 tonnes and were valued at just under £152 million.

Total fish consumption was running at a level of approximately 6·7 kg a head in 1979. Home production provided about 70 per cent of supplies.

Freshwater Fisheries

The most valuable freshwater fish are salmon and sea-trout. Sea fishing for salmon is prohibited in a wide area around the British Isles outside the 12-mile zone. Within the zone, drift netting and certain other methods are prohibited off the coast of Scotland but are permitted under licence off England, Wales and Northern Ireland. In Scotland, salmon fishing is a private right. In England and Wales, water authority licences are required for coastal and estuary netting. The landed value of the salmon catch in 1979 was approximately £2 million in England and Wales, about £5·3 million in Scotland, and some £419,000 in Northern Ireland. Eels worth about £1·5 million were caught in Northern Ireland.

Distribution System

Fish is distributed through wholesalers located at the ports, who buy fish at quayside auctions and sell to inland wholesalers or retailers, and through processors who also buy at auctions and sometimes under contract arrangements with the owners of fishing vessels, particularly for fish frozen at sea.

Promotion and Regulation of the Industry

The government departments mainly responsible for the administration of legislation concerning the fishing industry and for fisheries research are the Ministry of Agriculture, Fisheries and Food, the Department of Agriculture and Fisheries for Scotland, the Welsh Office Agriculture Department and the Department of Agriculture for Northern Ireland. The safety and welfare of crews of fishing vessels and other matters common to shipping generally are provided for under the Merchant Shipping Acts administered by the Department of Trade.

The White Fish Authority administers grant and loan schemes providing financial assistance to the white fish industry. Financial aid is available for the purchase of new fishing vessels, vessel improvements, the provision and improvement of processing plants, cold stores and ice plants and towards the formation of fishermen's co-operatives. The Authority's other functions include research and development, training, dissemination of information, publicity and promotion and the provision of consultancy services including those to developing countries. The Herring Industry Board administers similar grant and loan schemes providing assistance for the industry towards the purchase of new, and the improvement of existing, vessels. The Authority and the Board have a joint administration. It is proposed that the two bodies be replaced by a single one.

The Department of Agriculture for Northern Ireland operates grant and loan schemes for the purchasing of new fishing vessels and engines and the improvement of existing vessels, and for processors, co-operatives and fish farmers.

In 1980, because of increased operating costs, falling prices and the absence of an agreed Community common fisheries policy, the Government gave £33 million in aid to the fishing industry.

FORESTRY

The estimated total area of woodland in Britain is 2·1 million hectares (5·2 million acres), or about 9 per cent of the total land area; 43 per cent of the area is in England, 43 per cent in Scotland, 11 per cent in Wales and the remainder in Northern Ireland.

The area of productive forest in Great Britain managed by the Forestry Commission, at 884,000 hectares (2·2 million acres), constitutes 51 per cent of this category. The annual rate of productive forest expansion is currently 11,800 hectares (29,150 acres) by the Commission mainly in Scotland, and some 8,100 hectares (20,000 acres) by private woodland owners. The Commission's programme includes considerable planting in upland areas, and consists mainly of conifers because of the difficult site conditions encountered.

Total employment in state and private forests in Great Britain was estimated at 19,000 in 1979.

Except for the periods of the two world wars, when felling was abnormally heavy, home woodlands have until recent years made only a limited contribution to the nation's consumption of wood and wood products, as less than half of the Commission's woodlands are yet in production. Britain imports 91 per cent of its needs, the total import cost of wood and wood products, including pulp and paper, being over £2,800 million in 1979. Roundwood removals in 1979 amounted to 4 million cubic metres.

The Forestry Commission and Forestry Policy

The Forestry Commission is the national forestry authority charged with promoting the interests of forestry, the development of afforestation and the production and supply of timber in Great Britain. The Commissioners comply with directions given by the forestry ministers, who are the Minister of Agriculture, Fisheries and Food and the Secretaries of State for Scotland and Wales. Northern Ireland has its own separate organisation (see below). In pursuing its main objective, timber production, Great Britain's forestry policy also takes into account amenity, environmental and employment criteria. Thus the Commission's activities include wildlife conservation, the landscaping of plantations, and the provision of facilities for recreation. The Commission has also encouraged the setting up of some 20 major new timber-using industries.

Finance

The Forestry Commission is financed partly by the State and partly by receipts from sales of produce, rentals and other sources. Income from timber is expected to increase as production doubles in the next 20 years, probably leading to a reduction in its grant-in-aid.

Private Forestry

Privately owned woods comprise 56 per cent of the total forest area in Great Britain. About half of the private woodland area is in ownerships of under 100 hectares (250 acres) in extent.

The effective management of private woodlands is encouraged by the provision of grants administered by the Forestry Commission, in return for which owners accept a continuing obligation to manage their woodlands in accordance with sound forestry practice.

Forestry Education and Research

Degree courses in forestry and associated studies are provided at three universities and there are supervisory, craft and managerial level courses.

The Forestry Training Council, set up by the Forestry Commission, assists the development of systematic training and the co-ordination of training in the state and private sectors.

The Furniture and Timber Industry Training Board is concerned with training for private-sector employees in the home timber trade.

Forestry research is carried out by the Forestry Commission, universities and other institutions.

Forestry in Northern Ireland

The Department of Agriculture is the forest authority for Northern Ireland. The Department may acquire land for afforestation and give financial and technical assistance for private planting. It has introduced measures to control felling, fires near plantations and damage by certain animals. Financial provision is made annually by Parliament.

The state forest area has grown steadily since the end of the second world war. By 1980 70,000 hectares (168,000 acres) of plantable land had been acquired, of which 53,000 hectares (130,000 acres) were planted. There were about 13,000 hectares (32,000 acres) of privately owned forest.

Some 1,200 people worked in state and private forests in 1980; of these, about 600 were employed under the Urban and Rural Improvement Campaign for developing recreational facilities, mostly in state forests.

16 Transport and Communications

The application of technological developments to Britain's transport and communications network is helping to make travel quicker and more convenient. Major improvements in the movement of passengers and freight have resulted from the construction of a network of motorways, the extension of fast inter-city rail services (such as those operated by high speed trains), the modernisation of many ports, the increased use of containers and other modern methods in shipping, the use by airlines of larger or speedier aircraft (such as the Concorde supersonic aircraft) and expansion schemes at many airports.

Transport and communications contribute 8 per cent of gross national product and are responsible for a rather higher proportion of gross domestic fixed capital formation. They employed some 1·5 million people in Great Britain in December 1979 and accounted for 7 per cent of the employed labour force. Of these, 205,300 employees were engaged in road passenger transport, 221,000 in road haulage, 204,400 in railways, 429,000 in postal services and telecommunications, 148,500 in sea transport, port and inland water transport, 91,300 in air transport and 173,100 in other transport services and storage.

INLAND TRANSPORT

Passenger and freight traffic is carried mainly by road. At the end of 1979 there were 18·6 million vehicles licensed for use on the roads of Great Britain, 3·9 per cent more than a year earlier. Of these 14·6 million were motor cars, 1·8 million road goods vehicles, 1·3 million motor cycles, scooters and mopeds, and 111,000 public road passenger vehicles (including taxis). Private ownership of cars has been growing rapidly for many years and the car is the most popular form of travel. Buses and coaches account for about 11 per cent of passenger mileage within Great Britain, rail for 7 per cent and air 0·5 per cent. Road haulage has a dominant position in the movement of inland freight, accounting for about 85 per cent of tonnage carried and for some three-quarters of tonne-kilometres. Railways and, to a lesser extent, pipelines and inland waterways are important in carrying certain types of freight, particularly bulk goods. The railways and much of the bus industry are publicly owned, but road haulage is almost entirely in the hands of private enterprise.

Transport policy rests on the fundamental aims of helping economic growth and higher national prosperity, and ensuring a reasonable level of personal mobility, while improving safety, particularly on the roads, minimising damage to the environment and taking account of energy considerations. Britain is taking an active part in the development of a common transport policy by the European Community.

ROADS

Motor vehicle traffic in Great Britain rose in 1979 by 0·6 per cent to a record 275,800 million vehicle-kilometres, of which cars and taxis accounted for 80 per cent. Improvements are continually being made in the network of trunk roads (which form a basic network linking major centres of population, industrial areas and ports) to accommodate the growth in traffic. A number of motorways (roads specially designed for high speed traffic) have been built, while other improvements, such as the construction of by-passes, have helped to make travelling easier and faster, particularly over long distances and between cities. Congestion on inter-urban roads has been reduced or eliminated and many towns and villages have been relieved of heavy through traffic. Although motorways account for less than 1 per cent of road mileage, they carry 10 per cent of traffic including over one-fifth of heavy goods vehicle traffic. In 1979 the road network totalled 224,567 miles (361,406 kilometres), of which some 1,611 miles (2,593 kilometres) were motorways. Motorways and other major roads are shown on the map at the end of the book.

TABLE 23: Road Mileage

	Public roads[a]	Trunk roads[a] (including motorways)	Trunk motorways[b]	
			in use[c]	under construction
England	160,113	6,177	1,339	55
Scotland	30,505	1,971	128	5
Wales	19,400	1,067	59	16
Northern Ireland	14,549	398	68	2
Britain	224,567	9,613	1,594	78

Sources: *Department of Transport, Northern Ireland Department of the Environment, Scottish Development Department and Welsh Office*
[a] As at April 1979.
[b] As at April 1980.
[c] In addition, there were 61 miles (98 kilometres) of local authority motorway in use in England and 13 miles (21 kilometres) in Scotland.

The main aims of the Government's programme to improve trunk roads are to meet the needs of industry and to keep heavy lorry traffic away from towns and villages. In England the main priorities are the M25 London orbital route and certain routes to serve industry and the major ports. In Wales the priorities are to complete the M4 motorway across south Wales, reconstruct the coast road in north Wales and improve roads which are important for industrial redevelopment. Most of the remaining links in the motorway/dual carriageway network in central Scotland have been completed. Accordingly, the programme is being directed mainly to the improvement of other strategic routes, particularly those in the north and north-east which are important for North Sea oil-related activities and some of the west-coast routes. In Northern Ireland the emphasis is on building new links to the motorway network, constructing more by-passes, and improving roads in the Belfast area and other urban areas. Priority for new roads in urban areas of Great Britain is being given to those designed to meet the needs of industry and commerce, serve new industrial or housing estates, provide links to the national trunk road network or to complement traffic management schemes.

Bridges and Tunnels

The suspension bridges across the Firth of Forth and the Severn Estuary, completed in the mid-1960s, both incorporated major advances in suspension bridge design. Their main spans are among the longest suspension bridge spans, but the bridge being built across the river Humber and due to be opened early in 1981 will have a span of 1,410 metres (4,626 feet), longer than any existing bridge span in the world. Other major bridges planned include a second bridge across the river Foyle at Londonderry, which is due to be completed by the end of 1983, and a bridge to carry the Ipswich by-pass across the river Orwell.

A few road tunnels have been built to cross major estuaries, notably the Mersey, the Thames, the Tyne and the Clyde. A second crossing of the Thames at Dartford (Kent) was opened in May 1980.

Administration Responsibility for trunk motorways and other trunk roads in Great Britain rests in England with the Minister of Transport, in Scotland with the Secretary of State for Scotland and in Wales with the Secretary of State for Wales. The costs of construction, improvement and maintenance are paid for by central Government. Work on major trunk road and motorway schemes in England is controlled by regional road construction units which include staff from the Department of Transport and county councils. The highway authority for non-trunk roads in England and Wales is, in general, the county council in whose area the roads lie, and in Scotland the regional or islands council. The Government is in the process of transferring to local authorities the responsibility for those trunk roads which have lost their importance as major through routes following the completion of nearby motorways.

In Northern Ireland the Northern Ireland Department of the Environment is responsible for public roads and their maintenance and construction.

Road Safety Great Britain's accident record is considerably better than that of most other countries even though it has one of the highest densities of road traffic in the world. In 1979, 6,300 people were killed on the roads, about 80,300 seriously injured and 247,100 slightly injured. A comprehensive framework of legislation embodied in the Road Traffic Acts and summarised in the *Highway Code* (which sets out the standard of conduct for road users) has contributed to the decline in casualty rates. Other factors have been modern roads, designed for present-day traffic and segregating vehicles from pedestrians, and campaigns conducted nationally by government departments and the Royal Society for the Prevention of Accidents and locally by local authorities to persuade people to take greater care on the roads. In recent years major publicity campaigns have been undertaken to increase the wearing of seat belts, to reduce casualties to child pedestrians and to riders of motor cycles, and to reduce the incidence of drinking and driving.

Comprehensive regulations govern the design of vehicles, their use on the roads, and the maintenance of their mechanical condition. Under a national 'type approval' scheme, all new cars must be of a type that has been certified as meeting the required standards. In Great Britain private cars and light vans which are three or more years old must be tested annually at private garages authorised as test stations. (In Northern Ireland private cars seven or more years old are tested at official vehicle inspection centres.) Heavy goods vehicles are tested annually at government test stations. Public service vehicles must be specially approved before being licensed to carry passengers, and are tested at regular intervals. Any vehicle may be stopped on the road at any time by the police and examined.

Minimum ages are laid down for driving: 16 for driving invalid carriages and mopeds; 17 for cars and other passenger vehicles with nine or fewer seats (including that of the driver), motorcycles and goods vehicles not over 3·5 tonnes maximum permissible weight; 18 for goods vehicles over 3·5 but not over 7·5 tonnes; and 21 for passenger vehicles with over nine seats and goods vehicles over 7·5 tonnes. All drivers of motor vehicles are required to pass the driving test before being granted a full licence to drive. Until they pass the test they must hold a 'provisional' licence, display 'L' (learner) plates on their vehicle and be accompanied while driving (with certain exceptions) by a qualified driver. In Northern Ireland a driver having passed the test is required to display an 'R' (restricted) plate for a one-year period during which he must not exceed 45 mph (72 km/h). There are schemes for special licensing and testing of drivers of heavy goods vehicles and public service vehicles.

Speed limits also contribute to road safety. There are national limits of 70 mph (113 km/h) on motorways and other dual carriageway roads, and 60 mph (97 km/h) on single carriageway roads, while in built-up areas a general limit of 30 mph (48 km/h) applies. To meet local needs the urban limit can be raised and the other limits lowered on specific stretches of road. A wide range of other measures directed primarily towards road safety include legislation and publicity to discourage drinking and driving (including a maximum permissible blood alcohol level for drivers of 80 milligrams of alcohol per 100 millilitres of blood), computer-controlled warning signals on most busy motorways to inform motorists of advisory speed limits in adverse conditions and of lane closures, and regulations governing the carriage of dangerous goods by road. The Government is proceeding with new measures designed to improve the safety of motorcycle riders and strengthen the law on drinking and driving. It has also undertaken a review of traffic law to consider the merits of replacing the totting-up procedure for driving offences by a points system varying according to the severity of the offence, and of extending and improving the fixed penalty system for minor traffic offences with the aim of reducing the burden on the police and the courts.

Traffic in Towns

Traffic in the centres of cities and towns in Britain is being managed so as to minimise congestion and its environmental effects, and to improve road safety. Local authorities have powers to introduce a range of measures which, when combined, form comprehensive traffic management schemes covering a particular area. Such schemes may include one-way systems, streets reserved for pedestrians, bus priority measures, parking controls and limited road construction. In most town centres parking is restricted and waiting limits apply. Major city centres often have controlled parking zones, where payment is required for on-street parking.

Several cities have new shopping precincts, some of them enclosed, which are specially designed for pedestrians and from which motor vehicles are excluded. In the centres of many towns, areas containing several streets have been wholly or partly converted to pedestrian use, and this has resulted in a more attractive environment.

Urban traffic control systems, which link traffic signals and some traffic signs to a central computer, represent an important addition to local authorities' ability to control traffic. A new method for large towns and cities of continuously adapting traffic signal response to the flow of traffic is being tested in Coventry, while a compact form of urban traffic control, sponsored by the Department of Transport and suitable for use in much smaller towns, is operating in Torbay and Hull.

Research

Research into all aspects of road construction, traffic engineering and safety, and into problems associated with transport is carried out by the Transport and Road Research Laboratory (TRRL), jointly responsible to the Department of Transport and the Department of the Environment. The TRRL provides technical and scientific advice and information to help in formulating, developing and implementing government policies relating to roads and transport, including their interaction with urban and regional planning. It employs nearly 850 people of whom about half are scientists and engineers.

ROAD HAULAGE Road haulage traffic in terms of tonne-kilometres has increased substantially and reached a record 104,600 million tonne-kilometres in 1979. Actual goods vehicle traffic has, however, grown much less because of a move towards larger and more efficient vehicles carrying heavier loads—over three-fifths of the traffic, in terms of tonne-kilometres, is carried in vehicles of over 28 tonnes gross laden weight. Much of the traffic is moved over short distances, with more than three-fifths of the tonnage being carried on hauls of 50 kilometres (31 miles) or less. Public haulage (private road hauliers carrying other firms' goods) accounts for 61 per cent of freight carried in Great Britain in terms of tonne-kilometres. The growth in road haulage has been concentrated on long-distance traffic, particularly international road haulage, and British hauliers are increasingly running goods vehicles to the rest of Europe. An independent inquiry, set up by the Minister of Transport, has been considering the growth in road haulage, especially its impact on people and the environment, and the best way of ensuring that future developments meet the public interest.

Structure of the Industry

Road haulage is predominantly an industry of small, privately owned businesses. Many of the 125,500 holders of an operator's licence in 1979 had only one vehicle and the average size of a vehicle fleet is only about four. The biggest operator in Great Britain is the National Freight Corporation (NFC). Turnover of the NFC's freight transport subsidiaries amounted to £417 million in 1979 and at the end of 1979 it owned or leased 18,400 vehicles, 11,200 additional trailers and 5,100 containers and demountable bodies. Under the Transport Act 1980 the status of the NFC has been changed from a publicly owned company into a company with shares. The Government intends to offer a majority of shares for sale to private investors. In Northern Ireland the biggest operator is Northern Ireland Carriers Ltd, owned jointly by the Northern Ireland Transport Holding Company and the NFC.

Licensing and Other Controls

Those operating goods vehicles of over 3·5 tonnes gross weight (with certain special exemptions) require an operator's licence, obtained on showing good repute and ability to maintain vehicles properly and control loading and drivers' hours. Licences are divided into restricted licences for firms carrying their own goods and standard licences, sub-divided into 'national only' and 'international', for hauliers operating for hire or reward. Proof of professional competence is required to obtain a standard licence.

Regulations control the emission of smoke and noise by lorries and the carriage of dangerous goods by road. There are limits on the hours worked by drivers of goods vehicles, and there are also minimum rest periods. The European Community regulation requiring the use of the tachograph (a device which automatically records a vehicle's speed and distance covered, driving time and stopping periods) in most goods vehicles over 3·5 tonnes gross weight in Great Britain is due to be phased in by December 1981. International road haulage is governed mainly by bilateral agreements, which are in force with 25 other European countries. These allow British road hauliers to carry goods to or through these countries. In some cases permits are required and these are usually limited to a quota negotiated annually. The demand for permits by

British road hauliers has been growing rapidly and for 1980 the Government negotiated substantial increases in the quotas with many countries.

PASSENGER SERVICES

Bus and urban railway services in Britain are provided mainly by publicly owned operators, coach services partly by publicly owned bodies, and taxis and hire cars almost entirely by privately owned businesses.

Buses and Coaches

In the public sector in Great Britain 22,000 vehicles are operated by the National Bus Company and the Scottish Transport Group, 11,000 by the seven passenger transport executives (responsible for the day-to-day management and operations of local transport in Greater Glasgow and the metropolitan counties of Greater Manchester, Merseyside, West Midlands, Tyne and Wear, South Yorkshire and West Yorkshire), 6,500 by the London Transport Executive and 6,000 by other local authority undertakings. There are some 5,600 privately owned undertakings (of which the majority have fewer than five vehicles) comprising about 28,500 vehicles; only a small proportion of these operators are concerned with scheduled bus services. Double-deck buses are an important feature of urban passenger transport in Britain and there are nearly 27,000 in operation. In addition, there are 47,000 single-deck buses and coaches, and nearly 100 trams (at Blackpool and Llandudno which have Britain's only remaining tramway systems).

The National Bus Company operates in England and Wales through locally based subsidiaries, such as the Western National Omnibus Company, Ribble Motor Services Ltd and Crosville Motor Services Ltd, and has a network of long-distance coach services. At the end of 1979 it owned some 17,500 vehicles and employed 63,400 people. In 1979 passenger journeys on the Company's buses amounted to 1,778 million, gross revenue was £498 million and the Company had a net surplus of £6.2 million.

The Scottish Transport Group (with about 3,800 vehicles) operates the main bus services in Scotland outside the major cities and also runs ferries to the islands off the west coast of Scotland.

In Northern Ireland almost all road passenger services are provided by subsidiaries of the Northern Ireland Transport Holding Company. Citybus Ltd operates services in the city of Belfast and Ulsterbus Ltd operates most of the services in the rest of Northern Ireland. These companies have 400 and 1,050 vehicles respectively.

Services

There has been a long-term decline in the use of bus and coach services (except in the area of contract and private hire), due primarily to the growth in ownership of private cars, and in 1978 some 7,305 million passenger road journeys were made in Great Britain, 29 per cent fewer than in 1968. Bus operators have taken action to contain costs and to improve productivity by introducing larger buses, increasing the proportion of bus services operated by one man and reducing or rationalising services. Many uneconomic bus services have been withdrawn, particularly in the rural areas. However, in some rural areas new 'postbus' services (Post Office minibuses carrying mail and passengers) or community-run minibus services have been introduced.

The Transport Act 1980 contains the biggest series of reforms in road passenger transport for 50 years and one of its aims is the encouragement of new types of service, especially in rural areas. It provides for fundamental changes in the road services licensing system, under which traffic commissioners are responsible for licensing public road passenger services. There are 11 traffic areas in Great Britain, each under the jurisdiction of an independent body of three commissioners. The Act provides for the removal of restrictions on operating long-distance express coach services and on excursions and tours, allowing free competition between operators. For those local services which remain subject to the commissioners' jurisdiction, the commissioners now grant an application for a licence unless satisfied that to do so would be against the public interest, thus making it easier for a new operator to start services. Restrictions on advertising car-sharing schemes have also been removed. Local authorities have been given the power to carry fare-paying adults on school buses where there is spare capacity. The Minister of Transport intends to designate a number of trial areas where no road service licences will be required and a minimum of restrictions will apply. A new system of safety and quality control will come into force early in 1981 involving the replacement of the present system of licensing each public service vehicle by a system of operator licensing, which will be administered by the traffic commissioners.

Taxis

There are about 37,000 taxicabs in Great Britain, mainly in urban areas, especially London where some 12,500 taxicabs that ply for hire in the streets are privately operated by companies or owner-drivers and are licensed annually by the Metropolitan Police. There are about 17,000 licensed cab drivers in London. Numerous car-hire firms are also in operation. Elsewhere taxis are licensed by local authorities. In Northern Ireland all taxis are licensed by the Northern Ireland Department of the Environment.

Urban Railways

There are underground railway services in three British cities: London, Glasgow and Liverpool. London Transport has 4,228 railway cars and serves 279 stations, while its trains operate over 260 miles (418 kilometres) of railway, of which about 100 miles (161 kilometres) are underground.

Urban rail projects are proceeding in several areas. A light rapid transit system under construction on Tyneside involves the electrification of two suburban railway lines, linked by new tunnels under Newcastle upon Tyne and Gateshead, and a new bridge over the Tyne. The first section was opened in August 1980 and the remainder of the system, which will eventually be 34 miles (55 kilometres) long with over 40 stations, will be brought into operation during the 1980s. The project is the largest provincial urban transport scheme to have been undertaken in Britain in the twentieth century. In Glasgow, as part of the 'Trans-Clyde' integrated public transport system, the Underground has been completely modernised and was reopened in April 1980, and a new rail link, the Argyle line, has been built. Recent additions to the London Underground were the extension of the Piccadilly line to Heathrow Airport in 1977, enabling passengers to travel directly between Heathrow and central London by the Underground; and the opening in 1979 of the Jubilee line, linking north-west and central London.

RAILWAYS

Railways were pioneered in Britain, and the Stockton and Darlington Railway, opened in 1825, was the first passenger public railway in the world to be worked by steam power. Under the Transport Act 1947 the four large railway companies in Great Britain were brought under public ownership and in 1963 the British Railways Board was set up to manage railway affairs and subsidiary activities. In Northern Ireland the Northern Ireland Railways Company Ltd, a subsidiary of the Northern Ireland Transport Holding Company, operates the railway service on 200 miles (322 kilometres) of track.

A high rate of progress in railway development has been maintained in recent years, notably on the inter-city passenger network where the introduction of faster trains, together with the raising of standards of track and signalling, has brought significant reductions in journey time on many routes. Inter-city rail services in Great Britain are among the best in the world in speed, frequency and comfort. Two major projects, the High Speed Train (HST) and the Advanced Passenger Train (APT), have been designed to raise speeds using existing track. A continuing important role is envisaged for the railways in Britain's transport system, especially in the provision of long-distance passenger transport, commuter services and essential local services, and in the movement of bulk freight.

Operations

British Rail's operating statistics are shown in Table 24. In 1979 the Board's turnover, including financial support and income from other activities but excluding internal transactions, was £2,306 million. It achieved a trading surplus of £62·3 million, although there was a net deficit of £0·4 million. Financial support for British Rail includes compensation for the financial burden of operating the rail passenger system as a public service and grants for level crossings. In 1979 the British Railways Board received £530 million from the Government and the passenger transport executives in respect of the public service obligation. At the end of 1979 the British Railways Board employed 244,100 people, of whom 182,000 were engaged on the railways.

TABLE 24: Railway Statistics

	1974	1977	1978	1979
Passenger journeys (*million*)	733	702	724	736
Passenger-miles (*million*)	19,200	18,200	19,100	19,900
Freight train traffic (*million tonnes*)	177	170	171	171
Freight train traffic (*million net tonne-miles*)	13,673	12,501	12,416	12,361
Assets (at end of year):				
Locomotives	3,971	3,610	3,580	3,571
HST power cars and passenger carriages	—	378	530	669
APT power cars and passenger carriages	—	—	8	20
Other coaching vehicles	23,238	21,580	21,031	20,963
Freight vehicles	241,429	166,935	150,371	137,589
Stations	2,790	2,848	2,837	2,821
Route open for traffic (*miles*)	11,289	11,168	11,123	11,020

Source: *British Railways Board*

Passenger Services

The passenger network (see map, p 310) comprises a fast inter-city network, linking the main centres of Great Britain; local stopping services; and commuter services in and around the large conurbations, especially London and south-east England. British Rail introduced the world's fastest diesel rail service, known as Inter-City 125 and operated by HSTs travelling at maximum sustained speeds of 125 mph (201 km/h), in 1976 on the route from London to Bristol and south Wales. Similar services were introduced on the London–Edinburgh route in 1978 and on the London–Plymouth–Penzance route in 1979. HSTs are due to enter service in 1981–82 on the route linking Edinburgh, Newcastle upon Tyne, Birmingham and south-west England or south Wales. The first of three pre-production electric APTs, capable of sustained speeds of 125 mph (201 km/h) over longer stretches than the HSTs, will be introduced on the London–Glasgow route later in 1980 covering the 400-mile (644-kilometre) journey in 4 hours 10 minutes. British Rail is proposing to order a further 50 to 60 APTs for services between London, Birmingham, Manchester, Liverpool and Glasgow.

Electrification is continuing, the latest project being a £130 million scheme,

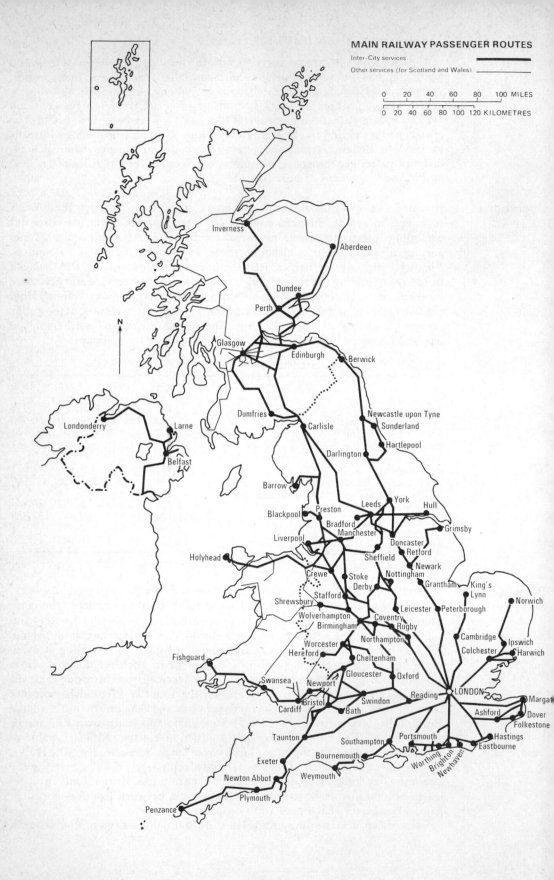

MAIN RAILWAY PASSENGER ROUTES

Inter-City services

Other services (for Scotland and Wales)

0 20 40 60 80 100 MILES

0 20 40 60 80 100 120 KILOMETRES

Inverness

Aberdeen

Dundee

Perth

Glasgow

Edinburgh

Berwick

Dumfries

Carlisle

Newcastle upon Tyne

Sunderland

Hartlepool

Darlington

Londonderry

Larne

Belfast

Barrow

Leeds

York

Hull

Preston

Blackpool

Bradford

Manchester

Grimsby

Liverpool

Doncaster

Retford

Sheffield

Holyhead

Crewe

Stoke

Derby

Newark

Nottingham

Shrewsbury

Stafford

Grantham

King's Lynn

Wolverhampton

Birmingham

Coventry

Leicester

Peterborough

Norwich

Rugby

Worcester

Northampton

Cambridge

Ipswich

Hereford

Fishguard

Cheltenham

Oxford

Colchester

Harwich

Swansea

Newport

Gloucester

Reading

LONDON

Margate

Cardiff

Bristol

Swindon

Bath

Ashford

Dover

Folkestone

Taunton

Southampton

Portsmouth

Hastings

Eastbourne

Exeter

Bournemouth

Worthing

Brighton

Newhaven

Newton Abbot

Weymouth

Plymouth

Penzance

to be completed in 1982, to electrify the line between London and Bedford. A review of the case for a programme of further main-line electrification is being conducted by the Government and the British Railways Board.

Passenger-mileage in 1979 was the highest since 1961 (when the rail network was 30 per cent larger), reflecting the extension of high-speed services and the wider range of promotional fares designed to encourage greater use of trains.

Freight

The most important freight commodities handled in 1979 were coal and coke (93·5 million tonnes) and iron and steel (25·1 million tonnes). British Rail is concentrating on traffic particularly suitable for carriage by rail, especially long-distance and bulk trainload traffic.

Increased efficiency is being obtained as new types of wagon are introduced with larger capacities and which are capable of higher speeds. A network of 'Speedlink' high-speed freight services using these new wagons is being established between the major industrial centres. In mid-1980 there were 48 Speedlink trains running each day and the number will be increased to about 100 by 1982. Freight traffic is being concentrated at fewer and better equipped and sited marshalling yards and terminals. A computer-based total operations processing system, which monitors all consignments and freight train and wagon movements in Great Britain, has reduced costs by allowing the more intensive use of rolling stock and the withdrawal of many obsolete wagons.

To encourage the use of railways for the carriage of freight, grants of 50 per cent are available towards the cost of construction or modernisation of privately owned rail freight facilities where this leads to significant environmental benefits by the removal of heavy goods vehicle traffic from the roads. By June 1980, 85 projects had been approved for grants totalling some £22·5 million.

Other Activities

British Rail has a group of other companies, of which British Rail Engineering Ltd (BREL) has the largest number of employees, about 36,200 at 13 engineering plants. BREL mainly constructs locomotives, coaches, wagons and containers for British Rail, and undertakes heavy maintenance and overhauls. It also carries out work for export. The Railway Technical Centre at Derby is the largest in the world; its most important achievement has been the development of the APT. Transmark provides consultancy services overseas on railway and associated operations. British Transport Hotels Ltd runs 29 hotels and controls Travellers-Fare, which is responsible for catering facilities at stations and on trains, and provides meals and snacks on more trains than any other railway company in Europe. British Rail also has various other activities including shipping and hovercraft (see p 315), ports (see p 312) and property. The British Railways Board proposes to establish a wholly-owned subsidiary company to hold the assets and shares of the main non-railway subsidiaries and to be responsible for introducing private capital into the individual businesses by the most appropriate means.

Channel Tunnel

Several proposals have been put forward for a fixed link across the English Channel between Britain and France. The British Railways Board and Société Nationale des Chemins de Fer Français (SNCF) have submitted a project, costing some £650 million, for a single-track rail-only tunnel and this is being considered by the Government.

Private Railways

There are a number of small privately owned passenger-carrying railways in Great Britain, mostly operated on a voluntary basis and providing limited services for tourists and railway enthusiasts; the principal aim of many of these railways is the preservation of steam traction. Most are standard gauge railways, but some which run mostly on British Rail track, mainly in Wales, are narrow gauge railways.

INLAND
WATERWAYS

Inland waterways are popular for recreation (see p 430), continue to carry freight and are important for land drainage and water supply. Of the 2,000 miles (3,219 kilometres) of canal and river navigations controlled by the publicly owned British Waterways Board, some 340 miles (547 kilometres) are maintained as commercial waterways for use by freight-carrying vessels. Freight traffic carried on the Board's waterways amounted to 84 million tonne-kilometres in 1979 and the tonnage carried was 5·2 million tonnes. In addition, some freight is carried on about 600 miles (966 kilometres) of inland waterways owned by other bodies. The Board also operates docks, warehouses and inland freight terminals, and has two barge fleets, although most of the traffic on its waterways is conveyed by independent carriers. In 1979 the Board's turnover amounted to £13·1 million, and it received government grants of £21·4 million, most of which were used to maintain its waterways to statutory standards. Completion of the Board's £14·2 million scheme to improve the Sheffield and South Yorkshire Navigation between Doncaster and Rotherham is expected in 1983. Improvements so far have already led to increased traffic on the canal and, when completed, the improvements will raise the barge capacity above Doncaster from 90 tonnes with the result that 700-tonne barges will be able to navigate as far as Mexborough and 400-tonne barges to reach Rotherham.

PORTS

There are some 250 port authorities or public wharf operators in Britain, and about 800 other undertakings engaged in operations such as stevedoring, towage, warehousing and lighterage. Port authorities are of four main types: nationalised bodies, public trusts, local authorities and statutory companies.

Ports run by nationalised undertakings represent over a fifth of total capacity, the majority, including Southampton, Hull, Grimsby/Immingham, Newport, Cardiff and Swansea, being owned by the British Transport Docks Board (Britain's largest port authority). In 1979 shipping arrivals and departures at the Board's docks totalled 141·4 million net registered tons (including fishing vessels) and total cargo handled was 82·2 million tonnes. The Board's revenue totalled £133·6 million, over one-quarter of revenue earned by British ports, and it achieved a net pre-tax profit of £13·6 million. Capital expenditure amounted to £13·3 million. The Government is considering ways of introducing private capital into the Board's operations. The British Railways Board controls certain ports, including Fishguard, Folkestone, Holyhead, Parkeston Quay (Harwich) and Stranraer, which are largely used for its shipping services, while the British Waterways Board owns Sharpness (Gloucester) and Weston Point in Runcorn. Major ports controlled by public trusts include London, Milford Haven, Tees and Hartlepool, Medway, Forth and Clyde. Local authorities own about one-third of Britain's ports, including Bristol and the new oil ports in Orkney and Shetland. Port undertakings owned by statutory companies include Manchester and Liverpool. Many private ports deal with the traffic of individual industrial firms in commodities such as china clay and petroleum.

Port authorities, in the main, operate with statutory powers and responsibilities set out in private Acts of Parliament. Most are members of the British Ports Association which aims to further the common interests of port authorities in their relations with the Government, shipowners and traders.

Port Traffic

Traffic through the ports of Great Britain rose by 8·8 per cent in 1979 to a record 384 million tonnes comprising 157 million tonnes of imports, 108 million tonnes of exports and 120 million tonnes of coastal traffic (mostly petroleum and coal). About 66 per cent of the traffic was in fuels, mainly petroleum and petroleum products, which rose by 10 per cent in 1979 reflecting growing oil exports.

Britain's main ports, in terms of total tonnage handled, are given in Table 25. Offshore oil developments have had a substantial effect on port traffic by greatly increasing the flow through certain North Sea ports, such as Tees and Hartlepool and the Forth ports, creating new oil ports at Flotta in Orkney and Sullom Voe in Shetland, and reducing oil traffic at traditional oil importing terminals such as Milford Haven and the Clyde. There has also been a switch in general cargo traffic from some of the traditional ports, such as London, Liverpool and Manchester, to smaller ports including Dover, Felixstowe and Harwich, partly because of the growth of container and roll-on traffic. While non-fuel traffic has been growing only slowly, container and roll-on traffic has trebled since 1970 to 41·7 million tonnes in 1979 and now accounts for almost one-third of non-fuel traffic. The leading ports for this type of traffic are Dover, Felixstowe, Southampton, London and Liverpool.

TABLE 25: Traffic through the Principal Ports of Great Britain[a]

million tonnes

	1969	1974	1977	1978	1979
London	56·2	46·2	43·1	41·7	40·2
Milford Haven	39·8	59·5	37·3	40·0	38·9
Tees and Hartlepool	21·8	25·0	28·2	30·7	37·1
Forth	8·0	9·8	24·9	28·5	28·8
Grimsby and Immingham	14·9	22·2	22·5	25·1	24·7
Southampton	29·1	27·5	23·7	20·0	22·6
Shetland	na	0·2	0·4	1·6	20·4
Medway	25·5	24·6	20·2	20·3	18·6
Orkney	na	na	9·0	15·6	17·8
Liverpool	29·3	27·8	17·7	14·8	13·1
Manchester	15·8	16·3	12·8	13·0	11·9

Source: *National Ports Council*
[a] Belfast is the main port in Northern Ireland and it handled 7·2 million tonnes in 1979.
na = not available.

Development

Modernisation of Britain's ports is in progress, primarily to accommodate the increase in the proportion of goods carried in container ships and roll-on vessels, and the changing nature and direction of Britain's trade. Most current developments are concerned with specific energy or industrial needs or to accommodate specialised container or roll-on services rather than with general purpose port facilities.

Major schemes completed in the last few years have included a £24 million container terminal, the world's largest terminal for refrigerated containers, at Tilbury (London); a terminal for handling iron ore and coal at Hunterston on the Clyde which can accommodate ships up to 350,000 deadweight tons and is the biggest of its type in Europe; the £37 million Royal Portbury Dock at Bristol, containing six berths and the largest entrance lock in Britain; and one of the world's biggest hoverports, a £12 million terminal at Dover to handle cross-Channel hovercraft. Major projects under construction or planned include a £27 million scheme to provide two deep-water container berths at Felixstowe, and a £12 million scheme for two roll-on berths, with multi-level access, at Dover, which will handle the most modern cross-Channel ferries. Work on a £20 million development scheme at Belfast, to provide two new unit load terminals, is expected to begin in 1981.

The first purpose-built terminal for oil from the British sector of the North Sea was completed at Hound Point on the Forth in 1975 and other terminals have been built on the Tees, at Flotta and Sullom Voe. Sullom Voe is expected to become the largest oil port in Europe in the early 1980s. Of the four jetties completed, three are able to handle oil tankers of up to 300,000 deadweight tons. With the growth of the offshore oil and gas industry, facilities for handling products for the petrochemical industry are planned. A natural gas liquids terminal is being built in the Firth of Forth and other major developments are being considered. Other developments related to offshore oil and gas include the construction of supply bases for offshore vessels at a number of ports mostly on the east coast; those include Great Yarmouth, Leith, Dundee, Montrose, Aberdeen, Peterhead, and Lerwick in Shetland.

SHIPPING

The British merchant fleet in mid-1979 at 28 million gross tons[1] (45·1 million deadweight tons) was the fourth largest after those of Liberia, Japan and Greece. The oil tanker fleet (13·3 million gross tons) was the third largest and the fleet of fully cellular container ships (1·8 million gross tons) was the largest, accounting for 18 per cent of the tonnage of vessels of this type. The fleet reached its peak of 33·2 million gross tons in 1975, but has declined since then, mainly owing to the world recession in shipping and increasing international competition, especially from ships operating under 'flags of convenience'. A large tonnage of ships, particularly of tankers, has been scrapped or sold. Nevertheless, the British fleet is still modern and technically advanced. About four-fifths of the fleet is less than ten years old compared with two-thirds of the world fleet.

THE MERCHANT FLEET

In July 1979, 39·3 million deadweight tons of trading vessels of 100 gross tons and over were both owned and registered in Britain. (This figure excludes non-trading vessels, such as fishing vessels, tugs and dredgers, and shipping registered in Britain but owned in other Commonwealth countries, which are included in the figure of 45·1 million deadweight tons.) These ships were usually employed as follows: 23·1 million deadweight tons as tankers; 11·6 million deadweight tons as tramps and 4·6 million deadweight tons as cargo or passenger liners.

Lloyd's Register of Shipping surveys and classifies ships with particular regard to their safety and operational efficiency.

Ownership

Nearly the whole of the British merchant fleet is privately owned. Over half of the tanker fleet belongs to the oil companies, although there are a few independent tanker operators. British liner tonnage is dominated by a relatively small number of large groups, the largest liner company being the Peninsular and

---

[1] One gross ton = 100 cubic feet (2·83 cubic metres). One deadweight ton = 1 tonne (1,000 kilogrammes or 2,205 lb). Gross tonnage indicates the total capacity of the enclosed space on a ship. Deadweight tonnage denotes the maximum load which a vessel can carry before submerging the load-line.

Oriental Steam Navigation Company (P & O). Some shipowners have delegated the management of their fleets to specialist ship management companies.
Several companies are participating in consortia, particularly where heavy
investment is required, as with container and bulk cargo vessels. Chartering of
ships of all nationalities takes place on the Baltic Exchange, the largest market
of its type in the world. The representative body for shipowners (excluding
owners of fishing vessels) is the General Council of British Shipping.

SERVICES

Almost all Britain's overseas trade by weight, about three-quarters by value,
is carried by sea, while the proportion of passengers travelling to or from
Britain by sea is about one-third, compared with about one-half in the early
1960s.

Cargo Services

In 1979 British seaborne trade amounted to 253 million tonnes (valued at
£69,586 million) or 851,617 million tonne-miles (1·4 million million tonne-
kilometres). Ships registered in Britain carried 29 per cent by weight, 25 per
cent in terms of tonne-miles and 41 per cent by value. Tanker cargoes
accounted for nearly half this trade by weight, but only about 13 per cent by
value, and foodstuffs and manufactured goods accounted for over three-
quarters by value.

Container and roll-on/roll-off vessels are responsible for a growing proportion of general cargo trade. Many of the deep-sea liner services from Britain
are operated by container ships. Roll-on services, accommodating passengers
and their cars and, in some cases, commercial vehicles are increasing in
number, particularly between Britain and the continent of Europe. Several
freight-only roll-on services operate to the Irish Republic, the continent of
Europe, and to more distant countries, especially in the Middle East, North
Africa and West Africa.

British shipping companies operating liner services have associated with
each other and with the companies of other countries operating on the same
routes in a series of 'conferences' designed to secure standardisation and
stability of rates, and to maintain frequency and regularity of services. The
essential principle of a conference is the establishment of a common tariff of
freight rates to be applied by each member line. There are about 100 conferences dealing with trade to and from Britain.

**Passenger
Services**

In 1979 some 21·3 million passengers arrived at or departed from British ports.
Nearly all of these travelled to or from the continent of Europe or the Irish
Republic, services on other routes having been withdrawn as a result of the
growth of air services. Remaining long-distance passenger ships are used for
cruising and in 1979 some 89,000 passengers embarked on pleasure cruises
from British ports. Services from British ports are shown on the map at the end
of the book.

Cross-Channel traffic accounts for a substantial proportion of traffic to the
continent of Europe. Sealink UK Ltd, a subsidiary of the British Railways
Board, is the largest short-sea ferry operator in Europe. The company and its
continental partners (SNCF of France, Régie des Transports Maritimes
Belges and Stoomvaart Maatschappij Zeeland of the Netherlands) operate
about 60 ships on short-sea routes. Sealink UK Ltd and the other major British
operators, including Townsend Thoresen and P & O's Normandy Ferries, are
or have been investing heavily in new ships, resulting in a substantial increase
in cross-Channel ferry capacity.

There are two operators providing cross-Channel hovercraft services:

Seaspeed (run by British Rail Hovercraft Ltd in conjunction with SNCF) with routes between Dover and Boulogne, and Dover and Calais; and Hoverlloyd Ltd between Ramsgate and Calais. A hovercraft crossing takes about one-third of the time taken by ships and hovercraft carry over one-quarter of the traffic on the short-sea crossings to the continent of Europe. Seaspeed operates the world's largest hovercraft, two British Hovercraft Corporation SR.N Super 4s which have been structurally enlarged so that each accommodates 424 passengers and 55 cars.

Passenger and freight ferry services are also operated to many of the offshore islands, such as the Isle of Wight, Orkney, Shetland and a number of other Scottish islands. The Government has issued a consultative document on the structure of subsidies for ferry services to the Scottish islands and is examining a system of support for these services based on road equivalent tariffs for the distance covered.

ROLE OF THE GOVERNMENT

The Department of Trade is the government department responsible for most matters connected with merchant shipping, including general policy towards the industry and Britain's relations with other governments and international organisations on shipping matters. The general policy is one of minimum intervention by the Government, while encouraging free and fair competition. Under the Merchant Shipping Acts the Department does, however, administer many regulations for marine safety and welfare, and for preventing and cleaning up pollution from ships (see p 185). For instance, it certifies the load-line (or Plimsoll line) that shows that a ship is not overloaded; ensures that standards of safety are observed in ship construction; ensures the provision of adequate life-saving, fire-fighting and radio equipment; and deals with the discipline, professional standards, health and accommodation of seamen. The Acts also contain certain reserve powers for protecting shipping and trading interests from measures adopted or proposed by overseas governments.

The Department's duties are carried out from marine survey offices and mercantile marine offices located at various ports. In the offices of the Registrar General of Shipping and Seamen, at Cardiff, a record is kept of all ships registered in Britain and its dependencies.

EMPLOYMENT OF SEAFARERS

Various qualifications are required for employment on board ship in certain grades. Responsibility for holding examinations and issuing certificates of competency rests with the Department of Trade, except in the case of radio officers where this is the function of the Home Office.

There are some 50 establishments providing full-time vocational training for seafarers. Most deck and catering junior ratings are trained at the National Sea Training College at Gravesend (Kent), the world's largest ratings' establishment, which can accommodate some 2,000 ratings a year.

Conditions of Employment

Wages and conditions of employment of most seafarers are negotiated by the National Maritime Board, composed of equal numbers of representatives of the General Council of British Shipping and seafarers' trade unions. Under the Merchant Navy Established Service Scheme, seafarers are employed either as 'registered seafarers' or they may enter into a company service contract, for a minimum of one year, for employment on the ships of a particular company. Registered seafarers receive special benefits between voyages in addition to the normal state benefits. The benefits paid to company service contract seafarers must be at least equivalent to those paid to registered seafarers.

SAFETY AT SEA The Department of Trade's responsibilities for safety include administration of the Marine Survey Service, the Coastguard Service, and certain administrative functions concerning lighthouses and pilotage. It makes regulations to implement international safety conventions and conducts inquiries into shipping casualties and accidents. Britain's merchant fleet is one of the safest in the world; it has a consistently lower record of ship losses than the world average.

Sea Rescue The Coastguard Service is responsible for initiating and co-ordinating civil marine search and rescue action in the United Kingdom Search and Rescue Region (SRR). This is divided into six coastguard SRRs, each controlled by a maritime rescue co-ordination centre supported by sub-centres, all of which maintain continuous telecommunications watch on marine distress frequencies. In addition, at times of casualty risk a watch is kept at some 250 other stations around the coast.

The Coastguard Service calls upon the lifeboats of the Royal National Life-boat Institution (RNLI), Ministry of Defence aircraft and helicopters, a long-range civilian helicopter based at Sumburgh (Shetland), and any other ships or aircraft available to assist in rescue action. In 1979 the Coastguard Service took action in 3,744 incidents (including cliff rescues) in which 6,870 people were assisted. The RNLI is supported entirely by voluntary contributions and depends for its operation on voluntary workers. In 1979 lifeboats were launched 2,593 times and rescued 1,537 people.

Lighthouses The general lighthouse authority for England and Wales, the Channel Islands and Gibraltar is the Corporation of Trinity House, which is administered by a board of Elder Brethren elected from the Royal Navy and the Merchant Navy. Lighthouses in Scotland and Ireland are the responsibility respectively of the Northern Lighthouse Board and the Commissioners of Irish Lights. These authorities control about 350 lighthouses, many minor lights and buoys, and a number of lightships, some of which are being replaced by unattended sea marks or by light towers.

Pilotage In Britain there are 47 pilotage authorities for the 87 pilotage districts and over 1,500 licensed pilots. Trinity House is the largest pilotage authority, licensing some 700 pilots in 41 districts in England and Wales. In some cases the harbour authority or local council is the pilotage authority. A Pilotage Commission has been established to advise on the organisation of pilotage.

Traffic Surveillance There are a number of traffic separation schemes around the shores of Britain, all of which have been adopted by the Inter-Governmental Maritime Consultative Organisation (a United Nations agency with headquarters in London). Compliance with these schemes is mandatory for all vessels of countries party to the 1972 International Collision Regulations. The most important scheme affecting British waters is in the Dover Strait, one of the world's busiest seaways. It consists of traffic lanes for shipping passing through the strait and inshore traffic zones for use by local shipping. The number of collisions has fallen considerably since the scheme was introduced. Britain and France operate radar surveillance of the strait to keep watch on ships not conforming to the scheme and, through the Channel Navigation Information Service, broadcast navigational information to ships in the Dover Strait. The Langdon Battery Operations Centre near Dover, opened in 1979, monitors ships passing through the strait. With the installation in 1981 of an automatic data processing system, which will be able to detect and track vessels automatically, it will probably be the most advanced maritime centre of its kind in the world. The Anglo-French Safety of Navigation Group, comprising representatives of British and French government departments, is responsible for reviewing and improving safety measures in the English Channel.

CIVIL AVIATION

Britain has a growing civil aviation industry which is continuing to develop to meet the increasing demand for air travel, particularly international travel. Airline services are operated by British Airways and by a number of independent airlines. Their fleets contain some of the most modern types of aircraft including wide-bodied aircraft and the Concorde supersonic aircraft with which British Airways inaugurated in 1976, jointly with Air France, the world's first supersonic passenger services. Many airports are being substantially modernised and new terminals installed.

Role of the Government The Secretary of State for Trade is responsible for international matters (including negotiation of air service agreements with more than 100 other countries, the licensing and control of public transport operations into Britain by overseas operators and British participation in the activities of international aviation bodies), airports policy, amenity matters (such as aircraft noise), aviation security policy and investigation of accidents.

Civil Aviation Authority The Civil Aviation Authority (CAA) is an independent statutory body responsible for the economic, technical and operational regulation of the industry; the provision by the National Air Traffic Services, jointly with the Secretary of State for Defence, of air navigation services and the aerodrome navigation services at certain British airports; and eight aerodromes in Scotland. Members of the CAA are appointed by the Secretary of State for Trade.

The Authority's primary objectives are to ensure that British airlines provide air services to satisfy all major categories of public demand at the lowest charges consistent with a high standard of safety and an economic return for efficient operators, and to further the reasonable interests of air transport users. Other duties are to ensure that British airlines compete effectively on international routes, to secure the most efficient use of airports in Britain and to have regard to the need to minimise the adverse effects of civil aviation on the environment. The CAA received a grant from the Government of £24·4 million in 1979–80 to cover its loss-making operations: the operation of its Scottish aerodromes (which are now subsidised by the Scottish Office) and the provision of air navigation services in British airspace (for which grants will continue to be paid until the arrangements for providing the services can be altered by international agreement).

Air Traffic In 1979 a total of some 41·7 million passengers travelled by air (international terminal passengers) to or from Britain, 6·4 per cent more than in 1978. British airlines have helped to pioneer new services and low fares, for example, Laker Airways' Skytrain services from London (Gatwick) to New York, Los Angeles and Miami, while a number of airlines are proposing new services combined with low fares to the continent of Europe. Total capacity offered on all services by British airlines amounted to 12,751 million capacity-tonne-kilometres in 1979, 6·5 per cent more than in 1978. British Airways accounts for some 87 per cent of scheduled services flown by British airlines, whereas the charter market is dominated by independent companies.

The value of overseas trade carried by air rose by 17 per cent in 1979 to £17,929 million, and the proportions of Britain's overseas trade carried by air amounted to 20 per cent of the value of exports and 17 per cent of imports. Air freight is important for the carriage of goods with a high value-to-weight ratio, especially where speed of movement is essential. Precious stones (particularly diamonds), live animals, medicinal and pharmaceutical products, clothing, leather and skins, and scientific instruments are major categories where a relatively high proportion of exports is sent by air.

British Airways

British Airways is one of the world's leading airlines, and in terms of international passengers carried and of international passenger-kilometres flown it is the largest in the world. During 1979–80 British Airways' turnover was £1,920 million (including £1,654 million from airline operations), and it made a net profit of £11 million. In March 1980 British Airways employed about 56,900 staff. Its assets of £1,037 million included £828 million of aircraft and spares and £121 million of land and buildings. The status of British Airways is to be changed from a nationalised industry to a private sector company. At the appropriate time the Government will effect this change and intends to sell a substantial minority of shares in the new company.

Airline Operations

British Airways' route network, covering some 590,738 kilometres (367,054 miles) of unduplicated route, is among the largest in the world. The airline serves nearly 170 destinations in 80 countries and in 1979–80 carried some 17·3 million passengers on scheduled services. International scheduled services are operated to the rest of Europe, the Middle East, the Far East, Australasia, East and South Africa, North America and Guyana in South America. Within Britain it runs 1,400 services a week to 16 towns and cities throughout the country. Scheduled Concorde services are operated from London (Heathrow) to New York, and to Washington, covering these routes in about half the time taken by subsonic aircraft. In 1975 British Airways inaugurated Europe's first air 'shuttle' service (a regular scheduled no-reservation service with back-up aircraft to carry extra passengers) between Heathrow and Glasgow, and similar services have been introduced from Heathrow to Edinburgh, Belfast and Manchester. Joint shuttle services with national airlines to a number of other European countries are being investigated.

Other activities carried out include helicopter services, engine overhaul work, airport technical services and investments in a number of hotel companies and air companies in other countries.

Aircraft

British Airways operated 203 aircraft and helicopters in 1980. Aircraft included 26 BAC One-Elevens, 20 Boeing 707s, 6 Boeing 737s, 27 Boeing 747s, 5 Concordes, 2 HS 748s, 15 Trident Ones, 16 Trident Twos, 25 Trident Threes, 14 TriStars, 10 Super VC10s and 11 Viscounts. Helicopters operated comprised 23 Sikorsky 61Ns, 1 Bell Jet Ranger and 2 Bell 212s. A large investment programme is under way to replace the older aircraft, and major orders for new aircraft include 22 Boeing 737s, 19 Boeing 757s, 9 TriStars and 3 Boeing Chinook helicopters.

Independent Airlines

The independent airlines carry 5 million passengers a year on scheduled services and nearly 11 million on charter flights. The main independent scheduled airline is British Caledonian Airways, which operates a fleet of 28 aircraft and carried 1·6 million scheduled service passengers in 1979. Its scheduled services are primarily to the continent of Europe, West and

Central Africa, South America and the United States. Other operators of scheduled passenger services include Air UK, British Midland Airways and Dan-Air Services. Dan-Air Services, Britannia Airways, Laker Airways and Monarch Airlines are the leading independent airlines running charter passenger services.

Helicopters are engaged on a variety of work, but are mainly employed on the large-scale operations connected with the development of Britain's offshore oil and gas resources. Bristow Helicopters, which operates a fleet of more than 50 helicopters in Britain, is the world's largest helicopter contracting business. There are a small number of scheduled helicopter passenger services in Britain, including a link between Heathrow and Gatwick airports, and routes between Penzance and the Isles of Scilly, and Glasgow and Fort William. Light aircraft and helicopters are also involved in other activities, such as charter operations, search and rescue services, crop-spraying, and aerial survey and photography.

Licensing

Under the CAA's air transport licensing system, British operators apply for licences for scheduled and charter services, or for revocation or variation of existing licences. The CAA also considers changes in fares, both for British carriers and for overseas carriers on services to and from Britain, and licenses air travel organisers who charter aircraft for inclusive tours. The Air Transport Users Committee, which is financed by the CAA but independent of it, makes reports and recommendations to the CAA for furthering the interests of air transport users including the investigation of complaints against airlines.

Safety

The CAA is responsible for the regulation of the safety of civil aircraft registered in Britain. Its Operations Division deals with the safety requirements concerning airline and general aviation operations, flight crew licensing and training, aerodromes, and fire and rescue services. The Airworthiness Division is responsible for the airworthiness certification of aircraft, the licensing of aircraft maintenance engineers and the approval of maintenance schedules for public transport aircraft. The CAA is advised in its duties by the Airworthiness Requirements Board.

Air Operators' Certificates

Every operator of aircraft used for public transport must possess an Air Operator's Certificate which is granted by the CAA when it is satisfied that the operator is competent to secure the safe operation of its aircraft. The CAA's flight operations inspectors (who are experienced airline pilots) check that satisfactory operating standards are maintained.

Flight Crew Qualifications and Training

Each member of the flight crew of a British registered aircraft must hold the appropriate official licence issued by the CAA. Except for pilots with acceptable military or other experience, all candidates for a first professional pilot's licence must have undertaken a full-time course of ground and flying instruction at a flying school approved by the CAA.

Air Traffic Control and Navigation Services

Responsibility for civil and military air traffic control over Britain and the surrounding seas rests with the National Air Traffic Services (NATS). The planning and provision of the facilities necessary for control of aircraft at the higher flight levels are carried out in conjunction with Eurocontrol, a European agency of which Britain is a member. The Controller of the NATS reports to both the CAA and the Ministry of Defence. The function of the NATS is to secure the safe, orderly and expeditious flow of air traffic within

British airspace. It also provides air traffic services for aircraft flying over the north-eastern quarter of the North Atlantic. At some 20 civil aerodromes, including most of the major British airports, the NATS provides the navigation services necessary for the operation of aircraft taking off and landing, and integrates them into the overall flow of traffic. To provide its services, the NATS uses radar, some 100 navigational beacons, landing aids, air-to-ground communications and an extensive telecommunications network.

Airports

Of the 140 licensed civil aerodromes in Britain, nearly one-quarter each handles more than 100,000 passengers a year. In 1979 Britain's civil airports handled a total of 57·8 million passengers (56·6 million terminal passengers and 1·2 million in transit), 8·4 per cent more than in 1978, and 795,300 tonnes of freight. London's Heathrow airport is the world's busiest airport for international travel, and is Britain's most important airport for passengers and air freight, handling 28·4 million passengers and 496,400 tonnes of freight in 1979. Gatwick, the second major airport in the London area, handled 8·8 million passengers in 1979. Other leading airports were Manchester, Glasgow, Luton, Birmingham, Edinburgh, Aberdeen and Belfast. While the number of passengers has, in general, risen in recent years, there has not been a corresponding increase in air transport movements owing to the growing use of wide-bodied aircraft.

Ownership and Control

The British Airports Authority (BAA), an independent statutory body operating on a commercial basis, owns and manages seven airports—Heathrow, Gatwick and Stansted in south-east England, and Glasgow, Edinburgh, Prestwick and Aberdeen in Scotland—which handle 76 per cent of air passengers and 89 per cent of air cargo traffic in Britain. In 1979–80 the BAA's income was £191·4 million and it recorded a pre-tax profit of £35·5 million.

Sumburgh airport and seven small aerodromes in the Highlands and Islands of Scotland are controlled by the CAA and Belfast's airport (Aldergrove) is managed by Northern Ireland Airports Ltd, a subsidiary of the Northern Ireland Transport Holding Company. Most of the other public airports are controlled by local authorities. Except for those controlled by the Government or by the CAA, all airports and all but a few minor private aerodromes must be licensed by the CAA. Stringent requirements, such as the provision of adequate fire-fighting, medical and rescue services, suitable runways, and of air traffic control services and visual aids, must be satisfied before a licence is granted. Strict security measures are in force at airports.

Development

The Government has decided that the growing demand for air transport facilities in south-east England should be met by the provision of additional capacity at existing airports, especially Heathrow, Gatwick and Stansted. It is also encouraging the maximum use of other main regional airports.

A fourth major terminal is to be built at Heathrow, raising the airport's capacity from 30 million to 38 million passengers a year. Its first stage is expected to be open in 1985. At Gatwick a £100 million redevelopment programme has been virtually completed, increasing the airport's annual capacity to some 16 million passengers. A public inquiry has been held into the BAA's plans for a second passenger terminal, which, if approved, would be in operation by the mid-1980s and would increase Gatwick's capacity to about 25 million passengers a year. The BAA is working on plans for a new terminal at

Stansted, which would be capable of handling 15 million passengers a year.

Work is in progress to develop facilities at several of Britain's other airports. A five-year development scheme, costing some £17 million, started in 1977 for the expansion of terminal facilities at Aldergrove. A new passenger terminal is planned at Birmingham airport. Offshore oil and gas activities have stimulated expansion schemes at airports in north-east Britain, such as at Aberdeen, where a new terminal was opened in 1977 and which has become one of the world's biggest heliports. At Sumburgh in Shetland the CAA has invested £30 million in developments including a new terminal for oil-related traffic.

THE POST OFFICE

The Post Office, founded in 1657, provides postal, telecommunications, data processing and Giro services. It was set up as a public authority under the Post Office Act 1969, having previously been a government department. The chairman and other members of the board are appointed by the Secretary of State for Industry. With some 400,000 employees, it is the largest commercial employer in Europe. The Government intends to separate the Post Office into two corporations, one for postal and banking services and the other for tele-communications, and legislation to create a new telecommunications corpora-tion is being prepared. The legislation will also contain provisions for relaxing the Post Office's monopoly position in postal and telecommunications services.

In 1979–80 the Post Office's income, excluding internal transactions, was £5,193 million and a profit of £297 million was recorded, with profits of £236·1 million on telecommunications and £49·3 million on posts. Capital expendi-ture on fixed assets amounted to £1,290 million in 1979–80. Over £80 million was spent on research and development, mostly at the Post Office's research centre at Martlesham Heath (Suffolk).

POSTAL
SERVICES

The Post Office pioneered postal services and was the first service to issue adhesive postage stamps as proof of advance payment for mail. It provides deliveries each working day to 22 million addresses. In 1979–80 the Post Office handled some 180 million parcels and 10,027 million items of other correspon-dence (including 9,609 million inland letters).

Postal operations are being mechanised and by 1982 there will be a national network of 83 mechanised high-speed sorting offices. Large parcel centres, each serving a group of counties, are gradually taking over the work of the 1,200 offices which handle parcels manually. Mechanised sorting is aided by the use of postcodes, of which there are 1·5 million; Britain's postcode system is one of the most sophisticated in the world.

Post Offices

Britain has 22,600 post offices, of which 1,580 are operated directly by the Post Office and the remainder on an agency basis by sub-postmasters. At a post office counter, besides making use of postal and telegraph facilities, a person may draw a pension or a family allowance, buy a dog licence, a television receiving licence, renew a motor vehicle licence, obtain a British visitor's passport, buy national insurance stamps, and use the facilities of the National Savings Bank (see p 361) and of the National Girobank (see p 359). In much of its counter service the Post Office acts as agent for government departments and local authorities.

Other Services   The Post Office provides a range of 40 specialist services, mainly for commerce. 'Datapost', a door-to-door overnight delivery service originally for computer data, has been expanded to include documents, medical samples and spare parts, and handles 3·8 million packets a year. There are International Datapost links with 16 countries. An 'Expresspost' messenger service provides a rapid delivery within or between certain main cities. About one-third of the Post Office's philatelic business, which mainly involves the sale of stamps to collectors or dealers, is conducted by the Philatelic Bureau in Edinburgh. The British Postal Consultancy Service offers advice and assistance on all aspects of postal business to overseas postal administrations, and over 20 countries have used its services.

**TELECOM-
MUNICATIONS**   Britain has some 26·7 million telephones, 17·6 million exchange connections, 86,000 telex connections and 67,000 data transmission modems (more than in any country except the United States). The Post Office's telecommunications business employs 240,000 people, has assets of £7,400 million, and runs eight factories and a fleet of nearly 54,000 telecommunications vehicles.

**Telephone
Services**   In 1979–80 some 20,079 million telephone calls were made in Britain comprising 16,600 million local calls, 3,257 million trunk calls and 222 million international calls. Subscribers dial virtually all local and trunk telephone calls, and about 90 per cent of international calls are dialled direct. Over 96 per cent of Britain's telephone subscribers can dial direct to 100 countries. To back up its nationwide system of cables, the Post Office has built a network of radio towers for transmitting telephone calls, television programmes and computer data over microwave channels.

*Special Telephone
Services*   Several specialised services are available by telephone, including the '999' emergency dialling service enabling subscribers to be connected rapidly and free of charge to the police, ambulance or fire brigade. Of the 599 million calls made to recorded information services in 1979–80, over 431 million were to the speaking clock. Other services include Dial a Disc, weather forecasts, sports results, motoring information, recipes, bedtime stories and Financial Times Index and Business News Summary.

Exchanges   Some 1,085 electronic exchanges are in use in Britain and 479 more have been ordered. They are more reliable than conventional electro-mechanical exchanges as they have very few moving parts and so require less maintenance. Most electronic exchanges are of the TXE2 type, with a capacity of up to 7,000 lines. Larger TXE4 exchanges, with a capacity of up to 40,000 lines, have been brought into service since 1976, and the first orders for an improved version, the TXE4A, have been placed. A series of new switching and associated systems for telephone exchanges, known as System X, using microelectronics technology, integrated digital transmission and switching, stored program (software) control and common channel signalling, has been developed. The first System X exchange, a junction tandem exchange in the City of London, entered service in July 1980 and the first local exchange, at Woodbridge (Suffolk), is due to be operating by the end of 1980.

Overseas Services   The demand for international calls is doubling every four or five years and the Post Office has increased the amount of equipment in its international exchanges substantially and raised the number of cable and satellite circuits linking Britain with other countries from nearly 3,000 in 1970 to nearly 16,000 in mid-1980. Nearly 70 per cent of the intercontinental telephone traffic to or from Britain is carried by satellite. Three aerials at the Goonhilly earth station in Cornwall provide commercial telecommunications services via high-capacity geostationary satellites positioned over the Atlantic and Indian Oceans. A fourth aerial is sending test speech and television signals to the European Space Agency's orbital test satellite, as the first step in the European Communications Satellite project (the responsibility of Eutelsat, an organisation set up by the telecommunication administrations of 17 European countries) intended to provide high-capacity links across Europe and the Mediterranean. Britain has the second largest interest in Intelsat, the world space communications satellite network. A second earth station at Madley near Hereford, opened in 1978, is helping the Post Office to cope with the growth in international traffic. It carries about 1 million calls a month between Britain and some 40 other countries. Its second aerial was completed in March 1980 and a third should be operating in mid-1981.

There are 17 submarine cables, covering a total of 19,000 nautical miles (35,200 kilometres), from Britain to the continent of Europe, the Irish Republic and the Faroe Islands, and three cables from Britain to North America.

In 1979 the Post Office set up BPO Telconsult as an international consultancy service to advise on the selection and installation of telecommunication systems.

Prestel

The Post Office's 'Prestel' service, the world's first public viewdata service, was inaugurated in 1979. It enables information to be obtained through the telephone network from a computer for display on a suitably equipped television set in words, figures and simple graphics. Some 150,000 'pages' of information are being provided from over 130 sources. Information is available on a wide range of subjects such as Government services, financial services, jobs and careers, housing, travel and sports results. Prestel is available in a number of cities including London, Birmingham, Nottingham, Edinburgh and Glasgow. The Post Office has sold Prestel software to telecommunications authorities in a number of countries. In 1980 the Post Office launched a trial international Prestel service for business users in Britain, Australia, the Federal Republic of Germany, the Netherlands, Sweden, Switzerland and the United States. ('Teletext' information services transmitted by broadcasting instead of the telephone network are operated by the British Broadcasting Corporation and the Independent Broadcasting Authority, see p 426.)

Maritime Communications

The Post Office provides communications links and radio services for shipping through one long-range and 11 medium-range radio stations around the coastline of Britain, while oil and gas production platforms in the North Sea are linked to Britain's telecommunications network by transhorizon radio. At all medium-range stations a continuous watch is maintained on the international distress frequencies. A number of remotely controlled short-range coast radio stations provide radiotelephone links with ships at sea at a range of up to 50 miles (80 kilometres). Britain, through the Post Office, has the third largest share in the International Maritime Satellite (INMARSAT) Organisation, which came into existence in 1979 and will provide satellite capacity to improve maritime communications. A fifth aerial will be built at Goonhilly in Cornwall.

Datel Services

Post Office Datel services provide for transmission of information for computers and other automatic processors. A wide variety of data transmission facilities, at speeds from 50 bits a second to 50,000 bits a second, including an internationally compatible service at 2,400 bits a second, are provided using Post Office circuits. The services consist of a suitable telegraph or telephone line and, when necessary, a modem (which converts digital signals into voice frequencies for transmission).

Telex

The British telex service is fully automatic. Demand for inland and international telex services is growing and the number of connections has more than doubled since 1971. Customers can dial direct to 155 countries and 98 per cent of all international calls are dialled direct. Britain's first computer-controlled telex exchange handling international automatic calls was installed in London in 1978 and a second is due to be brought into operation in 1981.

Telegrams

International telegrams are transmitted through the Post Office's computer-controlled Telegram Retransmission Centre in London. It is one of the largest in the world, and has direct access via satellite, cable and radio circuits to over 87 terminals in 75 countries.

Developments

The Post Office is developing several new telecommunications services. A national radiopaging service, providing direct dialling access over the public telephone network to small lightweight portable receivers, is to be established later in 1980 following trials in Greater London and the Thames Valley.

Intelpost, the world's first international public facsimile service transmitting letters and other documents by satellite, was inaugurated in June 1980 between Britain and Canada. Links with other countries are under consideration and there are plans to introduce an internal service within Britain.

The Post Office is participating in Euronet DIANE, a European Community project to provide access to computerised information on a wide range of subjects via a Community-wide data transmission network. It is responsible for the operation of the network management centre, in London, and for running an automated 'directory enquiry' service in six languages. Towards the end of 1980 the Post Office will inaugurate a fully commercial packet switching service for computer data in Britain; an international service is already available to the United States and Canada.

Optical fibres (very thin strands of glass capable of carrying large numbers of telephone calls simultaneously) are already installed in the telephone cable network on an experimental basis. They are being brought into service and are expected to result in substantial savings as they are smaller than conventional cables and require less amplifying equipment to boost long-distance calls. Work on laying the first optical fibre cables is in progress and by the end of 1982 the network, of over 3,500 kilometres (2,200 miles), will be the most comprehensive of its kind in the world.

DATA PROCESSING

The Post Office has a Data Processing Executive for internal services, and a comprehensive bureau service, known as National Data Processing, for industry and commerce. It operates some of the most comprehensive data processing systems in Europe and has implemented more than 1,800 projects.

17 Employment

As a major industrial country, Britain has a labour force with high levels of technical and commercial skills. To ensure as far as possible that people can find work best suited to their capabilities and that the working population, like the country's other economic resources, is fully utilised, the Government intervenes in the labour market in a number of ways: by providing employment services; by supplementing the training undertaken by employers; by policies to promote regional development and labour mobility; by measures to alleviate unemployment; through legislation to regulate terms and conditions of employment and improve industrial relations; and through legislation relating to health and safety at work.

THE WORKING POPULATION

The total working population of Britain at the middle of June 1979 was 26·4 million, about 48 per cent of the total population. If the unemployed, the self-employed, and the Armed Forces are omitted from the working population, there remained 22·8 million employees (13·3 million men and 9·5 million women) in employment. The percentage of women (particularly those working part-time) in the labour force continues to rise, although at a reduced rate compared with previous years. The great majority of the working population work for a wage or salary, but nearly 2 million are employers or self-employed. The working population increased slowly until 1966, then declined between 1966 and 1971, since when it has been rising again (see Table 26). One reason for the fall after 1966 was the increased number in full-time education. During the next few years both the male and female labour forces are expected to continue to increase. In June 1979 men accounted for 58 per cent of all employees and women for 42 per cent (about two-fifths of whom worked part-time).

TABLE 26: Manpower in Britain 1970–79   Thousands[a]

Year	Employees in employment[b]	Employers and self-employed	Unemployed[c]	Armed Forces[d]	Total working population[e]
1970	22,479	1,902	555	372	25,308
1971	22,122	1,909	724	368	25,123
1972	22,121	1,899	804	371	25,195
1973	22,664	1,947	575	361	25,547
1974	22,790	1,925	542	345	25,602
1975	22,710	1,886[e]	866	336	25,798
1976	22,543	1,886[e]	1,332	336	26,097
1977	22,619	1,886[e]	1,450	327	26,282
1978	22,666	1,886[e]	1,446	318	26,316
1979	22,825	1,886[e]	1,344	314	26,369

Source: *Department of Employment Gazette*
[a] Discrepancies between totals and the sums of their constituent parts are due to rounding.
[b] Part-time workers are counted as units.
[c] Excluding adult students.
[d] Including ex-Service personnel on leave after completing their service.
[e] Estimates.

The distribution of employees by industry in 1970 and 1979 is shown in Table 27.

The most notable trend in the employment pattern during the last decade has been the transfer of employment from manufacturing to service industries. Technological developments have increased automation, with a consequently reduced demand for manpower, and have assisted the growth of manufacturing capacity in other countries, particularly developing ones. New and, in some cases, cheaper services have been introduced through advances in technology, while improvements in living standards have led to an increasing demand for services. There is considerable public discussion of the social and economic effects of micro-electronic technology.

The high level of unemployment during the recession (see p 330) is also a major concern.

MANPOWER POLICY

In Great Britain the Department of Employment is generally responsible for employment policy, industrial relations and pay policy, and for the payment of unemployment benefit, but the Manpower Services Commission (MSC) advises the Government on manpower policy issues.

TABLE 27: Analysis of Civil Employment in Britain 1970 and 1979

Industry or Service	1970 Thousands	Per cent	1979[a] Thousands	Per cent
Agriculture, forestry and fishing	466	1·9	365	1·5
Mining and quarrying	410	1·7	337	1·4
Manufacturing industries	*8,342*	*34·2*	*7,155*	*29·0*
Chemicals and allied industries	442	1·8	440	1·8
Metals, engineering and vehicles	4,318	17·7	3,700	15·0
Textiles	678	2·8	479	1·9
Clothing and footwear	455	1·9	381	1·5
Food, drink and tobacco	792	3·2	699	2·8
Other manufactures	1,657	6·8	1,456	5·9
Construction	1,339	5·5	1,293	5·2
Gas, electricity and water	391	1·6	354	1·4
Transport and communications	1,572	6·4	1,482	6·0
Distributive trades	2,675	11·0	2,806	11·4
Professional, financial, scientific and miscellaneous services[b]	5,801	23·8	7,400	29·9
National and local government service	1,482	6·1	1,634	6·6
Total: employees	22,479	92·2	22,825	92·4
Employers and self-employed persons (all industries and services)	1,902	7·8	1,886[c]	7·6
Total in Civil Employment	24,381	100·0	24,711	100·0

Sources: *Department of Employment* and *Northern Ireland Department of Manpower Services*
[a] Provisional estimates.
[b] Excludes private domestic service.
[c] June 1975 estimate.
Discrepancies between totals and the sums of their constituent parts are due to rounding.

The MSC, which is separate from the Government but accountable to the Secretaries of State for Employment, Scotland and Wales, has a chairman and nine other members who are appointed after consultation with employers and employees, and local government and educational interests. Scottish and Welsh committees of the MSC consider special Scottish and Welsh aspects of manpower issues. Most of the MSC's activities are financed from public funds; expenditure in 1979–80 amounted to £609 million (plus £113 million on behalf of the Department of Employment). The MSC is advised by a network of district manpower committees on which employers, employees and other local interests are represented.

The MSC's main statutory duty is to make such arrangements as it considers appropriate, within a general policy framework agreed with Ministers, for assisting people to select, train for, obtain and retain employment, and for assisting employers to obtain suitable employees. The services in Northern Ireland are run on similar lines by the Department of Manpower Services.

EMPLOYMENT SERVICES

The main public employment services (other than the careers service) are provided in Great Britain by the MSC's Employment Service Division, the principal aim of which is to provide a comprehensive service for employers needing staff and for people, whether or not already in employment, seeking jobs. It operates through a network of about 1,000 local jobcentres and employment offices which handle all occupations except professional, scientific, technical and managerial, for which the MSC's Professional and Executive Recruitment is responsible. Jobcentres, where the provision of self-service facilities for job-seekers is a standard feature, are gradually replacing employment offices where such facilities do not always exist.

Though use of the service by both employers and job-seekers is voluntary, in the year to March 1980 over 6 million people registered for employment, 2·7 million vacancies were notified and 1·9 million were placed in employment.

Special Services

Special employment services include services for disabled people, services to assist the geographical mobility of workers, Professional and Executive Recruitment and the Careers Service.

Services for Disabled People

The public employment service has long provided a resettlement service to disabled people. This is provided by over 500 specially trained Disablement Resettlement Officers (DROs) who can advise on rehabilitation and training courses and on the comprehensive range of special schemes and facilities available. They can also advise employers on aspects of employing disabled people, including grants available for adaptation to premises and equipment in order to employ or retrain a specific disabled person. The DROs administer the quota scheme which, under the Disabled Persons (Employment) Act 1944, requires employers who employ 20 or more people to include 3 per cent registered disabled people among their workforce. Employment rehabilitation is provided at 27 centres (including one linked with a medical rehabilitation unit); in 1979 some 15,500 people attended the wide range of courses available. The MSC also gives financial assistance to voluntary and local authority bodies concerned with specific disabilities such as blindness, cerebral palsy and psychiatric disorders; in 1979 more than 600 people passed through these courses. As part of its 'Fit for Work' campaign to improve the employment prospects of disabled people, the MSC in 1979 instituted a scheme of annual awards to give public recognition to firms which excel in carrying out constructive policies on the employment of disabled people.

There are vocational training facilities for the disabled at 'skillcentres', educational institutions and employers' establishments. For the more seriously disabled there are special residential training colleges run by voluntary organisations with the help of the MSC's Training Services Division. Grants are available to disabled people qualified to undertake study or training for professional or comparable employment.

Sheltered employment is provided for the severely disabled in Great Britain by Remploy Ltd, a non-profit making company, and in Northern Ireland by Ulster Sheltered Employment Ltd, a company constituted similarly to Remploy, and by local authorities and voluntary organisations. Sheltered Employment Procurement and Consultancy Services is a unit of the MSC set up to offer consultancy, and other services to sheltered workshops. The MSC also works in close co-operation with the National Advisory Council on Employment of Disabled People.

In 1979 the MSC and the Northern Ireland Department of Manpower Services helped with the cost of providing places for over 14,000 severely disabled people, of whom approximately 1,900 were blind or partially sighted and some 280 were trainees.

Geographical Mobility Schemes

In order to ease regional imbalances in unemployment and job opportunities, the MSC provides financial assistance under the Job Search and Employment Transfer Scheme to enable people who are unemployed, or under threat of redundancy to look for and to move to jobs away from their homes. The assistance includes a range of grants and allowances to help with the cost of attending interviews, visiting new areas to look for work, and living away from home and moving home to the new area.

Similar schemes are operated in Northern Ireland by the Department of Manpower Services.

Professional and Executive Recruitment

Professional and Executive Recruitment (PER) is a specialist branch of the MSC which provides a recruitment service for employers who wish to engage professional, managerial, scientific or technical staff and assists people seeking employment at this level. PER operates nationally, through a network of offices and offers a comprehensive recruitment service which includes selection, interviewing and advertising. The service is free for job-seekers, while employers are charged a fee based on the type of service used. A broadly similar service, known as Professional and Executive Personnel and free to both employers and candidates, is operated in Northern Ireland.

Careers Service

Local education authorities have a statutory obligation under the Employment and Training Act 1973 to provide a careers service, a vocational guidance service for people attending all educational institutions (except universities) and an employment service for those leaving them. Authorities also provide an employment service for people, especially young people, in their early years at work. There is close co-operation with the MSC's employment service division which also caters for those who have left school and choose to use its facilities in preference to those of the careers service.

In Northern Ireland the careers service is an integral part of the Department of Manpower Services.

The MSC Careers and Occupational Information Centre publishes a wide range of material to help people looking for jobs to make an informed choice, and distributes careers literature to some 15,000 schools, careers offices and other centres.

Immigrant Workers

In general, people coming to Britain for employment (including Commonwealth citizens who do not have the right of abode, see p 12, but excluding nationals of other European Community countries and Gibraltar) need a work permit issued by the Department of Employment. This must be applied for by the prospective employer for a specific person and is issued for a specific job and for a fixed period not exceeding 12 months in the first instance. People admitted as holders of work permits may change their jobs only with the approval of the Department of Employment. Normally further leave to remain will be given on application to the Home Office if they remain in approved employment. The Home Office will consider an application to remove the conditions attached to their stay after four years in approved employment, and if granted, a worker may change employment without restriction. Among other conditions, work permits are issued only for work requiring a recognised professional qualification, or a high degree of skill or experience, where the Department of Employment is satisfied that the worker is necessary and there is no suitable worker in Britain or in other European Community countries to fill the post, and where the wages and conditions are not less favourable than for similar work. In general, the age limits for permits in most categories are 23–54 years. People coming for certain kinds of specialist employment (for example, doctors or dentists taking up professional appointments; ministers of religion; representatives of overseas newspapers, news agencies or broadcasting organisations; the self-employed) do not require work permits but may require entry clearances issued by a British Consulate or High Commission.

In addition, permits are issued under the Training and Work Experience Scheme for nationals of countries outside the European Community who are undertaking limited periods of training or work experience leading to the acquisition of a particular occupational skill or qualification. Permits are also issued for young people from outside the European Community to undertake short periods of employment intended to broaden their industrial or commercial experience and, if appropriate, to improve their knowledge of English.

European Community regulations establish the right of workers to move freely between member States for the purposes of employment. European Community workers entering another member State are entitled to be treated in the same way as nationals of that State as regards facilities of the national employment services, pay and working conditions, trade union rights, vocational training and retraining facilities, access to housing and property, and social security and industrial injury benefits. Workers who wish to remain in the United Kingdom for longer than an initial period of six months must apply to the Home Office for a residence permit. If they are in permanent employment the residence permit is normally valid for five years. If the employment is temporary (that is, for less than a year) the permit is valid for the expected duration of the employment.

Race Relations

The Department of Employment operates a Race Relations Employment Advisory Service with advisers based in the main areas where ethnic minorities have settled. Its general aim is to promote equal opportunity in employment regardless of race, colour, nationality, ethnic or national origin, and its advisers offer help and guidance to employers and unions on a wide range of issues which arise in the employment of a multi-racial workforce.

UN-EMPLOYMENT

As in many other industrial countries, unemployment in Britain rose sharply during the 1970s, with some fluctuations; by 1980 it had reached the highest level since the 1930s while remaining relatively low in the south-east of

England, it has been consistently higher in those parts of the country which have the greatest dependence on shipbuilding and certain branches of the heavy engineering and metal manufacturing industries, notably parts of Scotland and Wales, and north-east England and Merseyside. The general unemployment rate in Great Britain in August 1980 was 6·9 per cent: the areas with the highest rates were Wales and Scotland and the north of England. The unemployment rate in Northern Ireland has remained higher than in other parts of the United Kingdom. In August 1980 it was 12·7 per cent of all employees.

Government Action

Various measures have been introduced with the aim of mitigating the effects of high unemployment by providing job or training opportunities for people who would otherwise be unemployed.

The measures include: a scheme to encourage employers to use short-time working as an alternative to redundancies; a youth opportunities programme to provide a range of training and work experience opportunities to unemployed 16–18 year olds; a special temporary employment programme to provide worthwhile temporary jobs for adults in special development areas, development areas and designated inner city areas, who have been unemployed for a long time; a 'job release' scheme to encourage older workers, approaching pensionable age, to leave work early and release jobs for younger unemployed people; a 'job introduction' scheme for disabled people; and support for training places in industry. In August 1980 some 374,000 people were being helped through these measures and further measures are in hand.

The Government's general policy of helping small firms is also intended to alleviate unemployment.

TRAINING SERVICES

The main responsibility for carrying out industrial and commercial training lies with individual employers, but in recent years the MSC, with government support, has evolved a comprehensive strategy to help to improve the supply of trained manpower needed by the economy, to provide opportunities for individuals to acquire new skills, and to improve the efficiency and effectiveness of training generally. The MSC's Training Services Division is responsible for putting these programmes into effect.

Training in Industry

There are 23 industrial training boards and one industrial training committee, covering firms employing about 60 per cent of all employees, which are responsible for promoting training in their respective industries. They receive Exchequer funds to meet their advisory service and other costs and to enable them to pay grants to employers to encourage training activities of national importance (supplemented, during periods of economic recession, by special grants to support craft and technician training). The boards' five-year strategies and short-term operating plans and budgets are agreed with the MSC. The MSC also promotes training for some 10 million people employed in industries not covered by industrial training boards, maintaining liaison with major training organisations in this sector.

Training Opportunities Scheme

The Training Opportunities Scheme (TOPS) is intended to complement the training given in industry and commerce by providing individuals over the age of 19 with the opportunity to acquire new skills. Training is carried out at the Training Services Division's own skillcentres and annexes and at many colleges and employers' establishments. Skillcentre courses concentrate mainly on engineering, construction and automotive trades and those at colleges on clerical and commercial, management, technician and other skills.

Special priority has been given to expanding and developing technician training particularly for computer operations. In addition, electronics engineering courses biased towards micro-electronics and micro-processor applications have been established in several centres. In all about 500 different courses are available in a wide range of occupations. Trainees are paid allowances which vary with domestic responsibilities and may receive, among other things, an earnings-related supplement, travelling expenses and a lodging allowance. Some 74,500 adults were trained under TOPS in 1979–80.

Direct Training Services

The MSC also provides a number of other direct training services to employers.

The Training Within Industry scheme is intended to develop the skills of supervisors in developing leadership, instructing and communicating, improving methods and improving safety practices. Special courses are also available for supervisors employed in offices. Courses in international trade procedures are available for staff employed in export/import offices. Courses in instructional techniques are available to skillcentre staff and industrial and commercial firms at the MSC's two instructor training colleges (one in England and one in Scotland) and at three instructor training units attached to skillcentres. In-plant courses are also available.

Employers are able to sponsor their own employees for refresher and upgrading training at skillcentres, on courses designed specifically to meet the needs of the employer and of the employees concerned. There is also a complementary mobile instructor service for employers, which provides specific training for employees in their own workshops.

Training services at skillcentres and courses at instructor training colleges are also available to trainees from overseas. These facilities are increasingly being used by overseas governments and organisations, and in every case programmes are structured to meet agreed training objectives.

EMPLOYMENT PROTECTION LAW

Terms and Conditions of Employment

Britain has been a pioneer in the introduction of protective legislation for the safety, health and welfare of employees. The determination by statute of minimum wages, holidays and holiday pay is confined in principle to those trades and industries where the organisation of employers or workers, or both, is inadequate to negotiate collective agreements and to ensure their observance. However, recent legislation, consolidated in the Employment Protection (Consolidation) Act 1978, provides considerable safeguards for employees in their terms of employment.

An employer is required to give employees written information on their terms and conditions of employment, the disciplinary rules applicable to them and the procedure available where an employee has a grievance about his or her employment or is dissatisfied with any disciplinary decision; minimum periods of notice when employment is to be terminated are also laid down for both employers and employees. Employees with a minimum period of service of 104 weeks are entitled to lump-sum redundancy payments if their jobs cease to exist (for example, because of technological improvements or a fall in demand) and their employers cannot offer suitable alternative work, the cost being partly met from a fund subscribed to by industry. Protection against unfair dismissal is provided by machinery under which an employee may complain against an employer of unfair dismissal, and, if successful, obtain reinstatement, re-engagement or compensation; under the Employment Act 1980, however, new employees in firms employing 20 or fewer people must be employed for two years before they have the right to complain of unfair dismissal. Legal support is given to the right to trade union organisation by making it unfair to dismiss a person because of membership or participation in the activities of an independent trade union; rights of employees are also protected in regard to penalisation short of dismissal because of trade union membership or activities. Other rights which are maintained in the 1978 Act include limited payment when work is not available for reasons other than as a result of a trade dispute, and maternity rights for female employees, including protection from dismissal because of pregnancy, maternity pay, and the right, within certain limits, to return to work after confinement.

Discrimination   The Race Relations Act 1976 (see p 154) makes unlawful discrimination on grounds of colour, race, nationality (including citizenship) or ethnic or national origin, in employment, training and related matters. Employers may not discriminate when recruiting workers or in their treatment of employees in regard to their terms and conditions of employment, promotion, transfer, training and access to other benefits, or to their dismissal.

The employment provisions of the Sex Discrimination Act (see p 152) make sex discrimination unlawful in employment, training and related matters. An employer may not discriminate between men and women either in recruitment or in treatment of existing employees in such matters as promotion, training, transfer, benefits, facilities and dismissal. It is also unlawful for a married person to be treated less favourably than an unmarried person of the same sex.

PAY, HOURS OF WORK AND HOLIDAYS

Wage Rates and Earnings   Pay for manual occupations, and increasingly for non-manual occupations, is normally set by collective bargaining (see p 338). In a small number of industries and trades legally enforceable minimum rates are set by wages councils.

Basic rates of pay vary widely, though in private industry local rates normally exceed the rates specified in national agreements. Higher rates are usually paid for overtime and shift work, and weekly earnings may be further increased by incentive bonus schemes. Piecework, or payment-by-results, is still common, though of declining importance as production methods in many industries increasingly dictate employees' output.

According to the latest annual survey conducted by the Department of Employment into earnings and hours of work, the average weekly earnings of full-time male adult manual workers in manufacturing and some non-manufacturing industries in October 1979 were, including overtime, £96·94; while for full-time female adult manual workers they were £58·24. Women's earnings are thus markedly lower than those of men, partly because on average they work shorter hours, with less overtime paid at premium rates, and partly because they tend to be concentrated in the less well-paid jobs. The Equal Pay Act 1970 requires that a woman doing the same or broadly similar work as a man, or work that has been given equal value by job evaluation, should receive equal pay and conditions of employment.

Salaries and Fees   Remuneration in commercial, technical and professional careers is normally by annual salary paid monthly, often on a scale carrying annual increments, and such careers generally afford opportunities for promotion to posts with higher remuneration. Starting salaries may be in the range of £3,000 to £3,500 (lower for 16 to 18 year-old trainees and higher for some graduates entering industry).

Most of the senior posts in business, the professions and the Civil Service command salaries in the range of £14,000 to £20,000 a year gross before tax. The posts with salaries in the range of £20,000 to £40,000 a year include those of Cabinet Ministers, top-ranking judicial appointments, the highest positions in government departments and the largest municipal authorities, editors of daily newspapers, some persons outstanding in their professions and in the higher managerial posts in industry, commerce and banking. Salaries of chairmen of major companies may exceed £50,000 a year gross, and other people such as star entertainers often receive more through fees or fixed contracts. The range of net incomes in the country as a whole is, however, reduced by a system of progressive taxation.

Hours of Work

The normal working week in Britain is in the range 38–40 hours for manual work and 35–38 for non-manual work; a five-day week is usually worked. Actual hours worked in manual occupations differ from their standard hours; in October 1979 they were 44 for men compared with 37·4 for women. Men and women in non-manual occupations generally work less overtime than manual workers.

National legislation limits and defines permissible hours of work for women and young people in a number of industries or trades—the maximum, with limited exceptions, being 48 hours a week and 10 hours a day (9 hours a day for 6-day-week workers) in premises covered by the Factories Act for adult women over 18 and young people between 16 and 18. The employment of women and young people at night is prohibited in industrial undertakings, except for young men over 16 working in some continuous-process industries (subject to certain conditions). The Department of Employment can make exemptions from these restrictions on grounds of public interest. In general the hours of work of adult men, or of people not working in factories, are not restricted by statute.

Holidays with Pay and Public Holidays

Holiday entitlements are normally determined by collective agreements. These generally provide for at least three weeks paid holiday a year. However about half of manual workers covered by agreements have entitlements of four weeks. Non-manual workers generally have longer holidays than manual workers. Additional holidays, dependent upon length of service, are also quite common.

In addition to annual holidays, most agreements provide for bank holidays or public holidays. In England and Wales, in addition to Christmas Day and Good Friday, regular bank holidays take place on New Year's Day, Easter Monday, the first Monday in May, the last Monday in May, the last Monday in August and 26 December. In Scotland public holidays are declared locally; regular bank holidays are New Year's Day, 2 January, Good Friday, the first Monday in May, the last Monday in May, the first Monday in August, Christmas Day and 26 December. The English and Welsh bank holidays apply also to Northern Ireland, where in addition St Patrick's Day (17 March) and 12 and 13 July are public holidays; in certain areas the Tuesday after Easter is also a customary holiday for industry and trade.

Provision for an alternative day to be observed is made when any bank or public holiday falls on a Saturday or Sunday.

'Fringe' Benefits

A variety of additional benefits exist in varying degree. About half of employees in employment are covered by occupational pension schemes (see p 144). Many employees are also covered by occupational sick pay schemes, additional or complementary to the State schemes (see p 147), and by schemes to provide private medical treatment. A smaller number are covered by schemes for redundancy payments above the statutory minimum. Such benefits are more usual among clerical and professional employees receiving a standard salary than among manual workers, who have a chance to increase their pay—for example, by working overtime. Employees may have use of a company car and some firms provide profit-sharing and share-saving schemes. In accord with its view that share ownership and profit-sharing can help in developing employees' understanding of, and commitment to business and industry, the Government has extended fiscal measures designed to encourage profit-sharing.

Social Security

Social security benefits, which include unemployment, sickness and industrial injury benefits, are described in the Social Welfare chapter.

INDUSTRIAL RELATIONS

The structure of industrial relations in Britain has been established mainly on a voluntary basis. The system is based chiefly on the organisation of employees and employers into trade unions and employers' associations, and on freely conducted negotiations between them at all levels. The State is ready to provide assistance where the organisation of employees, employers, or both, is inadequate to conduct negotiations, or where the usual methods of resolving disagreements have failed. In all industries and services annual strike losses over the ten years 1969–78 averaged less than half a day per employee.

TRADE UNIONS

In nearly all industries and occupations some workers (and in some industries nearly all workers) are organised into trade unions. These have grown up gradually and independently over many years and, consequently, their form and organisation vary considerably, as do their traditions. In the last decade or so, trade unionism has again increased particularly among clerical, supervisory, technical and administrative workers. Trade unions may be organised either by occupation (for example, they may recruit clerks or fitters wherever employed) or by industry. Some are based on a combination of both principles. In some firms membership of the relevant trade union is required by agreement between the employer and union ('closed shops'). At the end of 1978 the total membership of British trade unions was 13 million. There were 480 unions, but nearly 80 per cent of all trade unionists were in the 26 largest unions, each with a membership of 100,000 or over, while only 0·6 per cent were in the 263 smallest unions with under 1,000 members each.

The Certification Officer appointed under the Employment Protection Act 1975 is required to maintain a list of trade unions. To be eligible for entry on the list a trade union must show that it consists wholly or mainly of workers and that its principal purposes include the regulation of relations between workers and employers, or between workers and employers' associations. Under the Employment Protection Act 1975 and other legislation, certain rights and privileges are reserved for independent trade unions. A trade union on the list may apply to the Certification Officer for a certificate that it is independent of employers.

The central organisation of most large unions consists of a national executive council, usually elected by and responsible to the annual conference of delegates from local branches. Between conferences, councils are the highest authority of unions, and carry out policy decisions made by the conference delegates. Most unions also have regional and district organisations. At the level of the individual member there are local branches, covering one or more workplaces. Members may attend branch meetings, make suggestions about terms and conditions of employment, discuss the work of the union, and take part in the election of the union's officers. The branch takes action on certain matters considered to be entirely, or mainly, of local interest and forwards its views on wider issues for action by the union's national or regional bodies. The organising of members in individual places of work, and the negotiation of local pay agreements with managements at the factory or plant, may be done by full-time district officials of the union, or, increasingly, by 'shop stewards', who are chosen by their fellow members in the place of work to represent them. Trade unions vary in the degree to which shop stewards are integrated into their organisation. Where two or more unions have members in the same workplace, shop stewards' committees may be formed to discuss matters of common concern.

Many unions provide 'strike pay' for members involved in official industrial action. They also provide legal advice for members who suffer injury or contract diseases at work, and may pay members' legal costs where a case for compensation goes to court. Some unions pay benefits in case of illness, accident, death and retirement (additional to those payable under the national insurance scheme) financed out of membership contributions. Many trade unions are affiliated to the Labour Party. Any trade union wishing to use money for political purposes must set up a separate fund, subject to special rules, one of which must allow any member who objects to contributing to the fund to opt out.

Trades Union Congress

In Britain the national centre of the trade union movement is the Trades Union Congress (TUC), which was founded in 1868. The TUC's objects are to promote the interests of its affiliated organisations and to improve the economic and social conditions of working people. Its affiliated membership comprises 111 trade unions which together represent 12·1 million workpeople, or 92 per cent of all trade unionists in Britain. The TUC deals with all general questions which concern trade unions both nationally and internationally and gives assistance on questions relating to particular trades or industries. Through membership of the National Economic Development Council (see p 203, it participates in discussions relating to the national economy.

The annual Congress convenes in September to discuss matters of concern to trade unionists and to employees generally. It elects a General Council which represents it between Congresses and is responsible for carrying out Congress decisions, watching economic and social developments, providing educational and advisory services to unions, and presenting to the Government the trade union viewpoint on economic, social and industrial issues. The council is also empowered to mediate in inter-union disputes in certain circumstances, and uses its authority to deal with unauthorised and unconstitutional stoppages of work, as well as official disputes.

The TUC, as well as many individual unions, conducts extensive educational services for members, mainly concerned with industrial subjects, trade unionism and the principles and practice of industrial relations.

The TUC plays an active part in international trade union activity, through its affiliations to the International Confederation of Free Trade Unions and the European Trade Union Confederation. It also nominates the British workers' delegation to the annual International Labour Conference.

There are eight TUC regional councils in England, based on the Government's eight planning regions (see p 175) with a further similar body for Wales known as the Wales Trades Union Council. These bodies, whose function is to make representations to the Government's various regional bodies, co-ordinate the activities of trade unions in the regions and keep them in touch with the policy of the TUC at national level.

Scotland and Northern Ireland Scottish trade unions also have their own national central body, the Scottish Trades Union Congress (STUC), which in many respects is similar in constitution and function to the TUC. Trade unions whose membership includes Scottish workers may affiliate to the STUC and a number of trade unions are in fact affiliated to both bodies. Trade unions in Northern Ireland are represented by the Northern Ireland Committee of the Irish Congress of Trade Unions (ICTU), though the majority of trade unionists in Northern Ireland belong to unions based in Great Britain. Almost 90 per cent of Northern Ireland trade unionists are members of organisations affiliated to the ICTU, while the majority belong to unions which are also affiliated to the TUC.

EMPLOYERS' ORGANISA- TIONS Many employers in Britain are members of employers' organisations, a large number of which are wholly or partly concerned with labour matters. The primary aims of such organisations are to help to establish suitable terms and conditions of employment, including a sound wage structure and proper standards of safety, health and welfare; to promote good relations with employees and the efficient use of manpower; and to provide means of settling any disputes which may arise. They may also represent members' points of view as manufacturers or traders to the Government on commercial matters.

Employers' organisations are usually organised on an industry basis rather than a product basis. A few are purely local in character or deal with a section of an industry; others are national in scope and are concerned with the whole of an industry. In some of the main industries there are local or regional organisations combined into national federations, while in others, within which different firms are engaged in making different principal products, there is a complex structure with national and regional federations for parts of an industry as well as for the industry as a whole. Altogether there are some 150 national employers' organisations, which negotiate the national collective agreements for their industry with the trade unions concerned. Many of these national organisations belong to the Confederation of British Industry.

The final authority of local or small national organisations may be a meeting where all member firms are directly represented; but in larger organisations some form of indirect representation is necessary, either through local organisations or through regions or sections into which these are grouped.

The representatives thus chosen, together with a number of office holders, form a general council or central committee, which meets perhaps once a quarter, mainly to make major policy decisions, to elect committees and to ratify their work. A paid staff under a director or secretary carries out the day-to-day work of the organisation. There is usually a small working group, consisting of senior officials and committee chairmen, which meets to deal with urgent questions and co-ordinate the work of committees. Employers' associations (as defined in the Trade Union and Labour Relations Act 1974) may apply to the Certification Officer for inclusion in the list of employers' associations maintained by the officer.

Confederation of British Industry

The central body of employers is the Confederation of British Industry (CBI) which deals with all matters affecting the interests of employers and represents them nationally to the Government and the public and also internationally, for instance, in the International Labour Organisation and in the various institutions of the European Community. It is also the British member of the Union of Industries of the European Communities and the Business and Industry Advisory Committee to the Organisation for Economic Co-operation and Development, and a member of the British national committee of the International Chamber of Commerce. Most national employers' organisations and nationalised industries and a large number of individual companies, both large and small, belong to the CBI, whose representatives or nominees sit on various official bodies and take part in the discussion of matters of importance to the national economy through their membership of the National Economic Development Council (see p 203).

Legal Framework

The Trade Union and Labour Relations Act 1974 defines the status of trade unions and employers' associations and sets out certain legal requirements which they must observe. The Act confers immunities on trade unions in respect of actions taken in support of a trade dispute, allows peaceful picketing, and also provides that collective agreements shall not be legally enforceable unless they are written agreements and specifically provide for this.

The Employment Protection Act 1975 placed the Advisory, Conciliation and Arbitration Service on a statutory basis, provided for the appointment of a Certification Officer and for the setting up of the Central Arbitration Committee; and established an Employment Appeal Tribunal to hear appeals concerning decisions of the Certification Officer and of industrial tribunals. (Industrial tribunals are independent judicial bodies which deal, in general, with complaints from employees on infringements of individual rights under a number of Acts concerning, for example, redundancy payments, contracts of employment, equal pay, unfair dismissals and sex discrimination.)

The Employment Act 1980 seeks to obtain a balance between rights and responsibilities in industrial relations. It enables the Government to make funds available to encourage the wider use of secret union ballots and to produce codes of practice to promote good industrial relations. It limits lawful picketing to the picket's own place of work and restricts the scope for secondary action such as blacking and sympathetic strikes. It provides greater protection for the individual in relation to the closed shop and makes a number of changes to employment protection legislation, particularly to help small firms. Draft codes of practice on the conduct of picketing and the closed shop were published in August 1980.

Northern Ireland

Northern Ireland has a similar but separate system of industrial relations under which certain responsibilities devolve upon the Labour Relations Agency. Industrial relations legislation enacted in 1976 has brought the province largely into line with similar legislation enacted in Great Britain since 1974.

COLLECTIVE BARGAINING AND JOINT CONSULTATION

In most industries terms and conditions of employment and procedures for the conduct of industrial relations are settled by negotiation and agreement between employers and trade unions. Agreements may be industry-wide, supplemented as necessary by informal local agreements in firms or factories, or at firm and factory level (plant bargaining). In the public sector agreements are generally reached at industry level. In some industries, firms and factories, negotiations are conducted by meetings held when necessary, while in others, joint negotiating councils or committees have been established on a permanent basis. The scope of the various joint bodies (from the national joint industrial councils for whole industries to the works councils and committees in individual workplaces) varies widely, and has frequently been extended to cover such additional matters as production plans, absenteeism, training, education and welfare. Normally these arrangements for collective bargaining suffice to settle all questions which are raised, but provision is sometimes made for matters not so settled to be referred for settlement to independent conciliation or arbitration. The Employment Protection Act 1975 made provision for information needed for collective bargaining purposes to be disclosed by employers to trade unions, subject to certain safeguards.

Standing arrangements exist for consultation at national level between the Government, the TUC, the CBI, and the nationalised industries through the National Economic Development Council on matters in which employers and workers have a common interest. The operation of collective bargaining has from time to time been restricted in an attempt to control inflation.

Advisory, Conciliation and Arbitration Service

The Advisory, Conciliation and Arbitration Service (ACAS) has the general duty of promoting the improvement of industrial relations, and in particular of encouraging the extension of collective bargaining and the development and (where necessary) reform of collective bargaining machinery.

In 1976 ACAS was placed on a statutory basis under the Employment Protection Act and is controlled by a council consisting of a chairman and nine other members experienced in industrial relations, of which three are nominated after consultation with the CBI, three after consultation with the TUC, and three are independent.

The service may offer conciliation in industrial disputes in both the public and private sectors of industry where this is thought to be helpful, and has discretion in meeting requests for conciliation subject only to the need to pay regard to agreed procedures in the industry or area of employment concerned.

At the joint request of the parties in dispute, and having regard to the need to safeguard negotiating procedures, ACAS may appoint single arbitrators or boards of arbitration to settle disputes on the basis of agreed terms of reference. Alternatively ACAS may refer cases for arbitration to the Central Arbitration Committee (see below). Some 395 joint requests for arbitration were made to ACAS during 1979.

Although ACAS has prime responsibility for intervention in disputes, the Secretary of State retains powers to appoint a court of inquiry or committee of investigation into a dispute, whether existing or foreseen.

The service gives advice on all aspects of industrial relations and personnel management. It conducts surveys to diagnose the causes of industrial relations problems and suggests remedial action to management and trade unions or employee representatives. It also carries particular responsibility for attempting conciliation on complaints of infringement of individual employee rights (such as individual complaints of unfair dismissal, complaints under the Equal Pay Act 1970 and complaints on employment matters under the Sex Discrimination Act 1975 and the Race Relations Act 1976).

The service is concerned with the long-term improvement of collective bargaining and, with the consent of the parties involved, conducts detailed inquiries in particular firms or industries. It also considers claims by independent trade unions that they should be recognised by an employer.

Central Arbitration Committee

The Central Arbitration Committee (CAC) is a permanent body for the settlement of disputes by voluntary arbitration. Disputes may be referred to the CAC by ACAS at the joint request of the employers and trade unions concerned.

The committee is also called upon to arbitrate on claims made under various Acts, including the Equal Pay Act 1970 and the Employment Protection Act 1975, and acts as the independent tribunal to which the Secretary of State for Employment refers questions relating to the payment of wages and conditions of employment observed by Government contractors.

Public Authorities

While industrial relations in government service and in the nationalised industries are, in general, organised on the same principles as in private industry, there are some special features.

Central and Local Government

Non-industrial employees in central Government service, are permitted and encouraged to join the appropriate Civil Service unions and there is a highly developed system of negotiation and joint consultation by means of the National and Departmental Whitley Councils. Unresolved disputes may, subject to certain limitations, be reported to the Secretary of State for reference to the Civil Service Arbitration Tribunal, an independent body appointed by the Secretary of State. Government industrial employees are similarly encouraged to belong to trade unions and there is machinery for joint consultation. Disputes on wages or conditions of employment that cannot be resolved by the existing machinery can be referred to the Central Arbitration Committee.

In local government service there are separate National Joint Councils for the main grades of employees (such as manual, clerical and technical employees) which deal with wages and conditions of service as well as other matters. There are corresponding regional and district councils.

Nationalised Industries

The major nationalised industries have a statutory duty to establish satisfactory arrangements for collective bargaining and for joint consultation with their employees; the British Steel Corporation has appointed worker directors.

Unlike firms in the private sector, the corporations are not usually members of employers' associations (although the majority are 'public sector members' of the CBI). In some industries they are sole or main employers, but even where part of the industry is in private hands, as for example in road transport, they are separately and directly represented on wage-negotiating bodies.

Wages and conditions of service in the nationalised industries are generally settled by negotiation between representatives of management and trade unions at the national level; in most cases there are also regional and local bodies, similarly representative, to deal with local issues but not normally to negotiate separate local agreements. Most of the industries use the facilities for arbitration offered to industry generally by the ACAS, but coalmining and rail transport have their own special arrangements. Consultation at all levels, including the workplace, has been arranged in all the nationalised industries.

Office of Manpower Economics

The Office of Manpower Economics, established in 1971 as an independent non-statutory body, acts as secretariat for the three review bodies set up to advise on the remuneration of certain groups in the public sector for which negotiating machinery is not appropriate, such as chairmen and members of boards of nationalised industries, the higher judiciary and senior civil servants; the armed forces; and doctors and dentists. It also services special inquiries on particular pay structures and related problems.

STATUTORY NEGOTIATING MACHINERY

In a number of industries and trades where the organisation of employers or employees or both is not strong enough to provide a basis for successful voluntary arrangements, there are statutory wage-regulating bodies, known as wages councils. These are composed of equal numbers of representatives of employers and employees in the respective sectors of industry, with three independent members. Wages councils publish proposals for minimum remuneration, holidays, holiday remuneration and other terms and conditions of employment. After considering any representations the councils make orders giving statutory force to such proposals. The Department of Employment's Wages Inspectorate enforces the provisions of these wages orders. About 2·7 million workers are covered by such arrangements.

The Secretary of State for Employment has power to convert a wages council into a statutory joint industrial council (SJIC), a body which functions in the same ways as a wages council, except that it has no independent members. Such conversion is intended to assist in the development of collective bargaining, an SJIC being seen as a half-way stage between the statutory system and full voluntary collective bargaining.

Agricultural wages boards (there are boards for England and Wales, for Scotland and for Northern Ireland) perform similar functions in relation to employment in agriculture.

HEALTH AND SAFETY AT WORK

Employers have a duty at common and criminal law to take reasonable care of their employees and provide a safe system of working, while employees have a duty of care towards each other and also to take care of their own safety. In addition, minimum required standards of safety in certain kinds of workplaces or work are laid down under a number of statutes; some of these also deal with health and welfare. The Health and Safety at Work etc. Act 1974 reorganised the system under which safety and health at work was safeguarded and extended it to cover everyone at work and to further the protection of the general public from industrial hazards.

Health and Safety Commission

The Health and Safety Commission, appointed by the Secretary of State for Employment after consultation with the TUC, CBI and local authorities, has responsibility for supervising the application and enforcement of health and safety legislation. Its operational arm is the Health and Safety Executive, consisting largely of the government inspectorates covering factories, mines and quarries, agriculture, explosives, nuclear installations and alkali works; the Employment Medical Advisory Service; and the Health and Safety Laboratories, which include the Safety in Mines Research Establishment.

The basic obligations laid down in the Act are supported by ministerial powers to make regulations dealing with a wide range of health and safety matters. Regulations may be supplemented where appropriate by codes of practice approved by the commission, and by guidance notes and other codes. In particular the Act gives inspectors the power to issue improvement and prohibition notices, which enable them to require practical improvements to be made within a specified time or to require preventive measures immediately without first having to obtain a court order. There are provisions for appeals to industrial tribunals against such notices.

Safety Regulations

About 207,000 industrial premises (factories, warehouses, shipyards, docks and construction sites) are regulated under the Factories Act 1961, which is enforced mainly by the Factory Inspectorate, part of the Health and Safety Executive. Likewise about 770,000 premises are subject to the Offices, Shops and Railway Premises Act 1963, whose enforcement is shared by the Factory Inspectorate, the Mines and Quarries Inspectorate, the Railway Inspectorate (see below) and local authorities.

The Acts and regulations made under them are designed to secure the health, safety and welfare of employees, and deal with such matters as the fencing of machinery; precautions against the exposure of people to toxic gases and dusts; precautions against fire, dangerous substances and special risks; the safe condition of premises; and cleanliness, lighting, temperature and ventilation. They also contain provisions concerning the employment of women. Anyone intending to employ other people in industrial or commercial premises to which either the Factories Act or the Offices, Shops and Railway Premises Act applies has to notify the enforcing authority of his intention and there is a statutory duty to report every accident which is either fatal or causes more than three days' incapacity. The Factories Act includes provisions for the compulsory notification and investigation of certain types of dangerous occurrence.

Comparable provision with appropriate variations covers mines and quarries, agriculture and transport (including aviation and shipping, the responsibility of the Department of Trade). As with the Factories Act these other provisions are, with some exceptions, enforced through inspectorates—the Mines and Quarries Inspectorate, the Agricultural Inspectorate, and the Railway Inspectorate of the Department of Transport. Safety requirements in all other places of work including hotels, places of entertainment and educational establishments but excluding domestic work in the home, are covered by the Health and Safety at Work etc. Act or (in respect of their offices and shops) by the Offices, Shops and Railway Premises Act, while fire authorities are responsible for general fire precautions and means of escape.

The Health and Safety Executive, through its Nuclear Installations Inspectorate, is the authority concerned with the granting of nuclear site licences for commercial nuclear installations. No such installation may be constructed or operated in Britain without a licence granted by the executive under sections of the Nuclear Installations Act 1965 which are relevant statutory provisions under the Health and Safety at Work etc. Act. Conditions attached to such licences in the interests of safety are imposed and enforced by the inspectorate.

The Health and Safety Commission also has responsibility under the Mineral Workings (Offshore Installations) Act 1971 and the Petroleum and Submarine Pipelines Act 1975 for the health and safety of all workers (including divers) engaged in the offshore oil and gas industry, by agency agreement with the Petroleum Engineering Directorate, Department of Energy.

Other Measures

Transport operators and ministries concerned with road and air travel give high priority to safety measures affecting crews and passengers. Every effort is made to counter the higher risks resulting from rising traffic densities by improving the design of vehicles and transport equipment, by control of standards of maintenance, by traffic regulations and by training crews in safety awareness.

To minimise the hazards which may arise from the use of pesticides, a voluntary scheme has been established under which pesticides are vetted by the Ministry of Agriculture, Fisheries and Food's Advisory Committee on Pesticides and Other Toxic Chemicals (see p 184) before being marketed. The committee gives clearance for specific uses, subject to its recommendations on such matters as safety precautions and labelling being agreed to.

There are also the Health and Safety Laboratories, which are concerned with research into health and safety problems in industry (see p 390).

Employment of Women and Children

Legislation forbids any employment of children under 14 years of age, and employment in any industrial undertaking of children who have not reached the statutory minimum school-leaving age (16); of women and young people underground in mines and in certain other dangerous occupations (for example, certain processes connected with lead manufacture); and of women in factories and workshops within four weeks after childbirth. It also limits and defines the permissible hours of employment for women and young people.

Promotion of Safety Measures

The Health and Safety Commission encourages the development of voluntary central organisation within each industry at national level for the consideration of safety matters and the formulation of policy and accident prevention. Its inspectorates, besides inquiring into notified accidents and safety aspects of machine design and specification, circulate expert advice to both sides of industry and to the general public. Recognised trade unions may appoint safety representatives to represent the employees in a workplace; also, two or more such representatives may make a written request to the employer to establish a safety committee, which must then be set up within three months.

Organisations in industry participate also in joint standing and advisory committees appointed by the Secretary of State for Employment, but these arrangements are being superseded. The Health and Safety Commission has appointed three subject advisory committees (on dangerous substances, toxic substances and medical matters), two committees concerned with particular hazards (major hazards and nuclear installations) and nine industry advisory committees (for agriculture, ceramics, construction, foundries, oil, paper and board, printing, railways and health services). The Royal Society for the Prevention of Accidents (RoSPA) and the British Safety Council are national bodies concerned with accident prevention and sponsor a number of local accident prevention groups.

Training and Research in Safety

Training is important in accident prevention and the Manpower Services Commission provides a course in job safety for supervisors in its Training Within Industry scheme (see p 332). The industrial training boards include specific provisions for safety training in their training recommendations.

RoSPA provides a variety of safety courses for special needs, mainly at its Industrial Safety Training Centre in Birmingham, and also helps the accident prevention movement by providing and organising conferences; its regional industrial safety officers work to promote safety activity among top-level managers. The British Safety Council also offers safety training courses. Other courses are organised by local accident prevention groups and organisations such as the Federation of Civil Engineering Contractors.

A substantial amount of research is being done by industry, universities and other academic bodies, and government research organisations into problems of guarding machines, ergonomics, safe handling, electrical hazards, nuclear safety, protective personal equipment, construction methods, explosions and fires, psychological factors and causes of accidents, both generally and in particular sectors of industry. Industrial research associations include among their more purely economic research projects the improvement of working conditions and the reduction of hazards.

The National Coal Board conducts courses of safety training for workmen and officials. Its research programme includes a number of projects with a direct bearing on safety. In addition, the Health and Safety Executive has a statutory responsibility for research concerning the safety and health of coal miners, largely exercised through its Safety in Mines Research Establishment.

The University of Aston in Birmingham runs degree and diploma courses for the training of safety officers and engineers whose careers will be concerned with the technical aspects of insurance and forensic work.

Employment Medical Advisory Service

The Employment Medical Advisory Service (EMAS), part of the Health and Safety Executive, provides a nation-wide service of advice on the medical aspects of employment problems to employers, employees, trade unions, doctors and others. It carries out medical examinations of workers in hazardous occupations and surveys of employment hazards, advises the staff of the Manpower Services Commission on medical aspects of job placement, rehabilitation and industrial training and co-operates with school medical officers and careers officers in helping to solve the employment problems of handicapped school leavers. The service, headed by the Health and Safety Executive's Director of Medical Services, has over 100 employment medical advisers based in the country's main industrial centres. The TUC, the CBI and other interested organisations are associated with the work of the service through advisory committees.

Scientific Support for Occupational Health

The Occupational Medicine and Hygiene Laboratories (which are part of the Health and Safety Laboratories, see p 343) at Cricklewood, north London, provide laboratory services and undertake research in the field of occupational health. The Factory Inspectorate also looks to the laboratories as a main source of laboratory assistance.

Research facilities are provided by government agencies such as the Medical Research Council; by university faculties of industrial health and social medicine; and by the research departments of various industries and large industrial concerns. Field investigations are carried out by the Factory Inspectorate, which has specialised technical branches, and by the EMAS.

Employers' Health Services

Many employers voluntarily maintain medical services for their employees over and above the statutory requirements. The big employers, including the State and the boards of nationalised industries, have taken the lead but a number of smaller factories also provide medical services and in a few cases have joined together in group medical services.

Other Amenities

An increasing number of firms pay part or all of the cost of recreational facilities. Some have their own rehabilitation centres or support convalescent homes. The provision of low-priced meals at the place of employment has become usual in large undertakings and quite common in smaller ones. Many offices and shops which are unable to provide canteen facilities for their staff have adopted luncheon voucher schemes.

Human Relations in Industry

Both official and voluntary organisations are concerned with promoting better human relationships in industry. Official research has sought to extend the available knowledge of the factors influencing human relations in industry and human efficiency. Such research is sponsored or conducted by the Social Science Research Council (see p 385) and the Medical Research Council (see p 383). In addition, the Department of Employment's Work Research Unit provides information on how particular jobs can be redesigned to create greater satisfaction, helps industry and others in initiating and evaluating changes in the content of work, and administers a research programme. Voluntary organisations include bodies which deal with management problems and provide a service to subscribing firms; professional associations, linking individuals with a common interest in particular functions of management; and bodies providing specialist services, usually on a fee-paying basis.

Safety, Health and Welfare in Northern Ireland
The safety, health and welfare of employees in Northern Ireland have been protected by legislation in the Factories Act (Northern Ireland) 1965 and the Office and Shop Premises Act (Northern Ireland) 1966. A number of firms voluntarily employ safety officers, and industrial safety groups, supported by representatives of industry, insurance companies and public authorities, make a valuable contribution to accident prevention.

The Health and Safety at Work (NI) Order 1978, which came into force early in 1979, extends health and safety legislation to all people at work except domestic workers in private employment. A Health and Safety Agency, roughly corresponding to the Health and Safety Commission, and an Employment Medical Advisory Service have been set up under the legislation.

18 Finance

Through the public finance system the Government raises money from individuals and companies by taxation, borrowing and other means, and spends it on behalf of the community in the provision of goods and services such as education, health and defence, in payments to people and organisations, and in capital investment. The term public finance also covers the raising of revenue and its expenditure by local authorities and certain other public bodies and the financial relationship between these agencies and the central Government.

THE PUBLIC SECTOR

PUBLIC EXPENDITURE

Public expenditure comprises the current and capital expenditure of central government and local authorities (collectively known as general government), excluding expenditure charged to the operating account of trading bodies; central government finance in the form of grants, loans or public dividend capital provided towards the cost of capital investment by the nationalised industries; the capital expenditure of other public corporations; the contingency reserve; and those debt interest payments which constitute a charge on taxation. Public expenditure, excluding the contingency reserve and debt interest, in 1979–80 amounted to nearly £72,000 million (at 1979 survey prices) of which 73 per cent was undertaken by the central Government and 26 per cent by local authorities, the remaining 1 per cent representing the capital expenditure of certain public corporations other than the nationalised industries. The social services programmes accounted for over 52 per cent of the total programmes, and defence expenditure for about 11 per cent. The wide range of functions and purposes of this expenditure and its distribution is shown in Table 28.

Out of the total public expenditure of £75,100 million in 1979–80 some £39,210 million or 52 per cent was spent by the public sector directly on goods and services (wages and salaries, other current expenditure on goods and services, gross domestic fixed capital formation and value of the physical increase in stocks and work in progress). Transfer payments to individuals, companies and other institutions in the private sector (for example, social security payments, capital grants, subsidies, and debt interest) made up the balance. Unlike public authorities' direct purchases of goods and services, transfer payments do not represent a direct demand on the nation's resources. The gross sums transferred create a proportionately lower indirect demand for goods and services because of taxes paid and savings made by the recipients.

Between 1974–75 and 1979–80 total public expenditure grew in real terms by nearly 5 per cent, but it is expected to fall progressively over the next few years in accordance with the Government's policy of reducing the claim of the public sector on national resources.

The Planning, Control and Monitoring of Public Expenditure

Major importance is attached to adequate planning and control of public expenditure. Planning is undertaken in the annual public expenditure survey, which leads to the publication of a document setting out the Government's plans for public expenditure over the next few years. Control is exercised through the Supply Estimates and cash limits. (Cash limits, see below, are derived from the plans decided in the public expenditure survey; they are not normally exceeded.) Effective control requires up-to-date information on the progress of expenditure, achieved through monitoring by the Treasury or other departments. These arrangements are described in more detail below.

TABLE 28: Public Expenditure 1979–80 and 1980–81

£ million at 1979 survey prices

	Outturn 1979–80 estimate	Plans 1980–81
Defence and external relations		
Defence	7,723	7,997
Overseas aid	794	779
European Community contributions	919	1,024
Other overseas services	432	406
Commerce and industry		
Agriculture, fisheries, food and forestry	944	877
Trade, industry, energy and employment	2,969	2,992
Government lending to nationalised industries	1,900	700
Environmental services		
Roads and transport	3,073	2,910
Housing	5,372	4,700
Other environmental services	3,273	3,192
Law, order and protective services	2,446	2,530
Social services		
Education and science, arts and libraries	9,654	9,225
Health and personal social services	9,067	9,186
Social security	18,890	19,354
Other services		
Other public services	1,014	976
Common services	1,047	1,066
Northern Ireland	2,200	2,136
Total programmes	71,716	70,051
Contingency reserve	84	1,000
Debt interest	3,300	3,500
Total Public Expenditure	75,100	74,551

Source: *The Government's Expenditure Plans 1980–81 to 1983–84*
Differences between totals and the sums of their constituent parts are due to rounding.

Public Expenditure Surveys

Each year a survey is made of the whole range of projected public expenditure. This covers the expected outturn for the current year and plans for the next three (until recently four) years.

The survey starts with a revaluation of the plans published in the previous report to a new constant price level (broadly, prices in the autumn of the preceding year). Proposals for changes in the existing plans are then brought together in order to provide ministers with a basis for decisions about the total and the composition of public expenditure in the period covered. This gives the Government the opportunity to plan any necessary changes without causing wasteful disruption in services, and to have regard to the general economic outlook when taking decisions.

A report on the survey is prepared in the first half of the year. This is followed by ministerial consideration of the report and then by the publication of the Government's public expenditure plans (see Bibliography) early in the following year. This provides the basis for an annual public expenditure debate in the House of Commons. The plans contain a contingency reserve to provide for additions to the programmes set out. Since 1976 this has been developed into a more operational instrument, as one of the means of securing that actual expenditure is kept within the plans. The object is, as far as possible, to limit claims on the reserve by meeting the cost of new measures, or increased estimates for existing measures, within existing departmental totals. Recourse to the reserve to meet additional expenditure is subject to the approval of Treasury ministers, who may refer the larger or more difficult claims for consideration by the Cabinet.

Estimates

In December each department submits its cash requirements for the financial year beginning on the following 1 April to the Treasury. Estimates cover central Government's own expenditure. (Not all this expenditure is classified as public expenditure—for example, payments to local authorities. Only when the money is spent by the local authorities is public expenditure recorded.) After they have been approved by the Treasury, the Supply Estimates are presented to Parliament shortly before the Budget (see p 350) and are approved by Parliament by means of an annual Appropriation Act in July (expenditure to this date from 1 April is covered by a Vote on Account approved by Parliament before the beginning of the financial year). There are 29 allotted days (known as supply days) in each session on which the choice of subject for debate rests with the Opposition and on which estimates can be debated. Broad issues of policy are normally discussed.

Other Government Funds

Certain expenditures are not approved annually, but are covered by Acts of Parliament allowing payments to continue from one year to another and are paid direct from the Consolidated Fund. These include the financial provision for members of the royal family, and salaries and pensions of judges. The Consolidated Fund, into which tax revenue and other receipts are paid, finances most of the central Government's expenditure; its balance is the Exchequer account at the Bank of England. The National Loans Fund covers most of the central Government's domestic lending and borrowing, and is operated as an official account at the Bank of England. The two funds deal only with sterling receipts and payments; official dealings in foreign exchange are carried out by the Exchange Equalisation Account (see p 357).

Cash Limits

Cash limits, first introduced on an extensive scale in 1976–77, have been applied to public spending wherever they can make a useful contribution to financial discipline. They also contribute to the Government's policy for reducing inflation and help in forecasting the Government's maximum financing requirements. To simplify the control of expenditure, the cash limits and those parts of the Supply Estimates to which they apply (accounting for about two-thirds of public expenditure) are presented in assimilated form. This has the advantage of making the Supply Estimates an effective control mechanism and subjects cash limits to parliamentary control. Spending departments and authorities are required to provide within their cash limits for increases in costs due to pay and price changes so there is no guarantee that the planned level of expenditure in real terms can be achieved.

Certain services such as social security payments are excluded because, once policy and rates of payment have been determined, cash spending in the short term depends on factors outside the Government's direct control such as the number of claimants. Local authority spending which is financed from local taxation (the rates, see p 66) is also outside the scope of cash limits, which apply only to central government expenditure. Financial assistance given by the central government to local authorities in the form of rate support grants (see p 65) comes from funds on which cash limits have been placed. Cash limits are also placed on local authority capital expenditure, which is financed by borrowing from the National Loans Fund. The estimates of the financing requirements of the nationalised industries are treated as a form of cash limit.

Monitoring

Expenditure by government departments is monitored by the Treasury and compared with profiles of expected expenditure prepared at the beginning of the financial year in accordance with the approved Public Expenditure Survey, Supply Estimate and cash limit provisions.

This process has been improved in recent years through the introduction of a computerised financial information system for both the Treasury and for spending departments.

Parliament and Audit

Parliamentary control of public expenditure is exercised not only through approval of the Supply Estimates but also through the work of the Comptroller and Auditor General, the Public Accounts Committee and the House of Commons Select Committee on the Treasury and the Civil Service.

The Comptroller and Auditor General

The Comptroller and Auditor General is appointed by the Crown and his independence of the Executive is secured by specific statutory provisions.

He has two functions: as Comptroller General he exercises his statutory duty to ensure that all revenue and other public moneys payable to the Consolidated Fund and the National Loans Fund are duly paid over and that all issues from these funds are authorised by statute; and as Auditor General, and in accordance with the Exchequer and Audit Departments Acts and the National Loans Act 1968, he audits, on behalf of the House of Commons, accounts of the transactions of the Consolidated Fund and National Loans Fund and every Appropriation Account, and submits his reports on them and other accounts to Parliament. For many years and with the encouragement of the Public Accounts Committee his statutory audit functions have been interpreted widely and his reports regularly examine and criticise matters of general financial administration, cost-effectiveness and cases of apparent waste or extravagance.

The Government has been reviewing the Exchequer and Audit Departments Acts and has issued a consultative document *The Role of the Comptroller and Auditor General* in order to carry forward its review. (See Bibliography.)

Parliamentary Control of Expenditure

A new structure of House of Commons Select Committees was established in 1979 (see also p 33). There are 14 committees which examine the expenditure (as well as the administration and policy) of the principal government departments. The objective of the new structure is to strengthen the accountability of ministers to the House of Commons and, to this end, the Government makes available to the select committees as much information as possible, including confidential information.

The Public Accounts Committee

The accounts of each department and the reports of the Comptroller and Auditor General upon them are considered by a House of Commons Select Committee called the Public Accounts Committee. This was established in 1861 to ensure that expenditure was only incurred in accordance with the purposes for which it was voted and with the relevant Acts of Parliament. The Committee's terms of reference are simply that it must examine and report upon the accounts laid before Parliament but these terms are widely interpreted. Successive committees have investigated whether full value has been obtained for the sums spent by departments and have reported in detail on cases in which administration appeared faulty or negligent. The Committee has become a powerful instrument for the exposure of waste or inefficiency and it embodies its findings in regular reports to Parliament. Although the Committee has no executive powers its reports to Parliament carry considerable weight and its recommendations are taken very seriously by departments and organisations that it examines. The Government's formal reply to these reports is presented to Parliament by the Treasury in the form of a Treasury Minute, and the reports and the Minute are made the subject of an annual debate in the House of Commons.

THE BUDGET

The Budget (an old word which meant a bag containing papers or accounts) is a set of proposals, usually put forward in March or April, for financing government expenditure and managing the economy. Supplementary budgetary measures may also be introduced at other times of the year. The proposals are described by the Chancellor of the Exchequer in the Budget speech, against the background of a statement on Britain and the world economy, the Government's past and prospective revenue and expenditure, and an assessment of the position and prospects of the economy.

The Budget speech is followed by the moving of a set of Ways and Means (or Budget) resolutions, in which the proposals are embodied. These resolutions, when passed by the House, become the foundation of the Finance Act, which expresses the proposals in statutory form.

A major function of the Budget is to act as an instrument of economic management, and the Budget statement is normally the main occasion for a review of general economic policy. The Budget is therefore concerned with the balance between the total of goods and services which are likely to be available to the nation and the total claims which are likely to be made on them. Through taxation the Government can exert a considerable influence on the volume of demand for goods and services; its measures can also have a broader influence on the pattern of demand and, through, for instance, increasing incentives, on the long-term performance of the economy.

The Budget deals with the means of financing expenditure and particularly with changes in taxation and not primarily with expenditure itself. On occasions, changes affecting expenditure, such as increases in pensions and family allowances, have been announced in the Budget statement, as have financial and monetary measures, such as changes in exchange control policies. Such measures, however, are not generally reflected in the resolutions or the Finance Act but are applied by the appropriate procedure, that is, separate legislation, statutory instruments or administrative action.

The scope of the Budget and that of the Finance Act which follows it are different although they are closely interrelated. The Budget is essentially concerned with the measures that give effect to the Chancellor's decision to increase or reduce to an appropriate extent the predicted level of demand on economic resources by use of the instruments at his disposal, and especially by increasing or reducing the yield of central government taxes. The tax changes proposed on the basis of the Budget judgment are enacted in the form approved by Parliament in the Finance Act, which also provides the annual opportunity for non-budgetary changes in the tax system and for certain other financial matters, such as provisions relating to Government borrowing.

The bulk of the taxation proposals in the Budget are concerned with changes in the rates of coverage of existing taxes, the introduction of new taxes or the abolition of existing ones, and changes in the administrative machinery relating to taxation. In two cases (income tax and corporation tax), however, annual Ways and Means resolutions followed by a Finance Act clause are necessary to maintain the taxes in existence at all, since they are annual taxes. Thus a Budget at or about the beginning of each financial year is a necessity.

New taxes and changes in certain existing taxes, like other changes in statute law, do not come into effect until the appropriate Bill—in this case the Finance Bill—has received Royal Assent (in the case of the spring Budget, normally about the end of July) or at some other date laid down in the Bill. Some changes, however, come into effect earlier, usually from Budget Day or from the start of the tax year, under the Provisional Collection of Taxes Act. This enables the Government to collect certain taxes provisionally, income tax, for example, either at the rates previously in operation or at new rates following the passing of the appropriate Ways and Means resolutions. Other ways of changing taxation are by special legislation or the use of the regulator, which permits limited changes between Budgets in the rates of value added tax (by up to 25 per cent) and the main groups of excise duties (by up to 10 per cent).

Public Sector Accounts
The economic background to the spring Budget and the transactions of the central government and the public sector as a whole are presented in the *Financial Statement and Budget Report* (see Bibliography) which is laid before the House of Commons by the Chancellor of the Exchequer when he presents the Budget. The report is in five parts: the Budget proposals; the medium-term financial strategy; the economic context of the Budget; the accounts of the public sector for the past financial year and the one immediately ahead; and the accounts of the central Government for the same two years. The accounts are designed to assist in assessing the impact of changes in revenue and public expenditure on the economy.

The accounts of the public sector show the transactions of the central government, local authorities, nationalised industries and other public corporations combined into a consolidated account covering the whole of the public sector. The transactions within the public sector cancel out on consolidation and the net balance on the consolidated account represents, therefore, the borrowing which is required by the public sector from the private and overseas sectors.

The accounts of the central government show transactions both on the conventional cash basis of Exchequer accounting and in accordance with the framework of the national income accounts.

To raise the money it requires over and above tax revenue and other receipts the Government offers a great variety of claims on itself designed to attract different types of lender. Broadly there is marketable debt and non-marketable debt. Marketable debt is made up of short-term floating debt consisting of Treasury bills, and funded or longer-term debt made up of government securities which are of varying maturities and publicly quoted on the Stock

Exchange. Non-marketable debt comprises the various forms of national savings designed to attract the smaller saver; certificates of tax deposits;[1] and ways and means advances, which basically are very short-term internal government borrowing. The bulk of public corporations' borrowing is met by central government through the National Loans Fund, although public corporations' temporary borrowing needs are met largely from the market under Treasury guarantee. That part of local authority borrowing met by central government is dealt with through the National Investment and Loans Office (set up in April 1980 as a result of the merger of the Public Works Loan Board and the National Debt Office) which has recourse to the National Loans Fund. The local authorities also borrow directly from the market, both short-term and long-term, through a range of different investments. Some public corporations and local authorities also borrow, under special statutory power and with Treasury consent, in foreign currencies.

After allowing for the changes introduced by the 1980 Budget the central government's borrowing requirement for 1980–81 was expected to be £9,313 million, compared with an estimated outturn of £8,227 million in 1979–80, and that for the public sector as a whole £8,536 million, compared with an estimated £9,795 million in 1979–80.

Table 29 shows total revenue from taxation and other sources in 1979–80 and the forecasts for 1980–81 together with the effects of the Budget changes.

SOURCES OF REVENUE

The three principal sources of tax revenue are first, taxes on income, which include income tax and corporation tax; second, taxes on capital, which include capital transfer tax and capital gains tax; and third, taxes on expenditure (including taxes on the ownership or use of certain assets), which include protective and excise duties, value added tax (VAT), the National Insurance Surcharge, local rates (see p 66), stamp duties and licence duties (for example, on motor vehicles). Taxes on individual incomes are progressive in that larger incomes bear a proportionately higher rate of tax. The Board of Inland Revenue assesses and collects the taxes on income and capital and the stamp duties; the Board of Customs and Excise collects the most important taxes on expenditure (the customs and excise duties and VAT) while a variety of authorities is responsible for the collection of the remainder. The Government has begun to shift the emphasis from taxes on income to taxes on expenditure.

Taxes on Income

Income Tax

Income tax is imposed for the year of assessment beginning on 6 April. The Finance Act 1980 abolished the lower rate band of 25 per cent for the first £750 of taxable income (total income less personal and other allowances) and altered the bands applicable to the other rates. The basic rate of 30 per cent now applies to the first £11,250 of taxable income. A rate of 40 per cent applies to the £11,251–£13,250 band of taxable income, 45 per cent to the £13,251–£16,750 band, 50 per cent to the £16,751–£22,250 band and 55 per cent to the £22,251–£27,750 band, ending with a maximum rate of 60 per cent on taxable income over £27,750. These rates apply to both earned and investment incomes. Investment incomes are also liable to a surcharge of 15 per cent on their excess over £5,500. The tax imposed on an individual is graduated by means of personal allowances and reliefs. In general the income of married

---

[1] The certificate of tax deposit scheme is operated by the Inland Revenue. Certificates may be purchased by individuals or corporate bodies to be tendered in settlement of a wide range of taxes.

TABLE 29: Taxation and Miscellaneous Receipts 1979–80 and 1980–81

£ million

	1979–80		1980–81
	Budget Forecast	Estimated Outturn	Budget Forecast
Taxation			
Inland Revenue:			
Income tax	19,655	20,500	23,830
Surtax	10	11	8
Corporation tax[a]	4,850	4,650	4,860
Petroleum revenue tax	730	1,435[b]	2,560
Capital gains tax	390	410	490
Development land tax	20	25	25
Estate duty	25	30	17
Capital transfer tax	360	400	400
Stamp duties	550	610	670
Total Inland Revenue	26,590	28,071	32,860
Customs and Excise:			
Value added tax	8,325	8,000	12,450
Oil	2,900	2,925	3,650
Tobacco	2,550	2,580	2,775
Spirits, beer, wine, cider and perry	2,400	2,395	2,825
Betting and gaming	410	400	475
Car tax	510	515	575
Other excise duties	10	10	10
European Community own resources[c]			
Customs duties, etc	860	935	950
Agricultural levies	285	240	290
Total Customs and Excise	18,250	18,000	24,000
Vehicle excise duties	1,148	1,137	1,411
National insurance surcharge	2,952	2,964	3,509
Total Taxation	48,940	50,172	61,780
Miscellaneous Receipts:			
Broadcast receiving licences	383	427	535
Interest and dividends	310	270	300
Other[d]	1,380	2,500	2,800
Total	51,013	53,369	65,415

Source: *Financial Statement and Budget Report 1980–81*

[a] Corporation tax receipts include advance corporation tax:

Gross	1,630	1,925	1,800
Net of repayments	1,580	1,815	1,700

[b] The Budget forecast did not include the receipts amounting to £709 million under the Petroleum Revenue Tax Act 1980.

[c] Customs duties and agricultural levies are accountable to the European Community as 'own resources'.

[d] Includes the 10 per cent of 'own resources' refunded by the Community to meet the costs of collection.

couples is taxed as one but the married man's allowance is higher than the single person's. A husband and wife may choose to have the wife's earnings charged separately for tax on condition that the husband receives the single instead of the married personal allowance. Even then they are taxed jointly on any investment income.

For 1980–81 a single person earning £5,000 a year pays £1,087 in income tax while a married man with the same earned income pays £856. The amount of tax payable by a single person varies from, for example, £37 on an earned annual income of £1,500 to £12,050 on one of £30,000.

Most wage and salary earners pay their income tax under a PAYE ('Pay as You Earn') system whereby tax is deducted (and accounted for to the Inland Revenue) by the employer, thus enabling them to keep as up to date as possible with their tax payments.

In general, income tax is charged on all income which originates in Britain and on all income arising abroad of persons resident in Britain. Interest on certain British government securities belonging to persons not ordinarily resident in Britain is exempt. Britain has entered into agreements with many countries providing for relief from double taxation; where such agreements are not in force unilateral relief is allowed.

Corporation Tax   Companies pay corporation tax on all their profits, whether distributed or not. Only a proportion of any capital gains is included in total profits, with the result that chargeable gains as a whole are subject to a lower effective rate of tax. Income tax is not deducted from dividends but a company which distributes profits to its shareholders is required to make to the Inland Revenue an advance payment of corporation tax. In general, this payment is set against a company's corporation tax bill and the recipient of the distribution in respect of which the advance payment was made is entitled to a tax credit, which satisfies his or her liability to income tax at the basic rate.

The rate of corporation tax is fixed retrospectively in the Budget for the past financial year; for the financial year 1979 (1 April 1979–31 March 1980) it is 52 per cent with a reduced rate of 40 per cent for small companies (such companies being defined in the relevant Finance Act). The tax is assessed on the profits of accounting periods, the rate of tax being the rate for the financial year in which the accounting period falls. Where an accounting period straddles 31 March the profits are apportioned on a time basis. Relief is given by an interim scheme for the rise in the value of stocks and work in progress between the beginning and the end of the accounting period. The Government is to consult with the accountancy profession and others on possible permanent scheme of relief following the profession's recent proposals for a system of inflation accounting. A consultative document is to be published reporting the results of the Government's general review of the present corporation tax provisions. Meanwhile deferred tax liability arising from stock relief for 1973–74 and 1974–75 has been written off. Outstanding relief for each subsequent year will also be written off after a six-year interval.

As part of its policy for encouraging small businesses, the Government has raised the qualifying profits limits for the small companies rate of corporation tax to £70,000 for full relief and £130,000 for marginal relief.

Petroleum Revenue Tax   Under the Oil Taxation Act 1975 a petroleum revenue tax (deducted in computing profits for corporation tax) is charged on profits from the winning, as opposed to refining or other form of processing, of hydrocarbons under licence in Britain and on its continental shelf. In 1980 the tax was raised from

60 per cent to 70 per cent. Each licensee of an oilfield is charged on the profits for that field, computed for half-yearly periods. The Petroleum Revenue Tax Act 1980 provides for payments of the tax in advance of assessment for liability.

Taxes on Capital

Capital Transfer Tax

A comprehensive tax, capital transfer tax, applies to transfer of personal wealth in three main areas: lifetime gifts; transfers on death; and transfers relating to settled property (that is, any property held in trust). The tax is chargeable in respect of a person's lifetime transfers as they occur and on a cumulative basis. The final stage of cumulation is the inclusion of the property 'passing' on an assumed transfer of the whole of the deceased's estate immediately before the death. The rates of tax applicable are progressively higher on successive slices of the cumulative total of chargeable transfers, with a lower scale of tax for lifetime transfers than for transfers on death. The higher scale applies to transfers made on death or up to three years before the transferer's death. Under both scales the first £50,000 of transfers is exempt. The rates on amounts over this figure rise from 30 per cent (higher scale) and 15 per cent (lower scale) on the slice between £50,000 and £60,000 to 75 per cent (both scales) on the excess over £2·01 million.

Capital Gains Tax

Capital gains accruing on the disposal of assets are liable to capital gains tax or, in the case of companies, to corporation tax. The rate of tax is normally 30 per cent, but in the case of individuals may be less, depending on their circumstances. For small businesses the tax on gifts and certain deemed disposals of business assets may be deferred until the assets are sold. Certain assets may be exempt from tax, including the principal private residence, chattels worth less than £2,000 (and any chattels, except those used for the purpose of a trade, with a predictable life of less than 50 years), private motor cars and National Savings Certificates. An individual is exempt from capital gains tax where the total net gains do not exceed £3,000 in any year. The excess over this amount is chargeable at a rate of 30 per cent. Gains on government securities are exempt from the tax if they have been held for more than 12 months.

Development Land Tax

The Development Land Tax Act 1976 introduced a development land tax (DLT) on development value in place of the charge on development gains and on first letting introduced in the Finance Act 1974. Any assessable development value raised on the disposal of an interest in land is chargeable to DLT at the rate of 60 per cent but the first £50,000 of any such development value realised in any financial year is completely exempt. Exemptions from DLT include the sale or development of owner-occupied residences.

Taxes on Expenditure

Value Added Tax

Value added tax (VAT) is a broadly-based tax, currently chargeable at 15 per cent. It is collected at each stage in the production and distribution of goods and services by taxable persons (generally a person carrying on a business with a turnover of more than £13,500 a year). The final tax is borne by the consumer. The taxable person is charged by suppliers of goods and services with VAT (input tax) who then charges the customer with VAT on goods and services supplied (output tax). It is the difference between output and input tax that is paid to Customs and Excise.

There are two methods by which certain goods and services are relieved from VAT: one is by charging VAT at a zero rate (a taxable person does not charge tax to a customer but reclaims any input tax paid to suppliers); the other is by exemption (a taxable person does not charge a customer any output tax and is not entitled to deduct or reclaim the input tax). Zero-rating applies to most types of food (except in the course of catering); books, newspapers and periodicals; fuel (except for petrol and other fuels for road use); construction of buildings; exports; public transport fares; young children's clothing and footwear; and drugs and medicines supplied on prescription. Exemption applies to land (including rents), insurance, postal services, betting, gaming other than by gaming machines and lotteries, finance, education, health, and burial and cremation.

Protective Duties   These are chargeable as customs duties in accordance with the Common Customs Tariff of the European Community (no such duties are chargeable on goods which qualify as Community goods). Special customs import and export procedures are operated under the common agricultural policy and community levies are chargeable on a wide range of agricultural products from non-community countries.

Excise Duties   Oils used for road fuel bear duty at the basic rate. Heavy oil not used for road fuel and light oil used for furnace fuel bear a lower duty and are zero-rated for VAT. Oil used as chemical feedstocks or otherwise than as a fuel or lubricant in manufacturing is relieved from the duty.

There are duties on spirits, beer, wine, madewine, cider and perry. Each is related to the alcoholic strength of the particular drink except for beer, where the rate of duty depends on the original gravity of the worts.

The cigarette duty is based partly on a charge per 1,000 cigarettes and partly on a percentage of retail price. Duty on other tobacco products is based on the weight of the finished product.

The principal betting duties are the general betting duty, which is charged at a rate of 7·5 per cent of the stake money, except for on-course betting, which is charged at 4 per cent; pool betting duty (which applies to football pools), charged at a rate of 40 per cent of the stake money; and bingo duty, charged at $7\frac{1}{2}$ per cent. Casino gaming machines are taxed mainly by licence duties.

The licence duty on a private motor car is £60 a year; motor cycles and three wheel vehicles etc., pay £6, £12 or £24 a year according to engine capacity. Goods vehicles are taxed by unladen weight and taxis and buses are taxed by seating capacity.

Car Tax   New cars and motor caravans, whether British made or imported, are chargeable with car tax at 10 per cent on the wholesale value. VAT falls on the price including car tax.

Stamp Duty   Transfers of property (other than of stocks and shares, which are liable to duty at 2 per cent) up to a value of £20,000 are exempt from stamp duty. Above this threshold stamp duty is chargeable at rates of 0·5 per cent, 1 per cent and 1·5 per cent on transfers valued up to £25,000, £30,000 and £35,000, respectively, with the full rate of 2 per cent applying to values above £35,000.

National Insurance Surcharge   The national insurance surcharge took effect from the start of the 1977–78 financial year. It is in the form of a levy paid by employers, along with their national insurance contributions, in respect of their employees and is equal to 3·5 per cent of employees' earnings up to £165 per week (earnings of less than £23 per week are exempt from the surcharge). Generally it is assumed that the incidence of this tax will be passed forward into prices, so that it ranks as a tax on expenditure.

The National Debt

On 31 March 1980 the total National Debt was estimated at £95,330 million, of which £3,950 million was repayable in currencies other than sterling, mainly to the United States Government. Of the £91,380 million of internal debt, £9,740 million was floating debt, while the long-term loans included a variety of stocks, bonds, loans and certificates carrying fixed rates of interest and with fixed or indeterminate dates of repayment. The National Debt relates only to the liabilities of the National Loans Fund (see p 352) which includes official holdings of central government debt by other central government funds.

PUBLIC FINANCE IN NORTHERN IRELAND

The general system of public finance in Northern Ireland is, in its main features, similar to that operating in Great Britain. The major sources of revenue are the main national taxes imposed by the United Kingdom Parliament over the whole country. The Northern Ireland share of the yield of United Kingdom taxes is paid out of the Consolidated Fund of the United Kingdom into that of Northern Ireland. Revenue also accrues from local resources such as the regional rate and from certain non-tax revenue. There is also an annual grant-in-aid voted by Parliament (£590 million in 1979–80 which, together with the attributed share of United Kingdom taxes, rates and miscellaneous sums, amounted to £1,858 million). Loans from the United Kingdom National Loans Fund are available (up to a limit of £1,000 million) to finance capital expenditure programmes in Northern Ireland.

Various funds have been established in Northern Ireland, in addition to statutory Reserve and Sinking Funds, for specific purposes. In general, these follow the pattern for Great Britain, the principal funds being those relating to national insurance and government loans. The latter constitutes a pool of money available mainly for local and public authority borrowers; on 31 March 1980 a sum of £338 million was outstanding against such borrowers.

FINANCIAL INSTITUTIONS

THE BANKING SYSTEM

The British banking system comprises a central bank; deposit banks which perform the usual main banking services: the National Girobank; the British offices of domestic and overseas banks whose main business is in other countries; merchant banks; and other specialised institutions.

The Central Bank

The Bank of England was established in 1694 by Act of Parliament and Royal Charter as a corporate body; the entire capital stock was acquired by the Government under the Bank of England Act 1946. As the central bank, the Bank acts as banker to the Government, to overseas central banks and to deposit banks and is the lender of last resort to the banking system; it is the note-issuing authority and the registrar for some 200 government, nationalised industry, local authority, public board and Commonwealth government stocks. On behalf of the Treasury it manages the Exchange Equalisation Account (EEA), which holds Britain's official reserves of gold, foreign exchange, Special Drawing Rights (SDRs) on the International Monetary Fund and European Currency Units (ECUs). Using the resources of the EEA, the Bank may intervene in the foreign exchange market both to prevent undue fluctuations in the exchange value of sterling and to conserve the means of making payments abroad.

As banker to the Government, the Bank examines and seeks to anticipate banking and financial problems and undertakes the appropriate operations in the money, capital and the foreign exchange markets; consequently it has a major responsibility for advising the Government on the formulation of monetary policy and for its subsequent execution. It is also the main channel of communication between the deposit banks and other financial institutions of the City of London on the one hand and the Government on the other.

The Bank's implementation of monetary policy is carried out primarily through control over interest rates although the banking system is subject to a number of more direct controls. The Bank administers directly the official discount rate, known as Minimum Lending Rate (MLR), which is the rate at which the Bank will normally provide funds to the discount market as a lender of last resort. MLR in turn can be expected to have an influence on other short-term interest rates. In addition, the authorities can influence interest rates through their daily operations in the money market and the terms on which they offer gilt-edged stock.

The Bank's direct controls over the banking system include the requirement that banks hold specified assets in minimum ratio to total eligible liabilities (broadly, sterling deposits drawn from outside the banking system). A number of changes to these requirements have been proposed in the Government's report on Monetary Control (see Bibliography) published in March 1980. The timetable of the changes will depend in part on discussion with the banks about new prudential and other requirements following the introduction of the Banking Act 1979. The Bank of England has also issued qualitative guidance on the direction of bank lending; this provides for priority to be given to the finance required by manufacturing industry, for the expansion of exports and for import saving.

Under the Banking Act 1979 all deposit-taking businesses which are not specifically excluded require authorisation from the Bank of England and are subject to its continuing supervision. Authorisation may take the form either of recognition as a bank or of a licence to take deposits. The Act also set up a deposit protection scheme to project the funds of depositors.

The Bank of England has the sole right in England and Wales of issuing bank notes. The note issue is fiduciary, that is to say, it is no longer backed by gold but by government and other securities. The Scottish and Northern Ireland banks have limited rights to issue notes; these issues, apart from an amount specified by legislation for each bank, must be fully covered by holdings of Bank of England notes. The provision of coin for circulation is the responsibility of the Royal Mint, a government department.

The Deposit Banks

The primary business of the deposit banks is the receipt, transfer and encashment of deposits. The principal deposit banks are the six London clearing banks, three Scottish clearing banks and two Northern Ireland banks. Mergers have resulted in the formation of six banking groups, four based in London and two in Scotland. The two Northern Ireland banks are owned by London clearing banks, but two groups of banks based in the Irish Republic also operate in Northern Ireland.

In July 1980 sterling sight and time deposits with these banks from non-bank customers in the British public and private sectors amounted to £34,160 million and accounted for 66 per cent of the total of such deposits with all banks in Britain, that is including the accepting houses, overseas banks, consortium banks, the National Girobank and other British banks. Sight deposits are repayable on demand and no interest is generally paid on them, but on time deposits interest is paid (at a rate below individual banks' base rates). The deposit banks provide full banking services throughout Britain, and operate through some 14,000 branches. Several of them have interests in British overseas and Commonwealth banks, and in other banks which have been formed specially to compete in international markets. They have also acquired substantial interests in hire-purchase finance houses, and some have set up their own unit trusts and merchant banks.

The deposit banks' main liquid assets consist of balances at the Bank of England, money at call (mainly loans to discount houses), their holdings of Treasury and some other bills and short-dated British government securities. The banks also hold a proportion of their assets as portfolio (mainly longer-dated British government securities) or trade investments.

The banks' profits are largely earned through their advances to customers, partly in the form of overdrafts[1] and partly in the form of loans (with or without collateral security). In July 1980 sterling advances by the London clearing banks amounted to 74 per cent of their sterling deposits.

The bank giro, a credit transfer scheme, and the direct debiting by which a creditor with a prior approval of the debtor may claim money due to him direct from the latter's banking account, have helped to improve the money transmission services. An increasing number of banks have automatic cash dispensing machines and many are also introducing more automated banking facilities. Credit cards are in widespread use for the settlement of accounts in retail shops; and cheque cards enable the card holder to cash a cheque up to a specified credit limit at any office of major British and Irish banks and at offices of many banks overseas.

Membership of the London Bankers' Clearing House, which deals with the clearing of cheques and drafts, consists of the Bank of England and the London clearing banks, together with the Co-operative Bank and the Central Trustee Savings Bank, which became members in 1975. In 1979 cheques and drafts worth over £3,615,000 million passed through the London clearing system.

National Girobank

The Post Office National Girobank (known as National Giro until 1978), which was introduced in 1968 to provide a low-cost current account banking and money transfer service, is operated through more than 20,000 post offices in Britain. All accounts and transactions are maintained by means of a computer complex at Bootle, Merseyside. In March 1980 Girobank had 820,000 accounts with balances of over £400 million. The number of transactions has risen from an annual rate of 80 million in March 1969 to one of about 300 million in March 1980. In addition to its services to individuals, Girobank's services to commerce, industry and the public utilities include a facility whereby organisations with dispersed branches, depots and representatives can rapidly channel receipts into their central account. Some 165 local authorities as well as voluntary housing associations use Girobank's rent collection services. Girobank's international services also provide money transfer facilities linking over 19 million account holders in the European Community and other countries.

The range of banking services provided by Girobank includes current accounts, personal loans, a cheque guarantee card, limited overdrawing for personal customers and overdrafts for corporate customers, deposit accounts, budget accounts, bridging loans, travellers' cheques and foreign currency, bureaux de change and a facility to draw cash at 80,000 post offices in Europe.

---

[1] Overdrafts are a short-term financial facility enabling customers to overdraw their accounts and were developed to cover fluctuating working capital requirements.

Overseas Banks

Altogether 430 overseas banks and financial institutions were represented in London in 1980 through branches, subsidiaries, representative offices and consortia. There were 380 banks directly represented in London, while 50 banks and financial institutions were represented through a stake in one or more of the 26 joint venture banks operating in London. Of those directly represented, 75 were from the United States, 25 from Japan and 115 from Europe, of which 55 were from the European Community. They provide a comprehensive banking service in many parts of the world and engage in the financing of trade not only between Britain and other countries but also between third countries.

The Merchant Banks

Merchant banks have traditionally been primarily concerned with acceptance credits[1] and with the sponsoring of capital issues on behalf of their customers. Today they have a widely diversified and complex range of activities with an important role in international finance and the short-term capital markets, the provision of expert advice and financial services to British industrial companies especially where mergers, takeovers and other forms of corporate reorganisation are involved, and in the management of investment holdings, including trusts, pensions and other funds.

The Discount Market

The discount market is an institution which is unique to the City of London. Its function in the monetary system is to provide a financial mechanism designed to promote an orderly flow of short-term funds. The market consists of 11 discount houses, five money traders, six Stock Exchange money brokers and two discount brokers, all of which borrow money 'at call' or short notice and lend for somewhat longer periods. The discount houses have recourse to the Bank of England as lender of last resort. The Bank lends to them generally overnight or for up to seven days at Minimum Lending Rate, although it may charge a higher rate. Most of the market's borrowed funds come from the banks, which are thus provided with a flexible means of earning a yield on surplus funds which they have at any given time.

The assets of the discount houses mainly consist of Treasury and commercial bills, government and local authority securities and negotiable certificates of deposit denominated in both sterling and United States dollars. The discount houses accept as a formal responsibility that they should cover the government's need to borrow on Treasury bills which are offered on tender each week.

National Savings

The Department for National Savings is responsible for the administration of government savings schemes: National Savings Bank accounts, National Savings Certificates, British Savings Bonds, Premium Savings Bonds and Save As You Earn contracts. Government policy is directed towards encouraging investment, primarily of personal savings, in these schemes, particularly as they represent a major source of funds for financing the public sector borrowing requirement. At April 1980 National Savings totalled £13,550 million. Facilities are provided by National Savings for the purchase of government stocks ('gilts'); a selection of about 50 stocks is held on the National Savings Stock Register. Gift tokens are also available at most post offices.

---

[1] Acceptance credits are usually short-term (90 days) arrangements to finance exports from, and imports to, Britain and other markets. The term is derived from the method of financing trade by which commercial bills are 'accepted' or guaranteed by a merchant bank against documents, after which they may be discounted for cash by a discount house or other intermediary.

National Savings Bank
The National Savings Bank provides a countrywide system for depositing and withdrawing small savings at post offices. There are about 21 million active accounts. Ordinary Accounts bear interest at 5 per cent and the first £70 of annual interest is tax-free. Up to £100 can be withdrawn on demand at any savings bank post office, but a few days' notice is required for larger amounts. The money is lodged with the National Debt Commissioners and is invested in government securities. Deposits bearing a higher rate of interest may be made in Investment Accounts. All deposits carry a government guarantee. At the end of April 1980 the sum of the two accounts totalled some £3,440 million.

National Savings Certificates
National Savings Certificates, in units of £10, are encashable at par at any time. Interest, which is free of income tax and capital gains tax, is paid only on encashment. The maximum permitted holding of the current Nineteenth Issue is £1,500. National Savings Certificates (second index-linked issue) are available only to those aged 60 and over at £10 for each one unit certificate. Interest does not accrue periodically but instead, subject to the certificate being held for one year, the repayment value is related to the movement of the general index of retail prices. If held for five years a bonus of 4 per cent of the purchase price is added to the repayment value. The maximum permitted holding is £3,000.

British Savings Bonds
The sale of British Savings Bonds ceased at the end of 1979. Bonds bought before then may be held to maturity at five years.

Premium Savings Bonds
Premium Savings Bonds are in units of £1 (minimum purchase is £5) and individual holdings are limited to £10,000. After a qualifying period of three months the bonds give investors a chance to win tax-free prizes. There is a weekly draw for prizes of £100,000, £50,000 and £25,000 and a monthly draw offering thousands of prizes ranging in value from £50 to £250,000. Total net sales of bonds to April 1980 were some £1,410 million.

Save As You Earn
The Third Issue of the Save As You Earn (SAYE) scheme introduced in 1975 is index-linked. The scheme enables savings to be made in fixed regular monthly amounts over five years, with a minimum of £4 and a maximum of £20 (to be raised to £50 in 1981), by means of deductions from pay or by other regular payments. At the end of five years, the repayment value is the total contributions plus any increase due to index-linking of monthly contributions. Completed savings which are not withdrawn qualify for fresh index-linking and a bonus equal to two monthly contributions at the end of seven years. Savers who wish to stop payments are able to withdraw the total sum saved (but there cannot be partial withdrawals). Tax-free compound interest is then paid at the rate of 6 per cent a year on amounts withdrawn after the first year.

Ulster Savings
Northern Ireland issues separately Ulster Savings Certificates on similar terms to National Savings Certificates.

Trustee Savings Banks
The Trustee Savings Banks (TSBs), most of which were founded in the nineteenth century, operate under their own trustees but are subject, under the Trustee Savings Banks Acts 1969, 1976 and 1978, to the supervision of the Trustee Savings Banks Central Board and the Treasury. Following a planned programme of amalgamations, there were 17 individual banks in June 1980 (compared with 67 in 1975) with about 1,640 branches, 14 million accounts and total deposits in excess of £5,300 million. The 1976 Act

empowered TSBs to provide a full range of banking services including credit services. The TSB credit services include personal loans, temporary overdrafts, bridging loans, mortgages and home improvement loans. The TSBs also have their own credit card, Trustcard, which operates within the VISA system. In addition, a range of life assurance and unit trust facilities are available. The TSBs are also in the process of introducing a national scheme for small scale commercial lending including overdrafts up to one year and medium term loans up to ten years.

OTHER
FINANCIAL
INSTITUTIONS

Many special financial facilities, which are supplementary to the credit facilities of the banks, are provided through institutions outside the banking system. These include institutions providing credit in specialised forms, such as hire purchase finance companies, and leasing and factoring companies; institutions which manage investments on behalf of the public, such as pension funds, life assurance companies, unit trusts and investment trusts; institutions which provide financial services, such as the Stock Exchange, with its associated stockbrokers; commodity markets; and the insurance market; and intermediaries which are less dependent on the financial markets in the City of London, such as building societies and credit unions.

Finance
Houses

Although there are a large number of firms engaged in the financing of hire purchase and other instalment credit transactions, about 85 per cent of all finance house business is accounted for by the 40 firms which constitute the Finance Houses Association (FHA). At the end of June 1980 the value of credit outstanding to the members of FHA amounted to £7,130 million. A substantial amount of new credit extended by finance houses related to cars and commercial vehicles, including motorcycles and caravans, the remainder relating to industrial and building equipment and other goods.

The leading finance houses comply with the authorities' policies on lending similar to those applied to banks, and all finance houses are required to observe term controls affecting the minimum deposits and maximum repayment period for specific goods financed by certain forms of lending.

Leasing
Companies

Leasing companies buy and own plant or equipment required and chosen by businesses and lease it at an agreed rental. This form of finance is growing in importance, partly because the leasing companies can take advantage of investment incentives to the benefit of customers whose tax position would otherwise make them unavailable. In 1979 new assets leased by the 55 members of the Equipment Leasing Association amounted to £1,800 million, some 11 per cent of British investment in capital equipment.

Factoring
Companies

Factoring companies purchase the trade debts due to a business and provide an accounting and debt collection service. The services available cover exports from and imports to Britain, as well as domestic trade. In 1978 the eight members of the Association of British Factors handled about £1,340 million worth of turnover.

Finance
Corporations

Finance corporations meet the need for medium- and long-term capital when such funds are not easily or directly available from traditional sources such as the Stock Exchange or the banks.

Finance for Industry Limited (FFI) was formed in 1973 as the holding company for two previously separate but related corporations, the Finance Corporation for Industry (FCI) and the Industrial and Commercial Finance

Corporation (ICFC). The purpose of the merger was to provide, in one specialist financial institution, the capacity to support investment programmes over the whole range of industry. The FCI provides medium-term funds at fixed and variable interest rates for large companies in excess of £2 million. During the year ended 31 March 1980 it advanced a total of £45 million and had commitments and guarantees at the end of the year of a further £44 million. The ICFC provides medium- and long-term funds at fixed interest rates for the small and medium sectors of industry. At the end of March 1980 the ICFC had gross facilities outstanding of £380 million in 3,340 companies. Its normal lending limits range from £5,000 to £2 million for periods between seven and 20 years. The shares in FFI are owned by the Bank of England (15 per cent) and the individual London and Scottish clearing banks.

Equity Capital for Industry Ltd (ECI) was formed in 1976 as a new specialist long-term institution with the primary purpose of providing equity or equity-type capital for industry in Britain which cannot appropriately be provided through the normal market mechanism. Its authorised capital is £50 million and the shares are largely held by insurance companies and life offices, investment trust companies, unit trusts and FFI. There is an unauthorised unit trust associated with ECI whose units are held by pension funds so as to enable them to participate in the provision of capital.

The Agricultural Mortgage Corporation was established in 1928 for the purpose of making loans to farmers. Its authorised share capital is £1·5 million and at 31 March 1980 loans and investments of the Corporation amounted to £415 million.

The Commonwealth Development Finance Company (CDFC) is no longer confined to the Commonwealth in its activities. It supports business enterprise overseas by providing finance in the form of share capital and loans on mutually acceptable terms. Its authorised share capital is £30 million, of which about 14½ million 'A' ordinary shares of £1 (£0·10 paid) are held by industrial, shipping, mining and banking interests in Britain, and 11¾ million 'B' ordinary shares of £1 (£0·50 paid) are held by the Bank of England and certain central banks in the Commonwealth. At 31 March 1980 the CDFC held investments of about £28 million spread over a wide range of industries in 36 countries.

The Commonwealth Development Corporation (CDC) was set up in 1948 and undertakes projects for the promotion and expansion of a wide range of enterprises within and outside the Commonwealth. At the end of 1979 the CDC had a total capital commitment of £449 million (see p 89).

The Crown Agents

The Crown Agents for Oversea Governments and Administrations provide financial, professional and commercial services for national governments, public authorities and international bodies. At the end of 1979 the Crown Agents did work for over 300 public organisations in nearly 100 countries. The members of the Board are appointed by the Secretary of State for Foreign and Commonwealth Affairs.

Under the provisions of the Crown Agents Act 1979 the Crown Agents operate as agents on behalf of government and public sector bodies in Britain and overseas in such areas as procurement, recruitment and investment management. They also carry on other activities such as consultancy work, in their own right. The Crown Agents Holding and Realisation Board has the duty of holding and realising on the best possible terms the remaining investments in property and banking entered into by the unincorporated agents on their own account.

Pension Funds

Pension funds are administered by trustees in order to invest members' pension contributions, either directly on the market or through intermediaries such as insurance companies. The total market value of funds managed, covering private employers and much of the public sector, was of the order of some £40,000 million at the end of 1979.

Investment Trust Companies and Unit Trusts

Investment trust companies and unit trusts enable investors to spread their risks and obtain the benefit of skilled management.

The usual type of investment trust company is constituted as a public company registered under the Companies Acts with limited liability; its business is to invest its capital in a range of stocks and shares. Like other companies, it may issue several types of stocks or shares and may retain part of its profits to build up reserves. Investment trust companies grew to importance in the latter half of the nineteenth century and have been prominent in directing capital towards overseas investment. At the end of 1979 members of the Association of Investment Trust Companies held assets worth some £6,500 million of which 33 per cent was held overseas.

Unit trusts are constituted by trust deed between a management company and a trustee company which holds the assets. Normally, the managers sell units to the public and must invest the proceeds in a fairly wide range of Stock Exchange securities. The costs of running the trust are defrayed partly by an initial charge which forms part of the price of a unit and partly by a half-yearly service charge which is usually taken out of the trust's income. Authorisation by the Department of Trade is needed before units can be offered to the public; this is only granted if the trust deed meets the Department's requirements.

The first British unit trust was formed in 1931. In June 1980 there were 1·75 million unit holdings. The value of funds invested in authorised trusts depends on the value of the underlying securities. This had risen from only £60 million at the end of 1958 to £4,500 million by June 1980. There is a wide variety of trusts both in the range of investment covered and in the ways of catering for the differing needs of investors.

Building Societies

Building societies are non-profit-making mutual institutions which borrow mainly short-term from individual savers, who are generally able to withdraw their money on demand, although fixed-term investments at higher rates of interest are becoming increasingly popular, and provide long-term loans at variable rates of interest on the security of private dwellings purchased for owner occupation. They also lend to a limited extent to house builders and on the security of business or commercial property. Most societies pay and charge interest on the basis of a structure of rates recommended periodically by The Building Societies Association, the movement's representative body.[1]

Building societies have existed in Britain for some 200 years and have been subject to specific legislation governing their operations (now consolidated in the Building Societies Act 1962) since 1836. The present legislation is administered by the Chief Registrar of Friendly Societies, to whom the societies must provide regular statements of their financial position and who has discretionary powers to restrict or suspend a society's operations if he considers that the

---

[1] The income tax on interest is paid by the society on behalf of individual investors, at a rate equal to their average tax rate (21 per cent for 1979–80). This means that while those not liable to tax cannot reclaim the tax paid on their behalf, investors who pay at the basic rate receive a better return than would otherwise be the case.

way in which its business is being conducted may put investors' money at risk.

Building societies account for about 90 per cent of all lending for house purchase in Britain and in recent years they have overtaken the banks as the principal repository for the personal sector's total liquid assets. This growth has been accompanied by a concentration of most of the business in the hands of a few large societies. At the end of 1979 there were 289 registered building societies with total assets of £45,600 million; over half this amount was accounted for by the five largest societies and about 83 per cent of it by the 17 largest. The amount lent on mortgages in 1979 was a record £8,860 million.

Credit Unions

A recent development in Great Britain has been the creation of credit unions, of which there are 48. Credit unions are small savings and loan clubs where members agree to pool part of their savings in order to provide themselves with low cost credit. The Credit Unions Act 1979 requires that members of a credit union should have a 'common bond', such as working in the same factory, and provides a system for their registration and supervision by the Chief Registrar of Friendly Societies.

In Northern Ireland they have grown successfully since the Industrial and Provident Societies Act (Northern Ireland) was introduced in 1969.

The Insurance Market

The British insurance industry provides a comprehensive and competitive service domestically and internationally. It has been estimated that British insurers handle some 20 per cent of business placed on the world market. The London market is the world's leading centre for insurance where, in addition to most British companies and Lloyd's, a large number of overseas companies are also represented. It is the world centre for the placement of international reinsurance and, partly as a consequence of this, many British companies have formed close relationships with overseas companies. A certain amount of insurance is provided by friendly societies, banks and trade unions but most insurance services in Britain are in the hands of mutual or joint stock insurance companies or Lloyd's underwriters.

Insurance Companies

Although some British insurance companies confine their activities to domestic business, the majority of the large companies undertaking general business, together with underwriters at Lloyd's, regard themselves primarily as international insurers, the largest proportion of their premium income and claims being attributable to international risks. Without such a wide range of interest, the British market would not be able to respond to the high level of demand made on it in respect of very large single risks such as specially designed ships for carrying liquefied gas and offshore oil production platforms. There are about 820 companies authorised to carry on one or more classes of insurance business in Britain, of which about 170 are overseas companies.

Some 300 companies belong to the British Insurance Association and these account for about 95 per cent of the world-wide business of the British insurance companies market.

Life assurance is available from 281 authorised insurance companies and from certain friendly societies: a very limited range of contracts is obtainable from certain Lloyd's underwriters. The main types of life policy are whole-life, endowment, unit-linked term assurance and annuities. Many life assurance policies are a form of savings contract as well as financial protection against premature death.

Lloyd's

Lloyd's, established in the seventeenth century, is an incorporated society of private insurers in London. Although its activities were originally confined to the conduct of marine insurance business, a very considerable world-wide market for the transaction of other classes of insurance business in non-marine, aviation and motor markets has been built up.

Lloyd's is regulated by a series of special Acts of Parliament starting in 1871 (further legislation, following the Fisher Report, see Bibliography, is being considered). The affairs of the Society of Lloyd's in its corporate capacity are administered by the Committee of Lloyd's. The Society does not accept insurance itself.

Lloyd's is not a company but a market for insurance, where business is transacted by individual underwriters for their own account and risk and in competition with each other. Insurance may only be placed through Lloyd's brokers, who negotiate with Lloyd's underwriters on behalf of the insured. Only elected underwriting members of Lloyd's, who must transact insurance with unlimited liability and who have met the most stringent financial regulations laid down by the Committee, are permitted to transact business at Lloyd's; these safeguards give security to the Lloyd's policy.

There are over 18,000 underwriting members of Lloyd's grouped into about 400 syndicates and represented at Lloyd's by underwriting agents who accept risks on behalf of the members of their syndicates.

Alongside its marine insurance business Lloyd's has built up a world-wide organisation for the collection and diffusion of shipping intelligence.

Insurance Brokers

The insurance market is completed by the insurance brokers, acting on behalf of the insured; brokers are an essential part of the Lloyd's market and a valuable part of the company market. Many brokers specialise in reinsurance business, acting as intermediaries in the exchange of contracts between companies, both British and overseas, and often acting as London representatives of the latter. The Insurance Brokers (Registration) Act 1977 provides for the registration of insurance brokers by a Registration Council.

International Insurance Services

Some 55 per cent of the general (that is, non-life) business of members of the British Insurance Association is carried on overseas, partly by reinsurance on the London market and partly through branches and agencies established in over 100 countries. The basic principle of this international business is that resources capable of meeting any potential loss are instantly available for use in any part of the world.

Behind this large and international volume of business stand the very substantial assets of the companies, in addition to substantial reserves of uncalled capital, and the deposits, underwriting trust funds and other resources of Lloyd's underwriters.

In accordance with the Treaty of Rome, insurance and reinsurance in the European Community are regulated by directives addressed to the governments of member states and intended to harmonise the legislation of the various member countries, thus providing a 'common market', which would avoid distortion of competition. Directives in operation cover freedom of establishment to provide services in respect of reinsurance, compulsory motor insurance, freedom of establishment in non-life insurance, and insurance intermediaries. A directive on the co-ordination of regulations relating to Community co-insurance operations came into force in 1980. The Commission has submitted proposals for directives on insurance contract law and insurance in areas of legal expenses, credit and suretyship.

The Stock Exchange

The stock exchanges of the United Kingdom and Irish Republic amalgamated in 1973 to become 'The Stock Exchange' with its main trading floor and central administration in London. There are also trading floors in Glasgow, Liverpool, Manchester, Birmingham and Dublin.

The number and variety of securities officially listed on the Stock Exchange are greater than in any other market in the world and its turnover of company securities is roughly equivalent to that of all the European exchanges combined. Some 8,000 securities are quoted on the Stock Exchange; at the end of March 1980 these had a total market value of £280,330 million. About 6,000 securities of companies were quoted, including a number of leading overseas securities. Company issues represented more than four-fifths of the securities at market valuation, the remainder being British, Irish Republic and other overseas government and corporation stocks. Institutional investors, such as pension funds, now own a higher proportion of ordinary shares than individuals. A market in unlisted securities (generally those of small companies which have been unable hitherto to obtain a Stock Exchange listing) is under consideration.

A market in traded share options opened in 1978 on the Stock Exchange. The market, initially in the shares of ten prominent British companies (now increased to 15), enables investors not only to buy options to purchase shares in future at pre-fixed prices but also to trade in the options themselves.

The Foreign Exchange Market

The market consists of banks and several firms of foreign exchange brokers which act as intermediaries between the banks. It provides those engaged in international trade with foreign currencies for their transactions. The foreign exchange banks are in close contact with financial centres abroad and are able to quote buying and selling rates for both spot and future delivery. An important function of the market is to engage in arbitrage transactions which serve to eliminate differentials in exchange rates between different centres. The forward market enables traders, who at a given date in the future are due to receive or make a specific foreign currency payment, to contract in advance to sell or buy the foreign currency involved for sterling at a precise fixed exchange rate. The Bank of England is responsible for granting recognition to broking houses which wish to provide services to the foreign exchange and currency deposit markets in 'scheduled currencies', that is, in those currencies for which a specific brokerage scale is laid down by the Bank.

The London Gold Market

Anyone may deal in gold but, in practice, dealings are largely concentrated in the hands of the five members of the London gold market. The five members meet twice daily to establish a London fixing price for gold. This price provides a reference point for world-wide dealings in gold. Although much interest centres upon the fixings, active dealing takes place throughout the day. Forward prices may also be quoted on request.

Commodity Markets

Britain remains the principal international centre for transactions in a large number of commodities, although most of the sales negotiated in London relate to consignments which never pass through the ports of Britain. The need for close links with sources of finance and with shipping and insurance services often determined the location of these physical markets in the City of London. There are also futures markets in cocoa, coffee, grains (wheat and barley), rubber, soya bean meal, sugar, wool and non-ferrous metals (aluminium, copper, lead, nickel, silver, tin and zinc).

19 Overseas Trade and Payments

Although small in area and accounting for only about 1·4 per cent of the world's population, Britain is the fifth largest trading nation in the world—and, as a member of the European Community, part of the world's largest trading area, which accounts for more than one-third of all trade.

For hundreds of years, and especially since the mid-nineteenth century, when the rapid growth of industry, commerce and shipping was accompanied by Britain's development as an international trading centre, overseas trade has been of vital importance to the economy. Britain exports goods to the value of about £40,700 million, about one-quarter of the gross domestic product. It is a major supplier of machinery, vehicles, aerospace products, metal manufactures, electrical equipment, chemicals and textiles, and a growing oil exporter. Britain relies upon imports for almost half of its total consumption of foodstuffs, and for most of the raw materials needed for its industries. It is among the world's largest importers of foodstuffs, timber and paper, metals and ores, and other raw materials. Invisible trade is also of great significance to the economy, and Britain's net earnings are second only to those of the United States.

A sound commercial banking system and a wide range of financial institutions ensure that commercial needs are met for both short- and long-term finance for international trade. The facilities provided by merchant banks and accepting houses, for example, have long been used to finance shipments of goods not only to and from Britain, but also between overseas countries.

This chapter describes the pattern of Britain's overseas trade (including its distribution by commodity and area). It also summarises the main aspects of Britain's invisible transactions, commercial policy, controls on trade and payments and government services to exporters. The chapter ends with a description of Britain's balance of payments and its external assets and liabilities.

OVERSEAS TRADE

PATTERN OF TRADE

Changes in the value, volume, composition and geographical distribution of exports and imports are outlined in the following paragraphs.

Value and Volume

In 1979 Britain's exports of goods were valued at about £40,700 million and its imports of goods at about £44,100 million (both values are free on board, defined in Table 30, and are on a balance of payments basis, as distinct from an overseas trade statistics basis, which for imports includes the cost of insurance and freight, and for both exports and imports includes returned goods). Between 1978 and 1979 the value of exports rose by 16 per cent while that of imports increased by 20 per cent. Over the same period the volume index of exports increased by 3·6 per cent and of imports by 11·6 per cent; the unit value index of exports rose by 11 per cent and of imports by 10 per cent.

The value and volume of exports and imports, together with the terms of trade index, from 1970 to 1979 are shown in Table 30.

Commodity Composition

Exports

Over three-quarters of Britain's exports consist of manufactured goods, both finished and semi-manufactured. By far the most important group of goods is machinery and transport equipment, which in 1979 accounted for 34 per cent of total exports. Exports of machinery alone accounted for 23 per cent of total exports in 1979. The share of chemicals has grown fairly steadily, to reach 11 per cent in 1979. The share of textiles has fallen from 19 per cent in 1948 to 7 per cent in 1960 and 3 per cent in 1979.

Imports

Although Britain is still one of the largest importers of food in the world the value of its imported food supplies has been growing less rapidly than the value of total imports and the ratio of imported food, beverages and tobacco to total imports, on an overseas trade statistics basis, has fallen from 39 per cent in 1954 to 13 per cent in 1979. There has been a similar downward trend in the proportion accounted for by basic materials—from 31 per cent in 1954 to about 8 per cent in 1979.

TABLE 30: Exports and Imports 1970–79[a]

	1970	1976	1977	1978	1979
Value (£ million)					
Exports f.o.b.[bc]	8,151	25,193	31,734	35,071	40,689
Exports f.o.b.[bd]	8,170	26,162	33,331	37,382	42,804
Imports f.o.b.[bc]	8,183	29,120	34,013	36,617	44,093
Imports c.i.f.[de]	9,163	31,584	36,978	40,930	48,467
Volume Index Nos (1975 = 100)[c]					
Exports	81·1	109·9	118·4	121·5	125·9
Imports	81·8	105·9	107·9	112·6	125·7
Unit Value Index Nos (1975 = 100)[c]					
Exports	50·8	119·6	141·5	155·1	171·9
Imports	42·8	122·1	141·4	147·0	162·3
Terms of Trade (1975 = 100)[cf]	118·8	98·0	100·1	105·5	105·9

Sources: *British business* and *United Kingdom Balance of Payments 1980 edition*
[a] Figures for recent years are subject to slight revision from year to year.
[b] 'Free on board', that is all costs accruing up to the time of placing the goods on board the exporting vessel having been paid by the seller.
[c] On a balance of payments basis.
[d] On an overseas trade statistics basis.
[e] 'Cost, insurance and freight', that is including shipping, insurance and other expenses incurred in the delivery of goods as far as their place of importation in Britain. Some of these expenses represent earnings by companies resident in Britain and are more appropriate to the invisibles account.
[f] Export unit value index as a percentage of import unit value index.

Imports of petroleum and petroleum products amounted to about 11 per cent of the total value of imports during 1979. A fall of 12 per cent in the volume of crude oil imports, reflecting increasing production of North Sea oil, was more than offset by rising oil prices, and value increased by 5 per cent.

In the past 25 years there has been a significant rise, in Britain as in the other main industrial countries, in the proportion of imports accounted for by finished manufactures. Such imports rose from about 5 per cent of total imports in 1954 to 36 per cent in 1979 when they were valued at £17,560 million. Imports of semi-manufactures have also been increasing and since 1962 have formed a larger part of the total import bill than basic materials, partly the result of a shift of the early stages of the manufacturing processes to the supplying countries. Imports of chemicals and other semi-manufactures totalled £13,882 million in 1979 and accounted for 29 per cent of total imports.

TABLE 31: Commodity Composition of Trade 1979[a]

Exports (f.o.b.)[b]	£ million	Per cent
Food, beverages and tobacco	2,947	6·9
Basic materials	1,249	2·9
Fuels	4,319	10·1
All manufactures	33,095	77·3
Manufactures (excluding erratic items[d])	*28,621*	*66·9*
Chemicals	4,914	11·5
Other semi-manufactures	6,653	15·5
Passenger motor cars	837	2·0
Other consumer goods	3,115	7·3
Intermediate goods	6,887	16·1
Capital goods	6,213	14·5
Miscellaneous	1,194	2·8
Total	42,804	100·0

Imports (c.i.f.)[c]		
Food, beverages and tobacco	6,521	13·4
Basic materials	3,965	8·2
Fuels	5,779	11·9
All manufactures	31,441	64·9
Manufactures (excluding erratic items[d])	*27,402*	*56·5*
Chemicals	3,404	7·0
Other semi-manufactures	7,814	16·1
Passenger motor cars	2,594	5·4
Other consumer goods	4,508	9·3
Intermediate goods	4,646	9·6
Capital goods	4,435	9·2
Miscellaneous	762	1·6
Total	48,467	100·0

Source: *British business*
[a] On an overseas trade statistics basis.
[b] See footnote *b* under Table 30.
[c] See footnote *e* under Table 30.
[d] Ships, aircraft, North Sea production installations and precious stones. These are high value items, irregular trade in which can have a misleading effect on the trade figures.
Differences between totals and the sums of their component parts are due to rounding.

Geographical Distribution of Trade

Although Britain's trade has, in general, grown fastest in recent years with the rest of the European Community, its largest market, there was a marked change in the pattern of British exports following the large rise in the price of oil at the end of 1973. This generated substantial reserves of foreign exchange for the oil-exporting countries, and British exports to them rose in value by 52 per cent between 1973 and 1974. On the other hand, the slowdown in activity in most of the developed economies during 1974 and 1975 reduced the rate of growth of British exports to these economies in 1975.

In 1976 and 1977 there was a return to growth in world trade and exports to the developed industrial countries continued the recovery which began in the latter part of 1975. Slower growth in world trade in 1978 was similarly reflected in Britain's export performance. World trade appears to have expanded rather faster in 1979 but British export performance was adversely affected by a loss of price competitiveness, political developments in Iran, a change of import regulations in Nigeria, and industrial disputes at home. In 1979 the Federal Republic of Germany replaced the United States as Britain's largest single export market. Details of Britain's principal export markets and sources of supply in 1978 and 1979 are given in Tables 32 and 33.

TABLE 32: Principal British Markets 1978–79

Exports to (f.o.b.)[a]	1978 (£ million)	1979 (£ million)	Percentage change 1978–79
Federal Republic of Germany	3,103	4,244	+37
United States[b]	3,524	4,047	+15
France	2,523	3,071	+22
Netherlands	2,255	3,063	+36
Irish Republic	2,042	2,555	+25
Belgium–Luxembourg	2,200	2,468	+12
Switzerland	1,913	2,407	+26
Sweden	1,173	1,542	+31
Italy	1,123	1,469	+31
Denmark	839	1,016	+21
Saudi Arabia	786	894	+14
Australia	854	840	− 2
Norway	650	769	+18
Canada	739	766	+ 4
South Africa	666	713	+ 7
Developed countries	26,414	32,208	+22
European Community	*14,084*	*17,885*	*+27*
Rest of Western Europe	*5,709*	*7,015*	*+23*
North America	*4,291*	*4,835*	*+13*
Other[c]	*2,330*	*2,474*	*+ 6*
Developing countries	9,798	9,260	− 5
Oil-exporting countries[d]	*4,769*	*3,793*	*−20*
Other	*5,029*	*5,467*	*+ 9*
Centrally planned economies[e]	1,070	1,191	+11

Source: *British business*
[a] On an overseas trade statistics basis.
[b] Including dependencies.
[c] Australia, New Zealand, South Africa, Japan.
[d] Algeria, Bahrain, Brunei, Ecuador, Gabon, Indonesia, Iran, Iraq, Kuwait, Libya, Nigeria, Oman, Qatar, Saudi Arabia, Trinidad and Tobago, United Arab Emirates, Venezuela.
[e] Soviet Union, Poland, German Democratic Republic, Hungary, Czechoslovakia, Albania, Bulgaria, Romania, China, North Korea, Vietnam, Mongolia.
Differences between totals and the sums of their component parts are due to rounding.

Invisible Transactions

As far back as estimates have been made (for nearly two centuries) Britain has usually earned a surplus from its invisible transactions. These fall into three main groups: services (receipts and payments arising from services, as distinct from goods, supplied to and received from overseas residents); interest, profits and dividends (income arising from outward and inward investment); and transfers between Britain and other countries. Table 34 shows the breakdown of the figures from 1970 to 1979. Services of the private sector (and public corporations) include sea transport and civil aviation, travel, financial services (including insurance) and 'other services' which include commissions on imports, royalties, services between related companies, construction work overseas, agency expenses and many other services.

The balance on invisibles in 1979 was £1,541 million. Gross earnings of £22,397 million from invisible exports were over half the total of £40,689 million from visible exports. The surplus in 1979 was lower than the surplus of £2,166 million in 1978, mainly owing to increased earnings by foreign oil companies in Britain associated particularly with increased oil production in the North Sea, higher travel expenditure overseas and increased payments to the European Community.

The deficits on government services have related notably to military services overseas, which have remained fairly steady in recent years, though currency

Table 33: Britain's Principal Sources of Supply 1978–79

Imports from (c.i.f.)[a]	1978 (£ million)	1979 (£ million)	Percentage change 1978–79
Federal Republic of Germany	4,511	5,799	+29
United States[b]	4,220	4,920	+17
France	3,215	4,064	+26
Netherlands	2,523	3,446	+37
Switzerland	2,155	2,565	+19
Italy	1,931	2,491	+29
Belgium–Luxembourg	1,829	2,325	+27
Irish Republic	1,605	1,689	+ 5
Sweden	1,344	1,606	+19
Japan	1,283	1,490	+16
Norway	1,445	1,327	− 8
Canada	1,086	1,260	+16
Saudi Arabia	870	1,109	+27
Denmark	962	1,081	+12
Soviet Union	692	828	+20
Developed countries	31,730	38,141	+20
European Community	*16,576*	*20,896*	*+26*
Rest of Western Europe	*6,986*	*8,110*	*+16*
North America	*5,337*	*6,221*	*+17*
Other[c]	*2,831*	*2,914*	*+ 3*
Developing countries	7,834	8,698	+11
Oil-exporting countries[d]	*3,449*	*3,375*	*− 2*
Other	*4,385*	*5,323*	*+21*
Centrally planned economies[e]	1,303	1,536	+18

Source: *British business*
[a] On an overseas trade statistics basis.
[b] Including dependencies.
[c] See footnote [c] under Table 32.
[d] See footnote [d] under Table 32.
[e] See footnote [e] under Table 32.

changes have caused the sterling value to rise. Substantial government transfer payments relate to economic grants to developing countries (see p 88) and subscriptions to international organisations including, since 1973, Britain's contribution to the common budget for the financing of European Community expenditure.

COMMERCIAL POLICY

Britain has long been an advocate of the removal of artificial barriers to trade, and to this end has taken a leading part in the activities of such organisations as the General Agreement on Tariffs and Trade (GATT) (since 1973 as part of the European Community, which operates as a single unit), the International Monetary Fund (IMF), the Organisation for Economic Co-operation and Development (OECD) and the United Nations Conference on Trade and Development (UNCTAD) (see p 91). As a member of the European Community, Britain participates in the development of the Community's commercial policy. The Community's common customs tariff is, on average, at a similar level to the tariffs of other major industrial countries.

General Agreement on Tariffs and Trade

Protective tariffs have been considerably modified in recent years as a result of negotiations held under the auspices of the GATT, which also seek to reduce tariffs and other barriers to trade and to eliminate discrimination in international commerce.

In the latest series of the GATT Multilateral Trade Negotiations, the 'Tokyo Round' (1973–79), a number of agreements dealing with both tariff and non-tariff barriers to trade were concluded. The non-tariff agreements have the common aim of reducing or eliminating existing non-tariff barriers to trade and preventing the erection of new obstacles. They cover areas such as technical barriers (calling for the use of international standards whenever

TABLE 34 Britain's Invisible Overseas Transactions 1970–79

£ million

	1970	1976	1977	1978	1979
Total invisibles	5,082	14,741	16,503	18,559	22,397
Credits	4,269	11,930	14,508	16,393	20,856
Debits	+813	+2,811	+1,995	+2,166	+1,541
Invisible balance					
Constituent items					
Services:					
General government*a*	−309	−667	−726	−698	−800
Private sector (and public corporations):					
SEA TRANSPORT	−80	+48	+60	−27	+63
CIVIL AVIATION	+46	+218	+219	+296	+262
TRAVEL	+50	+700	+1,166	+958	+673
FINANCIAL SERVICES	+439	+1,286	+1,371	+1,519	+1,579
OTHER SERVICES	+291	+679	+971	+1,438	+1,802
Interest, profits and dividends:					
General government	−269	−648	−715	−574	−473
Private sector (and public corporations)	+823	+1,953	+761	+1,094	+762
Transfers:					
General government	−177	−786	−1,112	−1,704	−2,074
Private sector	−1	+28	—	−136	−253

Source: *United Kingdom Balance of Payments 1980 Edition*
a Central government and local authorities.

possible), government procurement (calling for liberalisation of government purchasing), customs valuation (aiming at greater uniformity for customs valuation methods), and an agreement on subsidies and countervailing duties. Developed countries have undertaken not to grant export subsidies and all signatories undertake not to apply countervailing duties unless it can be demonstrated that a subsidy causes or threatens material injury to the domestic market.

Anti-Dumping

The GATT Anti-Dumping Code, to which the European Community is a signatory, is implemented by a Community regulation which controls the anti-dumping action that may be taken to protect British industry (as part of Community industry) against unfair competition and determines the criteria by which allegations of dumping are judged.

Community Trade Agreements

All tariffs on trade between Britain and the other European Community countries have been eliminated. Britain applies the common customs tariff to all countries neither belonging to, nor having any special arrangement with, the Community, subject to special arrangements for some industrial materials.

Community Preference

The Community has reciprocal preferential trading agreements with the European Free Trade Association (EFTA) countries, Cyprus, Israel, Malta and Spain and non-reciprocal agreements with Algeria, Morocco, Tunisia, Egypt, Jordan, Lebanon, Syria, Yugoslavia, and a group of African, Caribbean and Pacific countries (the ACP states, see below). Tariff preference is also given to other developing countries under the Generalised System of Preferences, the Faroe Islands, the overseas countries and territories of member countries, and to Greece and Turkey under the association agreements between them and the Community.

Commonwealth and Developing Countries

Former Commonwealth preferential agreements have been phased out and replaced, in the case of 29 developing Commonwealth countries in Africa, the Caribbean and the Pacific (ACP), by the trade provisions of the Convention of Lomé which came into effect in 1975. This was succeeded by a second convention, Lomé II, in March 1980. A further 29 non-Commonwealth developing countries within the same geographical area are also signatories.

Developing and industrial countries, including Britain, have agreed to establish a common fund to help to maintain stabilised prices of raw materials (see p 91). Work is in hand in UNCTAD to finalise the detailed arrangements for this new institution. It is envisaged that the fund will have capital of up to $750 million, to which Britain's contribution will be approximately $20 million.

CONTROLS ON PAYMENTS AND TRADE

There are now very few restrictions maintained by Britain on overseas transactions. Exchange controls on capital movements (originally introduced as an emergency measure at the beginning of the second world war) were abolished during 1979. As a result, British residents are free to purchase and use foreign currency for any purpose, including direct or portfolio investment abroad, and remittances and gifts abroad, and to maintain foreign currency bank accounts. Controls on the lending of sterling abroad have also been removed. Gold may be freely bought and sold. These measures enable Britain to meet in full its obligations on capital movements under European Community provisions and also those under the OECD Code on Capital Movements. Controls on trade in goods are described below.

Import and Export Control

Under the Import, Export and Customs Powers (Defence) Act 1939 the Department of Trade is empowered to prohibit or regulate the import or export of goods. Most goods may be imported freely under the provisions of the Open General Import Licence. Only a narrow range of goods is subject to export control. Several other government departments have separate powers to control imports and exports for specific purposes.

Import Controls

In accordance with its international obligations under the GATT, and to the IMF and the European Community, Britain has progressively removed quantitative restrictions from almost all its imports from the market economies. Those controls which do exist predominantly affect textile goods (usually having been imposed in accordance with the provisions of the GATT Multi-Fibre Arrangement, approved by the European Community in 1977). There are comparatively few quantitative restrictions on imports from centrally planned economies, and progress towards liberalisation continues to be made wherever possible. In accordance with its obligations to the European Community, Britain has also removed all quantitative restrictions on imports of goods of Community origin, with the exception of certain internationally recognised restrictions on a few goods such as arms, ammunition and radioactive materials. Some further restrictions or prohibitions are applied by other departments for the prohibition of goods bearing false or misleading indications of origin or improperly bearing a registered trade mark, for the protection of health or public safety, in the interest of conservation, and for other non-economic reasons (for example, on animals, drugs and explosives).

Export Controls The great majority of British exports are not subject to any government control or direction. The controls that are in operation are imposed to supervise exports of military and strategic significance. They also apply to certain metals, metal products (including certain British coins), waste and scrap; on cattle, sheep, pigs, horses, asses and mules, for humanitarian purposes and on cattle, swine and certain meat exported to another member State of the European Community, for health certification purposes; on endangered species of animals and plants, in accordance with international agreements; on photographic material over 60 years old and valued at £200 or more per item and all other articles over 50 years old, to restrict the export of items of national importance; on salmon and trout, to inhibit out-of-season fishing; on dangerous drugs; on British spirits (beverages) in casks of less than nine gallons; and on Common Agricultural Policy (CAP) products.

GOVERNMENT SERVICES The Government assists exporters by its efforts to create conditions favourable to the export trade and by providing information and advice about opportunities for trade in other countries and credit insurance facilities. Export promotion is also assisted by the Scottish Council (Development and Industry), the Development Corporation for Wales and in Northern Ireland by the Department of Commerce.

British Overseas Trade Board The British Overseas Trade Board (BOTB) directs Britain's official export promotion services, which include the provision of export intelligence assistance to British exporters in appointing agents and locating potential customers, help to exporters at trade fairs and other promotional events overseas, and support for firms participating in missions overseas and for inward commercial visits to Britain. It includes representatives of commerce and industry, the Trades Union Congress, the Department of Trade and the Foreign and Commonwealth Office and operates under the general authority of the Secretary of State for Trade, who is the president.

Information and Advice to Exporters Exporters wanting assistance and advice can consult the offices of the BOTB throughout Britain and, through these offices, the commercial posts of the British Diplomatic Service overseas. Overseas officers work closely with the BOTB in the provision of services for exporters. They regularly report on local economic and commercial conditions and generally assist the exporter to overcome any difficulties he encounters in trade with the country in question, particularly those arising out of governmental regulations.

Export Credit Insurance The Export Credits Guarantee Department (ECGD) provides credit insurance for about a third of the country's export trade and insures exports of both goods and services. The main risks covered include insolvency or protracted default of the buyer, governmental action which stops the British exporter receiving payment, new import restrictions, and war or civil disturbance in the buyer's country. Cover may commence from the date of contract or (at lower premiums) from the date of shipment.

This insurance may be supplemented by unconditional guarantees of repayment given direct to banks financing exporters, whether in sterling or foreign currencies. Alternatively, for contracts over £1 million ECGD will guarantee loans direct to overseas buyers enabling them to pay on cash terms, or 'lines of credit' similarly covering an agreed buying programme of an overseas country. The banks provide finance against these guarantees. ECGD is also prepared to support the issue of performance bonds in the commercial market in respect of cash or near-cash contracts worth over £250,000.

Investment insurance is provided for new British investment overseas against expropriation, war damage and restrictions on remittances.

Trade Fairs   Britain stages many exhibitions and trade fairs and British products are shown at many of the international specialist trade fairs throughout the world. Participation in trade fairs and store promotions overseas are forms of export promotion for which the Government provides information and financial assistance to exporters.

BALANCE OF PAYMENTS

Britain's balance of payments has usually been characterised by a deficit on visible trade partially offset by a surplus on invisible earnings. Estimates of the balance of payments and its main constituent items from 1970 to 1979 are given in summary in Table 35 and in greater detail since 1977 in Tables 36 and 37. The balance of payments statistics contain two indicators of particular importance. The first is the balance on current account, covering both visible (exports and imports of goods) and invisible (trade in services, investment income and transfers) transactions. This, together with capital transfers, provides a measure of how far Britain is paying its way abroad and thus adding to or using up overseas assets. The second indicator is the balance for official financing. This is the net result of all external transactions, that is the current account, capital transfers, investment and other capital transactions (including official long-term capital transactions, investment flows, trade credit, and changes in non-residents' balances held in London in sterling and in overseas currencies) and other flows, including unidentified transactions reflected in the balancing item. The balance for official financing shows the impact of all external transactions on the reserves and official debt position, that is, how much is available to add to the reserves and repay any official borrowing in the case of a net surplus, or how much must be financed by drawing on the reserves or by borrowing if there is a net deficit. Table 36 gives details of the current account since 1977. Increased production of North Sea oil was largely responsible for the fall in the visible deficit from £3,927 million in 1976 to £1,546 million in 1978 when there was a current account surplus of £620 million. The balance on current account deteriorated in 1979, however, a deficit of £1,863 million reflecting a worsening of the non-oil balance and a fall in the invisibles surplus.

The balance for official financing showed a surplus of £1,710 million in 1979 compared with a deficit of £1,126 million in 1978 and a surplus of £7,362 million in 1977. Although the abolition of exchange controls towards the end of 1979 resulted in substantial capital outflows (an estimated total effect of £2,000 million outflow in the second half of the year), this was more than offset by identified inflows of £3,600 million, resulting from a marked improvement in the attractiveness of sterling. The inflow went principally into private holdings of British Government stocks and sterling deposits with British banks. Overseas investment in the private sector amounted to £2,883 million while British private investment overseas totalled £6,401 million.

TABLE 35: Britain's Balance of Payments 1970–79

£ million

	Current balance	Balance for official financing	SDR allocation/ gold subscription to IMF[a]	Official financing		
				Total	Official borrowing[b]	Official reserves[c]
1970	+781	+1,287	+133	−1,420	−1,295	−125
1971	+1,076	+3,146	+125	−3,271	−1,735	−1,536
1972	+176	−1,265	+124	+1,141	+449	+692
1973	−1,056	−771	—	+771	+999	−228
1974	−3,379	−1,646	—	+1,646	+1,751	−105
1975	−1,674	−1,465	—	+1,465	+810	+655
1976	−1,116	−3,628	—	+3,628	+2,775[d]	+853
1977	−284	+7,362	—	−7,362	+2,226	−9,588
1978	+620	−1,126	—	+1,126	−1,203	+2,329
1979	−1,863	+1,710	+195	−1,905	−846	−1,059

Source: *United Kingdom Balance of Payments 1980 Edition*
[a] Gold subscription to IMF in 1970 was −£38 million.
[b] Drawings (+)/repayments (−).
[c] Drawings on (+)/additions to (−).
[d] Includes a credit of £1,113 million from the IMF.

TABLE 36: Britain's Current Account 1977–79

£ million

	1977	1978	1979
Visible trade:			
Exports (f.o.b.)	31,734	35,071	40,689
Imports (f.o.b.)	34,013	36,617	44,093
Visible balance	−2,279	−1,546	−3,404
Invisibles:			
Credits	16,503	18,559	22,397
Debits	14,508	16,393	20,856
Invisible balance	+1,995	+2,166	+1,541
Of which:			
Services	+3,061	+3,486	+3,579
Interest, profits and dividends	+46	+520	+289
Transfers	−1,112	−1,840	−2,327
Current balance	−284	+620	−1,863

Source: *United Kingdom Balance of Payments 1980 Edition*

The direct benefit of the United Kingdom Continental Shelf oil and gas programme to the balance of payments has increased substantially. Sales of oil and gas (valued at contract prices) exceeded £6,200 million in 1979. Identified net balance of payments items resulted in a net outflow of about £1,250 million in 1979 compared with about £570 million in 1976.

Britain participates in the Special Drawing Rights (SDRs) scheme which came into effect in 1970 in order to supplement world reserves. SDRs are reserve assets created and distributed by decision of the members of the IMF. Any member of the IMF may join the scheme, and its share is based on its IMF quota. Participants in the scheme accept an obligation to provide convertible currency, when designated by the IMF to do so, to another participant in exchange for SDRs up to a total amount equal to twice the net amount of their own allocation of SDRs. Only those countries with a sufficiently strong balance of payments are so designated by the IMF. SDRs may also be used in certain direct payments between participants in the scheme and for payments of various kinds to the IMF. The role of SDRs as a central standard of value in international transactions (see p 209) is being enhanced.

EXTERNAL ASSETS AND LIABILITIES

The significance of any inventory of Britain's aggregate external assets and liabilities is limited because a variety of claims and obligations are included that are very dissimilar in kind, in degree of liquidity and in method of valuation. By the end of 1979 Britain's external assets exceeded liabilities by about £6,400 million, compared with about £3,000 million at the end of 1978 and a net debtor position for the previous three years.

TABLE 37: Analysis of Capital Flows and Official Financing 1977–79

£ million

	1977	1978	1979
Current balance	−284	+620	−1,863
Investment and other capital transactions:			
Official long-term capital	−319	−336	−384
Overseas investment in the British public sector[a]	+2,182	−99	+900
Overseas investment in the British private sector	+3,188	+2,640	+2,883
British private investment overseas	−2,222	−4,414	−6,401
Overseas currency borrowing or lending (net) by British banks[a, b, c]:			
Borrowing to finance British investment overseas	+550	+835	−470
Other borrowing or lending (net)	−181	−1,271	+2,043
Exchange reserves in sterling[d]:			
British government stocks	+5	−115	+247
Banking and money market liabilities	−24	−4	+518
Other external banking and money market liabilities in sterling	+1,481	+293	+2,580
Import credit[e]	+297	+349	−133
Export credit[e]	−638	−839	−710
Other short-term transactions	+141	−557	+97
Total investment and other capital transactions	+4,460	−3,518	+1,170
Balancing item	+3,186	+1,772	+2,403
Allocation of SDRs	—	—	+195
Balance for official financing	+7,362	−1,126	+1,710
Net transactions with IMF	+1,113	−1,016	−596
Foreign currency borrowing (net):			
By the British Government	+871	+191	—
By public bodies under the exchange cover scheme	+242	−378	−250
Drawings on (+)/additions to (−) official reserves	−9,588	+2,329	−1,059
Total official financing	−7,362	+1,126	−1,905

Source: *United Kingdom Balance of Payments 1980 Edition*

[a] Excluding foreign currency borrowing by public bodies under the exchange cover scheme.
[b] Including certain other financial institutions.
[c] Excluding changes in levels resulting from changes in sterling valuation.
[d] Sterling reserves of overseas countries and international organisations, other than the IMF, reported by banks, etc. in Britain.
[e] Excluding trade credit between related firms; after deducting advance and progress payments to suppliers.

External Assets Britain's assets arising from private investment overseas are estimated to have been £35,767 million at the end of 1979. Direct investment[1] excluding banking and insurance, other than in the United States, and oil accounted for £19,147 million of the total, portfolio investment for £9,500 million and oil for £6,350 million.

British banking and commercial claims at the end of 1979 totalled £11,121 million. Within this total banking claims were £5,656 million; suppliers' export credit to unrelated firms was £4,611 million. Official external assets, including re-financed export credit, amounted to £4,877 million, which included outstanding inter-government loans by Britain of £1,281 million. These assets, with official reserves of £13,220 million (valuing gold at the market price rather than at the value included in the published levels), resulted in aggregate identified external assets at the end of 1979 of some £64,985 million.

Outward Private Investment The dismantling of the exchange control regulations in 1979 meant that foreign currency became available without limit for direct and portfolio investment overseas. The weight of evidence is that overseas investment strengthens the current account of the balance of payments by helping to keep and expand markets for British exports (many investments are in distribution and similar export-promoting sectors, or create demand abroad for other British goods and services) to the benefit of output and jobs at home. The balance of payments will also be strengthened by invisible earnings flowing from additional overseas investment; this will be particularly important in the future when the overseas earnings from North Sea oil begin to decline.

Direct investment outflow, excluding oil, was £2,738 million in 1979 compared with £2,394 million in 1978. (The latest available area analysis indicates that in 1978, £484 million was placed in developing countries, £543 million in other member countries of the European Community and £799 million in North America.) With the inclusion of oil, portfolio and other investment, aggregate private investment outflows totalled £6,401 million in 1979 compared with £4,414 million in 1978.

External Liabilities Identified external liabilities at the end of 1979 are estimated to have been some £58,559 million. Net drawing on the IMF accounted for £480 million of this sum and foreign currency borrowing by the Government for a further £1,955 million. Foreign currency borrowing by public bodies under the exchange cover scheme[2] totalled £4,202 million. Inter-governmental loans to Britain, mainly a consequence of the second world war and its aftermath, totalled £1,547 million of which £1,262 million was owed to the United States and £284 million to Canada. Other public sector liabilities of £7,093 million comprised mainly overseas holdings of British government securities. Treasury bills and notes and other borrowing by British public corporations and local authorities from overseas. British banking and commercial liabilities, including liabilities in sterling and in foreign currencies, totalled £16,802 million. Liabilities in the form of direct overseas investment in Britain's private sector excluding banking and insurance totalled £26,480 million.

---

[1] Direct investment refers mainly to the establishment of subsidiary companies and banks, while portfolio investment refers to investment in company securities.

[2] A scheme first introduced in 1969 whereby local authorities and public corporations raise foreign currency from overseas residents either directly or through British banks and surrender it to the Exchange Equalisation Account in exchange for sterling for use to finance expenditure in Britain. The Treasury sells the borrower foreign currency to service and repay the loan at the exchange rate that applied when the loan was taken out.

Since the 1960s London has been the centre of the euro-currency business, whereby banks and other institutions accept deposits and extend credit in foreign currencies. At the end of 1979 liabilities of British banks in foreign currencies amounted to £126,726 million (of which the equivalent of £98,871 million was in United States dollars) and claims were £121,351 million.

The 'sterling balances', or foreign holdings in Britain of sterling in the form of British government securities, bank deposits, deposits with local authorities and finance houses, and Treasury bills totalled £11,145 million. Of this, £2,793 million was held by residents of oil-exporting countries, £1,935 million by residents of other member countries of the European Community and £6,417 million by other holders. About 30 per cent of the balances were official holdings (mostly those of central monetary institutions) and 70 per cent were private holdings used by overseas residents to finance their international transactions. The total of these liabilities (excluding the counterpart of borrowing) remained broadly constant between the end of 1945 and 1970, then rose sharply in the early 1970s. As trade and payments arrangements have become more diversified in recent years the relative importance of sterling as a reserve currency has declined.

Inward Private Investment

Overseas liabilities arising from investment in the private sector of the British economy rose from £7,385 million in 1970 to £26,480 million at the end of 1979. Overseas investors in Britain are free to repatriate the proceeds of the sale of their investments, including any capital gains that may have accrued. Earnings and dividends are transferable irrespective of their size. In 1979 the inflow of direct, portfolio and other private investment, including oil, amounted to £2,883 million.

The value of overseas investment in the private sector at the end of 1979 comprised: the book value of direct investment in Britain by companies incorporated abroad (excluding oil, banking and insurance)—£11,907 million (this figure has been extrapolated from the book value at the end of 1974, taking account of subsequent annual transactions); portfolio holdings of British securities—£4,530 million; the book value of the net assets in Britain of overseas oil companies—£6,950 million; and borrowing by British companies overseas—£3,093 million.

Of the 1,241 million inflow of direct investment excluding oil into Britain in 1978 (the latest year for which detailed figures are available), £787 million originated in North America and £275 million in other member countries of the European Community. Foreign investment inflow brings a number of benefits to British industry, including technological development, which in turn will strengthen the economy and the balance of payments.

20 Promotion of the Sciences

Britain has for centuries provided an atmosphere of learning congenial to its scientists, whose record of achievements in relation to size of population is in many respects unsurpassed. This record has been maintained throughout the twentieth century and British scientists remain in the forefront in many areas. One recent example was the research carried out by two British scientists which made possible the birth of the world's first 'test-tube' baby in Britain in July 1978. Nobel prizes for science have been won by 62 British citizens, a number exceeded only by the United States.

The Government keeps under review facilities for training scientists and ensures that adequate research is devoted to matters of national interest, which include defence (see Chapter 4), industrial innovation, health, environmental protection, use and conservation of natural resources, the provision of good food, shelter and energy and of efficient transport and communications.

Expenditure

Total expenditure in Britain on scientific research and development in 1978 was £3,250 million, or 2 per cent of the gross domestic product. About half was financed by the Government which carries out about a quarter of Britain's research and development in its establishments. Remaining government expenditure on research went mainly to industry and the universities. Funds for research are also provided by private and public enterprises and by private endowments and trusts.

THE GOVERNMENT AND SCIENTIFIC RESEARCH

Central responsibility for basic civil science rests with the Secretary of State for Education and Science, while responsibility for technology rests mainly with the Secretary of State for Industry. In some cases the Prime Minister has a co-ordinating role. Other government departments are responsible for research and development related to their executive responsibilities. In 1972 the Government extended the customer-contractor approach to all its applied research and development, whereby each department as customer, with advice from its Chief Scientist, defines requirements and the work is undertaken by contractors (government laboratories, research councils, research associations, industry and the universities). Most departments have a Chief Scientist's Organisation, which formulates requirements, selects the most suitable contractors and co-operates with them to obtain the best value for money.

An Advisory Council for Applied Research and Development provides a central forum of external advice to ministers on the deployment of applied research and development in both the public and private sectors, on the future development and application of technology, and on the role of Britain in international collaboration in such activities. It has published a number of reports on aspects of new technology.

A Committee of Chief Scientists and Permanent Secretaries is responsible for ensuring that scientific questions are brought before ministers as appropriate and that scientific priorities reflect those of the Government as a whole.

The Department of Education and Science

The Department of Education and Science discharges its responsibilities for basic and applied civil science mainly through the five research councils to which it allocates funds from its science budget (the budget totals £383 million in 1980–81). The budget is intended to further scientific knowledge, to maintain a fundamental capacity for research and to support higher education. The councils and their allocations are: the Agricultural Research Council (£35 million), the Medical Research Council (£71·8 million), the Natural Environment Research Council (£45 million), the Science Research Council (£201·1 million) and the Social Science Research Council (£19·7 million). Science budget grants are also made to the British Museum (Natural History) and to the Royal Society. About one-fifth of the budget usually goes on research grants and contracts to universities, polytechnics and elsewhere, over two-fifths to research units and other establishments of the research councils, about one-seventh to postgraduate support and one-sixth to subscriptions to international scientific organisations. The Department is also responsible for some aspects of international scientific relations and helps to co-ordinate government policy regarding scientific and technical information.

The Advisory Board for the Research Councils

The Advisory Board for the Research Councils advises the Secretary of State on responsibilities for civil science with special reference to the research council system, the support of postgraduate students and the proper balance between national and international scientific activities, and on the allocation of the science budget between research councils and other bodies; and promotes close liaison between the councils and users of their research. Its membership includes the chairman or secretary of each of the research councils, the chairman of the University Grants Committee, the Chief Scientists from departments with a major interest in the work of the research councils, the Chief Scientist to the Central Policy Review Staff, and independent members drawn from universities, industry and the Royal Society.

RESEARCH COUNCILS' FUNCTIONS

Each of the five research councils is an autonomous body established under Royal Charter with membership drawn from the universities, professions, industry and the Government. They conduct research through their own research establishments and by supporting selected research in universities and other higher education bodies. As well as being financed from the science budget, three of the councils receive commissions, estimated at £73 million in 1980–81, from departments under the customer-contractor principle. The Agricultural Research Council receives 47 per cent of its income from commissions, the Natural Environment Research Council 32 per cent and the Medical Research Council 17 per cent.

Agricultural Research Council

The Agricultural Research Council (ARC) has eight institutes under its direct control: the Animal Breeding Research Organisation, at Edinburgh; the Institute for Research on Animal Diseases, at Newbury (Berkshire); the Institute of Animal Physiology, at Cambridge; the Food Research Institute, at Norwich; the Letcombe Laboratory, at Wantage (Oxfordshire), dealing with the growth of crops in relation to soil conditions and cultivation; the Meat Research Institute, at Bristol; the Poultry Research Centre, at Edinburgh; and the Weed Research Organisation, at Yarnton, near Oxford. There are six ARC units under distinguished scientists associated with universities. The ARC is also responsible for 15 independent state-aided agricultural research institutes, notably the Rothamsted Experimental Station, at Harpenden (Hertfordshire), which is the largest agricultural research institute in Britain and deals with research on soils, fertilisers, crop physiology and crop husbandry; and the National Institute of Agricultural Engineering, at Silsoe (Bedfordshire). There are also eight independent institutes in Scotland financed by the Department of Agriculture and Fisheries for Scotland with advice from the ARC on their scientific programmes, staffing and equipment.

The ARC is planning to devote additional sums to research in a number of areas including the study of photosynthesis with the aim of increasing crop yields, the breeding of plants which could make their own nitrogen and so bring savings in the use of fertilisers, and work on studying animal behaviour and diseases to obtain healthier and more productive livestock.

Medical Research Council

The main research establishments of the Medical Research Council (MRC) are the National Institute for Medical Research at Mill Hill, London, which carries out fundamental research relevant to medicine, the Clinical Research Centre at Northwick Park Hospital, London, and the Laboratory of Molecular Biology at Cambridge. In addition, the Council has over 60 research units, mostly located in university departments, medical schools and hospitals in Britain. These include a Radiobiology Unit, a Toxicology Unit, a Pneumoconiosis Unit and a Clinical and Population Cytogenetics Unit.

The Council is assisted by four advisory boards: the Neurobiology and Mental Health Board; the Cell Biology and Disorders Board; the Physiological Systems and Disorders Board; and the Tropical Medicine Research Board. In addition, the MRC is advised by committees concerned with particular aspects of its work and with research grants. The MRC's arrangements for the support of research fall under four main headings: investigations by members of its scientific staff, mostly working in its own establishments; short-term ('project') grants to workers in universities and elsewhere; long-term grants in support of specific research programmes in university departments ('programme grants'); and research training awards (fellowships and studentships) tenable both at home and overseas.

The Natural Environment Research Council

The Natural Environment Research Council (NERC) is responsible for encouraging, planning and executing research in the physical and biological sciences relating to man's natural environment and its resources. These researches are broadly grouped and defined as: the Solid Earth—its physical properties and mineral resources; Seas and Oceans—their behaviour and living and mineral resources; Inland Waters—their behaviour and living resources; Terrestrial Environments—wildlife communities and their resources; Atmosphere—its structure and interactions; and a number of interdisciplinary studies including pollution and the physical and biological properties of the Antarctic environment. Research programmes which the NERC is planning to expand include those on geological work in connection with deep drilling and mapping, which is important for future mineral and energy exploration; new means of insect pest control using viruses harmless to man; the climate; remote sensing by satellite, for resource and ecological surveys; and modelling the behaviour of British estuaries.

The Council's research institutes are: the British Antarctic Survey, the Institute of Geological Sciences, the Institute of Hydrology, the Institute of Marine Biochemistry, the Institute for Marine Environmental Research, the Institute of Oceanographic Sciences, the Institute of Terrestrial Ecology, the Institute of Virology and the Sea Mammal Research Unit. The Council also maintains central scientific and technical services which include research vessel services, an experimental cartography unit, and computing services.

Research institutes aided by council grants are: the Freshwater Biological Association, the Marine Biological Association of the United Kingdom, the Scottish Marine Biological Association, the Unit of Marine Invertebrate Biology, the Unit of Comparative Plant Ecology and some university units.

Science Research Council

The Science Research Council (SRC) supports basic research in astronomy, geophysics, the biological sciences, chemistry, mathematics, physics, engineering and applied sciences, in furthering its primary purpose of sustaining standards of education and research in the universities and polytechnics. Most of the SRC's resources are devoted to helping university and polytechnic staff to carry out basic research at the forefront of their subjects, in their institution, in one of the Council's research establishments, or elsewhere; to encouraging active collaboration in research between the higher education institutions and industry; to identifying and supporting areas of special importance and to enabling suitable graduates to receive further training in methods of research or a specialised branch of science or engineering of importance to British industry. The SRC provides grants for research projects, and awards studentships for training in methods of research or advanced courses of study and fellowships to promising scientists or engineers to enable them to carry out their own independent research programmes.

Research Establishments

The SRC maintains four research establishments: the Daresbury Laboratory at Warrington (Cheshire), the Royal Greenwich Observatory at Herstmonceux (East Sussex), the Royal Observatory, Edinburgh, and the Rutherford and Appleton Laboratories, with headquarters at Chilton in Oxfordshire (which are being merged). The establishments are each centres of specialised research, but are also used for the development and operation of research equipment beyond the resources of an academic institution. They provide support for scientists whose research needs access to facilities run by international research organisations, such as the powerful particle accelerators at the European Organisation for Nuclear Research (CERN) and the high-flux neutron source at the Institut Laue-Langevin (ILL).

International Collaboration

The SRC provides national contributions to CERN, the civil science programme of the North Atlantic Treaty Organisation, the Anglo Australian Telescope, the European Incoherent Scatter Project and part of the European Space Agency contribution. It also contributes to, and shares with its French and German partners, the control of the ILL reactor at Grenoble.

Engineering

Developments in engineering research and training geared to the needs of industry are major concerns of the SRC. Special programmes are being supported in three areas—polymer engineering, marine technology and production engineering—within a general effort to develop research and postgraduate training in university engineering departments. Other subjects receiving major support include microelectronics and computer applications (such as industrial robotics), materials and energy conservation, information and communication systems, biotechnology, medical engineering and coal technology. A network to provide an interactive computing facility to universities has been built up and is serviced at Chilton.

Astronomy

Astronomy uses both ground-based techniques, such as optical and radio telescopes, and space-based methods (see p 396). Optical astronomy is carried out in university departments and, within the SRC, at the Royal Greenwich

Observatory and the Royal Observatory, Edinburgh. Instruments include the Royal Greenwich Observatory's Isaac Newton Telescope, of diameter 2·5 metres (8 feet), which is being installed at a new site on the island of La Palma in the Canary Islands; the Anglo Australian Telescope, of diameter 3·9 metres (13 feet), at Siding Spring, Australia, in a joint project with the Australian Government; a 1·2-metre (4-ft) Schmidt telescope on the same site; and optical telescopes operated by the South African Astronomical Observatory, to which the SRC contributes. A 3·8-metre (12-ft) infra-red telescope, the largest telescope in the world designed specifically to make infra-red observations, was inaugurated at Mauna Kea, Hawaii, in 1979.

Cambridge and Manchester Universities are the main centres for research in radio astronomy with substantial support from the SRC.

Nuclear Physics The SRC establishments concerned with the provision of facilities for university research in nuclear physics are at Chilton, which supports university teams engaged in experiments in particle physics at CERN and other centres, and the Daresbury Laboratory, where a 30 million volt tandem accelerator for research into nuclear structure is due for completion in 1981.

Science Support is provided for high-quality research in biological and natural sciences, mathematics and science-based archaeology. Where experimental facilities are too expensive to be provided for individual universities and polytechnics, central facilities have been provided. For example, at the Daresbury Laboratory a new synchrotron storage ring came into operation in 1980. It provides high intensity electromagnetic radiation used in a wide range of experiments in materials science, surface physics, crystallography and molecular biology. Other central facilities include a spallation neutron source being built at Chilton to provide a pulsed beam of neutrons, and a high-powered laser facility, also at Chilton, which is used to study plasmas.

The Social Science Research Council The Social Science Research Council (SSRC) encourages, supports and carries out research in, and disseminates knowledge about, the social sciences. The SSRC's areas of interest include economics; political science; psychology; social anthropology; social and economic history; sociology and social administration; social sciences and the law; education; management and industrial relations; human geography; linguistics; planning; and various aspects of a wide range of other disciplines. It initiates research into such topics as health policy, energy policy, population studies, central and local government, young people in society, transmitted deprivation, and the social impact of North Sea oil. Grants are provided for research projects at universities and other institutions, and awards made to postgraduate students. The SSRC also has four research units: the Industrial Relations Research Unit at Warwick University; the Cambridge Group for the History of Population and Social Structure; the Research Unit on Ethnic Relations at Aston University (Birmingham); and the Centre for Socio-legal Studies at Oxford University.

THE UNIVERSITIES AND INSTITUTIONS OF UNIVERSITY STATUS Of the total estimated university expenditure on scientific research in the academic year 1978–79 (over £274 million), the largest government contribution (over £160 million) was through the University Grants Committee.

Scientific research in the universities and other institutions of higher education is also supported through the research councils. This support takes two forms. First, nearly two-thirds of the postgraduate students in science and technology receive maintenance awards from the research councils, through postgraduate studentships. These awards are in some cases for periods of up to three years of training in research work and in others for shorter periods for advanced studies. Second, grants and contracts are given to the universities and other institutions by the research councils for specified projects, particularly in new or developing areas of research. The ARC, MRC and SSRC maintain a number of research units within universities. In addition, the research councils provide central facilities in their own establishments for use by university research workers. The other main channels of support for scientific research in the universities are various government departments, the Royal Society, industry and the independent foundations.

Universities in industrial centres have tended to acquire outstanding reputations in studies relating to their local industries, and on a national scale close relationships are fostered between the universities, industries and the Government in numerous joint projects. Britain has two 'science parks', established by Trinity College, Cambridge, and Heriot-Watt University, Edinburgh. These are sites containing science-based industries and are designed to facilitate commercial developments in advanced technology in consultation with and to the benefit of local scientists.

DEPARTMENTAL RESEARCH AND DEVELOPMENT   In 1980–81 total Government research and development expenditure is estimated to be some £2,700 million. The largest departmental research and development budget is that of the Ministry of Defence (see p 100). The main civil departments involved are the Department of Education and Science, whose estimated research expenditure of £607 million in 1980–81 is mostly related to expenditure by the research councils and the universities; the Department of Energy (£229 million in 1980–81); the Department of Industry (£159 million); the Ministry of Agriculture, Fisheries and Food and the Department of Agriculture and Fisheries for Scotland (a total of £85 million); and the Department of the Environment and the Department of Transport (a total of £71 million).

The Department of Energy   The Department of Energy is responsible for the United Kingdom Atomic Energy Authority (UKAEA); research in support of the exploitation of North Sea oil and gas; research into alternative sources of energy and conservation of energy; co-ordination of energy research within government departments; general approval of the research programmes of the coal, gas and electricity supply industries; and co-ordination of British contributions to energy research and development programmes sponsored by international bodies.

An Advisory Council on Research and Development for Fuel and Power advises the Secretary of State on the general programme of research and development of the nationalised energy industries and on other matters related to energy research and development. An Energy Technology Support Unit at Harwell (Oxfordshire) assists the Department in assessing technological possibilities in energy policy, advises on long-term research and development programmes, and assists in their management.

An Offshore Energy Technology Board advises the Secretary of State for Energy on research and development in offshore oil and gas technology and is responsible for programmes designed to ensure the safety and efficiency of offshore operations and improve the competitive efficiency of the offshore equipment industry in Britain.

Nuclear Energy   The Secretary of State for Energy is responsible for promoting and controlling the development of nuclear energy and ensuring that the proper degrees of importance are attached to its various applications. The UKAEA is the main body carrying out relevant research and development. Its programme includes work in support of the Government's nuclear power programme, and it builds and operates experimental and prototype reactors (see p 277). The Authority also works outside the nuclear field. Research and development work is undertaken at the Atomic Energy Research Establishment at Harwell and at the Culham Laboratory, also in Oxfordshire; at the Atomic Energy Establishment at Winfrith (Dorset) and at establishments of the Authority's northern division at Risley (Cheshire), Dounreay (Highland), Springfields (Lancashire) and Windscale (Cumbria). The Safety and Reliability Directorate at Culcheth (Cheshire) is the focal point of the UKAEA's work in relation to the safety of nuclear reactors and related plants and processes.

Co-operation in nuclear energy between Britain and other countries takes place within a framework of intergovernmental agreements and membership of bodies such as the International Atomic Energy Agency (operating under the aegis of the United Nations) and the Nuclear Energy Agency of the Organisation for Economic Co-operation and Development, and through research links between the UKAEA and counterpart organisations in other countries.

Euratom

Britain takes part in the co-operative research programmes of the European Atomic Energy Community (Euratom, see p 73) including that concerned with thermonuclear fusion (the release of controlled nuclear energy from the joining of nuclei of light elements to form heavier ones). Britain's centre for fusion research is the UKAEA's Culham Laboratory whose work forms part of a co-ordinated European programme under the auspices of Euratom. A major component of this programme is the Joint European Torus (JET) project which is being built at Culham; the construction phase is due to be completed by 1983. The JET experiment is intended to demonstrate the feasibility of controlled nuclear fusion at the experimental level by producing plasma in the conditions needed in a fusion reactor.

The Department of the Environment and the Department of Transport

The Departments' research programmes are the responsibility of the Directorate General of Research which provides a common service to both Departments. They are formulated by seven research requirement committees, which bring together the main customer-contractor and research policy interests.

About 40 per cent of the Departments' programmes are carried out at their research establishments: the Building Research Establishment (see p 256), the Transport and Road Research Laboratory (see p 305) and the Hydraulics Research Station, the remainder being undertaken by outside organisations. About 50 per cent of the Department of the Environment's programme is devoted to environmental protection (including radioactive waste management, water resources and pollution), nearly 30 per cent to housing and construction, and the remainder to planning, the appraisal of mineral resources and the countryside. Some 45 per cent of the Department of Transport's programme is concerned with highways, 20 per cent with railways and inter-urban transport, 6 per cent with road safety and the remainder with local and urban transport, freight and ports. Research associations receiving financial assistance from the Departments include the Construction Industry Research and Information Association, the Building Services Research and Information Association, the Timber Research and Development Association and the Water Research Centre.

The Department of Industry

The Department of Industry is responsible for the sponsorship of manufacturing industries and for technical services to industry, and for six research establishments: the National Physical Laboratory (NPL) at Teddington (Greater London); the National Engineering Laboratory (NEL) at East Kilbride (Strathclyde); the Warren Spring Laboratory (WSL) at Stevenage (Hertfordshire); the National Maritime Institute (NMI) at Feltham (Greater London); the Computer Aided Design Centre at Cambridge; and the Laboratory of the Government Chemist in London. The NPL has responsibilities for the national system of measurement, for technical aspects of standards (including the British Calibration Service) and for research in computing, numerical analysis, chemical standards and materials applications. The NEL carries out research in mechanical engineering aimed at helping industry improve designs and production processes by the application of improved technology. Research at the WSL is particularly concerned with control engineering, materials handling, metals extraction, mineral processing, waste materials processing and environmental technology. The NMI has special facilities and expertise relating to the characteristics and performance of ships and offshore structures, marine traffic and navigation safety, wind and water forces on structures and in conducting marine trials and measurements at sea. The NMI is to be converted into a non-governmental research body. The Computer Aided Design Centre is concerned with increasing and optimising the use of computer aided design by industry. Analytical services and scientific advice to government departments are provided by the Laboratory of the Government Chemist. These establishments undertake contract research for British industry and overseas firms.

The Department sponsors research by extra-mural contracts with industry, universities and research associations. In accordance with the Government's customer-contractor principle, the Department administers a number of requirements boards to determine the objectives and balance of the relevant research and development programmes, to further the practical application of technology and to advise on science and technology matters in their fields. They cover ship and marine technology; mechanical engineering and machine tools; engineering materials; computers, systems and electronics; chemicals and minerals; metrology and standards; garment and allied industries; and electrical technology. They are responsible to the Secretary of State for Industry and include representatives from other departments, industry and bodies in the public sector. The Chief Scientist's Requirements Board covers other branches of technology.

Agricultural, Food, Fisheries and Forestry Research

Agricultural research is carried out mainly by the Agricultural Research Council, the government agricultural departments and by private industry. Fisheries research is conducted by the government fisheries departments, the White Fish Authority, and the Natural Environment Research Council. Advice is given to the government agricultural departments and to the ARC on state-aided research and development in agriculture and food in Great Britain by a joint consultative organisation.

Government Agricultural and Food Departments

The Agricultural Development and Advisory Service of the Ministry of Agriculture, Fisheries and Food does both applied and basic research. At its Central Veterinary Laboratory at Weybridge, research and laboratory investigations are carried out into most diseases affecting farm livestock, and the making and supplying of certain biological products. The Harpenden Laboratory is concerned with research and development on plant health problems, and also on the detection of pesticide residues in treated crops and crop products, and on the formulation of pesticides. Research work on insects, mites and fungi affecting food storage and on harmful mammals and birds is carried out at laboratories at Slough (Berkshire) and Tolworth and Worplesdon (both in Surrey). They are also concerned with the safe use of pesticides in food storage and in animal husbandry, and with the effect on wildlife of pesticides of all kinds.

The Chief Scientific Adviser (Food) and the Food Science Division provide advice on scientific and technical aspects of food. Particular attention is paid to the safety, quality and nutritive value of food, including consideration of food additives and contaminants. Close liaison is maintained with the Department of Health and Social Security and with other government departments and agencies. The Division has laboratories in Norwich and London.

In Scotland research work at East Craigs, Edinburgh, by the Department of Agriculture and Fisheries, is mainly concerned with the problems of cultivar taxonomy, seed testing, healthy seed potato production, plant pathology, pesticides, and the ecology of birds, mammals and insects harmful to agriculture and stored products. In Northern Ireland the Department of Agriculture is responsible for promotion of research in agriculture and in veterinary and food sciences with the aim of improving efficiency of production, marketability of foods and the health of plants and animals. The Department is also responsible for work on forest science, ecology of freshwater and marine fish as well as on the biology of freshwater resources.

Government Fisheries Departments

The Ministry of Agriculture, Fisheries and Food's research work is carried out by the Directorate of Fisheries Research at Lowestoft and by the Torry Research Station in Aberdeen. The former includes a Marine Fisheries Laboratory and Fisheries Radiobiological Laboratory at Lowestoft, a Shellfish and Marine Pollution Laboratory at Burnham-on-Crouch (Essex), a Salmon and Freshwater Fisheries Laboratory in London, a Shellfish Cultivation Station at Conwy (Gwynedd) and a Fish Disease Centre at Weymouth. Torry Research Station and an outstation at Hull are concerned with the investigation of all aspects of fish technology. There are seven research vessels engaged on sea-going, inshore and estuarine work. The Department of Agriculture and Fisheries for Scotland maintains a Marine Research Laboratory and five sea-going research ships at Aberdeen, and a Freshwater Fisheries Research Laboratory at Pitlochry.

A Fisheries Research and Development Board, representative of government departments and the industry, advises on research programmes, objectives and priorities. A Controller of Fisheries Research and Development, responsible jointly to the Minister of Agriculture, Fisheries and Food and the Secretary of State for Scotland, co-ordinates the laboratories' programmes.

Forestry

Forestry research is carried out by the Forestry Commission at the Forest Research Station, Alice Holt Lodge, Surrey, and the Northern Research Station, Roslin, near Edinburgh. By means of grants, aid is also given for forestry research work undertaken by various universities and other institutions, including the Commonwealth Forestry Institute, Oxford. Expenditure by the Commission on research work in Great Britain amounted to £4 million in 1978–79. Research into the quality and uses of home-grown timber is carried out by Princes Risborough Laboratory in Buckinghamshire, and also by grant-aided associations. Research on Dutch elm disease is being carried out by the Commission.

The Royal Botanic Gardens at Kew (founded in 1759), covering 120 hectares (300 acres), and its 200-hectare (500-acre) estate at Wakehurst Place, Ardingly (West Sussex) are part of the Ministry of Agriculture, Fisheries and Food. The Herbarium houses one of the largest collections of specimens in the world and is primarily concerned with research into the classification of plants and the preparation of plant lists as well as the classification of about 50,000 specimens a year from overseas. A Conservation Unit gathers and provides information on endangered species of plant on a worldwide basis. The study of plant anatomy, plant biochemistry, cytology and genetics is undertaken in the Jodrell Laboratory. The laboratory's plant physiology section is based at Wakehurst Place where research is being carried out into seed germination and storage. A wide range of living plants, comprising some 3,100 types representing 340 families of plant, is displayed at Kew.

The Royal Botanic Garden at Edinburgh was founded in 1670 and is administered by the Department of Agriculture and Fisheries for Scotland. Associated gardens are the Logan Botanic Garden at Ardwell near Stranraer, the Younger Botanic Garden at Benmore near Dunoon, and Dawyck Garden at Stobo near Peebles. The large collection of living plants, both out of doors and in greenhouses, is used for taxonomic research (into plant classification).

Other Government-sponsored Research

The Procurement Executive of the Ministry of Defence engages in research for defence purposes at its research and development establishments and through contracts placed with industry and universities (see p 100). It also undertakes certain research for civil purposes, including meteorology (being responsible for financing the Meteorological Office at Bracknell in Berkshire, which compiles weather forecasts and undertakes research in meteorology and some aspects of geophysics), civil aviation and space research.

The Department of Health and Social Security spent £26 million on research and development in 1979–80 of which £11·4 million was on biomedical research through the Medical Research Council. The Department's Chief Scientist is supported by a group of independent advisers covering a wide range of scientific disciplines. The Department is involved in international research and development, and is participating in the European Community's medical and public health research programme.

The Health and Safety Executive carries out research in its Health and Safety Laboratories and by using appropriate outside contractors. Its area of research covers all matters affecting the health and safety of people at work, and the risks arising from work activities to the public. Fields of study include explosion risks, fires, protective equipment, methods for monitoring and measuring airborne contaminants, occupational medicine and hygiene, and the safety of engineering systems.

The Department of Employment has an Economic and Social Division to conduct and advise on its programme of research on socio-economic problems including industrial relations and general manpower issues. Assistance is given in social research by the Office of Population Censuses and Surveys and close contact is maintained with the Social Science Research Council.

Nearly all of the Home Office's expenditure on research and development, of about £9 million a year, is concerned with law and order.

PUBLIC SECTOR RESEARCH

Some of the public corporations which run the nationalised industries have their own research organisations, in particular those concerned with energy (see Chapter 14), steel and transport. These organisations also give support to other organisations concerned with research on matters of interest to them.

Covent Garden

The buildings and surrounding area of what was previously London's principal fruit, flower and vegetable market have been restored and developed into a new shopping and entertainments centre.

New Agricultural Equipment

A self-propelled sprout harvester, which can strip up to 200 stalks a minute, has three separate cleaning systems to remove waste and a 1,250 kg (2,756 lbs) storage hopper.

A portable tanker, with a specially developed polyethylene body mounted on flotation wheels, can carry anything from water or oil to liquid fertilisers.

A four-wheel drive telescopic handler, designed to accept a wide range of agricultural implements.

A soil loosener causes less damage to soil structures than traditional ploughing methods, encourages the increase in levels of organic matter and earthworms, and leaves the surface suitable for immediate direct drilling.

Sport

A new dinghy, with built-in buoyancy, designed to give the newcomer a safe introduction to sailing.

An 'electronic line monitor' signals, when the tennis ball is out of court, by a bleep in the earpiece worn by the line judge at Wimbledon.

NATIONAL RESEARCH DEVELOPMENT CORPORATION

The National Research Development Corporation (NRDC) is an independent public corporation which was set up in 1949 to promote the development and the exploitation of new technology. Its two main activities are to exploit inventions developed in the universities and research council and government establishments, and to provide finance for innovation by industrial companies. The NRDC has a portfolio of 6,000 British and overseas patents and about 500 licensees, and also some 600 investments in development projects of which about 300 are joint ventures with industrial companies. It is expected to operate as a commercial organisation and has been profitable for many years. Some of the major technical achievements which it has exploited or supported include cephalosporin antibiotics, pyrethroid insecticides, glass-reinforced cement, carbon fibres, printed circuit boards, computers and computer software, computer-aided design, electric motors and hovercraft.

PRIVATELY FINANCED RESEARCH

A considerable amount of research is undertaken and financed by private sector firms and learned bodies (see below). Virtually all industrial research work is carried out within industry by firms in their own laboratories and by research associations. Important contributions to the support of medical research in particular subjects are made by industry, especially the pharmaceutical industry, and by the many private charities or voluntary organisations which raise money for particular branches of research. Charities and voluntary bodies between them contribute approximately £25 million a year to medical research.

Industrial Research

Within the total expenditure of £2,324 million on research and development carried out within private industry in 1978, expenditure by private industry accounted for £2,061 million, public corporations for £213 million and research associations for £51 million. The main industries involved included electronics (which spent £650 million), chemicals and allied products (£432 million), aerospace (£425 million), mechanical engineering (£182 million) and motor vehicles (£130 million). Firms in science-based industries commit large private funds to research and development in the course of business.

A number of institutes for sponsored research have been established to extend the facilities for private research for industrial firms by studying problems which are not within the scope of the average industrial laboratory.

Research Associations

A scheme by which the Government helped firms with similar interests to form organisations known as research associations, to carry out industrial research co-operatively, was started in 1917. Encouragement by government grants, related to the contributions made by the industries concerned, has lately been phased out in favour of extra-mural contract support, such as that offered by the Department of Industry's Research and Development Requirements Boards (see p 388). About 30 of these research associations operate in areas of interest to the Department of Industry. In addition there are four (buildings services; construction industry; timber; and water) linked with the Department of the Environment and four (Flour Milling and Baking; Campden Food Preservation; British Food Manufacturing Industries; and British Industrial Biological Research) linked with the Ministry of Agriculture, Fisheries and Food. Among the largest of the industrial research associations are those dealing with production engineering, welding, electrical manufacturing, cotton and man-made fibres, non-ferrous metals and motor manufacturing. (See also Chapter 13.)

**THE LEARNED
SOCIETIES**

Although today most research is conducted under other auspices, the learned societies, of which there are more than 300, have retained their traditional function of facilitating the spread of knowledge. The most eminent of those concerned with science in its broadest aspects (as distinct from those societies with specialised interests and activities) are the Royal Society, Royal Society of Arts, Royal Institution and British Association.

Royal Society

The Royal Society, or, more fully, the Royal Society of London for Improving Natural Knowledge, founded in 1660, occupies a unique place in Britain's scientific affairs and is equivalent to national academies of sciences in other countries. It is the oldest such academy in the world to have enjoyed continuous existence. There are today three main categories of Fellowship: Royal Fellows, Foreign Members, of whom there are about 85, and the main body of Fellows numbering about 900. Election to the Fellowship, which is for life, is restricted to 40 persons a year. The Royal Society is governed by a council of 21 members. The President of the Society is consulted on scientific appointments to research councils and Fellows serve on most governmental advisory councils and committees concerned with research.

The Royal Society recognises the highest standards of scientific and technological achievements through its elections to the Fellowship and the award of its medals and endowed lectureships. It awards 14 medals (not all annually) including the Copley Medal (its highest award) and three Royal Medals, while there are seven endowed lectureships. The Society encourages research through the award of grants and research appointments. It administers 18 research professorships, of which four are supported from private funds and the remainder from its parliamentary grant. A further 12 senior research fellowships and 30 other research fellowships are supported in British universities. Grants for research are made from its private funds and from its parliamentary grant, and particular funds are available for scientific investigations and expeditions, for travel by individual scientists, for studies in the history of science and for scientific publications. The dissemination of scientific knowledge is encouraged by a programme of scientific discussion meetings and through its publications. It has an extensive library of works relating to the history of science. The council tenders advice to the Government and other bodies on matters relating to science and technology and their application, and study groups on particular aspects of science are established at intervals to prepare reports which are widely distributed to the scientific community. A number of committees of the council, some of them jointly with other bodies, promote improvements in education in science subjects and emphasise the importance of the applied sciences and engineering in industry. A joint committee with the British Academy has been established to keep under review the activities of learned societies in Britain and to assist them.

The international relations of the Royal Society are extensive. As the national academy of science, it represents Britain in all but one of the 18 international unions comprising the International Council of Scientific Unions. The Society also represents Britain on the Council of the International Institute for Applied Systems Analysis. It is a member of the European Science Foundation and certain other organisations, and also plays a leading part in international scientific programmes. It has agreements for exchange visits by scientists and co-operative research with many academies throughout the world, and maintains informal relations to promote scientific co-operation with many other countries. The largest formal scheme is the European Science Exchange Programme, which provides for fellowships (usually of one year) and study visits (lasting about two months) with 16 other countries in Western Europe.

Royal Society of Arts

The Royal Society of Arts (properly, the Royal Society for the Encouragement of Arts, Manufactures and Commerce) is concerned with arts, architecture and design, science and technology, industry and commerce, the environment and education. Since its foundation in 1754, one of the Society's principal objects has been to promote the progress of all branches of practical knowledge, chiefly by means of lectures and conferences, and by the publication of a monthly journal designed to enable leading authorities to report on developments of public as well as specialist interest.

Royal Institution

The Royal Institution was founded in 1799 as a public body for facilitating the introduction of useful mechanical inventions and improvements, and for teaching the application of science to everyday life. Later it undertook the 'promotion of chemical science by experiments and lectures for improving arts and manufactures', and 'the diffusion and extension of useful knowledge'. Its character, however, was largely determined by the work of Sir Humphry Davy and Michael Faraday, who established a tradition of research. Today the Royal Institution has extensive laboratories which undertake research on subjects including fast chemical kinetics, photosynthesis and solar energy. Lectures are given on recent developments in science and other branches of knowledge with particular emphasis on encouraging young people to take an interest in science.

British Association

The British Association for the Advancement of Science was founded in 1831 to promote general interest in science and its applications. One of its chief activities is the annual meeting, attended by many young students as well as by eminent scientists. In addition the Association plans special lectures, exhibitions and discussions (some designed for young audiences), the publication of pamphlets, the organisation of conferences, and the appointment of study groups. The Association has area committees and three lectureships for young scientists (dealing with the physical, biological and sociological sciences) to encourage scientists to make their activities known to wider audiences. The British Association has made an important contribution to the development of science by taking or recommending action to remove obstacles to the discovery and application of scientific knowledge.

Professional Institutions

There are numerous technical institutions and professional associations, many of which promote their own disciplines or are interested in the education and professional well-being of their members. The Council of Engineering Institutions, the federal body for the chartered engineering institutions, promotes the co-ordination of the engineering profession. The Council of Science and Technology Institutes is a federal body with five member institutes representing biologists, chemists, mathematicians, metallurgists and physicists.

A Fellowship of Engineering, envisaged as complementary to the Royal Society and forming an independent and authoritative forum of eminent engineering opinion, was set up in 1976. The founder members were Fellows of the Royal Society, together with a number of other distinguished engineers who were selected by the chairman of the Council of Engineering Institutions and the presidents of the individual engineering institutions. Further Fellows, up to a total of 1,000, but not more than 60 in one year, are being elected.

Science and Society

There are at least two bodies primarily concerned with the relationship between science and society: the British Society for Social Responsibility in Science; and the Council for Science and Society, formed by specialists in the natural and social sciences, the law, and medicine to support and stimulate research into the social effects of scientific and technological development.

Zoological Gardens

The Zoological Society of London, whose main function is as a scientific organisation, runs the world-famous London Zoo, opened in 1828, which occupies 14 hectares (36 acres) of Regent's Park, London. In 1931 the Society opened Whipsnade Park Zoo near Dunstable (Bedfordshire) where over 2,000 animals roam a 200-hectare (500-acre) park. Comparative studies are undertaken in pathology, biochemistry, radiology and infectious diseases, and in the reproductive processes of mammals. The Society also organises scientific meetings and symposia for zoologists, publishes scientific journals and maintains one of the largest zoological libraries in the world. At the end of 1979 the Society's collections at London Zoo and Whipsnade included 2,153 mammals, 2,037 birds, 379 reptiles, 208 amphibians, 2,896 fishes and 3,822 invertebrates. Other well-known zoos are those at Edinburgh, Bristol, Chester, Dudley, Chessington and Jersey. There are also a number of 'safari parks' containing reservations of wild animals through which the public can pass in closed motor cars.

Scientific Museums

The British Museum (Natural History) is one of the world's principal centres for the general study of natural history, particularly for specialised research into taxonomy. It has five scientific departments: botany, entomology, mineralogy, palaeontology and zoology. It possesses extensive collections of extant and fossil animals and plants and of minerals, rocks and meteorites. The Science Museum illustrates the development of pure and applied science in all countries, but chiefly in Britain. The geology of Britain is probably known in more exact detail than that of any other country in the world, and the Institute of Geological Sciences has an outstanding collection of exhibits in its Geological Museum. These three museums are in South Kensington, London. Other important collections are those of the Museum of Science and Industry, in Birmingham, and the Museum of the History of Science, at Oxford.

INTER-NATIONAL SCIENTIFIC RELATIONS

Britain is represented on the European Community's Scientific and Technical Research Committee, the object of which is to co-ordinate national policies on these matters and to implement joint projects of interest to the Community, and the Committee for Scientific and Technological Policy of the Organisation for Economic Co-operation and Development (OECD). Other intergovernmental organisations involved in scientific co-operation with which Britain is concerned include: European Co-operation in Science and Technology; specialised agencies of the United Nations such as the United Nations Educational, Scientific and Cultural Organisation; the International Atomic Energy Agency; the Nuclear Energy Agency and the International Energy Agency of the OECD; the European Organisation for Nuclear Research; the European Space Agency; the European Molecular Biology Laboratory; the International Agency for Research on Cancer; and the North Atlantic Treaty Organisation Science Committee. Among non-governmental organisations Britain is represented in the international unions comprising the International Council of Scientific Unions (see p 392). The five research councils, the Royal Society and the British Academy were founder members of the European Science Foundation set up in 1974. Since 1968 Britain has signed over 30 intergovernmental agreements with other countries on co-operation in science and technology or technical co-operation. These agreements are usually intended to promote mutually beneficial exchanges and are administered by various government departments.

There are scientific counsellors in the British Embassies in Washington, Paris, Bonn, Moscow and Tokyo who among other things promote contacts in science and technology between Britain and the countries to which they are accredited. These counsellors serve all central government departments concerned in overseas scientific affairs, as well as the research councils and the Royal Society, which is the main representative of Britain in areas of non-governmental collaboration. Administrative support for the counsellors is provided in Britain by the Department of Industry's Overseas Technical Information Unit.

The Overseas Development Administration

The Overseas Development Administration (ODA) of the Foreign and Commonwealth Office promotes scientific activities in the interests of developing countries. These include research covering a wide range of disciplines, specialist advice from Britain, advisory visits, conferences for exchange of information, training scientists from overseas in universities and research institutions in Britain, recruiting scientific staff from Britain, and providing support for existing research services and research projects overseas. Equipment is sometimes provided for research purposes and to encourage scientific training. The ODA has four scientific units which are wholly engaged on aid to developing countries: the Centre for Overseas Pest Research, the Directorate of Overseas Surveys, the Land Resources Development Centre and the Tropical Products Institute. In 1979 the ODA spent £11·1 million on scientific activities including research for the benefit of developing countries. Over 700 research and development projects to improve life in the developing countries are being supported; many are concerned with agriculture or medicine.

The British Council

The principal aims of the British Council (see p 71) in science (including agriculture, medicine and technology) are to foster co-operation between British scientists and scientists of other countries, to promote among overseas specialists a better understanding and knowledge of Britain and its scientific achievements, and, in the developing countries, to identify and manage development projects in the technological, scientific and educational sectors.

There are 70 staff overseas with science qualifications who work to advance technological, educational and scientific development, and collaboration with Britain. One of their priorities is to make British expertise available, increasingly through consultancy schemes; others are to establish research and development facilities, to provide trained manpower, and to assist with the establishment of technical teaching institutes.

Interchange of scientists, technologists and educationalists is considered to be of prime importance. British specialists in a very wide range of subjects are sent overseas to advise on research and development and on teaching, and to give courses of lectures, while scientists, technologists and technical teachers are recruited or seconded to posts in overseas universities, technical teaching institutes, teacher training colleges, education authorities, schools or curriculum reform centres.

The Council invites senior overseas people to Britain and arranges programmes of visits or attachments. It makes its own awards for postgraduate study in Britain and supervises programmes for senior specialists and students who come to Britain through the United Nations agencies or bilateral technical assistance schemes. The Council administers the Academic Links and Inter-change Scheme, the Academic Links with Eastern Europe Scheme and a number of smaller programmes in support of academic collaboration between institutions of higher education in Britain and other countries. Professional courses organised by the Council in various parts of Britain for overseas specialists include science and medicine. At the Council's headquarters in London, extensive professional, advisory and information facilities covering education, medicine, science, technology and science education support its work overseas.

SPACE ACTIVITIES

Government responsibility for space activities is undertaken by the Secretary of State for Education and Science (through the Science Research Council), the Secretary of State for Defence and the Secretary of State for Industry according to the nature of the project. Expenditure on space activities in 1979 was about £60 million.

Britain is a member of the European Space Agency (ESA) together with Belgium, Denmark, France, the Federal Republic of Germany, the Irish Republic, Italy, the Netherlands, Spain, Sweden and Switzerland. The Department of Industry is responsible for leading the British delegation to the ESA and for British participation in the space application programmes of the Agency consisting of the development of telecommunication, meteorological and maritime satellites and Spacelab, a manned laboratory to be carried aboard the United States Space Shuttle. Development and production of equipment for the ESA's 'Ariane' launcher is undertaken through a bilateral agreement with France. The Department of Industry is also responsible for industrial sponsorship of Britain's space industry. It participates in a joint departmental industry technology programme designed to improve Britain's industrial capability in space application systems; the programme is supervised on behalf of the Department by the Procurement Executive of the Ministry of Defence. The Space Department of the Royal Aircraft Establishment at Farnborough also undertakes long-term research and development to assist industry, and collates and disseminates data on remote sensing.

The Department of Industry, through the Post Office, is responsible for the use of satellites for civil communications purposes and undertakes research work in connection with communications systems using satellites, including those of Intelsat (see p 324).

The British civil scientific space research programme is the responsibility of the Department of Education and Science through the SRC. The latter provides Britain's representatives and financial contribution for the ESA's scientific satellite programme. Scientific research, notably in astronomy, space and the earth's atmosphere, using satellites, rockets and balloons, is supported by the SRC (see p 385). There are bilateral arrangements with other countries, notably the United States through its National Aeronautics and Space Administration (NASA). British experiments have provided information which has helped to increase scientific knowledge, especially in astronomy and astrophysics, and to interpret climatic patterns. The British Ariel V scientific satellite found several hundred new X-ray sources in space and the Ariel VI satellite, launched in 1979, produced more detailed information on these sources. The SRC's Rutherford and Appleton Laboratories provide support and services for the universities' space-based experiments and also operate the NASA Spaceflight Tracking and Data Network station at Winkfield (Berkshire). Winkfield is also the home of one of the three World Data Centres for space research.

21 Promotion of the Arts

Artistic and cultural activity in Britain ranges from the highest standards of professional performance to the enthusiastic support and participation of amateurs. London is one of the leading world centres for music, drama, opera and dance; and festivals held in Bath, Cheltenham, Edinburgh and other towns and cities are also well known. Many British playwrights, composers, sculptors, painters, writers, actors, singers, choreographers and dancers enjoy international reputations. At an amateur level, activities which make use of local talent and resources take many forms. Amateur choral, orchestral, operatic, dramatic and other societies for the arts abound; and increasing numbers of people take an interest in crafts such as pottery, weaving and woodwork.

Promotion and patronage of the arts are the concern of both official and unofficial bodies. The Government and local authorities take an active part, and a substantial and increasing amount of help also comes from private sources, including trusts and commercial concerns. Policies towards support for the arts are broadly similar, however, and there are two main aims. One is to maintain and improve the traditional arts and cultural heritage, and to make them more accessible to greater numbers of people. The other is to provide financial aid to working artists and craftsmen, and to encourage more people to take part in creative leisure pursuits.

Ministerial responsibility for general arts policy is borne by the Chancellor of the Duchy of Lancaster, a member of the Cabinet, at the Office of Arts and Libraries; the Secretaries of State for Wales, Scotland and Northern Ireland are also concerned with cultural matters. In addition, the Government is responsible for the upkeep of ancient monuments and historic buildings, and grants are made towards the maintenance of privately owned historic buildings (see p 178).

The main educational functions concerning the arts are carried out through the central government education departments. They are concerned, in partnership with local education authorities and voluntary bodies, with arts education in schools, further education colleges, polytechnics, evening institutes and community centres, and with the public library service.

Arts Councils   Most government support for the arts takes the form of grants to independent agencies. The most important of these is the Arts Council of Great Britain, established by Royal Charter in 1946, whose main objects are to develop and improve the knowledge, understanding and practice of the arts, to increase their accessibility to the public, and to advise and co-operate with government departments, local authorities and other organisations.

Government allocations to the Arts Council in 1980–81 amount to £70 million. The Council gives financial help and advice to large numbers of organisations, from the major opera, dance and drama companies, orchestras and festivals, to the smallest touring theatres and experimental groups.

The Council encourages such diverse interests as contemporary dance, photography and art films, and helps professional creative writers, choreographers, composers, artists and photographers through bursary and award schemes. It promotes art exhibitions and tours of opera, dance and drama companies. Funds are provided for specialist training courses in the arts and for help with the construction of new buildings or improvements to existing theatres, concert halls and other arts buildings under its 'Housing the Arts' scheme.

Members of the Council are appointed by the Chancellor of the Duchy of Lancaster. Advised by panels responsible for different aspects of the arts, the Council itself allocates subsidies to the main professional arts-promoting organisations. Organisations in Scotland and Wales receive their subsidies from the Scottish and Welsh Arts Councils which are committees of the Arts Council of Great Britain with a large measure of autonomy.

In Northern Ireland there is an independent Arts Council with aims and functions similar to those of the Arts Council of Great Britain. It receives an annual grant from the Northern Ireland Department of Education.

British Council The British Council promotes knowledge of British culture and literature overseas (see p 71), and maintains libraries in most of the countries in which it is represented. The Council may initiate or support overseas tours by British theatre companies, orchestras, choirs and opera and dance companies, as well as by individual actors, musicians and artists. It promotes fine arts and other exhibitions overseas, and organises British participation in international exhibitions. The Council distributes overseas a wide range of specialised films, many of them on the arts, and encourages professional interchange in all cultural fields between Britain and other countries.

Broadcasting Organisations A major contribution to the arts (particularly music and drama) is made by the British Broadcasting Corporation (BBC) and, to a lesser extent, by the independent television and radio programme companies and the Independent Broadcasting Authority (IBA). The BBC has orchestras employing many of the country's full-time professional musicians, and each week it broadcasts some 80 hours of serious music (both live and recorded) on its Radio 3 channel. It regularly commissions new music, particularly by British composers, and sponsors concerts, competitions and festivals. Independent television companies make grants for the promotion of the arts in their regions, particularly to regional arts associations, and transmit general magazine programmes on the arts. Both the BBC and IBA broadcast a wide range of new drama together with adaptations of novels and stage plays. They also screen a variety of feature films including British and overseas productions.

Local Support Local authorities support the arts in many ways. In addition to their responsibilities for education (including specialised art education) and the public library service, many provide and maintain local museums and art galleries. In Great Britain the authorities have power to incur expenditure on entertainment in all its forms. Many authorities make contributions to regional arts associations (see below) and towards the expenses of professional symphony orchestras and local theatre companies. Grants are often made towards the capital cost of new arts buildings, especially theatres; the Greater London Council, for example, made a substantial contribution towards the cost of the National Theatre.

Voluntary Contributions It is part of the Government's arts policy to give firm encouragement to voluntary sponsorship of the arts. Valuable support comes from many voluntary sources including charitable trusts and foundations, and supporters' organisations of the major national institutions. Industrial and commercial concerns offer a growing source of patronage, and the Association for Business Sponsorship of the Arts and the Arts Council both advise interested companies. Sponsorship may take the form of grants to local arts festivals, theatres and orchestras, and donations towards individual cultural events. Tax advantages and exemptions are available to encourage such support.

Regional Arts

Regional co-operation in arts patronage is encouraged through 17 regional arts associations in England and Wales whose aim it is to ensure that the whole range of the arts is more widely available to people throughout their areas. They can offer financial assistance to local and other regional arts organisations and advise on and promote all sorts of local arts activities. They are financed by a combination of local authority, Arts Council and private funds; local authorities and a wide range of other interests are represented on the associations. Other examples of co-operative patronage are the orchestra boards which support symphony and chamber orchestras and the societies formed to present some of the many arts festivals in Britain.

Festivals

Considerable interest and enthusiasm is shown for more than 200 professional arts festivals which take place each year. Most are subsidised by a combination of local authority, regional arts association and private funds, while the major ones receive direct Arts Council assistance. Some arts festivals concentrate particularly on music. These include: the Three Choirs Festival which has taken place annually for more than 250 years in Gloucester, Worcester or Hereford; the Cheltenham Festival which is largely devoted to contemporary British music; and the Aldeburgh and Bath festivals. Others cater for a number of art forms; among the better known are the Edinburgh International Festival, the Royal National Eisteddfod of Wales, and those held in Bath, Brighton, Buxton, Malvern, Harrogate, Salisbury, Windsor and York. A festival is held in Belfast under the auspices of Queen's University.

Arts Centres

There are some 200 arts centres in Great Britain and the number is increasing steadily. They provide opportunities for enjoyment of and participation in the arts. The centres are supported mainly by regional arts associations and local authorities with some help from the Arts Council and other organisations. They may be small centres for amateur activities or they may offer a professional programme. A growing number of theatres and art galleries also provide a focal point for the community by offering facilities for other arts.

Authors' Copyright

The author of any original literary, dramatic, musical or artistic work is automatically protected by the Copyright Act 1956 and its related international conventions[1] from the unauthorised reproduction of the work both before and after publication. The author of the work is the first owner of the copyright, and the normal term of copyright in published original works is the life of the author and a period of 50 years after his or her death.

DRAMA

Britain is one of the world's major theatre centres. As well as theatre in London and the regions a network of informal touring companies has developed, which visit many of the new arts centres and community festivals.

---

[1] A copyright work first published in Britain has automatic copyright in all countries which are members of the Berne Copyright Convention and the Universal Copyright Convention.

Support for much of this development in British drama comes jointly from the Government, through the Arts Councils of Great Britain and Northern Ireland, from local authorities and regional arts associations, and from some private sponsorship. In particular the Arts Council assists developments in new drama by encouraging co-operation between theatres and playwrights by means of bursaries, commissions and guaranteed royalties. Schemes are also in operation to train stage designers, directors, technicians, actors and those wishing to take up theatre administration.

Professional Theatre

Over 250 theatres in professional use in Britain can each accommodate more than 200 people. Some are owned or rented by non-profit-distributing companies, the majority of which receive Arts Council subsidies, while the remainder are operated commercially or owned by local authorities.

London is the centre of theatrical activity with some 50 principal theatres in or near the centre and 20 in the suburbs. Most are let to producing managements on a commercial basis, but five are occupied by major subsidised companies. These include the National Theatre which stages classical and modern plays from various countries in its three auditoria on the south bank of the River Thames, the Royal Shakespeare Company which presents Shakespearean plays at Stratford-upon-Avon and a mixed repertoire in London, and the Old Vic Company, Britain's major theatrical touring company, which has a London base in the famous Old Vic theatre.

Outside London there are a number of theatres which accommodate pre- and post-West End tours of the major London productions and performances by companies specially formed for touring. (Both the National Theatre and Royal Shakespeare companies have toured in Britain and overseas.) A decline in the number of these theatres has been checked in response to the demand by audiences outside London for the larger opera, dance and drama companies. Some theatres have been bought by local authorities. Many non-repertory theatres outside London present all kinds of drama and many also put on variety shows and other entertainments. There has, however, been a growth in the activities of over 40 resident theatre companies which receive financial support from the Arts Council and the local authorities. These companies employ leading producers, designers and actors, and standards are high. Some companies have their own theatres, others rent from local authorities.

There is no censorship of plays, but the Theatres Act 1968 makes it an offence to present or direct an obscene performance of a play in public or in private (including theatre clubs), an obscene performance being defined as one which tends to 'deprave and corrupt persons who are likely ... to attend it'. Provision is made for a defence against an obscenity charge on the grounds that the performance is for the public good in the interests of, for example, drama, opera or literature.

Amateur Theatre

There are several thousand amateur dramatic societies in Britain; they are encouraged by local education authorities, other public bodies, and four special organisations—the British Theatre Association, the National Drama Conference, the Scottish Community Drama Association and the Association of Ulster Drama Festivals. Most universities have active amateur drama clubs and societies; an International Festival of University Theatre is held annually.

Dramatic Training

Training for the theatre is provided mainly in drama schools. Among the best known are the Royal Academy of Dramatic Art, the Central School of Speech and Drama, the London Academy of Music and Dramatic Art, and the

Guildhall School of Music and Drama, all of which are in London; and the Old Vic School in Bristol. There is the Royal Scottish Academy of Music and Drama in Glasgow; and in Cardiff, the Welsh College of Music and Drama. Several universities offer major courses in drama.

Theatre for Young People

Theatre for young people is becoming increasingly popular and concessionary ticket schemes are operated to encourage young people to attend theatres. In 1970 the Young Vic was opened as a theatre for young people, the National Youth Theatre is based in London, and the Scottish Youth Theatre was established in 1970. There are some 10 specialist companies, including the Unicorn Theatre for Young People, Theatre Centre and the Polka Company, some of which are supported by the Arts Council. Outside London about 30 repertory companies provide programmes and other types of theatre activity for young people.

Most of the many amateur youth theatres in Britain are supported by local authorities. Many schools and youth clubs put on plays and provide some education in drama. The London education service provides special drama centres for young people.

MUSIC, OPERA AND DANCE

Music plays an important role in British cultural life. Pop music, folk music, jazz, light music and brass bands all have substantial followings while the widespread interest in classical music is reflected in the large audiences at choral and orchestral concerts and at performances of opera, dance and chamber music.

The Arts Council offers subsidy (together with financial assistance from local authorities and commercial sponsors) to orchestras, opera and dance companies, music societies and festivals. It also provides bursaries and commissions for composers, musicians, designers and choreographers. The Master of the Queen's Music holds an office within the Royal Household, with responsibility for organising and writing music for State occasions.

Music

Seasons of orchestral concerts are promoted every year in many of the large towns and cities. In central London the principal concert halls are the Royal Festival Hall, adjacent to which are the Queen Elizabeth Hall and the Purcell Room accommodating smaller-scale performances; the Royal Albert Hall, where the annual summer season of Promenade Concerts is given; the Wigmore Hall, a recital centre; and St John's, Smith Square.

Orchestras

The leading symphony orchestras are the London Philharmonic, the London Symphony, the Philharmonia, the Royal Philharmonic, the Royal Liverpool Philharmonic, the Hallé (Manchester), the City of Birmingham Symphony, the Bournemouth Symphony, the Ulster and the Scottish National. The BBC runs a number of orchestras, including four symphony orchestras, providing broadcast concerts which are often open to the public. There are also specialised string and chamber orchestras such as the English Chamber Orchestra, the Academy of St Martin-in-the-Fields, the London Mozart Players, the Bournemouth Sinfonietta, the Northern Sinfonia (Newcastle upon Tyne), the Scottish Baroque Ensemble and the Scottish Chamber Orchestra. Most orchestras (other than those of the BBC) receive financial aid from the Arts Councils, local authorities and industrial sources.

Choral Societies

Among the principal choral societies are the Bach Choir, the Royal Choral Society, the Swansea Philharmonic Choir, the Edinburgh Royal Choral Union and the Belfast Philharmonic Society. Almost all the leading orchestras have close links with particular choirs, such as the Philharmonia Chorus and the London Symphony Chorus, though these choirs are mostly independent of the orchestras. The majority of choral societies are affiliated to the National Federation of Music Societies.

Amateur Interest   Interest in amateur music-making is encouraged by county music committees (some of them voluntary and some sub-committees of local education authorities), which are aided by the Carnegie United Kingdom Trust and united in the Standing Conference for Amateur Music. The National Federation of Music Societies (the organisation for chamber music societies, amateur choirs and orchestras) receives Arts Council funds to help affiliated societies with the cost of engaging professional musicians. Some 1,200 music societies are members of the Federation, which advises them on concert planning and promotion. The Welsh Amateur Music Federation, funded by the Welsh Arts Council, assists amateur music-making in Wales.

Opera and   Regular seasons of opera and ballet are given at the Royal Opera House,
Dance   Covent Garden, London, which receives financial assistance from the Arts Council and from private and business sponsorship. The Royal Opera House has a permanent orchestra which plays for the Royal Opera and the Royal Ballet. Both organisations have a high international reputation. Seasons of opera and operetta in English are given by the English National Opera which performs in the London Coliseum, and makes provincial tours supplemented by the English National Opera North based in Leeds. Sadler's Wells Theatre houses most of the London performances of visiting opera and dance companies and the Sadler's Wells Royal Ballet which performs in London and the regions. Scottish Opera has regular winter seasons at its permanent home, the Theatre Royal in Glasgow, and tours mainly in Scotland and northern England, while the Welsh National Opera has four quarterly seasons at the New Theatre, Cardiff and at the Hippodrome Theatre, Birmingham, and tours chiefly in Wales and the west of England.

Other Opera   An opera season, for which international casts are specially assembled, is held
Groups   every summer at Glyndebourne in Sussex; this is followed with an autumn tour by Glyndebourne Touring Opera with different casts. Other opera companies include Kent Opera, the English Music Theatre Company which specialises in the performance of works by British composers, and the New Opera Company. Opera in Northern Ireland is promoted by the Northern Ireland Opera Trust and the Studio Opera Group. A new touring company, Opera 80, financed mainly by the Arts Council, started production in 1980.

Dance Companies   Dance companies also include London Festival Ballet, Ballet Rambert (Britain's oldest ballet company, which re-formed in 1966 as a leading modern dance company), Scottish Ballet, based in Glasgow, London Contemporary Dance Theatre (which provides regular seasons of contemporary dance in London besides touring extensively) and Northern Ballet Theatre (which concentrates its activities in the north of England, although it makes periodic tours elsewhere).

There are several modern dance groups based in the regions with support from their regional arts associations. They include Ludus, East Anglian Dance Theatre, Merseyside Dance Trust, and Lynx Dance in Education

Team. About a dozen mime groups or soloists are assisted by the Arts Council.

Training in Music, Opera and Dance

Professional training in music is given at colleges of music, of which the Royal Academy of Music, the Royal College of Music and Trinity College of Music in London, and the Royal Scottish Academy of Music and Drama in Glasgow are grant-aided. Other leading colleges include the Guildhall School of Music and Drama in London, the Royal Northern College of Music in Manchester and the Birmingham School of Music. The National Opera Studio provides advanced training courses. The leading dance schools are the Royal Ballet School, the Rambert School of Ballet and the London School of Contemporary Dance which, with many private schools, have helped in raising British dance to its present high standard. Dance is now a subject for degree studies.

Youth and Music, an organisation affiliated to the international *Jeunesses Musicales*, encourages attendances by young people at opera, dance and concert performances. Ballet for All, previously a branch of the Royal Ballet and now run by the Royal Academy of Dancing, presents lecture-demonstrations on classical ballet to young audiences. Scottish Ballet Workshop, the educational branch of Scottish Ballet, works in schools throughout Scotland.

Many children learn to play musical instruments at school, and some take the examinations of the Associated Board of the Royal Schools of Music. The National Youth Orchestras of Great Britain and of Wales and other youth orchestras are noted for their high standards. Almost a third of the players in the European Community Youth Orchestra come from Britain.

FILMS

British films, actors and the creative and technical services which support them have achieved successes in international film festivals and other events. Cinema and television films are exported to most countries.

There are about 1,600 cinema screens in Great Britain, and estimated attendances in 1979 amounted to 112 million. Cinema attendance figures have been declining since the mid-1950s as television has become generally accessible. In 1953 the average weekly cinema audience was some 25 million; by 1979 it was less than 10 per cent of that figure.

An Interim Action Committee is studying the future of the film industry. Among the ideas being considered is the establishment of a British Film Authority.

The Government does not invest directly in films but the National Film Finance Corporation lends money for production and distribution of feature films from capital advanced by the Government and private interests, and also provides loans for script-writing and other pre-production costs.

A levy on cinema admissions, the Eady Levy, provides a fund to benefit the makers of eligible films. Grants from the levy can be made to the Children's Film Foundation, the British Film Institute Production Board, the National Film School, and the National Film Finance Corporation. The rest of the fund is distributed to makers of eligible films in proportion to a film's takings.

A specified number of British or European Community films must be shown in British cinemas each year. For main feature films the quota is 30 per cent and for supporting programmes, 25 per cent.

Cinema Licensing and Film Censorship

Local authorities have powers to license cinemas and censor films. They have a legal duty to prohibit the admission of children under the age of 16 to unsuitable films, and may also exercise censorship over films for adults. In considering the suitability of films the authorities normally rely on the judgment of an independent body, the British Board of Film Censors, to which most films for public showing are submitted.

The British Board of Film Censors was set up in 1912, on the initiative of the cinema industry, to ensure that a proper standard was maintained in the films offered to the public. The Board, which does not use any written code of censorship, may require cuts to be made before granting a certificate to a film; very rarely, it refuses a certificate. Films passed by the board are put into one of four categories: 'U' (for general exhibition); 'A' (for general exhibition but parents are advised that the film contains material which they may not wish children under the age of 14 years to see); 'AA' (for persons of not less than 14 years of age); and 'X' (for persons of not less than 18 years of age).

The Government is considering the report, published in December 1979, of the Committee on Obscenity and Film Censorship (see Bibliography).

Documentary Films

The documentary tradition in short film production in Britain was founded in 1929 when a group of directors began making factual films of a distinctive and imaginative kind for the Government, and later for commercial organisations. The war years saw a big expansion in this field and, since then, British documentary technicians have continued to produce, for both cinema and television, high quality factual films which have won numerous international awards. The British Industrial and Scientific Film Association promotes the use of films in industry, science and commerce. The Federation of Specialised Film Associations is the trade association of documentary, short, industrial, advertising and cartoon film makers. The National Panel for Film Festivals, under the aegis of the British Council, is responsible for the selection of British entries for international short and documentary film festivals.

The Government sponsors a wide range of documentary films for use non-theatrically and on television in Britain and overseas. They are produced through the Central Office of Information (COI), and the majority are commissioned from private companies. There are several major documentary film libraries, including the COI's Central Film Library, which provides films on hire or free of charge to a wide variety of educational, industrial and other users. The Films of Scotland Committee promotes the production of films covering the industries and cultural traditions of Scotland.

Children's Films

Cinemas which give children's shows require a special licence from local authorities which may impose conditions. There are about 220 cinemas providing programmes for children on Saturday mornings. An important contribution to these programmes is made by the Children's Film Foundation, which, with aid from the British Film Fund Agency, produces and distributes entertainment films specially designed for children.

British Film Institute

The development of the film and television as an art is promoted by the British Film Institute, founded in 1933 and financed mainly by a government grant, and by the Scottish Council for Educational Technology which also receives a government grant. The Institute offers financial and technical help to new and experienced film makers who cannot find support elsewhere. The Institute administers the National Film Theatre in London and the National Film Archive and has a library from which films may be hired; it also has a library of scripts and books on the film and television, a British National Film Catalogue recording all non-fiction and short films available in Britain, and an information service. It makes grants to the Federation of Film Societies, the British Universities Film Council and the Society for Education in Film and Television. The Institute's Educational Department offers guidance to teachers in formal education at all levels on film and television courses, and its Editorial Department produces a range of publications including a critical journal *Sight and Sound* and the *Monthly Film Bulletin*.

The National Film Archive contains nearly 40,000 films, including newsreels and other miscellaneous items, and 5,000 television programmes, besides art designs and posters; it also has over 1 million photographic stills, selected to illustrate the history and the art of the film and television.

The National Film Theatre has two cinemas showing films of outstanding historical, artistic or technical interest. It is unique as a cinema offering regular programmes unrestricted by commercial considerations or by the age or nationality of the films shown. Each year it organises the London Film Festival. The British Film Institute has promoted the development of some 50 regional film theatres on the lines of the National Film Theatre and may make grants towards their costs. In Scotland the Scottish Film Council, as a committee of the Scottish Council for Educational Technology, is responsible for regional film theatres and administers the Scottish Central Film Library. Grants in Northern Ireland are made by the Arts Council of Northern Ireland.

Training in Film Production

An independent National Film School financed primarily by grants from the Office of Arts and Libraries and the British Film Fund Agency, offers three-year courses for writers, directors, producers and cameramen. Training in film production is also given at the London International Film School, the Royal College of Art, and at some polytechnics and other institutions.

VISUAL ARTS

A number of modern British painters and sculptors have a high international reputation, and have received many international prizes and commissions for major works in foreign cities. The growth of interest in the visual arts at home has been fostered by improved methods of display in museums and galleries, and by the activities of many institutions, societies, private galleries and the growing number of local arts centres.

State support for painting and sculpture mainly takes the form of maintenance and purchase grants for the national museums and galleries, purchase grants for municipal museums and galleries, and grants towards the cost of art education. The Government also encourages high standards of industrial design and craftsmanship through grants to the Design Council.

In addition to direct State assistance, the Arts Council runs the Hayward Gallery in London, where major loan exhibitions are shown, and the Serpentine Gallery, which mainly presents the work of young artists. The Council maintains its own collection of contemporary British art, and organises or offers grants or guarantees for a variety of touring and other exhibitions. It also supports art societies and independent galleries, and provides commissions and awards for artists. A number of photography galleries receive Arts Council support, including the Side Gallery in Newcastle upon Tyne, the largest gallery in Britain devoted entirely to photography. The Scottish and Welsh Arts Councils have art galleries in Edinburgh, Glasgow, and Cardiff respectively, and the Northern Ireland Arts Council owns a gallery in Belfast.

The Art Market

London is a major centre for the international art market and regular sales of works of art take place in the main auction houses. Certain items are covered by export control: these are works of art and collectors' items over 50 years old and worth more than £8,000 (more than £2,000 in the case of British historical portraits); photographic material over 60 years old and worth more than £200;

documentary material over 50 years old; and British archaeological material over 50 years old. A licence is required before such items can be exported, but this is granted automatically in the case of objects imported into Britain within the last 50 years. In other cases the application for a licence is considered by the Department of Trade, and if the Department's expert advisers recommend the withholding of a licence, the matter is referred to the Reviewing Committee on the Export of Works of Art. If the Committee considers a work to be of national importance it can advise the Government to withhold the export licence for a specified time to give a public museum or art gallery an opportunity to offer to buy the object at a fair price.

Museums and Art Galleries

About 1,000 museums and art galleries are open to the public including the major national collections and a wide variety of municipally and independently owned institutions.

National Collections

Taken together, the national museums and art galleries in London contain among the most comprehensive collections of objects of artistic, archaeological, scientific, historical and general interest to be found within any one city. They are the British Museum, the Victoria and Albert Museum, the National Gallery, the Tate Gallery, the National Portrait Gallery, the Imperial War Museum, the National Army Museum, the Royal Air Force Museum, the National Maritime Museum, the Museum of London, the Wallace Collection, the British Museum (Natural History), the Geological Museum and the Science Museum.

Some of these national museums have also opened branches outside London, examples being the National Railway Museum at York which is administered by the Science Museum, and portrait collections at Montacute House (Somerset) and Beningborough Hall (Yorkshire), administered by the National Portrait Gallery in collaboration with the National Trust.

There are three national museums and art galleries in Edinburgh: the National Museum of Antiquities of Scotland, the Royal Scottish Museum (including the Scottish United Services Museum), and the National Galleries of Scotland (comprising the National Gallery of Scotland, the Scottish National Portrait Gallery, and the Scottish National Gallery of Modern Art). The National Museum of Wales, in Cardiff, has a branch at St. Fagan's Castle where the Welsh Folk Museum is housed and has recently opened an Industrial and Maritime Museum in Cardiff's dockland. It also has a branch museum (the North Wales Quarrying Museum) at Llanberis in Gwynedd. In Northern Ireland there are two national museums: the Ulster Museum in Belfast and the Ulster Folk and Transport Museum, County Down.

Most of the national collections are administered by trustee bodies, but the Victoria and Albert and Science Museums are the responsibility of the Office of Arts and Libraries; the Royal Scottish Museum is the responsibility of the Scottish Education Department.

Other Collections

Other important collections in London include the Armouries (housed in the Tower of London), the Public Record Office and Sir John Soane's Museum. In Buckingham Palace the Queen's Gallery has exhibitions of pictures from the extensive royal collections.

Most cities and towns have museums devoted to art, archaeology and natural history, usually administered by the local authorities, but sometimes by local learned societies or by individuals or trustees. Both Oxford and Cambridge are rich in museums, many of them associated with the universities (for example, the Ashmolean Museum in Oxford, founded in 1683, the oldest in the country, and the Fitzwilliam Museum in Cambridge). There are important museums and art galleries in Aberdeen, Belfast, Birmingham, Bristol, Cardiff, Dundee, Glasgow, Leeds, Leicester, Liverpool, Manchester, Norwich, Reading, Sheffield, Southampton and York. Many private art collections housed in historic family mansions, including those owned by the National Trust, are open to the public. An increasing number of open air museums depict the regional life of an area or preserve early industrial remains (for example, the Weald and Downland Museum in Sussex, the North of England Open Air Museum in Durham, and the Ironbridge Gorge Museum in Shropshire which won the first European Museum of the Year Award in 1978).

Finance

All national collections are financed chiefly from government funds. Besides meeting administrative and maintenance costs, the Government provides annual purchase grants (£10·4 million in 1980–81). It may also provide special purchase grants. An independent National Heritage Memorial Fund provides assistance to organisations wishing to acquire land, buildings, works of art and other objects associated with the national heritage. Ministerial responsibility for accepting pre-eminent works of art in place of capital transfer tax is shared by the Chancellor of the Duchy of Lancaster and the Secretary of State for the Environment.

Local museums and art galleries, which are maintained from rates or endowments, receive help in building up their collections through the annual government grants administered by the Victoria and Albert, Science and Royal Scottish Museums. Financial and practical assistance is also given to museums and galleries by trusts and voluntary bodies, including the Calouste Gulbenkian Foundation, the National Art-Collections Fund, the Contemporary Art Society and the Association for Business Sponsorship of the Arts.

Policy and Co-ordination

The Government is advised on policy matters by the Standing Commission on Museums and Galleries, which also promotes co-operation between national and provincial institutions. Eight area museum councils, grant-aided by the Government, provide technical services and advice on conservation, display, documentation and publicity.

The Museums Association, to which museums and art galleries and their staffs throughout the country belong and which also has many overseas members, is an independent organisation. It serves as a focus for the collection of information and discussion of matters relating to museum administration, and as a training and examining body for professional qualifications.

Exhibitions

Temporary exhibitions provided by the Arts Councils, the national museums and galleries, the Art Exhibitions Bureau and the area museum councils are a regular feature of many museums. In London the Hayward Gallery, the Tate Gallery, the British Museum, the Victoria and Albert Museum and the Royal Academy are the main centres for loan exhibitions; these are also held at the Whitechapel Art Gallery, the Camden Arts Centre and the Institute of Contemporary Arts. Commercial exhibitions are held in the galleries of the London dealers. The Serpentine Gallery in London's Kensington Gardens houses Arts Council exhibitions of contemporary artists, and another small gallery in London is run by the Crafts Council.

There are a number of national art exhibiting societies, some of which, notably the Royal Academy at Burlington House, have their own galleries in London. The Royal Scottish Academy holds annual exhibitions in Edinburgh.

An increasing number of amateur art societies throughout Britain hold local exhibitions and encourage local interest in the fine arts. There are also children's exhibitions, including the National Exhibition of Children's Art.

Training in Art and Design   Art and design education is provided in maintained colleges of art, further education colleges and polytechnics, which are administered by local education authorities. Other institutions offering art and design courses include universities, the Royal Academy Schools and some private art schools. At postgraduate level there is the Royal College of Art which awards its own degrees. Art is also taught at an advanced level at the four Scottish Central (Art) Institutions administered by the Scottish Education Department.

The leading academic institutions for the study of the history of art are the Courtauld and Warburg Institutes of the University of London, and the Department of Classical Art and Archaeology in University College, London.

Art has a place in all school curricula, and the Society for Education through Art encourages, among other activities, the purchase by schools of original works of art by organising an annual Pictures for Schools exhibition. Pictures may also be borrowed from many public libraries.

Crafts   Government grants for the crafts, amounting to some £1·2 million in 1980–81, are administered in England and Wales by the Crafts Council (formerly the Crafts Advisory Committee). Set up in 1971 to advise the minister responsible for the arts on the needs of artist-craftsmen, the Council holds regular exhibitions of work at its gallery in London and also publishes the bi-monthly magazine *Crafts* which features crafts activities in Britain and abroad. It also gives financial assistance to enable craftsmen to be trained and to establish or expand their businesses. Its activities include crafts associated with conservation and restoration. It runs a comprehensive information service and houses a slide-index. The Council manages the craft shop at the Victoria and Albert Museum which sells a selection of works by British artist-craftsmen. Scotland receives a separate government grant which is similarly administered by the Joint Crafts Committee. The British Craft Centre in London, which receives an annual grant from the Crafts Council, aims to increase public recognition, enjoyment, and support of the work of artist-craftsmen, and holds ten exhibitions a year (most of the contents of which are for sale).

Architecture   Official responsibility towards the nation's architecture is concerned mainly with encouraging the best in new building and conserving the best that has been inherited from the past (for conservation, see p 178).

Several government departments, notably the Department of the Environment, provide advice on building and architecture. In collaboration with the Royal Institute of British Architects, the Secretary of State for the Environment makes annual awards for good housing design in both the public and private sectors. Royal Fine Art Commissions for England and Wales and for Scotland advise the departments, planning authorities and other public bodies on questions of public amenity or artistic importance.

The Royal Institute of British Architects is the leading professional institution with a membership of 21,216 in Britain and 5,216 overseas. It exercises control over standards in architectural education, and maintains one of the largest architectural libraries in the world. The Royal Incorporation of Architects in Scotland is allied to it.

Other bodies with an interest in architecture include the Civic Trust (see p 188) which promotes high standards in civic building and planning, and the

National Trusts (see p 188) which acquired land and buildings in order to protect them from harmful development for the benefit of the public. The number of people visiting National Trust properties rose from just over a million in 1960 to more than 6·2 million in 1979.

LITERATURE AND LIBRARIES

The study of literature is included in the curricula of all schools, colleges and universities. There are free public libraries throughout the country, private libraries and many private literary societies. Book reviews are featured in the press and on television and radio and there are numerous periodicals concerned with literature. Recognition of outstanding literary merit is provided by a number of awards, including the Booker, W. H. Smith & Son, and Whitbread prizes and Arts Council National Book Awards. Awards to encourage young writers are made for instance, by the Somerset Maugham Trust Fund and the E. C. Gregory Trust Fund.

Government help is given through the Arts Councils which support literature in a number of ways, including grants awarded to writers, translators, publishers, small presses and magazines. Legislation passed in 1979 provides for a scheme to give authors the right to receive payment from government funds for the use of their books borrowed from public libraries. Payments are expected to start in 1982. The title Poet Laureate is conferred on a poet who receives a stipend as an officer of the Royal Household.

Literary and Philological Societies

Societies for the promotion of literature include the English Association and the Royal Society of Literature. The British Academy for the Promotion of Historical, Philosophical and Philological Studies (known as the British Academy) is the leading society of humanistic studies and receives a government grant.

Other specialist societies include the Early English Text Society, the Bibliographical Society, the Harleian Society, the Saltire Society, and several societies devoted to particular authors, the largest of which is the Dickens Fellowship. A number of societies, for example, the Poetry Society and the Apollo Society, sponsor poetry readings and recitals. There are also a number of clubs and societies, such as the New Fiction Society and the Poetry Book Society, which distribute selected new books to their members.

Books

In 1979 British publishers issued nearly 42,000 separate titles: more than 32,000 new ones, and over 9,000 reprints and new editions. An increasing proportion of books—including specialised non-fiction—is sold in paperback form. Book clubs make available hardback books at a lower price.

Leading organisations representing the interests of those concerned with book production and distribution are the Publishers' Association and the Booksellers' Association. The British Council also publicises British books and periodicals through its libraries in 63 countries, its programme of book exhibitions (287 exhibitions were mounted in 1979–80) and its bibliographical publications including the monthly *British Book News*. The Book Development Council promotes British books overseas. (For sales and exports of books in 1979 see p 253). The National Book League has a membership including authors, publishers, booksellers, librarians and readers. It encourages an interest in books and arranges exhibitions in Britain and overseas.

Libraries

The British Library, created in 1973 from a merger of the British Museum Library with other libraries and institutions, is organised in three divisions. The Reference Division, which receives a copy of each new book, pamphlet or newspaper published in Britain and acquires significant literature from other countries, includes the Department of Printed Books holding about 10 million titles, the Department of Manuscripts, the Department of Oriental Manuscripts and Printed Books, and the Science Reference Library, which is the national centre for patent documentation and contains more than 20 million specifications worldwide. The Lending Division at Boston Spa, West Yorkshire, has 3·2 million volumes including some 54,000 current periodicals available on loan to other libraries in Britain and overseas. It also has access to many millions of books in other libraries and is the national centre for inter-library lending within Britain and between Britain and foreign countries. The Bibliographic Services Division processes the acquisitions of the British Library for inclusion in its catalogues and publishes the *British National Bibliography* which lists all new books and new editions published in Britain, the *British Catalogue of Music* and other bibliographic records. It also provides automated information services of bibliographic data for libraries and their users throughout Britain. The Research and Development Department is a major source of funding for the support of research and development in library and information services in Britain. Plans for a new headquarters of the British Library in London are under review. Under copyright legislation, the national libraries of Scotland and of Wales, the Bodleian Library of Oxford University and the Cambridge University Library are also entitled to claim copies of all new British publications.

Some of the national museums also have large libraries, and many government departments have well-established libraries of considerable size and importance. The Public Record Office contains the records of the superior courts of law and of most government departments, as well as such famous historical documents as Domesday Book. In Scotland the Scottish Record Office serves the same purpose. The National Register of Archives (maintained by the Historical Manuscripts Commission) contains particulars of local and private records.

Besides the few great private collections, such as that of the London Library, there are the rich resources of the learned societies and institutions (for scientific societies and institutions, see p 392). Examples are the libraries of the Royal Institute of International Affairs, the Royal Commonwealth Society, the Royal Geographical Society, the Royal Society of Edinburgh, the British Theatre Association, the Royal Academy of Music, the National Library for the Blind and the National Book League.

Libraries in Education

The ancient university libraries of Oxford and Cambridge are unmatched by any of the more recent foundations, although the combined library resources of the colleges and institutions of the University of London total some 6 million volumes, the John Rylands University Library in Manchester contains some 2 million volumes, and the university libraries of Edinburgh, Birmingham, Glasgow and Leeds each have over 1 million volumes and a substantial number have over half a million each. Many universities have built up large and important research collections in special subjects; for example, the Barnes Medical Library at Birmingham, and the British Library of Political and Economic Science at the London School of Economics. Other universities and the polytechnics are also building collections.

The importance of good libraries is recognised at all levels of the education system. School libraries, most of which are maintained by local education authorities, often receive important support services from the public library service, including loans of books.

Public Libraries   Britain is served by a network of public libraries, administered by local public library authorities. These libraries have a total stock of some 132·5 million books (not including the libraries in publicly maintained schools).

Qualified and specialist staff are available for consultation in all but the smallest service points. About one-third of the total population are members of public libraries. The Chancellor of the Duchy of Lancaster is responsible for the supervision of the public library service in England and is advised by the Library Advisory Council for England. The Secretary of State for Wales has responsibility for supervising of the public library service in Wales and is advised by the Library Advisory Council for Wales. Public library authorities in England and Wales have a duty to provide (with some limitations) a free lending and reference library service of books and periodicals. In Scotland local authorities must provide library facilities. In Northern Ireland the public library service is the responsibility of the education and library boards which also have a duty to make library services available to schools. There are some 5,700 public library service points in Britain; some areas are served by mobile libraries of which about 700 are in service, and domiciliary services cater for people who are unable to visit a library.

Many libraries have collections of records and musical scores for loan to the public. Notable examples are the City of Westminster Central Music Library and the Henry Watson Music Library at Manchester Central Library. A number of libraries also lend from collections of works of art, either originals or reproductions. Nearly all libraries provide children's departments, while reference sections and art, music, commercial and technical departments meet the growing and more specific demands in these fields. Most libraries hold a significant collection of books and documents on the history of their localities.

The public library is often a centre for local cultural activities; these may include film shows, lectures, adult education classes, book-week exhibitions, drama groups, record recitals and children's story hours.

A voluntary system of library co-operation exists in England and Wales under which eight regional library bureaux (consisting mainly of public libraries in each area) aim to be largely self-sufficient in the interlending of current British books, achieved in some regions by a system of co-operative subject specialisation.

A number of local schemes for the exchange of specialist titles and information involve industrial, commercial and sometimes university libraries, and are normally centred on a major public or technical college library.

The National Libraries of Scotland and of Wales carry out functions similar to those of the regional bureaux and the Lending Division of the British Library. In Northern Ireland access to the stocks of all co-operating libraries is available to the libraries controlled by the five education and library boards and to the libraries of Queen's University and the New University of Ulster.

Library Associations   The principal professional organisation is the Library Association. It maintains a Register of Chartered Librarians, publishes books, pamphlets and official journals, and holds regular conferences. There are also associations of libraries, for example, the Association of Special Libraries and Information Bureaux and the Standing Conference of National and University Libraries.

22 The Press

More daily newspapers, national and regional are sold per person in Britain than in most other developed countries. Despite a slow but continuous decline in national newspaper sales, on an average day nearly three out of four adults over the age of 15 read a national morning newspaper and about one in two read an evening newspaper. National papers have a total circulation of about 14·5 million on weekdays and 19 million on Sundays though the total readership is considerably greater.

The press caters for a variety of political views, interests and levels of education. It is subject neither to State control nor to censorship.

Although pronounced views may be expressed in some newspapers and their political leanings may be obvious, they are almost always financially independent of any political party and are not obliged to follow any specific party line. In order to preserve their character and traditions, a few newspapers and periodicals are governed by arrangements which vest ownership of the undertaking in trustees, or operate it in accordance with a deed of trust, or provide that the transfer of shares be controlled by trustees. Others have management arrangements to ensure editors' authority and independence.

Unlike most of its European counterparts the British press receives no subsidies and relatively few tax and postal concessions. Newspaper and magazine sales and advertising receipts are zero-rated for value-added tax purposes. Registered newspapers receive a concession on postal rates, and there are concessions on 'per-word' rates for international press telegrams and photo-telegrams. In common with all postal customers, newspaper and magazine publishers can obtain reductions in charges for regular bulk postings.

There are 124 daily (Monday to Saturday) and Sunday newspapers and over 1,000 weekly newspapers are published. These figures include certain specialised papers with circulations limited not by region but by interest; for instance, business newspapers, sporting newspapers, newspapers in foreign languages for people of other countries resident in Britain and religious newspapers. Newsprint forms roughly a third of average national newspaper costs. Three-quarters of Britain's requirements are imported. The national newspaper industry is faced with a number of problems. Financial difficulties (alleviated to some extent by improvements in advertising revenue) are further complicated by problems of labour relations, often associated with the introduction of new production techniques.

Ownership

Newspaper ownership, as it affects the national, London-evening and regional daily newspapers, is concentrated mainly in the hands of a comparatively small number of large press publishing groups (the groups controlling the national press are listed in Table 38), but there are, in addition, some 200 independent regional and local newspaper publishers.

Although most enterprises are organised as limited liability companies, individual and partner proprietorship survives. The large national newspaper and periodical publishers are major corporations with diversified interests over the whole field of publishing and communications; some have shares in independent television and radio contracting companies; and others are involved in industrial and commercial activities which have no connection with publishing or the mass media.

The law provides safeguards against the risks inherent in undue concentration of the means of communication. For instance, if it appears that newspaper shareholdings in television programme companies have led or are leading to results which are contrary to the public interest, the Independent Broadcasting Authority may, with the consent of the Home Secretary, notify the companies that their programmes may cease to be transmitted. There is a similar stipulation for independent local radio; if a local newspaper has a monopoly in the area, it is not allowed to have a controlling interest in the local radio station. In addition, it is unlawful to transfer a newspaper or newspaper assets to a proprietor whose newspapers have an average daily circulation amounting, with that of the newspaper to be taken over, to 500,000 or more unless the Secretary of State for Trade gives written consent. Except in certain limited cases, which include transfers of very small newspapers, consent may be given only after the Secretary of State has referred the matter to the Monopolies and Mergers Commission and received its report.

The 'National' Press

Ten morning daily papers and seven Sunday papers (see Table 38) circulate throughout the country, and are known as national newspapers. All but one are produced in London (where Fleet Street is the traditional centre for the press), but six of the dailies and four of the Sundays also print northern editions in Manchester (accounting for about a quarter of the total production of the national press). An edition of the *Financial Times* is also printed in Frankfurt. Prices of the national newspapers vary from 10p to 25p for the dailies and 18p to 30p for the Sundays.

The leading Scottish papers, *The Scotsman* and the *Glasgow Herald*, have a considerable circulation outside Scotland.

National newspapers are often thought of as either 'quality' or 'popular' papers on the basis of differences in format (broadsheet or tabloid, though this is not a rigid distinction), style and content. Four dailies and three Sundays are usually described as quality newspapers. The three Sunday qualities produce colour supplements which are distributed as part of the paper.

The slow decline in newspaper circulations as a whole (from 37 million in 1970 to 33·5 million in 1980), conceals the different experiences of individual papers and the fact that the circulation of some newspapers has remained generally steady, while that of others has increased.

English Regional Newspapers

The regional newspapers of England (outside London, over 70 morning or evening dailies and Sundays and some 700 newspapers appearing once or twice a week) provide mainly regional and local news. The daily newspapers also give coverage to national affairs, and a number co-operate to provide their own foreign news service. Generally, regional evening newspapers are non-political, while the morning newspapers adopt a more positive political stance and tend to be independent or conservative in outlook.

Circulation

The total circulation of the regional morning and evening papers is estimated at over 7 million. Of the morning papers the *Yorkshire Post* (Leeds) and the *Northern Echo* (Darlington) have circulations of over 100,000 and two provincial Sunday papers—the *Sunday Sun* (Newcastle upon Tyne) and the *Sunday Mercury* (Birmingham)—have circulations of over 140,000 and 190,000 respectively. Individual circulation figures of regional evening papers start at about 15,000; most are in the 30,000–100,000 range, although the *Manchester Evening News* and the *Birmingham Evening Mail* have circulations of over 330,000 and the *Liverpool Echo* of over 240,000. Weekly papers are mainly of local appeal; they are also a valuable medium for local advertising. Most have circulations in the 5,000–40,000 range.

There are also many free distribution advertising newspapers (mostly weekly), some published by orthodox newspaper publishers.

London Suburban Papers

The London local weeklies (about 120) include papers for every district in Greater London. They circulate in as many as six to eight local editions of individual papers, affiliated in some cases to larger groups.

A number of evening newspapers, using the latest production technology, are published in the outer metropolitan area.

Wales

Wales has one daily morning newspaper, the *Western Mail*, published in Cardiff; its circulation of just under 100,000 is mainly in south Wales. In north Wales the *Liverpool Daily Post* gives wide coverage to events in the area. Evening papers published in Wales are the *South Wales Echo*, Cardiff; the *South Wales Argus*, Newport; the *South Wales Evening Post*, Swansea; and the *Evening Leader*, Wrexham. Their circulation range is between 29,000 and 117,000. North Wales is also served by the *Liverpool Echo*, the *Shropshire Star* covers parts of mid- and north Wales, and there is coverage to a smaller extent by the *Manchester Evening News*.

Weeklies

The weekly press (over 50) includes English language papers, some of which carry articles in Welsh, bilingual papers, and Welsh language papers.

Scotland

Scotland has six morning, six evening and three Sunday newspapers. The morning papers, with circulations of between 92,000 and 720,000 are *The Scotsman* published in Edinburgh; the *Glasgow Herald*; the *Daily Record* (sister paper to the *Daily Mirror*); the Dundee *Courier and Advertiser*; the Aberdeen *Press and Journal*; and the *Scottish Daily Express* (published in Manchester). The evening papers have circulations in the range of 16,000 to 192,000 and are the *Evening News* of Edinburgh, Glasgow's *Evening Times*, Dundee's *Evening Telegraph and Post*, Aberdeen's *Evening Express*, the *Paisley Daily Express* and the *Greenock Telegraph*. The Sunday papers are the *Sunday Mail*, the *Sunday Post* and the *Scottish Sunday Express* (published in Manchester).

Weeklies

Weekly and local newspapers number about 140, of which the *Hamilton Advertiser* and the *Falkirk Herald* have the largest circulations.

Northern Ireland

Northern Ireland has two morning newspapers, one evening and one Sunday paper, all published in Belfast with circulations ranging from 50,000 to 156,000. They are the *News-Letter* (Unionist) and the *Irish News* (Nationalist), the evening *Belfast Telegraph* and the *Sunday News*. There are 40 weekly newspapers.

New Technology

The size of the labour element in the costs of national and provincial newspapers continues to encourage publishers to look for ways of increasing productivity, often by use of the new composing technology which dispenses with traditional 'hot metal' typesetting, with type set in molten lead, and employs photographic methods to produce an image. It can combine photo-

TABLE 38: National and London-Evening Newspapers

Title and foundation date	Controlled by	Circulation[a] average Jan.–June 1980
NATIONAL MORNINGS 'Populars'		
Daily Express (1900)	Trafalgar House Investments	2,325,099
Daily Mail (1896)	Associated Newspapers Group Ltd	1,984,804
Daily Mirror (1903)	Reed International Ltd	3,650,636
Daily Star (1978)	Trafalgar House Investments	1,033,168
Morning Star (1966)	The People's Press Printing Society Ltd	33,793
The Sun (1969)	News International Ltd	3,837,215
'Qualities'		
The Daily Telegraph (1855)	Telegraph Newspaper Trust	1,445,833
Financial Times (1888)	Pearson Longman Ltd	197,698
The Guardian (1821)	The Guardian and Manchester Evening News Ltd	375,179
The Times (1785)	The Thompson Organisation Ltd	315,724
NATIONAL SUNDAYS 'Populars'		
News of the World (1843)	News International Ltd	4,472,283
The Sunday People (1881)	Reed International Ltd	3,899,802
Sunday Express (1918)	Trafalgar House Investments	3,100,338
Sunday Mirror (1963)	Reed International Ltd	3,856,267
'Qualities'		
The Observer (1791)	The Atlantic Richfield Co. and The Observer Trust	1,017,631
Sunday Telegraph (1961)	Telegraph Newspaper Trust	1,031,811
The Sunday Times (1822)	The Thompson Organisation Ltd	1,418,516
LONDON EVENINGS[b]		
Evening News (1881) Monday–Friday	Associated Newspapers Group Ltd	462,493
Evening Standard (1827) Monday–Friday	Trafalgar House Investments	371,903

[a] Circulation figures are those of the Audit Bureau of Circulations (founded in 1931 and consisting of publishers, advertisers and advertising bureaux) and are certified average daily or weekly net sales for the period. The circulation figure of the Morning Star is otherwise audited.

[b] A merger of London's two evening papers under the Evening Standard title has been announced.

composition with computer storage and handling of data, and substitutes electronic for manual methods. It presents possibilities for reorganisation which can have effects throughout a newspaper office and may raise difficult problems of manning levels; the introduction of the 'on-line' system, for example, under which text can be fed at electronic speeds to the computer store (and recalled for checking on visual display units) and can be passed between the store and the photosetters, can affect all the traditional departments of a newspaper up to the printing stage. The provincial press has generally led the way in adopting the new techniques.

The Periodical Press

The 4,900 periodical publications (including local freesheets) are classified as 'general', 'specialised', 'trade', 'technical' and 'professional'. There are also about 640 'house magazines' produced by industrial undertakings, business houses or public services for their employees and/or clients. The 'alternative' press probably includes a further 500 titles, most of which are devoted to radical politics, community matters, religion, the occult, science or ecology.

General and specialised periodicals include magazines of general interest; women's magazines; publications for children; religious periodicals for all denominations; fiction magazines; magazines dealing with sport, gardening, hobbies and humour; journals specialising in various subjects such as politics, finance and economics, science, agriculture, medicine and the arts; and the publications of learned societies, trade unions, regiments, universities and other organisations.

The weekly periodicals with the highest sales are: *Radio Times* and *TV Times* which have circulations approaching 4 million and *Woman's Weekly*, *Woman's Own*, *Woman*, *Weekly News* (which sells mainly in Scotland) and *My Weekly* with circulations in the 800,000 to 1·6 million range. The leading journals of opinion are *The Economist*, a politically independent publication covering topics from a wider angle than its title implies; the *New Statesman*, which is a review of politics, literature and the arts with an independent socialist political tendency; the *Spectator*, which covers much the same subjects from an independent conservative standpoint; *Tribune*, which represents the views of the left-wing of the Labour Party; *New Society*, covering the sociological aspects of current affairs; and *New Scientist*, which reports on science and technology in terms which the non-specialist can understand. *Punch*, traditionally the leading humorous periodical, and *Private Eye*, a satirical fortnightly, also devote attention to public affairs. More recent publications include *Financial Weekly*, a periodical for businessmen and investors and *Now!*, a weekly news magazine.

Literary and political journals and those specialising in international and Commonwealth affairs, published monthly or quarterly, appeal generally speaking to the more serious reader.

The publication of trade, technical, business, scientific and professional journals (covering hundreds of subjects, many of them in considerable depth) has become one of the more important aspects of the British publishing industry. In addition to circulating in Britain, these journals have a considerable circulation overseas and are an important medium for selling British goods. Their publication ranges in frequency from weekly to quarterly.

Periodicals published in England circulate throughout Britain. In Wales there are also several monthly and quarterly journals published in both Welsh and English; in Scotland there are three monthly illustrated periodicals, a weekly paper devoted to farming interests, a number of literary journals (of which the most famous is probably *Blackwood's*), and numerous popular magazines; and Northern Ireland has weekly, monthly and quarterly publications covering farming, the linen industry, building, motoring, politics and social work.

News Agencies

There are three principal British news agencies registered in Britain: Reuters Ltd; The Press Association Ltd; and The Exchange Telegraph Company Ltd.

Reuters Ltd, a world news organisation, is owned by four associations: the Newspaper Publishers Association; The Press Association; the Australian Associated Press; and the New Zealand Press Association. They are parties to a trust deed which safeguards the independence and integrity of the news service. Founded in Aachen in 1850 and transferred to London in 1851,

Reuters employs 558 journalists and correspondents in 69 countries and territories, and has links with about 120 national or private news agencies, which give it access to coverage by many hundreds of local reporters. Some 700,000 words of general news, sports, and economic reports are received in London every day and are retransmitted to 153 countries and territories over a global network of leased teleprinter lines, satellite links and cable and radio circuits. These news services are specially tailored to the needs of recipients in Britain and overseas, and are distributed to information media, either direct or through national news agencies. Reuters Economic Services, one of the world's largest financial and business news services, supplies information to banks, brokers and other commercial undertakings throughout the world by means of computer-based video display units, teleprinters and bulletins.

The Press Association Ltd, the British national news agency founded in 1868, is co-operatively owned by the principal newspapers of the United Kingdom outside London, and of the Irish Republic. It provides newspapers, the broadcasting organisations, Reuters and other international agencies with a complete service of home news, including general and parliamentary news, legal reports, and all branches of financial, commercial and sports news; and includes in its services to regional papers the world news of Reuters and the Associated Press. News is teleprinted 24 hours a day from head office in London over a network of lines leased from the Post Office—certain items being available in teletypesetting form. Through its photographic department The Press Association serves London and regional newspapers with a daily picture service from home and overseas; these are wired to the regional press. Its Special Reporting Service supplies reports of local or special interest to daily and weekly papers and periodicals. Press Association Features provides exclusive rights to syndicated articles and visual features.

The Exchange Telegraph Company Ltd (Extel), an independent news agency founded in 1872, is a wholly owned subsidiary of The Exchange Telegraphy Company (Holdings) Ltd, a public company. It supplies financial and sporting news to newspapers and broadcasting organisations, and to private subscribers. In conjunction with The Press Association Ltd, racing services are also supplied by telephone and video terminals to subscribers in London and the provinces from offices throughout Britain.

The British press and broadcasting organisations are also served by Associated Press Ltd, and by United Press International, which are British subsidiaries of United States news agencies.

A number of other British, Commonwealth and foreign agencies and news services have offices in London, and there are minor agencies in other cities, mostly specialising in various aspects of newspaper and periodical requirements. Syndication of features is not as common in Britain as in some countries, but a few agencies specialise in this type of work.

Training for Journalism

The National Council for the Training of Journalists (NCTJ), which represents the principal press organisations, sets and conducts examinations, and organises short training courses for journalists.

The two methods of entry into newspaper journalism are selection for a one-year NCTJ pre-entry course or direct recruitment by a regional or local newspaper. Both categories of entrant take part in an apprenticeship scheme consisting of 'on-the-job' training, and block release courses for those who have not attended a pre-entry course. A number of centres provide courses for reporters. Other training facilities include one-year postgraduate courses in journalism at the University College of South Wales in Cardiff, and at the City

University (London), and courses provided by the Newspaper Society Training Service for regional newspapers in such subjects as circulation, advertising, industrial relations and management. The NCTJ co-operates closely with the Printing and Publishing Industry Training Board (PPITB) which is responsible for training in printing, publishing and professional photography.

Under the Commonwealth Press Union Harry Brittain Memorial Fellowship Scheme, several young Commonwealth journalists each year spend three months working and studying in Britain. The Thomson Foundation holds training courses for journalists from all parts of the world and provides consultants and tutors for courses in journalism held overseas.

Training for work with periodicals was traditionally done 'on the job' but formal courses of instruction are becoming more widely available. The London College of Printing offers a one-year pre-entry course in periodical journalism as well as block- and day-release courses for those who have already started work as trainees. In addition, several of the larger publishing houses provide systematic training which includes periods in the classroom to supplement work experience. For publishers who do not offer training independently, a training group has been established under the auspices of the PPITB.

Press Institutions

The most important organisations to which employers in the industry belong are the Newspaper Publishers Association, whose members publish national newspapers in London and Manchester; the Newspaper Society, which represents the regional, local and London suburban press; the Scottish Daily Newspaper Society, which represents the interests of daily and Sunday newspapers in Scotland; the Scottish Newspaper Proprietors Association, which represents the owners of weekly newspapers in Scotland; Associated Northern Ireland Newspapers, whose members are the proprietors of weekly newspapers in Northern Ireland; and the Periodical Publishers Association, whose membership embraces the independent publishers of trade and technical publications and general magazines.

Organisations representing journalists are the Institute of Journalists (IOJ), with about 2,250 members, and the National Union of Journalists (NUJ), with more than 32,000 members. All practising journalists (including those engaged in radio, television, public relations, freelance journalism and book publishing editorial work) are eligible for membership of either. Four main printing unions are concerned with the press.

The Guild of British Newspaper Editors with about 500 members aims to maintain the professional status and independence of editors, defend the freedom of the press, and improve the education and training of journalists. The British Association of Industrial Editors is the professional organisation to which most editors of house journals belong.

The Press Council

The Press Council has a membership consisting of equal numbers of press and non-press members, with an independent chairman. Its aims are: to preserve the established freedom of the press; to maintain the character of the press in accordance with the highest professional and commercial standards; to keep under review any developments likely to restrict the supply of information of public interest and importance; to deal with complaints about the conduct of the press or the conduct of persons and organisations towards the press (the Council's complaints committee comprises equal numbers of press and non-press members); to report on developments in the press which may tend towards greater concentration or monopoly; to make representation on appropriate occasions to the Government, to organs of the United Nations and to press organisations abroad; to publish its adjudications and periodic reports recording its work; and to review from time to time developments in the press and the factors affecting them. The Council publishes annual reports, which include statistics of the newspaper and periodical press and a series of articles examining the structure of the leading press groups.

The Press and the Law

The press has generally the same freedom as the individual to comment on matters of public interest.

Apart from the requirements to register newspapers and periodicals under the Newspaper Libel and Registration Act 1881, there are no specific press laws but certain statutes include sections which apply to the press.[1] These relate to such matters as the extent of newspaper ownership in television and radio companies; the transfer of newspaper assets; restrictions on the reporting of preliminary hearings of indictable offences (in England, Wales and Northern Ireland); the right of press representatives to be admitted to meetings of local authorities; restrictions on the publication of (a) certain details of divorce, domestic and rape proceedings in courts of law, (b) legal proceedings involving children, (c) advertisement and investment circulars, which are governed by Acts dealing with the publication of false or misleading descriptions of goods and services and with fraud, and (d) advertisements of remedies for certain diseases, which are covered by public health legislation; agreements between the Post Office and newspaper proprietors on telegraphic communications, which must comply with telegraphs legislation; restrictions on certain types of prize competition; and copyrights, which come under copyright laws. In certain circumstances, if the defence authorities and press representatives in the Defence, Press and Broadcasting Committee agrees that publication of information on particular topics would be detrimental to the national interest, defence notices ('D' notices) are circulated confidentially to the news media requesting that such information should not be published. Compliance with these requests is expected, but they have no legal force. An internal review of the 'D' notice system is being conducted by the committee.

Of particular relevance to the press are the laws on libel and contempt of court. A newspaper may not publish comments on the conduct of judicial proceedings which are likely to prejudice their reputation for fairness before or during the actual proceedings nor may it publish before or during a trial anything which might tend to influence the result. The obtaining and publication of information from state and official sources of a confidential or security nature is affected by the official secrets legislation. Newspapers are also liable to proceedings for seditious libel and incitement to disaffection. The majority of legal proceedings against the press are libel actions brought by private individuals. In such cases, the editor, proprietor, publishers, printer and distributor of the newspaper, as well as the author of the article concerned, may all be held responsible.

[1] A Government draft code of conduct on trade union closed shops has been issued under the Employment Act 1980 (see p 338). In relation to the press the code considers the position of editors and journalists and the essential freedom of the press to collect and publish information and to publish comment and criticism.

23 Television and Radio

All British broadcasting is based on the tradition that it is a public service accountable to the people through Parliament. Television and radio are the responsibility of two broadcasting authorities, the British Broadcasting Corporation (BBC) and the Independent Broadcasting Authority (IBA), which work to broad requirements and objectives placed on them by Parliament, but are quite independent in the day-to-day conduct of business. This independence carries with it certain obligations as to programmes and programme content. Each authority must ensure that its programmes display, as far as possible, a proper balance and wide range of subject matter, impartiality in matters of controversy and accuracy in news coverage, and also that programmes do not offend against good taste. Codes of guidance on violence in television programmes, particularly during hours when large numbers of children are likely to be viewing, are operated by both authorities. A code of advertising standards and practice is also operated by the IBA. There is no advertising on BBC television and radio.

The Home Secretary regulates broadcasting generally under the Wireless Telegraphy Acts 1949 and 1967 which prohibit the sending or receiving of wireless communications except under licence. The Minister is answerable to Parliament on broad policy questions, and may issue directions on a number of technical and other matters.

Television viewing is by far the most popular leisure pastime in Britain, and some 98 per cent of the population have access to television. It is estimated that about 10 per cent of households have two or more receivers. Average viewing time per person is over $17\frac{1}{2}$ hours a week. Practically every home also has radio, and car radios and portable transistors have made radio, national and local, one of the country's major day-time diversions.

Citizens' band radio has been publicly discussed for some time. In May 1980 the Home Secretary announced that a system known as 'Open Channel' would be introduced following administrative and technical studies.

Households with television must buy a licence each year; they cost £12 for black and white and £34 for colour. Of over 18 million licences current in May 1980 approximately 13 million were for colour and 5·3 million for black and white television. The revenue from licences meets most of the cost of the BBC's domestic services. Independent television and independent local radio are self-supporting, with revenue drawn from the sale of advertising time.

The British Broadcasting Corporation

The constitution and finances of the BBC are governed by the Royal Charter and by a Licence and Agreement. The Corporation consists of 12 governors (including a chairman, a vice-chairman and separate national governors for Scotland, Wales and Northern Ireland), each appointed by the Queen on the advice of the Government. The governors are responsible for all aspects of broadcasting. Committees advise them on such matters as the social effects of television, religious broadcasting, music, agriculture, schools broadcasting, further education, programmes for immigrants, science and engineering and charitable appeals. There is also a programme complaints commission.[1] The governors appoint the Director General who is chairman of the BBC's board of management, which also includes the managing directors for television, radio and external broadcasting, and the directors of personnel, finance, public affairs and engineering.

The National Broadcasting Councils for Scotland and Wales control the policy and content of television and radio programmes intended primarily for reception in their respective countries. Local radio councils, representative of the local community, are appointed by the BBC to advise on the development and operation of local radio stations.

The domestic services of the BBC are financed principally by the income from the sale of television licences. This is supplemented by profits from trading activities, including television programme exports, the sale of records and publications connected with BBC programmes, the hire and sale of educational films, film library sales and exhibitions based on programmes and other BBC activities. Nearly three-quarters of the BBC's expenditure on domestic services relates to television. The BBC meets the cost of local radio stations but some local education authorities help to make educational programmes. The BBC's External Services are financed by a grant determined each year by the Government. The general rise in costs is causing the BBC to make a number of economies and reduce its output of both radio and television.

The Independent Broadcasting Authority

The IBA's constitution and finances are governed by the Independent Broadcasting Authority legislation and a Licence. It consists of a chairman, a deputy chairman and ten other members (three of whom have responsibility for Scotland, Wales and Northern Ireland) appointed by the Home Secretary. The IBA does not produce radio or television programmes; these are provided by commercial programme companies. Its main functions are to appoint the companies, to supervise programme arrangements, to control advertising and to build, own and operate transmitting stations. The chief executive officer of the IBA, the Director General, is supported by a headquarters and regional office staff covering all technical and administrative services.

The IBA is advised by a General Advisory Council, by Scottish, Northern Ireland and Welsh committees, and by committees on educational broadcasting, religious broadcasting, charitable appeals and advertising. A specialist panel advises on medical and allied advertisements. A Complaints Review Board reviews reports of complaints received and investigated by the IBA's staff.[1] Local committees advise on local radio services.

The IBA's finance comes from annual rental payments made by the television and radio programme companies. The television programme companies also pay to the IBA, for transfer to the Government, a levy related to their profits. A similar levy on the profits of local radio contractors is proposed.

The Programme Companies

Fifteen television programme companies hold contracts to provide television programmes in the 14 independent television regions; two companies share the contract for London, one providing programmes during the week and the other at the weekend. (New television contracts to run from January 1982 are to be awarded by the IBA in December 1980.) The companies operate on a commercial basis, deriving their revenue from the sale of advertising time. The financial resources, advertising revenue and programme production of the

---

[1] It is proposed to establish a single complaints commission to deal with complaints of unfair treatment or infringement of privacy against both the BBC and IBA.

companies vary considerably, depending largely on the size of population in the areas in which they operate. Although newspapers can acquire an interest in programme companies, there are safeguards to protect public interest.

In consultation with the IBA, each company plans the content of the programmes to be broadcast in its area. These consist partly of material produced by the company itself, partly of that produced by the other programme companies, and partly of that purchased from elsewhere. The five largest companies (Thames, ATV, Granada, Yorkshire and London Weekend) provide more programmes for broadcast elsewhere on the national network than do the smaller ones. A common news service is provided by Independent Television News Ltd., a non-profit-making company in which all the programme companies are shareholders. The negotiations concerning the supply, exchange and purchase of programmes and their co-ordinated transmission through the independent television network take place largely on the Network Planning Committee which consists of representatives of all the programme companies and of the IBA.

Local radio is broadcast by independent stations on the same principles. The programme companies are under contract to the IBA, operate under its control and are financed by advertising revenue. News coverage is supplied as a common service by Independent Radio News.

Television

Three television channels are in operation: BBC-1 and ITV broadcasting on both 405 lines very high frequency (vhf) and 625 lines ultra high frequency (uhf), and BBC-2 which broadcasts on 625 lines uhf only. Some 99 per cent of the population live within range of vhf, and almost 98 per cent within range of uhf transmissions, which are still being extended. The vhf transmissions are expected to cease within a few years. Most television sets are designed to receive four channels, and the Government has decided that the IBA shall be given responsibility for broadcasting on the fourth channel (see below).

Apart from a break during the war years the BBC has been providing regular television broadcasts since 1936. All BBC-2 programmes and the majority of those on BBC-1 are broadcast on the national network. Of the BBC's 1978–79 television output over 44 per cent was produced in London and 35 per cent elsewhere in Britain; about 14 per cent comprised feature films and series, and 13·5 per cent Open University programmes. Current affairs, features, documentary, news, schools, further education, Open University and religious programmes comprised about 45·5 per cent of the total.

Through co-ordinated planning of programmes on its two services the BBC is able to cater simultaneously for people of differing interests. While both services cover the whole range of television output, BBC-1 presents a higher proportion of programmes of general interest, such as light entertainment, sport, current affairs, children's programmes and outside broadcasts, while BBC-2 places greater emphasis on minority interests, providing a larger element of documentaries, travel programmes, serious drama, music, programmes on pastimes and international films.

The first regular independent television broadcasts began in London in 1955. ITV services are provided by the regional programme companies.

On average each of the 14 ITV areas transmitted about 100 hours of television programmes a week in 1979–80, nearly two-fifths of which comprised informative programmes—including news, documentaries, current affairs, education and religion. Three-quarters of the programmes seen on ITV are produced by the programme companies themselves. There is a maximum of six minutes of advertising an hour on average, in three short breaks.

Legislation has been introduced to establish a fourth television channel to be operated by the IBA; the service is expected to begin in the autumn of 1982. The IBA will be expected to ensure that the channel caters for tastes and interests not normally provided for by the existing independent service. It must provide a suitable proportion of educational programmes, encourage innovation and experiment, and ensure that a substantial proportion of programmes are provided otherwise than by the independent television companies. The companies will, however, finance the new service and in return will have the right to sell advertising time in fourth channel programmes broadcast in their region. In Wales the fourth channel is to be operated by a new Welsh Fourth Channel Authority. A substantial proportion of programmes will be in Welsh; evening broadcasting will be mainly in Welsh.

British Television Overseas

British television programmes have won many international awards, and the country is one of the world's foremost exporters of television productions. It is estimated that Britain exported about £38 million-worth of television programmes in 1978, and there are few countries in the world where British programmes have not been shown.

Cable Services

Over 14 per cent of households with television rely on cable systems for the reception of programmes. The systems are usually used to improve reception quality, to avoid 'screening' by buildings or the local topography, or because external aerials are not allowed in some residential buildings. There are cable networks in almost every urban area; some cover a whole town, some homes scattered throughout an area, and others individual housing estates. Of some 2·7 million subscribers to cable networks in 1980 about 1·5 million subscribed to commercial systems, 995,000 to systems operated by local authorities and other non-commercial bodies, and some 99,000 to housing associations' systems. Commercial relay operators are represented by The Cable Television Association of Great Britain. All operators of cable systems are licensed by the Home Secretary and the Post Office.

Since 1972 six experiments have been authorised by the Home Secretary for local stations to distribute locally-originated television programmes by cable systems to subscribers. Three stations are still in operation. At Greenwich in London funds are provided by the local commercial cable television company, while at Swindon they are provided by a number of non-commercial bodies and from the promotion of a weekly lottery. At Milton Keynes the experimental station provides a locally-originated programme service over the Post Office cable system. All the experiments enable people to see programmes about local activities and to have access to programme-making facilities under the guidance of the station staff. There are proposals for a Pay-TV experiment among cable operators.

Radio

BBC Radio's four national channels each have a distinct character. Radio 1 provides a programme of pop music, while Radio 2 provides light music as well as being the principal channel for the coverage of sport. Radio 3 provides mainly classical music (much of which is in stereo) and in the evening offers, in addition, adult education programmes and works of artistic and intellectual interest. Radio 4 is the main speech programme, providing the principal news and information service and a wide range of drama, music, talks, entertainment and schools broadcasts. There are many stereo programmes.

Local radio is provided by 20 BBC stations in England and by 19 independent stations distributed throughout Britain. Another 18 local radio stations (nine BBC and nine IBA) are being established and approval has been given for a further 15 (one BBC and 14 IBA). Local broadcasts provide a comprehensive service of local news and information, music and other entertainment, education, consumer advice and coverage of local events, and offer residents a chance to air their views, often by using the phone-in technique.

Four experiments in locally-initiated sound programmes over cable distribution systems have been authorised. As in the case of the local community cable television experiments an advertising service may be included if a station elects to do so.

External Services

The BBC broadcasts to most countries overseas (in 39 languages, including English) for a total of some 705 hours a week. The main objectives are to give unbiased news, to reflect British opinion and to project British life and culture. News bulletins, current affairs programmes, political commentaries and topical magazine programmes form the main part of the output. A full sports service, music, drama, and general entertainment are also included.

The languages in which the External Services broadcast and the length of time each language is on the air are prescribed by the Government. Apart from this the BBC has full responsibility and it is completely independent in determining the content of news and other programmes.

The foreign language services are divided into areas: the African, Arabic, Eastern, Far Eastern, Latin American, French (to Europe and Africa), Central European, South European, German and East European Services. Broadcasts range from 63 hours a week in Arabic to 35 minutes in Maltese.

The BBC's English by Radio and Television Service is the most extensive language teaching undertaking in the world. English lessons are broadcast weekly by radio with explanations in 30 other languages, and recorded lessons are supplied to between 250 and 300 stations in over 100 countries. English by Television programmes are shown in more than 100 countries.

The BBC World Service broadcasts for 24 hours a day in English and is supplemented at peak listening times by additional series of programmes designed to be of special interest to Africa.

BBC news bulletins and other programmes are rebroadcast by the domestic radio services of many countries. Rebroadcasting involves direct relays from BBC transmissions and the use of recorded programmes supplied through the BBC tape and disc transcription service. There are some 3,000 rebroadcasts weekly of World Service programmes in about 50 countries. The Transcription Service offers programmes to over 100 countries.

Another part of the External Services, the Monitoring Service, listens to and reports on foreign broadcasts, supplying a daily flow of significant news and comment from overseas to the BBC, the press, and the Government.

Radio for overseas is also produced by the radio services of the Central Office of Information (COI). A wide range of material is recorded on tape and sent to radio stations in over 70 countries for transmission. In addition, COI television services provide material such as documentary and magazine programmes for distribution to overseas television stations.

Transmitters and Studios

The BBC's domestic television and radio services operate more than 1,200 transmitters, and its external services from some 47 transmitters in Britain and 32 overseas. Most of the circuits used to link studios and transmitters are rented from the Post Office. For its domestic radio, the BBC uses 100 studios in London and the regions, and for its external services 30 in London. In addition, there are semi-automatic studios which can be operated by programme officials without engineering staff. Each of the BBC's 20 local radio stations has at least two studios. BBC television productions come from main studios at the Television Centre in west London and other studios in various parts of London, and six fully-equipped regional studio centres and eight television studios in other towns. Outside broadcasting is covered by a number of mobile units.

The IBA uses a total of 500 television and sound radio transmitting stations throughout Britain, programme links being rented from the Post Office. Independent television programmes are produced at 17 studio centres throughout the country, reflecting the IBA's policy of encouraging regional television, and are designed for either local broadcasting or for national transmission. All companies have facilities for colour transmission.

Advertising

The BBC does not give publicity to any individual firm or organised interest by mentioning its name or branded products, except when it is necessary in order to provide effective and informative programmes. Under the terms of its Licence and Agreement it must not broadcast any commercial advertisement or sponsored programme.

Advertisements are broadcast on independent television but there is no sponsoring of programmes by advertisers. Advertisements must be clearly distinguishable and separate from programmes, and the amount of time given to advertising must not be so great as to detract from the value of the programmes as a medium of information, education and entertainment. In any one hour of broadcasting the amount of advertising time on independent television is normally limited to seven minutes. Averaged over the day's programmes it must not exceed six minutes per hour. The independent local radio stations are normally limited to up to nine minutes of advertising each hour. The IBA has drawn up a code governing standards and practice in advertising on television and radio and giving guidance about the types and methods of advertisement that may not be used. Some advertising is prohibited, notably that with a political or religious object or on behalf of cigarettes or betting. Advertisements may not be inserted in certain types of programme, such as broadcasts to schools.

Government publicity material designed to support non-political campaigns may be broadcast on independent radio and television. It is prepared through the COI and is broadcast and paid for on a normal commercial basis. Short public service items, mainly about health, safety and welfare themes, are also produced by COI for free transmission by the BBC and independent television and radio. The Government has no general access to radio or television.

Parliamentary and Political Broadcasting

Parliamentary reporting includes a daily factual and impartial account of proceedings in Parliament, transmitted on BBC's Radio 4 when Parliament is in session. Since 1978 proceedings of Parliament, including its committees, have been broadcast on radio. Some occasions are broadcast live, and recorded sound extracts may be included in both radio and television news and current affairs programmes.

There is also frequent coverage of political subjects in news bulletins and current affairs programmes on both radio and television. Ministerial and party political broadcasts are transmitted periodically under the rules agreed between the major political parties, the BBC and the IBA.

Technical Developments

Research into technical problems is carried out by scientific and engineering staffs of the BBC, the IBA, the Home Office, other government departments and the radio industry. One of the most important recent developments has been the introduction of smaller, lighter cameras and video recorders for use on outside locations. 'Electronic news gathering' (ENG) equipment, whereby pictures can be transmitted directly to a studio or recorded on videotape on location, reduces significantly the time before an item can be broadcast. Other developments include the use of magnetic tape on videotape recorders, the increasing use of computers to generate graphical shapes such as captions and credits, and the improvement of the quality of videotape pictures.

Advances by the BBC have included the electronic conversion of mono-chrome and colour television pictures between the European and the American systems, and the development of a sound-and-vision system known as 'sound-in-syncs' which enables the television sound and picture to be carried over a single 625-line vision circuit, eliminating the operational complexity and expense of a separate circuit for sound. IBA engineers were the first in the world to introduce a fully digital field rate standards converter (DICE) to improve the interchange of programmes between areas using the 525-lines system (for example, North America) and those using the 625-lines system (for example, Europe). Current IBA research projects include the development of the first digital video tape recorder with economical use of tape, and a pro-gramme of research into the future use of space satellites for broadcasting. (The Home Secretary has initiated a study into the implications of establishing a direct broadcasting satellite service in Britain by about 1985. The study covers the technical, financial and resource implications of such a service, the implications for the existing broadcasting system and services, the possible industrial benefits and likely developments in Europe.)

Both the BBC and IBA have produced 'teletext' systems, known respectively as CEEFAX and ORACLE, which allow the broadcasting of written and simple graphical information to television receivers fitted with special adap-tors. Both systems enable viewers to select a display of 'pages' of written information on the television screen; the system also allows sub-titles to appear in conjunction with programmes, which is of great benefit to the deaf and hard of hearing. The Post Office's public viewdata service, Prestel, offers a wide range of information which is transmitted through telephone lines and may be viewed on appropriately equipped television receivers (see p 324).

International Relations

The BBC and the IBA (together with the Independent Television Companies Association) are active members of the European Broadcasting Union (EBU), which was established to advance international broadcasting projects. The EBU manages Eurovision, is responsible for the technical and administrative arrangements for co-ordinating the exchange of programmes over that network and for intercontinental satellite links, and maintains a technical monitoring station where frequency measurements and other observations on broadcast-ing stations are carried out.

The BBC belongs to the Commonwealth Broadcasting Association whose members extend to each other such facilities as the use of studios, recording channels, and programme contributions. The BBC also provides technical aid, particularly in training the staff of other broadcasting organisations through-out the world; members of the BBC's staff are seconded for service overseas.

The BBC is a partner in Visnews, which supplies a service of world news-film to some 200 television organisations in over 90 countries and is the most widely used newsfilm agency in the world. The BBC is also a member of the

International Television Federation (Intertel), which produces high-quality information programmes which are exchanged overseas. United Press International, Paramount Pictures and Independent Television News jointly provide an international newsfilm service to more than 100 overseas television organisations via the Eurovision network and by satellite.

The Government spends a considerable amount each year on training in broadcasting for overseas students and largely finances the British Council (see p 71), which includes in its activities training in educational television and radio for members of broadcasting organisations overseas. Training in television work is also provided for overseas trainees at the Thomson Television College in Glasgow, run by the Thomson Foundation, a charitable trust.

The BBC and the IBA participate in the work of the International Telecommunications Union, the United Nations agency responsible for the regulation and control of all international telecommunication services (including radio and television), for the allocation and registration of all radio frequencies and, through its international consultative committees, for the promotion and co-ordination of the international study of technical problems in broadcasting. The BBC is also represented on the United Kingdom Committee of the International Special Committee on Radio Interference.

24 Sport and Recreation

There is widespread interest in sport in Britain. Large crowds attend occasions such as the association football 'Cup Final' at Wembley Stadium, the international rugby matches at Twickenham, Murrayfield and Cardiff Arms Park, the Wimbledon lawn tennis championships, the classic horse races, Grand Prix motor racing and the cricket Test Matches; millions also watch them on television. Many people take part in active recreation such as climbing, rambling, riding, boating, angling and other water-based sports, keep fit, movement and dance activities. Indoor sports like darts, billiards and snooker are also popular.

An important feature of British sport and recreation is its amateur element (the people who devote time and energy to the organising, teaching and training of individual activities).

ORGANISATION
AND
PROMOTION

A Parliamentary Under-Secretary of State in the Department of the Environment is responsible for co-ordinating government policy on sport and active recreation. The Secretaries of State for Wales, Scotland and Northern Ireland exercise similar responsibilities in their areas.

The Government provides financial and other assistance through a number of official bodies. Some of these, such as the Sports Councils (see below) and the Countryside Commissions, have specific responsibilities for sport and recreation, and assist other public and private bodies in the provision of facilities. Others, for example, the Forestry Commission, the British Waterways Board, the Nature Conservancy Council and the regional water authorities, provide recreational amenities in addition to their main functions.

Sports
Councils

The main responsibility for the general development of sport in Great Britain rests with three independent bodies—the Sports Council (for England and for general matters affecting Britain as a whole), the Sports Council for Wales and the Scottish Sports Council. Members of the councils are appointed by the Government. The Councils have the task, subject only to general ministerial directives, of allocating funds made available by the Government (in 1980–81 amounting to some £24·7 million). They award grants for sports development, coaching and administration to the governing bodies of sport and other national organisations; and administer the national sports centres. Grants and loans are made to voluntary organisations and local authorities to assist the provision of sports facilities. In some circumstances grants are also given to commercial organisations. The Councils also assist British representatives at international sports meetings and encourage links with international and overseas organisations. The Sports Council consults with the Central Council of Physical Recreation, comprising members of the national governing and representative bodies of sport and physical recreation in England. There are nine regional councils for sport and recreation in England, on each of which are represented the sporting, countryside and local authority interests of the region. The Scottish Sports Council consults with the Scottish Standing Conference of Sport which comprises representatives of the national governing bodies of sport in Scotland; and the Sports Council for Wales maintains, through a standing committee, a close liaison with the governing bodies of sport in Wales.

In Northern Ireland the Department of Education provides financial assistance to local authorities and voluntary sports bodies for the provision of facilities.

The Sports Council for Northern Ireland, which is financed by the Department of Education for Northern Ireland, advises the Government on sport and physical recreation and gives financial assistance to sports organisations for training and coaching, equipment and administration. In order to reduce the overlapping of functions between the Council, the Department of Education and district councils, the Government has proposed that the Council's role should become advisory only.

A bibliographic service about sport is provided by the National Documentation Centre, set up by the Sports Council and based at the University of Birmingham. The Council also has an information centre providing data on a wide range of sports topics; similar services are provided by the Sports Council for Wales and the Scottish Sports Council. The Sports Council's Technical Unit for Sport gives technical advice on the design and layout of sports halls and playing areas and carries out research.

Organisations Individual sports are run by independent governing bodies whose functions usually include drawing up the rules of the sport, holding events, handling membership, selecting and training national teams and promoting international links.

There are also organisations which represent people who take part in more informal physical recreation, such as walking, or cycling for pleasure; others, for example the National Trusts (see p 188), are concerned with leisure interests as part of a wider concern.

The British Olympic Association The British Olympic Association, founded in 1905, organises the participation of British teams in the Olympic Games. The Association's committee consists of representatives of the 26 sports in the programme of the Olympic Games (summer and winter). It determines the size of the British team; raises funds; makes all the arrangements for the team's travel and comfort at the games; organises the provision and transport of clothing and equipment; and provides a headquarters staff for the management of the team.

The National Playing Fields Association The National Playing Fields Association aims to encourage the provision of playing fields, playgrounds and recreational facilities. It maintains a technical advisory service, and specialises in the play and recreational needs of children and young people including young handicapped people. The Association is a national charity established by Royal Charter, and depends mainly on voluntary contributions with some support from public funds. It is helped by its eight regional play advisers and by affiliated associations in Scotland and Northern Ireland and in English and Welsh counties.

Sport for the Disabled The British Sports Association for the Disabled, founded in 1961, aims to encourage greater opportunities for the physically handicapped to take part in sport and active recreation. The Association receives an annual Sports Council grant and provides advice on physical recreation for the disabled, arranges sports meetings and encourages the provision of facilities (including sports clubs) for disabled people. Regional and branch committees of the Association organise local, regional and national games. Annual national and international paraplegic games are arranged by the British Paraplegic Sports Society. At Stoke Mandeville Hospital, the first sports stadium in the world designed for the disabled was opened in 1969. In Scotland, Wales and Northern Ireland there are similar associations which co-ordinate sporting activities and facilities for disabled people. The Sports Council has been instrumental in forming the United Kingdom Sports Association for People with Mental Handicap. This brings together organisations concerned with mentally handicapped people in order to increase their opportunities to take part in sport.

Private Sponsorship

Increasing numbers of sports receive financial sponsorship from commercial organisations. Sponsorship may take the form of financing specific events, or it may be granted to individual sports organisations.

A Sports Aid Foundation has responsibility for raising and distributing funds from industry, commerce and private sponsors in order to assist the training of talented individual sportsmen and sportswomen. The Foundation makes grants on the recommendation of the governing bodies of sport. In Northern Ireland this is done by the Ulster Sports and Recreation Trust. The Sports Council also runs a sponsorship advisory service which links potential sponsors with suitable sports.

PROVISION OF FACILITIES

Local authorities are the main providers of land and large-scale facilities for community recreation; their total expenditure on sport and outdoor recreation in England and Wales amounted to some £375 million in 1979–80, and in Scotland about £76·8 million. The facilities provided include parks, playing fields, sports halls, tennis courts, golf courses, lakes, swimming baths and sports centres catering for a wide range of indoor and outdoor activities.

Publicly maintained schools are required by law to provide for the physical education of their pupils. All (except those solely for infants) must have a playing field, or the use of one, and most secondary schools have a gymnasium. Some have other amenities such as swimming pools, sports halls and halls designed for dance and movement. In many areas, physical education facilities in schools are available to the whole community outside school hours. Sport and recreation facilities are likewise provided at universities (some of which have departments of physical education), and there are 'centres of sporting excellence' at universities and other colleges enabling selected young athletes to develop their talents and also providing for their educational needs.

Opportunities for outdoor recreation in national parks, nature reserves, forest parks and country parks are provided by public bodies (see p 180). Water-based activities on canals, rivers, lakes and reservoirs are increasingly popular. The British Waterways Board, for example, maintains about 1,760 kilometres (1,100 miles) of cruising waterways for navigation, about 1,450 kilometres (900 miles) of other waterways and some 90 reservoirs. An Inland Waterways Amenity Advisory Council advises the Board on the use of its waterways for pleasure purposes, and a Water Space Amenity Commission gives advice on the recreational use of water in England generally.

In addition to the recreational facilities provided by public authorities, many facilities are made available by local voluntary clubs. Some of these cater for indoor recreation, but more common are those providing sports grounds, particularly for games such as cricket, association and rugby football, hockey, tennis and golf. Clubs linked to industrial business firms often cater for a wide range of activities, and in many cases make their facilities available to members of the public. Commercial facilities, provided as profit-making businesses, include tenpin bowling centres, ice- and roller-skating rinks, squash courts, golf driving ranges and riding stables.

Sports Centres   National sports centres, some of which were initially financed by funds from voluntary sources, are maintained by the sports councils and provide facilities and a wide range of courses for instructors and performers in many recreational activities. As well as making residential courses available for enthusiasts from all over Britain, the centres are used extensively by local clubs and by the community generally.

There are seven national centres in England and Wales. Combined facilities for a range of sports are provided at three centres: the Crystal Palace National Sports Centre in London and the Bisham Abbey in Buckinghamshire and Lilleshall National Sports Centre in Shropshire. The centre at Crystal Palace has a main stadium seating 17,000 spectators, a sports hall seating 2,000 spectators, a swimming hall with pools meeting Olympic requirements and seating 2,000, two teaching pools, ten squash courts, an indoor cricket school, practice rooms for most indoor sports and a hostel for 132 residents. These facilities are available for international competitions as well as for training purposes, and are supported by a grant from the Greater London Council in addition to the Sports Council grant. The other four are specialist centres: the Plas-y-Brenin National Centre for Mountain Activities in north Wales, the Cowes National Sailing Centre in the Isle of Wight, the Holme Pierrepont National Water Sports Centre in Nottinghamshire, and Harrison's Rocks, a small rock-climbing centre in Sussex. Work has begun on the construction of a National Outdoor Pursuits Centre at Plas-y-Deri in Gwynedd which is expected to be completed in 1982, and there are plans for the construction of a National Ice Skating Centre in Manchester. In addition there is a National Sports Centre for Wales in Cardiff which is supported by local authorities but financed mainly from the Sports Council for Wales grant.

The Scottish Sports Council operates three national sports training centres: Glenmore Lodge near Aviemore for outdoor sports, Inverclyde at Largs for general sports, and a national water sports training centre in Cumbrae Isle on the Firth of Clyde.

As well as the national sports centres, other centres (such as the Meadowbank Sports Centre administered by Edinburgh District Council) cater for a wide range of recreational activities and often attract more than purely local interest. Over 300 indoor sports centres serve local rather than national needs; more are planned, some as 'dual' projects on school sites. There are also several centres catering for specialised interests and generally administered by the sponsoring organisations. These include the National Equestrian Centre, run by the British Equestrian Federation, and the Stoke Mandeville Sports Stadium for the Paralysed and Other Disabled, run by the British Paraplegic Sports Society (see p 429).

Northern Ireland has 12 indoor sports centres, 11 of which include swimming pools. Three others, which will also include pools, are being built.

POPULAR SPORTS   Some of the major sports in Britain are described below. Sportsmen may be professionals (paid players) or amateurs. Some sports, such as rugby union football, hockey and rowing, are entirely amateur but in others the distinction between amateur and professional status is less strictly defined.

Association Football   Probably the most popular spectator sport is association football, dating as an organised game from the nineteenth century, and controlled by separate football associations in England, Wales, Scotland and Northern Ireland. In England over 400 clubs are affiliated to the English Football Association (FA) and some 37,000 clubs to regional or district associations.

The principal clubs in England and Wales belong to the Football League (92 clubs) and in Scotland to the Scottish Football League (38 clubs); the clubs play in four divisions in England and Wales and three in Scotland. During the season attendances at Football League matches total about 25 million.

The annual competitions for the FA Challenge Cup, the Football League Cup, the Scottish FA Cup and the Scottish League Cup are organised on a knock-out basis, and the finals (four of the most important matches of the year) are played at Wembley Stadium, London, and at Hampden Park, Glasgow.

National teams representing England, Wales, Scotland and Northern Ireland compete against one another annually and take part in European competitions, the World Cup competition and other international matches.

Attempts have been made to give football clubs closer links with the community in order to overcome problems of hooliganism. The Sports Council, using specially allocated funds, has made grants to a number of clubs to enable them to modernise or expand football and other sporting facilities which will attract young people.

Athletics

In England amateur athletics (including track, road and cross-country running, relay racing, jumping, vaulting, hurdling, steeplechasing, throwing and race walking) are governed, for men, by the Amateur Athletic Association and, for women, by the Women's Amateur Athletic Association. Scotland, Wales and Northern Ireland have their own associations and, as in England, there are separate women's associations. The various organisations encourage the development of the sport, establish uniform rules and regulations and promote regional and national championships. Hundreds of clubs are affiliated to the various national associations.

International athletics and the selection of British teams are the concern of the British Amateur Athletic Board which is composed of representatives of the national associations. For the Olympic Games one team represents the United Kingdom but England, Wales, Scotland and Northern Ireland compete separately in the Commonwealth Games and also organise their own international meetings. The Board also administers coaching schemes.

The Highland Games

The Highland Games, traditional gatherings of local people in the Highlands of Scotland, at which sports (including tossing the caber, putting the weight and throwing the hammer) and dancing and piping competitions take place, are unique spectacles which attract large numbers of spectators from all over the world. Among better-known Highland Games are the annual Braemar Gathering (traditionally attended by the Royal Family), the Argyllshire and Cowal Gatherings and the meeting at Aboyne.

Boxing

Boxing as a British sport is one of the oldest, probably originating in Saxon times. Its modern form, also adopted in many overseas countries, dates from 1865 when the Marquess of Queensberry drew up a set of rules eliminating much of the brutality that had characterised prize fighting and making skill the basis of the sport. Boxing is both amateur and professional; and in both, strict medical regulations are observed.

The Amateur Boxing Association controls all amateur boxing in England including schoolboy, club and association boxing, and boxing in the armed services. There are separate associations in Scotland and Wales. Northern Ireland forms part of the Irish Amateur Boxing Association. The associations organise various amateur boxing competitions, and teams from England, Wales, Scotland and Northern Ireland take part in international competitions.

Professional boxing is controlled by the British Boxing Board of Control, founded in 1929. The Board appoints inspectors, medical officers and representatives to ensure that regulations are observed and to guard against over-matching and exploitation.

Cricket

Cricket is among the most popular of summer sports and is sometimes called the English national game. It is known to have been played as early as the 1550s. Among the many clubs founded in the eighteenth century is the Marylebone Cricket Club (MCC) which was founded in London and which reframed the laws of the game. Cricket in Britain is now governed by the Cricket Council which consists of representatives of the MCC, the Test and County Cricket Board (representing first class cricket) and the National Cricket Association (representing club and junior cricket).

The game is played in schools, colleges and universities, and in most towns and villages there are amateur teams which play weekly games from late April to the end of September. In the Midlands and the north of England there is a network of League cricket contested by teams of Saturday afternoon players reinforced by professionals, some of whom come from overseas.

Some of the best supported games are the annual series of five-day sponsored Test Matches played between England and a touring team from Australia, New Zealand, India, Pakistan or the West Indies. A team representing England usually tours one or more of these countries in the British winter. One-day international games also attract large crowds. A World Cup is played every four years, with some of the smaller cricketing nations as well as the major countries competing. There is also a sponsored First Class County Championship of three-day games played by 17 county teams who also take part in three one-day sponsored competitions—two of these are knock-out competitions and the other is a Sunday League.

Cricket is also played by women and girls, the governing body being the Women's Cricket Association, founded in 1926. Women's cricket clubs have regular week-end fixtures, and junior sides play largely six-a-side competitions. Test match series are played against Australia, New Zealand and the West Indies and other international games take place.

Field Sports

The British Field Sports Society looks after the interests of all field sports (including hunting, game shooting, falconry and hare coursing). The Society is a member of the British Shooting Sports Council which is the representative body of recreational shooting.

Fox hunting on horseback with a pack of hounds is the most popular British hunting sport but there is also stag hunting, and hunting the hare. The fox hunting season lasts from early November to April; there are over 320 packs of hounds of all kinds in Britain. The sport is not without its critics, but a large number of people take a keen interest in it.

Game shooting as an organised country sport probably originated in the early part of the nineteenth century. Game consists of grouse, black-grouse, partridge, pheasant and ptarmigan, species which are protected by law during a close season when they are allowed to breed on numerous estates supervised by game-keepers who are employed on private property as well as by bodies such as the Forestry Commission. It is necessary to have a licence to kill game, and a certificate must be obtained from the local police by anyone who owns, buys or acquires a shot gun. The Game Conservancy, formed by landowners, farmers and others interested in game conservation, collects information and studies factors controlling game population.

The most popular country sport is fishing, and there are about 4 million anglers in Britain. Many fish for salmon and trout particularly in the rivers and lochs of Scotland, but in England and Wales the most widely practised form of fishing is for coarse fish such as pike, perch, carp, roach, dace, tench, chub and bream. Angling clubs affiliate to the National Federation of Anglers and many clubs organise angling competitions. National championships are organised by the Federation which also enters a team in the World Angling Championship. Freshwater fishing usually has to be paid for; most coarse fishing is let to angling clubs by private owners, while trout and salmon fishermen either rent a stretch of river, join a club, or pay for the right to fish by the day, week or month. Coastal and deep sea fishing are free to all (apart from salmon and sea trout fishing which is by licence only). In Northern Ireland the Ulster Provincial Council of the Irish Federation of Sea Anglers, the Ulster Coarse Angling Federation and the Ulster Angling Federation look after the interests of the sport. In Wales all angling is the responsibility of the Welsh Anglers Council.

Golf

Golf originated in Scotland where it has for centuries borne the title of the Royal and Ancient Game, the headquarters of the Royal and Ancient Golf Club being situated at St. Andrews on the east coast. The Club is the international governing body of the sport. Golf is played throughout Britain and there are golf courses in the vicinity of most towns, some of them owned by local authorities. The main event of the golfing year is the Open Golf Championship; other important events include the Walker Cup match for amateurs and the Ryder Cup match for professionals, both of which are played between Britain and the United States.

Lawn Tennis

The modern game of lawn tennis was first played in England in 1872 and the first championships at Wimbledon in 1877. The controlling body, the Lawn Tennis Association, was founded in 1888. The main event of the season is the annual Wimbledon fortnight, widely regarded as the most important tennis event in the world; this draws large crowds, with the grounds at the All-England Club accommodating over 30,000 spectators. There are also county championships and national competitions for boys' and girls' schools. International events include the Davis Cup and Kings Cup for men and the Federation Cup for women. Women from Britain and the United States compete for the Wightman Cup.

Motor Sports

Among the most popular spectator sports are motor racing and motor rallying. The governing body, RAC (Royal Automobile Club) Motor Sports Association, issues competition licences to motor clubs registered with it covering all events from hill climbs to full international race meetings. It also organises the British Grand Prix which counts towards the Formula One World Motor Racing Championship, and the RAC Rally which counts towards the World Rally Championship.

Motor cycle racing is governed by the Auto-Cycle Union and the most important events of the year are the Isle of Man Tourist Trophy races, the British Grand Prix, and the TT Formula 1 World Championship. Motor cycle speedway racing is governed by the Speedway Control Board.

Racing

Horse racing takes two forms—flat racing (from late March to early November) and steeplechasing and hurdle racing (from August to June). The Derby, run at Epsom, is the outstanding event in the flat racing calendar. Other classic races are: the Two Thousand Guineas and the One Thousand Guineas, both run at Newmarket; the Oaks, run at Epsom; and the St. Leger, run at Doncaster. The most important steeplechase and hurdle race meeting is the National Hunt Festival Meeting at Cheltenham. The Grand National, run at Aintree near Liverpool, is the best known steeplechase.

The Jockey Club administers all horse racing in Britain. Its rules are the basis of turf procedure and it also licenses racecourses. Racing takes place on most weekdays throughout the year and about 12,400 horses are in training.

The racing of greyhounds after a mechanical hare (considered to be among Britain's most popular spectator sports) takes place at 105 tracks licensed by local authorities. Meetings are usually held two or three times a week at each track, up to a maximum of 130 days a year. Rules for the sport are drawn up by the National Greyhound Racing Club; overall administration and organisation is the responsibility of the British Greyhound Racing Board.

Riding

The authority responsible for equestrian activities (other than racing) at international level is the British Equestrian Federation which co-ordinates the work of the British Horse Society and the British Show Jumping Association.

At national level the British Horse Society promotes the welfare of horses and ponies, the interests of horse and pony breeding and the art of riding. It provides information, publications, a film library, courses and examinations and, together with riding schools approved by it, helps to promote horse-mastership. It also runs the British Equestrian Centre at Kenilworth, Warwickshire, where activities take place throughout the year. With some 30,000 members the Society is the parent body of the Pony Club and the Riding Club movement. These hold rallies, meetings and competitions, culminating in their annual national championships at the British Equestrian Centre.

Horse trials are held during the spring and summer under the auspices of the Society. The three-day events held each year are at Badminton (Avon) in April, Windsor (Berkshire) in May, Bramham (Yorkshire) in June, Burghley House (Lincolnshire) in September, and Wylye (Wiltshire) in October, and include dressage, cross-country riding and show jumping.

Show jumping is promoted by the British Show Jumping Association which draws up competition rules and prescribes the general standards and height of obstacles. The Association keeps a register of horses and ponies taking part in shows and seeks to improve the standard of jumping and to provide for British representation in international competitions. It has over 16,000 members and 1,250 shows are affiliated to it. The major show jumping events each year include the Royal International Horse Show, the Horse of the Year Show, and the Birmingham International Show Jumping Championships.

Rugby Football

Rugby football is played according to two different sets of rules: Rugby Union (a 15-a-side game) is played by amateurs while Rugby League (a 13-a-side game) is played by professionals as well as amateurs.

Rugby Union is played throughout Britain under the auspices of the Rugby Football Union (in England), the Welsh Rugby Union, the Scottish Rugby Union and the Irish Rugby Football Union. International matches between England, Scotland, Wales, Ireland and France are played each year and there are tours by international teams.

Rugby League is played mostly in the north of England. The governing body of the professional game is the Rugby Football League which sends touring teams to Australia and New Zealand. Annual matches are also played against France. The Challenge Cup Final, the major match of the season, is played at Wembley Stadium in London. The amateur game is governed by the British Amateur Rugby League Association. An international championship is played annually between England, Scotland and Wales (competing as one team), Ireland and France.

Sailing

Sailing has always been popular on Britain's inland and coastal waters. The Royal Yachting Association has over 1,450 affiliated clubs, 65,000 personal members and approximately 600 recognised teaching centres in the country, including the National Sailing Centre at Cowes in the Isle of Wight where courses are available in all branches of the sport. One of the world's principal regattas takes place each year at Cowes, and major events are held at other British sailing centres.

Swimming

Swimming is enjoyed by millions of people in Britain, many of whom learn to swim at public baths, schools or swimming clubs. Instruction and coaching is provided by qualified teachers who hold certificates awarded by the Amateur Swimming Association, to which over 1,700 clubs are affiliated. The Association also draws up and enforces regulations for amateur swimming, diving, synchronised swimming and water polo championships and competitions in England. Separate associations control the sport in Scotland and Wales. Northern Ireland forms part of the Irish Amateur Swimming Association.

Underwater swimming (sub-aqua) is governed nationally by the British Sub-Aqua Club which promotes underwater exploration, science and sport. Formed in 1953, the club has become the largest in the world with some 30,000 members and more than 1,000 branches in Britain and overseas.

Other Sports

The governing bodies of some other sports played in Britain are given below. Most are organised on the basis of clubs and regional organisations linked to a national body. Many of the sports have separate national bodies for England, Scotland, Wales and Northern Ireland.

Sport	Governing Body
Aerosports:	
Private Flying	Aircraft Owners and Pilots Association
Gliding	British Gliding Association
Hang Gliding	British Hang Gliding Association
Parachuting	British Parachuting Association
Archery	Grand National Archery Society
Badminton	Badminton Association of England
Basket Ball	British and Irish Basketball Federation
Billiards and Snooker	Billiards and Snooker Control Council
Bowls	British Isles Bowling Council
Canoeing	British Canoe Union
Croquet	Croquet Association
Curling	Royal Caledonian Curling Club
Cycling:	
Cycle Racing	British Cycling Federation
Touring	Cyclists' Touring Club
Darts	British Darts Organisation

Fencing	Amateur Fencing Association
Gymnastics	British Amateur Gymnastics Association
Hockey	Hockey Association (men)
	All England Women's Hockey Association
Jogging	National Jogging Association
Judo	British Judo Association
Karate	British Karate Control Commission
Lacrosse	All England Women's Lacrosse Association
	English Lacrosse Union (men)
Mountaineering	British Mountaineering Council
Netball	All England Netball Association
Orienteering	British Orienteering Federation
Polo	Hurlingham Polo Association
Race Walking	Race Walking Association
Rowing	Amateur Rowing Association
Shooting (Target)	British Shooting Sports Council
	National Rifle Association
	National Small-Bore Rifle Association
	Clay Pigeon Shooting Association
Skateboarding	Skateboard Association
Skating	National Skating Association of Great Britain
Skiing	National Ski Federation of Great Britain
Squash Rackets	Squash Rackets Association
Surfing	British Surfing Association
Table Tennis	English Table Tennis Association
Tenpin Bowling	British Tenpin Bowling Association
Volleyball	British Volleyball Federation
Water Skiing	British Water Ski Federation
Weightlifting	British Amateur Weightlifters' Association
Wrestling	English Olympic Wrestling Association

GAMBLING   Various forms of betting and commercial gaming are permitted under strict regulations and the total money staked in Great Britain in 1979 was about £5,100 million. It is estimated that some 94 per cent of adults gamble at some time or another, 39 per cent regularly.

Gaming includes the playing of casino and card games, gaming machines and licensed bingo, thought to be played by about 5 to 6 million people on a fairly regular basis. Betting takes place mainly on horse and greyhound racing, and on football matches (usually through football pools). Racing bets may be made at racecourses and greyhound tracks, or through some 12,000 licensed off-course betting offices which take nearly 90 per cent of the money staked. A form of pool betting (totalisator betting) is organised on, and off, course by the Horserace Totalisator Board (HTB). Bookmakers and the HTB contribute a 'betting levy' to the Horserace Betting Levy Board which promotes the improvement of horseracing and horsebreeding and the advancement of veterinary science.

In addition legislation allows local authorities and certain bodies to hold lotteries.

Appendix

Currency

The unit of currency is the pound sterling divided into 100 new pence (p). There are six denominations: 50p; 10p; 5p; 2p; 1p; and ½p.

Bank of England notes are issued for sums of £1, £5, £10 and £20. A £50 note is to be introduced in 1981.

Metric Equivalents for British Weights and Measures

Length

		1 inch	=	2·54 centimetres
12 inches	=	1 foot	=	30·48 centimetres
3 feet	=	1 yard	=	0·914 metre
1,760 yards	=	1 mile	=	1·609 kilometres

Area

		1 square inch	=	6·451 square centimetres
144 square inches	=	1 square foot	=	929·03 square centimetres
9 square feet	=	1 square yard	=	0·836 square metre
4,840 square yards	=	1 acre	=	0·405 hectare
640 acres	=	1 square mile	=	2·59 square kilometres

Capacity

		1 pint	=	0·568 litre
2 pints	=	1 quart	=	1·136 litres
4 quarts	=	1 gallon	=	4·546 litres
8 gallons	=	1 bushel	=	36·37 litres
8 bushels	=	1 quarter	=	2·909 hectolitres

Weight (Avoirdupois)

	=	1 ounce (oz.)	=	28·35 grammes
16 oz.	=	1 pound (lb.)	=	0·454 kilogramme
14 lb.	=	1 stone (st.)	=	6·35 kilogrammes
112 lb.	=	1 hundredweight (cwt.)	=	50·8 kilogrammes
20 cwt. (2,240 lb.)	=	1 long ton	=	1·016 tonnes
2,000 lb.	=	1 short ton	=	0·907 tonne

Double Conversion Tables for Measures and Weights

(Note: the central figures represent either of the two columns beside them, as the case may be, for example, 1 centimetre = 0·394 inch, and 1 inch = 2·540 centimetres.)

Centi-metres		inches	Metres		Yards	Kilo-metres		Miles	Hec-tares		Acres
2·540	1	0·394	0·914	1	1·094	1·609	1	0·621	0·405	1	2·471
5·080	2	0·787	1·829	2	2·187	3·219	2	1·243	0·809	2	4·942
7·620	3	1·181	2·743	3	3·281	4·828	3	1·864	1·214	3	7·413
10·160	4	1·575	3·658	4	4·374	6·437	4	2·485	1·619	4	9·884
12·700	5	1·969	4·572	5	5·468	8·047	5	3·107	2·023	5	12·355
15·240	6	2·362	5·486	6	6·562	9·656	6	3·728	2·428	6	14·826
17·780	7	2·756	6·401	7	7·655	11·266	7	4·350	2·833	7	17·298
20·320	8	3·150	7·315	8	8·749	12·875	8	4·971	3·237	8	19·769
22·860	9	3·543	8·230	9	9·843	14·484	9	5·592	3·642	9	22·240
25·400	10	3·937	9·144	10	10·936	16·094	10	6·214	4·047	10	24·711

Kilo-grammes		Av. Pounds	Litres		Pints	Litres		Gallons	Metric Quintals per Hectare		Hun-dred-weight per Acre
0·454	1	2·205	0·568	1	1·760	4·546	1	0·220	1·255	1	0·797
0·907	2	4·409	1·136	2	3·520	9·092	2	0·440	2·511	2	1·593
1·361	3	6·614	1·705	3	5·279	13·638	3	0·660	3·766	3	2·390
1·814	4	8·818	2·273	4	7·039	18·184	4	0·880	5·021	4	3·186
2·268	5	11·023	2·841	5	8·799	22·730	5	1·100	6·277	5	3·983
2·722	6	13·228	3·409	6	10·559	27·276	6	1·320	7·532	6	4·780
3·175	7	15·432	3·978	7	12·319	31·822	7	1·540	8·787	7	5·576
3·629	8	17·637	4·546	8	14·078	35·368	8	1·760	10·043	8	6·373
4·082	9	19·842	5·114	9	15·838	40·914	9	1·980	11·298	9	7·169
4·536	10	22·046	5·682	10	17·598	45·460	10	2·200	12·553	10	7·966

Thermometrical Table

0° Centigrade = 32° Fahrenheit.

100° Centigrade = 212° Fahrenheit.

To convert °Fahrenheit into °Centigrade: subtract 32, then multiply by $\frac{5}{9}$; °Centigrade into °Fahrenheit: multiply by $\frac{9}{5}$, then add 32.

Bibliography

This bibliography is in no sense comprehensive: it is intended only as a guide to further reading on the subjects covered in this handbook.

Readers are asked to note that in Britain the Central Office of Information reference documents marked with an asterisk (*) may be obtained, on payment of a charge, from the Central Office of Information, Publications Division Distribution Unit, Hercules Road, London SE1 7DU; and overseas they may be obtained from British Information Offices. Entries marked with a dagger (†) are also published in paperback form. Those marked with a double dagger (‡) are overseas publications and the prices given apply only to Britain.

Certain reference pamphlets produced by the Central Office of Information can be purchased from Her Majesty's Stationery Office and its agents overseas. These pamphlets are listed here with their respective prices (postage extra).

Acts of Parliament referred to in the text can be obtained at various prices from H.M. Stationery Office and its agents overseas.

International Standard Book Numbers (ISBN) should be quoted when ordering publications. So that readers will be supplied with the latest edition no ISBNs are given for annual and periodical publications.

1 The Land and the People

Physical Background

	ISBN		£
Chandler, T. J. and Gregory, S., *Editors.* The Climate of the British Isles *Longman*	0 582 48558 4	1976	8·25
Cheatle, J. R. W. A Guide to the British Landscape *Collins*	0 00 219240 3	1976	3·95
Martin, W. Keble. A Concise British Flora in Colour *Sphere Books*	0 7221 0503 7	1979	4·50
Peterson, Roger; Mountfort, Guy and Hollom, P. A. D. A Field Guide to the Birds of Britain and Europe *Collins*	0 00 219177 6	1974	5·50
Phillips, R. Wild Flowers of Britain *Pan*	0 330 25183 X	1977	4·95
Stamp, L. Dudley and Beaver, S. H. The British Isles: A Geographic and Economic Survey, 6th rev. edn. *Longman*	0 582 48144 9	1971	13·50
Trueman, A. E. Geology and Scenery in England and Wales, Rev. edn. *Penguin*	0 14 020185 8	1972	2·50
British Regional Geology Handbooks. *HMSO*		1947 to 1978	0·40 to 2·25
Meteorological Office Annual Report. *HMSO*		Annual	

Demographic Background

	ISBN		£
Halsey, A. H. Change in British Society			
Oxford University Press	0 19 289119 7	1978	1·95
Kelsall, R. K. Population, 4th edn.			
Longman	0 582 29005 8	1979	2·95
Census 1971, various reports. *HMSO*			Various
Demographic Review. *HMSO*	0 11 690680 4	1978	2·75
Population Trends. *HMSO*		Quarterly	
Ulster Year Book. *Belfast, HMSO*		Annual	
1981 Census of Population. Cmnd 7146. *HMSO*	0 10 171460 2	1978	0·40

Annual Reports and Statistics:
Family Expenditure Survey. *HMSO*
General Household Survey. *HMSO*
Office of Population, Censuses and Surveys Annual Series
of Statistics: A series of volumes covering medical and
population statistics. *HMSO*
Registrar General, Northern Ireland
Belfast, HMSO
Registrar General, Scotland:
Part I. Mortality Statistics. *HMSO*
Part II. Population and Vital Statistics. *HMSO*
Social Trends. *HMSO*

2   Government

General Survey

	ISBN		£
Alderman, G. British Elections: Myth and Reality			
Batsford	0 7134 0196 6	1978	3·50
Bromhead, P. Britain's Developing Constitution			
Allen & Unwin	0 04 320100 8	1974	3·95
Butler, David and Sloman, Anne.			
British Political Facts, 1900–1979			
Macmillan	0 333 25591 7	1980	20·00
de Smith, S. A. Constitutional and Administrative Law.			
3rd edn.			
Penguin	0 14 080223 1	1977	4·50
Hartley, T. C. and Griffith, J. A. G. Government and the			
Law. *Weidenfeld & Nicolson*	0 297 76792 5	1975	5·50
Keir, *Sir* D. Lindsay. The Constitutional History of			
Modern Britain since 1485. 9th edn.			
A & C Black	0 7136 0939 7	1969	5·00
Minogue, M., *Editor.* Documents on Contemporary			
British Government: Vol. 1. British Government and			
Constitutional Change			
Cambridge University Press	0 521 29148 8	1977	4·95
Vol. 2. Local Government in Britain			
Cambridge University Press	0 521 29147 X	1977	4·95
Phillips, O. H. and Jackson, P. O. Hood Phillips'			
Constitutional and Administrative Law. 6th edn.			
Sweet and Maxwell	0 421 23980 8	1978	6·00
Yardley, D. C. M. Introduction to British Constitutional			
Law. 5th edn.			
Butterworth	0 406 69006 5	1978	4·95
The Government of Northern Ireland. Proposals for			
Further Discussion. Cmnd 7950. *HMSO*	0 10 179500 9	1980	1·50

The Monarchy

	ISBN		£
Burke's Guide to the Royal Family			
Burke's Peerage	0 85011 015 7	1973	12·50
Howard, Philip. The British Monarchy			
in the Twentieth Century			
Hamish Hamilton	0 241 89564 2	1977	7·50
Longford, Elizabeth. The Royal House of Windsor			
Sphere Books	0 7221 5599 9	1976	2·50

Parliament

	ISBN		£
The Monarchy in Britain. (COI Reference Pamphlet R5526/77) No. 118. *HMSO*	0 11 700915 6	1977	0·90
The BBC Guide to Parliament (in association with *The House Magazine*) *BBC*	0 563 17748 9	1979	4·50
Dod's Parliamentary Companion *Dod's Parliamentary Companion Ltd.*		Annual	
May, Erskine. Parliamentary Practice. 19th edn. *Butterworth*	0 406 29102 0	1976	25·00
Raison T. Power and Parliament *Blackwell*	0 631 11301 0	1979	5·95
Robinson, A. Parliament and Public Spending. The Expenditure Committee of the House of Commons, 1970–76 *Heinemann*	0 435 83750 8	1978	8·75
Rose, Richard. Politics in England: An Interpretation for the 1980s *Faber*	0 571 8023 X	1980	4·95
——The Problem of Party Government *Penguin*	0 14 021954 4	1976	1·60
Stacey, F. Ombudsmen Compared *Oxford University Press*	0 19 827420 3	1978	10·00
Taylor, Eric. The House of Commons at Work *Macmillan*	0 333 23319 0	1979	7·95†
Walkland, S. A. and Ryle, M., *Editors.* The Commons in the 70's *Fontana*	0 00 634497 6	1977	1·50
Bond, Maurice. Guide to the Records of Parliament *HMSO*	0 11 700351 4	1971	3·25
——**and Beamish, David**. The Lord Chancellor *HMSO*	0 11 700573 8	1977	1·25
The British Parliament. (COI Reference Pamphlet 56/RP/80) No. 33. *HMSO*	0 11 701006 5	1980	3·30
Factsheets on various aspects of the House of Commons and its work. *House of Commons Public Information Office*		1979 to 1980	Free
House of Commons. First Report from the Select Committee on Procedure, Session 1977–78. (Contains proposals for new system of select committees) *HMSO*	0 10 297878 6	1978	3·25
Organisation of Political Parties in Britain. Reference Paper R4769/77. *COI*		1977	*
Parliamentary Elections in Britain. (COI Reference Pamphlet R5513/78) No. 159. *HMSO*	0 11 700977 6	1978	0·65

The Prime Minister, The Cabinet, Government Departments, the Civil Service

	ISBN		£
Blake, Robert. The Office of Prime Minister *British Academy*	0 85672 119 0	1975	4·00
Brown, R. G. S. and Steel, D. R. The Administrative Process in Britain. 2nd edn. *Methuen*	0 416 85890 2	1979	8·50†
Hanson, A. H. and Walles, M. Governing Britain *Fontana*	0 00 632374 X	1976	1·75
Headey, Bruce. British Cabinet Ministers *Allen & Unwin*	0 04 320098 2	1974	12·50
Mackintosh, John P. The British Cabinet. 3rd edn. *Stevens*	0 420 44680 X	1977	6·70
——The Government and Politics of Britain. 4th edn. *Hutchinson University Library*	0 09 131341 4	1977	2·95
Central Government of Britain. (COI Reference Pamphlet 21/RP/79) No. 40. *HMSO*	0 11 701002 2	1979	2·25
The Civil Service. Report of the Committee 1966–68 [Fulton Report]. Cmnd 3638. *HMSO*	0 10 136380 X	1968	0·87½

	ISBN		£
House of Commons. Eleventh Report from the Expenditure Committee, Session 1976–77. The Civil Service: Vol. 1. Report. *HMSO*	10 10 297477 2	1977	1·60
Government Observations on the Eleventh Report from the Expenditure Committee, Session 1976–77. Cmnd 7117. *HMSO*	0 10 171170 0	1978	0·50
The United Kingdom's Overseas Representation. Cmnd 7308. *HMSO*	0 10 173080 2	1978	1·35

Annual Reports:
Her Majesty's Civil Service Commissioners, *CSC*
Parliamentary Commissioner for Administration. *HMSO*

Local Government

Arnold-Baker, Charles. The Local Government Act 1972 *Butterworth*	0 406 11280 0	1973	8·00
Cross, C. A. Principles of Local Government Law *Sweet & Maxwell*	0 421 19240 2	1974	5·45
Hepworth, N. P. The Finance of Local Government. 4th edn. *Allen & Unwin*	0 04 352072 3	1978	5·50
Minogue, Martin, *Editor.* A Consumer's guide to Local Government *Macmillan*	0 333 23763 3	1977	1·95
Municipal Year Book and Public Services Directory *Municipal Publications*		Annual	
Redcliffe-Maud, *Lord* **and Wood, Bruce**. English Local Government Reformed *Oxford University Press*	0 19 888091 X	1974	1·75
Richards, Peter G. The Reformed Local Government System. 4th edn. *Allen & Unwin*	0 04 352090 1	1980	3·95
——and **Keith-Lucas, Bryan**. A History of Local Government in the Twentieth Century *Allen & Unwin*	0 04 352071 5	1978	3·50
Schofield, A. N. Local Government Elections. 8th edn. *Shaw and Sons*	0 7219 0343 6	1979	17·50
Local Government Finance [The Layfield Report]. Cmnd 6453. *HMSO*	0 10 164530 9	1976	5·75
Local Government Finance (the Government's response to the report of the Layfield Committee). Cmnd 6813 *HMSO*	0 10 168130 5	1977	0·70
Local Government Finance in Scotland. Cmnd 6811 *HMSO*	0 10 168110 0	1977	0·55
Local Government in Britain (COI Reference Pamphlet 12/RP/79) No. 1. *HMSO*	0 11 701003 0	1979	2·50
Relations between Central Government and Local Authorities. Report by the Central Policy Review Staff *HMSO*	0 11 700574 6	1977	1·75

The Fire Service

Annual Reports:
H.M. Chief Inspector of Fire Services (England and Wales). *HMSO*
H.M. Inspector of Fire Services for Scotland. *HMSO*

3   Overseas Relations

General

Barber, James, Who makes British Foreign Policy *Open University Press*	0 335 01962 5	1976	2·50
Wallace, William. The Foreign Policy Process in Britain *Allen & Unwin for the Royal Institute of International Affairs*	0 04 327057 3	1977	3·95

	ISBN		£
House of Commons. Fourth Report from the Expenditure Committee, Session 1977–78. The Central Policy Review Staff Review of Overseas Representation:			
Vol. 1. Report. *HMSO*	0 10 283678 7	1978	2·10
Vol. 2. Minutes of Evidence and Appendices. *HMSO*	0 10 283778 3	1978	7·60
House of Commons. Second Report from the Foreign Affairs Committee, Session 1979–80. Foreign and Commonwealth Office Organisation. *HMSO*	0 10 251180 2	1980	4·50
Review of Overseas Representation. Report by the Central Policy Review Staff. *HMSO*	0 11 630803 6	1977	8·50
The United Kingdom's Overseas Representation. Cmnd 7308. *HMSO*	0 10 173080 2	1978	1·35
Britain's Overseas Relations (COI Reference Pamphlet 1/RP/80) No. 163. *HMSO*	0 11 701005 7	1980	2·70

The European Community

	ISBN		£
Paxton, John. A Dictionary of the European Economic Community *Macmillan*	0 333 25854 1	1978	3·95
Swann, Dennis. The Economics of the Common Market *Penguin*	0 14 080189 8	1978	1·95
Wallace, William *Editor.* Britain in Europe. *Heinemann*	0 435 83919 5	1980	10·50†
Britain in the European Community: The Developing Countries. (COI Reference Pamphlet R6030/77) No. 154. *HMSO*	0 11 700938 5	1977	0·75
Developments in the European Communities. *HMSO*		Biennial	
Noel, Emile. The European Community: How it works. *EEC/HMSO*	92 825 1015 8	1979	2·60‡
Treaty establishing the European Economic Community. Cmnd 7460. *HMSO*	0 10 174600 8	1979	3·00
Treaty establishing the European Coal and Steel Community. Cmnd 7461. *HMSO*	0 10 174610 5	1979	1·75
Treaty establishing the European Atomic Energy Community. Cmnd 7462. *HMSO*	0 10 174620 2	1979	1·75
Treaty of Accession to the European Economic Community and the European Atomic Energy Community. Cmnd 7463. *HMSO*	0 10 174630 X	1979	5·00

The Commonwealth

	ISBN		£
Commonwealth Institute Report *Commonwealth Institute*		Annual	
Commonwealth Institute Review. *Commonwealth Institute*		Annual	
Commonwealth Organisations *The Commonwealth Secretariat*		1979	2·00
The Commonwealth Today *The Commonwealth Secretariat*		1977	Free
Report of the Commonwealth Secretary-General 1977–79 *The Commonwealth Secretariat*		1979	Free
A Year Book of the Commonwealth. *HMSO*		Annual	
Britain and the Commonwealth. (COI Pocket Booklet PB 5935/77). *HMSO*	0 11 700923 7	1977	0·90
Britain's Associated States and Dependencies. (COI Pocket Booklet PB 5917/76). *HMSO*	0 11 700795 1	1976	0·40

International Security

	ISBN		£
Arms Control and Disarmament. (COI Reference Pamphlet R6031/77) No. 155. *HMSO*	0 11 700939 3	1977	1·00
Berlin and East-West Relations. (COI Reference Pamphlet R6035/78) No. 157. *HMSO*			
(See also Defence bibliography: p 445)			

The United Nations

	ISBN		£

Annual Report:
Foreign and Commonwealth Office. Report on the proceedings
of the United Nations General Assembly and Security Council
(including British statements on important issues). *HMSO*

Development Assistance

	ISBN		£
Britain and the Developing Countries: Overseas Aid. A Brief Survey. (COI Reference Pamphlet R5762/78) No. 77. *HMSO*	0 11 700980 6	1978	1·00
Britain in the European Community: the Developing Countries. (COI Reference Pamphlet R6030/77) No. 154. *HMSO*	0 11 700938 5	1977	0·75
British Aid Statistics. *HMSO*		Annual	
Development Co-operation. Efforts and Policies of the Members of the Development Assistance Committee. 1979 Review. *OECD/HMSO*	92 64 12019 X	1979	8·40‡
The Second ACP-EEC Convention of Lome. Cmnd 7895. *HMSO*	0 10 178950 5	1980	5·50

Annual Reports:
Commonwealth Development Corporation. *HMSO*
The British Council. *BC/HMSO*
The Crown Agents. *CA*

4 Defence

NATO Facts and Figures *NATO Information Service, Brussels*	1978	
NATO Handbook *NATO Information Service, Brussels*	1979	
Jane's All the World's Aircraft, edited by John W. R. Taylor *Macdonald and Jane's*	Annual	
Jane's Fighting Ships, edited by J. E. Moore *Macdonald and Jane's*	Annual	
Jane's Weapon Systems, edited by R. T. Pretty *Macdonald and Jane's*	Annual	
RUSI and Brassey's Defence Yearbook *Brassey's Publishers Ltd*	Annual	
The Military Balance *International Institute for Strategic Studies*	Annual	
Supply Estimates, Defence. *HMSO*	Annual	
Statement on the Defence Estimates. *HMSO*	Annual	

5 Justice and the Law

The Law

	ISBN		£
Burney, E. Magistrate, Court and Community *Hutchinson*	0 09 139480 5	1979	6·95
Collins, Lawrence. European Community Law in the United Kingdom *Butterworth*	0 406 26920 3	1975	7·80
Draycott, A. T. and Richman, J., *Editors.* Stone's Justices' Manual *Butterworth*		Annual	
Halsbury, Lord. Laws of England. 4th edn. *Editor-in-Chief* Lord Hailsham. 56 vols. *Butterworth*		Various	
Jackson, R. M. The Machinery of Justice in England. 7th edn. *Cambridge University Press*	0 521 29231 X	1977	9·95
James, Philip S. Introduction to English Law *Butterworth*	0 406 60497 5	1976	3·60

	ISBN		£
Kiralfy, A. K. R. The English Legal System			
Sweet & Maxwell	0 421 23890 9	1978	4·25
Owens, Joan Llewelyn. The Law Courts			
Dent	0 460 06665 X	1976	3·60
Pollock, Seton. Legal Aid: the First 25 years			
Oyez	0 85120 263 2	1975	4·50
Walker, D. M. The Scottish Legal System. 4th edn.			
William Green	0 414 00591 0	1976	7·50
——*Editor.* The Oxford Companion to Law			
Oxford University Press	0 19 866110 X	1980	17·50
Wraith, R. E. and Hutchesson, P. G. Administrative Tribunals			
Allen & Unwin	0 04 347002 5	1973	15·00
Criminal Justice in Britain. (COI Reference Pamphlet R5984/78) No. 129. *HMSO*	0 11 700978 4	1978	1·50
The Legal System of Scotland. *HMSO*	0 11 491332 3	1977	1·15
The Legal Systems of Britain. (COI Reference Pamphlet R6000/76) No. 141. *HMSO*	0 11 700792 7	1976	1·10
Royal Commission on Legal Services. Final Report:			
Vol. 1. Report. Cmnd 7648. *HMSO*	0 10 176480 4	1979	12·00
Vol. 2. Surveys and Studies. Cmnd 7648–1. *HMSO*	0 10 176481 2	1979	11·00
Royal Commission on Legal Services in Scotland. Report:			
Vol. 1. Report. Cmnd 7846. *HMSO*	0 10 178460 0	1980	8·50
Vol. 2. Appendices. Cmnd 7846–1. *HMSO*	0 10 178461 9	1980	12·50

Annual Reports and Statistics:
Judicial Statistics (England and Wales). *HMSO*
Civil Judicial Statistics (Scotland). *HMSO*
Council on Tribunals. *HMSO*
Criminal Statistics, England and Wales. *HMSO*
Criminal Statistics, Scotland. *HMSO*
The Law Commission. *HMSO*
The Law Society of Scotland on the Legal Aid Scheme. *HMSO*
Legal Aid – The Law Society and the Lord Chancellor's Advisory Committee. *HMSO*
Scottish Law Commission. *HMSO*

The Police Service

	ISBN		£
Alderson, J. Policing Freedom: A Commentary on the Dilemmas of Policing in Western Democracies			
Macdonald & Evans	0 7121 1815 2	1979	7·50
Critchley, T. A. A History of Police in England and Wales			
Constable	0 09 461490 3	1978	5·50
Leigh, L. H. Police Powers in England and Wales			
Butterworth	0 406 84540 9	1975	5·60
Whitaker, B. The Police in Society			
Eyre Methuen	0 413 34200 X	1979	9·95

Annual Reports:
Commissioner of Police of the Metropolis. *HMSO*
H.M. Chief Inspector of Constabulary. *HMSO*
H.M. Chief Inspector of Constabulary for Scotland. *HMSO*

Penal Systems

	ISBN		£
Bochel, Dorothy. Probation and After-Care: its Development in England and Wales			
Scottish Academic Press	0 7073 0192 0	1976	7·50
Jones, Howard and Cornes, Paul (assisted by **Stockford, Richard**). Open Prisons			
Routledge & Kegan Paul	0 7100 8602 4	1977	8·50
Prisons and the Prisoner: the work of the Prison Service in England and Wales. *HMSO*	0 11 340759 9	1977	5·25

	ISBN		£
Report of the Committee of Inquiry into the United Kingdom Prison Services. Cmnd 7673. *HMSO*	0 10 176730 7	1979	6·00
The Sentence of the Court. A Handbook for Courts on the Treatment of Offenders. *HMSO*	0 11 340146 9	1978	2·00

Annual Reports:
Criminal Injuries Compensation Board. *HMSO*
Parole Board. *HMSO*
Parole Board for Scotland. *HMSO*
Prisons in Scotland. *HMSO*
The Work of the Prison Department. *HMSO*

6   Social Welfare

General

	ISBN		£
Brown, Muriel. Introduction to Social Administration in Britain			
Hutchinson	0 09 131351 1	1977	3·25
Brown, R. S. G. The Management of Welfare: a Study of British Social Service Administration			
Martin Robertson	0 85520 109 6	1975	7·75
Family Welfare Association. Charities Digest			
FWA		Annual	
——Guide to the Social Services			
Macdonald and Evans		Annual	
Hall, Phoebe; Land, Hilary; Parker, Roy and Webb, Adrian. Change, Choice and Conflict in Social Policy			
Heinemann	0 435 82671 9	1975	2·90
Mays, John; Forder, Anthony and Keidan, Olive. Penelope Hall's Social Services of England and Wales. 9th edn.			
Routledge & Kegan Paul	0 7100 8252 5	1975	3·50
National Council of Social Service. Voluntary Social Services: A Directory of National Organisations			
NCSS	0 7199 0956 2	1979	2·95
Oswin, Maureen. Holes in the Welfare Net			
Bedford Square Press/National Council of Social Service	0 7199 0940 6	1978	2·95
Watkin, Brian. Documents on Health and Social Services: 1834 to the present day			
Methuen	0 416 18080 9	1975	2·50
Wilmott, Phyllis. Consumer's Guide to the British Social Services			
Penguin	0 14 020871 2	1978	1·25
Wolfenden Committee. The Future of Voluntary Organisations			
Croom Helm	0 85664 660 1	1978	2·95

Health and Personal Social Services

	ISBN		£
Abel-Smith, Brian. Value for Money in Health Services			
Heinemann	0 435 82006 0	1976	2·95
Barnard, Keith and Lee, Kenneth, *Editors.* Conflicts in the National Health Service			
Croom Helm	0 85664 420 X	1977	6·95
Darnbrough, Ann and Kinrade, Derek (Compilers). Directory for the Disabled: a handbook of information and opportunities for the disabled and handicapped			
Woodhead-Faulkner	0 85941 066 8	1977	4·25
Hall, Phoebe. Reforming the Welfare: the Politics of Change in the Personal Social Services			
Heinemann	0 435 82400 7	1976	5·50
Levitt, Ruth. The Reorganised National Health Service			
Croom Helm	0 85664 657 1	1977	3·50
Pringle, M. L. Kellmer and Naidoo, Sandhya. Early Child Care in Britain			
Gordon and Breach	0 677 05200 6	1975	9·70

	ISBN		£
Sainsbury, Eric. The Personal Social Services			
Pitman	0 273 01097 2	1977	5·95
Patients First. *HMSO*	0 11 320720 4	1979	1·00
Prevention and Health. Cmnd 7047. *HMSO*	0 10 170470 4	1977	1·60
Priorities for Health and Personal Social Services in England *HMSO*	0 11 320654 2	1976	1·60
Report of the Royal Commission on the National Health Service. Cmnd 7615. *HMSO*	0 10 176150 3	1979	8·00
The School Health Service 1908–74. *HMSO*	0 11 270409 3	1976	1·00
Sharing Resources for Health in England: Report of the Resource Allocation Working Party. *HMSO*	0 11 320227 X	1976	1·70
Care of the Elderly in Britain. (COI Reference Pamphlet R5858/77) No. 121. *HMSO*	0 11 700809 5	1977	0·90

Annual Reports:
Central Health Services Council. *HMSO*
Department of Health and Social Security. On the
State of the Public Health. *HMSO*
Health Education Council. *The Council*
Scottish Education Department. Social Work in Scotland. *HMSO*
Scottish Home and Health Department. Health
Services in Scotland. *HMSO*
Scottish Health Service Planning Council. *HMSO*
Supplementary Benefits Commission. *HMSO*

Social Security

Calvert, Harry. Social Security Law			
Sweet & Maxwell	0 421 22120 8	1978	7·25
The Reform of the Supplementary Benefits Scheme. Cmnd 7773. *HMSO*	0 10 177730 2	1979	0·40
Supplementary Benefits Handbook. 6th edn. *HMSO*	0 11 760679 0	1979	1·70

Community Relations

Ethnic Minorities in Society. A Reference Guide *British Council of Churches and the Runnymede Trust*	0 902397 39 7	1976	0·40
Five Views of Multi-Racial Britain: talks on race relations broadcast by BBC TV. *Commission for Racial Equality*	0 902355 79 1	1978	1·00
Smith, David J. Racial Disadvantage in Britain: the PEP Report *Penguin*	0 14 021979 X	1977	1·25
Reflections on Race: Analysis by three prominent churchmen *Community and Race Relations Unit, British Council of Churches*		1980	0·70
Immigration into Britain: Notes on Regulations and Procedures. (COI Reference Pamphlet 62/RP/80) No. 164. *HMSO*	0 11 7010081	1980	2·10
Race Relations in Britain. (COI Reference Pamphlet R5934/77) No. 108. *HMSO*	0 11 700929 6	1977	1·25

Annual Reports:
Commission for Racial Equality. *HMSO*
Control of Immigration: Statistics. *HMSO*

7 Education

Association of Commonwealth Universities. Commonwealth Universities Yearbook *The Association*			Annual
——Awards for Commonwealth University Staff *The Association*			Biennial
——(For the Committee of Vice-Chancellors and Principals of the Universities of the United Kingdom.)			

	ISBN		£
The Compendium of University Entrance Requirements for First-Degree Courses in the United Kingdom			
The Association		Annual	
——Financial Aid for First-Degree Study at Commonwealth Universities			
The Association		Irregular	
——Grants for Study Visits by University Administrators and Librarians			
The Association		Irregular	
——Scholarships Guide for Commonwealth Postgraduate Students			
The Association		Biennial	
British Council and the Association of Commonwealth Universities. Higher Education in the United Kingdom: A Handbook for Students from Overseas and their Advisers			
Longman		Biennial	
Cantor, L. M. Further Education Today. A Critical Review			
Routledge & Kegan Paul	0 7100 0413 3	1979	4·25
——**and Roberts, I. F.** Further Education in England and Wales. 2nd edn.			
Routledge & Kegan Paul	0 7100 7359 3	1972	3·75
Council for National Academic Awards. Directory of First-Degree and Diploma of Higher Education Courses			
CNAA		Annual	Free
——Directory of Postgraduate and Post-Experience Courses			
CNAA		Annual	Free
Dent, H. C. Education in England and Wales			
Hodder & Stoughton	0 340 21488 0	1977	2·45
Education Year Book			
Councils & Education Press		Annual	
Evans, K. The Development and Structure of the English Educational System			
Hodder & Stoughton	0 340 17606 7	1975	5·60†
Furneaux, Barbara. The Special Child: The Education of Mentally Handicapped Children			
Penguin	0 14 080092 1	1969	0·75
Lawson, John and Silver, Harold. A Social History of Education in England			
Methuen	0 416 08680 2	1973	4·95
National Association of Teachers in Further and Higher Education. Handbook of Institutions Providing Both Teacher Training and other Full-time Advanced Courses. *NATFHE/Lund Humphries*		Annual	
National Institute of Adult Education. Yearbook of Adult Education			
National Institute of Adult Education		Annual	
O'Connor, Maureen. Your Child's Primary School			
Pan	0 330 25153 8	1977	0·75
——Your Child's Comprehensive School			
Pan	0 330 25152 X	1977	0·75
Perry, Walter. Open University. A personal account by the first Vice-Chancellor			
Open University Press	0 335 00042 8	1976	8·50
Rutter, Michael. Fifteen Thousand Hours			
Open Books	0 7291 0113 4	1979	3·50
Van der Eyken, William, *Editor.* Education, the Child and Society: A Documentary History 1900–1973			
Penguin	0 14 080341 6	1973	1·20
Wardle, D. English Popular Education 1780–1975			
Cambridge University Press	0 521 29073 2	1976	2·95
Adult Literacy in 1977–78: A remarkable educational advance. *HMSO*	0 11 270480 8	1978	1·75
Bristow, Adrian. Inside the Colleges of Further Education. 2nd edn. *HMSO*	0 11 270331 3	1976	1·20
Aspects of Secondary Education in England. *HMSO*	0 11 270498 0	1979	6·75
Education in Britain. (COI Reference Pamphlet 15/RP/79) No. 7. *HMSO*	0 11 701001 4	1979	1·50

	ISBN		£
Educational Disadvantage and the Educational Needs of Immigrants. Cmnd 5720. *HMSO*	0 10 157200 X	1974	0·15
A Framework for the School Curriculum. *Department of Education and Science*		1980	Free
Health Education in Schools. *HMSO.*	0 11 270456 5	1977	2·50
A Language for Life. Report of the committee on reading and the use of English [Bullock Report]. *HMSO*	0 11 270326 7	1975	7·00
Primary Education in England: A Survey by HM Inspectors of Schools. *HMSO*	0 11 270484 0	1978	3·50
Special Educational Needs (Report of the Warnock Committee). Cmnd 7212. *HMSO*	0 10 172120 X	1978	5·65
University-Industry Relations. Cmnd 6928. *HMSO*	0 10 169280 3	1977	0·50

Annual Reports and Statistics:
British Council. *BC/HMSO*
Council for National Academic Awards. *CNAA*
Education Statistics for the United Kingdom. *HMSO*
Department of Education and Science. *HMSO*
Department of Education for Northern Ireland: Education in Northern Ireland. *Belfast, HMSO*
Northern Ireland Education Statistics. *Belfast, HMSO*
Scottish Education Department: Education in Scotland. *HMSO*
Statistics of Education (6 volumes) England and Wales:
Vol. 1. Schools. *HMSO*
Vol. 2. School Leavers, CSE and GCE. *HMSO*
Vol. 3. Further Education. *HMSO*
Vol. 4. Teachers. *HMSO*
Vol. 5. Finance and Awards. *HMSO*
Vol. 6. Universities. *HMSO*
Statistics of Education in Wales. *HMSO*
Universities Central Council on Admissions (and Statistical Supplement). *UCCA*
University Grants Committee. Annual Survey. *HMSO*

The Youth Service

Eggleston, J. Adolescence and Community. The Youth Service in Britain *Edward Arnold*	0 7131 5887 5	1976	3·50
Jeffs, Anthony J. Young People and the Youth Service *Routledge & Kegan Paul*	0 7100 0347 1	1979	7·50
Thomas, Michael and Perry, Jane. National Voluntary Youth Organisations. PEP Broadsheet No. 550 *Political and Economic Planning*	0 85374 132 8	1975	2·60
The Youth Service and Similar Provision for Young People. *HMSO*			

8   Planning and the Environment

Aldridge, Meryl. The British New Towns: a programme without a policy *Routledge & Kegan Paul*	0 7100 0356 0	1979	10·50
Burke, Gerald. Townscapes *Penguin*	0 14 021821 1	1976	3·50
Civic Trust. Environmental Directory *Civic Trust*	0 900849 89 4	1978	1·20
Cullingworth, J. B. Town and Country Planning in Britain. 6th edn. *Allen & Unwin*	0 04 352060 X	1976	7·95
Garner, J. F. and Crow, R. K. Clean Air—Law and Practice. 4th edn. *Shaw and Sons*	0 7219 0680 X	1976	6·00
Hall, Peter. Urban and Regional Planning *Penguin*	0 14 021725 8	1975	2·25
Heap, Sir Desmond. Outline of Planning Law *Sweet & Maxwell*	0 421 22800 8	1978	7·50

	ISBN		£
Taylor, Ray; Cox, Margaret and Dickins, Ian,			
Editors. Britain's Planning Heritage			
Croom Helm	0 85664 192 8	1975	5·75
An Outline of Planning in the United Kingdom. *HMSO*	0 11 750902 7	1976	2·00
Digest of Environmental Pollution Statistics. No. 2. *HMSO*	0 11 751433 0	1980	5·25
Environmental Planning in Britain. (COI Reference			
Pamphlet R6037/78) No. 9. *HMSO*	0 11 700981 4	1978	1·50
Historic Buildings and Conservation Areas: Policy and			
Procedure. *HMSO*	0 11 751172 2	1977	0·75
Planning in the United Kingdom			
Department of the Environment	0 903197 61 8	1976	10·00
Pollution Control in Great Britain: How it Works. *HMSO*	0 11 751367 9	1978	2·25
River Pollution Survey of England and Wales. *HMSO*	0 11 751020 3	1978	16·00
Royal Commission on Environmental Pollution:			
First Report. Cmnd 4585. *HMSO*	0 10 145850 9	1971	0·95
Second Report. Cmnd 4894. *HMSO*	0 10 148940 4	1972	0·45
Fifth Report: Air Pollution Control: An Integrated			
Approach. Cmnd 6371. *HMSO*	0 10 163710 1	1976	1·75
Sixth Report: Nuclear Power and the Environment.			
Cmnd 6618. *HMSO*	0 10 166180 0	1976	2·65
Seventh Report: Agriculture and Pollution. Cmnd 7644.			
HMSO	0 10 176440 5	1979	6·00

Annual Reports:
Commission for the New Towns. *HMSO*
Countryside Commission (E & W). *HMSO*
Countryside Commission for Scotland. *HMSO*
Nature Conservancy Council. *The Council/HMSO*

9 Housing

	ISBN		£
Hoath, David. Council Housing			
Sweet & Maxwell	0 421 23860 7	1978	4·45
Merrett, Stephen. State Housing in Britain			
Routledge & Kegan Paul	0 7100 0265 3	1979	6·95
Tiplady, David. Housing Welfare Law			
Oyez	0 85120 262 4	1975	4·95
Housing and Social Policies: Some Interactions.			
Report by the Central Policy Review Staff			
HMSO	0 11 630809 5	1978	1·50
Housing Design Bulletins. *HMSO*		Various	
Housing Summary Tables. Census 1971,			
Great Britain. *HMSO*	0 11 690411 9	1974	0·95
National Dwelling and Housing Survey. *HMSO*	0 11 751382 2	1979	8·50

Annual Reports and Statistics:
Digest of Housing Statistics for Northern Ireland
Belfast, HMSO   Biannual
Housing and Construction Statistics, Great Britain
HMSO   Quarterly
Housing Corporation Report
The Corporation   Annual
Local Housing Statistics, England and Wales
HMSO   Quarterly
Report on Research and Development:
Departments of the Environment and Transport
HMSO   Annual
Scottish Housing Statistics
Edinburgh, HMSO   Quarterly

10 The Churches

Handbooks and reports published by
the religious denominations

11   The National Economy

	ISBN		£
Blackaby, F. T., *Editor*. British Economic Policy 1960–74			
Cambridge University Press	0 521 22042 4	1978	20·00
Morris, Derek, *Editor*. The Economic System in the			
United Kingdom. *Oxford University Press*	0 19 877141 X	1980	12·00†
Murphy, Brian. A History of the British Economy			
1086–1970: Part 1. 1086–1740			
Longman	0 582 35033 6	1973	2·75
Part 2. 1740–1970			
Longman	0 582 35034 4	1973	5·25
National Institute Economic Review			
National Institute of Economic and Social Research		Quarterly	
Prest, A. R. and Coppock, D. J. The UK Economy:			
A Manual of Applied Economics			
Weidenfeld & Nicolson	0 297 77533 2	1978	4·95
Wright, John. Britain in the Age of Economic Management.			
Oxford University Press	0 19 219148 9	1980	5·50†
An A to Z of Income and Wealth. *HMSO*	0 11 730118 3	1980	1·25
Economic Trends. *HMSO*		Monthly	
Royal Commission on the Distribution of Income and			
Wealth:			
Report No. 8. Fifth Report on the Standing			
Reference. Cmnd 7679. *HMSO*	0 10 176790 0	1979	7·00

Statistics:
Regional Statistics. *HMSO*		Annual
Annual Abstract of Statistics. *HMSO*		Annual
Digest of Welsh Statistics. *HMSO*		Annual
Monthly Digest of Statistics. *HMSO*		Monthly
National Income and Expenditure. *HMSO*		Annual
Northern Ireland Digest of Statistics. *HMSO*		Biannual
Scottish Abstract of Statistics. *HMSO*		Annual

12   The Framework of Industry

Organisation and Production

Allen, G. C. British Industry and Economic Policy			
Macmillan	0 333 25972 6	1979	12·00
British Standards Institution. Year Book			
BSI		Annual	
Johnson, P. S. *Editor* The Structure of			
British Industry. *Granada*	0 246 11211 5	1980	20·00
Historical Record of the Census of Production			
1907 to 1970. Business Statistics Office,			
Department of Industry. *HMSO*	0 11 512132 3	1979	10·00

Annual Report:
Census of Production. Business Statistics Office,
Department of Industry. *HMSO*
Design Council. *DC*

The Government and Industry

Financial incentives and assistance for Industry		
(and supplements). 3rd edn.		
Arthur Young McClelland Moores and Co.	1980	Free
Guide to Regional Industrial Policy Changes.		
Department of Industry	1980	Free

Annual Reports:
British Tourist Authority. *BTA*
Industries Development Assistance. *Department of
Commerce, Northern Ireland*
Industry Act 1972. Annual Report by the Secretaries
of State for Industry, Scotland and Wales. *HMSO*

National Economic Development Council: sector
working party annual reports. *NEDC*
National Enterprise Board. *NEB*
Scottish Development Agency. *SDA*
Scottish Development Department. *HMSO*
Welsh Development Agency. *WDA*

Consumer Protection and Competition Policy

	ISBN		£
Consumers' Association. The Buyer's Right			
Consumers' Association	0 85202 152 6	1978	3·45
Lowe, R. and Woodroffe, G. Consumer Law and Practice			
Sweet and Maxwell	0 421 23630 2	1980	17·95†
Medawar, Charles. Social Audit Consumer Handbook			
Macmillan	0 333 21666 0	1978	3·95
Swann, Dennis. Competition and Consumer Protection			
Penguin	0 140809 33 3	1979	2·95
A Review of Restrictive Trade Practices Policy. A			
Consultative Document. Cmnd 7512. *HMSO*	0 10 175120 6	1979	2·00

Annual Report:
Office of Fair Trading. *HMSO*

13 Manufacturing and Service Industries

	ISBN		£
Allen, G. C. British Industries and their Organisation			
Longman	0 582 48002 7	1970	4·75
Society of Motor Manufacturers and Traders.			
The Motor Industry of Great Britain			
SMMT		Annual	
British Industry Today: Aerospace. (COI Reference			
Pamphlet R5890/79) No. 104. *HMSO*	0 11 701000 6	1979	2·25
British Industry Today: Chemicals. (COI Reference			
Pamphlet R6025/78) No. 151. *HMSO*	0 11 700933 4	1978	1·75

Annual Reports:
British Aerospace. *HMSO*
British Shipbuilders. *HMSO*
British Steel Corporation. *BSC/HMSO*

Construction

	ISBN		£
House's Guide to the Construction Industry			
House Information Services	0 903716 14 3	1978	14·00
National Economic Development Office. Before you build:			
what a client needs to know about the Construction			
Industry. *HMSO*	0 11 700539 8	1974	1·00

Annual Report:
Building Research Establishment. *HMSO*

Distributive and Service Trades

	ISBN		£
Channon, Derek F. The Service Industries			
Macmillan	0 333 19807 7	1979	20·00
Dawson, John A. The Marketing Environment			
Croom Helm	0 85664 513 3	1979	14·95
Medlik, S. Profile of the Hotel and Catering Industry			
Heinemann	0 434 91248 4	1978	4·95
Advertising and Public Relations in Britain. (COI Reference			
Pamphlet R6016/76) No. 146. *HMSO*	0 11 700803 6	1976	0·65

14   Energy and Natural Resources

Energy

	ISBN		£
Energy Papers, Department of Energy *HMSO*		1975 to 1980	Various
The Windscale Inquiry: Report by the Hon. Mr Justice Parker. Vol. 1. Report and Annexes 3–5. *HMSO*	0 11 751314 8	1978	3·75

Annual Reports and Statistics:
British Gas Corporation. *HMSO*
British National Oil Corporation. *BNOC*
Central Electricity Generating Board. *CEGB/HMSO*
Central Electricity Generating Board. Statistical Yearbook. *CEGB*
Development of the Oil and Gas Resources of the United Kingdom. *HMSO*
Digest of United Kingdom Energy Statistics. *HMSO*
Electricity Council. *EC*
Electricity Council. Statement of Accounts and Statistics. *HMSO*
Electricity. Department of Energy. *HMSO*
National Coal Board. Annual Report and Accounts. *NCB/HMSO*
Northern Ireland Electricity Service. *NIES*
North of Scotland Hydro-Electric Board. *NSHEB*
South of Scotland Electricity Board. *SSEB*
Statistical Review of the World Oil Industry. *British Petroleum Co.*

Non-fuel Minerals

Mineral Resources Consultative Committee: Reports on individual minerals. *HMSO*	1971 to 1979	Various

Annual Reports and Statistics:
Mineral Exploration and Investment Grants Act 1972. Annual Report by the Department of Industry. *HMSO*
United Kingdom Mineral Statistics. Institute of Geological Sciences. *HMSO*

Water

	ISBN		£
Kirby, Celia. Water in Great Britain *Penguin*	0 14 022152 2	1979	1·50
Ground Water. Department of the Environment Water Data Unit. *HMSO*	0 11 751147 1	1978	21·00
Surface Water. Department of the Environment Water Data Unit. *HMSO*	0 11 751244 3	1978	21·50
Water Data 1978. *Department of the Environment Water Data Unit*	0 904871 23 1	1980	Free

Annuals:
National Water Council. *NWC/HMSO*
Reports of the Regional Water Authorities and the Welsh Water Authority. *Water Authorities*

15   Agriculture, Fisheries and Forestry

Agriculture

	ISBN		£
Wormell, P. Anatomy of Agriculture *Harrap*	0 245 53302 8	1978	12·50
The Agricultural Research Service *Agricultural Research Council*		1978	Free
Agriculture in Britain. (COI Reference Pamphlet 55/RP/80) No. 43. *HMSO*			

	ISBN		£
Agriculture into the 1980s: A set of six reports. EDC for Agriculture. *NEDO*	Various	1977	Various
The Common Agricultural Policy *Commission of the European Communities*		1977	Free
Output and Utilisation of Farm Produce in the United Kingdom *Ministry of Agriculture, Fisheries and Food*		Annual	

Annual Reports and Statistics:
Agricultural Development and Advisory Service. *HMSO*
Agricultural Marketing Schemes. *HMSO*
Agricultural Statistics, England and Wales. *HMSO*
Agricultural Statistics, Scotland. *HMSO*
Animal Health. *HMSO*
Annual Review of Agriculture. *HMSO*
Department of Agriculture and Fisheries for Scotland:
Agriculture in Scotland. *HMSO*
Department of Agriculture, Northern Ireland. *Belfast, HMSO*
Farm Incomes in England and Wales. *HMSO*
National Food Survey Committee: Household Food Consumption and Expenditure. *HMSO*

Fisheries

Annual Reports:
Fisheries of Scotland. *HMSO*
Herring Industry Board. *HMSO*
White Fish Authority (and Accounts). *HMSO*

Annual Statistical Tables:
Scottish Sea Fisheries. *HMSO*
Sea Fisheries. *HMSO*

Forestry

Strategy for the UK Forest Industry. *Centre for Agricultural Strategy*	0 7049 0613 9	1980	8·10
Forestry Policy Consultative Document. *HMSO*	0 11 710125 7	1972	0·18
Forestry Commission Guides. *HMSO*			Various

Annual Reports:
Forestry Commission. *HMSO*
Forest Research. *HMSO*

16 Transport and Communications

Inland Transport

Barker, T. C. and Robbins, M. A History of London Transport. Vol. 1. The Nineteenth Century *Allen & Unwin*	0 04 385066 9	1976	3·75
Vol. 2. The Twentieth Century to 1970 *Allen & Unwin*	0 04 385067 7	1976	4·50
Hadfield, Charles. British Canals *David & Charles*	0 7153 6700 5	1980	7·50†
Haresnape, Brian. British Rail 1948–78: A Journey by Design *Ian Allan*	0 7110 0982 1	1979	7·95
Nock, O. S. 150 Years of Main Line Railways *David & Charles*	0 7153 7881 3	1980	5·95
——Two Miles a Minute: The Story behind the Conception and Operation of Britain's High Speed and Advanced Passenger Trains *Patrick Stephens*	0 85059 412 X	1980	7·95

	ISBN		£
British Industry Today: Freight Transport. (COI Reference Pamphlet R5900/79) No. 101. *HMSO*	0 11 700991 1	1979	1·10
Drinking and Driving [Blennerhassett Report]. *HMSO*	0 11 550396 X	1976	1·05
The Highway Code. *HMSO*	0 11 550433 8	1978	0·25
Policy for Roads: England 1980. Cmnd 7908. *HMSO*	0 10 179080 5	1980	3·50
Report of the Advisory Committee on Trunk Road Assessment [Leitch Report]. *HMSO*	0 11 550458 3	1978	7·25
Review of Main Line Electrification: Interim Report. *HMSO*	0 11 550508 3	1979	1·75
Road Haulage Operators' Licensing: Report of the Independent Committee of Inquiry. *HMSO*	0 11 550496 6	1979	4·00
Town Traffic in Britain. (COI Reference Pamphlet R5860/77) No. 130. *HMSO*	0 11 700967 9	1977	0·75

Annual Reports and Statistics:
Basic Road Statistics. *British Road Federation*
British Railways Board. *BRB/HMSO*
British Waterways Board. *HMSO*
London Transport Executive. *LTE*
National Bus Company. *NBC/HMSO*
Northern Ireland Transport Holding Company. *NITHC*
Railway Accidents. *HMSO*
Road Accidents Great Britain. *HMSO*
Scottish Transport Group. *STG*
Transport and Road Research Laboratory. *HMSO*
Transport Statistics Great Britain. *HMSO*

Ports

Annual Reports and Statistics:
Annual Digest of Port Statistics. 2 vols. *National Ports Council*
British Transport Docks Board. *BTDB*

Shipping

	ISBN		£
British Shipping Statistics 1979–80 *General Council of British Shipping*		1980	7·50
International Shipping and Shipbuilding Directory *Benn*		Annual	
United Kingdom Maritime Search and Rescue Organisation 1979. *HMSO*	0 11 512467 5	1979	3·25

Annual Reports and Statistics:
Casualties to Vessels and Accidents to Men. *HMSO*
General Council of British Shipping. *GCBS*

Civil Aviation

	ISBN		£
'Flight' Directory of British Aviation *IPC*	0 617 00283 5	1979	8·50
Report of the Advisory Committee on Airports Policy: The Need for Third London Airport. *HMSO*	0 11 512920 0	1979	2·50
Report of the Study Group on South East Airports: Possible Sites for a Third London Airport. *HMSO*	0 11 512921 9	1979	10·00

Annual Reports:
British Airports Authority. *BAA*
British Airways Board. *BAB/HMSO*
Civil Aviation Authority. *CAA*
CAA Annual Statistics. *CAA*

The Post Office

	ISBN		£
Corby, Michael. The Postal Business 1969–79: A Study in Public Sector Management			
Kogan Page	0 85038 227 0	1979	11·50
Prestel 1980. *Post Office*		1980	4·00
Report of the Post Office Review Committee. Cmnd 6850			
HMSO	0 10 168500 9	1977	2·35

Annual Reports and Accounts:
Cable and Wireless Ltd. *CW*
Post Office. *HMSO*

---

17   Employment

	ISBN		£
Clegg, H. A. The System of Industrial Relations in Great Britain. 3rd edn.			
Blackwell	0 631 17160 6	1976	5·95
Kahn-Freund, Otto. Labour and the Law. 2nd edn.			
Stevens	0 420 45220 6	1977	6·15
Mitchell, Ewan. The Employer's Guide to the Law on Health, Safety and Welfare at Work. 2nd edn.			
Business Books	0 220 66341 6	1979	12·00
Slade, Elizabeth. Tolley's Employment Handbook			
Tolley	0 510 49352 1	1978	6·50
Smith, C. T. B. & others. Strikes in Britain. Manpower Paper No. 15. *HMSO*	0 11 361142 0	1978	6·00
Taylor, Robert. The Fifth Estate: Britain's Unions in the Modern World			
Pan	0 330 25943 1	1980	1·95
Department of Employment Gazette. *HMSO*		Monthly	
Manpower and Employment in Britain: The Role of Government. (COI Reference Pamphlet R5943/77) No. 152. *HMSO*	0 11 700935 0	1977	0·75

Annual Reports and Statistics:
Advisory, Conciliation and Arbitration Service. *ACAS*
British Labour Statistics. Year Book. *HMSO*
Central Arbitration Committee. *CAC*
Certification Office for Trade Unions and Employers' Associations. *COTUEA*
Health and Safety Commission. *HMSO*
Manpower Services Commission. *MSC/HMSO*
Time Rates of Wages and Hours of Work. *HMSO*

---

18   Finance

	ISBN		£
Atkinson, A. B.; Harrison, A. J. and Stark, T. Wealth and Personal Income: Vol. VI. Reviews of United Kingdom Statistical Sources			
Pergamon Press	0 08 022450 4	1978	12·50
Boddy, M. The Building Societies			
Macmillan	0 333 27150 5	1980	10·00†
Clarke, William M. Inside the City			
Allen & Unwin	0 04 332070 8	1979	8·50
Hockley, Graham Charles. Public Finance: an introduction			
Routledge & Kegan Paul	0 7100 0149 5	1979	5·95
Kay, J. A. and King, M. A. The British Tax System			
Oxford University Press	0 19 877105 3	1978	2·95
McRae, H. and Cairncross, F. Capital City, London as a Financial Centre			
Eyre Methuen	0 417 01620 4	1974	0·85
Meade, G. E. The Structure and Reform of Direct Taxation [The Meade Report]			
Allen & Unwin	0 04 336064 5	1978	8·50†

	ISBN		£
Prest, A. R. and Barr, N. A. Public Finance in theory and practice. 6th edn.			
Weidenfeld & Nicolson	0 297 77649 5	1979	8·95
Pringle, Robin. A Guide to Banking in Britain			
Methuen	0 416 81220 1	1975	3·25
Revell, Jack. The British Financial System			
Macmillan	0 333 14925 4	1973	3·95
Self-regulation at Lloyd's. Report of the Fisher Working Party			
Corporation of Lloyd's		1980	20·00
Committee to Review the Functioning of Financial Institutions: Evidence on the Financing of Industry and trade. *HMSO*		1977 to 1979	Various
——Report and Appendices. Cmnd 7937. *HMSO*	0 10 179370 7	1980	10·50
Financial Statement and Budget Report. *HMSO*		Annual	
Financial Statistics. *HMSO*		Monthly	
The Government's Expenditure Plans. *HMSO*		Annual	
Guide to Public Sector Financial Information. No. 1. 1979. H.M. Treasury, Central Statistical Office. *HMSO*	0 11 630759 5	1979	2·50
Insurance Business, Department of Trade. *HMSO*		Annual	
Insurance in Britain. (COI Reference Pamphlet R5787/78) No. 133. *HMSO*	0 11 700984 9	1978	1·25
Monetary Control. Cmnd 7858. *HMSO*	0 10 178580 1	1980	2·50
The Role of the Comptroller and Auditor General. Cmnd 7845. *HMSO*	0 10 178450 3	1980	2·25
Supply Estimates. *HMSO*		Annual	

Annual Reports:
Commissioners of Customs and Excise. *HMSO*
Commissioners of Inland Revenue. *HMSO*
Royal Mint. *Royal Mint*

19   Overseas Trade and Payments

	ISBN		£
Davies, Brinley. The United Kingdom and the World Monetary System			
Heinemann	0 435 84350 8	1975	1·20
Export Credits Guarantee Department. A History of ECGD: 1919–1979			
ECGD		1979	Free
Tew, Brian. The Evolution of the International Monetary System 1945–77			
Hutchinson	0 09 129211 5	1977	3·25
Whiting, D. P. International Trade and Payments			
Macdonald & Evans	0 7121 0952 8	1978	2·95
Overseas Trade Statistics of the United Kingdom. *HMSO*		Monthly	
United Kingdom Balance of Payments. *HMSO*		Annual	

20   Promotion of the Sciences

	ISBN		£
Cameron, Ian. To the Farthest Ends of the Earth: The History of the Royal Geographical Society 1830–1980			
Macdonald General Books	0 354 04478 8	1980	10·95
Cardwell, D. S. L. The Organisation of Science in England. (Rev. edn. 1972)			
Heinemann	0 435 54154 4	1972	1·25
Government Organisation of Science and Technology in Britain. *British Council*	0 900229 22 5	1976	1·50
Highlights of British Science			
The Royal Society	0 85403 104 9	1978	8·25 (8·00 in UK)
Industrial Research in Britain. 8th edn.			
Francis Hodgson	0 85280 171 8	1976	60·00
A Survey of Learned Societies			
The Royal Society	0 85403 086 7	1976	2·00
Biotechnology. Report of a joint working party of the Advisory Council for Applied Research and Development, the Advisory Board for the Research Councils and the Royal Society. *HMSO*	0 11 630816 8	1980	3·00

	ISBN		£
Britain and International Scientific Co-operation. (COI Reference Pamphlet R5814/77) No. 81. *HMSO*	0 11 700970 9	1977	1·75
Framework for Government Research and Development. Cmnd 5046. *HMSO*	0 10 150460 8	1972	0·13
Review of the Framework for Government Research and Development (Cmnd 5046). Cmnd 7499. *HMSO*	0 10 174990 5	1979	1·25
Third Report of the Advisory Board for the Research Councils 1976–1978. Cmnd 7467. *HMSO*	0 10 174670 9	1979	0·70
University-Industry Relations. Cmnd 6928. *HMSO*	0 10 169280 3	1977	0·50

Annuals:
Agricultural Research Council. *HMSO*
Cabinet Office, Government Research and Development.
A Guide to Sources of Information. *HMSO*
Departmental Research:
   Agriculture, Fisheries and Food. *HMSO*
   Employment. *HMSO*
   Energy. *HMSO*
   Environment and Transport. *HMSO*
   Health and Social Security. *HMSO*
   Overseas Development. *HMSO*
   Research and Development Requirements and
   Programmes Report. *Department of Industry*
   Research Establishments Review. *Department of Industry*
Health and Safety Research. *HMSO*
Medical Research Council. *HMSO*
National Research Development Corporation. *NRDC*
Natural Environment Research Council. *HMSO*
Research in British Universities, Polytechnics and Colleges:
Vol. 1. Physical Sciences. *British Library*
Vol. 2. Biological Sciences. *British Library*
Science Research Council. *HMSO*
Social Science Research Council. *HMSO*
United Kingdom Atomic Energy Authority. *HMSO*
Yearbook of the Royal Society of London. *The Royal Society*

21   Promotion of The Arts

The Arts

	ISBN		£
Minihan, Janet. The Nationalisation of Culture. The development of state subsidies to the arts in Great Britain *Hamish Hamilton*	0 241 89537 5	1977	10·00
Redcliffe-Maud, *Lord*. Support for the Arts in England and Wales *Calouste Gulbenkian Foundation*	0 903319 06 3	1976	1·50
White, E. W. The Arts Council of Great Britain *Davis-Poynter*	0 7067 0108 9	1975	8·00

Annual Reports:
Arts Council of Great Britain. *Arts Council/HMSO*
British Council. *HMSO*
Export of Works of Art. Report of the Reviewing
Committee. *HMSO*

Drama

	ISBN		£
Elsom, John. Post-war British Theatre *Routledge & Kegan Paul*	0 7100 0168 1	1979	3·95
Kerensky, Oleg. The New British Drama *Hamish Hamilton*	0 241 89628 2	1977	6·95
Taylor, John Russell. The Penguin Dictionary of the Theatre. *Penguin*	0 14 051033 8	1970	1·25
The Oxford Companion to the Theatre. *Editor,* Phyllis Hartnoll. 3rd edn. *Oxford University Press*	0 19 211531 6	1967	10·00

Music

	ISBN		£
Scholes, Percy. The Oxford Companion to Music. 10th edn.			
Oxford University Press	0 19 311306 6	1970	9·50

Films

	ISBN		£
Betts, Ernest. The Film Business: A History of British Cinema, 1896–1972			
Allen & Unwin	0 04 791028 3	1973	5·50
Screen Violence and Film Censorship (Home Office Research Unit Report). *HMSO*	0 11 340680 0	1977	2·75

Annual Reports:
British Film Fund Agency. *HMSO*
Cinematograph Films Council. *HMSO*
National Film Finance Corporation (and Statement of Accounts). *HMSO*

Visual Arts

	ISBN		£
Guide to Stately Homes, Museums, Castles and Gardens			
Automobile Association	0 86145 010 8	1980	2·50
Historic Houses, Castles and Gardens in Great Britain and Ireland			
ABC Historic Publications		Annual	
Jencks, Charles. Modern Movements in Architecture			
Penguin	0 14 021534 4	1973	2·95
Museums and Art Galleries in Great Britain and Ireland			
ABC Historic Publications		Annual	
Sunderland, John. Painting in Britain 1525–1975			
Phaidon Press	0 7148 1716 3	1976	12·95
Wilson, Simon. British Art: from Holbein to the Present Day. *Bodley Head*	0 370 30131 5	1979	10·00

Literature

	ISBN		£
Atkinson, F. The Public Library			
Routledge & Kegan Paul	0 7100 6690 2	1970	1·80
Harvey, Sir Paul, *Editor.* The Oxford Companion to English Literature. 4th edn.			
Oxford University Press	0 19 866106 1	1967	9·50
Saunders, W. L., *Editor.* British Librarianship Today			
Library Association	0 85365 498 0	1976	8·25

Annual Report:
The British Library. *The British Library*

22   The Press

	ISBN		£
Jenkins, Simon. Newspapers: The Power and the Money			
Faber	0 571 11468 7	1979	1·95
Lee, Allan J. The Origins of the Popular Press in England, 1855–1914			
Croom Helm	0 85664 392 0	1976	9·50
Smith, Robin Callender. Press Law			
Sweet & Maxwell	0 421 23450 4	1978	3·05
Contempt of Court: a Discussion Paper. Cmnd 7145. *HMSO*	0 10 171450 5	1978	0·45
Royal Commission on the Press:			
Final Report. Cmnd 6810. *HMSO*	0 10 168100 3	1977	4·25
Final Report: Appendices. Cmnd 6810–1. *HMSO*	0 10 168101 X	1977	2·60
Interim Report: the National Newspaper Industry. Cmnd 6433. *HMSO*	0 10 164330 6	1976	1·50

	ISBN		£
Industrial Relations in the National Newspaper Industry. Cmnd 6680. *HMSO*	0 10 166800 7	1976	5·00
Industrial Relations in the Provincial Newspaper and Periodical Industries. Cmnd 6810–2. *HMSO*	0 10 168102 X	1977	2·60
Analysis of Newspaper Content. Cmnd 6810–4. *HMSO*	0 10 168104 6	1977	5·25
Attitudes to the Press. Cmnd 6810–3. *HMSO*	0 10 168103 8	1977	5·50
Concentration of Ownership in the Provincial Press. Cmnd 6810–5. *HMSO*	0 10 168105 4	1977	2·10
Periodicals and the Alternative Press. Cmnd 6810–6. *HMSO*	0 10 168106 2	1977	1·35
New Technology and the Press. *HMSO*	0 11 730073 X	1975	0·85
Review of Sociological Writing on the Press. *HMSO*	0 11 730074 8	1976	1·05
Studies on the Press. *HMSO*	0 11 730075 6	1977	5·50
The Women's Periodical Press in Britain 1946–76. *HMSO*	0 11 730076 4	1977	1·50

Annuals:
Benn's Press Directory. *Benn*
Press Council Annual Report. *The Council*
Willing's Press Guide. *Thomas Skinner Directories*
Writers' and Artists' Year Book. *A. & C. Black*

23   Television and Radio

	ISBN		£
Briggs, Asa. The History of Broadcasting in the United Kingdom: Vol. I. The Birth of Broadcasting *Oxford University Press*	0 19 212926 0	1961	3·50
Vol. II. The Golden Age of Wireless *Oxford University Press*	0 19 212930 9	1965	4·75
Vol. III. The War of Words *Oxford University Press*	0 19 212956 2	1970	8·00
Vol. IV. Sound and Vision *Oxford University Press*	0 19 212967 8	1979	25·00
Curran, Charles. A Seamless Robe *Collins*	0 00 211864 5	1979	8·95
Goldie, Grace Wyndham. Facing the Nation: Television and Politics 1936–1976 *Bodley Head*	0 370 01383 2	1977	7·50
Television and Radio: Guide to Independent Television and Independent Local Radio. *IBA*		Annual	
Windlesham, Lord. Broadcasting in a Free Society *Blackwell*	0 631 11371 1	1980	7·95
Broadcasting. Cmnd 7294. *HMSO*	0 10 172940 5	1978	1·25
Report of the (Annan) Committee on the Future of Broadcasting. Cmnd 6753. *HMSO*	0 10 167530 5	1977	7·25

Annual Reports:
British Broadcasting Corporation. BBC Handbook. *BBC*
Independent Broadcasting Authority. *IBA/HMSO*

24   Sport and Recreation

	ISBN		£
Arlott, J., *Editor*. The Oxford Companion to Sports and Games. *Oxford University Press*	0 19 211538 3	1975	8·50
Coppock, J. R. and Duffield, B. S. Recreation in the Countryside: A Spatial Analysis *Macmillan*	0 333 15170 4	1975	3·95
Indoor Sports Centres (Sports Council Study). *HMSO*	0 11 750393 2	1972	1·20
Royal Commission on Gambling. Final Report. Cmnd 7200 *HMSO*	0 10 172000 9	1978	7·50

Annual reports are published by the Sports Council, the Scottish Sports Council, the Sports Council for Wales and the Sports Council for Northern Ireland. In addition, most of the organisations concerned with sport publish year-books covering results and records of the previous season and future prospects. Many weekly or monthly periodicals on sport are also published.

Index

Bold type in a sequence of figures indicates main references.

As the main purpose of this book is to inform readers overseas about Britain, organisations and societies are generally indexed under their subject matter rather than under *Association of, British, National, Royal,* etc. (*that is, Accidents, Royal Society for the Prevention of; Archives, National Register of*). In cases where the first word is not separable, however (*for example, Royal Air Force, Royal Society*), entries will be found appropriately.

Items are indexed under England, Northern Ireland, Scotland or Wales only where they are matters peculiar to these countries; otherwise they are indexed under the relevant subject headings.

A

Aberdeen 165, 221, 298, 315, 323, 389
Abingdon 268
Abortion 136
Academic Awards, Council for National 166
Accepting houses 360
Accession Council 21
Accidents:
Industrial 147
road users 304, 305
Royal Society for the Prevention of (RoSPA) 304, 343
Administration Management, Institute of 214
Administrative tribunals 124–5
Admiralty:
Board 94
Court 121
Adoption *see* Children
Adult Education *see* Education
Advertising 47, 180, 260, 414, 420
Association 260
broadcasting 420, 421, 422, 423, **425**
Advisory Committees and Councils *see* relevant subject matter
Advocates 109, 119, 127, 129
Faculty of (Scotland) 127
Aerodromes 318, 320, 321
Aero-engines *see* Aircraft
Aeronautical Research 245, 390, 396
After-care:
prisoners 115, 116, **118**
young offenders 118, 119, 120
Age concern 151
Age distribution *see* Population
Agricultural:
and Horticulture Co-operation, Central Council for 291
colleges and institutes 296, **297**, 301
Common Policy (CAP) 43, 55, 73, 75, 291, **292–3**, 375
Credit Corporation Ltd. 293

Agricultural—*contd.*
Development and Advisory Service (ADAS) **293**, 295, 296
Engineering, National College of 297
Engineers' Association 240
Guidance and Guarantee Fund, European (FEOGA) **43–4**, 77
industry 43, 200, 217, 218, 219, 285, 286–7, 289–90
Inspectorate 341, 342
Intervention Board for, Produce **43–4**, 291, 292
Land Tribunal 294
machinery industry 217, 218, 239–40, 286
Mortgage Corporation Ltd. 293, 363
Produce, Intervention Board for **43–4**, 291, 292
Research Council (ARC) 44, 296, **382–3**, 386, 388
Scientific Services Station 296, 388, 389
Training Board 297
wages boards 341
workers:
 earnings 291
 health and safety 285, 341–3
 numbers 200, 285
 protective legislation 290–1, 292, 342
Agriculture **66–7**, 73, 77, 200, 217, 218, 219, **285–301**
advisory services 286, 295, 296
animal disease control 43, 289, **295**
annual reviews 292
artificial insemination (AI) 287, 289
chemicals, toxic 183, 184, 296
crops 285, 286, **287**, 289, **290**, 389
dairying 285, 286, **288–9**
education and training 296–7
employment in 200, 285, 291
exports 285, 292
farms, number, size and types 4–5, **285–6**
feedingstuffs **287**, 289, 291
Fisheries and Food, Ministry of 43–4, 52, 139, 183, 186, **291**, 292, 295, 296, 300, 301, 388, 389
food supplies, home grown 200, **286**, 287, 288, 289, 290, 291

Agriculture —contd.
grassland 5, 285, **287**, 289
hill farming 285, 286, 289, 293
horticulture **289–90**, 293
infestation control 295, 388, 389
land drainage 5, 43, **294**
levies 292, 294
livestock 285, 286, **287–8**, 289, 291, 295
  imports 291
marketing boards and schemes **290–1**, 292, 293
mechanisation 240, **286**, 291
milk production and distribution **288–9**, 293
pest clearance 295, 296
policy of Government 43–4, 291–2, 295
See also **European Community**, Agricultural price guarantees 77, 293–4
production 200, 285, **286–90**
research see **Research, scientific**
subsidies and grants 291, 292, **293**, 294
veterinary services 295, **296**, 388
Aid to overseas countries see **Finance**
Air:
Force see **Defence** and **Royal Air Force**
freight traffic **319**, 320, 321
operators certificate 320
pollution, prevention of 52, 183, **186–7**, 390
safety 320
Air Transport Users Committee 320
traffic:
  control of 320–1
  Services, National 320
Transport see **Civil Aviation**
Aircraft:
and aero-engines industry 201, 211, 216, 218, 222, 242, 243, 244
aerospace industry 47, 200, 210, 217, **243–5**, 391, 396
  British Aerospace (BAe) 47, 203, 243, 244
  Society of British Aerospace Companies 245
civil 319–23, 390
Establishments, Royal 396
military 99, 243, **244**
research 244, 390
Airdrie 221
Airmail services see **Civil Aviation**
Airports see **Civil Aviation**
Airways, British 204, 318, **319**
Albert Hall, Royal 401
Alcoholics:
drinks:
  consumption 16
  duties on 356
treatment for 135
Aldeburgh (festival) 399
Aldergrove 321, 322
Aldershot 217
Aliens 12
See also **Foreigners**
Allied Command Europe Mobile Forces 95
Ambulance services 136
Amlwch 268
Ancient Monuments 45, 178, 188, 397
Society 188
Angle Bay 268
Anglesey 1, 221
Anglican
Communion 197
Consultative Council 197
Roman Catholic Commission 199
See also **Church**: of England
Angling 428, **434**

Animals 5, 43, **287–9**, 388, 389
Advisory Committee on Animal Experiments 295
control of diseases and pests 43, 289, **295**, 388, 389
imports of 287, 295
Appellate courts 111, 112, 121, 122
Appleton Laboratory 384, 396
Archbishops 25, 37, 196, 197
Architects 408
associations and societies 408
Institute of British, Royal (RIBA) 408
Architectural Heritage Society 178
Architecture 162, 166, 178, **408–9**
Archives, National Register of 410
Area Boards:
electricity 274, 275, 277, 278, 279
gas 268
Argyll 181
Armed Forces see **Defence**
Armenian Church 199
Arms control and disarmament 81–3
Army 93, 94, 95, 96, 97, 98
arms and services 95, 96, 98
Board 94
equipment 99
Museum 406
Reserve Forces 99–100
Staff College 96, 97
See also **Defence**
Airports 217, 219, 318, 321
See also **Civil Aviation**
Arson 114
Art:
collections and exhibitions 398, 406, **407–8**
colleges and schools 164, 165, 166, 397, **408**
Commissions, Royal Fine 408
Exhibitions Bureau 407
galleries and museums 53, 63, **406**
market 405–6
National Exhibition of Children's 408
Royal College of 408
Society for Education through 408
  Pictures for Schools Exhibition 408
Arts 397–411
centres 399
Council of Great Britain **397–8**, 399, 400, 401, 402
festivals 397, **399**, 400
Government support for the 44, 397, 398, 400, 402, 403, 404, 405, 406, 407, 408, 409
regional associations 398, **399**
Royal Academy of 408
Royal Society of 215, **393**
Ashford 297
Ashridge College of Management 214
Associated Press Ltd. 417
Associations see relevant subjects
Astronomy 384–5
Athletics 432
Atomic:
Energy Authority, United Kingdom (UKAEA) 45, 105, 275, 278, 386, **387**
Energy Community European (EURATOM) 73, **387**
See also **Nuclear energy**
Attendance centre (young offenders) 119
Attorney-General 38, **48–9**, 109, 110, 111, 125, 126
Automation 213, 239, 240, 242, 252, 273, 317, 324, 325
Automobile Club, Royal (RAC) 434
Automobiles see **Motor**

Aviation *see* **Civil Aviation**
Aviemore 431
Avonmouth 237
Aylesbury 177

B

Bacon-curing industry 249
Bail 108, 109
Bakery products 249
Balance of Payments 200, 201, 202, 208, 368, 369, **376–80**
Ballet and ballet companies 402, 403
schools 402
Baltic Exchange 315
Bank:
credit cards 259, 359, 362
Deposit 357, **358–9**, 361
European Investment 230
Merchant 360
National Girobank 322, **359**
notes 358, 438
of England 49, 348, **357–8**, 367
rate 358
Bank Holidays 334
Banking system 357–62, 368
Baptist Church 198
Barnsley 219
Barristers 123, 126, **127**, 128
Barry 220
Basingstoke 177, 217
Bath 164, 217, 397, 399
Bedford and Bedfordshire 296, 311, 383
Belfast 11, 50, 165, 178, 197, 244, 245, 296, 303, 307, 314, 319, 321, 405, 406, 407
Ben Nevis 2
Berkeley Laboratories 279, 389
Berkshire 382, 389, 390
Betting and Gambling 47, 121, 356, **437**
Beverage industries 218, 221, 248, **249–50**
Bicycle industry *see* **Cycle industry**
Billingsgate Market 260
Bills, parliamentary *see* **Parliament**
Biochemistry 383, 390, 394
Biology 383, 389, 391
Birds 5–6, 389, 394
Birmingham 11, 50, 164, 199, 218, 243, 260, 309, 321, 322, 324, 343, 344, 394, 401, 402, 403, 407, 410, 429
Birth rate 7, 8–9
Births, registration of 7
Biscuit and cake industry 249
Bisham Abbey Sports Centre 431
Bishops 25, 196, 197
Blackburn 218
Blackpool 219
Black Rod 26
Blind:
education 159
National Library for the 410
supplementary benefits 149
Blood transfusion service 136
Board of Customs and Excise *see* **Customs and Excise**
Board of Inland Revenue *see* **Inland Revenue**
Boating 428, 431
Boilers and boilerhouse plant 218, 239
Bolton 218
Book:
Development Council 409
exhibitions 409
League, National 409

Books 71, 253, **409**
See also **Libraries** *and* **Publishing**
Booksellers' Association 409
Border Forest Park 181
Borough Councils *see* **Local Government, councils**
Borstal institutions and training 119, 120
Boston Spa 410
Botanic Gardens, Royal 390
Botany 390, 394
Bothamsall 267
Boundary Commissions 27, 61
Bournemouth 401
Boxing 432–3
Boys' Clubs, National Association of 172
Bracknell 96, 390
Bradford 11, 164, 219
Bread and flour confectionery industry 249
Brecon Beacons 180
Brewing industry 211, 218, 221, 249
Brickmaking industry 252, 281
Bridges and tunnels 256, 304–5, 312
Brighton 260, 399
Bristol 2, 3, 11, 50, 164, 217, 309, 312, 313, 401, 407
Britannia Royal Naval College 96
British:
Academy 392, 409
Agro Chemical Supply Industry Scheme 184
Airways 204, 318, **319**
    See also **Civil Aviation**
Archaeology Council for 188
Army of the Rhine (BAOR) 95, 98
Association for the Advancement of Science 393
Broadcasting Corporation (BBC) 37, 161, 168, 171, 199, 324, 398, **420–1**, 422, 423, 424, 425, 426, 427
    Monitoring Service 424
    orchestras 398
    radio services 199, **423–4**
    Transcription Service 424
    World Service 424, 426
    See also **Broadcasting**
Council 27, 48, 71–2, **169**, 171, **395–6**, **398**, 404, 409, 427
    scholarships and fellowships 89, 171
Isles:
    area and definition of 1
    climate 3–4, 5
    demographic background 6–12
    fauna 5–6
    geology and topography 2–3
    languages 11–12
    physical background 1–6
    seas 1
    social framework 13–18
    soil and vegetation 4–5
    See also **Population**
Library **409–10**, 411
Museum 382, 394, 406, 407, 409
Overseas Trade Board 48, 50, 71, 375
Standards Institution (BSI) 215
For other organisations with British *as first word of their title see relevant subject*
Brixham 298
Broadcasting: television and radio 48, 161, 165, 168, 169, 171, 398, **420–7**, 428
advertising on 260, 420, 421, 422, 423, 424, **425**
advisory councils and committees 199, 420, 421
authorities 420
channels 422, 423

Broadcasting: television and radio—*contd.*
colour transmission 420, 426
Councils, National 421
educational 161, 165, **168**, 169, 171, 420, 421,
422, 423, 424
Eurovision 426
films 397, 403
frequencies 422, 426
international relations 426–7
licences 420, 421
local stations 420, 421, 422, 423, 424, 425
political 30, 425
press and 417, 419, 424
programme companies 417, 421–2
publications 421
regional 421–2, 425
religious 199, 420, 421, 422
research 426
services:
　cable television 423
　domestic television and radio 18, 168, 420,
　421, 422, 424–5
　external 421, 424
　independent radio 413, 422, 424
　local radio 413, 421, 422, 424, 425
　studios 424–5
　television 18, 161, 165, 168, 413, 422, 423
　transcription 424
　transmitting stations 424–5
technical developments 426
'Teletext' 325
Training in 426, 427
See also **British**: Broadcasting Corporation *and*
independent: Television
Brush industry 254
Buckingham 165
Palace 23, 406
　art gallery 406
Buckinghamshire 389, 431
Buddhists 199
Buddhist Society 199
Budget 202, 348, **350–2**, 353, 354
Community 76
Building:
Agency, National 190, 256
Agrément Board 256
Centres, Association of 256
and civil engineering 256
contractors' plant 256
design and construction 45, 162, 190, 191, 192,
255
employment in 255
industrialised 162, 255, 256
by local authorities 190, 191–2, 194
new towns 190
overseas 256
private 190, 191, 255, 256
production 201
Property Services Agency 45, 255
Regulations 190
research 45, 190, 256, 387
　Establishment (BRE) 69, 90, 190, 256, 387
school 162
societies 191, 260, 364–5
standards 191, 192
　National House Building Council (NHBC) 191
safety regulations 342
Services Research and Information Association
387
See also **Construction** *and* **Engineering**, Civil
Burnley 218
Burton-on-Trent 218
Bury 218

Bus and coach services 51, **307**, 308
National Bus Company 204, 307
Business Statistics Office (BSO) 40
By-elections 26, 28
Byker 185
By-laws 47, 102

C

COI *see* **Information, Central Office of**
Cabinet 20, 23, 35–6, **38–9**, 41, 48, 203
Office 39, **42**, 71
　Central Policy Review Staff 42
　Central Statistical Office 40, 42, 205
　Historical Section 42
　Secretariat 42
Cable:
Television Association of Great Britain 423
Cables *see* **Post Office**
Cables and wires (insulated) industry 217, 241
Calder Hall 277
Calibration Service, British 216, 388
Camberley 96
Camborne 217
Cambridge 36, 104, 165, 217, 382, 385, 386,
388, 406, 407, 410
Cambridgeshire 285
Canals 219, 312
Canning industry, *see* **Food, processing**
Cannock Chase 218
Canterbury, Province of 196
Canvey Island 270
Capenhurst (research centre) 278, 279
Capital gains tax *see* **Taxation**
Caravan
and Camping Sites 180
manufacturing industry 220, 243
Caravanning 17
Cardiff 11, 50, 199, 215, 220, 312, 316, 402, 405,
406, 407, 428, 431
Carnegie United Kingdom Trust 402
Carpets industry 218, 219, 221, 222, **251**
Cars *see* **Motor vehicles**
Car tax 356
Castlewellan 181
Catering trades 210, 239, 257, 260, 261
education 166
Catholic *see* **Church, Roman**
Cell Biology and Disorders Board 383
Celtic language 7, 11–12
Cement industry 217, **252**
Census of:
Population 7, 50, 196
Production 234
Central:
Computer and Telecommunications Agency 42
Council of Physical Recreation 428
Criminal Court 109, 125
Directorate on Environmental Pollution 183
Policy Review Staff 42, 327
Statistical Office (CSO) 40, 41, 205
Cereals:
Authority Home-Grown 287
crops 285, **287**, 290
industry 249
Chambers of Commerce 214, 338
Association of British 214
Chancellor *see* **Lord Chancellor**
Chancellor of the:
Duchy of Lancaster 37, 44, 397, 411
Exchequer 43, 44, 48, 350, 351

Chancellor of the Exchequer—*contd.*
See also **Finance,** Exchequer
Chancery Division (High Court) 121, 122
Channel Islands:
area 1
legislature **19–20**, 24, 36
population 7
reciprocity (national health benefits) 47
relationship with UK and Crown 20, 24, 36, 47
See also **Guernsey** *and* **Jersey**
Chapel Cross 277
Charity Commission 151
Charter services (aircraft) 318, 319, 320
Cheltenham 217, 397, 399
Chemical:
industries 201, 210, 211, 213, 216, 217, 218,
220, 222, 235, 236, **246–7**, 388
plants 216, 239
See also **Engineering**
Cheque cards 359
Cheshire 218, 219, 267, 268, 278, 384, 387
Chief of the Defence Staff 93
Chiefs of Staff Committee 93
Child:
benefit 143, 145, 146
special allowance 146
Children:
adoption of 121, 122, **143**
allowances for 143, **146**, 149
art, drama, films and music 401, 403, 404, 408
care 118, 119, 140, **141–3**
child guidance 136
cinema attendance and clubs 404
employment 343
foster homes 118, 142
handicapped 136, 140, 151
National Society for Mentally Handicapped
151
health centres and clinics 134, 136
homes for 142
in care 46, 118
in trouble 112, **118–20**, 142
National Society for the Prevention of Cruelty
to 142, 151
nurseries 141
orphans 141, 146
school transport 162
voluntary child care organisations 142, 151
Children's:
carriage industry 254
Committee 140
Film Foundation 403, 404
Chilton 384, 385
China:
clay industry 217, 252, 281, 312
manufacture 217, 252, 281
Chiropodists 133, 138
Chocolate and confectionery 217, 219, 248, **249**
Christian Scientists 198
Christchurch 217
Church:
Anglican Communion 197
Anglican Consultative Council 197
Commissioners 197
in Ireland (Presbyterian) 118, 198
in Scotland, Episcopal (Anglican) 118, 145, 197
in Wales (Anglican) 197
of England 21, 25, 27, 37, **196–7**
appointment of senior clergy 37, 196
archbishops 25, 37, 196, 197
bishops 25, 37, 196, 197
Children's Society 151
clergy 27, 196

Church
of England—*contd.*
colleges 197
ecclesiastical courts 197
finance 197
General Synod 196
Laity 196
Lambeth Conference 197
parishes 196
parochial councils 196
provinces and dioceses 196, 197
relations with Monarch 21, 196, 197
relations with State 196
schools 157, 160, 198, 199
social and welfare work 118
of Ireland (Anglican) 27, 196, 197
of Scotland (Presbyterian) 27, 118, 196, 197
General Assembly 37, 197
relations with Monarch 197
social and welfare work 118, 151
of Wales (Presbyterian) 198
Roman Catholic 27, 118, 196, **198–9**
archbishops 198
parishes and dioceses 198
schools 157, 160, 198
social and welfare work 118, 152, 199
Churches 196–9
British Council of 199
co-operation among 199
Council of Christians and Jews 199
Free (non-conformist) 118, **197–8**, 199
Free Church Federal Council 199
social and welfare work 118, 151–2
World Council of 199
Churchill Scholarships 171
Cinemas 403, 404, 405
Citizens Advice Bureau 128, 152, 232
Citizenship 12, 46, 188
Civic Trust 188, 408
Civil:
Courts 121–3
Defence 100
See also **Defence**
engineering *see* **Engineering**
Justice 121–4
law 102, 121
science 44–5, 381, 382, 384
Service 37, 41, 42, **56–60**
administration 40
Arbitration Tribunal 340
categories and classes 57–9
College 42, 58–9
Commission **42**, 58
conditions of service 42, **58–9**
Department 40, **42–3**
earnings 59, 334
labour relations 340
manual workers 57, 59
political and private activities 59–60
recruitment and training 42, **58–9**
security 58
staff associations 59, 340
structure 57
Civil Aviation 51, 200, **318–22**, 371
aircraft 242, 318, **319–20**
aircrew qualifications 320
air freight 319, 320, 321
airports 217, 219, 318, **321**
ownership and control 321
air services 318, 319, 320, 321
Authority (CAA) 318, 320, 321, 322
Airworthiness Division 320
Bristow Helicopters 321

Civil Aviation—*contd.*
British Airports Authority (BAA) 321
British Airways 204, 318, **319**
 Divisions:
 European 319
 Overseas 319
 Travel 319
British Caledonian Airways 319
charter operations 319, 320
earnings 319, 321
Eurocontrol 320
government responsibility 318, 321
helicopter service 319, 320
independent airline companies 319–20
licensing 318, **320**, 321
ministerial responsibility for 51, 318, 321
National Air Traffic Services 319, 321, 322
navigational aids 242, 321, 322
noise control 187, 318
safety measures 320, 342
 Air Transport Users Committee 320
traffic control 318, 320, 342
training 320, 342
See also **Aircraft** *and* **Research**
Clean Air 4, 15, 177, **186–7**
Alkali and, Inspectorate 186, 341
National Society for 15, 188
Clerk:
of the House of Commons 26
of the Parliaments 26
Clerks to the Justice 110, 125
Cleveland 220, 237, 278, 281
Climate 3–4, 5
Climbing 421, 428
Clinical Research Centre 383
Clinics 136, 152
Clock and watch industry 221, 240
Cloth industry 218, 219, 221, 250
Clothing:
Export Council 252
industry 216, 218, 219, 221, **250**, 251, 252
shops 257
Clubs:
social 18, 140
youth 171, 172
Clyde and Clydeside 3, 11, 178, 221, 274, 313
Coal:
and Steel Community, European (ECSC) 72, 77
Board, National (NCB) 203, 210, 262, **271**, 273,
274, 344
 non-mining activities 271
capital investment **273**
coalfields and mines 2, 218, 219, 220, 262, 271,
273
consumption 263, 274
exports and imports 271, 274, 313
financial structure 273
industry 45, 201, 210, 218, 219, 220, 262, 271,
273, 311
 co-operation with European Community 263,
 273
production and manpower 72, 211, 212, **271–2**
research 274, 344, 386
 associations and establishments 274
Coastal preservation 179, 180, 300
Coastguard Service 185, 317
Coinage 358, 375, 438
Coke 243, 262, 274, 311
Coleraine 165
Colleges 155, 156, 163, 164, 165, 166, 168
agricultural 296–7
arts 397, 403, 408
correspondence 163

Colleges—*contd.*
Instructor Training 332
of education 155, 156, 163, 164, 165, 166, 171,
408
residential (adult education) 167–8
Secretarial 163
Services 96–7
technical 166, 167, 256, 385, 386, 388
theological 197
World, United 171
See also **Education**
Combine harvesters 286, 287
Commercial:
associations 215, 228
Banking Systems 358–60
policy 372
premises, health and welfare in 342, 343, 344
Commissioners:
of Irish Lights 317
of Police 103, 106
Committees *see* relevant subjects
Commodity:
composition 369–70
Markets 367
prices 370
Common:
Agricultural Policy (CAP) 43–4, 73, 76, 291,
292–3
fisheries policy 297–8
Market *see* **European Community**
Services Agency (Scotland) 132, 137
Commons and village greens 181
Commonwealth, The 77–81
Action Programme of Industrial Co-operation
79
ACP countries 76, 374
Agricultural Institutes and Bureaux 395
aid to 46, 48, 79, 88–9, 374
banks 358, 363
Broadcasting Associations 80
citizens 12, 153
 adopted persons 143
 employment of 12, 153–4
consultation 78
co-operation:
 and developing countries **86–92**, 374
 education 78, 79, 169, 170
 financial and trade 86–90, 374
 research 395
Development Corporation (CDC) 79, 88, 363
Development Finance Company Limited
(CDFC) 363
Education Conferences 78
Education Liaison Committee 170
Foundation 79
Fund for Technical Co-operation 78, **79**
Games 432
immigration 7, 12, 17, 47
Institute 79
Forestry 389
Medical Conferences 78
member states 20, 77
Parliamentary Association 80
Press Union 80, 418
 Travelling Scholarship Scheme 418
Queen as Head of 20
Royal, Society 79
Scholarship and Fellowship Plan 79, 89, 170,
418
Secretariat 78–9
Technical Co-operation 79
Universities, Association of 170
Youth Exchange Council 80

Communications *see* Post Office, Research *and* Telecommunications
Community:
Centres 14, 397
Environment Programme 184
homes for children 118, 142
Service Volunteers 151, 173
Company law 233
Comprehensive education 158
Comptroller and Auditor General 349
Computers 161, 168, 212, 213, 218, 241, 242, 273, 305, 323, 324, 325, 332, 384, 388, 391, 417
See also Data *and* Post Office
Computer Aided Design Centre 388
Computing Centre, National 212
Concert Halls 398, 401
Confectionery industry 217, 219, **249**
Confederation of British Industry (CBI) 176, 213, 215, 338, 339, 340, 341
Conference:
Centres 260
on International Economic Co-operation 76
Conservation:
areas 178
Society 188
Conservative Party 28
Consolidated Fund 349
Constabulary, Inspectors of 103, 106
Construction:
equipment 218, **239**
industries 45, 210, 211, 227, **255–6**
research 45, 256, 387
industry:
Research and Information Association 387
materials 280–1
work overseas 256
Consumer:
Council, National 232
councils 232–3
expenditure *see* Expenditure
goods industries 247, 248, 249, 250, 251, 252
see also individual industries
Groups, National Federation of 233
Minister for Consumer Affairs 51, 230
organisations 232–3
protection, 63, **232–3**
Fair Trading, Director of 231, 232
Consumers:
Association (CA) 233
Contemporary Arts, Institute of 407
Conurbations 218, 309
Convalescent homes 134
Conversion tables 438–9
Co-operative:
Bank 359
marketing (agricultural) 290–1
Retail Services Ltd. 260
societies 260
Wholesale Society (CWS) 260
Copyright, authors' 399
Cornwall 2, 7, 12, 24, 217, 237, 280, 324
Coronation 21
Coroners' Courts 113–14
Corporation tax *see* Taxation
Cotton:
industry 250, **251**
Shirley Institute 250
textiles 250
Councils of counties, districts, etc. *see* Local Government
Councils, Other, *see* relevant subject
Counsel, *see* Law, legal profession
Counsellors of State 23

Countryside:
access to 180, 181
Commissions 179, **180–1**, 428
responsibility for 45
County courts 112, **121**, 123
Court of:
Appeal 111, 112, 121, 122
Justice (European Community) 102
Session (Scotland) **122–3**, 124, 125
Courts martial 114
Appeals Court 129
Courts of Law *see* Law
Covent Garden Market 260
Covent Garden Opera 402
Coventry 11, 218, 273, 305
Cowley 216
Crafts: 408
Advisory and Joint, Committee 408
Council and Centres 215, 408
Cranwell 96
Crawley 217
Credit Cards 259, 359, 362
Cricket 428, 430, **433**
Criminal:
Central, Court 109, 125
Courts 109–10
Injuries Compensation 104
Investigation departments 107
law 47, 48, 103, 109
Law Revision Committee 129
records 103, 107
Criminals, treatment of 47, 103, 108, **114–21**
Criminological Research and Studies 103–4
Crofters' Commission 294
Crown:
Agents for Overseas Governments and Administrations 71, 363
Courts **110**, 111, 117, 121, 123
Dependencies, 1, 20, 80, 95
mineral rights 262
Office, Edinburgh 54, 110
Crown, The *see* Monarchy *and* Royal Family
Cruden Bay 268
Crystal Palace National Sports Centre 431
Culcheth 387
Culham Laboratory 387
Cumbria 3, 218, 220, 277, 278, 387
Currency 200, 208
transactions 374, 375, 377, 378
See also Finance
Customs and Excise:
Board of 40, **44**, 49, 352, 355
duties *see* Taxation
Cutlery and flatware industry 219, 246
Cycle and motor cycle industry 218, **243**

D

Dagenham 216
Dancing 397, 398, 401, **402**, **403**, 430
Royal Ballet and School 403
Daresbury (nuclear physics) 384, 385
Darlington 308, 413
Dartford 304
Dartmoor 2, 180
Dartmouth 96
Data:
Datapost 324
Processing 242, 317, 322, 325
Service, National 325
See also Computers *and* Post Office
World, Centres for Space Research 396

Deaf 151
Deans 196
Death:
causes of 9, 109, 114, 129, 304
duty see Taxation, estate duty
grant and allowances 148
rate 7, 8, 9
registration of a 7
Defence 44, 93–101, 204
Armed Forces 44, 96–100, 326
    officers in 23, 96, 97
boards 94
Chiefs of Staff Committee 93
Civil see Civil Defence
College, National 97
colleges 96, 97
combat forces 97, 98–9
Commands 95, 96, 97
co-operation 93
Council 93
deployment 94–5
engagements 96
expenditure 94, 100, 101, 346
Fire services 68
Forces vote 27
international organisations 93, 94, 95
manpower 95, 96, 97
Ministry of and Secretary of State for 39, 44–5,
48, 71, 93, 96, 97, 100, 172, 317, 318, 320, 386,
390, 396
National Defence Industries Council 101
national projects 101
NATO strategy 93, 94–5, 97, 99, 100, 101
nuclear power 98
    Strategic Force 97
Ordnance Factories, Royal 101
overseas commitments 93, 95, 97–8
personnel 96
planning and control 93–4
policy and commitments 44, 93, 95
Procurement 44, 93, 100–1, 390, 396
ranks 93, 96
research and development 100–1, 390,
396
reserve and auxiliary force 99–100
Staff colleges 96, 97
strategic force 93, 97
Studies, Royal College of 97
training 96–7
warning systems 99, 100
weapons and equipment 98, 99, 244
    collaborative projects 101
    export controls 375
women's services 96
See also Army, Royal Air Force, Royal Navy
and Research
Demography 6–12
Dental services 132, 133, 135–6, 137
British Dental Association 137
dentists 132, 137
for school children 162
General Dental Council 137
Dependencies and Associated States 80
population 81
Deposit banks see Banks
Derby and Derbyshire 218
Design:
and Industries Association (DIA) 215
associations 215
awards for 215
Centres 215
Computer Aided Centre, 212, 388
Councils 215, 405

Design—contd.
education in 166, 408
Index 215
Detention centres 119, 120
Detergents 247, 248
Devaluation see Sterling
Development:
areas and districts 223, 226, 227–9
Boards, Regional 227, 228, 229
Commission 228
Corporation for Wales 214
councils 214
See also Economic and Research
grants and loans 223, 226, 228, 229, 230
organisation see Industry
plans 174–5
Devolution 19
Devon 2, 5, 249, 252
Dioceses see Church of England, provinces
and
Diplomatic Service 57–8, 375
Director of Public Prosecutions 48, 109,
126
Disabled:
British Sports Association for the 429
education 159, 168
employment of 328–9
housewives 148
mentally handicapped 134, 141, 159, 430
physically handicapped 134, 140, 159, 429
rehabilitation of 134, 141, 328
sports stadium 430, 431
welfare services for 47, 130, 140, 147–8, 151–2
Disablement:
benefit 147–8, 149
mobility allowance 148
pensions (war) 47, 143, 149–50
Resettlement Service 328–9
Vocational training 329
Disarmament Committee on 82
Discount market and houses 359, 360
Diseases, control of 134, 139–40
Distributive trades 200, 204, 207, 210,
256–61
District courts (Scotland) see Law and
Local Government
District Nurses 133, 137
Divorce 121, 123, 128
rate 10, 13
Docks see Ports
Dockyards, naval 101, 217
Doctors:
British Medical Association 137
general practitioner services 133
in industry 344
in National Health Service 135, 137, 139
Documentation Centre, National 429
Domestic:
electrical appliances industry 220, 241
help 140, 141
product gross 94, 156, 200, 202, 203, 204, 207,
210, 234, 255, 256, 302
utensils industry 218
Doncaster 185, 219, 312
Dorset 267, 277, 387
Dounreay 277, 387
Dover 3, 217, 313, 314, 316, 317
Drama 397, 398, 399–401
Conference, National 400
schools and colleges 400–1
See also Theatres
Dramatic Art, Royal Academy of 400
Drinks industries 218, 221, 239, 246, 249–50

Drugs 46, 135, 137, 247
Committee on Safety of Medicines 137
dependence 135
Dry Cleaning 261
Duchy of Lancaster 24, 37, 44, 397, 411
Duchy of Cornwall 24
Dudley 218, 394
Duke of Edinburgh 23
Duke of Edinburgh's Award Scheme 172
Dumbarton 274
Dumfries 277
Dundee 164, 221, 251, 314, 414
Dungeness 278
Dunnet Head 1
Dunstable 216, 394
Durham 164, 220, 407
'Dutch' elm disease 389
Dyestuffs 218, 246, 248
Dyfed 273

E

Earnings 15, 202, **333–4**
See also **Wages**
East Anglia 5, 11, 164, 175, 290
East and West Relations 81–2
Economic:
and Social Affairs 85–6
and Social Pattern 15
Commission for Europe 185
Co-operation and Development, Organisation
for (OECD) 86, 87, 89, 185, 263, 372, 374, 394
Development 200–2
Development Council, National (NEDC) 203,
214, 222, 293, 338, 339
growth 200–2
Integration with Europe *see* **European
Community**
Management 203–4
planning, regional 229
policy 202–3
Economy, national 200–9
economic development 200–2
external position 207–9
gross domestic product 94, 156, 200, 202, 203,
204, 207, 210, 234, 255, 256, 285, 302, 368, 381
gross national product 70, 87, 88, 204, 302
incomes and prices 201, 202, 205–6
investment 200, 207
measures against inflation 201, 202, 203, 348
personal incomes and expenditure 16, 205–6,
333–4
policy 43, **202–3**, 222, 223
See also **Balance of Payments, Finance,
Industry** *and* **Trade**
Edinburgh 11, 50, 111, 122, 165, 221, 296, 309,
319, 321, 323, 324, 384, 385, 386, 390, 394, 397,
399, 401, 405, 406, 407, 414, 431
Education 13–15, 18, 44, 65, 117, 155–73, 200,
204
administration 155–6
adult 162, 163, 164, 167–8, 422
 Literacy Unit 161, 168
 National Institute of 168
agricultural 296–7
and Science, Department of *and* Secretary of
State for **44–5**, 156, 158, 159, 160, 163, 168,
169, 171, 183, 381, 382, 386, 396, 398
architectural 166
art and design 166, 397, 398, 405, 408
broadcasting to schools 161, 420, 422

Education—*contd.*
building programme 44, 162
Business, Council 167
colleges *see* **Colleges**
commercial and management 166, 167, 214
curricula and courses **159–60**, 165, 166, 167,
168, 169, 170, 212, 214–15, 301, 397
 correspondence 163, 165, 167
 day release 59, 164, 418
 sandwich 163, 164, 166, 297
 secretarial 163, 167
development 155
evening classes **161–2**, 168, 397
examinations 161, 162, 165
finance of 155, 156, 157, 158, 159, **163**, 164,
168, 170, 171, 172, 173
forestry 301, 397
'further' 155, 156, 162–3, 166–8, 169, 170, 214,
397, 408, 422
 advanced courses 166
General Certificate of *see* examinations, *above*
grants *see* finance of, *above* 161
higher 155, 156, 162, 163, **164–7**, 168, 170
inspectorate 159, 160
local education authorities 63, 155, 156, 157,
158, 159, 162, 163, 164, 167, 168, 169, 171, 172
Micro Electronics 155
music 403
National Certificates and Diplomas 166–7
physical and games 117, 120, 162, 430
polytechnics 155, 163, 164, 166, 167, 214, 397,
405, 408
priority areas 155
prisoners 117, 119
religious 160
research on 160, 168, 169
scholarships and awards 155, 159, 161, 164,
165, 166, 171
schools 44, 155, **158–9**
 community 168, 169
 comprehensive 158
 Council 161, 169
 Council for Curriculum and Examinations 160
 county 157, 160
 denominational 157, 160, 196, 198–9
 fees 156, 157, 159
 'first' 156
 health and welfare 140, 142, 162
 independent (public) 155, 156, 157, **158–9**
 Tribunal 158
 leaving age 155, 156
 management 157
 meals service 150, 162
 'middle' 158
 nursery 157
 preparatory 159
 primary 155, 156, 157–8
 pupil numbers 155, 156, 157
 secondary 157, 158, 159, 161
 voluntary 156, 157, 160, 163
special educational treatment 159
teachers 117, 155, 156, 159, 161, 169, 170
 exchange schemes 170
training 156, 164, 166, 167, 172
Teaching Council for Scotland, General 166
Teaching Methods 168
technical and technological 163, 166, 167, 382
 Technician Education Council 167
Technical Education and Training Organisation
for Overseas Countries 71
See also **Industry**, education and training for
trade unions and 336
visual aids in 161

Education—*contd.*
Council for Educational Technology 161
 Educational Foundation for 161
vocational 117, 120, 155, 167, 168, 329
See also **Universities**
Educational:
Assistance programme 71, 161
Foundation for Visual Aids 161
Research, National Foundation for 169
Scientific and Cultural Organisation (UNESCO) 394
Technology, Council for 161
Visits and Exchanges, Central Bureau for 169–70
Eggs 289, 291
Authority 291
Egmanton 267
Eisteddfod 399
Elderly people:
Age Concern 10
Centres for 177
homes for 141
housing for 141, 192, 193, 195
proportion in population 10
welfare 46, 130, 134, **140–1**
See also **Pensions**
Elections:
to the European Parliament 74
local government 61–2
parliamentary 25, 26, **27–9**
Electrical:
and Allied Manufacturers' Association, British 241
Appliances, Association of Manufacturers of Domestic 241
appliances industries 200, 217, 218, 220, 241, 242
engineering *see* **Engineering**
ERA Technology Ltd 241
Industry 201, 211, 241
machinery industry 218, 220
Research Association 241
Electricity 45, 203, 210, 211, 212, 241, 262, 263, **274–7**
area boards and councils 274, 275, 277, 278
Board, South of Scotland (SSEB) 274, 275, 278, 279
consumption 263, 279
Council 274, 279
Generating Board, Central (CEGB) 274, 275, 277, 278, 279, 283
generation 241, 244, 274, 275–7
manpower 275
North of Scotland Hydro-Electric Board (NSHEB) 274, 275, 277, 278, 279
power stations 274, 275, 277
 hydro-electric 221, 263, 274, 275
 nuclear 221, 262, 275, 277–8
production 210
research 279
Service (NI) 274, 275, 279
transmission lines 274, 278
Electronic:
Engineering Association 241, 245
equipment:
 industry 211, 217, 218, 221, 241, **242**
 micro electronics 155, 213, 240, 242, 324, 384
 post office 242, 323, 324, 325
 X-ray scanner systems 242
Ellesmere Port 219, 268
Elm trees 5
Emigration 9–10

Employers' organisations 212, 213, 214, 335, 337–8
Employment 17, 45, 56, 58, 210, 212, 213, 216, 217, 218, 220, 221, 226, 227, 234, 236, 252, 255, 256, 260, 261, 285, 298, 302, 308, 311, 316, 322, 326–45
Advisory, Conciliation and Arbitration Service (ACAS) 338, 339–40
arbitration and conciliation 338, 339, 340
Careers Service 328, 329
Central Arbitration Committee 340
Department of *and* Secretary of State for 40, 45, 149, 153, 203, 212, 236, 327, 328, 330, 333, 334, 340, 341, 343, 345
Disablement Resettlement Service 134, 328–9
Economic and Social Division 390
'fringe' benefits 335, 341–5
health in 341–5
holidays 17–18, 334
industrial relations 45, 335–41
 Statutory Joint Industrial Council 341
Instructor Training:
 Colleges 332
 Units 332
Jobcentres 328
Job search schemes 329
Law 332–3, 338
manpower:
 deployment 327, 329
 mobility of 72, 226, 329, 330
 Services Commission (MSC) 51, 56, 134, 214, 327–8, 329, 331, 332, 343, 344
Medical Advisory Service (EMAS) 341, 344
National Joint Council 340
offices 328
of immigrants 12, 330
permits 12, 330
Professional and Executive Recruitment 329
protective legislation **332–3**, 334, 335, 338, 339, 340, 341, 342, 343
redundancy 332
safety in 341–5
 regulations 342
sex discrimination 121, 152–3, 333, 339
sheltered 329
Skill centres (SCs) 329, 331–2
Training Opportunities Scheme (TOPS) 331
training services 329, 331–2
 colleges 331–2
Transfer Scheme 329
women 152–3, 326, 333, 334, 343
work, hours of 334
Work Research Unit 345
working conditions 332–3
See also individual industries, **Manpower, Trade Unions, Unemployment, Wages** *and* **Work**: hours of
Energy:
conservation 190, 263–4
 advisory council on 264
 measures 264
consumption 263, 267, 270–1, 274
Department of *and* Secretary of State for 44, 183, 203, 222, 262, 264, 268, 279, 283, 284, 386
efficiency 262
Government's policy 263, 267
industries 262, 264, 267, 268, 271, 274, 278, 279
 employment in 262, 267, 271, 275, 280
 European Community co-operation 263
international relations 267
and Natural Resources 262–84
production and distribution 270, 271, 273, 275, 278, 280

Energy—*contd.*
renewable sources of 279–80
research and development 268, 271, 274, 279, 284, 386
  advisory council 264
  Offshore Energy Technology Board 268, 386
smokeless fuel 271
sources of 262, 264, 265, 267, 270, 271, 274, 277, 279
Standing Commission on the Environment 183
technology support unit 45, 264, 386
See also **Coal, Electricity, Gas, Hydro-electric, Nuclear energy** *and* **Petroleum**
Engineering 211, 216, 217, 218, 219, 220, 221, 222, 244, 245
aeronautical 216, 222, 244
chemical 388
civil 256, 343
electrical 211, 217, 218, 219, 220, 241, 388
electronic 211, 216, 217, 218, 219, 221, 222, 241, 332, 386, 388
Fellowship of 393
Institutions, Council of 393
Instrument 240–1
Laboratory, National 388
marine 221
mechanical 220, 238, 240, 388
Engines, industrial 239
England:
area 1
population, figures 7, 11, 12
English:
Association 409
Channel 2, 318
language 11, 17, 71, 73, 160, 163, **171**, 424
Music Theatre Company 402
National Opera 402
Tourist Board 229
Enterprise
Board, National 228, 234
Zones 178, 226
Environment:
Department of the *and* Secretary of State for the 40, 45, 49, 51, 53, 61, 64, 67, 174, 175, 179, 182, 183, 186, 190, 203, 222, 255, 256, 280, 281, 283, 284, 305, 387, 408, 428
Ministers for 45, 46
Property Services Agency 45, 255
Research Council, Natural (NERC) 296, 382, 383–4, 388
Environmental:
Amenity Societies 188
Conservation, Council for 189
Health 139, 174
planning and conservation 45, 174–89
pollution 14, 179, 182–8
  Administration 183
  Royal Commission on 15, 183
protection 178, 179, 180
Equal opportunities 16–17, 56, 152–3, 330, 333
commission 56, 152, 153
complaints 153
Equity Capital for Industry Ltd 363
Essex 164
Estate Duty *see* **Taxation**
Ethnic relations *see* **Race relations**
Europe, trade with 72–3, 232, 237, 238, 244, 245, 247, 249, 263
Council of 86
European:
Agricultural Guidance and Guarantee Fund (FEOGA) 43–4, 77, 292

European—*contd.*
Atomic Energy Community (EURATOM) 73, 387
Broadcasting Union (EBU) 426
Coal and Steel Community (ECSC) 72, 77
Communities 19, 24, 33, 35, 71, 102, 237, 338
  Act 73
Convention on Human Rights 86
Co-operation in Science and Technology (COST) 394
Council 75
Court of Justice 74, 102
Currency Units (ECUs) 292
Economic Community (EEC) 72, 73
Free Trade Association (EFTA) 373
Investment Bank 77, 230
Molecular Biology Laboratory 394
Monetary:
  Co-operation Fund 208
  Fund 77
  System 77, 208
Organisation for Nuclear Research (CERN) 384, 385, 394
Parliament 24, **74**
Regional Development Fund 77, 229–30
Science Exchange Programme 292
Science Foundation (ESF) 392, 394
Social Fund 77
Space:
  Agency (ESA) 245, 325, 384, 396
  programme 396
See also subject headings
European Community, The 19, 24, 33, 35, 43, 47, 52, 70, 72–7, 138, 150, 169, 207, 208, 232, 237, 245, 247, 251, 255, 262, 263, 290, 291, 292, 293, 297, 298, 307, 330, 360, 368, 370, 371, 372, 373, 375
Accession, Treaty of 73
Agricultural 43, 51, 55, 73, 76
  Guidance and Guarantee Fund (FEOGA) 44, 77
  policy 43, 55, 73, 76, 291, **292–3**, 375
Budget 73, 372
coal and steel 72, 230
Commission 48, 73, 74, 232
  President of 74
Common Customs Tariff 72, 372
Community law 74
  Court of Auditors 74
  Court of Justice 74, 102
  courts of appeal 74
Council of Ministers 73, 74, 75
currency 76, 208
Economic and Social Committee 74
educational co-operation 169
Environment Programme 184
external relations 75–6
'Euronet' project 325
finance:
  aid to Commonwealth and developing countries 75–6
  capital movement 72
  grants and loans 72, 230, 292, **293**
  insurance 366
fisheries policy 297, 298
food hygiene 43
institutions 73–5, 169
internal policies 76–7
legislation 23, 33, 44, 73, 233, 306
Lomé Convention 76, 91, 92, 287, 374
manpower:
  mobility of 72, 330
  training 77, 330

European Community, The—*contd.*
Medical and Health Research Programme 390
Membership 19, **72–7**, 368
nuclear energy activities 73, 387, 394
Parliament, European 24, 74
policies 75, 302
publications, 50
reciprocal agreements, health and social
security 138, 150
regional development 229–30
    Fund 299
Representatives, Committee of Permanent
(COREPER) 73
revenue:
    budget 76, 371
    sources of 76
Scientific and Technical Research Committee
(CREST) 394
schools and colleges 169
tariffs 72, 75, 373, 374
trade:
    agreements 72, 232, 298, 375
    development 72, 360, 374
    price controls 292, 293, 298, 374–5
    restrictive practices, control of 232
treaties 72, 73, 232, 366
Exchange control 208, 373–4
Exchange Equalisation Account (EEA) 348, 357
Exchange rates 208
Exchange reserves 376
Exchange Telegraph Company Ltd (Extel) 416,
417
Exchequer *see* **Finance**
excise duties *see* **Taxation**
Exeter 164
Exhibition Centre, National 218, 243, 260
Exmoor 5, 180
Expenditure:
committees 34, 349, 350
consumer 205, 206
estimates 348
pattern of 15–16
public 43, 94, 102, 106, 155, 156, 189, 203,
206–7, **346–50**
public authorities 130, 206–7
royal income and 23–4
Surveys, Public 347, 348, 349
Taxes on 355–6
See also **Defence, Finance, Research,**
Agriculture: subsidies, *and* **Housing**:
subsidies
Export 200, 201, 207–8, 234, 236, 237, 238, 239,
243, 246, 247, 248, 250, 252, 253, 267, 285, 292,
313, 319, **368–9**, 375–6, 423
controls 357, 374, 375, 405
Credits Guarantee Department (ECGD) **46**, 71,
87, 375
insurance 46, 375
licensing and restrictions 406
Overseas Trade Board, British 71, **375**
See also **Trade** *and* individual industries

F

Factories:
building 176, 226, 227
Inspectorate 183, 341, 342, 344
legislative provisions 341, 342, 343
See also **Employment** *and* individual industries
Fair Trading 230, 231, 232
Falkirk (newspaper) 414
Falmouth 217, 298

Families 13–14
welfare services for 46, 130, 133, 140, **141**, 149
Family:
Division (High Court) 121, 122
Income Supplement 47, 149
planning 136, 137
Practitioner Services 133
Royal *see* **Monarchy**
Welfare Association 151
Farming *see* **Agriculture**
Farnborough 217, 245, 396
Fauna 5–6, 182
Fawley 267
Fen district 5, 285
Fertilisers 220, 247, **248**
Festival Hall, Royal 401
Field Sports 433–4
Fife 221, 271
Film:
Archive, National 404, 405
Authority, British 403
Censors, British Board of 403–4
Council, for Educational Technology, Scottish
404, 405
Eady Levy 403
Festivals 403, 404, 405
    National Panel for 404
Finance Corporation, National 403
Fund Agency, British 404, 405
Industrial and Scientific Film Association,
British 404
industry 403
Institute, British 44, 403, **404–5**
library 404
production 403, 404
quota system 403
School, National 403
Theatre, National 405
Films 397, **403–5**
children's 404
documentary 404
educational 404
feature 398, 403
licensing 403
of Scotland Committee 404
Finance 76, 94, 106, 163, 200, 204, 206–7,
346–67
aid to overseas countries 43–4, 46, 86–90
banking 357–62, 368
Budget 202–3, 348, **350–1**, 353, 354
cash limits 348–9
Comptroller and Auditor General 349
corporations 203–4, **362–3**
currency reserves 208, 374, 376, 377, 378
estimates 348
Exchange Equalisation Account 348, 357
Exchequer 48, 49, 67, 144, 331, 348, 349, 350,
351
See also **Treasury**
financial institutions 357–67
financing of international trade 360
for Industry Ltd. 362
Houses Association 362
Inflation, measures against 202–3, 348
International Monetary System 207–9
local government 65–8, 206–7
monetary policy 202–3
National Debt 357
National Loans Fund 50, 348, 349, 352, 357
public:
    Accounts Committee 350
    corporations 203–4
    expenditure 346–50

Finance—*contd.*
public—*contd.*
 Expenditure Survey 347, 348, 349
 sector accounts 351–2
sources of revenue 352–7
Special Drawing Rights (SDRs) 209, 357, 377, 378
See also **Balance of Payments, Exchange Control, Expenditure, Income, Investment, Revenue, Sterling, Taxation** *and* **Trade**
Finnart 268
Fire:
Central, Brigades Advisory Council 68, 69
equipment 68–9
Joint, Prevention Committee 69
personnel 68
prevention research 69
Research, Joint Committee on 69
Research Station 69
Service Technical College 69
Services 47, **68–9**, 320
Fishing:
European Community:
 Common Fisheries Policy 297–8
 Involvement 297, 298
 Limits 297
fleets 299
freshwater 6, **299**, 389
grounds 2, 297, 298
Herring Industry Board 300
industry 43, 220, 300
 employment in 298–9
 imports and exports 298, 299
 processing 299, 300
 subsidies and loans 300
licences 299
methods of sea 299
ports 298, 312
research 300, 388, 389, 391
 and Development Board, Fisheries 389
rights 298, 299
sport 434
White Fish Authority 300
Fleetwood 298
Float glass 253
Floor coverings 251, 254
Flora *see* **Vegetation**
Flour milling 219, 249, 287, 391
and Baking Research Association 249, 391
Fog 4, 186–7
Folkestone 217, 312
Food:
biscuits 249
bread 249
chocolate and confectionery 217, 219, 249
consumption 16, 205, 287, 288, 368
Contamination, prevention of 183
exports 248, 249, 292
frozen 16, 217, 249, 299
home grown supplies 285, 286, 287, 289, 290
Hygiene Laboratory 140
imports 291, 292, 298, 368, 369, 370
industries 210, 217, 219, 222, 249
Manufacturing Industries, Research Association, British 391
poisoning, control of 139
poisoning, control of 139
processing 217, 219, 222, 239, 249, 289, 290, 299
purity 43, 139, 389, 391
research 382, 388, 389, 391
safety of 139

Food—*contd.*
sales 249, 259, 260
Science Laboratory 389
Food and Agriculture Organisation (FAO) 85
Football 428, 430, 431–2
pools 356, 437
Rugby 428, 430, 431, **435–6**
Footpaths and bridleways 180, 181
Footwear:
industry 217, 218, 250, **252**
shops and repairers 257, 261
Foreign:
and Commonwealth Office **46**, 57, 70, 375
Diplomatic Service 57, 71
Exchange Market **367**, 374–5
Policy 81–3
See also **Overseas**
Foreigners:
employment of 153–4, 330
naturalisation of 12, 47
Forensic science 107
Forest:
area 4–5, 181, 182, 285, **300–1**
of Dean 181
parks 181, 430
Forestry 5, 181, 182, **300–1**, 428, 433
Commission 300, **301**, 389
education, training and research 301
 Princes Risborough Laboratory 389
 Training Council 301
employment in 300
policy 301
Forth:
bridge 303
river and firth 221, 273, 303, 312, 313
Forties Field 265
Fowl pest 295
Fox hunting 433
Fraud Squad 107
Freezing (food) 217, 220, 249
Freight:
Corporation, National 204, 306
services 51, 67, 302, **306**, **311**, 312, 313, 314, 315, 319
Freshwater Biological Association 384, 389
Friendly Societies, Registrar of 364
Friends of the Earth 188
Frigg (gasfield) 270
Fruit and vegetable products and preserves 249, 289, **290**
Fruit, production and distribution 249, 260, **290**
Fuel and Power *see* **Energy, Coal, Electricity, Gas, Hydro-electric, Nuclear energy, North Sea, Petroleum** *and* **Research**
Furniture and Timber Industry Training Board 301
Furniture Development Council 254
Furniture Industry 235, **254**
Research Association 254

G

GATT *see* **General Agreement on Tariffs and Trade**
Gaelic 12, 160
Gainsborough 267
Gambling *see* **Betting and Gambling**
Games equipment industry 254
Game shooting 433–4
Gardens 18
Botanic 390

Gas 2, 45, 200, 202, 203, 204, 217, 262, **268–71**
British 203, 268, 270, 271
consumption 270–1
natural 45, 217, 262, 263, 268, 270, 271
    development and production 239, **270**
    indigenous supplies 270, 279
    location 268, **270**
    Offshore Energy Technology Board 268
    operations 268, 270
pipeline system 270
production and distribution 45, 202, 270
research and development 271, 386
structure 268
terminals 270
turbines 239, 275, 277
transmission and storage 270
Gateshead 308
Gatwick (airport) 217, 318, 320, 321
General:
Agreement on Tariffs and Trade (GATT) 75, 86,
252, **372–3**, 374
Electric Company 210
Register Offices 53
Registrar 50, 53
Geological Museum and Survey 394, 406
Geological Sciences, Institute of 48, 90, 280,
383, 394
Geology 2–6, 182, 383, 394
Geophysics 384
Georgian Group 188
Gin industry 249
Girl Guides 151, 172
Girobank 145, 322, 359
Glasgow 11, 45, 111, 164, 165, 178, 187, 199,
221, 237, 307, 308, 309, 319, 320, 321, 367, 401,
402, 405, 407, 410, 414, 432
Glass industry 219, 220, 247, 252, **253**
Research Association, British 253
Glenariff 181
Glenmore 181
Gloucester and Gloucestershire 217, 274, 277,
279, 312, 399
Glyndebourne (opera) 402
Godalming 274
Gold and convertible currency reserves 209,
374, 376, 377, 379
Gold and silver ware industry 246, 262
Gold Market (London) 367
Golf 430, **434**
Goole 220
Goonhilly 324
Gorton Glenn 181
Gosford 181
Government 19–69
Actuary, Department of 40
    advisory committees and councils 41
Chemist, Laboratory of 388
composition of 37–8
departments of 20, 37, 39, **40–56**
economic management 203–4
employment services 327–32
National Loans Fund 348, 349, 352, 357
relations with industry 47, **210**, 222–3, 226–9,
273, 322–5, 327–32
relations with overseas countries 46, 48, 50,
395
Statistical Service 40, 42
See also **Civil Service, Expenditure, Finance,
Local Government, Ministers, Monarchy,
Parliament, Privy Council** *and* **Research**
Grangemouth 221, 268
Grants *see* **Education, Housing, Local
Government** *and* **Industry**

Gravesend 316
Great Britain:
area 1
definition 1
population 7–11
Greater London Council *see* **London**
Great Seal 49
Green Belts 179
Greenock 414
Greenwich 1, 96, 384, 385, 423
Greyhound racing 435, 437
Grimsby 220, 298, 312
Grocery trade 259, 260, 261
Guardian's allowance 146
Guernsey:
population 7
reciprocity (national health benefits) 47
See also **Channel Islands**
Guided weapons 98, 243, 244
Gymnastics 162, 430
Gymnasts, remedial 134, 138
Gwynedd 268, 277, 389

H

HMSO *see* **Stationery Office**
Habeas Corpus 108, 109
Hairdressing establishments 257, 261
Hamilton (newspaper) 414
Hampshire 245
Handicapped persons *see* **Disabled** *and*
Welfare
Hand tools industry 246
'Hansard' 30
Harbours *see* **Ports**
Harpenden 296, 382, 388
Harrogate 260, 399
Hartlepool 220, 278, 312
Harwell 45, 386, 387
Harwich 312, 313
Hatfield 216
Hayward Gallery 405, 407
Health 15, 130–40, 200, 204
advisory councils and other committees 132,
133, 137, 140, **341–2**, 390
and Safety:
    at work 183, 337, **341–5**
    Commission 214, 341, 342, 343
    Executive 183, 186, 187, 341, 342
and Social Security, Department of **46–7**, 125,
131, 135, 143, 149, 150, 162, 184, 389, 390
and social services 130–53
authorities and boards 119, 130, 131, 132, 137,
138, 139
    area 131, 132
centres **134**, 135
community services 130, 133–7, 139–40
control of infectious diseases 139–40
education 133, 135, **137**
Employment Medical Advisory Service 344
environmental 45, 139
home nursing 133, 136
laboratories **139–40**, 344
primary, care 133
private medical treatment 133, **138–9**
professions 137–8
public 55, 65, 130, 131, 132, 139
research 139
safety of medicines 137
School:
    children 136, 141–2, 162
    service 136

Health—*contd.*
Service Commissioners 132
Service, National 53, **130–40**
  administration 46, **131–2**
  agreements with other countries 138
  authorities 131–2
  charges 132–3
  commissioners 132
  finance 132–3
  general practitioner services 133, 138
    community physicians 139
    group practices and health centres 134
  help to families 141
  hospital and specialist services 134–6
  mental services 141
  Northern Ireland 131, 132, 133, 135
  organisation 131–3
  reciprocal agreements 130, 138
  specialist services 133, 134–7
  visiting 135, 140
Supplementary Benefits Commission 47, 144
Heathrow (airport) 217, 308, 319, 321
Heating appliances 240, 241, 243
Hebrides 2, 3, 4
Helicopters 99, 243, 317, 319, **320**
air-sea rescue 317, 320
Henley-on-Thames 214, 284
Herbaria 390
Hereford 277, 399
Heritage Coasts 179, 186
Hertfordshire 296
Hewett 270
Heysham 278
High Court of Justice 109, 111, 112, **121**, 122, 125
High Court of Justice (Northern Ireland) 108, 123, 127
High Court of Justiciary (Scotland) 109, 111, 112, 122, 126, 127
Highland Games 432
Highlands and Islands, Scotland 2, 3, 4, 5, 7, 12, 53, 111, 221, 229, 321
aerodromes and airways 321
Development Board 53, 229
Highway Code 304
Highway construction 63, 175, 255, 303, 304
See also **Roads**
Hindus 199
Hire purchase finance companies 362
Historical Manuscripts Commission 410
Historic buildings and monuments 45, **178**, 397
building preservation notices 178
Churches Preservation Trust 188
building preservation notices 178
Council 178
Monuments, Royal Commission on 178
towns 45
Hockey 430, 431
Holidays 18, 334
Hollow-ware industry 246
Holyhead 221, 313
Home help 135, 140
Homeless people 194
Home:
Office *and* Home Secretary **47**, 49, 68, 69, 103, 104, 105, 106, 107, 112, 116, 119, 125, 129, 135, 151, 316, 390, 413, 420, 421, 423, 426
Office Voluntary Service Unit 151
Honours 21, 37, 46
Hop growing 287
Horse:
racing 428, **435**, 437
riding 435

Horse—*contd.*
show jumping 435
trials 435
Horsemanship 435
British Equestrian Federation 431, 435
Horserace:
Betting Levy Board 437
courses 435, 437
Totalisator Board (HTB) 437
Horticulture *see* **Agriculture**
Hosiery:
and Allied Trades Research Association 250
and knitwear industry 218, 221, 251
Hospices 135
Hospital:
advisory committees 132
Friends, Leagues of 151
laboratories 136, 139–40
Hospitals:
and specialist services 134–6
construction 134
maternity services 133
number of 134
ophthalmic services 133
prisons 117
psychiatric 117
staff 134
teaching 137
voluntary help in 151, 152
Households 13–14, 189, 197
House of Commons 21, 24, 25, **26–7**, 28, 29, 30, 31, 32, 33, 34, 35, 36, 37, 38, 39, 126, 196
broadcasting proceedings 30
committees 31, **32–3**
election to **27**, 28
financial control 29, 32
officers **26–7**, 29, 33
party composition 28–9
privileges 35
See also **Parliament** *and* **Speaker**
House of Lords 21, 24, **25–6**, 27, 28, 29, 30, 31, 32, 33, 35, 37, 39, 49, 62, 111, 112, 122, 125, 126, 129
Appellate Committee of 33, 49
as Court of Appeal 111, 112, 122, 123
committees 32, **33–4**
eligibility to 25, 26
officers 25, 26, 28
privileges 35
Record Office 30
Housing 13–14, 17, 65, 177, 189–95
administration 196
advisory centres 152, 190
and Construction, Minister for 45–6
associations and societies 190, 193, 195
authorities, local 189, 190, 191–2, 193, 194
Community leasehold 193
construction and design 13–14, 45, 190, 191, 192, 194, **255–6**, 408
Co-ownership 193, 195
Corporation 193
finance 45, 65–6, 189, 191
furnished accommodation 193
Homeloan Scheme 193, 195
home ownership 14, 189, **191**, 192, 195
improvement 14–15, 255, **193–4**, 195
ministerial responsibility for 45–6, 190
number of dwellings 190, 191, 192, 194
Option Mortgage Scheme 191, 195
policy 13–14, 190, 192, 195
privately rented 14, 189–90, 192–3, 195
public authorities 189, 190, **191–2**
renovation grants 193

Housing—contd.
rent rebates 66, 192
rent restrictions 192
research and development 190
shared ownership 191, 195
'shorthold' letting 193
slum clearance 65, 192, **194**
standards 191, 192
subsidies 65–6, 177, 190, 192
town development schemes 177
unfurnished accommodation 14
Hovercraft 315, 316, 391
British Rail Hovercraft Ltd. 316
Hoverlloyd Ltd. 316
Hull 164, 220, 298, 305, 312
Human Rights 86
Commission on 86
Humber and Humberside 3, 10, 219, 227, 236,
238, 256, 285
bridge 303
Hunterston 278, 313
Hunting 433
Hydraulics Research Station (HRS) 90, 284, 387
Hydrocarbons tax 354
Hydro-electric:
Board, North of Scotland (NSHEB) 274, 275,
277, 279
power 221, 275, 277
See also **Electricity**
Hydrological research 284, 383

I

IBA see **Independent Broadcasting Authority**
Ice Skating Centre, National 431
Immigrants:
Commission for Racial Equality 154
Community Relations 154
Culture 17
Race Relations 153–4, 330
Welfare of 45, 153–4, 177
Immigration 9, **12–13**, 17, 47, 153–4
Immingham 219, 312
Immunisation 139
Imperial Chemical Industries Ltd 210, 247
Imperial War Museum 406
Imports 200, 202, 219, 220, 265, 299, 301, 313
licensing and restrictions 47, 295, 374
See also individual industries and **Trade**
Improvement grants, housing 193–4
Income:
and expenditure, national 204–7
local government 65–7
personal 15, 18, 205–6, 333, 334
sources of 205, 333–4
Incomes and prices 201, 202, 205–6
Income Tax see **Taxation**
Indefatigable (gasfield) 270
Independent:
airline companies 319–20
Broadcasting Authority (IBA) 161, 324, 398,
413, 420, **421–2**, 423, 424, 425, 426, 427
Television 168, 413, **421–2**, 423, 425
advertising 420, 421, **425**
Companies Association 426
local radio 413, 420, 421, 422, 424, 425
News Ltd. 422, 427
programme companies 413, 421–2
Radio News 422
Industrial:
Advisory, Conciliation and Arbitration Service
(ACAS) 339–40

Industrial—contd.
Arbitration Committees 339–40
Artists and Designers, Society of 215
association 213–14
automation 213, 239, 240
building 226, 227, 255, 256
design 215, 405
Councils 215, 405
Development 222, 223, 226, 227, 228, 229
Advisory Agencies 227, **228**
Advisory Boards 227
Boards, Regional 227, 229
Fund, European Regional 229
Unit 228
disputes 339, 340
films 404
information 212, 213, 214, 222, 223
injuries benefits 143, 144, 147
minerals 280, 281
negotiating machinery 338, 339, 340, **341**
plant and steelworks manufacture 216, 217,
218, 219, 220, 221, 236, 237, **239**
policy 47–8, 202–3, 210, 222, 223, 226, 228
property 215
relations 47–8, 212, 213, **335–41**
councils and committees 336, 337, 338–40,
341
practice, code of 233
Unit 385
research establishments 48, 237, 238, 239, 240
241, 245, 381, 384, 386, 388, 391, 396
Safety regulations 341–3
Industry 47–8, 50–1, 200–2, 204, **210–33**,
234–61
advisory councils and committees 40, 203
associations **213–14**, 215, 216
Confederation of British (CBI) 213, 215, **338**,
339, 340, 341
Department of and Secretary of State for 47,
52, 67, 203, 211, 218, 222, 226, 227, 228, 236,
238, 280
development areas and districts 223, 226,
227–9
development organisations 222, 227, 228
education and training for 155, 166–7, 214,
329, 330, **331–2**
Enterprise Board, National 228, 234
finance corporations 362–3
grants and loans to 223, **226**, 228, 229, 230,
237, 362–3
health and welfare services 341–5
investment in see **Investment**
location 174, **216–22**, 223, 226–7
management **214–15**, 222–3
British Institute of (BIM) 214
Council of Industry for, Education 214
Education, Foundation for 215
Industrial Society 214
Institute of Directors 214
training for 214–15
manufacturing 47, 200, 204, 207, 210, 211, 212
216–22, **234–61**
employment in 210, 212, 216–22, 226, 227,
332–3
mergers and re-grouping 203, 211, 231, 241
micro-electronics 213, 240
organisation 210–22
regional 226–7
ownership 210, 222–3
plant and machinery 212
production and productivity in 204, 210,
211–12, 234, 236, 237, 238, 239, 240, 241, 242
British Productivity Council 212

Industrial—*contd.*
public enterprise 222–3
relations with Government 47, 210, 222–3, 226–9, 327–32
restrictive trade practices 230, **232**
  Fair Trading 230, 231, 232
safety in 341–5
standards in 215–16
structure 210–11
training 214, 329, 330, **331–2**
  boards 331, 343
  Instructor, Colleges and Units 332
  Manpower Services Commission (MSC) 214, 327–8, 329, 331, 332, 343, 344
  Opportunities Scheme (TOPS) 331–2
  Skillcentres (SCs) 329, 331–2
  Within Industry (TWI) 331–2, 343
See also **Employment, Exports**, individual industries, **Public corporations, Research** *and* Trade
Infectious diseases, control of 9, 139
Inflation *see* **Finance**
Information:
and advice to exporters 375
Central Office of 40, 48, 404, 424, 425
services overseas 48
Inland Revenue
Board of 40, **48**, 49, 66, 352
sources of *see* **Taxation**
Inland transport 51, **302–12**
Inland waterways 302, **312**
Amenity Advisory Council 430
British Waterways Board 312, 430
development 312
recreation 430
Inns of Court 127
Inquests 114
Insecticides 248, 389, 391
Insects 6, 389
Inspectorates:
constabulary 103, 106
factory 183, 341, 342, 344
fire service 342
mines and quarries 341, 342
Nuclear Installations 187, 342
railway employment 342
wages 341
Institutes *and* **Institutions** *see* relevant subjects
Insurance 200, 206, **365–6**
Association, British 365
brokers 200, **366**
companies 190, 363, **365**
export credit 46, 375
international services 365–6
marine 366
market 365
underwriters 200
See also **National Insurance**
Instrument engineering 240–1
Inter-Governmental Maritime Consultative Organisation (IMCO) 185, 317
International:
Agency for Research on Cancer (IARC) 394
agricultural research centres 395
Atomic Energy Agency (IAEA) 387, 394
Civil Aviation Organisation 187
Confederation of Free Trade Unions 337
Conference on, Economic Co-operation 76
Council of Scientific Unions (ICSU) 392, 394
Criminal Police Organisation (Interpol) 107
Development Issues (Brandt Report) 91
Economic Co-operation 91

International—*contd.*
Energy Agency (IEA) **263**, 274, 394
Fellowship Scheme 392
Festival of University Theatre 400
Institute of Applied Systems Analysis 392
Labour:
  Conference 337
  Organisation 85, 338
Machine tools exhibition 238
Maritime Satellite (INMARSAT) Organisation 324
Monetary:
  agreements 208, 209, 357
  Fund (IMF) 78, 86, 208, **209**, 372, 377, 378
  Special Drawing Rights (SDRs) 209, 357, 377, 378
  system 207–9
North–South Dialogue 90–2
peace and security 81–3
Royal Institute of, Affairs 410
Telecommunication Union (ITU) 427
Telecommunications Satellite Organisation (INTELSAT) 324, 396
Telegraph Service 325
Television Federation (Intertel) 427
Telex Exchange, London 325
Voluntary Service 173
Inter-University Council for Higher Education Overseas 71
Invention 392
Investment 200, 201, 202, **207**, 210, 212–13, **227–8**, 230, 234–5, 237
Bank, European 230
in fuel and power industries 263, 273, 275
grants and loans 223, **226**, 228, 229, 230, 273
in industry 202, 207, **213–13**, 227–8, 234, 235, 237
National Enterprise Board **228**, 234
overseas 200, 371, 372, 373, 376, 378, 379, 380
  in Britain 228
private sector 212, 213, 378, 379, 380
trust companies 364
See also individual industries *and* **Savings**
Invisible transactions *see* **Trade**
Ipswich 217
Irish Republic 1, 19, 62, 104, 198, 315, 358, 417
citizens' status in UK 12
citizens' voting rights in UK 27, 62
population: migration 17
stock exchanges 367
trade with UK 253, 371, 372, 417
Iron:
and steel
  exports 236, 237
  industry 201, 219, 220, **236–7**
  research 237
castings 218, **237**
ore 220, 237
See also **Steel**
Ironbridge Gorge Museum 407
Isaac Newton optical telescope 385
Islamic Centres 199
Isle of Man:
area 1
language 7
legislature **19**, 24, 36
population 7
races (TT) 434
relationship with UK Government and Crown 20, 24, 47
Tynwald Court 24
Isle of Wight 1, 3, 4, 61, 316, 431, 436
Isles of Scilly 1, 326

J

Jams and marmalades industry 249
Jersey:
population 7
See also **Channel Islands**
Jewellery industry 218, 246
Jewry 199
'Jobcentres' 328
Job Search Scheme 328
Jockey Club 435
Jodrell Laboratory 390
John o'Groats 1
Journalists:
Institute of (IOJ) 418
National Council for the Training of (NCTJ) 417–18
National Union of (NUJ) 418
See also **Press**
Judge Advocate General's Department 49
Judges 21, 102, 108, 110, 112, 115, **121–2**, 123, 124, 125, **126–7**
Judicial Committee of the Privy Council 36, 49
Judicial procedure 112, 113, 121, 126
Judiciary *see* **Law**
Jury *see* **Law**
Justice:
administration of 47, 121–9
and the Law 102–29
Criminal 102–21
Civil 121–5
Court of (European Community) 74, 102
See also **Law**
Justices of the Peace 110, 111, 126
Jute industry 221, 251
Juvenile Courts 110, 112, 118
informal children's hearings (Scotland) 112, 119

K

Keele University 164
Keep Britain Tidy Group 188
Kent 164, 267, 268, 277, 290, 304, 316
Kew:
Observatory 4, 187
Royal Botanic Gardens 390
Kidderminster 218
Kielder Reservoir 220, 284
Kilkeel 298
Kimmeridge 267
King George's Jubilee Trust 172
Kingsnorth 277
Kingston-upon-Hull 219
Kirkintilloch 278
Knighthoods 21
Knitwear industry 218, 221, 250, **251**

L

Labour *see* **Employment**
Labour Party 28, 34, 336
Lace industry 218
Lake District 2, 4, 180
Lancashire 11, 218, 278, 285
Lancaster 219
Duchy of 24, 37, 44, 397, 398, 407
University 164

Land:
acquisition and disposal 64
control of pollution 184–5
drainage 298
reclamation **182**, 226, 227
Development Agencies 226
Registry 49
Resources Development Centre 395
use 5–8, 45, 53, 174, 176, 179, 180, 181, 182, **285**, 286, 289, 290
Lands:
Tribunals 66, 294
Land's End 3
Language 6–7, **11–12**, 73, 160, 161, 163, 168, 169, 170, **171**
Laundries and launderettes 257
Law 19, 20, 23, 24, 48, 49, 102–29
administration of the 47, 48, 125–9
arrest, law of 107, **108–9**
civil justice 121–5
Commissions 49, 129
common 20, 24, 102
Community 74, 102
Court of Justice 74, 102
courts (criminal and civil) 48, **109–14**, 115, 119, **121–5**, 129
district (Scotland) 110, **111**, 126, 129
Restrictive Practices 124
criminal appeals 111, 112
Criminal Injuries Compensation Board 104
criminal justice 102–21
divorce 48, 50, 121, 123, 128
employment 332–3
evidence, rules of 112, 113, 123
expenditure on 128–9
General Council of the Bar 128
Habeas Corpus 108, 109
Judges' Rules 108
judiciary 20, 21, 49, 50, 109, 111, 113, **121–2**, **125–6**
jury 110, 111, 112, **113**, 123
legal aid and advice 47, 112, 125, **128**, **129**
Fund 128
legal profession 127–8
Council of Legal Education 127
legislation *see* **Parliament**
military 49
Officers' Department 48–9
Officers of the Crown 38, 47, 48, 126, 127
Official Solicitor 48, 49, 52
penalties 114–18
press (legal requirements) 413, **419**
prosecutions 109–10, 112, 113
Reform Committees 129
Society 127, 128
Society of Northern Ireland, Incorporated 128
Society of Scotland 127
sources of 102
Statute Law Committee 50
trials and verdicts *see* prosecutions, *above*
Lawn Tennis 428, 430, **434**
Lawyers 111, 112, 127, 128
Learned societies **392**, 393, 406, 410
Leatherhead (laboratories) 279
Leather industry 252, 319
British Leather Manufacturers' Research Association 252
Leeds 11, 164, 402, 407, 410
Leicester and Leicestershire 164, 218, 273, 407
Leisure trends 18
Leith 314
Leman Bank 270
Lerwick 4, 298, 314

Liberal Party 28
Libraries 44, 53, 63, 64, 71, 397, 398, 404, **409–11**
Arts and, Office of 44, 397, 405
Aslib 411
mobile 411
private collections 410, 411
public 55, 397, 398, **409–11**
school 410
university 410, 411
Library:
Advisory Councils 411
Association 411
Boards 156, 157, 411
British 409–10
co-operation 410, 411
Film 404, 405
National:
  of Scotland 53, 410, 411
  of Wales 51, 410, 411
Licences:
aircrews, aircraft and aerodromes 318, **320**, 321
animals 47, 295, 296, 322, 375
betting 47, 121, 437
broadcasting 47, 322, 420, 421
cinemas and films 403–4
clubs 56, 121
driving 305, 306
drugs 47, 135
firearms 47
fishing 299, 434
game and gun 47, 433
gaming and lotteries 47, 437
import 44, 250, 295, 374
issue of, by Post Office 322
motor vehicles 304, **306–7**, 308, 322
oil and gas prospecting 264
public houses 47, 53, 121
race courses 435
works of art 405–6
Life:
expectation of 8–9
peerages 25–6
Lifeboats 317
Royal National Life-boat Institution 317
Lighthouses 317
Lilleshall National Sports Centre 431
Limestone 281
Lincolnshire 5, 218, 267, 285
Linen industry 251
Linwood 221
Literary societies and prizes 409
Literature 409–11
associations and societies 409
awards 409
Royal Society of 409
Litter 184
Liverpool 11, 164, 219, 309, 312, 313, 401, 407
Livestock *see* **Agriculture**
Lizard Peninsula 1
Llandarcy 220, 268
Lloyd's, Society of 366
Local Administration, Commission for 68
Local Government 19, 20, 45, 55, **60–6**, 150
authorities, types of 60–8, 130, 131, 139
Boundary Commissions 61
complaints system 68
councillors 61, 62, 65
councils:
  borough 61, 62, 63, 66, 190
  community 63, 64
  county and metropolitan county 61, 62, 63, 139, 174, 175, 181, 184

Local Government—*contd.*
Councils—*contd.*
  district 61, 62, 63, 64, 66, 139, 174, 175, 190
  London see **London**
  parish and rural areas 62, 63
  regional authorities and islands 61, 63, 64, 131, 139, 174, 175, 184, 190
election 61–3
employment in 64–5, 340
environmental health 61, 63, 139
finance **65–7**, 130, 348, 352, 357
functions and services **63–4**, 130
grants and loans 65–6
internal:
  committees 64
  organisation 64
labour relations 340
loans 67
National Joint Councils 340
officers and employees 64–5
rates 66–7
relations with central Government 61, 130
responsibility for:
  amenities 63–4
  arts, encouragement of 63, 397, 398, 399, 400, 401, 408
  child care 118, **141–2**
  education see **Education**
  fire services 68–9
  handicapped 141
  health 61, 63, 64, 130, 139
  housing and planning 61, 64, 65, 141, 174–80, 182, 190
  licensing of films 403
  mentally ill 141
  pollution control 183, 185, 187
  public libraries 64, 410–11
  roads 64, 65, 304, 305
  social services 64, 65, 131
  sport 430
  traffic control 63
  welfare 341, 342
  youth services 171
Locomotives:
industry **243**, 311
types in use 309
Lomé, Convention of 76, 91, 92, 287, 372
London:
airports 217, 319, 320, 321
art, drama, music 397, 398, 400, 401, 403, 405, 406, 407, 408
  schools and colleges 400, 401, 403
Bankers' Clearing House 359
bishop of 196
borough councils 63, 66, 174, 190
Broadcasting:
  company 421, 422
  studios 425
Business Studies, Graduate School of 164
Central Mosque 199
City of 21, 61, 62, 67, 105, 106, 107, 125, 174, 190, 200, 323, 358, 360, 365, 366, 367
  Common Council of the 190
  Corporation of the 63
  police 105, 106, 107
Commodity Exchanges 367
design centre 215
Discount Market 367
food markets 260
Gold Market 367
Greater London 61, 62, 63, 216
  area 11

London—*contd.*
Greater London Council (GLC) 61, 62, 63, 174, 184, 398, 431
housing and planning 62, 174
industries 216–17
libraries 410
Lord Mayor 21, 62
Metropolitan Area, Outer 216
museums and art galleries 406, 407
newspapers 412, 413, 414, 415
police 64, 103, 105, 106, 107
population 8–11
port of and docks 313
religious centres 199
Sports Centre 431
Stock Exchange 367
taxicabs 308
telephone information service 323, 325
theatres 399, 400, 401
traffic 303, 305, 313
Transport 307
Transport Executive 307
  Underground rail services 308
Universities 44, 164, 408, 410, 411, 418
  libraries 411
Zoo 394
Londonderry 222
Longannet 277
Lord:
Advocate 38, 52, 53, 54, 109, 115, 119, 125, 126, 129
Advocate's Department 43, 54
Chancellor 26, 37, 38, 39, 48, 49, 50, 104, 110, 112, 114, 121, 122, 124, 125, 126, 128
  as Speaker of the House of Lords 26, 36–7, 49
Chancellor's Departments 49
Chief Justice (England) 37, 122
High Commissioner 37, 197
Justice Clerk 111, 122, 126
Justice General (Scotland) 111, 122
Lieutenants of Counties 37
President of the Council 37, 42
President of the Court of Session 122, 124, 126
Privy Seal 37, 46
Lords:
Commissioners (Treasury) 29, 38, 43
House of *see* **House of Lords**
Justices of Appeal 37, 122
of Appeal 25, 37, 122
Spiritual 21, 25
Temporal 21, 25
Lothian 221, 273, 278
Lotteries 437
Loughborough 164
Lowestoft 217, 298, 389
Luncheon voucher schemes 344
Luton 216
Lutheran Church 199

M

Machine Tool:
industry 218, 220, **238**
Research Association 238
Trades Association 238
See also **Tools**
Magazines *see* **Periodicals**
Magistrates and Magistrates' courts 49, 108, 110, 111, 112, 121, 123, 124
Mail order sales 258
Malting industry 249, 287

Malvern 399
Management *see* **Industry**
Manchester 11, 50, 164, 178, 218, 268, 307, 309, 312, 313, 319, 321, 385, 401, 403, 407, 413, 414, 418
Man-made fibres 218, 221, 222, 247, **250**, 251, 391
Manpower 210, 211, 212, 216, 252, 285, 298, 302, 322, 326, 327, 340–1
Conciliation and Arbitration Service 339–40
distribution of 326, 327
Economics, Office of 340–1
Qualified 334–5, 395–6
Services Commission (MSC) 51, 56, 134, 148, 214, **327–8**, 329, 331, 332, 343, 344
See also **Employment** *and* individual industries
Manslaughter 114
Manufacturers' associations 241
Manufacturing:
establishments, size of 210–11
industries:
  output and exports 200, 202, 211, **234–61**
See also **Industry** *and* Individual industries
Marchwood (laboratories) 279
Marine:
Biological Associations 384
Dumping at sea 186
Engineering *see* **Engineering** *and* **Shipbuilding**
Pollution 185–6, 389
Safety and Welfare 300, 314, 316
Technology 383, 384, 388
Maritime:
Board, National 316
Institute, National 388
International, Satellite Organisation (INMARSAT) 245, 324
Museum, National 406
Market gardening *see* **Agriculture**
Marketing:
Boards, agricultural *see* **Agriculture**
Institute of 215
Markets:
commodity 367
discount 360
exchange 367
fish and fish meal 260, 299
food (London) 259, 260
gold 367
insurance 365–6
Marriage 10, 13, 16
guidance centres 151, 152
rates 10, 13
Marshall Scholarships 171
Marshlands 5
Martlesham Heath 322
Master of Rolls 122
Maternity services 133, 136, 145, 146
Matrimonial proceedings (law) 121, 122
Mayors and Lord Mayors 21, 62
Meadowbank Sports Centre 431
Meals, provision of:
at place of employment 344
for old people 140, 152
for school children 149, 162
Meat and Livestock Commission 291
Mechanical engineering 218, 220, 237, **238**, 240
handling equipment 238, 239
Medical:
Advisory Service, Employment 341, **344**
Association, British 137
Council, General 137
Electronic X-ray Scanner systems 242
private insurance schemes 138

Medical—contd.
profession see Doctors
research 382, **383**, 386
  Council (MRC) 44–5, 344, 345, 382, **383**, 386, 390
  National Institute for 383
  in universities 383, 386
schools 164, 383
services:
  in industry 344
  in prisons 117
  for school children 136, 162
social workers 135, **143**
Medicines
Commission 137
safety of 137
Medmenham 284
Medway 216, 312, 313
Mental health services 117, **141**, 151
Merchant:
banks 360
Fleet 314
  ownership 314
Navy:
  conditions of employment 316
  Established Service Scheme 316
seafarers 316
shipbuilding 245–6
Merseyside 11, 177, 218, 223, 307, 331
tunnel 304
Metal manufacture 217, 236–9, 243
Meteorological Office 284, 390
Methodist Church 197
Metric conversion tables 438–9
Metropolitan Police Force 105, 106, 107, 308
Midlands 11, 217, 218, 223, 237, 268
Midwifery 133, 137
Midwives:
Board 137
Royal College of 137
Migration 9
Milford Haven 220, 268, 298, 312, 313
Milk:
in schools 162
marketing 290, 293
  Boards 290
production 288, 289
safety regulations 139
Milton Keynes 259, 423
Minerals 45, 262, 271, 383
industrial 262, 271, 280
Indigenous resources 280
non-fuel 262, **280–1**
  exploration **280**, 281
  ownership 262
  production 262, 280–1
  trade 280–1
Mines and quarries:
employment in 271, 273
industry 211, 218, 219, 220, 262, 271, 273
Inspectorate 341, 342
mining machinery 239
research 274, 344
safety measures 342, 344
See also **Coal**
Mining Research and Development Establishment 274
Ministers:
Council of 73, 74
of the Crown 20, 21, 23, **36–40**
  ministerial responsibility 23, 37, 39–40, 203
  salaries 38

Ministers—contd.
of State 37, **38**, 39, 42, 43, 44, 45, 46, 47, 48, 51, 52, 55
See also **Prime Minister** *and* individual government departments
Monarchy 19, **20–4**
accession 21
ceremonial 21, **22**
Civil List 23
  pensions 37
coronation 21
Privy Council 23, 24, **35–6**
relations with:
  armed forces 21
  churches 21, 37, 196, 197
  Commonwealth 20, 21
  foreign governments 21, 23
  Home Office 47
  judiciary 21, 125, 126
  Parliament 21, 23, 24, 25, 26, 32, 34, 35, 36, 37, 38
Royal:
  income and expenditure 23–4, 348
  Prerogatives 21, 23, 25, 36, 47
  Proclamations 25, 36
  title 20
succession 20–1
See also **Royal family**
Monetary Policy *see* **Finance** *and* **Economic, National**
Monopolies 231
and Mergers Commission 203, 231, 413
Montrose 314
Moorland 5
Motor:
cycle racing 434
cycles 243, 302
dealers and repair services 243
Manufacturers and Traders, Society of (SMMT) 243
racing 428, 434
shows 243
sports 434
vehicles:
  design standards 304
  industry 200, 201, 211, 216, 217, 218, 219, 220, 221, 243
  licensing 304, 305, **306**, 307, 308
  noise levels 187
  numbers licensed 305
  owners 14
  parking 64, 258, 305
  safety measures 304–5
  taxation 356
  tests 304
Motorways 51, 219, 303, 304, 305
Mountains 2, 3, 4, 5
Murder 109, 114, 129
Museums 37, 44, 53, 63, **394, 406–7**
and Galleries Standing Commission on 407
Association 407
Councils 407
finance 407
Mushrooms 289, 290
Music 398, 399, **401–3**
Amateur, Standing Conference for 402
choral societies 401–2
college and schools 403
Committees, County 402
concerts 398, 401
festivals 399, 401
folk 401
jazz 401

Music—*contd.*
Library, Central 410, 411
Master of the Queen's 401
orchestras 397, 398, 399, **401**, 403
'pop' 401
records 398, 411
Societies, National Federation of 403
Muslims 199

N

NATO *see* **North Atlantic Treaty Organisation**
National:
Anti-Waste Programme 184
Debt 357
  Office 40
Economy *see* **Economy** *and* **Finance**
Enterprise Board 228, 234
Equestrian Centre 431, 435
Exhibition Centre 218, 243, 260
Gallery 406
Insurance
  benefits and allowances 46–7, **143–9**
  contributions 47, **144–5**, 206
  pension scheme 145–6
  reciprocal agreements 47, 130, 138
  stamps 145, 322
  supplementary benefits 47, **148–9**
  Commission 47, 144
  surcharge 352, 356
Joint Councils 339, 340
Loans Fund 50, 348, 349, 352, 357
Maritime Museum 406
Maritime Museum Institute 388
parks 180, 219
  Council for 188
product, gross (GNP) 87, 88, 204, 302
Trusts 14–15, 179, 188, 429
  See relevant subject matter for organisations,
  etc. having National *as first word of their titles*
Nationalised Industries 200, 203–4, 210, 222,
234, 236, 237, 262, 263, 264, 265, 267, 268, 270,
271, 274
finance and investment 273, 275
labour relations of 340
research 268, 271, 274
See also individual industries
Nationality 12–13, 47
Natural:
beauty, areas of 180–1
Environment Research Council (NERC) 284,
296, 382, 383–4, 388
gas *see* **Gas** *and* **Energy**
History, British Museum 382, 394
Institute of Terrestrial Ecology 383
resources 262–84
Sciences 166
Naturalisation 12, 47
Nature:
Conservancy Council 180, 182, 428
conservation 178–82
  Society for the Promotion of 188
  voluntary organisations 188
Council for 15
reserves 182, 430
Navigational Aids 242, 314, 317, **324**
Navy *see* **Defence, Ministry of, Merchant**
Fleet and **Royal Navy**
Needles 3
Neurobiology and Mental Health Board 383
Newburgh 275

Newcastle upon Tyne 178, 259, 308, 309, 401,
405
Newhaven 217
Newlyn 298
New
Forest 181
Opera Company 402
Newport 220, 312, 414
News Agencies 416–17
Newspaper:
Circulation 412, **413–14**, 415
Editors:
  British Association of Industrial 418
  Guild of British Newspaper 418
industry 51, 412
new technology 414–15
owners 412–13
Publishers Association 416, **418**
Society 418
See also **Press**
Newspapers:
evening 413, 414, 415
national 412, **413**, 414, 415
regional 412, 413–14, 415
Newsprint, supply of 412
New towns 45, **176–7**
Development Corporations 176
Noise:
abatement 187
  Society 15, 188
Advisory Council on 15
  zones 187
control of 187, 318
Non-ferrous metals industry 211, 217, **237–8**
Northampton 177, 218
North Atlantic Treaty Organisation (NATO)
70, 81, 83, 93, **94–5**, 97, 98, 99, 100, 101, 244,
384
Northern Ireland (*see also* subject headings)
administration 54–6
agriculture and horticulture 55, 286, 287, 288,
289, 290, 291, 292, 389
Airports Ltd 321
area 1
art, drama and museums 397, 398, 400, 402,
405, 406, 411
Arts Council of 398, 400, 405
broadcasting councils and committees 420,
421
Chamber of Commerce and Industry 214
Civil Service 55, 58
Commissioner for Complaints 68, 132
constitution 19, 54, 55
Constitutional Convention 54
Co-ownership Housing Association 195
Council for Educational Research 169
Courts of Law 110, 112, 123, 126
Economic Council 176
education 55, 156, 157, 158, 160, 162, 163, 164,
165, 166, 167, 169, 171
Electricity Service 275, 279
Equal Opportunities Commission 152
Fair Employment Agency 56
Fire Authority and Services 68
forest parks and scenic drives 181
forestry 55, 301
gas supply 268
Government departments 40, 41, **54–6**
Department of Agriculture **55**, 181, 183, 192,
295, 296, 297, 300, 301
Department of the Civil Service 55
Department of Commerce **55**, 227, 229, 245,
375

Northern Ireland—*contd.*
Department of Education 40, **55**, 156, 160, 164, 429
Department of the Environment 40, **55**, 61, 67, 174, 175, 176, 178, 182, 183, 184, 186, 194, 283, 304, 308
Department of Finance **56**, 67
Department of Health and Social Service **56**, 119, 131, 135, 143
 Supplementary Benefits Commission 144
Department of Manpower Services **56**, 134, 149, 236, 328, 329
Government Loans Fund 67
health and welfare services 56, 63, 134, 139, 143
holidays, statutory 334
Housing 194–5
 Executive 194
industrial safety 345
industry 55, 56, 222, 227, 228, 229
 Local Enterprise Development Unit (*LEDU*) 228
Labour Relations Agency 56, 338
law courts 102, 104, 109, 123, 126, 128
legislation 19, 53–4, 57, 102, 104, 119–20
libraries 55, 64, 411
library boards 156, 157, 411
local government 55, 61, 62, 63, 64, 65, 66, 67, 68
maintenance of law and order 95, 102, 104, 105, 106, 108, 110, 123, 124
motorway system 303, 304
music, opera and dance 401, 402
national insurance 143
national parks 181
Nature Resources Committee 182
Newspapers, Associated 418
Nurses and Midwives, Council of 137
Office 48, **55**, 126
police 103, 104, 105
population 7, 11
ports and harbours 55, 298
press 414, 418
public finance 357
railways 308
registers 56
representation in United Kingdom Parliament 20, 54
roads 54, 64, 303, 304
Secretary of State for 54, 55, 105, 126, 128, 397, 428
social services 56, 62, 131, 141, 149, 151
Sports Council 429
trade unions 337
transport 56, 304, 305, 306, 307, 308
Transport Holding Company 306, 307, 308
unemployment 331
universities and colleges 156, 165, 166
voting 63
water pollution 184
water supply 55, 61, **283**, 284
workers 329
See also **Ulster**
North of Scotland Hydro-Electric Board (NSHEB) 274, 275, 277, 278, 279
North Sea 52, 186, 200, 202, 204, 207, 217, 220, 221, 237, 263, **265**, 268, 270, 304, 386
See also **Gas, Petroleum** *and* **Energy**
Northumberland 180, 220
North York Moors 180
Norwich 217, 382, 389
Nottingham and Nottinghamshire 218, 259

Nuclear:
Fuels Ltd., British 277, **278**
Disposal, Radio Active Waste 278
Installation Inspectorate of Health and Safety Executive 187
Safety and Reliability Directorate 387
Nuclear Energy:
advisory committees and boards 264, 387
Agency (NEA) 387, 394
Industry 219, 220, 262, **277**, 278, 386–7
international agencies 387, 394
power stations 220, 239, 257, 262, **277**, 278
Programme 262, **277–8**
reactors 239, 277, 387
research 279, 386–7
Nuclear weapons 82
weapons and equipment *see* **Defence**
See also **Atomic Energy Authority**
Nursery schools *see* **Education**
Nursing and nurses 96, 133, 136, 137
associations 137
Council of Nurses and Midwives 137
General Nursing Councils 137
in Armed Forces 96
in the home 133, 141
Royal College of Nursing 137

O

Observatory:
Edinburgh, Royal 384, 385
Royal Greenwich (RGO) 1, 384, 385
Occupational therapists 134, 138
Oceanography 383
Offenders:
children 112, **118–20**
treatment of 102, **114–18**, 125, 126
Office machinery industry 240
Office
machinery industry 221, 240
of Fair Trading 203
Official Solicitor 49
Offshore:
buoy 317
Energy Technology Board 268, 386
equipment industry 264
oil and gas 185, **264**, 342
Supplies Office 45, 264
Oil *see* **Petroleum**
Oldham 218
Old people *see* **Elderly**
Olympic Games 429, 432
British Olympic Association 429
Open University 117, 163, **165**, 169, 422
Opera and opera companies 397, 401, **402–3**
English National 402
Royal Opera House 402
training 403
Ophthalmic services 133, 138
Opposition, parliamentary 28, 29, 34, 60
Optical and radio astronomy 384, 385
observatories 384, 385
telescopes 385
Opticians 133, 138
General Optical Council 138
Orders in Council 36, 42
Ordnance Survey 49
Organisation for Economic Co-operation and Development (OECD) 86, 87, 89, 185, 263, 372, 374, 394
Orkney Islands 1, 61, 64, 294, 312, 313

Overseas:
aid programme 86–92
banks 360
broadcasting 423, 424, 426–7
constructional work 256
dependent territories, public services 58
détente 81–2
Development Administration **46**, 57, 70–1,
86–7, **395**
educational assistance 71–2, 169
Inter-University Council for Higher Education
170
North-South Dialogue 90–2
Pest Research Centre 90, 395
relations 70–92
  Administration 70–1
  Britain and the United Nations 83–7
  Commonwealth 77–81
  development co-operation 86–92, 395
  international peace and security 81–3
  membership of the European Community 72–7
scientific relations 395
students 169–70
  Affairs, UK Council for 170
teachers' exchange schemes 169, 170
Trade Board, British 48, 50, 71
  See also **Trade**
Voluntary agencies 90
Oxford 165, 216, 387, 389, 394, 406, 410

P

Packaging 217, 240, 247, 251, 253
Paint industry 220, 247, 248
Paisley 221, 414
Paper and board industry 217, 219, 221, 235,
253, 301
Paraplegic Sports Society, British 430, 431
Paramount Pictures 427
Parkeston Quay 313
Parks 180, 430
Countryside Commissions 180
forest 181
national 180, 219
Parliament 19, 20, 21, 23, **24–35**, 36, 37, 38, 39,
40, 43, 48, 50, 52, 54, 55, 56, 61, 102, 103, 122,
127, 132, 149, 222, 290, 301, 313, 318, 348, 349,
366, 420, 425
Bills, parliamentary 21, 25, **30–4**, 43, 50, 54, 351
  procedure **28–38**, 43
  Royal Assent to 21, 32
committees **32–4**, 349–50
control of:
  armed forces 93
  finance 29, 33, 34, 40, 49, 349
  Government in power 28, 29–30, 31, **32–4**
  public corporations 203–4, 222
dissolution of 23, 25, 36
duration of 25
elections 24, 26, **27–8**
European 24, 74
functions 25
legislation 24, **30–2**, 34, 35, 39, 50
Opposition 28, 29, 34, 60
party system 24–5, 26, 27, **28–9**, 39
privileges 35
procedure 29–30
prorogation of 21, 25
relations with:
  the Church 196, 197
  local authorities 61, 63

Parliament—*contd.*
relations with—*contd.*
  the Monarchy 20, 21, 23, 24, 25, 26, 32, 36, 37,
  38, 47
  sessions 25
  Standing Orders Committee 33
  State opening of 23, 26
  Statutory Instruments 32, 350
  summoning of 21, 36
  Whips **29**, 38, 43
  See also **House of Commons** *and* **House of
  Lords**
Parliamentary:
Commissioner 35, 132
Committees 32–3, 406
control 34–5, 349
Counsel:
  on Bills 50
  Office 43
political broadcasting 425
Secretaries 29, 37, 38, 39, 42, 43, 44, 45, 46, 47,
48, 51, 52, 53, 54, 55
Parole Boards 116, 125, 126
Patent Office 215
Paymaster General 37, **49**
Peers and Peeresses 22, 25, 27
Pembrokeshire 180
Peak District 180
Penal systems 125
Advisory Council 125
Pennines 2, 4, 11
Pensions:
attendance allowance 148
earnings-related pension scheme 144
graduated pension scheme 144, 145
inflation-linked 145
invalidity allowance 147
occupational 144, 145, 364
payment of, by Post Office 322
public service 49, 57
retirement 144, **145–6**
State pension scheme 145–6
supplementary, old persons' 149
war 47, 143, **149–50**
widows 144, **146–7**
Penzance 309, 320
Periodical Publishers Association 416, 418
Periodicals 392, 393, 405, 409, 410, 411, 412,
416, 418
Permanent Boundary Commissions 27
Personal social services 64, 65, 140–3
Personnel Management, Institute of 215
**Pesticides and Other Toxic Chemicals,
Advisory Committee on** 184, 343
Pesticides Safety Precautions Scheme 184,
296, 343, 389
Pest Infestation Control Laboratory 389
Peterborough 177, 217
Peterhead 298, 314
Petroleum and petroleum products 45, 186,
200, 201, 202, 203, 204, 207, 209, 211, 220, 221,
246, 248, 261, 262, 263, 264, **265**, **267–8**, 313,
314
British Petroleum Ltd 210, 234, 265
chemicals industry 210, 213, 218, 235, **246**, 247
equipment industry 45, 203–4, 221, 237, 239,
240, 264
exports 265, 267, 314, 368
imports and consumption 262, 265, **267**, 269, 314
industry 45, 203, 224, 234, 264, 265, 320
National Oil Corporation, British (BNOC) 45,
203, 267
oilfields 262, 264, 265, 267, 268, 355

Petroleum and petroluem products—*contd.*
Offshore:
  equipment industry 221, 264
  oil and gas 45, 185, 234, **264**, 314
  Supplies Office 45, 264
  Technology Board 268, 386
pipelines **267–8**
prevention of sea pollution by 179, **185**
production platforms 185, 221, 265, 325
refineries and refining 211, 216, 220, 239, 262, **267**
research 268, 386
revenue tax 200, 265, 354–5
tankers 268, 314
terminals 220, 221, 268, 314, 323
Pharmaceuticals 218, 220, **247**
Committee on Review of Medicines 137
Committee on Safety of Medicines 137
Pharmaceutical Society of Great Britain 138
Pharmacists 133, 138
Philatelic Bureau 323
Photographic:
equipment 241
Manufacturers Association, British 241
Physical Laboratory, National 216, 388
Physical Recreation, Central Council of (CCPR) 428
Physically handicapped *see* **Disabled**
Physiological Systems and Disorders Board 383
Physiotherapists 134, 138
Pig industry 285, **289**, 291, 295
Pilotage 318
Pipelines:
gas 270
oil 267–8
Pitlochry 278, 389
Planning:
Association, Town and Country 188
boards and councils, economic 175
development areas and schemes 174–5, 223, 226–7
environmental 63, 64, 174, 222, 255
inner cities 177–8
inquiry commissions 175
policies 174, 177
public participation 175
regional **175–6**, 222, 223
research 45, 385
voluntary planning organisations 188
Plant health 43, 296, 388, 389
Pathology Laboratory 388
Plastics 219, 220, 238, 246, **247**, 254
Plas-y-Brenin National Centre for Mountain Activities 431
Plas-y-Deri National Outdoor Pursuits Centre 431
Playing fields 162, 429
Association, National (NPFA) 429
Plimsoll line 316
Plymouth 217, 298, 309
Poet Laureate 37, 409
Poetry festivals and societies 409
Polaris **vessels** 95, 97
Police 47, 53, 63, 64, 102, 103, **104–5**, 106, 107
associations 105, 107
Authorities 65, **105–6**
cadets 106
committees 105
Negotiating Board 105
Research Services Unit 107
Royal Commission on 102
Scientific Development Branch 107

Political:
broadcasts 30, 425
party system 28–9
Pollution, prevention of:
air 14, 45, 139, 183, 184, **186–7**, 390
land 14, 183, 184
noise 14, 139, 183, 184, **187**
research 45, 383, 387, 390
rivers 45, 185, 283, 284
sea (by oil) 179, 183, 185–6, 316
water supply 45, 183, 184, **283**, 284
Polytechnics *see* **Education**
Pony Club 435
Poole 11, 217
Population 7–9, 10–11, 176, 326, 368, 385
age distribution 10
birth and death rates 7, 8–9
censuses 7, 50
  and Surveys, Office of 40, 50, 390
Commonwealth 77
density 8, 10–12
Dependencies **80**
ethnic minorities 9, 12
households 13–14, 191
increase in 7
migration 9
mortality, causes of 9
nationalities 12, 17
regional distribution 11–12
sex ratio 10
trends 7–8
vital statistics 7
working 11, 15, 234, 262, 285, 302
Portavogie 298
Portrait Galleries, National 406
Ports and docks 51, 139, 216, 217, 219, 255, 298, **312–13**
authorities 312, 313
  British Ports Association 313
container facilities 312, 313
development 177, 313–14
ownership 312
transport industry 312, 313
Portsmouth 217
Port Talbot 220
Post Office 47, 203–4, 210, 233, 242, 307, **322–5**, 396, 417, 419, 423, 424, 426
cable and wireless services 323, 324, 325, 423
counter services 322
'Datapost' 323
Data Processing Service, National 325
Datel Services 324–5
Development 326
Employment 322
Exchanges 323
finance 322
mail services 322
Martlesham Heath (Research Centre) 322
mechanisation 322, 323, 324, 325
micro-electronics 323
mini buses 307
National Girobank 145, 322, 359
organisation 322
Packet Switches Services 325
Postal Consultancy Service, British 323
'Postbus' 307
'Prestel' 242, **324**, 426
radio paging service 325
research 322, 325, 396, 426
satellites 324–5, 396
System 'X' 323
telegrams 325

Post Office—*contd.*
telegraph services 322, 325
telephone services 242, 322, 323, 325
  special services 324
telex service 242, **325**
teletext 242, 324
See also **Telecommunications**
Potato production and marketing 261, 286,
287, 290, 293, 389
Marketing Board 290, 292
Pottery industry 218, **252–3**, 281, 397
Poultry:
diseases 295, 382, 389
industry 285, **289**
Power stations *see* **Electricity** *and*
Nuclear Energy
Preservation:
councils and societies 188
of buildings 178, 188, 397, 408
of coastal areas 179
of rural amenities 180
of trees 178–9, 180
Press 412–19
Association Ltd. 416, 417
broadcasting and the 413, **417**, 419, 426
Council 418–19
institutions 418
legal requirements 413, 419
London suburban 414, 418
'National' 412, **413**, 414, 415
ownership 412–13
Periodical 416
regional 412, **413–14**
training for journalism 417–18
  Thomson Foundation 418
Preston 218
Prestwick (airport) 321
Price:
guarantees (agricultural) 43–4, 293
restriction by traders 232
Prime Minister 21, 23, 25, 28, 29, 36, **37**, 38, 39,
42, 43, 59, 60, 196, 381
Prince of Wales 23, 24
Committee 188
Printing:
and Publishing Industry Training Board
(PPITB) 418
industry 213, 216, 217, 234, **253**
Prisons and prisoners 114, **116–18**, 120, 125
chaplains 118
education 117
employment 117
medical service 117
privileges and discipline 117–18
psychological services 117
remission of sentence **116–17**, 120
training and employment 117, 118, 120
visitors 117, 118
  boards of 117, 118, 125
welfare and after-care 116, **118**, 125
Privy Council 23, 24, **35–6**, 38
Committees 36
Counsellors 36, 37
devolution policy 36
Probation 47, 114, **115–16**, 120, 125
officers 115, 116, 118
service to the community, scheme 114, 115
Procurator General 50
Procurators Fiscal 54, 110, 114
Production and productivity *see* **Industry**
Professional:
and Executive Recruitment (PER) 329
Institutions and associations 383–4, **393**

Property:
Law 121
Service Agency 45, 255
Protection of Ancient Buildings, Society for
189
Animals and Birds 5–6, 182
Birds, Royal Society for 189
Rural
  England, Council for 188
  Scotland, Association for 188
  Wales, Council for 188
Psychiatric social work 115, 117, 134, 135, 136
Public:
Accounts Committee 349, 350
administration 200
authorities 255, 340
corporations 20, 203–4, 207, 210, 222–3, 228,
381, 390
See also **Nationalisation** *and*
individual corporations
Finance *see* **Finance**
holidays 18, 334
houses (pubs) 18
libraries 64, 397, 398, 409, 410, 411
passenger transport 307, 308, **309**, 318, 319
Prosecutions, Director of 48, 110, 126
Record Office 38, 48, 406, 410
services of overseas dependent territories 58
Works Loan Board 67, 191, 352
Publishers' Association 418
Publishing 50, 213, 221, 234, 236, **253**, 392, 409,
411, 412
Pumps and industrial valves 221, 238, 239

Q

Quakers 198
'Quangos' 41
Queen *see* **Monarchy**
Queen Elizabeth
Country Park 181
Forest Park 181
Hall 401
Queen's:
Bench Division (England and Wales) 121, 122
Courts 126
Printer 50
Proctor 48, 50
Silver Jubilee Trust 172, 173
University 165, 296, 399, 411

R

Race Relations 45, **153–4**, 330, **333**
Employment Advisory Service 330
Ethnic Relations Research Unit 385
Racial Equality, Commission for 154
Radar 242, 244, 317, 321
Radio:
astronomy 385
communications 241, 242, 324
  See also **Broadcasting, Navigational Aids**
  and **Satellites**
  industry 241, 242, 426
  Interference, UK Committee of the
  International Special Committee on
  (CISPR) 427
with offshore installations 324
telegraphy 323
telescopes 384
transhorizon 324

Radioactive Waste Management Advisory Committee 188
Radioactivity 187–8, 278
Radiochemical Centre Ltd 247
Radiography 138
Radioisotopes 234, 247
Radiological Protection Board, National 188
Radiopaging Service 325
Railways 51, 204, 219, 302, **308–12**
Board, British 105, 308, 309, 311, 312
British Rail Engineering Ltd. (BREL) 312
development 309
diesel traction 309
electrification 308, 309, 311
Employment Inspectorate 342
Freight:
  Services 51, 302, **311**
  'Speedlink' 311
grants 309, 311
hotels and catering 311
inter-city 308–9
mechanisation 308–9
operations 309
  Processing System, Total 311
passenger service 308, **309**, 310
private 311–12
safety measures 342
underground (London) 309
vehicles industry 217, 218, **243**, 311
workshops 219, 243
Rainfall 4, 284
Rambling 428
Ramsgate 316
Rates 66–7
rebates 66, 177
support grants 66
valuation courts 66
water 281
Ravenscraig 237
Raw materials, trade in 200, 219, 280
Reactors *see* **Nuclear energy**
Reading 164, 217, 296, 407
Recorders (law) 110, 121
Recreation 18, 45, 179, 180, **428–37**
facilities for 179, 180, 181, **430–1**
Physical 162, 428, 430–1
  Central Council of (CCPR) 428
See also **Clubs, Leisure** *and* **Sports**
Red Cross Society, British 151
Redditch 218
Redruth 217
Referendum on European Community membership 72
Refineries *see* **Petroleum**
Refractory goods 252
Refrigeration machinery 239
Refuse, collection and disposal of 63, 64, 139, 184, 185
Regional:
Arts 398, 399
development 223–8
  agencies 228
  assisted areas 223–6
  grants and loans 226, 227, 229
employment incentives 226, 228, 329
industrial
  incentives 226, 228
  policy 222, 226
planning boards and councils 175–6
policy, industrial and 222, 223, 226, 228
Water Authorities 281, **283, 295**, 428
Regions, standard 216–22

Registrar:
General of Shipping and Seamen 316
Registrars:
General 50, 53
of births, deaths and marriages 50
Religion *see* **Churches** *and also* **Broadcasting** *and* **Education**
Remploy Ltd 329
Rent:
allowances 150, 195
restrictions 194–5
tribunals 124, 195
Reptiles 6
Rescue services, sea and air 317, 320, 321, 324
Research, scientific 381–96
advisory councils and committees 381, 382, 383, 386, 388, 390
agricultural 296, 382–3, 388, 395
  consultative organisation 388
aircraft 390
associations 381, 387, 391, 392
astronomy 384, 385
biological 182, 383, 384, 385, 389, 391, 393
botanical 390
building and civil engineering 45, 190, 256, 387
chemical 388, 391, 393
civil aviation 100, 391
Commonwealth 387, 389
communications 381, 387, 384
construction 45, 256, 387
councils 44–5, 381, 382, 383, 384, 385
  Advisory Board for 381, 382
Council, Science (SRC) 384, 385
criminology 103–4
defence **100–1**, 390
Development Corporation, National (NRDC) 391
ecological 383, 384, 389
electronics 388, 391
engineering 384, 388, 391, 393
environmental 383–4, 387
establishments 48, 381, 382, 383, 384, 385, 387, 388
expenditure on 381, 382, 384, 385, 386, 387, 389, 390, 391, 392, 396
fellowships and studentships 383, 384, 385, 386, 392, 393, 395
fire prevention 69, 390
fisheries 388, 389
forestry 301, 389
fuel and power 268, 271, 274, 279, 385, 386–7
  Advisory Council on Research and Development 386
furniture 254
geological 49, 383, 394
Government responsibility 381–96
industry 48, 245, 287, 388, 391, 396
See also individual industries
in universities and technical colleges 382, 383, 384, 385–6, 391
land use and planning 383, 395
lectureships and awards 383, 384, 386, 392, 393
medical 383, 390, 391, 394
meteorological 388, 390, 394
microelectronic 384
mining 274, 388, 394
nuclear 73, 279, 385, 386–7, 394
optical astronomy 384, 385
pest control 248, 296, 383, 389, 395
  Centre for Overseas Pest Research 395
petroleum 268, 386
pharmaceuticals 391
plant 383, 384, 388, 390

Research, scientific—contd.
policy 381
pollution 45, 183, 383, 387, 390
private institutes for 391, 393
radio-astronomy 384, 385
results, information on 391
roads 51, 305–6, 387
social 382, 385, 390, 394
solar energy 279
space 384, 396
technological 380, 385, 386, 391, 393
telecommunications 396
television and radio 426
textiles 391
timber, uses of 387, 389
tropical products 383, 395
universities 383, 384, **385, 386**
veterinary 389
water supplies 383
zoological 394
Restrictive practices 124, **232**
Court 124, 232
Fair Trading 231, 232
Retail:
organisation and turnover 257–9
  types of 257, 258, 259
trade 257–9
Reuters Ltd 416, 417
Revenue 43, 200, 265, 307, 352–7, 412
Rhodes Scholarships 171
Riding (horse) 428, 435
Show jumping 435
Rights of way 181
Risley 278, 287
River authorities 312
See also **Water**: boards and authorities
Road:
freight 302, 306
  Corporation, National 204, 306
haulage 51, 302, **306**
  European Community rules 306
passenger transport 302, 307
  authorities 307
  Executives (PTEs) 307
  grants 307
Research Laboratory, Transport and (TRRL) 90,
305, 387
Roads 51, 55, 63, **302–3**, 304, 305
authorities 304
classification 304, 305
development and construction 51, 55, 303,
304, 387
motorways and trunk roads 51, 219, 302, 303,
304
Northern Ireland 55, 304
research 305, 387
safety 51, 304–5, 306
transport on 302, 303, 304, 305, 306, 307, 308,
387
Rochdale 218
Roman Catholic Church see **Church**
Rope-making 220, 251
Roslin 389
Rotherham 312
Rough (gasfield) 270
Royal:
Air Force 93, 95, 99, 100
  College 96
  Museum 406
  Regiment 99
  reserve and auxiliary forces 99
  Staff College 96
  Volunteer Reserve 100

Royal—contd.
See also **Defence**
ceremonial 23
Commissions 41, 102, 127, 178, 183
  appointment and function of 41
Constitution 19–20
Courts of Justice 122
Dockyards 57, 97, 101
Family 20, 21, 22, 23, 24
  income and expenditure 23–4
  visits 23
Institution 396
Jubilee Trusts 172
Marines 95, 96, 98
  Reserve 100
Military Academy 96
Mint 40, 57, 345, 358
Naval:
  College 96
  Reserve 100
  Staff College 96
Navy 93, 95, 96, 97, 98
  nuclear submarines 95, 97, 98
See also **Defence**
observatories 385
Observer Corps 100
Ordnance Factories 57, 97, 101
Prerogatives see **Monarchy**
Proclamations see **Monarchy**
Smithfield Show 240
Society 382, 386, **392**, 393, 394, 395
  of Arts 393
  See relevant subject matter for organisations,
  etc., having Royal as first word of their title
Royston 273
Rubber industry 217, 218, 219, 247, **254**
Rugby 218
football 428, 430, 431, **435–6**
Runcorn 219, 312
Rural:
amenities, preservation of 180, 181, 182
Councils 228
districts:
  councils 61, 62, 63, 64
  population 11
industries 228–9
Preservation Societies 15, 188
Rutherford Laboratory 384

S

Sadler's Wells Company and Theatre 402
Safety:
and Reliability Directorate 387
Commission, Health and 214, **241–2**, 343
Council, British 343
in Mines Research Establishment (SMRE) 341,
344
measures 294
  Royal Society for the Prevention of Accidents
  (RoSPA) 304
See also **Agricultural workers, Civil Aviation,
Mines and quarries, Railways** and **Roads**
Sailing 436
National, Centre 431, 436
St. Andrews University 164
St. Austell 217
St. Bees Head 3
St. Fergus 270
St. Helens 219
St. John Ambulance 151
Salford University 164

Salmon fishing 299, 434
Salvation Army 151, 198
Samaritans 151
Sand and gravel industry 280, 281
Sandstone 281
Sandwell 218
Satellites 245, 323, 324, 396, 417, 426, 427
Save as You Earn (SAYE) 361
Savings 205, 322, 352, **360–1**
National
  banks 322, 360, 361
  bonds 361
  Certificates 355, 360, 361
  contractual 360
  Department for 40, 57, 360
  gift tokens 360
  Stock Register 360
Scafell Pike 2
Schools *see* Education
Science:
Advisory Board for Research Councils 382
and Society, Council for 394
and Technology:
  Council of, Institutes 393
  Institutes of 383, 384
awards 381, 392, 393
British Society for Social Responsibility in 394
Department of Education and *see* Education
Museum 394, 406
promotion of 381–96
publications 381, 392, 393
Research Council (SRC) 45, 382, **384**, 394, 396
See also **Research** *and* **Universities**
Scientific:
and industrial instruments industry 220, 241
  Control and Automation Manufacturers
    Association 241
  Sira Institute 241
co-operation:
  between industry and universities 381, 382,
    384, 385, 386, 390, 396
  government and industry 381, 382, 388, 395
  with overseas countries **394, 395**, 396
counsellors 395
Film Association, British Industrial and 404
Instruments Manufacturers Association 241
museums **394**, 406, 407
overseas organisations 89
Parliamentary and, Committee 381, 391
research *see* Research
Scientists:
number employed 383, 384, 392
training of 381, 382, 384, **385–6**
Scotland (*see also* subject headings):
administration 19, 51–4
aerodromes and airways 318, 320, 321
area 1
botanic gardens 390
broadcasting councils and committees 421
Common Services Agency 132, 137
devolution 19
economic planning 51, 52–3, 227, 228
education 53, 156, 157, 158, 160, 161, 163, 164,
165, 166, 167, 168, 169, 171, 172
energy 51, 265, 270, 274, 275, 277, 278
Government departments 40, 43, **50–4**
  Agriculture and Fisheries **52**, 183, 186, 291,
    296, 300, 383, 386, 389, 390
  Central Services 53
  Development 53–4, 179
  Economic Planning **52–3**, 176, 227
  Education 40, **52**, 156, 164, 171, 405, 408
  Environment 40

Scotland—*contd.*
Central Services—*contd.*
  Home and Health 53, 68, 131, 184
  Law Officers 53–4
  Lord Advocate's 38, 52, 53
  Record Office 53, 410
  Registers of Scotland 53
holidays, statutory 334
industry 53, **221–2**, 226, 227, 228, 237, 251
local government 61, 66, 67
Lands Valuation Appeal Court 66
Lord Provost 62
Ministers of State for 51, 52
museums and art galleries 53, 406, 407
music and opera 401, 402
National:
  Library of 53, 411
  Trust for 179, 188
Parliamentary Draftsmen for 54, 126
population 7, 11, 12
ports (fishing) 298
press 413, **414**, 418
river purification boards 184
Royal Observatory 384, 385
Secretary of State 49, 51, 52, 53, 67, 104, 105,
106, 156, 174, 176, 178, 181, 190, 263, 283, 291,
301, 389, 397, 428
unemployment 223, 331
water supply **283**, 284
Scotland Yard, New 105
Scottish:
Academy of Music and Drama, Royal 401, 403
Agricultural Securities Corporation 293
Arts Council 398, 405
Business Education Council 167
Chamber of Commerce 214
Community Drama Association 400
Council:
  Development and Industry 214, 375
  Economic 184
  of Social Service 151
Courts Administration **53–4**, 111, 122
Craft Centre 215
Crime Squad 107
Daily Newspaper Society 418
Development Agency 52–3, 182, 227, 228, 229
Development Department **52**, 61, 174, 186, 190
Gallery of Modern Art 406
Grand Committee (parliamentary) 33
Health Service Planning Council 132
Joint Crafts Committee 408
Land Court **122–3**, 294
Law Commission 54, 129
Newspaper Proprietors Association 418
Office 48, 52, 179, 222, 226, 228
Opera Company 402
orchestras 401
Special Housing Association (SSHA) 190
Sports Council 53, 428, 431
Standing Conference of Sport 428
Tourist Board 53, 229
Transport Group 52, 307
Universities 36, 164–5, 410
Wildlife Trust 189
Scouts 151, 172
Scunthorpe 220, 237
Sealink UK Ltd 315
Seamen:
conditions of employment 316
number and qualifications 316
Safety and Welfare 317
training 316
  College, National Sea 316

Seas 1– 2, 316, 317
Seaspeed 316
Sea transport 312, 313, 314, 315, 316
Selby 219, 273
Service trades 210, **260–1**
Severn bridge 303
Severn river 280, 303
Sewerage and sewage disposal 45, 51, 184, 185, 239, 283, 284
Sex Discrimination 121, **152–3**, 333, 339
Sheffield 11, 164, 187, 219, 253, 312, 407
Sheriffs and Sheriff Courts 54, 109, **111**, 113, 114, 119, 122, 124
Shetland Islands 1, 4, 64, 294, 312, 313, 316, 317, 322
Shipbuilders, British 203
Shipbuilding:
and marine engineering 217, 220, 221, 222, 245–6, 331
British Ship Research Association 246
Shipowners 313, **314–5**
Shipping 200, 302, 312, **314–18**
and Seamen, Registrar-General 316
coastal 312, 313
conferences 315
container facilities and services 302, 313, 314
dry bulk carrier vessels 313, 314, 315
employers' and employees' organisations 316, 317
employment of 316
exports 246
fishing fleet 299
General Council of, British 315
liners, passenger and cargo 315, 316
Lloyd's Register of 314
merchant fleet, composition 314
merchant seafarers 316
Navy see **Royal Navy**
on inland waterways 312
ore terminals 313, 314
organisations 316, 317
ports 216, 217, 219, 312–13
radar surveillance 317
radio communications 316, 324
relations with Government 317
safety **317**, 324
tankers and terminals 268, 312, 313, 314
tonnage 312, 313, 314
traffic control and zones 317
tramps 31, 315
Shops:
cash and carry, wholesale 260
co-operative societies 260
department stores 260
hypermarkets and superstores 258–9
independent 258–60
multiple stores 257, 258, 259
number of 258, 259, 260, 261
sales promotion 260–1
self-service 258, 259
supermarkets 258, 259
Shropshire 407, 431
Sickness benefit 147, 335
Sikhs 199
Silsoe 297, 383
Silverware 238, 246
Silviculture see **Forestry**
Skillcentres (SCs) 329, 331
Slieve Donard 2
Slough 217, 389
Small Firms Information Centres 228
Smallholdings see **Agriculture**
Smithfield Market 260

Smoke control 4, 186
Snowdon 2, 4
Snowdonia 180
Soap production 248
Soccer see **Football**
Social:
attitudes 13
life 13–18
Science Research Council (SSRC) 45, 169, 345, 385, 390
research units 385
Security 46, **143–50**, 207, 335
benefits 145–50
contributions 144–5
Department of Health and Social Security see Health
expenditure on 130
reciprocal agreements with other countries 47, 130, **138**
Services 130, 140–50
Services 46–7, 140–3, 207, 346, 347
personal 63, 64, 130, 140–3
Secretary of State for 46, 131
voluntary organisations 143, 151–2
Volunteer Centre 152
Training in 143
welfare 130–54
Work, Central Council for Education and Training in 143
workers 135, **143**, 150–2
See also **Health Service, National** and **National Insurance**
Soft drinks industry 249–50
Soil 4–5, 285, 382
Solar Energy 279, 393
Solicitor:
General 48, 49, 125, 126
for Scotland 38, 52, 53, 109, 126
Official 49
Solicitors 126, **127**, 128, 129
Solihull 218
Somerset 5, 278, 406
Southampton 164, 217, 267, 278, 312, 313, 407
South of Scotland Electricity Board see **Electricity**
Sovereign see **Monarchy**
Space Activities 396
Space Research:
Council (SRC) 396
European:
programme 396
Space Agency (ESA) 324, 396
See also **Research**
Speaker:
House of Commons 26, 27, 29, 34
House of Lords 29, 30, 49
Special constables 106
Spectacles 133
Opticians 133, 138
Speed limits 306
Speedlink Trains 311
Sport 46, 47, 428–37
facilities for 52, 430–1
government responsibility 46, 428
National Playing Fields Association 429
organisation and promotion 428–9
private sponsorship 430
voluntary organisations 428, 430
Sports:
Aid Foundation 430
Association for the Disabled, British 429
bodies 436–7
British Paraplegic Society 430, 431

Sports—contd.
centres, national 421, 428, 431
Councils 180, **428–9**, 430, 431, 432
equipment industry 254–5
United Kingdom Association for People with
Mental Handicap 430
See also **Recreation**
Springfield 278, 387
Staff colleges (armed forces) 96
Stafford and Staffordshire 218, 252, 273, 274
Stag hunting 433
Stamp trading 259
Standards Institution, British 215–16
Standing Committees see **Parliament,**
committees
Stanhope Bretby 274
Stanlow 267, 268
Stansted (airport) 321
Stationery Office, Her Majesty's (HMSO) 40, 59
Statistical Office, Central (CSO) **40**, 205
Office, Business 40
publications 41
Statutory:
Instruments 32, 350
Publications Office 50
Steel:
Community, European Coal and (ECSC) **72**, 77,
230
Corporation, British (BSC) 47, 202, 220, 236,
237, 238, 340
Producers' Association British Independent
236
Steelwork plant industry 219, 220, **236–9**
Sterling 201, 203, 207, 208, 357, 358, 360, 372,
374, 375, 376, 378, 379, **380**
devaluation 201
exchange rates 207, 208, 209, 372
Stevenage 284
Stirling University 164
Stock Exchange 67, 352, **367**
Stockport 218
Stockton 308
Stoke Mandeville:
Hospital 430
Sports Stadium for the Paralysed and Disabled
430, 431
Stoke-on-Trent 218
Stoke Orchard 274
Stranraer 312, 390
Stratford-upon-Avon 218, 400
Strathclyde 221, 229, 278, 294
University (Glasgow) 165
Strikes see **Industrial disputes**
Students 163–**4**, 166, 167
from overseas 89, 170, 395, 396, 418
grants 164
See also **Education** and **Universities**
Submarines 97, 98, 241, 267, 324
Sugar 219, 287
beet 287
Corporation Ltd., British 287
Sullom Voe (oil terminal) 221, 313, 314
Sumburgh 317, 321, 322
Sunbury-on-Thames 268
Sunshine 4
**Supreme Court of Judicature in Northern
Ireland** 123
Surgical instruments 240, 241
Surrey 164, 388, 389
Surtax see **Taxation**
Sussex 164, 407, 431
Swansea 178, 220, 312, 414
Swimming 430, **436**

Swindon 177, 217, 423
Synthetic fibres 218, 221, 222, 250, **251**
Synthetic rubber 222, 247, 254

T

Tables, statistics (in chapter order):
The Land and the People
 Area of the United Kingdom 1
 Populations 1901–79 7
 *Size and Population of some of the Main
 Urban Areas Mid-1979* 11
Government
 *Percentages of Votes Cast, and Members
 Elected, in the May 1979 General Election* 28
Overseas Relations
 *Official Development Assistance to
 Development Countries 1976–79* 88
Justice and the Law
 *Indictable Offences Recorded
 by the Police per 100,000
 Population (England and Wales) 1979* 103
National Economy
 *Gross Domestic Product by Industry (at
 current prices* 204
 *Distribution of Total Supplies of Goods and
 Services* 205
 *Changes in Pattern of Consumers' Spending
 (at current prices)* 206
Framework of Industry
 Index of Output 1974–79 (1975 = 100) 211
 *Index of Output per head 1974–79
 (1975 = 100)* 212
 *Gross Domestic Fixed Capital Formation
 1974–79 (1975 prices)* 212
Manufacturing and Service Industries
 Manufacturing Industry: Net Output 1976–78
 235
 *Index of Manufacturing Production 1974–79
 (1975 = 100)* 236
 *Retail Trades in Great Britain
 1978* 258
Energy and Natural Resources
 *Inland Energy Consumption (in terms of
 primary sources)* 263
 Oil Statistics 265
 Coal Statistics 273
 *Generation by and Capacity of Public Supply
 Power Stations* 275
 *Output of Some of the Main
 Non-fuel Minerals* 281
Agriculture, Fisheries and Food
 *British Production as Percentage of Total
 Supplies* 286
 Manpower, Land Use, Produce and Livestock
 288
Transport and Communications
 Road Mileage 303
 Railway Statistics 309
 *Traffic Through the Principal Ports of
 Great Britain* 313
Employment
 Manpower in Britain 1970–79 326
 *Analysis of Civil Employment in Britain
 1970 and 1979* 327
Finance
 Public Expenditure 1979–80 and 1980–81 347
 *Taxation and Miscellaneous Receipts
 1979–80 and 1980–81* 353
Overseas Trade and Payments
 Exports and Imports 1970–79 369
 Commodity Composition of Trade 1979 370

Tables, statistics—*contd.*
Overseas Trade and Payments—*contd.*
 Principal British Markets 1978–79 371
 British Principal Sources of Supply 1978–79
 372
 Britain's Invisible Overseas Transactions
 1970–79 373
 Britain's Balance of Payments 1970–79 377
 Current Account 1977–79 377
 Analysis of Capital Flows and Official
 Financing 1977–79 378
The Press:
 National and London-Evening Newspapers 415
Tachograph 307
Tankers and terminals *see* Shipping
Tape recorders industry 242
Tariff policy 298, **372**, **373**, 374
Tate Gallery 406, 407
Taxation 15, 32, 48, 200, 202–3, 205, 228, 350,
351, **352–6**
betting and gaming duties 356
capital gains tax 48, 353, 355
capital transfer tax 48, 353, 355, 407
car tax 353, 356
corporation tax 48, 353, 354
customs and excise duties 44, 351, 352, 353, 356
development land tax 48, 355
expenditure, taxes on 227–8, 352, 355–6
income tax 48, 202, 206, 351, **352–4**
 relief and exemptions 227–8, 352, 354
National Insurance Surcharge 352, 353, 356
Northern Ireland 357
PAYE 144, 354
Petroleum revenue tax 48, 353, **354–5**
protective and revenue duties 352, 353
stamp duties 48, 352, 353, 356
value added tax (VAT) 44, 351, 352, 353, **355–6**,
412
vehicle excise duty 353, 356
Taxicabs 308, 309
Tayside 274
Teachers and Teaching *see* Education
Technical:
assistance 45, 89, 170, 382, 384, 385, 386
assistance programmes, British 170, 394, 395
British Volunteer Programme 89
education *see* Education
Technology *see* Education, Research, Science,
Universities *and* relevant industries
Teesside 11, 220, 312, 313, 314
Telecommunications:
equipment industry 222, 241, **242**
Exchanges 323
maritime communications 317, 324
'Prestel' 242, 324
satellites 245, 323, 324, 396
submarine cables 241, 324
telegraphs 322, 325
telephones 322, **324**
 specialised services 324
Teletext 242, 325
Telex 242, 325
Viewdata service 324
Telegraph and telephone equipment industry
241, 242
Telescopes, optical and radio 384, 385
Television *see* Broadcasting, Independent
Television *and* Licences
Telford 218
Temperature 4
Tennis *see* Lawn
Territorial and Army Volunteer Reserve (T &
AVR) 99

Textile industries 200, 201, 217, 218, 219, 220,
222, 250
machinery industry 222, 239
research 388
Thames:
river and valley 3, 6, 11, 216, 285, 290, 325
tunnels 304
Theatre Association, British 400, 410
Theatre 398, **400**, 401
amateur 400
for young people 401
National Theatre 398, 400
Shakespeare Companies, Royal 400
See also Drama
Thermometrical Table 439
Thetford 177
Thomson Foundation 418, 427
Thomson Television College 427
Tilbury 216, 313
Timber:
industry 221, 301
Research and Development Association 387,
389
Tin industry 217, 220, 237
Tinplate industry 217, 220
Tobacco:
industry 211, 213, 217, 218, 235, **250**
revenue duty 353, 356
Toilet preparations industry 248
Tolworth 389
Tools industries:
exhibition 238
hand 219, 246
machine 211, 220, **238**
 Research Association 238
small (engineers) 246
Topography 2–6
Totalisators 437
Tourist:
Authority, British 229
boards 229
trade 51, 217, 219, 220, 222, 227
Town Development Schemes 177
Planning Institute, Royal 188
Toy industry 254
Tractors 219, 243, **286**
Trade 75, 200, 201, 202, 207–8
associations 213–14, 240, 241, 253, 260, 404
commercial policy 325
controls on 374–5
Department of *and* Secretary of State for 46,
48, 50, 51, 52, 71, 183, 185, 202, 230, 231, 233,
316, 318, 375, 406, 413
Fairs 376
overseas 75, 207–8, 237, 238, 239, 241, 242,
243, 244, 246, 253, 254, **256**, 267
 area distribution 368, **370–1**
 balance of payments 200, 201, 208, **376–80**
 Board, British 48, 50, **375**
 commodity composition 368, **369**
 exports 200, 201, 202, 207, 236, 238, 240, 241,
243, 246, **369**, 370, 374, 375
 financing of 372–3, 374
 Government assistance to 371–2, 375
 imports 200, **369**, 370, 374–5
 international 200, 201, 207–9
 invisible transactions 200, 201, 368, **371–2**,
373, 376
 markets 372–3
 pattern of 368–70
 statistics 370, 371, 372
 tariffs 372, 373
 value and volume of 368–9

Trade—*contd.*
restriction and controls 231, 232
  Fair Trading 230–2
retail 257–9
wholesale 259–60
  Cash and Carry Warehouses 260
Trade Fairs 376
Trades Union Congress 176, 336–7, 339, 341, 375
Scottish 337
Trades unions 41, 212, 213, **335–6**, 337
affiliations 336
Certification Officer 335, 338
Civil Service 59, 340
educational facilities 212, 336
Speedlink trains 311
International Confederation of Free Trade Unions 337
press 418
Trading:
Director-General of Fair 231, 232
Standards Departments 216
Traffic:
air 318–19
Commissioners 307
congestion 303, 305
control 175, 303, 304, 305, 306
inland waterways 302, **312**
in towns **305**, 313
London 303, 308
Northern Ireland 304, 308
ports 312–3
rail and road 302, 303, 304, 305, 306, 307, 308, 309
research and development **305–6**, 316, 317–18
sea 302, 314, 315, 316
wardens 106
Training:
for industry 155, 163, 164, 212, 214–15, 331–2
  boards 301, 331, 343
  Instructor, Training:
    Colleges 332
    Units 332
  Opportunities Schemes (TOPS) 331–2
  Within Industry (TWI) 331–2, 343
Transport 14, 51, 66, 203, 211, 212, **302–22**
air 302, **318–22**
and Road Research Laboratory (TRRL) 90, 305
Authorities, Passenger (PTAs) boards 308, 309, 311, 312
bus and coach 15, 51, **307**
  National Bus Company 204, 307
Department of *and* Secretary of State for **51**, 175, 183, 203, 222, 304, 305, 306, 308
Docks Board, British 312
Executives 307
for school children 162
Helicopters 318, 321
Holding Company (Northern Ireland) 306, 307, 320
Hotels Ltd., British 311
hovercraft 314, 315, 316
Hoverport 315
inland 292–312
London 243, 307, 308, 309, 312, 313, 318, 321
nationalised 302, 307, 308, 311, 312, 313
  National Freight Corporation (NFC) 204, 306
Northern Ireland 56, 304, 306, 307, 308
planning 174
police 105
policy 302, 316
rail 51, **308–12**
research 305–6, 387

Transport—*contd.*
research—*contd.*
  Advisory Council Planning and 387
road 51, **302–3**, 387
safety measures 304–5, 306–7
  tachograph 306
Scottish Transport Group 307
sea 312–18
services, public 302, 304, 306, **307**, 308, **309**, 313, 315–16
European Trade Union Confederation 337
subsidies and grants 177, 304, 309, 312, 314
See also **Civil Aviation** *and* **Shipping**
Travel *see* **Tourist trade**
Treason 114
Treasury 37, 38, 40, 41, **43**, 44, 50, 56, 71, 203, 348, 349, 350, 351, 352, 357, 359
bills 351, 359, 360
Chancellor of the Exchequer 37, 43, 44, 350, 351
Chief Secretary to the 43
Counsel 109
Solicitor's Department 40, 50
Treatment of Offenders 114–18
Treaty of:
Accession 73
Rome 72, 73
Trees 5, 178, 180
Tribunals 41, 48, 49, 124–5
Council on 49, 125
Trinity House, Corporation of 317
Trooping the Colour 23
Tropical:
Medicine Research Board 383
Products Institute 90, 395
Trust companies 364
Trustee Savings Banks 359, **361–2**
Tunnels *see* **Bridges and**
Tyne and Wear 11, 185, 220, 307
Tyneside and Tyne ports 220, 237, 308

U

Uddingston 221
Ulster:
Architectural Heritage Society 188
Constabulary, Royal (RUC) 105, 106
Countryside Committee 181
Defence Regiment 100
Drama Festivals, Association 400
museums and art galleries 55, 406
New University (Coleraine) 165, 411
Orchestra 401
Polytechnic 156, 163, 167, 172
savings certificates 361
Sheltered Employment Ltd 329
See also **Northern Ireland**
Ulsterbus Ltd 307
Underground railways 308
Unemployment 201, 202, 223, **330–1**
benefit (insurance) 45, 144, 145, **148**
Unicorn Theatre for Young People 401
United Kingdom:
area and composition 1, 19
citizenship 12–13
constitution 19–20
See also subject headings
United Nations:
agencies:
  Committee on Disarmament 82
  Committee on Human Rights 83, **84–5**

United Nations–contd.

agencies–contd.

Conference on Trade and Development (UNCTAD) 91, 372, 374

contributions to 90

Educational, Scientific and Cultural Organisation (UNESCO) 85, 394

Food and Agriculture Organisation (FAO) 85

Inter-Governmental Maritime Consultative Organisation (IMCO) 185, 317

International Atomic Energy Agency 387, 394

International Telecommunication Union (ITU) 427

World Health Organisation (WHO) 47, 85

arms control and disarmament 82–3

Britain and the 83–6

economic and social affairs 85–6

General Assembly 75, 86

relations with 70, 95, 395

Security Council 70

Universal Declaration of Human Rights 84

United Press International 417, 427

United:

Reformed Church 198

States:

  educational and research co-operation 395

  exchange rates 208

  nuclear disarmament with 82–3

  trade with 242, 248, 254, 368

World College 171

Unit Trusts 362, 364

Universities 44, 155, 156, 163, **164–5**, 166, 167, 168, 169, 170, 171, 214, 296, 297, **385–6**, 395, 401, 406, 407, 408, 410, 411

agricultural degree courses 293, **296–7**

Central Council on Admission 165

degrees, diplomas and certificates 127, 163, 165, 166, 167, 296, 301

drama clubs and societies 401

extra-mural courses 168, 382, 386, 388, 389

Film Council, British 404

finance 156, **163**, 164

forestry courses 301

halls of residence 165

museums and libraries 406, 410, 411

physical education at 430

Privy Council committees for 36

research 104, 256, 382, 383, 385, 386, 395

scholarships and research fellowships 161, 164, 170, 382, 383, 384, 385, 392

Special Commonwealth Awards 170

sport 430

staff 165

students **163–4**, 165, 170

technological education 166, 167, 256, 385, 386

University:

colleges 156, 163, **164**, 165

Grants Committee 44, 156, 163, 382, 385

interchange schemes 169–70, 395–6

Open 117, 163, **165**, 169

Unmarried mothers 141

Urban:

affairs 45

aid programme 177–8

planning 174–8

population 11

Transport 303, 305, 307, **308**

V

Vaccination 139, 289, 295

Vaccines 131, 289

Valuation for rating 66–7

Value added tax see **Taxation**

Valves, industrial 239

Vegetables:

crops 285, 290

processing 249, 290

Vegetation 4–5, 285, 383

Vehicle:

licensing 51, 304, **306**, 356

safety 51

Vehicles industries 211, 216, 218, 219, 220, 221, 240, **243**

Vending machines, automatic 240

Ventilation equipment 240

Veterinary:

Laboratory, Central 295, 388

medical products 296

service and research **296**, 388

state service 295

surgeons 295

Victoria and Albert Museum 406, 407, 408

Victorian Society 188

Viewdata service 324

Viking (gasfield) 270

Virological laboratories 139

Visibility 4

Visnews 426

Visual arts 405

Vocational guidance and training 117, 120, 155, **167**, 212, 316, 329

Voluntary:

agencies 89, **90**

organisations 118, 130, **142–3**, 151–2, 172, 188, 397, **428**

  child care 142–3, 151–2

  clubs 430

  education 156, 157, 160, 162, 167, 169, 171, 172

  preservation societies 188

  prisoners' aid 118

  sport 428, 430

  welfare 130, 135, 137, 140, 151–2

  youth services 172, 173

Service International 89

Service Overseas 89

Service Unit 151

Volunteer

Centre (social services) 152

Programme, British 89

Voting:

in House of Commons 31

in House of Lords 31

in local government elections 61–3

in parliamentary elections 27

W

Wages:

Councils 333, **341**

Inspectorate 341

and salaries 16–17, 202, 206, 326, **333–4**

  equal pay 16–17, 152, 153, 340

  negotiations 333, 336, 338

  statutory regulations 152, 338–9, 340

Wales:

administration 1, 19, 51

area 1

Atlantic College 171

broadcasting councils and committees 421

Countryside Commission 180

development

  Board for Rural 176, 190

  Corporation 214, 375

Wales—*contd.*
devolution 19
environmental planning 174, 176, 177
industry 48, 51, **220–1**, 227, 228, 229, 237, 268, 272
local government 61, 62
National
  Library 51, 410, 411
  Museum of 51, 406
  Sports Centre for 431
  Youth Orchestra 403
population 7, 11, 220
ports 220, 312
press **414**, 416
Prince of 23, 24
Royal National Eisteddfod 399
Secretary of State for 51, 131, 174, 178, 182, 190, 227, 304, 397, 411, 428
Sports Council for 428, 429, 431
Tourist Board 51
Trades Union Council 337
University of 164
See also subject headings
Wallingford 284
Walsall 218
War Museum, Imperial 406
War pensioners 47, 143, **149–50**
Warren Spring Laboratory 238, 388
Warrington 177, 219, 384
Warwick and Warwickshire 164, 218
Waste:
Management Advisory Council 184
radioactive 187–8, 278, 387
reclamation and recycling 184–5, 278, 388
Water:
companies, statutory 283
conservation 281, 283
consumption 281, 283
Council, National 281
Development Board, Central Scotland 283
pollution 45, 139, 179, 183, 184, 185, 283, 284
rate 281
recreation 179, 428, 430, 431
regional, authorities 283, 428
Research 284, 388, 391
  Centre 284, 387
  Laboratory 284
sources of 262, 281, 284
Space Amenity Commission 430
supply 45, 55, 64, 139, 204, 220, 222, 283–4
Waterways:
Amenity Advisory Council, Inland 430
Board, British 313, 428, 430
Weald and Downland Museum 407
Wealth, distribution of 15, 204–7
Weapons *see* **Defence**
Weather 3–4
bulletins for ships 324
forecast services 323
Weedkillers 248
Weed Research Organisation 382
Weights and Measures 438
Welfare:
blind, deaf and disabled 47, 134–5, 140, 148, 150, 151
centres 134, 135, 140
children 46, 118–19, 132, 135–6, 140, 141–2, 150, 151
  Youth treatment centres 119
elderly 130, 134, 135, **140–1**, 143, 145–6, 149, 150, 152
family 46, 146, 149
immigrants 17, 47, 153–4

Welfare—*contd.*
industrial 341–5
mentally ill 134, **141**
mothers **146**, 151
prisoners and probationers 115, 116, 117, **118**, 119
Social 130–52
See also **National Insurance** *and* **Health**
Welsh:
Amateur Music Federation 402
Arts Council 393, 405
Assembly 19
College of Music and Drama 401
Development Agency 51, 65, 182, 214, 227, 229
Folk Museum 406
Grand Committee 33
Industrial Development Advisory Board 227
language 6–7, 11–12, 159, 160, 416
  Council 11
National Opera Company 402
Office 48, **51**, 61, 174, 179, 186
Water Authority 283
Wembley:
Conference Centre 260
Stadium 428, 432, 436
Western Isles 61, 64
Westminster Abbey 21
Weybridge 216, 388
Whisky industry 221, 249
Whitley Councils, National 59
Whole House, Committee 33
Wholesale trade 259, 260
Widnes 219
Widows' benefits and pensions 144, 145, 146, 150
Wigmore Hall 401
Winds 3–4
Windscale 277, 278, 387
Windsor 399
Winfrith 277, 387
Winkfield 396
Wires and cables (insulated) industry 217, 241
Wolverhampton 218
Women:
in armed Forces 96
complaints of discrimination 153
employment 16–17, 152–3, 326, 333, 334, **343**
equal:
  Opportunities Commission 56, 152, **153**
  opportunities 152–3
  pay for 16–17, 333
  rights 16, 152–3, 333
periodicals for 416
proportion in population 7, 10, 326
sex discrimination 16, 152–3, 333, 339
United Nations Commission on the Status of Women 85
Women's:
Institutes, National Federation of 168
Royal Air Force 96
Royal Army Corps 96
Royal Naval Service 96
Royal Voluntary Service 151, 152
Woodlands 5, 178, 179, 181, 285, 300
Woodbridge (Suffolk) 323
Woodstock (Kent) 268
Wool 289, 292
Industries Research Association 250
industry 219, 221, **250**
Marketing Board, British 290
See also **Knitwear** *and* **Textile** industries
Worcester 399

Work:
health and safety at 294, 341–5
hours of 333, **334**
See also **Employment**
Workers:
immigrant 12, 17, **330**
manual 333, 334
professional, managerial and clerical 214–15,
329, 333–4
Workers' Educational Association (WEA) 168
Works councils and committees 339
World:
Bank 46
Council of Churches 199
Data Centres (for space research) 396
Health Organisation (WHO) 47, 85
United, Colleges 171
Worplesdon 389
Worsted industry 219, 251
Wrexham 221, 414

Young Men's Christian Association,
National Council of (YMCA) 152, 168
Young offenders 112, **118–20**
Young Women's Christian Association (YWCA)
152
Youth:
and Music 403
careers service 329
centres and clubs 171–2, 401
  National Association of Youth Clubs
  172
Hostels Associations 172
orchestras 403
organisations:
  voluntary 151–2, 171, 172
services 171–3
  National Council for Voluntary (NCVYS) 172
Theatre, National 401
Treatment Centres 119
workers 172

Y

Yarmouth, Great 217
York 164, 399, 406
Province of 196
Yorkshire 11, 175, 180, 219, 236, 273, 410

Z

Zoological Society 394
library 394
research 394
Zoos and safari parks 394

Printed in England for Her Majesty's Stationery Office
by Fakenham Press Limited
Fakenham, Norfolk

Dd 698152   Pro. 14353   K140   12/80

ISBN 0 11 701004 9